INTERNATIONAL CRIMINAL
LAW DESKBOOK

Cavendish
Publishing
Limited

Sydney • London

INTERNATIONAL CRIMINAL LAW DESKBOOK

John P Grant and J Craig Barker

Cavendish
Publishing
Limited

Sydney • London

First published in Great Britain in 2006 by
Cavendish Publishing Limited, The Glass House
Wharton Street, London WC1X 9PX, United Kingdom
Website: www.cavendishpublishing.com

Published in the United States by Cavendish Publishing
c/o International Specialized Book Services,
5824 NE Hassalo Street, Portland,
Oregon 97213-3644, USA

Published in Australia by Cavendish Publishing (Australia) Pty Ltd
45 Beach Street, Coogee, NSW 2034, Australia

© 2006 John P Grant and J Craig Barker

British Library Cataloguing in Publication Data
A Catalogue record for this book is available

Library of Congress Cataloguing in Publication Data
A Catalogue record for this book is available

ISBN 10: 1-85941-979-8
ISBN 13: 978-1-85941-979-3

1 3 5 7 9 10 8 6 4 2

Printed and Bound in Great Britain

To Elaine and Kim, wives whose support and forbearance are beginning to reach Olympic proportions

In so many respects, the Nuremberg trials were a landmark in international law, heralding an era in which individuals could, in theory at least, be accountable for the commission of international crimes. But the identification of international crimes, beyond war crimes, was slow to evolve; and tended to be, as in the terrorism conventions, a response to some real or perceived international crisis. The evolution of courts or tribunals, in which to try those charged with international crimes, was even slower, dating only from the *ad hoc* international criminal tribunals for Yugoslavia and Rwanda in the early 1990s.

The Nuremberg legacy became instead part of the bedrock of the international human rights movement. That movement was concerned not with international crime and international criminal jurisdiction, but with providing international guarantees for a wide variety of rights for individuals. Human rights are now articulated in a vast number of international and regional instruments and explained in a voluminous scholarly and practical literature.

The new 'growth' area of international law is clearly international criminal law. The genesis, structure, operation and prospects of the International Criminal Court have already attracted more scholarly interest than its achievements will ever warrant. The truth, sad to some, is that international crimes will be predominantly adjudicated within the courts of States. Again, the terrorism conventions are a model. While they define various specific (international) crimes, they mandate that each State party enact the necessary legislation and establish the necessary jurisdiction, leaving it to the State party with custody of an alleged offender to institute criminal proceedings in its own courts or, through extradition, to transfer that person to the jurisdiction of another State party.

The present international criminal law régime is focused on, and directed towards, domestic criminal law and domestic criminal courts – and no amount of wishful thinking will make it different in the future. The predominance of domestic law and jurisdiction is well established in the existing conventional régime and will be unaffected by the functioning of the International Criminal Court, whose Statute recognises that the ICC has jurisdiction only when a State with custody of an alleged offender cannot or will not prosecute.

While international criminal law can be viewed as part of – and an offshoot from – human rights, it is nonetheless emerging as a discipline in its own right. That trend will continue.

The *International Criminal Law Deskbook* is intended to be a comprehensive collection of the core documents in the area. The focus is entirely on international instruments and not on any implementing or enabling domestic legislation. Equally, the focus is entirely on those parts of those instruments that bear upon international criminal law, and nothing else.

In relation to Part I of the book dealing with Substantive International Criminal Law, the extracts encompass the definition of the offence(s), the potential offenders (perpetrators, attempters, accomplices, etc), the requirement to criminalise the offence(s) in domestic law and to assert jurisdiction, the jurisdictional reach permitted to domestic courts, any prosecute-or-extradite obligation, any fair trial requirements and any co-operation obligations. In Part II, which deals with Proceducal International Criminal Law, the extracts in relation to courts and tribunals are generally much more inclusive in order to give as full a picture of the relevent bodies as possible. These extracts include, in particular, provisions relative to jurisdiction, structure and composition and procedural matters. In relation to the instruments dealing with extradition and judicial assistance, the extracts include, *inter alia*, provisions relating to the definition of relevant offences, grounds for refusal and procedural matters. In both Parts of the book, the extracts include preambulary statements as an aid to understanding and contextualising the actual text of the instruments. The extracts do not include any final clauses, such as those dealing with reservations and entry into force.

In order to make some sense of the naked wording of instruments, the editors have written short explanatory and contextualising introductions to each of the 79 instruments. These introductions contain references to official and semi-official sources of the instruments and extensive linkages between the documents themselves.

Some considerable thought was put into the ordering of the documents. It was decided that an overly complicated classification scheme was inappropriate and less than helpful to the reader. The editors opted for a simple classification scheme, international criminal law being divided first into the substantive and the procedural. Within each of these, a further simple division was made into four, reflecting the major generally recognised subdivisions. Within these subdivisions, documents are arranged chronologically, save that, when the one document has related successors, the successors are set out immediately following the initial document.

Thanks are due to the staff at the Boley Law Library at Lewis & Clark School of Law. Particular thanks are due to the immensely talented and indefatigable Erin Uhlemann, who was the first-named's research assistant in the autumn of 2004, and to research librarian Wendy Hitchcock. Elaine and Kim (not forgetting Megan and McKenzie) have our enduring gratitude for their support and forbearance.

John P Grant

Portland, Oregon

J Craig Barker

Brighton, England

May 2005

CONTENTS

PART II PROCEDURAL INTERNATIONAL CRIMINAL LAW

TABLE OF ABBREVIATIONS

AJIL	American Journal of International Law
CETS	Council of Europe Treaty Series (from No 194)
Cm	Command Paper
CTS	Consolidated Treaty Series
Dept of State Bull	Department of State Bulletin
ETS	European Treaty Series (to No 193)
ICAO	International Civil Aviation Organization
ICJ Rep	International Court of Justice Reports
ILC Yb	Yearbook of the International Law Commission
ILM	International Legal Materials
JC	Justiciary Cases (Scotland)
LNTS	League of Nations Treaty Series
OASTS	Organization of American States Treaty Series
PCIJ	Permanent Court of International Justice Reports
PCNICC	Preparatory Committee for the International Criminal Court
Reach Kram	Cambodian Legislation
SLT	Scots Law Times
TIAS	Treaties and other International Acts of the United States of America
UKTS	United Kingdom Treaty Series
UN Doc	United Nations Document
UNTS	United Nations Treaty Series

PART I

SUBSTANTIVE INTERNATIONAL CRIMINAL LAW

LAWS OF WAR

DOCUMENT I

Geneva Convention I (for the Amelioration of the Condition of the Wounded and Sick in Armed Forces in the Field) 1949
75 UNTS 31

This Convention was drafted during the Diplomatic Conference held in Geneva from 21 April to 12 August 1949. The Convention was adopted on 12 August 1949 and entered into force on 21 October 1950.

There are 192 parties, making the Convention virtually universal.

When the Convention was adopted in 1949, it replaced three earlier conventions of the same name (Article 59), the first of which, having been adopted on 22 August 1864 (129 CTS 361), was replaced, as between the parties, by the Convention of 6 July 1906 (11 LNTS 440). The First World War made apparent the need to for a new convention to address modern warfare issues. As a result, the Geneva Convention for the Relief of the Wounded and Sick in Armies in the Field was adopted on 27 July 1929 (118 LNTS 303) and was accompanied by another convention on the Treatment of Prisoners of War (118 LNTS 343). The 1949 Diplomatic Conference revised and expanded the two 1929 Conventions to create the four Geneva Conventions: this Convention, Convention II for the Amelioration of the Condition of Wounded, Sick and Shipwrecked Members of the Armed Forces at Sea (Document 2), *Convention III relative to the Treatment of Prisoners of War* (Document 3) *and Convention IV relative to the Protection of Civilian Persons in Time of War* (Document 4).

Like the other three Geneva Conventions, this Convention is broadly applicable. It applies to all cases of declared war or other armed conflict, even if the state of war is not recognised by one of the parties, and to territorial occupations, even if the occupation meets with no armed resistance (Article 2). Certain minimum provisions of the Convention apply to non-international armed conflicts (Article 3).

Parties are obliged to enact the legislation necessary to ensure effective penal sanctions for those committing or ordering grave breaches of the Convention, as defined in Article 50 (Article 49). Such persons are to be pursued and brought to trial, regardless of their nationality (Article 49). Parties are also obliged to suppress all acts contrary to the Convention that are not grave breaches (Article 49). There is provision for safeguards for proper trial and defence, which are to be no less favourable than those prescribed in Article 105 of Geneva Convention III (Document 3)*(Article 49). All laws and regulations enacted by parties to give effect to these requirements are to be transmitted to the Swiss Government (Article 48).*

See the other three Geneva Conventions (Documents 2–4) *and the two Protocols of 8 June 1977* (Documents 6–7).

See Final Record of the Diplomatic Conference of Geneva of 1949 *(3 volumes, 1949);* Pictet et al, The Geneva Conventions of 12 August 1949: A Commentary *(4 volumes,*

1952–60); Draper, The Red Cross Conventions *(1958); Friedman,* The Law of War: A Documentary History *(1972).*

The undersigned Plenipotentiaries of the Governments represented at the Diplomatic Conference held at Geneva from April 21 to August 12, 1949, for the purpose of revising the Geneva Convention for the Relief of the Wounded and Sick in Armies in the Field of July 27, 1929, have agreed as follows:

Article 3

In the case of armed conflict not of an international character occurring in the territory of one of the High Contracting Parties, each Party to the conflict shall be bound to apply, as a minimum, the following provisions:

1. Persons taking no active part in the hostilities, including members of armed forces who have laid down their arms and those placed hors de combat by sickness, wounds, detention, or any other cause, shall in all circumstances be treated humanely, without any adverse distinction founded on race, colour, religion or faith, sex, birth or wealth, or any other similar criteria. To this end, the following acts are and shall remain prohibited at any time and in any place whatsoever with respect to the above-mentioned persons:

    (a) violence to life and person, in particular murder of all kinds, mutilation, cruel treatment and torture;

    (b) taking of hostages;

    (c) outrages upon personal dignity, in particular humiliating and degrading treatment;

    (d) the passing of sentences and the carrying out of executions without previous judgment pronounced by a regularly constituted court, affording all the judicial guarantees which are recognized as indispensable by civilized peoples.

2. The wounded and sick shall be collected and cared for.

An impartial humanitarian body, such as the International Committee of the Red Cross, may offer its services to the Parties to the conflict.

The Parties to the conflict should further endeavour to bring into force, by means of special agreements, all or part of the other provisions of the present Convention.

The application of the preceding provisions shall not affect the legal status of the Parties to the conflict.

Article 12

Members of the armed forces and other persons mentioned in the following Article, who are wounded or sick, shall be respected and protected in all circumstances.

They shall be treated humanely and cared for by the Party to the conflict in whose power they may be, without any adverse distinction founded on sex, race, nationality, religion, political opinions, or any other similar criteria. Any attempts upon their lives, or violence to their persons, shall be strictly prohibited; in particular, they shall not be murdered or exterminated, subjected to torture or to biological experiments; they shall not wilfully be left without medical assistance and care, nor shall conditions exposing them to contagion or infection be created.

Only urgent medical reasons will authorize priority in the order of treatment to be administered.

Women shall be treated with all consideration due to their sex. The Party to the conflict which is compelled to abandon wounded or sick to the enemy shall, as far as military considerations permit, leave with them a part of its medical personnel and material to assist in their care.

Article 18

The military authorities may appeal to the charity of the inhabitants voluntarily to collect and care for, under their direction, the wounded and sick, granting persons who have responded to this appeal the necessary protection and facilities. Should the adverse Party take or retake control of the area, he shall likewise grant these persons the same protection and the same facilities.

The military authorities shall permit the inhabitants and relief societies, even in invaded or occupied areas, spontaneously to collect and care for wounded or sick of whatever nationality. The civilian population shall respect these wounded and sick, and in particular abstain from offering them violence.

No one may ever be molested or convicted for having nursed the wounded or sick.

The provisions of the present Article do not relieve the occupying Power of its obligation to give both physical and moral care to the wounded and sick.

Article 19

Fixed establishments and mobile medical units of the Medical Service may in no circumstances be attacked, but shall at all times be respected and protected by the Parties to the conflict. Should they fall into the hands of the adverse Party, their personnel shall be free to pursue their duties, as long as the capturing Power has not itself ensured the necessary care of the wounded and sick found in such establishments and units.

The responsible authorities shall ensure that the said medical establishments and units are, as far as possible, situated in such a manner that attacks against military objectives cannot imperil their safety.

Article 20

Hospital ships entitled to the protection of the Geneva Convention for the Amelioration of the Condition of Wounded, Sick and Shipwrecked Members of Armed Forces at Sea of 12 August 1949, shall not be attacked from the land.

Article 23

In time of peace, the High Contracting Parties and, after the outbreak of hostilities, the Parties thereto, may establish in their own territory and, if the need arises, in occupied areas, hospital zones and localities so organized as to protect the wounded and sick from the effects of war, as well as the personnel entrusted with the organization and administration of these zones and localities and with the care of the persons therein assembled.

Upon the outbreak and during the course of hostilities, the Parties concerned may conclude agreements on mutual recognition of the hospital zones and localities they have created. They may for this purpose implement the provisions of the Draft Agreement annexed to the present Convention, with such amendments as they may consider necessary.

The Protecting Powers and the International Committee of the Red Cross are invited to lend their good offices in order to facilitate the institution and recognition of these hospital zones and localities.

Article 32

Persons designated in Article 27 [medical personnel of a neutral country] who have fallen into the hands of the adverse Party may not be detained.

Unless otherwise agreed, they shall have permission to return to their country, or if this is not possible, to the territory of the Party to the conflict in whose service they were, as soon as a route for their return is open and military considerations permit.

Pending their release, they shall continue their work under the direction of the adverse Party; they shall preferably be engaged in the care of the wounded and sick of the Party to the conflict in whose service they were. On their departure, they shall take with them their effects personal articles and valuables and the instruments, arms and if possible the means of transport belonging to them.

The Parties to the conflict shall secure to this personnel, while in their power, the same food, lodging, allowances and pay as are granted to the corresponding personnel of their armed forces. The food shall in any case be sufficient as regards quantity, quality and variety to keep the said personnel in a normal state of health.

Article 36

Medical aircraft, that is to say, aircraft exclusively employed for the removal of wounded and sick and for the transport of medical personnel and equipment, shall not be attacked, but shall be respected by the belligerents, while flying at heights, times and on routes specifically agreed upon between the belligerents concerned.

They shall bear, clearly marked, the distinctive emblem prescribed in Article 38, together with their national colours on their lower, upper and lateral surfaces. They shall be provided with any other markings or means of identification that may be agreed upon between the belligerents upon the outbreak or during the course of hostilities.

Unless agreed otherwise, flights over enemy or enemy-occupied territory are prohibited.

Medical aircraft shall obey every summons to land. In the event of a landing thus imposed, the aircraft with its occupants may continue its flight after examination, if any.

In the event of an involuntary landing in enemy or enemy-occupied territory, the wounded and sick, as well as the crew of the aircraft shall be prisoners of war. The medical personnel shall be treated according to Article 24 and the Articles following.

Article 37

Subject to the provisions of the second paragraph, medical aircraft of Parties to the conflict may fly over the territory of neutral Powers, land on it in case of necessity, or use it as a port of call. They shall give the neutral Powers previous notice of their passage over the said territory and obey all summons to alight, on land or water. They will be immune from attack only when flying on routes, at heights and at times specifically agreed upon between the Parties to the conflict and the neutral Power concerned. The neutral Powers may, however, place conditions or restrictions on the passage or landing of medical aircraft on their territory. Such possible conditions or restrictions shall be applied equally to all Parties to the conflict.

Unless agreed otherwise between the neutral Power and the Parties to the conflict, the wounded and sick who are disembarked, with the consent of the local authorities, on neutral territory by medical aircraft, shall be detained by the neutral Power, where so required by international law, in such a manner that they cannot again take part in operations of war. The cost of their accommodation and internment shall be borne by the Power on which they depend.

Article 44

With the exception of the cases mentioned in the following paragraphs of the present Article, the emblem of the red cross on a white ground and the words "Red Cross" or "Geneva Cross" may not be employed, either in time of peace or in time of war, except to indicate or to protect the medical units and establishments, the personnel and material protected by the present Convention and other Conventions dealing with similar matters. The same shall apply to the emblems mentioned in Article 38, second paragraph, in respect of the countries which use them. The National Red Cross Societies and other societies designated in Article 26 shall have the right to use the distinctive emblem conferring the protection of the Convention only within the framework of the present paragraph.

Furthermore, National Red Cross (Red Crescent, Red Lion and Sun) Societies may, in time of peace, in accordance with their rational legislation, make use of the name and emblem of the Red Cross for their other activities which are in conformity with the principles laid down by the International Red Cross Conferences. When those activities are carried out in time of war, the conditions for the use of the emblem shall be such that it cannot be considered as conferring the protection of the Convention; the emblem shall be comparatively small in size and may not be placed on armlets or on the roofs of buildings.

The international Red Cross organizations and their duly authorized personnel shall be permitted to make use, at all times, of the emblem of the red cross on a white ground.

As an exceptional measure, in conformity with national legislation and with the express permission of one of the National Red Cross (Red Crescent, Red Lion and Sun) Societies, the emblem of the Convention may be employed in time of peace to identify vehicles used as ambulances and to mark the position of aid stations exclusively assigned to the purpose of giving free treatment to the wounded or sick.

Article 46

Reprisals against the wounded, sick, personnel, buildings or equipment protected by the Convention are prohibited.

Article 49

The High Contracting Parties undertake to enact any legislation necessary to provide effective penal sanctions for persons committing, or ordering to be committed, any of the grave breaches of the present Convention defined in the following Article.

Each High Contracting Party shall be under the obligation to search for persons alleged to have committed, or to have ordered to be committed, such grave breaches, and shall bring such persons, regardless of their nationality, before its own courts. It may also, if it prefers, and in accordance with the provisions of its own legislation, hand such persons over for trial to another High Contracting Party concerned, provided such High Contracting Party has made out a prima facie case.

Each High Contracting Party shall take measures necessary for the suppression of all acts contrary to the provisions of the present Convention other than the grave breaches defined in the following Article.

In all circumstances, the accused persons shall benefit by safeguards of proper trial and defence, which shall not be less favourable than those provided by Article 105 and those following, of the Geneva Convention relative to the Treatment of Prisoners of War of 12 August 1949.

Article 50

Grave breaches to which the preceding Article relates shall be those involving any of the following acts, if committed against persons or property protected by the Convention: wilful killing, torture or inhuman treatment, including biological experiments, wilfully causing great suffering or serious injury to body or health, and extensive destruction and appropriation of property, not justified by military necessity and carried out unlawfully and wantonly.

Article 51

No High Contracting Party shall be allowed to absolve itself or any other High Contracting Party of any liability incurred by itself or by another High Contracting Party in respect of breaches referred to in the preceding Article.

Article 53

The use by individuals, societies, firms or companies either public or private, other than those entitled thereto under the present Convention, of the emblem or the designation "Red Cross" or "Geneva Cross" or any sign or designation constituting an imitation thereof, whatever the object of such use, and irrespective of the date of its adoption, shall be prohibited at all times.

By reason of the tribute paid to Switzerland by the adoption of the reversed Federal colours, and of the confusion which may arise between the arms of Switzerland and the distinctive emblem of the Convention, the use by private individuals, societies or firms, of the arms of the Swiss Confederation, or of marks constituting an imitation thereof, whether as trademarks or commercial marks, or as parts of such marks, or for a purpose contrary to commercial honesty, or in circumstances capable of wounding Swiss national sentiment, shall be prohibited at all times.

Nevertheless, such High Contracting Parties as were not party to the Geneva Convention of 27 July 1929, may grant to prior users of the emblems, designations, signs or marks designated in the first paragraph, a time limit not to exceed three years from the coming into force of the present Convention to discontinue such use provided that the said use shall not be such as would appear, in time of war, to confer the protection of the Convention.

The prohibition laid down in the first paragraph of the present Article shall also apply, without effect on any rights acquired through prior use, to the emblems and marks mentioned in the second paragraph of Article 38.

Article 54
The High Contracting Parties shall, if their legislation is not already adequate, take measures necessary for the prevention and repression, at all times, of the abuses referred to under Article 53.

DOCUMENT 2

Geneva Convention II (for the Amelioration of the Condition of Wounded, Sick and Shipwrecked Members of Armed Forces at Sea) 1949
75 UNTS 85

This Convention was drafted during the Geneva Diplomatic Conference held in Geneva from 21 April to 12 August 1949. The Convention was adopted on 12 August 1949 and entered into force on 21 October 1950.

There are 192 parties, making the Convention virtually universal.

*The wounded, sick and shipwrecked members of armed forces at sea first received protection when the Geneva Convention of 22 August 1864 (129 CTS 361) was supplemented by the 1868 Additional Articles Relating to the Conditions of the Wounded in War (138 CTS 189), although the latter never entered into force through failure of ratification. The Hague Convention III for the Adaptation of Maritime Warfare of the Principles of the Geneva Convention of 22 August 1864 was adopted in 1899 (187 CTS 443) and was soon replaced by the Hague Convention X of the same name of 1907 (15 LNTS 340). The First World War made apparent the need to revise these instruments to address modern warfare issues. This Convention was revised and scheduled for consideration in Geneva in early 1940. However, the Second World War intervened, and a new agreement was not drafted until the Diplomatic Conference in 1949, which adopted, in addition to this Convention, three other Conventions: Convention I for the Amelioration of the Condition of the Wounded and Sick in Armed Forces in the Field (**Document 1**), Convention III relative to the Treatment of Prisoners of War (**Document 3**), and Convention IV relative to the Protection of Civilian Persons in Time of War (**Document 4**).*

Like Geneva Conventions I, III and IV, the Convention applies in all cases of declared war or other armed conflict, even if the state of war is not recognised by one of the parties, and to territorial occupations, even if the occupation meets with no armed resistance (Article 2). Certain minimum provisions of the Convention apply to non-international armed conflict (Article 3).

Parties are obliged to enact the legislation necessary to ensure effective penal sanctions for those committing or ordering grave breaches of the Convention, as defined in Article 51 (Article 50). Such persons are to be pursued and brought to trial, regardless of their nationality (Article 50). Parties are also obliged to suppress all acts contrary to the Convention that are not grave breaches (Article 50). There is provision for safeguards for proper trial and defence, which are to be no less favourable than those prescribed in Article 105 of Geneva Convention III **(Document 3)***(Article 50). All laws and regulations enacted by parties to give effect to these requirements are to be transmitted to the Swiss government (Article 49).*

See the other three Geneva Conventions **(Documents 1 and 3–4)** *and the two Protocols of 8 June 1977* **(Documents 6–7)**.

See Final Record of the Diplomatic Conference of Geneva of 1949 *(3 volumes, 1949);* Pictet et al, The Geneva Conventions of 12 August 1949: A Commentary *(4 volumes, 1952–60); Draper,* The Red Cross Conventions *(1958); Friedman,* The Law of War: A Documentary History *(1972).*

The undersigned Plenipotentiaries of the Governments represented at the Diplomatic Conference held at Geneva from April 21 to August 12, 1949, for the purpose of revising the Xth Hague Convention of October 18, 1907 for the Adaptation to Maritime Warfare of the Principles of the Geneva Convention of 1906, have agreed as follows:

Article 3

In the case of armed conflict not of an international character occurring in the territory of one of the High Contracting Parties, each Party to the conflict shall be bound to apply, as a minimum, the following provisions:

1. Persons taking no active part in the hostilities, including members of armed forces who have laid down their arms and those placed hors de combat by sickness, wounds, detention, or any other cause, shall in all circumstances be treated humanely, without any adverse distinction founded on race, colour, religion or faith, sex, birth or wealth, or any other similar criteria.

    To this end, the following acts are and shall remain prohibited at any time and in any place whatsoever with respect to the above-mentioned persons:

    (a) violence to life and person, in particular murder of all kinds, mutilation, cruel treatment and torture;

    (b) taking of hostages;

    (c) outrages upon personal dignity, in particular, humiliating and degrading treatment;

    (d) the passing of sentences and the carrying out of executions without previous judgment pronounced by a regularly constituted court, affording all the judicial guarantees which are recognized as indispensable by civilized peoples.

2. The wounded, sick and shipwrecked shall be collected and cared for.

An impartial humanitarian body, such as the International Committee of the Red Cross, may offer its services to the Parties to the conflict.

The Parties to the conflict should further endeavour to bring into force, by means of special agreements, all or part of the other provisions of the present Convention.

The application of the preceding provisions shall not affect the legal status of the Parties to the conflict.

Article 12

Members of the armed forces and other persons mentioned in the following Article, who are at sea and who are wounded, sick or shipwrecked, shall be respected and protected in all circumstances, it being understood that the term "shipwreck" means shipwreck from any cause and includes forced landings at sea by or from aircraft. Such persons shall be treated humanely and cared for by the Parties to the conflict in whose power they may be, without any adverse distinction founded on sex, race, nationality, religion, political opinions, or any other similar criteria. Any attempts upon their lives, or violence to their persons, shall be strictly prohibited; in particular, they shall not be murdered or exterminated, subjected to torture or to biological experiments; they shall not wilfully be left without medical assistance and care, nor shall conditions exposing them to contagion or infection be created.

Only urgent medical reasons will authorize priority in the order of treatment to be administered.

Women shall be treated with all consideration due to their sex.

Article 22

Military hospital ships, that is to say, ships built or equipped by the Powers specially and solely with a view to assisting the wounded, sick and shipwrecked, to treating them and to transporting them, may in no circumstances be attacked or captured, but shall at all times be respected and protected, on condition that their names and descriptions have been notified to the Parties to the conflict ten days before those ships are employed. The characteristics which must appear in the notification shall include registered gross tonnage, the length from stem to stern and the number of masts and funnels.

Article 23

Establishments ashore entitled to the protection of the Geneva Convention for the Amelioration of the Condition of the Wounded and Sick in Armed Forces in the Field of August 12, 1949 shall be protected from bombardment or attack from the sea.

Article 24

Hospital ships utilized by National Red Cross Societies, by officially recognized relief societies or by private persons shall have the same protection as military hospital ships and shall be exempt from capture, if the Party to the conflict on which they depend has given them an official commission and in so far as the provisions of Article 22 concerning notification have been complied with.

These ships must be provided with certificates from the responsible authorities, stating that the vessels have been under their control while fitting out and on departure.

Article 25

Hospital ships utilized by National Red Cross Societies, officially recognized relief societies, or private persons of neutral countries shall have the same protection as military hospital ships and shall be exempt from capture, on condition that they have placed themselves under the control of one of the Parties to the conflict, with the previous consent of their own governments and with the authorization of the Party to the conflict concerned, in so far as the provisions of Article 22 concerning notification have been complied with.

Article 26

The protection mentioned in Articles 22, 24 and 25 shall apply to hospital ships of any tonnage and to their lifeboats, wherever they are operating. Nevertheless, to ensure the maximum comfort and security, the Parties to the conflict shall endeavour to utilize, for the transport of wounded, sick and shipwrecked over long distances and on the high seas, only hospital ships of over 2,000 tons gross.

Article 27

Under the same conditions as those provided for in Articles 22 and 24, small craft employed by the State or by the officially recognized lifeboat institutions for coastal rescue operations, shall also be respected and protected, so far as operational requirements permit.

The same shall apply so far as possible to fixed coastal installations used exclusively by these craft for their humanitarian missions.

Article 36

The religious, medical and hospital personnel of hospital ships and their crews shall be respected and protected; they may not be captured during the time they are in the service of the hospital ship, whether or not there are wounded and sick on board.

Article 37

The religious, medical and hospital personnel assigned to the medical or spiritual care of the persons designated in Articles 12 and 13 shall, if they fall into the hands of the enemy, be respected and protected; they may continue to carry out their duties as long as this is necessary for the care of the wounded and sick. They shall afterwards be sent back as soon as the Commander-in-Chief, under whose authority they are, considers it practicable. They may take with them, on leaving the ship, their personal property.

If, however, it prove necessary to retain some of this personnel owing to the medical or spiritual needs of prisoners of war, everything possible shall be done for their earliest possible landing.

Retained personnel shall be subject, on landing, to the provisions of the Geneva Convention for the Amelioration of the Condition of the Wounded and Sick in Armed Forces in the Field of August 12, 1949.

Article 47

Reprisals against the wounded, sick and shipwrecked persons, the personnel, the vessels or the equipment protected by the Convention are prohibited.

Article 50

The High Contracting Parties undertake to enact any legislation necessary to provide effective penal sanctions for persons committing, or ordering to be committed, any of the grave breaches of the present Convention defined in the following Article.

Each High Contracting Party shall be under the obligation to search for persons alleged to have committed, or to have ordered to be committed, such grave breaches, and shall bring such persons, regardless of their nationality, before its own courts. It may also, if it prefers, and in accordance with the provisions of its own legislation, hand such persons over for trial to another High Contracting Party concerned, provided such High Contracting Party has made out a *prima facie* case.

Each High Contracting Party shall take measures necessary for the suppression of all acts contrary to the provisions of the present Convention other than the grave breaches defined in the following Article.

In all circumstances, the accused persons shall benefit by safeguards of proper trial and defence, which shall not be less favourable than those provided by Article 105 and those following of the Geneva Convention relative to the Treatment of Prisoners of War of August 12, 1949.

Article 51

Grave breaches to which the preceding Article relates shall be those involving any of the following acts, if committed against persons or property protected by the Convention: wilful killing, torture or inhuman treatment, including biological experiments, wilfully causing great suffering or serious injury to body or health, and extensive destruction and appropriation of property, not justified by military necessity and carried out unlawfully and wantonly.

Article 52

No High Contracting Party shall be allowed to absolve itself or any other High Contracting Party of any liability incurred by itself or by another High Contracting Party in respect of breaches referred to in the preceding Article.

DOCUMENT 3

Geneva Convention III (relative to the Treatment of Prisoners of War) 1949
75 UNTS 135

This Convention was drafted during the Diplomatic Conference held in Geneva from 21 April to 12 August 1949. It was adopted on 12 August 1949 and entered into force on 21 October 1950.

There are 192 parties, making the Convention virtually universal.

Despite a long-standing concern about the treatment of prisoners of war, it was not until relatively late that there were any binding legal protections: there were provisions on prisoners of war in the Regulations annexed to Hague Convention II of 1899 (187 CTS 429) and Hague Convention IV of 1907 (187 CTS 227). The deficiencies in this régime became apparent during the First World War. In consequence, a dedicated convention, the Convention relative to the Treatment of Prisoners of War, was adopted at Geneva on 27 July 1929 (118 LNTS 343). The deficiencies in the 1929 Convention became apparent during the Second World War. At the 1949 Diplomatic Conference, the 1929 Convention – along with the Geneva Convention for the Relief of the Wounded and Sick in Armies in the Field of the same year (118 LNTS 303) – was revised and extended to create, in addition to this Convention, three other Conventions: Convention I for the Amelioration of the Condition of the Wounded and Sick in Armed Forces in the Field **(Document 1)**, *Convention II for the Amelioration of the Condition of the Wounded, Sick and Shipwrecked Members of Armed Forces at Sea* **(Document 2)** *and Convention IV relative to the Protection of Civilian Persons in Time of War* **(Document 4)**.

Like Geneva Conventions I, II and IV, the Convention applies in all cases of declared war or other armed conflict, even if the state of war is not recognised by one of the parties, and to territorial occupations, even if the occupation meets with no armed resistance (Article 2). Certain minimum provisions of the Convention apply to non-international armed conflict (Article 3).

Parties are obliged to enact the legislation necessary to ensure effective penal sanctions for those committing or ordering grave breaches of the Convention, as defined in Article 130 (Article 129). Such persons are to be pursued and brought to trial, regardless of their nationality (Article 129). Parties are also obliged to suppress all acts contrary to the Convention that are not grave breaches (Article 129). There is provision for safeguards for proper trial and defence, which are to be no less favourable than those prescribed in Article 105 of Geneva Convention III **(Document 3)** *(Article 129). All laws and regulations enacted by* *parties to give effect to these requirements are to be transmitted to the Swiss government (Article 128).*

See the other three Geneva Conventions **(Documents 1–2 and 4)** *and the two Protocols of 8 June 1977* **(Documents 6–7).**

See Final Record of the Diplomatic Conference of Geneva of 1949 *(3 volumes, 1949);* Pictet et al, The Geneva Conventions of 12 August 1949: A Commentary *(4 volumes, 1952–60);* Draper, The Red Cross Conventions *(1958);* Friedman, The Law of War: A Documentary History *(1972).*

The undersigned Plenipotentiaries of the Governments represented at the Diplomatic Conference held at Geneva from April 21 to August 12, 1949, for the purpose of revising the Convention concluded at Geneva on July 27, 1929, relative to the Treatment of Prisoners of War, have agreed as follows:

Article 3

In the case of armed conflict not of an international character occurring in the territory of one of the High Contracting Parties, each Party to the conflict shall be bound to apply, as a minimum, the following provisions:

1. Persons taking no active part in the hostilities, including members of armed forces who have laid down their arms and those placed hors de combat by sickness, wounds, detention, or any other cause, shall in all circumstances be treated humanely, without any adverse distinction founded on race, colour, religion or faith, sex, birth or wealth, or any other similar criteria. To this end the following acts are and shall remain prohibited at any time and in any place whatsoever with respect to the above-mentioned persons:

    (a) violence to life and person, in particular murder of all kinds, mutilation, cruel treatment and torture;

    (b) taking of hostages;

    (c) outrages upon personal dignity, in particular, humiliating and degrading treatment;

    (d) the passing of sentences and the carrying out of executions without previous judgment pronounced by a regularly constituted court affording all the judicial guarantees which are recognized as indispensable by civilized peoples.

2. The wounded and sick shall be collected and cared for.

An impartial humanitarian body, such as the International Committee of the Red Cross, may offer its services to the Parties to the conflict.

The Parties to the conflict should further endeavour to bring into force, by means of special agreements, all or part of the other provisions of the present Convention. The application of the preceding provisions shall not affect the legal status of the Parties to the conflict.

Article 13

Prisoners of war must at all times be humanely treated. Any unlawful act or omission by the Detaining Power causing death or seriously endangering the health of a prisoner of war in its custody is prohibited, and will be regarded as a serious breach of the present Convention. In particular, no prisoner of war may be subjected to physical mutilation or to medical or scientific experiments of any kind which are not justified by the medical, dental or hospital treatment of the prisoner concerned and carried out in his interest.

Likewise, prisoners of war must at all times be protected, particularly against acts of violence or intimidation and against insults and public curiosity.

Measures of reprisal against prisoners of war are prohibited.

Article 14

Prisoners of war are entitled in all circumstances to respect for their persons and their honour.

Women shall be treated with all the regard due to their sex and shall in all cases benefit by treatment as favourable as that granted to men.

Prisoners of war shall retain the full civil capacity which they enjoyed at the time of their capture. The Detaining Power may not restrict the exercise, either within or without its own territory, of the rights such capacity confers except in so far as the captivity requires.

Article 129

The High Contracting Parties undertake to enact any legislation necessary to provide effective penal sanctions for persons committing, or ordering to be committed, any of the grave breaches of the present Convention defined in the following Article.

Each High Contracting Party shall be under the obligation to search for persons alleged to have committed, or to have ordered to be committed, such grave breaches, and shall bring such persons, regardless of their nationality, before its own courts. It may also, if it prefers, and in accordance with the provisions of its own legislation, hand such persons over for trial to another High Contracting Party concerned, provided such High Contracting Party has made out a prima facie case.

Each High Contracting Party shall take measures necessary for the suppression of all acts contrary to the provisions of the present Convention other than the grave breaches defined in the following Article.

In all circumstances, the accused persons shall benefit by safeguards of proper trial and defence, which shall not be less favourable than those provided by Article 105 and those following of the present Convention.

Article 130

Grave breaches to which the preceding Article relates shall be those involving any of the following acts, if committed against persons or property protected by the Convention: wilful killing, torture or inhuman treatment, including biological experiments, wilfully causing great suffering or serious injury to body or health, compelling a prisoner of war to serve in the forces of the hostile Power, or wilfully depriving a prisoner of war of the rights of fair and regular trial prescribed in this Convention.

Article 131

No High Contracting Party shall be allowed to absolve itself or any other High Contracting Party of any liability incurred by itself or by another High Contracting Party in respect of breaches referred to in the preceding Article.

DOCUMENT 4

Geneva Convention IV (relative to the Protection of Civilian Persons in Time of War) 1949
75 UNTS 287; 50 AJIL (Supp) 724 (1956)

The Convention was drafted during the Diplomatic Conference held in Geneva from 21 April to 12 August 1949. It was adopted on 12 August 1949 and entered into force on 21 October 1950.

There are 192 parties, making it virtually universal.

The 19th century codifications of the laws of war made scant mention of civilians, the preoccupation being with combatants. The Regulations annexed to Hague Convention II of 1899

(187 CTS 429) and Hague Convention IV of 1907 (187 CTS 227) mention civilians, but only in the context of enemy occupation and in basic terms. The impact of the First World War on civilians prompted moves for a dedicated convention to protect civilians, but the 1929 Diplomatic Conference could only agree to further study towards that end (www1.umn.edu/humanrts/ instree/1929a.htm). By 1938, a convention had been drafted (www1.umn.edu/humanrts/ instree/1938a.htm). The Second World War, with profound effect on civilians, intervened to prevent further action on that draft convention, although it was resurrected, refined and elaborated at the 1949 Diplomatic Conference, to be adopted along with three other conventions: Convention I for the Amelioration of the Condition of the Wounded and Sick in Armed Forces in the Field **(Document 1)**, *Convention II for the Amelioration of the Condition of the Wounded, Sick and Shipwrecked Members of Armed Forces at Sea* **(Document 2)** *and Convention III relative to the Treatment of Prisoners of War* **(Document 3)**.

Like Geneva Conventions I, II and III, the Convention applies in all cases of declared war or other armed conflict, even if the state of war is not recognised by one of the parties, and to territorial occupations, even if the occupation meets with no armed resistance (Article 2). Certain minimum provisions of the Convention apply to non-international armed conflict (Article 3).

Parties are obliged to enact the legislation necessary to ensure effective penal sanctions for those committing or ordering grave breaches of the Convention, as defined in Article 147 (Article 146). Such persons are to be pursued and brought to trial, regardless of their nationality (Article 146). Parties are also obliged to suppress all acts contrary to the Convention that are not grave breaches (Article 146). There is provision for safeguards for proper trial and defence, which are to be no less favourable than those prescribed in Article 105 of Geneva Convention III **(Document 3)** *(Article 146). All laws and regulations enacted by parties to give effect to these requirements are to be transmitted to the Swiss government (Article 145).*

See the other three Geneva Conventions **(Documents 1–3)** *and the two Protocols of 8 June 1977* **(Documents 6–7)**.

See Final Record of the Diplomatic Conference of Geneva of 1949 *(3 volumes, 1949);* Pictet *et al,* The Geneva Conventions of 12 August 1949: A Commentary *(4 volumes, 1952–60);* Draper, The Red Cross Conventions *(1958);* Friedman, The Law of War: A Documentary History *(1972).*

The undersigned Plenipotentiaries of the Governments represented at the Diplomatic Conference held at Geneva from April 21 to August 12, 1949, for the purpose of establishing a Convention for the Protection of Civilian Persons in Time of War, have agreed as follows:

Article 3

In the case of armed conflict not of an international character occurring in the territory of one of the High Contracting Parties, each Party to the conflict shall be bound to apply, as a minimum, the following provisions:

1. Persons taking no active part in the hostilities, including members of armed forces who have laid down their arms and those placed hors de combat by sickness, wounds, detention, or any other cause, shall in all circumstances be treated humanely, without any adverse distinction founded on race, colour, religion or faith, sex, birth or wealth, or any other similar criteria.

   To this end the following acts are and shall remain prohibited at any time and in any place whatsoever with respect to the above-mentioned persons:

   (a) violence to life and person, in particular murder of all kinds, mutilation, cruel treatment and torture;

(b) taking of hostages;

(c) outrages upon personal dignity, in particular humiliating and degrading treatment;

(d) the passing of sentences and the carrying out of executions without previous judgment pronounced by a regularly constituted court, affording all the judicial guarantees which are recognized as indispensable by civilized peoples.

2.   The wounded and sick shall be collected and cared for.

An impartial humanitarian body, such as the International Committee of the Red Cross, may offer its services to the Parties to the conflict. The Parties to the conflict should further endeavour to bring into force, by means of special agreements, all or part of the other provisions of the present Convention. The application of the preceding provisions shall not affect the legal status of the Parties to the conflict.

Article 146

The High Contracting Parties undertake to enact any legislation necessary to provide effective penal sanctions for persons committing, or ordering to be committed, any of the grave breaches of the present Convention defined in the following Article.

Each High Contracting Party shall be under the obligation to search for persons alleged to have committed, or to have ordered to be committed, such grave breaches, and shall bring such persons, regardless of their nationality, before its own courts. It may also, if it prefers, and in accordance with the provisions of its own legislation, hand such persons over for trial to another High Contracting Party concerned, provided such High Contracting Party has made out a prima facie case.

Each High Contracting Party shall take measures necessary for the suppression of all acts contrary to the provisions of the present Convention other than the grave breaches defined in the following Article.

In all circumstances, the accused persons shall benefit by safeguards of proper trial and defence, which shall not be less favourable than those provided by Article 105 and those following of the Geneva Convention relative to the Treatment of Prisoners of War of 12 August 1949.

Article 147

Grave breaches to which the preceding Article relates shall be those involving any of the following acts, if committed against persons or property protected by the present Convention: wilful killing, torture or inhuman treatment, including biological experiments, wilfully causing great suffering or serious injury to body or health, unlawful deportation or transfer or unlawful confinement of a protected person, compelling a protected person to serve in the forces of a hostile Power, or wilfully depriving a protected person of the rights of fair and regular trial prescribed in the present Convention, taking of hostages and extensive destruction and appropriation of property, not justified by military necessity and carried out unlawfully and wantonly.

DOCUMENT 5

Protocol I Additional to the Geneva Conventions of 12 August 1949, and relating to the Protection of Victims of International Armed Conflicts 1977
1125 UNTS 3; 16 ILM 1391 (1977)

This Protocol was the product of the Diplomatic Conference on the Reaffirmation and Development of International Humanitarian Law Applicable in Armed Conflicts, held at

Geneva in four annual sessions between 1974 and 1977. It was adopted on 8 June 1977 and entered into force on 7 December 1978.

There are 162 parties, including all the major powers, except the USA.

As modern warfare changed following the adoption of the four Geneva Conventions of 1949, the international community began to recognise the need to add further protections for victims of international armed conflicts. Because the Geneva Conventions did not specifically address a number of issues, including wars of national liberation, it was necessary to expand the laws of war covered by the Conventions. Two draft protocols were prepared by the International Committee of the Red Cross in 1971 and 1972 in Geneva. In February 1974, the Swiss Government convened the Diplomatic Conference on the Reaffirmation and Development of International Humanitarian Law Applicable in Armed Conflicts to discuss these draft protocols.

Protocol I expressly supplements the Geneva Conventions and applies the Conventions to situations in which peoples engage in fighting against colonial domination, cases of alien occupation, and the presence of racist regimes in the exercise of the right of self-determination (Article 1(4)).

The provisions of the Geneva Conventions of 1949 on grave breaches, as extended by Article 85(2)–(4), and breaches are extended to the Protocol (Article 85(1)). Thus, parties are obliged to enact the legislation necessary to ensure effective penal sanctions for those committing or ordering grave breaches of the Convention; such persons are to be pursued and brought to trial, regardless of their nationality. Parties are also obliged to suppress all acts contrary to the Conventions and Protocol that are not grave breaches. There must be safeguards for proper trial and defence, which are to be no less favourable than those prescribed in Article 105 of Geneva Convention III **(Document 3)**.

Parties are under an express duty repress grave breaches of the Conventions and Protocol and to take measures to suppress all other breaches (Article 86(1)). An act of a subordinate does not absolve superiors of penal or disciplinary responsibility if the superiors had knowledge or reliable incriminating information of the breach and did nothing to prevent it (Article 86(2)). Military commanders have responsibilities, among which is to prevent and, where necessary, suppress breaches and to report them to competent authorities (Article 87(1)). Parties are required to afford one another the greatest measure of mutual assistance in criminal proceedings in respect of grave breaches (Article 88(1)); and to co-operate in requests for extradition (Article 88(2)).

The Protocol establishes an International Fact-Finding Commission (Article 90(1)(a)) to enquire into alleged grave breaches and to facilitate, through its good offices, the restoration of respect for the Conventions and the Protocol (Article 90(2)(c)). The Commission is open only to those parties which make a declaration (akin to a declaration under the 'Optional Clause' of Article 36(2) of the Statute of the International Court of Justice) recognising its competence to undertake enquiries (Article 90(2)(a)); 67 parties have made such declarations.

See the four Geneva Conventions of 1949 **(Documents 1–4)** *and the Second Protocol of 8 June 1977* **(Document 6)**.

See Official Records of the Diplomatic Conference on the Reaffirmation and Development of International Humanitarian Law Applicable in Armed Conflicts (ICRC, 17 volumes, 1978); ICRC, Commentary on the Additional Protocols of 8 June 1977 to the Geneva Conventions of 12 August 1949 (1987).

The High Contracting Parties,

Proclaiming their earnest wish to see peace prevail among peoples,

Recalling that every State has the duty, in conformity with the Charter of the United Nations, to refrain in its international relations from the threat or use of force against the sovereignty, territorial integrity or political independence of any State, or in any other manner inconsistent with the purposes of the United Nations,

Believing it necessary nevertheless to reaffirm and develop the provisions protecting the victims of armed conflicts and to supplement measures intended to reinforce their application,

Expressing their conviction that nothing in this Protocol or in the Geneva Conventions of 12 August 1949 can be construed as legitimizing or authorizing any act of aggression or any other use of force inconsistent with the Charter of the United Nations,

Reaffirming further that the provisions of the Geneva Conventions of 12 August 1949 and of this Protocol must be fully applied in all circumstances to all persons who are protected by those instruments, without any adverse distinction based on the nature or origin of the armed conflict or on the causes espoused by or attributed to the Parties to the conflict,

Have agreed on the following:

Article 10 Protection and care

1. All the wounded, sick and shipwrecked, to whichever Party they belong, shall be respected and protected.

2. In all circumstances they shall be treated humanely and shall receive, to the fullest extent practicable and with the least possible delay, the medical care and attention required by their condition. There shall be no distinction among them founded on any grounds other than medical ones.

Article 11 Protection of persons

1. The physical or mental health and integrity of persons who are in the power of the adverse Party or who are interned, detained or otherwise deprived of liberty as a result of a situation referred to in Article 1 shall not be endangered by any unjustified act or omission. Accordingly, it is prohibited to subject the persons described in this Article to any medical procedure which is not indicated by the state of health of the person concerned and which is not consistent with generally accepted medical standards which would be applied under similar medical circumstances to persons who are nationals of the Party conducting the procedure and who are in no way deprived of liberty.

2. It is, in particular, prohibited to carry out on such persons, even with their consent:

    (a) physical mutilations;

    (b) medical or scientific experiments;

    (c) removal of tissue or organs for transplantation, except where these acts are justified in conformity with the conditions provided for in paragraph 1.

3. Exceptions to the prohibition in paragraph 2 (c) may be made only in the case of donations of blood for transfusion or of skin for grafting, provided that they are given voluntarily and without any coercion or inducement, and then only for therapeutic purposes, under conditions consistent with generally accepted medical standards and controls designed for the benefit of both the donor and the recipient.

4. Any wilful act or omission which seriously endangers the physical or mental health or integrity of any person who is in the power of a Party other than the one on which he depends and which either violates any of the prohibitions in paragraphs 1 and 2 or fails to comply with the requirements of paragraph 3 shall be a grave breach of this Protocol.

5. The persons described in paragraph I have the right to refuse any surgical operation. In case of refusal, medical personnel shall endeavour to obtain a written statement to that effect, signed or acknowledged by the patient.

6. Each Party to the conflict shall keep a medical record for every donation of blood for transfusion or skin for grafting by persons referred to in paragraph I, if that donation is made under the responsibility of that Party. In addition, each Party to the conflict shall endeavour to keep a record of all medical procedures undertaken with respect to any person who is interned, detained or otherwise deprived of liberty as a result of a situation referred to in Article I. These records shall be available at all times for inspection by the Protecting Power.

Article 12 Protection of medical units

1. Medical units shall be respected and protected at all times and shall not be the object of attack.

2. Paragraph I shall apply to civilian medical units, provided that they:

   (a) belong to one of the Parties to the conflict;

   (b) are recognized and authorized by the competent authority of one of the Parties to the conflict; or

   (c) are authorized in conformity with Article 9, paragraph 2, of this Protocol or Article 27 of the First Convention.

3. The Parties to the conflict are invited to notify each other of the location of their fixed medical units. The absence of such notification shall not exempt any of the Parties from the obligation to comply with the provisions of paragraph I.

4. Under no circumstances shall medical units be used in an attempt to shield military objectives from attack. Whenever possible, the Parties to the conflict shall ensure that medical units are so sated that attacks against military objectives do not imperil their safety.

Article 13 Discontinuance of protection of civilian medical units

1. The protection to which civilian medical units are entitled shall not cease unless they are used to commit, outside their humanitarian function, acts harmful to the enemy. Protection may, however, cease only after a warning has been given setting, whenever appropriate, a reasonable time-limit, and after such warning has remained unheeded.

2. The following shall not be considered as acts harmful to the enemy:

   (a) that the personnel of the unit are equipped with light individual weapons for their own defence or for that of the wounded and sick in their charge;

   (b) that the unit is guarded by a picket or by sentries or by an escort;

   (c) that small arms and ammunition taken from the wounded and sick, and not yet handed to the proper service, are found in the units;

   (d) that members of the armed forces or other combatants are in the unit for medical reasons.

Article 14 Limitations on requisition of civilian medical units

1. The Occupying Power has the duty to ensure that the medical needs of the civilian population in occupied territory continue to be satisfied.

2. The Occupying Power shall not, therefore, requisition civilian medical units, their equipment, their *matériel* or the services of their personnel, so long as these resources are necessary for the provision of adequate medical services for the civilian population and for the continuing medical care of any wounded and sick already under treatment.

3. Provided that the general rule in paragraph 2 continues to be observed, the Occupying Power may requisition the said resources, subject to the following particular conditions:

   (a) that the resources are necessary for the adequate and immediate medical treatment of the wounded and sick members of the armed forces of the Occupying Power or of prisoners of war;

   (b) that the requisition continues only while such necessity exists; and

   (c) that immediate arrangements are made to ensure that the medical needs of the civilian population, as well as those of any wounded and sick under treatment who are affected by the requisition, continue to be satisfied.

Article 15 Protection of civilian medical and religious personnel

1. Civilian medical personnel shall be respected and protected.

2. If needed, all available help shall be afforded to civilian medical personnel in an area where civilian medical services are disrupted by reason of combat activity.

3. The Occupying Power shall afford civilian medical personnel in occupied territories every assistance to enable them to perform, to the best of their ability, their humanitarian functions. The Occupying Power may not require that, in the performance of those functions, such personnel shall give priority to the treatment of any person except on medical grounds. They shall not be compelled to carry out tasks which are not compatible with their humanitarian mission.

4. Civilian medical personnel shall have access to any place where their services are essential, subject to such supervisory and safety measures as the relevant Party to the conflict may deem necessary.

5. Civilian religious personnel shall be respected and protected. The provisions of the Conventions and of this Protocol concerning the protection and identification of medical personnel shall apply equally to such persons.

Article 16 General protection of medical duties

1. Under no circumstances shall any person be punished for carrying out medical activities compatible with medical ethics, regardless of the person benefiting therefrom.

2. Persons engaged in medical activities shall not be compelled to perform acts or to carry out work contrary to the rules of medical ethics or to other medical rules designed for the benefit of the wounded and sick or to the provisions of the Conventions or of this Protocol, or to refrain from performing acts or from carrying out work required by those rules and provisions.

3. No person engaged in medical activities shall be compelled to give to anyone belonging either to an adverse Party, or to his own Party except as required by the law of the latter Party, any information concerning the wounded and sick who are, or who have been, under his care, if such information would, in his opinion, prove harmful to the patients concerned or to their families. Regulations for the compulsory notification of communicable diseases shall, however, be respected.

Article 20 Prohibition of reprisals

Reprisals against the persons and objects protected by this Part are prohibited.

Article 24 Protection of medical aircraft

Medical aircraft shall be respected and protected, subject to the provisions of this Part.

Article 35 Basic rules

1. In any armed conflict, the right of the Parties to the conflict to choose methods or means of warfare is not unlimited.

2. It is prohibited to employ weapons, projectiles and material and methods of warfare of a nature to cause superfluous injury or unnecessary suffering.

3. It is prohibited to employ methods or means of warfare which are intended, or may be expected, to cause widespread, long-term and severe damage to the natural environment.

Article 37 Prohibition of perfidy

1. It is prohibited to kill, injure or capture an adversary by resort to perfidy. Acts inviting the confidence of an adversary to lead him to believe that he is entitled to, or is obliged to accord, protection under the rules of international law applicable in armed conflict, with intent to betray that confidence, shall constitute perfidy. The following acts are examples of perfidy:

    (a) the feigning of an intent to negotiate under a flag of truce or of a surrender;

    (b) the feigning of an incapacitation by wounds or sickness;

    (c) the feigning of civilian, non-combatant status; and

    (d) the feigning of protected status by the use of signs, emblems or uniforms of the United Nations or of neutral or other States not Parties to the conflict.

2. Ruses of war are not prohibited. Such ruses are acts which are intended to mislead an adversary or to induce him to act recklessly but which infringe no rule of international law applicable in armed conflict and which are not perfidious because they do not invite the confidence of an adversary with respect to protection under that law. The following are examples of such ruses: the use of camouflage, decoys, mock operations and misinformation.

Article 38 Recognized emblems

1. It is prohibited to make improper use of the distinctive emblem of the red cross, red crescent or red lion and sun or of other emblems, signs or signals provided for by the Conventions or by this Protocol. It is also prohibited to misuse deliberately in an armed conflict other internationally recognized protective emblems, signs or signals, including the flag of truce, and the protective emblem of cultural property.

2. It is prohibited to make use of the distinctive emblem of the United Nations, except as authorized by that Organization.

Article 39 Emblems of nationality

1. It is prohibited to make use in an armed conflict of the flags or military emblems, insignia or uniforms of neutral or other States not Parties to the conflict.

2. It is prohibited to make use of the flags or military emblems, insignia or uniforms of adverse Parties while engaging in attacks or in order to shield, favour, protect or impede military operations.

3. Nothing in this Article or in Article 37, paragraph 1 (d), shall affect the existing generally recognized rules of international law applicable to espionage or to the use of flags in the conduct of armed conflict at sea.

Article 40 Quarter

It is prohibited to order that there shall be no survivors, to threaten an adversary therewith or to conduct hostilities on this basis.

Article 41 Safeguard of an enemy hors de combat

1. A person who is recognized or who, in the circumstances, should be recognized to be *hors de combat* shall not be made the object of attack.

2. A person is *hors de combat* if:

    (a) he is in the power of an adverse Party;

   (b) he clearly expresses an intention to surrender; or

   (c) he has been rendered unconscious or is otherwise incapacitated by wounds or sickness, and therefore is incapable of defending himself; provided that in any of these cases he abstains from any hostile act and does not attempt to escape.

3. When persons entitled to protection as prisons of war have fallen into the power of an adverse Party under unusual conditions of combat which prevent their evacuation as provided for in Part III, Section I, of the Third Convention, they shall be released and all feasible precautions shall be taken to ensure their safety.

Article 42 Occupants of aircraft

1. No person parachuting from an aircraft in distress shall be made the object of attack during his descent.

2. Upon reaching the ground in territory controlled by an adverse Party, a person who has parachuted from an aircraft in distress shall be given an opportunity to surrender before being made the object of attack, unless it is apparent that he is engaging in a hostile act.

3. Airborne troops are not protected by this Article.

Article 44 Combatants and prisoners of war

1. Any combatant, as defined in Article 43, who falls into the power of an adverse Party shall be a prisoner of war.

2. While all combatants are obliged to comply with the rules of international law applicable in armed conflict, violations of these rules shall not deprive a combatant of his right to be a combatant or, if he falls into the power of an adverse Party, of his right to be a prisoner of war, except as provided in paragraphs 3 and 4.

3. In order to promote the protection of the civilian population from the effects of hostilities, combatants are obliged to distinguish themselves from the civilian population while they are engaged in an attack or in a military operation preparatory to an attack. Recognizing, however, that there are situations in armed conflicts where, owing to the nature of the hostilities an armed combatant cannot so distinguish himself, he shall retain his status as a combatant, provided that, in such situations, he carries his arms openly:

   (a) during each military engagement, and

   (b) during such time as he is visible to the adversary while he is engaged in a military deployment preceding the launching of an attack in which he is to participate. Acts which comply with the requirements of this paragraph shall not be considered as perfidious within the meaning of Article 37, paragraph I (c).

4. A combatant who falls into the power of an adverse Party while failing to meet the requirements set forth in the second sentence of paragraph 3 shall forfeit his right to be a prisoner of war, but he shall, nevertheless, be given protections equivalent in all respects to those accorded to prisoners of war by the Third Convention and by this Protocol. This protection includes protections equivalent to those accorded to prisoners of war by the Third Convention in the case where such a person is tried and punished for any offences he has committed.

5. Any combatant who falls into the power of an adverse Party while not engaged in an attack or in a military operation preparatory to an attack shall not forfeit his rights to be a combatant and a prisoner of war by virtue of his prior activities.

6. This Article is without prejudice to the right of any person to be a prisoner of war pursuant to Article 4 of the Third Convention.

7. This Article is not intended to change the generally accepted practice of States with respect to the wearing of the uniform by combatants assigned to the regular, uniformed armed units of a Party to the conflict.

8.   In addition to the categories of persons mentioned in Article 13 of the First and Second Conventions, all members of the armed forces of a Party to the conflict, as defined in Article 43 of this Protocol, shall be entitled to protection under those Conventions if they are wounded or sick or, in the case of the Second Convention, shipwrecked at sea or in other waters.

Article 45 Protection of persons who have taken part in hostilities

1.   A person who takes part in hostilities and falls into the power of an adverse Party shall be presumed to be a prisoner of war, and therefore shall be protected by the Third Convention, if he claims the status of prisoner of war, or if he appears to be entitled to such status, or if the Party on which he depends claims such status on his behalf by notification to the detaining Power or to the Protecting Power. Should any doubt arise as to whether any such person is entitled to the status of prisoner of war, he shall continue to have such status and, therefore, to be protected by the Third Convention and this Protocol until such time as his status has been determined by a competent tribunal.

2.   If a person who has fallen into the power of an adverse Party is not held as a prisoner of war and is to be tried by that Party for an offence arising out of the hostilities, he shall have the right to assert his entitlement to prisoner-of-war status before a judicial tribunal and to have that question adjudicated. Whenever possible under the applicable procedure, this adjudication shall occur before the trial for the offence. The representatives of the Protecting Power shall be entitled to attend the proceedings in which that question is adjudicated, unless, exceptionally, the proceedings are held in camera in the interest of State security. In such a case the detaining Power shall advise the Protecting Power accordingly.

3.   Any person who has taken part in hostilities, who is not entitled to prisoner-of-war status and who does not benefit from more favourable treatment in accordance with the Fourth Convention shall have the right at all times to the protection of Article 75 of this Protocol. In occupied territory, any such person, unless he is held as a spy, shall also be entitled, notwithstanding Article 5 of the Fourth Convention, to his rights of communication under that Convention.

Article 47 Mercenaries

1.   A mercenary shall not have the right to be a combatant or a prisoner of war.

2.   A mercenary is any person who:

(a) is specially recruited locally or abroad in order to fight in an armed conflict;

(b) does, in fact, take a direct part in hostilities;

(c) is motivated to take part in the hostilities essentially by the desire for private gain and, in fact, is promised, by or on behalf of a Party to the conflict, material compensation substantially in excess of that promised or paid to combatants of similar ranks and functions in the armed forces of that Party;

(d) is neither a national of a Party to the conflict nor a resident of territory controlled by a Party to the conflict;

(e) is not a member of the armed forces of a Party to the conflict; and

(f) has not been sent by a State which is not a Party to the conflict on official duty as a member of its armed forces.

Article 51 Protection of the civilian population

1.   The civilian population and individual civilians shall enjoy general protection against dangers arising from military operations. To give effect to this protection, the following rules, which are additional to other applicable rules of international law, shall be observed in circumstances.

2.   The civilian population as such, as well as individual civilians, shall not be the object of attack. Acts or threats of violence the primary purpose of which is to spread terror among the civilian population are prohibited.

3. Civilians shall enjoy the protection afforded by this Section, unless and for such time as they take a direct part in hostilities.

4. Indiscriminate attacks are prohibited. Indiscriminate attacks are:

    (a) those which are not directed at a specific military objective;

    (b) those which employ a method or means of combat which cannot be directed at a specific military objective; or

    (c) those which employ a method or means of combat the effects of which cannot be limited as required by this Protocol; and consequently, in each such case, are of a nature to strike military objectives and civilians or civilian objects without distinction.

5. Among others, the following types of attacks are to be considered as indiscriminate:

    (a) an attack by bombardment by any methods or means which treats as a single military objective a number of clearly separated and distinct military objectives located in a city, town, village or other area containing a similar concentration of civilians or civilian objects; and

    (b) an attack which may be expected to cause incidental loss of civilian life, injury to civilians, damage to civilian objects, or a combination thereof, which would be excessive in relation to the concrete and direct military advantage anticipated.

6. Attacks against the civilian population or civilians by way of reprisals are prohibited.

7. The presence or movements of the civilian population or individual civilians shall not be used to render certain points or areas immune from military operations, in particular in attempts to shield military objectives from attacks or to shield, favour or impede military operations. The Parties to the conflict shall not direct the movement of the civilian population or individual civilians in order to attempt to shield military objectives from attacks or to shield military operations.

8. Any violation of these prohibitions shall not release the Parties to the conflict from their legal obligations with respect to the civilian population and civilians, including the obligation to take the precautionary measures provided for in Article 57.

Article 52 General protection of civilian objects

1. Civilian objects shall not be the object of attack or of reprisals. Civilian objects are all objects which are not military objectives as defined in paragraph 2.

2. Attacks shall be limited strictly to military objectives. In so far as objects are concerned, military objectives are limited to those objects which by their nature, location, purpose or use make an effective contribution to military action and whose total or partial destruction, capture or neutralization, in the circumstances ruling at the time, offers a definite military of advantage.

3. In case of doubt whether an object which is normally dedicated to civilian purposes, such as a place of worship, a house or other dwelling or a school, is being used to make an effective contribution to military action, it shall be presumed not to be so used.

Article 53 Protection of cultural objects and of places of worship

Without prejudice to the provisions of the Hague Convention for the Protection of Cultural Property in the Event of Armed Conflict of 14 May 1954, and of other relevant international instruments, it is prohibited:

(a) to commit any acts of hostility directed against the historic monuments, works of art or places of worship which constitute the cultural or spiritual heritage of peoples;

(b) to use such objects in support of the military effort;

(c) to make such objects the object of reprisals.

Article 54 Protection of objects indispensable to the survival of the civilian population

1. Starvation of civilians as a method of warfare is prohibited.

2. It is prohibited to attack, destroy, remove or render useless objects indispensable to the survival of the civilian population, such as foodstuffs, agricultural areas for the production of foodstuffs, crops, livestock, drinking water installations and supplies and irrigation works, for the specific purpose of denying them for their sustenance value to the civilian population or to the adverse Party, whatever the motive, whether in order to starve out civilians, to cause them to move away, or for any other motive.

3. The prohibitions in paragraph 2 shall not apply to such of the objects covered by it as are used by an adverse Party:

   (a) as sustenance solely for the members of its armed forces; or

   (b) if not as sustenance, then in direct support of military action, provided, however, that in no event shall actions against these objects be taken which may be expected to leave the civilian population with such inadequate food or water as to cause its starvation or force its movement.

4. These objects shall not be made the object of reprisals.

5. In recognition of the vital requirements of any Party to the conflict in the defence of its national territory against invasion, derogation from the prohibitions contained in paragraph 2 may be made by a Party to the conflict within such territory under its own control where required by imperative military necessity.

Article 56 Protection of works and installations containing dangerous forces

1. Works or installations containing dangerous forces, namely dams, dykes and nuclear electrical generating stations, shall not be made the object of attack, even where these objects are military objectives, if such attack may cause the release of dangerous forces and consequent severe losses among the civilian population. Other military objectives located at or in the vicinity of these works or installations shall not be made the object of attack if such attack may cause the release of dangerous forces from the works or installations and consequent severe losses among the civilian population.

2. The special protection against attack provided by paragraph 1 shall cease:

   (a) for a dam or a dyke only if it is used for other than its normal function and in regular, significant and direct support of military operations and if such attack is the only feasible way to terminate such support;

   (b) for a nuclear electrical generating station only if it provides electric power in regular, significant and direct support of military operations and if such attack is the only feasible way to terminate such support;

   (c) for other military objectives located at or in the vicinity of these works or installations only if they are used in regular, significant and direct support of military operations and if such attack is the only feasible way to terminate such support.

3. In all cases, the civilian population and individual civilians shall remain entitled to all the protection accorded them by international law, including the protection of the precautionary measures provided for in Article 57. If the protection ceases and any of the works, installations or military objectives mentioned in paragraph 1 is attacked, all practical precautions shall be taken to avoid the release of the dangerous forces.

4. It is prohibited to make any of the works, installations or military objectives mentioned in paragraph 1 the object of reprisals.

5. The Parties to the conflict shall endeavour to avoid locating any military objectives in the vicinity of the works or installations mentioned in paragraph 1. Nevertheless, installations

erected for the sole purpose of defending the protected works or installations from attack are permissible and shall not themselves be made the object of attack, provided that they are not used in hostilities except for defensive actions necessary to respond to attacks against the protected works or installations and that their armament is limited to weapons capable only of repelling hostile action against the protected works or installations.

6. The High Contracting Parties and the Parties to the conflict are urged to conclude further agreements among themselves to provide additional protection for objects containing dangerous forces.

7. In order to facilitate the identification of the objects protected by this article, the Parties to the conflict may mark them with a special sign consisting of a group of three bright orange circles placed on the same axis, as specified in Article 16 of Annex I to this Protocol. The absence of such marking in no way relieves any Party to the conflict of its obligations under this Article.

Article 57 Precautions in attack

1. In the conduct of military operations, constant care shall be taken to spare the civilian population, civilians and civilian objects.

2. With respect to attacks, the following precautions shall be taken:

   (a) those who plan or decide upon an attack shall:

   (i) do everything feasible to verify that the objectives to be attacked are neither civilians nor civilian objects and are not subject to special protection but are military objectives within the meaning of paragraph 2 of Article 52 and that it is not prohibited by the provisions of this Protocol to attack them;

   (ii) take all feasible precautions in the choice of means and methods of attack with a view to avoiding, and in any event to minimizing, incidental loss of civilian life, injury to civilians and damage to civilian objects;

   (iii) refrain from deciding to launch any attack which may be expected to cause incidental loss of civilian life, injury to civilians, damage to civilian objects, or a combination thereof, which would be excessive in relation to the concrete and direct military advantage anticipated;

   (b) an attack shall be cancelled or suspended if it becomes apparent that the objective is not a military one or is subject to special protection or that the attack may be expected to cause incidental loss of civilian life, injury to civilians, damage to civilian objects, or a combination thereof, which would be excessive in relation to the concrete and direct military advantage anticipated;

   (c) effective advance warning shall be given of attacks which may affect the civilian population, unless circumstances do not permit.

3. When a choice is possible between several military objectives for obtaining a similar military advantage, the objective to be selected shall be that the attack on which may be expected to cause the least danger to civilian lives and to civilian objects.

4. In the conduct of military operations at sea or in the air, each Party to the conflict shall, in conformity with its rights and duties under the rules of international law applicable in armed conflict, take all reasonable precautions to avoid losses of civilian lives and damage to civilian objects.

5. No provision of this Article may be construed as authorizing any attacks against the civilian population, civilians or civilian objects.

Article 59 Non-defended localities

1. It is prohibited for the Parties to the conflict to attack, by any means whatsoever, non-defended localities.

2. The appropriate authorities of a Party to the conflict may declare as a non-defended locality any inhabited place near or in a zone where armed forces are in contact which is open for occupation by an adverse Party. Such a locality shall fulfil the following conditions:

    (a) all combatants, as well as mobile weapons and mobile military equipment must have been evacuated;

    (b) no hostile use shall be made of fixed military installations or establishments;

    (c) no acts of hostility shall be committed by the authorities or by the population; and

    (d) no activities in support of military operations shall be undertaken.

3. The presence, in this locality, of persons specially protected under the Conventions and this Protocol, and of police forces retained for the sole purpose of maintaining law and order, is not contrary to the conditions laid down in paragraph 2.

4. The declaration made under paragraph 2 shall be addressed to the adverse Party and shall define and describe, as precisely as possible, the limits of the non-defended locality. The Party to the conflict to which the declaration is addressed shall acknowledge its receipt and shall treat the locality as a non-defended locality unless the conditions laid down in paragraph 2 are not in fact fulfilled, in which event it shall immediately so inform the Party making the declaration. Even if the conditions laid down in paragraph 2 are not fulfilled, the locality shall continue to enjoy the protection provided by the other provisions of this Protocol and the other rules of international law applicable in armed conflict.

5. The Parties to the conflict may agree on the establishment of non- defended localities even if such localities do not fulfil the conditions laid down in paragraph 2. The agreement should define and describe, as precisely as possible, the limits of the non-defended locality; if necessary, it may lay down the methods of supervision.

6. The Party which is in control of a locality governed by such an agreement shall mark it, so far as possible, by such signs as may be agreed upon with the other Party, which shall be displayed where they are clearly visible, especially on its perimeter and limits and on highways.

7. A locality loses its status as a non-defended locality when it ceases to fulfil the conditions laid down in paragraph 2 or in the agreement referred to in paragraph 5. In such an eventuality, the locality shall continue to enjoy the protection provided by the other provisions of this Protocol and the other rules of international law applicable in armed conflict.

Article 60 Demilitarized zones

1. It is prohibited for the Parties to the conflict to extend their military operations to zones on which they have conferred by agreement the status of demilitarized zone, if such extension is contrary to the terms of this agreement.

2. The agreement shall be an express agreement, may be concluded verbally or in writing, either directly or through a Protecting Power or any impartial humanitarian organization, and may consist of reciprocal and concordant declarations. The agreement may be concluded in peacetime, as well as after the outbreak of hostilities, and should define and describe, as precisely as possible, the limits of the demilitarized zone and, if necessary, lay down the methods of supervision.

3. The subject of such an agreement shall normally be any zone which fulfils the following conditions:

    (a) all combatants, as well as mobile weapons and mobile military equipment, must have been evacuated;

    (b) no hostile use shall be made of fixed military installations or establishments;

    (c) no acts of hostility shall be committed by the authorities or by the population; and

    (d) any activity linked to the military effort must have ceased.

The Parties to the conflict shall agree upon the interpretation to be given to the condition laid down in sub-paragraph (d) and upon persons to be admitted to the demilitarized zone other than those mentioned in paragraph 4.

4. The presence, in this zone, of persons specially protected under the Conventions and this Protocol, and of police forces retained for the sole purpose of maintaining law and order, is not contrary to the conditions laid down in paragraph 3.

5. The Party which is in control of such a zone shall mark it, so far as possible, by such signs as may be agreed upon with the other Party, which shall be displayed where they are clearly visible, especially on its perimeter and limits and on highways.

6. If the fighting draws near to a demilitarized zone, and if the Parties to the conflict have so agreed, none of them may use the zone for purposes related to the conduct of military operations or unilaterally revoke its status.

7. If one of the Parties to the conflict commits a material breach of the provisions of paragraphs 3 or 6, the other Party shall be released from its obligations under the agreement conferring upon the zone the status of demilitarized zone. In such an eventuality, the zone loses its status but shall continue to enjoy the protection provided by the other provisions of this Protocol and the other rules of international law applicable in armed conflict.

Article 62 General protection

1. Civilian civil defence organizations and their personnel shall be respected and protected, subject to the provisions of this Protocol, particularly the provisions of this Section. They shall be entitled to perform their civil defence tasks except in case of imperative military necessity.

2. The provisions of paragraph 1 shall also apply to civilians who, although not members of civilian civil defence organizations, respond to an appeal from the competent authorities and perform civil defence tasks under their control.

3. Buildings and materiel used for civil defence purposes and shelters provided for the civilian population are covered by Article 52. Objects used for civil defence purposes may not be destroyed or diverted from their proper use except by the Party to which they belong.

Article 75 Fundamental guarantees

1. In so far as they are affected by a situation referred to in Article 1 of this Protocol, persons who are in the power of a Party to the conflict and who do not benefit from more favourable treatment under the Conventions or under this Protocol shall be treated humanely in all circumstances and shall enjoy, as a minimum, the protection provided by this Article without any adverse distinction based upon race, colour, sex, language, religion or belief, political or other opinion, national or social origin, wealth, birth or other status, or on any other similar criteria. Each Party shall respect the person, honour, convictions and religious practices of all such persons.

2. The following acts are and shall remain prohibited at any time and in any place whatsoever, whether committed by civilian or by military agents:

    (a) violence to the life, health, or physical or mental well-being of persons, in particular:

        (i)   murder;

        (ii) torture of all kinds, whether physical or mental;

        (iii) corporal punishment; and

        (iv) mutilation;

    (b) outrages upon personal dignity, in particular humiliating and degrading treatment, enforced prostitution and any form of indecent assault;

    (c) the taking of hostages;

    (d) collective punishments; and

    (e) threats to commit any of the foregoing acts.

3. Any person arrested, detained or interned for actions related to the armed conflict shall be informed promptly, in a language he understands, of the reasons why these measures have been taken. Except in cases of arrest or detention for penal offences, such persons shall be released with the minimum delay possible and in any event as soon as the circumstances justifying the arrest, detention or internment have ceased to exist.

4. No sentence may be passed and no penalty may be executed on a person found guilty of a penal offence related to the armed conflict except pursuant to a conviction pronounced by an impartial and regularly constituted court respecting the generally recognized principles of regular judicial procedure, which include the following:

    (a) the procedure shall provide for an accused to be informed without delay of the particulars of the offence alleged against him and shall afford the accused before and during his trial all necessary rights and means of defence;

    (b) no one shall be convicted of an offence except on the basis of individual penal responsibility;

    (c) no one shall be accused or convicted of a criminal offence on account of any act or omission which did not constitute a criminal offence under the national or international law to which he was subject at the time when it was committed; nor shall a heavier penalty be imposed than that which was applicable at the time when the criminal offence was committed; if, after the commission of the offence, provision is made by law for the imposition of a lighter penalty, the offender shall benefit thereby;

    (d) anyone charged with an offence is presumed innocent until proved guilt according to law;

    (e) anyone charged with an offence shall have the right to be tried in his presence;

    (f) no one shall be compelled to testify against himself or to confess guilt;

    (g) anyone charged with an offence shall have the right to examine, or have examined, the witnesses against him and to obtain the attendance and examination of witnesses on his behalf under the same conditions as witnesses against him;

    (h) no one shall be prosecuted or punished by the same Party for an offence in respect of which a final judgment acquitting or convicting that person has been previously pronounced under the same law and judicial procedure;

    (i) anyone prosecuted for an offence shall have the right to have the judgment pronounced publicly; and

    (j) a convicted person shall be advised on conviction of his judicial and other remedies and of the time-limits within which they may be exercised.

5. Women whose liberty has been restricted for reasons related to the armed conflict shall be held in quarters separated from men's quarters. They shall be under the immediate supervision of women. Nevertheless, in cases where families are detained or interned, they shall, whenever possible, be held in the same place and accommodated as family units.

6. Persons who are arrested, detained or interned for reasons related to the armed conflict shall enjoy the protection provided by this Article until their final release, repatriation or re-establishment, even after the end of the armed conflict.

7. In order to avoid any doubt concerning the prosecution and trial of persons accused of war crimes or crimes against humanity, the following principles shall apply:

    (a) persons who are accused of such crimes should be submitted for the purpose of prosecution and trial in accordance with the applicable rules of international law; and

    (b) any such persons who do not benefit from more favourable treatment under the Conventions or this Protocol shall be accorded the treatment provided by this Article, whether or not the crimes of which they are accused constitute grave breaches of the Conventions or of this Protocol.

8. No provision of this Article may be construed as limiting or infringing any other more favourable provision granting greater protection, under any applicable rules of international law, to persons covered by paragraph 1.

Article 76 Protection of women

1. Women shall be the object of special respect and shall be protected in particular against rape, forced prostitution and any other form of indecent assault.

2. Pregnant women and mothers having dependent infants who are arrested, detained or interned for reasons related to the armed conflict, shall have their cases considered with the utmost priority.

3. To the maximum extent feasible, the Parties to the conflict shall endeavour to avoid the pronouncement of the death penalty on pregnant women or mothers having dependent infants, for an offence related to the armed conflict. The death penalty for such offences shall not be executed on such women.

Article 77 Protection of children

1. Children shall be the object of special respect and shall be protected against any form of indecent assault. The Parties to the conflict shall provide them with the care and aid they require, whether because of their age or for any other reason.

2. The Parties to the conflict shall take all feasible measures in order that children who have not attained the age of fifteen years do not take a direct part in hostilities and, in particular, they shall refrain from recruiting them into their armed forces. In recruiting among those persons who have attained the age of fifteen years but who have not attained the age of eighteen years, the Parties to the conflict shall endeavour to give priority to those who are oldest.

3. If, in exceptional cases, despite the provisions of paragraph 2, children who have not attained the age of fifteen years take a direct part in hostilities and fall into the power of an adverse Party, they shall continue to benefit from the special protection accorded by this Article, whether or not they are prisoners of war.

4. If arrested, detained or interned for reasons related to the armed conflict, children shall be held in quarters separate from the quarters of adults, except where families are accommodated as family units as provided in Article 75, paragraph 5.

5. The death penalty for an offence related to armed conflict shall not be executed on persons who had not attained the age of eighteen years at the time the offence was committed.

Article 85 Repression of breaches of this Protocol

1. The provisions of the Conventions relating to the repression of breaches and grave breaches, supplemented by this Section, shall apply to the repression of breaches and grave breaches of this Protocol.

2. Acts described as grave breaches in the Conventions are grave breaches of this Protocol if committed against persons in the power of an adverse Party protected by Articles 44, 45 and 73 of this Protocol, or against the wounded, sick and shipwrecked of the adverse Party who are protected by this Protocol, or against those medical or religious personnel, medical units or medical transports which are under the control of the adverse Party and are protected by this Protocol.

3. In addition to the grave breaches defined in Article 11, the following acts shall be regarded as grave breaches of this Protocol, when committed wilfully, in violation of the relevant provisions of this Protocol, and causing death or serious injury to body or health:

   (a) making the civilian population or individual civilians the object of attack;

   (b) launching an indiscriminate attack affecting the civilian population or civilian objects in the knowledge that such attack will cause excessive loss of life, injury to civilians or damage to civilian objects, as defined in Article 57, paragraph 2(a)(iii);

(c) launching an attack against works or installations containing dangerous forces in the knowledge that such attack will cause excessive loss of life, injury to civilians or damage to civilian objects, as defined in Article 57, paragraph 2(a)(iii);

(d) making non-defended localities and demilitarized zones the object of attack;

(e) making a person the object of attack in the knowledge that he is hors de combat;

(f) the perfidious use, in violation of Article 37, of the distinctive emblem of the red cross, red crescent or red lion and sun or of other protective signs recognized by the Conventions or this Protocol.

4. In addition to the grave breaches defined in the preceding paragraphs and in the Conventions, the following shall be regarded as grave breaches of this Protocol, when committed wilfully and in violation of the Conventions of the Protocol;

(a) the transfer by the Occupying Power of parts of its own civilian population into the territory it occupies, or the deportation or transfer of all or parts of the population of the occupied territory within or outside this territory, in violation of Article 49 of the Fourth Convention;

(b) unjustifiable delay in the repatriation of prisoners of war or civilians;

(c) practices of apartheid and other inhuman and degrading practices involving outrages upon personal dignity, based on racial discrimination;

(d) making the clearly-recognized historic monuments, works of art or places of worship which constitute the cultural or spiritual heritage of peoples and to which special protection has been given by special arrangement, for example, within the framework of a competent international organization, the object of attack, causing as a result extensive destruction thereof, where there is no evidence of the violation by the adverse Party of Article 53, sub-paragraph (b), and when such historic monuments, works of art and places of worship are not located in the immediate proximity of military objectives;

(e) depriving a person protected by the Conventions or referred to in paragraph 2 of this Article of the rights of fair and regular trial.

5. Without prejudice to the application of the Conventions and of this Protocol, grave breaches of these instruments shall be regarded as war crimes.

Article 86 Failure to act

1. The High Contracting Parties and the Parties to the conflict shall repress grave breaches, and take measures necessary to suppress all other breaches, of the Conventions or of this Protocol which result from a failure to act when under a duty to do so.

2. The fact that a breach of the Conventions or of this Protocol was committed by a subordinate does not absolve his superiors from penal or disciplinary responsibility, as the case may be, if they knew, or had information which should have enabled them to conclude in the circumstances at the time, that he was committing or was going to commit such a breach and if they did not take all feasible measures within their power to prevent or repress the breach.

Article 88 Mutual assistance in criminal matters

1. The High Contracting Parties shall afford one another the greatest measure of assistance in connexion with criminal proceedings brought in respect of grave breaches of the Conventions or of this Protocol.

2. Subject to the rights and obligations established in the Conventions and in Article 85, paragraph 1, of this Protocol, and when circumstances permit, the High Contracting Parties shall co-operate in the matter of extradition. They shall give due consideration to the request of the State in whose territory the alleged offence has occurred.

3. The law of the High Contracting Party requested shall apply in all cases. The provisions of the preceding paragraphs shall not, however, affect the obligations arising from the provisions of any other treaty of a bilateral or multilateral nature which governs or will govern the whole or part of the subject of mutual assistance in criminal matters.

DOCUMENT 6

Protocol II Additional to the Geneva Conventions of 12 August 1949, and relating to the Protection of Victims of Non-International Armed Conflicts 1977
1125 UNTS 609; 16 ILM 1442 (1977)

This Protocol was the product of the Diplomatic Conference on the Reaffirmation and Development of International Humanitarian Law Applicable in Armed Conflicts, held at Geneva in four annual sessions between 1974 and 1977. It was adopted on 8 June 1977 and entered into force on 7 December 1978.

There are 157 parties, including all the major powers, except the USA.

As modern warfare changed following the adoption of the four Geneva Conventions of 1949, the international community began to recognize the need to add further protections for victims of international armed conflicts. Because the Geneva Conventions did not adequately address a number of issues, including the limited guarantees in common Article 3 of these Conventions in respect of non-international armed conflicts, it was necessary to expand the laws of war covered by the Conventions. Two draft protocols were prepared by the International Committee of the Red Cross in 1971 and 1972 in Geneva. In February 1974, the Swiss Government convened the Diplomatic Conference on the Reaffirmation and Development of International Humanitarian Law Applicable in Armed Conflicts to discuss these draft protocols.

Protocol II is a short document, containing only 25 articles, compared with the 101 articles found in Protocol I **(Document 5)**. *It expressly develops and supplements common Article 3 of the Geneva Conventions and Protocol I. It is striking that Protocol II contains no provisions on its execution, nor on the repression of grave breaches and the suppression of breaches. It is therefore to be regarded as an authoritative – indeed definitive as between the parties – interpretation of common Article 3 and enforceable through the obligations and mechanisms of the Geneva Conventions and Protocol I.*

See the four Geneva Conventions **(Documents 1–4)** *and the first Protocol of 8 June 1977* **(Document 5)**.

See Official Records of the Diplomatic Conference on the Reaffirmation and Development of International Humanitarian Law Applicable in Armed Conflicts *(ICRC, 17 volumes; 1978)*; ICRC, Commentary on the Additional Protocols of 8 June 1977 to the Geneva Conventions of 12 August 1949 *(1987)*.

The High Contracting Parties,

Recalling that the humanitarian principles enshrined in Article 3 common to the Geneva Conventions of 12 August 1949 constitute the foundation of respect for the human person in cases of armed conflict not of an international character,

Recalling furthermore that international instruments relating to human rights offer a basic protection to the human person,

Emphasizing the need to ensure a better protection for the victims of those armed conflicts,

Recalling that, in cases not covered by the law in force, the human person remains under the protection of the principles of humanity and the dictates of the public conscience,

Have agreed on the following:

Article 4 Fundamental guarantees

1. All persons who do not take a direct part or who have ceased to take part in hostilities, whether or not their liberty has been restricted, are entitled to respect for their person, honour and convictions and religious practices. They shall in all circumstances be treated humanely, without any adverse distinction. It is prohibited to order that there shall be no survivors.

2. Without prejudice to the generality of the foregoing, the following acts against the persons referred to in paragraph 1 are and shall remain prohibited at any time and in any place whatsoever:

    (a) violence to the life, health and physical or mental well-being of persons, in particular murder as well as cruel treatment such as torture, mutilation or any form of corporal punishment;

    (b) collective punishments;

    (c) taking of hostages;

    (d) acts of terrorism;

    (e) outrages upon personal dignity, in particular humiliating and degrading treatment, rape, enforced prostitution and any form of indecent assault;

    (f) slavery and the slave trade in all their forms;

    (g) pillage;

    (h) threats to commit any of the foregoing acts.

3. Children shall be provided with the care and aid they require, and in particular:

    (a) they shall receive an education, including religious and moral education, in keeping with the wishes of their parents, or in the absence of parents, of those responsible for their care;

    (b) all appropriate steps shall be taken to facilitate the reunion of families temporarily separated;

    (c) children who have not attained the age of fifteen years shall neither be recruited in the armed forces or groups nor allowed to take part in hostilities;

    (d) the special protection provided by this Article to children who have not attained the age of fifteen years shall remain applicable to them if they take a direct part in hostilities despite the provisions of sub-paragraph (c) and are captured;

    (e) measures shall be taken, if necessary, and whenever possible with the consent of their parents or persons who by law or custom are primarily responsible for their care, to remove children temporarily from the area in which hostilities are taking place to a safer area within the country and ensure that they are accompanied by persons responsible for their safety and well-being.

Article 5 Persons whose liberty has been restricted

1. In addition to the provisions of Article 4, the following provisions shall be respected as a minimum with regard to persons deprived of their liberty for reasons related to the armed conflict, whether they are interned or detained:

    (a) the wounded and the sick shall be treated in accordance with Article 7;

(b) the persons referred to in this paragraph shall, to the same extent as the local civilian population, be provided with food and drinking water and be afforded safeguards as regards health and hygiene and protection against the rigours of the climate and the dangers of the armed conflict;

(c) they shall be allowed to receive individual or collective relief;

(d) they shall be allowed to practise their religion and, if requested and appropriate, to receive spiritual assistance from persons, such as chaplains, performing religious functions;

(e) they shall, if made to work, have the benefit of working conditions and safeguards similar to those enjoyed by the local civilian population.

2. Those who are responsible for the internment or detention of the persons referred to in paragraph 1 shall also, within the limits of their capabilities, respect the following provisions relating to such persons:

(a) except when men and women of a family are accommodated together, women shall be held in quarters separated from those of men and shall be under the immediate supervision of women;

(b) they shall be allowed to send and receive letters and cards, the number of which may be limited by the competent authority if it deems necessary;

(c) places of internment and detention shall not be located close to the combat zone. The persons referred to in paragraph 1 shall be evacuated when the places where they are interned or detained become particularly exposed to danger arising out of the armed conflict, if their evacuation can be carried out under adequate conditions of safety;

(d) they shall have the benefit of medical examinations;

(e) their physical or mental health and integrity shall not be endangered by an unjustified act or omission. Accordingly, it is prohibited to subject the persons described in this Article to any medical procedure which is not indicated by the state of health of the person concerned, and which is not consistent with the generally accepted medical standards applied to free persons under similar medical circumstances.

3. Persons who are not covered by paragraph 1 but whose liberty has been restricted in any way whatsoever for reasons related to the armed conflict shall be treated humanely in accordance with Article 4 and with paragraphs 1 (a), (c) and (d), and 2 (b) of this Article.

4. If it is decided to release persons deprived of their liberty, necessary measures to ensure their safety shall be taken by those so deciding.

Article 6 Penal prosecutions

1. This Article applies to the prosecution and punishment of criminal offences related to the armed conflict.

2. No sentence shall be passed and no penalty shall be executed on a person found guilty of an offence except pursuant to a conviction pronounced by a court offering the essential guarantees of independence and impartiality. In particular:

(a) the procedure shall provide for an accused to be informed without delay of the particulars of the offence alleged against him and shall afford the accused before and during his trial all necessary rights and means of defence;

(b) no one shall be convicted of an offence except on the basis of individual penal responsibility;

(c) no one shall be held guilty of any criminal offence on account of any act or omission which did not constitute a criminal offence, under the law, at the time when it was committed; nor shall a heavier penalty be imposed than that which was applicable at the time when the criminal offence was committed; if, after the commission of the offence, provision is made by law for the imposition of a lighter penalty, the offender shall benefit thereby;

(d) anyone charged with an offence is presumed innocent until proved guilty according to law;

(e)   anyone charged with an offence shall have the right to be tried in his presence;

(f)   no one shall be compelled to testify against himself or to confess guilt.

3.   A convicted person shall be advised on conviction of his judicial and other remedies and of the time-limits within which they may be exercised.

4.   The death penalty shall not be pronounced on persons who were under the age of eighteen years at the time of the offence and shall not be carried out on pregnant women or mothers of young children.

5.   At the end of hostilities, the authorities in power shall endeavour to grant the broadest possible amnesty to persons who have participated in the armed conflict, or those deprived of their liberty for reasons related to the armed conflict, whether they are interned or detained.

Article 7 Protection and care

1.   All the wounded, sick and shipwrecked, whether or not they have taken part in the armed conflict, shall be respected and protected.

2.   In all circumstances they shall be treated humanely and shall receive, to the fullest extent practicable and with the least possible delay, the medical care and attention required by their condition. There shall be no distinction among them founded on any grounds other than medical ones.

Article 9 Protection of medical and religious personnel

1.   Medical and religious personnel shall be respected and protected and shall be granted all available help for the performance of their duties. They shall not be compelled to carry out tasks which are not compatible with their humanitarian mission.

2.   In the performance of their duties medical personnel may not be required to give priority to any person except on medical grounds.

Article 10 General protection of medical duties

1.   Under no circumstances shall any person be punished for having carried out medical activities compatible with medical ethics, regardless of the person benefiting therefrom.

2.   Persons engaged in medical activities shall neither be compelled to perform acts or to carry out work contrary to, nor be compelled to refrain from acts required by, the rules of medical ethics or other rules designed for the benefit of the wounded and sick, or this Protocol.

3.   The professional obligations of persons engaged in medical activities regarding information which they may acquire concerning the wounded and sick under their care shall, subject to national law, be respected.

4.   Subject to national law, no person engaged in medical activities may be penalized in any way for refusing or failing to give information concerning the wounded and sick who are, or who have been, under his care.

Article 11 Protection of medical units and transports

1.   Medical units and transports shall be respected and protected at all times and shall not be the object of attack.

2.   The protection to which medical units and transports are entitled shall not cease unless they are used to commit hostile acts, outside their humanitarian function. Protection may, however, cease only after a warning has been given setting, whenever appropriate, a reasonable time-limit, and after such warning has remained unheeded.

Article 13 Protection of the civilian population

1.   The civilian population and individual civilians shall enjoy general protection against the dangers arising from military operations. To give effect to this protection, the following rules shall be observed in all circumstances.

2. The civilian population as such, as well as individual civilians, shall not be the object of attack. Acts or threats of violence the primary purpose of which is to spread terror among the civilian population are prohibited.

3. Civilians shall enjoy the protection afforded by this Part, unless and for such time as they take a direct part in hostilities.

Article 14 Protection of objects indispensable to the survival of the civilian population

Starvation of civilians as a method of combat is prohibited. It is therefore prohibited to attack, destroy, remove or render useless, for that purpose, objects indispensable to the survival of the civilian population, such as foodstuffs, agricultural areas for the production of foodstuffs, crops, livestock, drinking water installations and supplies and irrigation works.

Article 16 Protection of cultural objects and of places of worship

Without prejudice to the provisions of The Hague Convention for the Protection of Cultural Property in the Event of Armed Conflict of 14 May 1954, it is prohibited to commit any acts of hostility directed against historic monuments, works of art or places of worship which constitute the cultural or spiritual heritage of peoples, and to use them in support of the military effort.

Article 17 Prohibition of forced movement of civilians

1. The displacement of the civilian population shall not be ordered for reasons related to the conflict unless the security of the civilians involved or imperative military reasons so demand. Should such displacements have to be carried out, all possible measures shall be taken in order that the civilian population may be received under satisfactory conditions of shelter, hygiene, health, safety and nutrition.

2. Civilians shall not be compelled to leave their own territory for reasons connected with the conflict.

CRIMES AGAINST HUMANITY

DOCUMENT 7

Slavery Convention 1926
(as amended by the Protocol of 1953)
60 LNTS 253 as amended by 182 UNTS 51

This Convention was adopted on 25 September 1926 and entered into force on 9 March 1927; the Protocol was adopted on 23 October 1953 and entered into force on 7 July 1955.

There are 95 parties, including China, France, Germany, the UK, and the USA.

There were a number of international instruments to suppress the slave trade in the 19th century, the most significant of which was Chapter 2 of the General Act of the Congo Conference, concluded at Berlin on 26 February 1885 (165 CTS 485). The Treaty of Saint-Germain-en-Lay of 10 September 1919 (8 LNTS 26) prohibited, as between the parties, slavery and the slave trade. The Slavery Convention was concluded under the auspices of the League of Nations and was intended to suppress the slave trade and bring about the progressive suppression of slavery on a global basis (Article 2). The 1953 Protocol substituted the United Nations and its organs for the League of Nations and its organs in the 1926 Convention (see Articles 7 and 8). The Supplementary Convention on the Abolition of Slavery, the Slave Trade, and Institutions and Practices Similar to Slavery of 7 September 1956 (266 UNTS 3) extended the ambit of the 1926 Convention to situations akin to slavery, eg debt bondage and serfdom. Slavery is prohibited by Article 4 of the Universal Declaration of Human Rights of 1948 (GA Res 217(III)) and by Article 8 of the International Covenant on Civil and Political Rights of 1966 (999 UNTS 171). 'Enslavement' is included among the crimes against humanity subject to the jurisdiction of the International Criminal Court (see Article 7(1)(c)) of the ICC Statute (Document 53). It is generally accepted that the prohibition of slavery is jus cogens, a fundamental principle of international law from which no derogation is possible.

Under the Slavery Convention, and, within the limits of their jurisdiction, parties are required to take steps to prevent and suppress the slave trade (Article 2(a)) and, to that end, to adopt the necessary measures in respect of their territory and vessels (Article 3), such measures mandating severe penalties for their breach (Article 6).

See also Article 99 of the UN Convention on the Law of the Sea 1982 (Document 36) and the Protocol on Trafficking in Persons, especially Women and Children 2000 (Document 41).

See UN Secretary-General, The Suppression of Slavery (1951 and 1954).

Whereas the signatories of the General Act of the Brussels Conference of 1889–90 declared that they were equally animated by the firm intention of putting an end to the traffic in African slaves,

Whereas the signatories of the Convention of Saint-Germain-en-Laye of 1919, to revise the General Act of Berlin of 1885 and the General Act and Declaration of Brussels of 1890, affirmed their intention of securing the complete suppression of slavery in all its forms and of the slave trade by land and sea,

Taking into consideration the report of the Temporary Slavery Commission appointed by the Council of the League of Nations on June 12th, 1924,

Desiring to complete and extend the work accomplished under the Brussels Act and to find a means of giving practical effect throughout the world to such intentions as were expressed in regard to slave trade and slavery by the signatories of the Convention of Saint-Germain-en-Laye, and recognising that it is necessary to conclude to that end more detailed arrangements than are contained in that Convention,

Considering, moreover, that it is necessary to prevent forced labour from developing into conditions analogous to slavery, have decided to conclude a Convention and have accordingly appointed as their Plenipotentiaries [names omitted],

Have agreed as follows:

Article 1

For the purpose of the present Convention, the following definitions are agreed upon:

(1)   Slavery is the status or condition of a person over whom any or all of the powers attaching to the right of ownership are exercised.

(2)   The slave trade includes all acts involved in the capture, acquisition or disposal of a person with intent to reduce him to slavery; all acts involved in the acquisition of a slave with a view to selling or exchanging him; all acts of disposal by sale or exchange of a slave acquired with a view to being sold or exchanged, and, in general, every act of trade or transport in slaves.

Article 2

The High Contracting Parties undertake, each in respect of the territories placed under its sovereignty, jurisdiction, protection, suzerainty or tutelage, so far as they have not already taken the necessary steps:

(a)   To prevent and suppress the slave trade;

(b)   To bring about, progressively and as soon as possible, the complete abolition of slavery in all its forms.

Article 3

The High Contracting Parties undertake to adopt all appropriate measures with a view to preventing and suppressing the embarkation, disembarkation and transport of slaves in their territorial waters and upon all vessels flying their respective flags.

The High Contracting Parties undertake to negotiate as soon as possible a general Convention with regard to the slave trade which will give them rights and impose upon them duties of the same nature as those provided for in the Convention of June 17th, 1925, relative to the International Trade in Arms (Articles 12, 20, 21, 22, 23, 24 and paragraphs 3, 4 and 5 of Section II of Annex II), with the necessary adaptations, it being understood that this general Convention will not place the ships (even of small tonnage) of any High Contracting Parties in a position different from that of the other High Contracting Parties.

It is also understood that, before or after the coming into force of this general Convention, the High Contracting Parties are entirely free to conclude between themselves, without, however, derogating from the principles laid down in the preceding paragraph, such special agreements as, by reason of their peculiar situation, might appear to be suitable in order to bring about as soon as possible the complete disappearance of the slave trade.

Article 4

The High Contracting Parties shall give to one another every assistance with the object of securing the abolition of slavery and the slave trade.

Article 5

The High Contracting Parties recognise that recourse to compulsory or forced labour may have grave consequences and undertake, each in respect of the territories placed under its sovereignty, jurisdiction, protection, suzerainty or tutelage, to take all necessary measures to prevent compulsory or forced labour from developing into conditions analogous to slavery.

It is agreed that:

(1)   Subject to the transitional provisions laid down in paragraph (2) below, compulsory or forced labour may only be exacted for public purposes.

(2)   In territories in which compulsory or forced labour for other than public purposes still survives, the High Contracting Parties shall endeavour progressively and as soon as possible to put an end to the practice. So long as such forced or compulsory labour exists, this labour shall invariably be of an exceptional character, shall always receive adequate remuneration, and shall not involve the removal of the labourers from their usual place of residence.

(3)   In all cases, the responsibility for any recourse to compulsory or forced labour shall rest with the competent central authorities of the territory concerned.

Article 6

Those of the High Contracting Parties whose laws do not at present make adequate provision for the punishment of infractions of laws and regulations enacted with a view to giving effect to the purposes of the present Convention undertake to adopt the necessary measures in order that severe penalties may be imposed in respect of such infractions.

Article 7

The High Contracting Parties undertake to communicate to each other and to the Secretary-General of the United Nations any laws and regulations which they may enact with a view to the application of the provisions of the present Convention.

Article 8

The High Contracting Parties agree that disputes arising between them relating to the interpretation or application of this Convention shall, if they cannot be settled by direct negotiation, be referred for decision to the International Court of Justice. In case either or both of the States Parties to such a dispute should not be Parties to the Protocol of December 16th, 1920, relating to the Permanent Court of International Justice, the dispute shall be referred, at the choice of the Parties and in accordance with the constitutional procedure of each State, either to the International Court of Justice or to a court of arbitration constituted in accordance with the Convention of October 18th, 1907, for the Pacific Settlement of International Disputes, or to some other court of arbitration.

DOCUMENT 8

Convention for the Prevention and Punishment of the Crime of Genocide 1948
78 UNTS 277; 45 AJIL (Supp) 7 (1951)

The Convention was adopted on 9 December 1948 as an annex to General Assembly Resolution 260(III) and entered into force on 12 January 1951.

There are 133 parties, including all the major powers.

While the practice of genocide predated Nazi Germany, it was the scale of the genocide during that era that prompted international action. On 11 December 1946, the UN General

Assembly of adopted Resolution 96 (I) which affirmed that genocide was a crime under international law and called for an international convention. A draft Convention was first prepared by the Secretary-General in 1947. After consideration of the first draft, a UN Ad Hoc Committee on Genocide prepared a second draft. This draft was presented to the General Assembly in 1948 and was adopted as an annex to Resolution 260(III). While not mentioned by name, genocide is clearly contrary to Article 3 of the Universal Declaration of Human Rights of 1948 (GA Res 217(III)) and Article 6 of the International Covenant on Civil and Political Rights of 1966 (999 UNTS 171). Genocide is one of the four major limbs of jurisdiction of the International Criminal Court (see Articles 5(1)(a) and 6 of the ICC Statute **(Document 53))**. *It is generally accepted that the prohibition of genocide is jus cogens, a fundamental principle of international law from which no derogation is possible.*

The Genocide Convention defines the crime of genocide (Article II) and associated acts (Article III). Parties are required to enact legislation to criminalise genocide and to subject those convicted of genocide to effective penalties (Article V). Such persons are to be prosecuted in the courts of the state in whose territory the genocide was committed or by an international penal tribunal (Article VI). In fact, there was no universal international penal tribunal until the creation of the International Criminal Court in 1998 **(see Document 53)**. *The Convention provides that there is to be no impunity for constitutionally appointed rulers or public officials (Article IV); and that genocide is not to be considered a political crime so as to exclude extradition (Article VII).*

The Contracting Parties,

Having considered the declaration made by the General Assembly of the United Nations in its resolution 96 (I) dated 11 December 1946 that genocide is a crime under international law, contrary to the spirit and aims of the United Nations and condemned by the civilized world,

Recognizing that at all periods of history genocide has inflicted great losses on humanity, and

Being convinced that, in order to liberate mankind from such an odious scourge, international co-operation is required,

Hereby agree as hereinafter provided:

Article I
The Contracting Parties confirm that genocide, whether committed in time of peace or in time of war, is a crime under international law which they undertake to prevent and to punish.

Article II
In the present Convention, genocide means any of the following acts committed with intent to destroy, in whole or in part, a national, ethnical, racial or religious group, as such:

(a)   Killing members of the group;

(b)   Causing serious bodily or mental harm to members of the group;

(c)   Deliberately inflicting on the group conditions of life calculated to bring about its physical destruction in whole or in part;

(d)   Imposing measures intended to prevent births within the group;

(e)   Forcibly transferring children of the group to another group.

Article III
The following acts shall be punishable:

(a)   Genocide;

(b)   Conspiracy to commit genocide;

(c)   Direct and public incitement to commit genocide;

(d)   Attempt to commit genocide;

(e)   Complicity in genocide.

Article IV

Persons committing genocide or any of the other acts enumerated in article III shall be punished, whether they are constitutionally responsible rulers, public officials or private individuals.

Article V

The Contracting Parties undertake to enact, in accordance with their respective Constitutions, the necessary legislation to give effect to the provisions of the present Convention, and, in particular, to provide effective penalties for persons guilty of genocide or any of the other acts enumerated in article III.

Article VI

Persons charged with genocide or any of the other acts enumerated in article III shall be tried by a competent tribunal of the State in the territory of which the act was committed, or by such international penal tribunal as may have jurisdiction with respect to those Contracting Parties which shall have accepted its jurisdiction.

Article VII

Genocide and the other acts enumerated in article III shall not be considered as political crimes for the purpose of extradition. The Contracting Parties pledge themselves in such cases to grant extradition in accordance with their laws and treaties in force.

Article VIII

Any Contracting Party may call upon the competent organs of the United Nations to take such action under the Charter of the United Nations as they consider appropriate for the prevention and suppression of acts of genocide or any of the other acts enumerated in article III.

Article IX

Disputes between the Contracting Parties relating to the interpretation, application or fulfilment of the present Convention, including those relating to the responsibility of a State for genocide or for any of the other acts enumerated in article III, shall be submitted to the International Court of Justice at the request of any of the parties to the dispute.

DOCUMENT 9

International Convention on the Suppression and Punishment of the Crime of Apartheid 1973
1015 UNTS 243; 13 ILM 51 (1974)

The Convention was adopted on 30 November 1973 as an annex to General Assembly Resolution 3668 (XXVIII) and entered into force on 18 July 1976.

There are 101 parties to the Convention. Among the notable non-parties are France, Germany, South Africa, the UK and the USA.

The term 'apartheid' comes from the Afrikaans name for the policy of racial segregation pursued by the minority South African government from the late 1940s until 1994. The first international instrument to name and condemn it was Article 3 of the International Convention on the Elimination of All Forms of Racial Discrimination of 21 December 1965 (660 UNTS 195). The moves to elaborate a dedicated apartheid convention were opposed by some states, essentially on the ground that the subject was already adequately addressed in the Racial Discrimination Convention. Being such a systematic and gross form of racial discrimination, and racial discrimination being a core human right, apartheid is a crime against humanity, and it is recognised as such by Article 7(1)(j) of the Statute of the International Criminal Court of 1998 **(Document 53)**.

For the purposes of the Convention, the crime of apartheid is defined in Article II in the specific context of the 'policies and practices of racial segregation and discrimination practiced in Southern Africa'. International criminal responsibility attaches to any individual who commits, participates in or directly incites, conspires in or abets the proscribed acts (Article III). The Convention requires States to establish jurisdiction in respect of these proscribed acts and to prosecute alleged offenders (Article IV(b)), but contains no provisions on extradition beyond the statement that the proscribed acts are not to be considered as political offences (Article XI). The Convention allows for the possibility of prosecution before an 'international penal tribunal' (Article V), although none such existed before the creation of the International Criminal Court. This Convention may now be largely of historical interest, as its clear focus was on apartheid as practised in South Africa and as, according to the UN High Commissioner for Human Rights in 1995, apartheid in South Africa is at an end (UN Doc E/CN.4/1995/176).

See also the International Convention against Apartheid in Sports of 10 December 1985 (1500 UNTS 161).

The States Parties to the present Convention,

Recalling the provisions of the Charter of the United Nations, in which all Members pledged themselves to take joint and separate action in co-operation with the Organization for the achievement of universal respect for, and observance of, human rights and fundamental freedoms for all without distinction as to race, sex, language or religion,

Considering the Universal Declaration of Human Rights, which states that all human beings are born free and equal in dignity and rights and that everyone is entitled to all the rights and freedoms set forth in the Declaration, without distinction of any kind, such as race, colour or national origin,

Considering the Declaration on the Granting of Independence to Colonial Countries and Peoples, in which the General Assembly stated that the process of liberation is irresistible and irreversible and that, in the interests of human dignity, progress and justice, an end must be put to colonialism and all practices of segregation and discrimination associated therewith,

Observing that, in accordance with the International Convention on the Elimination of All Forms of Racial Discrimination, States particularly condemn racial segregation and apartheid and undertake to prevent, prohibit and eradicate all practices of this nature in territories under their jurisdiction,

Observing that, in the Convention on the Prevention and Punishment of the Crime of Genocide, certain acts which may also be qualified as acts of apartheid constitute a crime under international law,

Observing that, in the Convention on the Non-Applicability of Statutory Limitations to War Crimes and Crimes against Humanity, "inhuman acts resulting from the policy of apartheid" are qualified as crimes against humanity,

Observing that the General Assembly of the United Nations has adopted a number of resolutions in which the policies and practices of apartheid are condemned as a crime against humanity,

Observing that the Security Council has emphasized that apartheid and its continued intensification and expansion seriously disturb and threaten international peace and security,

Convinced that an International Convention on the Suppression and Punishment of the Crime of Apartheid would make it possible to take more effective measures at the international and national levels with a view to the suppression and punishment of the crime of apartheid,

Have agreed as follows:

Article I

1. The States Parties to the present Convention declare that apartheid is a crime against humanity and that inhuman acts resulting from the policies and practices of apartheid and similar policies and practices of racial segregation and discrimination, as defined in article II of the Convention, are crimes violating the principles of international law, in particular the purposes and principles of the Charter of the United Nations, and constituting a serious threat to international peace and security.

2. The States Parties to the present Convention declare criminal those organizations, institutions and individuals committing the crime of apartheid.

Article II

For the purpose of the present Convention, the term "the crime of apartheid", which shall include similar policies and practices of racial segregation and discrimination as practised in southern Africa, shall apply to the following inhuman acts committed for the purpose of establishing and maintaining domination by one racial group of persons over any other racial group of persons and systematically oppressing them:

(a) Denial to a member or members of a racial group or groups of the right to life and liberty of person:

    (i) By murder of members of a racial group or groups;

    (ii) By the infliction upon the members of a racial group or groups of serious bodily or mental harm, by the infringement of their freedom or dignity, or by subjecting them to torture or to cruel, inhuman or degrading treatment or punishment;

    (iii) By arbitrary arrest and illegal imprisonment of the members of a racial group or groups;

(b) Deliberate imposition on a racial group or groups of living conditions calculated to cause its or their physical destruction in whole or in part;

(c) Any legislative measures and other measures calculated to prevent a racial group or groups from participation in the political, social, economic and cultural life of the country and the deliberate creation of conditions preventing the full development of such a group or groups, in particular by denying to members of a racial group or groups basic human rights and freedoms, including the right to work, the right to form recognized trade unions, the right to education, the right to leave and to return to their country, the right to a nationality, the right to freedom of movement and residence, the right to freedom of opinion and expression, and the right to freedom of peaceful assembly and association;

(d) Any measures, including legislative measures, designed to divide the population along racial lines by the creation of separate reserves and ghettos for the members of a racial group or groups, the prohibition of mixed marriages among members of various racial groups, the expropriation of landed property belonging to a racial group or groups or to members thereof;

(e) Exploitation of the labour of the members of a racial group or groups, in particular by submitting them to forced labour;

(f) Persecution of organizations and persons, by depriving them of fundamental rights and freedoms, because they oppose apartheid.

Article III

International criminal responsibility shall apply, irrespective of the motive involved, to individuals, members of organizations and institutions and representatives of the State, whether residing in the territory of the State in which the acts are perpetrated or in some other State, whenever they:

(a) Commit, participate in, directly incite or conspire in the commission of the acts mentioned in article II of the present Convention;

(b) Directly abet, encourage or co-operate in the commission of the crime of apartheid.

Article IV

The States Parties to the present Convention undertake:

(a) To adopt any legislative or other measures necessary to suppress as well as to prevent any encouragement of the crime of apartheid and similar segregationist policies or their manifestations and to punish persons guilty of that crime;

(b) To adopt legislative, judicial and administrative measures to prosecute, bring to trial and punish in accordance with their jurisdiction persons responsible for, or accused of, the acts defined in article II of the present Convention, whether or not such persons reside in the territory of the State in which the acts are committed or are nationals of that State or of some other State or are stateless persons.

Article V

Persons charged with the acts enumerated in article II of the present Convention may be tried by a competent tribunal of any State Party to the Convention which may acquire jurisdiction over the person of the accused or by an international penal tribunal having jurisdiction with respect to those States Parties which shall have accepted its jurisdiction.

Article XI

1. Acts enumerated in article II of the present Convention shall not be considered political crimes for the purpose of extradition.

2. The States Parties to the present Convention undertake in such cases to grant extradition in accordance with their legislation and with the treaties in force.

DOCUMENT 10

Convention against Torture and Other Cruel, Inhuman and Degrading Treatment and Punishment 1984
1465 UNTS 85; 23 ILM 1027 (1984)

The Convention was adopted on 10 December 1984 as an annex to UN General Assembly Resolution 39/46 and entered into force on 26 June 1987.

There are 137 parties, including all the major powers.

The prohibition on torture had found expression in international law some time before the 1984 Convention was adopted. Article 5 of the Universal Declaration on Human Rights of 1948 (GA Res 217(III)) and Article 7 of the International Covenant on Civil and Political Rights of 1966 (999 UNTS 171) expressly prohibit torture or 'cruel, inhuman or degrading treatment or punishment'. Common Article 3 to the four Geneva Conventions of 1949

(Documents 1–4) *prohibits parties from perpetrating violent acts, including 'mutilation, cruel treatment and torture'. The Torture Convention was preceded by a General Assembly Declaration on Protection from Torture of 9 December 1975 (GA Res 3452 (XXX)). Torture is a crime against humanity, as evidenced further by its inclusion among the crimes against humanity enumerated in the Statute of the International Criminal Court (Article 7(1)(f))* **(Document 53)**. *The prohibition on torture is jus cogens, a principle of international law from which no derogation is possible.*

Torture as defined in Article 1 of the Convention is to be prevented by each State party 'in any territory under its jurisdiction' (Article 2(1)). No exceptional circumstances whatsoever can be invoked to justify torture (Article 2(2)). Nor can superior orders be invoked to justify torture (Article 2(3)). Each state party is obliged to ensure that torture is criminalised under its domestic law and punishable by appropriate penalties (Article 4). Each party is also obliged to establish its jurisdiction over acts of torture for offences committed in its territory or on its ships, by its nationals and (if the party wishes) against its nationals (Article 5(1)). A party with custody of an alleged offender must either extradite that person or report that person to its competent authorities for prosecution – the aut dedere aut judicare *principle (Article 7(1)). For the purposes of extradition, the Convention provides that torture is to be deemed within existing extradition treaties and is to be added to future extradition treaties (Article 8(1)). The Convention itself may be used as a conventional basis for extradition (Article 8(2)) and torture is to be considered committed in the territories of all parties with jurisdiction under Article 5(1)) (Article 8(4)). No State may extradite or otherwise return a person to any State where that person might be tortured (Article 3(1)). There is no provision excluding the political offence exception to extradition. There is, however, an obligation on all parties to afford one another the greatest measures of assistance in criminal proceedings (Article 9(1)).*

See also the European Convention for the Prevention of Torture 1987 (ETS No 126); Inter-American Convention to Prevent and Punish Torture 1985 (OASTS No 67).

The States Parties to this Convention,

Considering that, in accordance with the principles proclaimed in the Charter of the United Nations, recognition of the equal and inalienable rights of all members of the human family is the foundation of freedom, justice and peace in the world,

Recognizing that those rights derive from the inherent dignity of the human person,

Considering the obligation of States under the Charter, in particular Article 55, to promote universal respect for, and observance of, human rights and fundamental freedoms,

Having regard to article 5 of the Universal Declaration of Human Rights and article 7 of the International Covenant on Civil and Political Rights, both of which provide that no one may be subjected to torture or to cruel, inhuman or degrading treatment or punishment,

Having regard also to the Declaration on the Protection of All Persons from Being Subjected to Torture and Other Cruel, Inhuman or Degrading Treatment or Punishment, adopted by the General Assembly on 9 December 1975 (resolution 3452 (XXX)),

Desiring to make more effective the struggle against torture and other cruel, inhuman or degrading treatment or punishment throughout the world,

Have agreed as follows:

Article 1

1. For the purposes of this Convention, torture means any act by which severe pain or suffering, whether physical or mental, is intentionally inflicted on a person for such purposes as obtaining

from him or a third person information or a confession, punishing him for an act he or a third person has committed or is suspected of having committed, or intimidating or coercing him or a third person, or for any reason based on discrimination of any kind, when such pain or suffering is inflicted by or at the instigation of or with the consent or acquiescence of a public official or other person acting in an official capacity. It does not include pain or suffering arising only from, inherent in or incidental to lawful sanctions.

2. This article is without prejudice to any international instrument or national legislation which does or may contain provisions of wider application.

Article 2

1. Each State Party shall take effective legislative, administrative, judicial or other measures to prevent acts of torture in any territory under its jurisdiction.

2. No exceptional circumstances whatsoever, whether a state of war or a threat or war, internal political instability or any other public emergency, may be invoked as a justification of torture.

   An order from a superior officer or a public authority may not be invoked as a justification of torture.

Article 3

1. No State Party shall expel, return ("refouler") or extradite a person to another State where there are substantial grounds for believing that he would be in danger of being subjected to torture.

2. For the purpose of determining whether there are such grounds, the competent authorities shall take into account all relevant considerations including, where applicable, the existence in the State concerned of a consistent pattern of gross, flagrant or mass violations of human rights.

Article 4

1. Each State Party shall ensure that all acts of torture are offences under its criminal law. The same shall apply to an attempt to commit torture and to an act by any person which constitutes complicity or participation in torture.

2. Each State Party shall make these offences punishable by appropriate penalties which take into account their grave nature.

Article 5

1. Each State Party shall take such measures as may be necessary to establish its jurisdiction over the offences referred to in article 4 in the following cases:

   (a) When the offences are committed in any territory under its jurisdiction or on board a ship or aircraft registered in that State;

   (b) When the alleged offender is a national of that State;

   (c) When the victim was a national of that State if that State considers it appropriate.

2. Each State Party shall likewise take such measures as may be necessary to establish its jurisdiction over such offences in cases where the alleged offender is present in any territory under its jurisdiction and it does not extradite him pursuant to article 8 to any of the States mentioned in Paragraph 1 of this article.

3. This Convention does not exclude any criminal jurisdiction exercised in accordance with internal law.

Article 6

1. Upon being satisfied, after an examination of information available to it, that the circumstances so warrant, any State Party in whose territory a person alleged to have committed any offence referred to in article 4 is present, shall take him into custody or take other legal measures to

ensure his presence. The custody and other legal measures shall be as provided in the law of that State but may be continued only for such time as is necessary to enable any criminal or extradition proceedings to be instituted.

2.   Such State shall immediately make a preliminary inquiry into the facts.

3.   Any person in custody pursuant to paragraph 1 of this article shall be assisted in communicating immediately with the nearest appropriate representative of the State of which he is a national, or, if he is a stateless person, to the representative of the State where he usually resides.

4.   When a State, pursuant to this article, has taken a person into custody, it shall immediately notify the States referred to in article 5, paragraph 1, of the fact that such person is in custody and of the circumstances which warrant his detention. The State which makes the preliminary inquiry contemplated in paragraph 2 of this article shall promptly report its findings to the said State and shall indicate whether it intends to exercise jurisdiction.

Article 7

1.   The State Party in territory under whose jurisdiction a person alleged to have committed any offence referred to in article 4 is found, shall in the cases contemplated in article 5, if it does not extradite him, submit the case to its competent authorities for the purpose of prosecution.

2.   These authorities shall take their decision in the same manner as in the case of any ordinary offence of a serious nature under the law of that State. In the cases referred to in article 5, paragraph 2, the standards of evidence required for prosecution and conviction shall in no way be less stringent than those which apply in the cases referred to in article 5, paragraph 1.

3.   Any person regarding whom proceedings are brought in connection with any of the offences referred to in article 4 shall be guaranteed fair treatment at all stages of the proceedings.

Article 8

1.   The offences referred to in article 4 shall be deemed to be included as extraditable offences in any extradition treaty existing between States Parties. States Parties undertake to include such offences as extraditable offences in every extradition treaty to be concluded between them.

2.   If a State Party which makes extradition conditional on the existence of a treaty receives a request for extradition from another State Party with which it has no extradition treaty, it may consider this Convention as the legal basis for extradition in respect of such offenses. Extradition shall be subject to the other conditions provided by the law of the requested State.

3.   States Parties which do not make extradition conditional on the existence of a treaty shall recognize such offences as extraditable offences between themselves subject to the conditions provided by the law of the requested state.

4.   Such offences shall be treated, for the purpose of extradition between States Parties, as if they had been committed not only in the place in which they occurred but also in the territories of the States required to establish their jurisdiction in accordance with article 5, paragraph 1.

Article 9

1.   States Parties shall afford one another the greatest measure of assistance in connection with civil proceedings brought in respect of any of the offences referred to in article 4, including the supply of all evidence at their disposal necessary for the proceedings.

2.   States Parties shall carry out their obligations under paragraph 1 of this article in conformity with any treaties on mutual judicial assistance that may exist between them.

Article 10

1.   Each State Party shall ensure that education and information regarding the prohibition against torture are fully included in the training of law enforcement personnel, civil or military, medical

personnel, public officials and other persons who may be involved in the custody, interrogation or treatment of any individual subjected to any form of arrest, detention or imprisonment.

2. Each State Party shall include this prohibition in the rules or instructions issued in regard to the duties and functions of any such persons.

Article 11

Each State Party shall keep under systematic review interrogation rules, instructions, methods and practices as well as arrangements for the custody and treatment of persons subjected to any form of arrest, detention or imprisonment in any territory under its jurisdiction, with a view to preventing any cases of torture.

Article 12

Each State Party shall ensure that its competent authorities proceed to a prompt and impartial investigation, wherever there is reasonable ground to believe that an act of torture has been committee in any territory under its jurisdiction.

Article 13

Each State Party shall ensure that any individual who alleges he has been subjected to torture in any territory under its jurisdiction has the right to complain to and to have his case promptly and impartially examined its competent authorities. Steps shall be taken to ensure that the complainant and witnesses are protected against all ill-treatment or intimidation as a consequence of his complaint or any evidence given.

Article 14

1. Each State Party shall ensure in its legal system that the victim of an act of torture obtains redress and has an enforceable right to fair and adequate compensation including the means for as full rehabilitation as possible. In the event of the death of the victim as a result of an act of torture, his dependents shall be entitled to compensation.

2. Nothing in this article shall affect any right of the victim or other person to compensation which may exist under national law.

Article 15

Each State Party shall ensure that any statement which is established to have been made as a result of torture shall not be invoked as evidence in any proceedings, except against a person accused of torture as evidence that the statement was made.

Article 16

1. Each State Party shall undertake to prevent in any territory under its jurisdiction other acts of cruel, inhuman or degrading treatment or punishment which do not amount to torture as defined in article 1, when such acts are committed by or at the instigation of or with the consent or acquiescence of a public official or other person acting in an official capacity. In particular, the obligations contained in articles 10, 11, 12 and 13 shall apply with the substitution for references to torture or references to other forms of cruel, inhuman or degrading treatment or punishment.

2. The provisions of this Convention are without prejudice to the provisions of any other international instrument or national law which prohibit cruel, inhuman or degrading treatment or punishment or which relate to extradition or expulsion.

TERRORISM

DOCUMENT 11

Tokyo Convention on Offences and Certain Other Acts Committed on Board Aircraft 1963
704 UNTS 171; 2 ILM 1042 (1963)

This Convention was concluded under the auspices of the International Civil Aviation Organization at Tokyo on 14 September 1963 and came into force on 4 December 1969.

There are 178 parties, including all the major powers.

Against a background of increasing acts committed against the safety of civil aviation, including hijackings, and doubt as to jurisdictional competences arising from such acts, the Tokyo Convention was adopted to settle the jurisdictional issues and has come to be regarded as the first terrorism (or counter-terrorism) convention. It applies to offences and 'acts which, whether or not they are offences, may or do jeopardize the safety of the aircraft or of persons or property therein or which jeopardize good order and discipline on board' (Article 1(1)). Jurisdiction is vested in the State of registration of the aircraft (Article 3(1)), as well as a State party in whose territory the offence has effect, whose nationals and permanent residents are either the culprits or victims, against whose security the offence is committed, whose flight rules or regulations are breached, or whose multilateral international obligations require action (Article 4). For the purposes of extradition, the offence is to be treated as committed, not only where it occurred, but also in the State of registration (Article 16(1)), although the Convention, unlike its successors, imposes no obligation to extradite (Article 16(2)).

See also the other global terrorism conventions (**Documents 12, 15–17, 20–26 and 28**).

The States Parties to this Convention,

Have agreed as follows:

Chapter 1: Scope of the Convention

Article 1
1. This Convention shall apply in respect of:

    (a) offences against penal law;

    (b) acts which, whether or not they are offences, may or do jeopardize the safety of the aircraft or of persons or property therein or which jeopardize good order and discipline on board.

2. Except as provided in Chapter III, this Convention shall apply in respect of offences committed or acts done by a person on board any aircraft registered in a Contracting State, while that aircraft is in flight or on the surface of the high seas or of any other area outside the territory of any State.

3. For the purposes of this Convention, an aircraft is considered to be in flight from the moment when power is applied for the purpose of take-off until the moment when the landing run ends.

4. This Convention shall not apply to aircraft used in military, customs or police services.

Article 2

Without prejudice to the provisions of Article 4 and except when the safety of the aircraft or of persons or property on board so requires, no provision of this Convention shall be interpreted as authorizing or requiring any action in respect of offences against penal laws of a political nature or those based on racial or religious discrimination.

Article 3

1. The State of registration of the aircraft is competent to exercise jurisdiction over offences and acts committed on board.

2. Each Contracting State shall take such measures as may be necessary to establish its jurisdiction as the State of registration over offences committed on board aircraft registered in such State.

3. This Convention does not exclude any criminal jurisdiction exercised in accordance with national law.

Article 4

A Contracting State which is not the State of registration may not interfere with an aircraft in flight in order to exercise its criminal jurisdiction over an offence committed on board except in the following cases:

(a) the offence has effect on the territory of such State;

(b) the offence has been committed by or against a national or permanent resident of such State;

(c) the offence is against the security of such State;

(d) the offence consists of a breach of any rules or regulations relating to the flight or manoeuvre of aircraft in force in such State;

(e) the exercise of jurisdiction is necessary to ensure the observance of any obligation of such State under a multilateral international agreement.

Article 12

Any Contracting State shall allow the commander of an aircraft registered in another Contracting State to disembark any person pursuant to Article 8, paragraph 1.

Article 13

1. Any Contracting State shall take delivery of any person whom the aircraft commander delivers pursuant to Article 9, paragraph 1.

2. Upon being satisfied that the circumstances so warrant, any Contracting State shall take custody or other measures to ensure the presence of any person suspected of an act contemplated in Article 11, paragraph 1 and of any person of whom it has taken delivery. The custody and other measures shall be as provided in the law of that State but may only be continued for such time as is reasonably necessary to enable any criminal or extradition proceedings to be instituted.

3. Any person in custody pursuant to the previous paragraph shall be assisted in communicating immediately with the nearest appropriate representative of the State of which he is a national.

4. Any Contracting State, to which a person is delivered pursuant to Article 9, paragraph 1, or in whose territory an aircraft lands following the commission of an act contemplated in Article 11, paragraph 1, shall immediately make a preliminary enquiry into the facts.

5. When a State, pursuant to this Article, has taken a person into custody, it shall immediately notify the State of registration of the aircraft and the State of nationality of the detained person and, if it considers it advisable, any other interested State of the fact that such person is in custody and of the circumstances which warrant his detention. The State which makes the preliminary enquiry contemplated in paragraph 4 of this Article shall promptly report its findings to the said States and shall indicate whether it intends to exercise jurisdiction.

Article 14

1. When any person has been disembarked in accordance with Article 8, paragraph 1, or delivered in accordance with Article 9, paragraph 1, or has disembarked after committing an act contemplated in Article 11, paragraph 1, and when such person cannot or does not desire to continue his journey and the State of landing refuses to admit him, that State may, if the person in question is not a national or permanent resident of that State, return him to the territory of the State of which he is a national or permanent resident or to the territory of the State in which he began his journey by air.

2. Neither disembarkation, nor delivery, nor the taking of custody or other measures contemplated in Article 13, paragraph 2, nor return of the person concerned, shall be considered as admission to the territory of the Contracting State concerned for the purpose of its law relating to entry or admission of persons and nothing in this Convention shall affect the law of a Contracting State relating to the expulsion of persons from its territory.

Article 15

1. Without prejudice to Article 14, any person who has been disembarked in accordance with Article 8, paragraph 1, or delivered in accordance with Article 9, paragraph 1, or has disembarked after committing an act contemplated in Article 11, paragraph 1, and who desires to continue his journey shall be at liberty as soon as practicable to proceed to any destination of his choice unless his presence is required by the law of the State of landing for the purpose of extradition or criminal proceedings.

2. Without prejudice to its law as to entry and admission to, and extradition and expulsion from its territory, a Contracting State in whose territory a person has been disembarked in accordance with Article 8, paragraph 1, or delivered in accordance with Article 9, paragraph 1 or has disembarked and is suspected of having committed an act contemplated in Article 11, paragraph 1, shall accord to such person treatment which is no less favourable for his protection and security than that accorded to nationals of such Contracting State in like circumstances.

Article 16

1. Offences committed on aircraft registered in a Contracting State shall be treated, for the purpose of extradition, as if they had been committed not only in the place in which they have occurred but also in the territory of the State of registration of the aircraft.

2. Without prejudice to the provisions of the preceding paragraph, nothing in this Convention shall be deemed to create an obligation to grant extradition.

Article 17

In taking any measures for investigation or arrest or otherwise exercising jurisdiction in connection with any offence committed on board an aircraft the Contracting States shall pay due regard to the safety and other interests of air navigation and shall so act as to avoid unnecessary delay of the aircraft, passengers, crew or cargo.

Article 18

If Contracting States establish joint air transport operating organizations or international operating agencies, which operate aircraft not registered in any one State those States shall, according to the circumstances of the case, designate the State among them which, for the purposes of this Convention, shall be considered as the State of registration and shall give notice thereof to the International Civil Aviation Organization which shall communicate the notice to all States Parties to this Convention.

DOCUMENT 12

Hague Convention for the Suppression of Unlawful Seizure of Aircraft 1970
860 UNTS 105; 10 ILM 133 (1971)

This Convention was concluded under the auspices of the International Civil Aviation Organization (ICAO) at The Hague, the Netherlands, on 16 December 1970 and came into force on 14 October 1971.

There are 177 parties, including all the major powers.

Aircraft hijackings became increasingly prevalent as a political statement and/or a bargaining counter in the 1960s, with a total of 27 hijackings worldwide in 1968 and 832 in 1969. As a response, ICAO, recognising the deficiencies of the Tokyo Convention on Offences and Certain Other Acts Committed on Board Aircraft of 14 September 1963 (**Document 11**)*, adopted the Hague Convention to deter such acts and to provide for the punishment of offenders (preamble).*

The Convention requires the Contracting States to criminalise specified acts set out in Article 1 and make them 'punishable by severe penalties' (Article 2). Each Contracting State has jurisdiction, inter alia*, where one of the Convention's offences is committed in its territory, against or on board an aircraft registered in that State, or where the aircraft lands in its territory (Article 4(1) and (2)). Each Contracting State is required to report an offender to its prosecution authorities or to extradite him (Article 7) – the* aut dedere aut judicare *principle. The Convention declares the specified offences to be extraditable offences under existing extradition treaties and to be included in future extradition treaties (Article 8(1)); if there is no extradition treaty, the Convention itself may be treated as such (Article 8(2)). The parties are obliged to afford one another the greatest measure of assistance in criminal proceedings (Article 10)).*

See also the other global terrorism conventions (**Documents 15–17, 20–26 and 28**)*.*

The States Parties to this Convention,

Considering that unlawful acts of seizure or exercise of control of aircraft in flight jeopardise the safety of persons and property, seriously affect the operation of air services, and undermine the confidence of the peoples of the world in the safety of civil aviation;

Considering that the occurrence of such acts is a matter of grave concern;

Considering that, for the purpose of deterring such acts, there is an urgent need to provide appropriate measures for punishment of offenders;

Have agreed as follows:

Article 1
Any person who on board an aircraft in flight:

(a) unlawfully, by force or threat thereof, or by any other form of intimidation, seizes, or exercises control of, that aircraft, or attempts to perform any such act, or

(b) is an accomplice of a person who performs or attempts to perform any such act commits an offence (hereinafter referred to as "the offence").

Article 2
Each Contracting State undertakes to make the offence punishable by severe penalties.

Article 3

1. For the purposes of this Convention, an aircraft is considered to be in flight at any time from the moment when all its external doors are closed following embarkation until the moment when any such door is opened for disembarkation. In the case of a forced landing, the flight shall be deemed to continue until the competent authorities take over the responsibility for the aircraft and for persons and property on board.

2. This Convention shall not apply to aircraft used in military, customs or police services.

3. This Convention shall apply only if the place of take-off or the place of actual landing of the aircraft on board which the offence is committed is situated outside the territory of the State of registration of that aircraft; it shall be immaterial whether the aircraft is engaged in an international or domestic flight.

4. In the cases mentioned in Article 5, this Convention shall not apply if the place of take-off and the place of actual landing of the aircraft on board which the offence is committed are situated within the territory of the same State where that State is one of those referred to in that Article.

5. Notwithstanding paragraphs 3 and 4 of this Article, Articles 6, 7, 8 and 10 shall apply whatever the place of take-off or the place of actual landing of the aircraft, if the offender or the alleged offender is found in the territory of a State other than the State of registration of that aircraft.

Article 4

1. Each Contracting State shall take such measures as may be necessary to establish its jurisdiction over the offence and any other act of violence against passengers or crew committed by the alleged offender in connection with the offence, in the following cases:

    (a) when the offence is committed on board an aircraft registered in that State;

    (b) when the aircraft on board which the offence is committed lands in its territory with the alleged offender still on board;

    (c) when the offence is committed on board an aircraft leased without crew to a lessee who has his principal place of business or, if the lessee has no such place of business, his permanent residence, in that State.

2. Each Contracting State shall likewise take such measures as may be necessary to establish its jurisdiction over the offence in the case where the alleged offender is present in its territory and it does not extradite him pursuant to Article 8 to any of the States mentioned in paragraph 1 of this Article.

3. This Convention does not exclude any criminal jurisdiction exercised in accordance with national law.

Article 5

The Contracting States which establish joint air transport operating organizations or international operating agencies, which operate aircraft which are subject to joint or international registration shall, by appropriate means, designate for each aircraft the State among them which shall exercise the jurisdiction and have the attributes of the State of registration for the purpose of this Convention and shall give notice thereof to the International Civil Aviation Organization which shall communicate the notice to all States Parties to this Convention.

Article 6

1. Upon being satisfied that the circumstances so warrant, any Contracting State in the territory of which the offender or the alleged offender is present, shall take him into custody or take other measures to ensure his presence. The custody and other measures shall be as provided in the law of that State but may only be continued for such time as is necessary to enable any criminal or extradition proceedings to be instituted.

2. Such State shall immediately make a preliminary enquiry into the facts.

3. Any person in custody pursuant to paragraph 1 of this Article shall be assisted in communicating immediately with the nearest appropriate representative of the State of which he is a national.

4. When a State, pursuant to this Article, has taken a person into custody, it shall immediately notify the State of registration of the aircraft, the State mentioned in Article 4, paragraph 1(c), the State of nationality of the detained person and, if it considers it advisable, any other interested States of the fact that such person is in custody and of the circumstances which warrant his detention. The State which makes the preliminary enquiry contemplated in paragraph 2 of this Article shall promptly report its findings to the said States and shall indicate whether it intends to exercise jurisdiction.

Article 7

The Contracting State in the territory of which the alleged offender is found shall, if it does not extradite him, be obliged, without exception whatsoever and whether or not the offence was committed in its territory, to submit the case to its competent authorities for the purpose of prosecution. Those authorities shall take their decision in the same manner as in the case of any ordinary offence of a serious nature under the law of that State.

Article 8

1. The offence shall be deemed to be included as an extraditable offence in any extradition treaty existing between Contracting States. Contracting States undertake to include the offence as an extraditable offence in every extradition treaty to be concluded between them.

2. If a Contracting State which makes extradition conditional on the existence of a treaty receives a request for extradition from another Contracting State with which it has no extradition treaty, it may at its option consider this Convention as the legal basis for extradition in respect of the offence. Extradition shall be subject to the other conditions provided by the law of the requested State.

3. Contracting States which do not make extradition conditional on the existence of a treaty shall recognize the offence as an extraditable offence between themselves subject to the conditions provided by the law of the requested State. 4. The offence shall be treated, for the purpose of extradition between Contracting States, as if it had been committed not only in the place in which it occurred but also in the territories of the States required to establish their jurisdiction in accordance with Article 4, paragraph 1.

Article 9

1. When any of the acts mentioned in Article 1(a) has occurred or is about to occur, Contracting States shall take all appropriate measures to restore control of the aircraft to its lawful commander or to preserve his control of the aircraft.

2. In the cases contemplated by the preceding paragraph, any Contracting State in which the aircraft or its passengers or crew are present shall facilitate the continuation of the journey of the passengers and crew as soon as practicable, and shall without delay return the aircraft and its cargo to the persons lawfully entitled to possession.

Article 10

1. Contracting States shall afford one another the greatest measure of assistance in connection with criminal proceedings brought in respect of the offence and other acts mentioned in Article 4. The law of the State requested shall apply in all cases.

2. The provisions of paragraph 1 of this Article shall not affect obligations under any other treaty, bilateral or multilateral, which governs or will govern, in whole or in part, mutual assistance in criminal matters.

Article 11

Each Contracting State shall in accordance with its national law report to the Council of the International Civil Aviation Organization as promptly as possible any relevant information in its possession concerning:

(a) the circumstances of the offence;

(b) the action taken pursuant to Article 9;

(c) the measures taken in relation to the offender or the alleged offender, and, in particular, the results of any extradition proceedings or other legal proceedings.

Article 12

1. Any dispute between two or more Contracting States concerning the interpretation or application of this Convention which cannot be settled through negotiations, shall, at the request of one of them, be submitted to arbitration. If within six months from the date of the request for arbitration the Parties are unable to agree on the organization of the arbitration, any one of those Parties may refer the dispute to the International Court of Justice by request in conformity with the Statute of the Court.

2. Each State may at the time of signature or ratification of this Convention or accession thereto, declare that it does not consider itself bound by the preceding paragraph. The other Contracting States shall not be bound by the preceding paragraph with respect to any Contracting State having made such a reservation.

3. Any Contracting State having made a reservation in accordance with the preceding paragraph may at any time withdraw this reservation by notification to the Depositary Governments.

DOCUMENT 13

OAS Convention to Prevent and Punish the Acts of Terrorism taking the Form of Crimes Against Persons and Related Extortion that are of International Significance 1971
OASTS No 37; 10 ILM 255 (1971)

This Convention was concluded under the auspices of the Organization of American States (OAS) at Washington, DC, on 2 February 1971 and came into force on 16 October 1973.

There are 17 parties (from an OAS membership of 34), including Canada but not including the USA.

The initial terrorist concern in the Americas was kidnappings and associated extortions. Even today, Colombia – shortly followed by Mexico, Brazil, Venezuela and Ecuador – has the highest kidnapping rate in the world. The OAS Convention is concerned with kidnappings and extortions that rise above the purely domestic to acts 'against persons entitled to special protection' (preamble, Articles 1–2).

The Convention identifies the proscribed acts, describing them as 'common crimes of international significance, regardless of motive' (Article 2). It adds the proscribed acts to existing extradition treaties (Article 3) and requires their inclusion in future extradition treaties (Article 7). A variant of the aut dedere aut judicare *principle is contained in Article 5. Those to whom the Convention is applied have fair trial guarantees (Article 8(c)). The OAS terrorism régime was expanded with the conclusion of the Inter-American Convention against Terrorism of 3 June 2002* **(Document 14)**.

See also the global terrorism conventions **(Documents 11–12, 15–17, 20–26 and 28)** *and the European terrorism conventions* **(Documents 18–19)**.

Whereas:

The defense of freedom and justice and respect for the fundamental rights of the individual that are recognized by the American Declaration of the Rights and Duties of Man and the Universal Declaration of Human Rights are primary duties of states;

The General Assembly of the Organization, in Resolution 4, of June 30, 1970, strongly condemned acts of terrorism, especially the kidnapping of persons and extortion in connection with that crime, which it declared to be serious common crimes;

Criminal acts against persons entitled to special protection under international law are occurring frequently, and those acts are of international significance because of the consequences that may flow from them for relations among states;

It is advisable to adopt general standards that will progressively develop international law as regards cooperation in the prevention and punishment of such acts; and

In the application of those standards the institution of asylum should be maintained and, likewise the principle of nonintervention should not be impaired,

The Member States of the Organization of American States have agreed upon the following articles:

Article 1

The contracting states undertake to cooperate among themselves by taking all the measures that they may consider effective, under their own laws, and especially those established in this convention, to prevent and punish acts of terrorism, especially kidnapping, murder, and other assaults against the life or physical integrity of those persons to whom the state has the duty according to international law to give special protection, as well as extortion in connection with those crimes.

Article 2

For the purposes of this convention, kidnapping, murder, and other assaults against the life or personal integrity of those persons to whom the state has the duty to give special protection according to international law, as well as extortion in connection with those crimes, shall be considered common crimes of international significance, regardless of motive.

Article 3

Persons who have been charged or convicted for any of the crimes referred to in Article 2 of this convention shall be subject to extradition under the provisions of the extradition treaties in force between the parties or, in the case of states that do not make extradition dependent on the existence of a treaty, in accordance with their own laws.

In any case, it is the exclusive responsibility of the state under whose jurisdiction or protection such persons are located to determine the nature of the acts and decide whether the standards of this convention are applicable.

Article 4

Any person deprived of his freedom through the application of this convention shall enjoy the legal guarantees of due process.

Article 5

When extradition requested for one of the crimes specified in Article 2 is not in order because the person sought is a national of the requested state, or because of some other legal or constitutional impediment, that state is obliged to submit the case to its competent authorities for prosecution, as if the act had been committed in its territory. The decision of these authorities shall be communicated to the state that requested extradition. In such proceedings, the obligation established in Article 4 shall be respected.

Article 6

None of the provisions of this convention shall be interpreted so as to impair the right of asylum.

Article 7

The contracting states undertake to include the crimes referred to in Article 2 of this convention among the punishable acts giving rise to extradition in any treaty on the subject to which they agree among themselves in the future. The contracting states that do not subject extradition to the existence of a treaty with the requesting state shall consider the crimes referred to in Article 2 of this convention as crimes giving rise to extradition, according to the conditions established by the laws of the requested state.

Article 8

To cooperate in preventing and punishing the crimes contemplated in Article 2 of this convention, the contracting states accept the following obligations:

(a) To take all measures within their power, and in conformity with their own laws, to prevent and impede the preparation in their respective territories of the crimes mentioned in Article 2 that are to be carried out in the territory of another contracting state.

(b) To exchange information and consider effective administrative measures for the purpose of protecting the persons to whom Article 2 of this convention refers.

(c) To guarantee to every person deprived of his freedom through the application of this convention every right to defend himself.

(d) To endeavor to have the criminal acts contemplated in this convention included in their penal laws, if not already so included.

(e) To comply most expeditiously with the requests for extradition concerning the criminal acts contemplated in this convention.

DOCUMENT 14

Inter-American Convention Against Terrorism 2002
OASTS No A–66; 42 ILM 19 (2003)

This Convention was concluded under the auspices of the Organization of American States (OAS) at Bridgetown, Barbados, on 3 June 2002 and came into force on 10 July 2003.

There are 12 parties, including Canada and Mexico, but not the USA.

In the aftermath of the 9/11 terrorist attacks on New York and Washington, the OAS adopted a more comprehensive, regional agreement than the OAS Convention of 2 February 1971 **(Document 13)** *and at the same time addressed issues arising from Security Council Resolution 1373 (2001) of 28 September 2001* **(Document 27).**

The Convention adopts as offences all the proscribed acts in the 10 principal, global terrorism conventions **(Documents 12, 14–17, 20–23, 25–26 and 28),** *excluding the Tokyo Convention on Offences and Certain Other Acts Committed on Board Aircraft of 14 September*

1963 **(Document 11)** *and the Convention on the Marking of Explosives for the Purpose of Detection of 1 March 1991* **(Document 24)** *(Article 2). States not already parties to these conventions are exhorted to become parties and to criminalise the offences in their domestic law (Article 3). The Convention enumerates and mandates measures to give effect to the obligations contained first in the International Convention for the Suppression of the Financing of Terrorism of 9 December 1999* **(Document 26)** *and Security Council 1373 (2001) (Articles 4– 6). For the purposes of extradition, the offences set out in Article 2 are not to be regarded as political offences (Article 11). As part of mutual legal assistance (Article 9), provision is made for anyone detained or sentenced in one party to be transferred, with consent, to another party to assist in the investigation or prosecution of terrorist offences (Article 10). The measures taken under the Convention must guarantee full respect for human rights (Article 15(1)), including a fair trial (Article 15(3)).*

See also the European terrorism conventions **(Documents 18–19)**.

The States Parties to this Convention,

Bearing in mind the purposes and principles of the Charter of the Organization of American States and the Charter of the United Nations;

Considering that terrorism represents a serious threat to democratic values and to international peace and security and is a cause of profound concern to all member states;

Reaffirming the need to adopt effective steps in the inter-American system to prevent, punish, and eliminate terrorism through the broadest cooperation;

Recognizing that the serious economic harm to states which may result from terrorist acts is one of the factors that underscore the need for cooperation and the urgency of efforts to eradicate terrorism;

Reaffirming the commitment of the states to prevent, combat, punish, and eliminate terrorism; and

Bearing in mind resolution RC.23/RES I/0I rev I corr I, "Strengthening Hemispheric Cooperation to Prevent, Combat, and Eliminate Terrorism," adopted at the Twenty-third Meeting of Consultation of Ministers of Foreign Affairs,

Have agreed to the following:

Article I Object and purposes
The purposes of this Convention are to prevent, punish, and eliminate terrorism. To that end, the states parties agree to adopt the necessary measures and to strengthen cooperation among them, in accordance with the terms of this Convention.

Article 2 Applicable international instruments
1. For the purposes of this Convention, "offenses" means the offenses established in the international instruments listed below:

    (a) Convention for the Suppression of Unlawful Seizure of Aircraft, signed at The Hague on December 16, 1970.

    (b) Convention for the Suppression of Unlawful Acts against the Safety of Civil Aviation, signed at Montreal on September 23, 1971.

    (c) Convention on the Prevention and Punishment of Crimes against Internationally Protected Persons, including Diplomatic Agents, adopted by the General Assembly of the United Nations on December 14, 1973.

    (d) International Convention against the Taking of Hostages, adopted by the General Assembly of the United Nations on December 17, 1979.

(e) Convention on the Physical Protection of Nuclear Material, signed at Vienna on March 3, 1980.

(f) Protocol on the Suppression of Unlawful Acts of Violence at Airports Serving International Civil Aviation, supplementary to the Convention for the Suppression of Unlawful Acts against the Safety of Civil Aviation, signed at Montreal on February 24, 1988.

(g) Convention for the Suppression of Unlawful Acts against the Safety of Maritime Navigation, done at Rome on March 10, 1988.

(h) Protocol for the Suppression of Unlawful Acts against the Safety of Fixed Platforms Located on the Continental Shelf, done at Rome on March 10, 1988.

(i) International Convention for the Suppression of Terrorist Bombings, adopted by the General Assembly of the United Nations on December 15, 1997.

(j) International Convention for the Suppression of the Financing of Terrorism, adopted by the General Assembly of the United Nations on December 9, 1999.

2. Upon depositing its instrument of ratification to this Convention, a state party that is not a party to one or more of the international instruments listed in paragraph 1 of this article may declare that, in application of this Convention to such state party, that particular instrument shall be deemed not to be included in that paragraph. The declaration shall cease to have effect as soon as that instrument enters into force for that state party, which shall notify the depositary of this fact.

3. When a state party ceases to be a party to one of the international instruments listed in paragraph 1 of this article, it may make a declaration, as provided in paragraph 2 of this article, with respect to that instrument.

Article 3 Domestic measures

Each state party, in accordance with the provisions of its constitution, shall endeavor to become a party to the international instruments listed in Article 2 to which it is not yet a party and to adopt the necessary measures to effectively implement such instruments, including establishing, in its domestic legislation, penalties for the offenses described therein.

Article 4 Measures to prevent, combat, and eradicate the financing of terrorism

1. Each state party, to the extent it has not already done so, shall institute a legal and regulatory regime to prevent, combat, and eradicate the financing of terrorism and for effective international cooperation with respect thereto, which shall include:

(a) A comprehensive domestic regulatory and supervisory regime for banks, other financial institutions, and other entities deemed particularly susceptible to being used for the financing of terrorist activities. This regime shall emphasize requirements for customer identification, record-keeping, and the reporting of suspicious or unusual transactions.

(b) Measures to detect and monitor movements across borders of cash, bearer negotiable instruments, and other appropriate movements of value. These measures shall be subject to safeguards to ensure proper use of information and should not impede legitimate capital movements.

(c) Measures to ensure that the competent authorities dedicated to combating the offenses established in the international instruments listed in Article 2 have the ability to cooperate and exchange information at the national and international levels within the conditions prescribed under its domestic law. To that end, each state party shall establish and maintain a financial intelligence unit to serve as a national center for the collection, analysis, and dissemination of pertinent money laundering and terrorist financing information. Each state party shall inform the Secretary General of the Organization of American States of the authority designated to be its financial intelligence unit.

2. When implementing paragraph 1 of this article, states parties shall use as guidelines the recommendations developed by specialized international and regional entities, in particular the Financial Action Task Force and, as appropriate, the Inter-American Drug Abuse Control Commission, the Caribbean Financial Action Task Force, and the South American Financial Action Task Force.

Article 5 Seizure and confiscation of funds or other assets

1. Each state party shall, in accordance with the procedures established in its domestic law, take such measures as may be necessary to provide for the identification, freezing or seizure for the purposes of possible forfeiture, and confiscation or forfeiture, of any funds or other assets constituting the proceeds of, used to facilitate, or used or intended to finance, the commission of any of the offenses established in the international instruments listed in Article 2 of this Convention.

2. The measures referred to in paragraph 1 shall apply to offenses committed both within and outside the jurisdiction of the state party.

Article 6 Predicate offenses to money laundering

1. Each state party shall take the necessary measures to ensure that its domestic penal money laundering legislation also includes as predicate offenses those offenses established in the international instruments listed in Article 2 of this Convention.

2. The money laundering predicate offenses referred to in paragraph 1 shall include those committed both within and outside the jurisdiction of the state party.

Article 7 Cooperation on border controls

1. The states parties, consistent with their respective domestic legal and administrative regimes, shall promote cooperation and the exchange of information in order to improve border and customs control measures to detect and prevent the international movement of terrorists and trafficking in arms or other materials intended to support terrorist activities.

2. In this context, they shall promote cooperation and the exchange of information to improve their controls on the issuance of travel and identity documents and to prevent their counterfeiting, forgery, or fraudulent use.

3. Such measures shall be carried out without prejudice to applicable international commitments in relation to the free movement of people and the facilitation of commerce.

Article 8 Cooperation among law enforcement authorities

The states parties shall work closely with one another, consistent with their respective domestic legal and administrative systems, to enhance the effectiveness of law enforcement action to combat the offenses established in the international instruments listed in Article 2. In this context, they shall establish and enhance, where necessary, channels of communication between their competent authorities in order to facilitate the secure and rapid exchange of information concerning all aspects of the offenses established in the international instruments listed in Article 2 of this Convention.

Article 9 Mutual legal assistance

The states parties shall afford one another the greatest measure of expeditious mutual legal assistance with respect to the prevention, investigation, and prosecution of the offenses established in the international instruments listed in Article 2 and proceedings related thereto, in accordance with applicable international agreements in force. In the absence of such agreements, states parties shall afford one another expeditious assistance in accordance with their domestic law.

Article 10 Transfer of persons in custody

1. A person who is being detained or is serving a sentence in the territory of one state party and whose presence in another state party is requested for purposes of identification, testimony, or

otherwise providing assistance in obtaining evidence for the investigation or prosecution of offenses established in the international instruments listed in Article 2 may be transferred if the following conditions are met:

(a) The person freely gives his or her informed consent; and

(b) Both states agree, subject to such conditions as those states may deem appropriate.

2. For the purposes of this article:

(a) The state to which the person is transferred shall have the authority and obligation to keep the person transferred in custody, unless otherwise requested or authorized by the state from which the person was transferred.

(b) The state to which the person is transferred shall without delay implement its obligation to return the person to the custody of the state from which the person was transferred as agreed beforehand, or as otherwise agreed, by the competent authorities of both states.

(c) The state to which the person is transferred shall not require the state from which the person was transferred to initiate extradition proceedings for the return of the person.

(d) The person transferred shall receive, for time spent in the custody of the state to which he or she was transferred, credit toward service of the sentence being served in the state from which he or she was transferred.

3. Unless the state party from which a person is to be transferred in accordance with the present article so agrees, that person, whatever his or her nationality, shall not be prosecuted or detained or subjected to any other restriction of his or her personal liberty in the territory of the state to which that person is transferred in respect of acts or convictions prior to his or her departure from the territory of the state from which said person was transferred.

Article 11 Inapplicability of political offense exception

For the purposes of extradition or mutual legal assistance, none of the offenses established in the international instruments listed in Article 2 shall be regarded as a political offense or an offense connected with a political offense or an offense inspired by political motives. Accordingly, a request for extradition or mutual legal assistance may not be refused on the sole ground that it concerns a political offense or an offense connected with a political offense or an offense inspired by political motives.

Article 12 Denial of refugee status

Each state party shall take appropriate measures, consistent with the relevant provisions of national and international law, for the purpose of ensuring that refugee status is not granted to any person in respect of whom there are serious reasons for considering that he or she has committed an offense established in the international instruments listed in Article 2 of this Convention.

Article 13 Denial of asylum

Each state party shall take appropriate measures, consistent with the relevant provisions of national and international law, for the purpose of ensuring that asylum is not granted to any person in respect of whom there are reasonable grounds to believe that he or she has committed an offense established in the international instruments listed in Article 2 of this Convention.

Article 14 Nondiscrimination

None of the provisions of this Convention shall be interpreted as imposing an obligation to provide mutual legal assistance if the requested state party has substantial grounds for believing that the request has been made for the purpose of prosecuting or punishing a person on account of that person's race, religion, nationality, ethnic origin, or political opinion, or that compliance with the request would cause prejudice to that person's position for any of these reasons.

Article 15 Human rights

1. The measures carried out by the states parties under this Convention shall take place with full respect for the rule of law, human rights, and fundamental freedoms.

2. Nothing in this Convention shall be interpreted as affecting other rights and obligations of states and individuals under international law, in particular the Charter of the United Nations, the Charter of the Organization of American States, international humanitarian law, international human rights law, and international refugee law.

3. Any person who is taken into custody or regarding whom any other measures are taken or proceedings are carried out pursuant to this Convention shall be guaranteed fair treatment, including the enjoyment of all rights and guarantees in conformity with the law of the state in the territory of which that person is present and applicable provisions of international law.

Article 16 Training

1. The states parties shall promote technical cooperation and training programs at the national, bilateral, subregional, and regional levels and in the framework of the Organization of American States to strengthen the national institutions responsible for compliance with the obligations assumed under this Convention.

2. The states parties shall also promote, where appropriate, technical cooperation and training programs with other regional and international organizations conducting activities related to the purposes of this Convention.

Article 17 Cooperation through the Organization of American States

The states parties shall encourage the broadest cooperation within the pertinent organs of the Organization of American States, including the Inter-American Committee against Terrorism (CICTE), on matters related to the object and purposes of this Convention.

Article 18 Consultations among the parties

1. The states parties shall hold periodic meetings of consultation, as appropriate, with a view to facilitating:

    (a) The full implementation of this Convention, including the consideration of issues of interest relating thereto identified by the states parties; and

    (b) The exchange of information and experiences on effective means and methods to prevent, detect, investigate, and punish terrorism.

2. The Secretary General shall convene a meeting of consultation of the states parties after receiving the 10th instrument of ratification. Without prejudice to this, the states parties may hold consultations as they consider appropriate.

3. The states parties may request the pertinent organs of the Organization of American States, including CICTE, to facilitate the consultations referred to in the previous paragraphs and to provide other forms of assistance with respect to the implementation of this Convention.

Article 19 Exercise of jurisdiction

Nothing in this Convention entitles a state party to undertake in the territory of another state party the exercise of jurisdiction or performance of functions that are exclusively reserved to the authorities of that other state party by its domestic law.

DOCUMENT 15

Montreal Convention for the Suppression of Unlawful Acts Against the Safety of Civil Aviation 1971
974 UNTS 177; 10 ILM 1151 (1971)

This Convention was concluded under the auspices of the International Civil Aviation Organization at Montreal, Canada, on 23 September 1971 and entered into force on 26 January 1973.

There are 180 parties, including all the major powers.

The Convention was adopted as a response to a spate of bombings of civil aircraft, particularly bombings of two aircraft hijacked to Dawson's Field, Jordan, and exploded on the ground and a third bombed on the ground at Cairo, all in September 1970. It is the third global terrorism Convention concerned with aircraft, following the Tokyo Convention on Offences and Certain Other Acts Committed on Board Aircraft of 1963 **(Document 11)** *and the Hague Convention for the Suppression of Unlawful Seizure of Aircraft of 1970* **(Document 12)**.

The Convention is directed against the sabotage of aircraft, and requires the Contracting States to criminalise specified acts set out in Article 1 and make them 'punishable by severe penalties' (Article 3). Each Contracting State has jurisdiction, inter alia, *where one of the Convention's offences is committed in its territory, against or on board an aircraft registered in that state, or where the aircraft lands in its territory (Article 5). Each Contracting State is required to report an offender to its prosecution authorities or to extradite him (Article 7) – the* aut dedere aut judicare *principle. The Convention declares the specified offences to be extraditable offences under existing extradition treaties and to be included in future extradition treaties (Article 8(1)); if there is no extradition treaty, the Convention itself may be treated as such (Article 8(2)).*

The Convention has been the subject of proceedings before the International Court of Justice. On 3 March 1992, Libya initiated proceedings against the UK and the USA in respect of disputes concerning the interpretation and application of the Montreal Convention arising from the destruction of Pan Am 103 over the town of Lockerbie in Scotland on 21 December 1988, resulting in the loss of 270 lives. On 14 April 1992, the Court declined to indicate provisional measures of protection for Libya: Questions of Interpretation and Application of the 1971 Montreal Convention Arising from the Aerial Incident at Lockerbie (Provisional Measures) 1992 ICJ Rep 3 *(Libya v UK) and* 1992 ICJ Rep 114 *(Libya v USA). After the UK and the USA raised preliminary objections to the jurisdiction of the Court and the admissibility of the applications, the Court, in two separate judgments of 27 February 1998, found that there existed a dispute between the parties, that the Court had jurisdiction to hear the case and that the Libyan application was admissible:* Questions of Interpretation and Application of the 1971 Montreal Convention Arising from the Aerial Incident at Lockerbie (Preliminary Objections) 1998 ICJ Rep 9 *(Libya v UK) and* 1998 ICJ Rep 115 *(Libya v USA). By two letters of 9 September 2003, the governments of Libya and the UK on the one hand, and of Libya and the USA on the other, notified the Court that they had agreed to 'discontinue with prejudice the proceedings'. By order of 10 September 2003, the president of the Court directed the removal of the case from the Court's list.*

The essential provisions of the Convention were extended to acts of sabotage at international airports by a Protocol of 24 February 1988 **(Document 16)**.

See also the other global terrorism conventions **(Documents 11–12, 16–17, 20–26 and 28)**.

The States Parties to this Convention,

Considering that unlawful acts against the safety of civil aviation jeopardize the safety of persons and property, seriously affect the operation of air services, and undermine the confidence of the peoples of the world in the safety of civil aviation;

Considering that the occurrence of such acts is a matter of grave concern;

Considering that, for the purpose of deterring such acts, there is an urgent need to provide appropriate measures for punishment of offenders;

Have agreed as follows:

Article 1

1. Any person commits an offence if he unlawfully and intentionally:

    (a) performs an act of violence against a person on board an aircraft in flight if that act is likely to endanger the safety of that aircraft; or

    (b) destroys an aircraft in service or causes damage to such an aircraft which renders it incapable of flight or which is likely to endanger its safety in flight; or

    (c) places or causes to be placed on an aircraft in service, by any means whatsoever, a device or substance which is likely to destroy that aircraft, or to cause damage to it which renders it incapable of flight, or to cause damage to it which is likely to endanger its safety in flight; or

    (d) destroys or damages air navigation facilities or interferes with their operation, if any such act is likely to endanger the safety of aircraft in flight; or

    (e) communicates information which he knows to be false, thereby endangering the safety of an aircraft in flight.

2. Any person also commits an offence if he:

    (a) attempts to commit any of the offences mentioned in paragraph 1 of this Article; or

    (b) is an accomplice of a person who commits or attempts to commit any such offence.

Article 2

For the purposes of this Convention:

(a) an aircraft is considered to be in flight at any time from the moment when all its external doors are closed following embarkation until the moment when any such door is opened for disembarkation; in the case of a forced landing, the flight shall be deemed to continue until the competent authorities take over the responsibility for the aircraft and for persons and property on board;

(b) an aircraft is considered to be in service from the beginning of the preflight preparation of the aircraft by ground personnel or by the crew for a specific flight until twenty-four hours after any landing; the period of service shall, in any event, extend for the entire period during which the aircraft is in flight as defined in paragraph (a) of this Article.

Article 3

Each Contracting State undertakes to make the offences mentioned in Article 1 punishable by severe penalties.

Article 4

1. This Convention shall not apply to aircraft used in military, customs or police services.

2. In the cases contemplated in subparagraphs (a), (b), (c) and (e) of paragraph 1 of Article 1, this Convention shall apply, irrespective of whether the aircraft is engaged in an international or domestic flight, only if:

(a) the place of take-off or landing, actual or intended, of the aircraft is situated outside the territory of the State of registration of that aircraft; or

(b) the offence is committed in the territory of a State other than the State of registration of the aircraft.

3. Notwithstanding paragraph 2 of this Article, in the cases contemplated in subparagraphs (a), (b), (c) and (e) of paragraph 1 of Article 1, this Convention shall also apply if the offender or the alleged offender is found in the territory of a State other than the State of registration of the aircraft.

4. With respect to the States mentioned in Article 9 and in the cases mentioned in subparagraphs (a), (b), (c) and (e) of paragraph 1 of Article 1, this Convention shall not apply if the places referred to in subparagraph (a) of paragraph 2 of this Article are situated within the territory of the same State where that State is one of those referred to in Article 9, unless the offence is committed or the offender or alleged offender is found in the territory of a State other than that State.

5. In the cases contemplated in subparagraph (d) of paragraph 1 of Article 1, this Convention shall apply only if the air navigation facilities are used in international air navigation.

6. The provisions of paragraphs 2, 3, 4 and 5 of this Article shall also apply in the cases contemplated in paragraph 2 of Article 1.

Article 5

1. Each Contracting State shall take such measures as may be necessary to establish its jurisdiction over the offences in the following cases:

(a) when the offence is committed in the territory of that State;

(b) when the offence is committed against or on board an aircraft registered in that State;

(c) when the aircraft on board which the offence is committed lands in its territory with the alleged offender still on board;

(d) when the offence is committed against or on board an aircraft leased without crew to a lessee who has his principal place of business or, if the lessee has no such place of business, his permanent residence, in that State.

2. Each Contracting State shall likewise take such measures as may be necessary to establish its jurisdiction over the offences mentioned in Article 1, paragraph 1(a), (b) and (c), and in Article 1, paragraph 2, in so far as that paragraph relates to those offences, in the case where the alleged offender is present in its territory and it does not extradite him pursuant to Article 8 to any of the States mentioned in paragraph 1 of this Article.

3. This Convention does not exclude any criminal jurisdiction exercised in accordance with national law.

Article 6

1. Upon being satisfied that the circumstances so warrant, any Contracting State in the territory of which the offender or the alleged offender is present, shall take him into custody or take other measures to ensure his presence. The custody and other measures shall be as provided in the law of that State but may only be continued for such time as is necessary to enable any criminal or extradition proceedings to be instituted.

2. Such State shall immediately make a preliminary enquiry into the facts.

3. Any person in custody pursuant to paragraph 1 of this Article shall be assisted in communicating immediately with the nearest appropriate representative of the State of which he is a national.

4. When a State, pursuant to this Article, has taken a person into custody, it shall immediately notify the States mentioned in Article 5, paragraph 1, the State of nationality of the detained

person and, if it considers it advisable, any other interested States of the fact that such person is in custody and of the circumstances which warrant his detention. The State which makes the preliminary enquiry contemplated in paragraph 2 of this Article shall promptly report its findings to the said States and shall indicate whether it intends to exercise jurisdiction.

Article 7

The Contracting State in the territory of which the alleged offender is found shall, if it does not extradite him, be obliged, without exception whatsoever and whether or not the offence was committed in its territory, to submit the case to its competent authorities for the purpose of prosecution. Those authorities shall take their decision in the same manner as in the case of any ordinary offence of a serious nature under the law of that State.

Article 8

1. The offences shall be deemed to be included as extraditable offences in any extradition treaty existing between Contracting States. Contracting States undertake to include the offences as extraditable offences in every extradition treaty to be concluded between them.

2. If a Contracting State which makes extradition conditional on the existence of a treaty receives a request for extradition from another Contracting State with which it has no extradition treaty, it may at its option consider this Convention as the legal basis for extradition in respect of the offences. Extradition shall be subject to the other conditions provided by the law of the requested State.

3. Contracting States which do not make extradition conditional on the existence of a treaty shall recognize the offences as extraditable offences between themselves subject to the conditions provided by the law of the requested State.

4. Each of the offences shall be treated, for the purpose of extradition between Contracting States, as if it had been committed not only in the place in which it occurred but also in the territories of the States required to establish their jurisdiction in accordance with Article 5, paragraph 1(b), (c) and (d).

Article 9

The Contracting States which establish joint air transport operating organisations or international operating agencies, which operate aircraft which are subject to joint or international registration shall, by appropriate means, designate for each aircraft the State among them which shall exercise the jurisdiction and have the attributes of the State of registration for the purpose of this Convention and shall give notice thereof to the International Civil Aviation Organization which shall communicate the notice to all States Parties to this Convention.

Article 10

1. Contracting States shall, in accordance with international and national law, endeavour to take all practicable measures for the purpose of preventing the offences mentioned in Article 1.

2. When, due to the commission of one of the offences mentioned in Article 1, a flight has been delayed or interrupted, any Contracting State in whose territory the aircraft or passengers or crew are present shall facilitate the continuation of the journey of the passengers and crew as soon as practicable, and shall without delay return the aircraft and its cargo to the persons lawfully entitled to possession.

Article 11

1. Contracting States shall afford one another the greatest measure of assistance in connection with criminal proceedings brought in respect of the offences. The law of the State requested shall apply in all cases.

2. The provisions of paragraph 1 of this Article shall not affect obligations under any other treaty, bilateral or multilateral, which governs or will govern, in whole or in part, mutual assistance in criminal matters.

Article 12
Any Contracting State having reason to believe that one of the offences mentioned in Article 1 will be committed shall, in accordance with its national law, furnish any relevant information in its possession to those States which it believes would be the States mentioned in Article 5, paragraph 1.

Article 13
Each Contracting State shall in accordance with its national law report to the Council of the International Civil Aviation Organization as promptly as possible any relevant information in its possession concerning:

(a) the circumstances of the offence;

(b) the action taken pursuant to Article 10, paragraph 2;

(c) the measures taken in relation to the offender or the alleged offender and, in particular, the results of any extradition proceedings or other legal proceedings.

Article 14
1. Any dispute between two or more Contracting States concerning the interpretation or application of this Convention which cannot be settled through negotiation, shall, at the request of one of them, be submitted to arbitration. If within six months from the date of the request for arbitration the Parties are unable to agree on the organization of the arbitration, any one of those Parties may refer the dispute to the International Court of Justice by request in conformity with the Statute of the Court.

2. Each State may at the time of signature or ratification of this Convention or accession thereto, declare that it does not consider itself bound by the preceding paragraph. The other Contracting States shall not be bound by the preceding paragraph with respect to any Contracting State having made such a reservation.

3. Any Contracting State having made a reservation in accordance with the preceding paragraph may at any time withdraw this reservation by notification to the Depositary Governments.

DOCUMENT 16

Protocol for the Suppression of Unlawful Acts of Violence at Airports serving International Civil Aviation 1988
ICAO Doc 9518; 27 ILM 672 (1988)

This Protocol was concluded under the auspices of the International Civil Aviation Organization at Montreal, Canada, on 24 February 1988 and entered into force on 6 August 1989.

There are 148 parties, including all the major powers.

The Protocol was adopted as a response to a spate of attacks and bombings at international airports, particularly the bombing at Frankfurt, Germany, in June 1985 and the co-ordinated attacks on Rome and Vienna international airports in December 1985, in the three of which some 20 people were killed and 150 injured. Essentially, the Protocol extends the provisions of the Montreal Convention for the Suppression of Unlawful Acts Against the Safety of Civil Aviation of 23 September 1971 **(Document 15)** *to any 'airport serving international civil aviation' (Article II).*

See also the other global terrorism conventions **(Documents 11–12, 17, 20–26 and 28)**.

The States Parties to this Protocol,

Considering that unlawful acts of violence which endanger or are likely to endanger the safety of persons at airports serving international civil aviation or which jeopardize the safe operation of such airports undermine the confidence of the peoples of the world in safety at such airports and disturb the safe and orderly conduct of civil aviation for all States;

Considering that the occurrence of such acts is a matter of grave concern to the international community and that, for the purpose of deterring such acts, there is an urgent need to provide appropriate measures for punishment of offenders;

Considering that it is necessary to adopt provisions supplementary to those of the Convention for the Suppression of Unlawful Acts against the Safety of Civil Aviation, done at Montreal on 23 September 1971, to deal with such unlawful acts of violence at airports serving international civil aviation;

Have agreed as follows:

Article I

This Protocol supplements the Convention for the Suppression of Unlawful Acts against the Safety of Civil Aviation, done at Montreal on 23 September 1971 (hereinafter referred to as "the Convention"), and, as between the Parties to this Protocol, the Convention and the Protocol shall be read and interpreted together as one single instrument.

Article II

1. In Article 1 of the Convention, the following shall be added as new paragraph 1 bis:

   "1 bis. Any person commits an offence if he unlawfully and intentionally, using any device, substance or weapon:

   (a) performs an act of violence against a person at an airport serving international civil aviation which causes or is likely to cause serious injury or death; or

   (b) destroys or seriously damages the facilities of an airport serving international civil aviation or aircraft not in service located thereon or disrupts the services of the airport, if such an act endangers or is likely to endanger safety at that airport."

2. In paragraph 2 (a) of Article 1 of the Convention, the following words shall be inserted after the words "paragraph 1": "or paragraph 1 bis".

Article III

In Article 5 of the Convention, the following shall be added as paragraph 2 bis:

"2 bis. Each Contracting State shall likewise take such measures as may be necessary to establish its jurisdiction over the offences mentioned in Article 1, paragraph 1 bis, and in Article 1, paragraph 2, in so far as that paragraph relates to those offences, in the case where the alleged offender is present in its territory and it does not extradite him pursuant to Article 8 to the State mentioned in paragraph 1(a) of this Article."

DOCUMENT 17

Convention on the Prevention and Punishment of Crimes Against Internationally Protected Persons, including Diplomatic Agents 1973
1035 UNTS 167; 13 ILM 43 (1974)

The Convention was adopted on 14 December 1973 as an annex to General Assembly Resolution 3166 (XXVIII) and came into force on 20 February 1977.

There are 131 parties, including all the major powers.

In the late 1960s, the international community became concerned at increasing attacks on diplomats in various parts of the world. As a consequence, this convention was drafted through the Sixth (Legal) Committee of the UN General Assembly.

The Convention is intended to protect 'internationally protected persons' as defined in Article 1. It requires the Contracting States to criminalise specified acts against such persons (Article 2(1)) and to make them punishable by appropriate penalties (Article 2(2)). Each Contracting State is to establish its jurisdiction, when one of the Convention's offences is committed in its territory or on one of its ships or aircraft when the offender is a national or when the victim is a national (Article 3(1)). Each Contracting State is required to report an offender to its prosecution authorities or to extradite him (Article 7) – the aut dedere aut judicare principle. The Convention declares the specified offences to be extraditable offences under existing extradition treaties and to be included in future extradition treaties (Article 8(1)); if there is no extradition treaty, the Convention itself may be treated as such (Article 8(2)). There are fair treatment guarantees for proceedings under the Convention (Article 9). Parties are to afford one another the greatest measure of assistance (Article 10).

See the other global terrorism conventions **(Documents 11–12, 15–16, 18, 20–26 and 28)**.

The States Parties to this Convention,

Having in mind the purposes and principles of the Charter of the United Nations concerning the maintenance of international peace and the promotion of friendly relations and co-operation among States,

Considering that crimes against diplomatic agents and other internationally protected persons jeopardizing the safety of these persons create a serious threat to the maintenance of normal international relations which are necessary for co-operation among States,

Believing that the commission of such crimes is a matter of grave concern to the international community,

Convinced that there is an urgent need to adopt appropriate and effective measures for the prevention and punishment of such crimes,

Have agreed as follows:

Article 1

For the purposes of this Convention:

1. "internationally protected person" means:

    (a) Head of State, including any member of a collegial body performing the functions of a Head of State under the constitution of the State concerned, a Head of Government or a

Minister for Foreign Affairs, whenever any such person is in a foreign State, as well as members of his family who accompany him;

(b) any representative or official of a State or any official or other agent of an international organization of an intergovernmental character who, at the time when and in the place where a crime against him, his official premises, his private accommodation or his means of transport is committed, is entitled pursuant to international law to special protection from any attack on his person, freedom or dignity, as well as members of his family forming part of his household.

2. "alleged offender" means a person as to whom there is sufficient evidence to determine prima facie that he has committed or participated in one or more of the crimes set forth in article 2.

Article 2

1. The intentional commission of:

(a) a murder, kidnapping or other attack upon the person or liberty of an internationally protected person;

(b) a violent attack upon the official premises, the private accommodation or the means of transport of an internationally protected person likely to endanger his person or liberty;

(c) a threat to commit any such attack;

(d) an attempt to commit any such attack; and

(e) an act constituting participation as an accomplice in any such attack shall be made by each State Party a crime under its internal law.

2. Each State Party shall make these crimes punishable by appropriate penalties which take into account their grave nature.

3. Paragraphs 1 and 2 of this article in no way derogate from the obligations of States Parties under international law to take all appropriate measures to prevent other attacks on the person, freedom or dignity of an internationally protected person.

Article 3

1. Each State Party shall take such measures as may be necessary to establish its jurisdiction over the crimes set forth in article 2 in the following cases:

(a) when the crime is committed in the territory of that State or on board a ship or aircraft registered in that State;

(b) when the alleged offender is a national of that State;

(c) when the crime is committed against an internationally protected person as defined in article 1 who enjoys his status as such by virtue of functions which he exercises on behalf of that State.

2. Each State Party shall likewise take such measures as may be necessary to establish its jurisdiction over these crimes in cases where the alleged offender is present in its territory and it does not extradite him pursuant to article 8 to any of the States mentioned in paragraph 1 of this article.

3. This Convention does not exclude any criminal jurisdiction exercised in accordance with internal law.

Article 4

States Parties shall co-operate in the prevention of the crimes set forth in article 2, particularly by:

(a) taking all practicable measures to prevent preparations in their respective territories for the commission of those crimes within or outside their territories;

(b) exchanging information and co-ordinating the taking of administrative and other measures as appropriate to prevent the commission of those crimes.

Article 5

1. The State Party in which any of the crimes set forth in article 2 has been committed shall, if it has reason to believe that an alleged offender has fled from its territory, communicate to all other States concerned, directly or through the Secretary-General of the United Nations, all the pertinent facts regarding the crime committed and all available information regarding the identity of the alleged offender.

2. Whenever any of the crimes set forth in article 2 has been committed against an internationally protected person, any State Party which has information concerning the victim and the circumstances of the crime shall endeavour to transmit it, under the conditions provided for in its internal law, fully and promptly to the State Party on whose behalf he was exercising his functions.

Article 6

1. Upon being satisfied that the circumstances so warrant, the State Party in whose territory the alleged offender is present shall take the appropriate measures under its internal law so as to ensure his presence for the purpose of prosecution or extradition. Such measures shall be notified without delay directly or through the Secretary-General of the United Nations to:

   (a) the State where the crime was committed;

   (b) the State or States of which the alleged offender is a national or, if he is a stateless person, in whose territory he permanently resides;

   (c) the State or States of which the internationally protected person concerned is a national or on whose behalf he was exercising his functions;

   (d) all other States concerned; and

   (e) the international organization of which the internationally protected person concerned is an official or an agent.

2. Any person regarding whom the measures referred to in paragraph 1 of this article are being taken shall be entitled:

   (a) to communicate without delay with the nearest appropriate representative of the State of which he is a national or which is otherwise entitled to protect his rights or, if he is a stateless person, which he requests and which is willing to protect his rights, and

   (b) to be visited by a representative of that State.

Article 7

The State Party in whose territory the alleged offender is present shall, if it does not extradite him, submit, without exception whatsoever and without undue delay, the case to its competent authorities for the purpose of prosecution, through proceedings in accordance with the laws of that State.

Article 8

1. To the extent that the crimes set forth in article 2 are not listed as extraditable offences in any extradition treaty existing between States Parties, they shall be deemed to be included as such therein. States Parties undertake to include those crimes as extraditable offences in every future extradition treaty to be concluded between them.

2. If a State Party which makes extradition conditional on the existence of a treaty receives a request for extradition from another State Party with which it has no extradition treaty, it may, if it decides to extradite, consider this Convention as the legal basis for extradition in respect of those crimes. Extradition shall be subject to the procedural provisions and the other conditions of the law of the requested State.

3. States Parties which do not make extradition conditional on the existence of a treaty shall recognize those crimes as extraditable offences between themselves subject to the procedural provisions and the other conditions of the law of the requested State.

4. Each of the crimes shall be treated, for the purpose of extradition between States Parties, as if it had been committed not only in the place in which it occurred but also in the territories of the States required to establish their jurisdiction in accordance with paragraph 1 of article 3.

Article 9

Any person regarding whom proceedings are being carried out in connection with any of the crimes set forth in article 2 shall be guaranteed fair treatment at all stages of the proceedings.

Article 10

1. States Parties shall afford one another the greatest measure of assistance in connection with criminal proceedings brought in respect of the crimes set forth in article 2, including the supply of all evidence at their disposal necessary for the proceedings.

2. The provisions of paragraph 1 of this article shall not affect obligations concerning mutual judicial assistance embodied in any other treaty.

Article 11

The State Party where an alleged offender is prosecuted shall communicate the final outcome of the proceedings to the Secretary-General of the United Nations, who shall transmit the information to the other States Parties.

Article 12

The provisions of this Convention shall not affect the application of the Treaties on Asylum, in force at the date of the adoption of this Convention, as between the States which are parties to those Treaties; but a State Party to this Convention may not invoke those Treaties with respect to another State Party to this Convention which is not a party to those Treaties.

Article 13

1. Any dispute between two or more States Parties concerning the interpretation or application of this Convention which is not settled by negotiation shall, at the request of one of them, be submitted to arbitration. If within six months from the date of the request for arbitration the parties are unable to agree on the organization of the arbitration, any one of those parties may refer the dispute to the International Court of Justice by request in conformity with the Statute of the Court.

2. Each State Party may at the time of signature or ratification of this Convention or accession thereto declare that it does not consider itself bound by paragraph 1 of this article. The other States Parties shall not be bound by paragraph 1 of this article with respect to any State Party which has made such a reservation.

3. Any State Party which has made a reservation in accordance with paragraph 2 of this article may at any time withdraw that reservation by notification to the Secretary-General of the United Nations.

DOCUMENT 18

European Convention on the Suppression of Terrorism 1977
ETS No 90; 15 ILM 1272 (1976)

The Convention was adopted under the auspices of the Council of Europe on 27 January 1977 and entered into force on 4 August 1978.

There are 44 parties, the Council of Europe having a total membership of 46.

The Member States of the Council of Europe, conscious of the growing menace of terrorism and of the international instruments to counter it, began to elaborate a European convention 1n 1973. The problem was seen as the political offence exception to extradition and the focus of the negotiations – and indeed the principal contribution of this convention – is the elimination of the political offence exception to extradition for terrorist offences.

Article 1 specifies five types of terrorist offence which are not to be regarded as political offences for the purpose of extradition, while Article 2 broadly states other offences which the parties may decide not to regard as political offences. Existing extradition treaties between the parties are modified to the extent that they are incompatible with the Convention (Article 3); see also Article 4. Extradition is precluded where its purpose is to prosecute or punish a person on the grounds of race, religion, nationality or political opinion (Article 5). A state with custody of a terrorist suspect is obliged to extradite that person or report him to its competent authorities for prosecution (Article 7) – the aut dedere aut judicare *principle.*

See the Protocol Amending the European Convention for the Suppression of Terrorism of 3 May 2002 **(Document 19)**.

See also the OAS terrorism conventions **(Documents 13–14)**.

The member States of the Council of Europe, signatory hereto,

Considering that the aim of the Council of Europe is to achieve a greater unity between its members;

Aware of the growing concern caused by the increase in acts of terrorism;

Wishing to take effective measures to ensure that the perpetrators of such acts do not escape prosecution and punishment;

Convinced that extradition is a particularly effective measure for achieving this result,

Have agreed as follows:

Article 1

For the purposes of extradition between Contracting States, none of the following offences shall be regarded as a political offence or as an offence connected with a political offence or as an offence inspired by political motives:

(a) an offence within the scope of the Convention for the Suppression of Unlawful Seizure of Aircraft, signed at The Hague on 16 December 1970;

(b) an offence within the scope of the Convention for the Suppression of Unlawful Acts against the Safety of Civil Aviation, signed at Montreal on 23 September 1971;

(c) a serious offence involving an attack against the life, physical integrity or liberty of internationally protected persons, including diplomatic agents;

(d) an offence involving kidnapping, the taking of a hostage or serious unlawful detention;

(e) an offence involving the use of a bomb, grenade, rocket, automatic firearm or letter or parcel bomb if this use endangers persons;

(f) an attempt to commit any of the foregoing offences or participation as an accomplice of a person who commits or attempts to commit such an offence.

Article 2

1. For the purpose of extradition between Contracting States, a Contracting State may decide not to regard as a political offence or as an offence connected with a political offence or as an offence inspired by political motives a serious offence involving an act of violence, other than one covered by Article 1, against the life, physical integrity or liberty of a person.

2. The same shall apply to a serious offence involving an act against property, other than one covered by Article 1, if the act created a collective danger for persons.

3. The same shall apply to an attempt to commit any of the foregoing offences or participation as an accomplice of a person who commits or attempts to commit such an offence.

Article 3

The provisions of all extradition treaties and arrangements applicable between Contracting States, including the European Convention on Extradition, are modified as between Contracting States to the extent that they are incompatible with this Convention.

Article 4

For the purpose of this Convention and to the extent that any offence mentioned in Article 1 or 2 is not listed as an extraditable offence in any extradition convention or treaty existing between Contracting States, it shall be deemed to be included as such therein.

Article 5

Nothing in this Convention shall be interpreted as imposing an obligation to extradite if the requested State has substantial grounds for believing that the request for extradition for an offence mentioned in Article 1 or 2 has been made for the purpose of prosecuting or punishing a person on account of his race, religion, nationality or political opinion, or that that person's position may be prejudiced for any of these reasons.

Article 6

1. Each Contracting State shall take such measures as may be necessary to establish its jurisdiction over an offence mentioned in Article 1 in the case where the suspected offender is present in its territory and it does not extradite him after receiving a request for extradition from a Contracting State whose jurisdiction is based on a rule of jurisdiction existing equally in the law of the requested State. This Convention does not exclude any criminal jurisdiction exercised in accordance with national law.

2. This Convention does not exculde any criminal jurisdiction exercised in accordance with national law.

Article 7

A Contracting State in whose territory a person suspected to have committed an offence mentioned in Article 1 is found and which has received a request for extradition under the conditions mentioned in Article 6, paragraph 1, shall, if it does not extradite that person, submit the case, without exception whatsoever and without undue delay, to its competent authorities for the purpose of prosecution. Those authorities shall take their decision in the same manner as any offence of a serious nature under the law of that State.

Article 8

1. Contracting States shall afford one another the widest measure of mutual assistance in criminal matters in connection with proceedings brought in respect of the offences mentioned in Article 1 or 2. The law of the requested State concerning mutual assistance in criminal matters shall apply in all cases. Nevertheless this assistance may not be refused on the sole ground that it concerns a political offence or an offence connected with a political offence or an offence inspired by political motives.

2. Nothing in this Convention shall be interpreted as imposing an obligation to afford mutual assistance if the requested State has substantial grounds for believing that the request for mutual assistance in respect of an offence mentioned in Article 1 or 2 has been made for the purpose of prosecuting or punishing a person on account of his race, religion, nationality or political opinion or that that person's position may be prejudiced for any of these reasons.

3. The provisions of all treaties and arrangements concerning mutual assistance in criminal matters applicable between Contracting States, including the European Convention on Mutual Assistance in Criminal Matters, are modified as between Contracting States to the extent that they are incompatible with this Convention.

Article 9

1. The European Committee on Crime Problems of the Council of Europe shall be kept informed regarding the application of this Convention.

2. It shall do whatever is needful to facilitate a friendly settlement of any difficulty which may arise out of its execution.

Article 10

1. Any dispute between Contracting States concerning the interpretation or application of this Convention, which has not been settled in the framework of Article 9, paragraph 2, shall, at the request of any Party to the dispute, be referred to arbitration. Each Party shall nominate an arbitrator and the two arbitrators shall nominate a referee. If any Party has not nominated its arbitrator within the three months following the request for arbitration, he shall be nominated at the request of the other Party by the President of the European Court of Human Rights. If the latter should be a national of one of the Parties to the dispute, this duty shall be carried out by the Vice-President of the Court or if the Vice-President is a national of one of the Parties to the dispute, by the most senior judge of the Court not being a national of one of the Parties to the dispute. The same procedure shall be observed if the arbitrators cannot agree on the choice of referee.

2. The arbitration tribunal shall lay down its own procedure. Its decisions shall be taken by majority vote. Its award shall be final.

DOCUMENT 19

Protocol Amending the European Convention on the Suppression of Terrorism 2002
ETS No 190

The Protocol was adopted under the auspices of the Council of Europe on 3 May 2002; it has not entered into force.

There are 13 parties; France, Germany, Russia and the UK are among Council of Europe Members which have not ratified the Protocol.

This Protocol to the European Convention of 1977 **(Document 18)** *was drafted as part of the post-9/11 measures against terrorism, at the same time ensuring due respect for human rights in combating terrorism. It extends the list of terrorist offences to be depoliticised by adding all the offences in the global terrorism conventions to date to Article 1 of the 1977 Convention (Article 1); see also Article 2. It leaves unchanged many of the other provisions of the 1977 Convention, including the* aut dedere aut judicare *obligation of Article 7. As a human rights matter, Article 4(2) precludes extradition where there is a risk or torture or exposure to the death penalty or life imprisonment without parole.*

See also the OAS terrorism conventions **(Documents 13–14).**

The member States of the Council of Europe, signatory to this Protocol,

Bearing in mind the Committee of Ministers of the Council of Europe's Declaration of 12 September 2001 and its Decision of 21 September 2001 on the Fight against International Terrorism, and the Vilnius Declaration on Regional Co-operation and the Consolidation of Democratic Stability in Greater Europe adopted by the Committee of Ministers at its 110th Session in Vilnius on 3 May 2002;

Bearing in mind the Parliamentary Assembly of the Council of Europe's Recommendation 1550 (2002) on Combating terrorism and respect for human rights;

Bearing in mind the General Assembly of the United Nations Resolution A/RES/51/210 on measures to eliminate international terrorism and the annexed Declaration to Supplement the 1994 Declaration on Measures to Eliminate International Terrorism, and its Resolution A/RES/49/60 on measures to eliminate international terrorism and the Declaration on Measures to Eliminate International Terrorism annexed thereto;

Wishing to strengthen the fight against terrorism while respecting human rights, and mindful of the Guidelines on human rights and the fight against terrorism adopted by the Committee of Ministers of the Council of Europe on 11 July 2002;

Considering for that purpose that it would be appropriate to amend the European Convention on the Suppression of Terrorism (ETS No. 90) opened for signature in Strasbourg on 27 January 1977, hereinafter referred to as "the Convention";

Considering that it would be appropriate to update the list of international conventions in Article 1 of the Convention and to provide for a simplified procedure to subsequently update it as required;

Considering that it would be appropriate to strengthen the follow-up of the implementation of the Convention;

Considering that it would be appropriate to review the reservation regime;

Considering that it would be appropriate to open the Convention to the signature of all interested States,

Have agreed as follows:

Article I

1. The introductory paragraph to Article 1 of the Convention shall become paragraph 1 of this article. In sub-paragraph b of this paragraph, the term "signed" shall be replaced by the term "concluded" and sub-paragraphs c, d, e and f of this paragraph shall be replaced by the following sub-paragraphs:

    "(c) an offence within the scope of the Convention on the Prevention and Punishment of Crimes Against Internationally Protected Persons, Including Diplomatic Agents, adopted at New York on 14 December 1973;

    (d) an offence within the scope of the International Convention Against the Taking of Hostages, adopted at New York on 17 December 1979;

    (e) an offence within the scope of the Convention on the Physical Protection of Nuclear Material, adopted at Vienna on 3 March 1980;

    (f) an offence within the scope of the Protocol for the Suppression of Unlawful Acts of Violence at Airports Serving International Civil Aviation, done at Montreal on 24 February 1988;"

2. Paragraph 1 of Article 1 of the Convention shall be supplemented by the following four sub-paragraphs:

    "(g) an offence within the scope of the Convention for the Suppression of Unlawful Acts Against the Safety of Maritime Navigation, done at Rome on 10 March 1988;

    (h) an offence within the scope of the Protocol for the Suppression of Unlawful Acts Against the Safety of Fixed Platforms Located on the Continental Shelf, done at Rome on 10 March 1988;

(i) an offence within the scope of the International Convention for the Suppression of Terrorist Bombings, adopted at New York on 15 December 1997;

(j) an offence within the scope of the International Convention for the Suppression of the Financing of Terrorism, adopted at New York on 9 December 1999."

3. The text of Article 1 of the Convention shall be supplemented by the following paragraph:

"2. Insofar as they are not covered by the conventions listed under paragraph 1, the same shall apply, for the purpose of extradition between Contracting States, not only to the commission of those principal offences as a perpetrator but also to:

(a) the attempt to commit any of these principal offences;

(b) the participation as an accomplice in the perpetration of any of these principal offences or in an attempt to commit any of them;

(c) organising the perpetration of, or directing others to commit or attempt to commit, any of these principal offences."

Article 2

Paragraph 3 of Article 2 of the Convention shall be amended to read as follows:

"3. The same shall apply to:

(a) the attempt to commit any of the foregoing offences;

(b) the participation as an accomplice in any of the foregoing offences or in an attempt to commit any such offence;

(c) organising the perpetration of, or directing others to commit or attempt to commit, any of the foregoing offences."

Article 3

1. The text of Article 4 of the Convention shall become paragraph 1 of this article and a new sentence shall be added at the end of this paragraph as follows: "Contracting States undertake to consider such offences as extraditable offences in every extradition treaty subsequently concluded between them."

2. The text of Article 4 of the Convention shall be supplemented by the following paragraph:

"2. When a Contracting State which makes extradition conditional on the existence of a treaty receives a request for extradition from another Contracting State with which it has no extradition treaty, the requested Contracting State may, at its discretion, consider this Convention as a legal basis for extradition in relation to any of the offences mentioned in Articles 1 or 2."

Article 4

1. The text of Article 5 of the Convention shall become paragraph 1 of this article.

2. The text of Article 5 of the Convention shall be supplemented by the following paragraphs:

"2. Nothing in this Convention shall be interpreted as imposing on the requested State an obligation to extradite if the person subject of the extradition request risks being exposed to torture.

3. Nothing in this Convention shall be interpreted either as imposing on the requested State an obligation to extradite if the person subject of the extradition request risks being exposed to the death penalty or, where the law of the requested State does not allow for life imprisonment, to life imprisonment without the possibility of parole, unless under applicable extradition treaties the requested State is under the obligation to extradite if the requesting State gives such assurance as the requested State considers sufficient that the death penalty will not be imposed or, where imposed, will not be carried out, or that the person concerned will not be subject to life imprisonment without the possibility of parole."

Article 5

A new article shall be inserted after Article 8 of the Convention and shall read as follows:

"Article 9

The Contracting States may conclude between themselves bilateral or multilateral agreements in order to supplement the provisions of this Convention or to facilitate the application of the principles contained therein."

Article 6

1. Article 9 of the Convention shall become Article 10.

2. Paragraph 1 of new Article 10 shall be amended to read as follows:

   "The European Committee on Crime Problems (CDPC) is responsible for following the application of the Convention. The CDPC:

   (a) shall be kept informed regarding the application of the Convention;

   (b) shall make proposals with a view to facilitating or improving the application of the Convention;

   (c) shall make recommendations to the Committee of Ministers concerning the proposals for amendments to the Convention, and shall give its opinion on any proposals for amendments to the Convention submitted by a Contracting State in accordance with Articles 12 and 13;

   (d) shall, at the request of a Contracting State, express an opinion on any question concerning the application of the Convention;

   (e) shall do whatever is necessary to facilitate a friendly settlement of any difficulty which may arise out of the execution of the Convention;

   (f) shall make recommendations to the Committee of Ministers concerning non-member States of the Council of Europe to be invited to accede to the Convention in accordance with Article 14, paragraph 3;

   (g) shall submit every year to the Committee of Ministers of the Council of Europe a report on the follow-up given to this article in the application of the Convention.".

3. Paragraph 2 of new Article 10 shall be deleted.

Article 7

1. Article 10 of the Convention shall become Article 11.

2. In the first sentence of paragraph 1 of new Article 11, the terms "Article 9, paragraph 2" shall be replaced by the terms "Article 10.e, or by negotiation". In the second sentence of this paragraph, the term "two" shall be deleted. The remaining sentences of this paragraph shall be deleted.

3. Paragraph 2 of new Article 11 shall become paragraph 6 of this article. The sentence "Where a majority cannot be reached, the referee shall have a casting vote" shall be added after the second sentence and in the last sentence the terms "Its award" shall be replaced by the terms "The tribunal's judgment".

4. The text of new Article 11 shall be supplemented by the following paragraphs:

"2. In the case of disputes involving Parties which are member States of the Council of Europe, where a Party fails to nominate its arbitrator in pursuance of paragraph 1 of this article within three months following the request for arbitration, an arbitrator shall be nominated by the President of the European Court of Human Rights at the request of the other Party.

3. In the case of disputes involving any Party which is not a member of the Council of Europe, where a Party fails to nominate its arbitrator in pursuance of paragraph 1 of this article within

three months following the request for arbitration, an arbitrator shall be nominated by the President of the International Court of Justice at the request of the other Party.

4. In the cases covered by paragraphs 2 and 3 of this article, where the President of the Court concerned is a national of one of the Parties to the dispute, this duty shall be carried out by the Vice-President of the Court, or if the Vice-President is a national of one of the Parties to the dispute, by the most senior judge of the Court who is not a national of one of the Parties to the dispute.

5. The procedures referred to in paragraphs 2 or 3 and 4 above apply, *mutatis mutandis*, where the arbitrators fail to agree on the nomination of a referee in accordance with paragraph 1 of this article."

DOCUMENT 20

International Convention Against the Taking of Hostages 1979
1316 UNTS 205; 18 ILM 1456 (1979)

The Convention was adopted on 17 December 1979 as an annex to General Assembly Resolution 34/146 and entered into force on 3 June 1983.

There are 138 parties, including all the major powers.

Related to concerns about offences against diplomats **(see Document 17)** *the international community viewed with alarm the increasing number of hostage-takings in the 1970s. The Sixth (Legal) Committee of the UN General Assembly was mandated to address the issue and produced a text that was markedly similar to that already enacted for diplomats.*

The Convention identifies and defines the proscribed acts in Article 1. It requires the Contracting States to criminalise these acts and to make them punishable by appropriate penalties (Article 2). Each Contracting State is to establish its jurisdiction, when one of the Convention's offences is committed in its territory or on one of its ships or aircraft, when the offender is a national, when the acts seeks to compel a State to do or abstain from doing some act and, if it chooses, when the victim is a national (Article 5(1)). Each Contracting State is required to report an offender to its prosecution authorities or to extradite him (Article 8) – the aut dedere aut judicare *principle. There may however be no extradition where the purpose is to prosecute or punish a person on account of his race, religion, nationality, ethnic origin or political opinion (Article 9(1)). The Convention declares the specified offences to be extraditable offences under existing extradition treaties and to be included in future extradition treaties (Article 10(1)); if there is no extradition treaty, the Convention itself may be treated as such (Article 10(2)). There may be no extradition where the purpose is to prosecute or punish a person on account of his race, religion, nationality, ethic origin or political opinion (Article 9(1)(a)). There are fair treatment guarantees for proceedings under the Convention (Article 8(2)) and, for aliens, consular access (Article 6(3)). Parties are to afford one another the greatest measure of assistance (Article 11). Because of the nature of hostage-taking, there is a specific obligation to secure the release of any hostage (Article 3).*

See the other global terrorism conventions **(Documents 11–12, 15–17, 21–26 and 28).**

The States Parties to this Convention,

Having in mind the purposes and principles of the Charter of the United Nations concerning the maintenance of international peace and security and the promotion of friendly relations and co-operation among States,

Recognising in particular that everyone has the right to life, liberty and security of person, as set out in the Universal Declaration of Human Rights and the International Covenant on Civil and Political Rights,

Reaffirming the principle of equal rights and self-determination of peoples as enshrined in the Charter of the United Nations and the Declaration on Principles of International Law concerning Friendly Relations and Co-operation among States in accordance with the Charter of the United Nations, as well as in other relevant resolutions of the General Assembly,

Considering that the taking of hostages is an offence of grave concern to the international community and that, in accordance with the provisions of this Convention, any person committing an act of hostage taking shall either be prosecuted or extradited,

Being convinced that it is urgently necessary to develop international co-operation between States in devising and adopting effective measures for the prevention, prosecution and punishment of all acts of taking of hostages as manifestations of international terrorism,

Have agreed as follows:

Article 1

1. Any person who seizes or detains and threatens to kill, to injure or to continue to detain another person (hereinafter referred to as the "hostage") in order to compel a third party, namely, a State, an international intergovernmental organization, a natural or juridical person, or a group of persons, to do or abstain from doing any act as an explicit or implicit condition for the release of the hostage commits the offence of taking of hostages ("hostage-taking") within the meaning of this Convention.

2. Any person who:
   (a) attempts to commit an act of hostage-taking; or
   (b) participates as an accomplice of anyone who commits or attempts to commit an act of hostage-taking likewise commits an offence for the purposes of this Convention.

Article 2

Each State Party shall make the offences set forth in article 1 punishable by appropriate penalties which take into account the grave nature of those offences.

Article 3

1. The State Party in the territory of which the hostage is held by the offender shall take all measures it considers appropriate to ease the situation of the hostage, in particular, to secure his release and, after his release, to facilitate, when relevant, his departure.

2. If any object which the offender has obtained as a result of the taking of hostages comes into the custody of a State Party, that State Party shall return it as soon as possible to the hostage or the third party referred to in article 1, as the case may be, or to the appropriate authorities thereof.

Article 4

States Parties shall co-operate in the prevention of the offences set forth in article 1, particularly by:

(a) taking all practicable measures to prevent preparations in their respective territories for the commission of those offences within or outside their territories, including measures to prohibit in their territories illegal activities of persons, groups and organizations that encourage, instigate, organize or engage in the perpetration of acts of taking of hostages;

(b) exchanging information and co-ordinating the taking of administrative and other measures as appropriate to prevent the commission of those offences.

Article 5

1. Each State Party shall take such measures as may be necessary to establish its jurisdiction over any of the offences set forth in article 1 which are committed:

    (a) in its territory or on board a ship or aircraft registered in that State;

    (b) by any of its nationals or, if that State considers it appropriate, by those stateless persons who have their habitual residence in its territory;

    (c) in order to compel that State to do or abstain from doing any act; or

    (d) with respect to a hostage who is a national of that State, if that State considers it appropriate.

2. Each State Party shall likewise take such measures as may be necessary to establish its jurisdiction over the offences set forth in article 1 in cases where the alleged offender is present in its territory and it does not extradite him to any of the States mentioned in paragraph 1 of this article.

3. This Convention does not exclude any criminal jurisdiction exercised in accordance with internal law.

Article 6

1. Upon being satisfied that the circumstances so warrant, any State Party in the territory of which the alleged offender is present shall, in accordance with its laws, take him into custody or take other measures to ensure his presence for such time as is necessary to enable any criminal or extradition proceedings to be instituted. That State Party shall immediately make a preliminary inquiry into the facts.

2. The custody or other measures referred to in paragraph 1 of this article shall be notified without delay directly or through the Secretary-General of the United Nations to:

    (a) the State where the offence was committed;

    (b) the State against which compulsion has been directed or attempted;

    (c) the State of which the natural or juridical person against whom compulsion has been directed or attempted is a national;

    (d) the State of which the hostage is a national or in the territory of which he has his habitual residence;

    (e) the State of which the alleged offender is a national or, if he is a stateless person, in the territory of which he has his habitual residence;

    (f) the international intergovernmental organization against which compulsion has been directed or attempted;

    (g) all other States concerned.

3. Any person regarding whom the measures referred to in paragraph 1 of this article are being taken shall be entitled:

    (a) to communicate without delay with the nearest appropriate representative of the State of which he is a national or which is otherwise entitled to establish such communication or, if he is a stateless person, the State in the territory of which he has his habitual residence;

    (b) to be visited by a representative of that State.

4. The rights referred to in paragraph 3 of this article shall be exercised in conformity with the laws and regulations of the State in the territory of which the alleged offender is present subject to the proviso, however, that the said laws and regulations must enable full effect to be given to the purposes for which the rights accorded under paragraph 3 of this article are intended.

5. The provisions of paragraphs 3 and 4 of this article shall be without prejudice to the right of any State Party having a claim to jurisdiction in accordance with paragraph 1(b) of article 5 to invite the International Committee of the Red Cross to communicate with and visit the alleged offender.

6. The State which makes the preliminary inquiry contemplated in paragraph 1 of this article shall promptly report its findings to the States or organization referred to in paragraph 2 of this article and indicate whether it intends to exercise jurisdiction.

Article 7

The State Party where the alleged offender is prosecuted shall in accordance with its laws communicate the final outcome of the proceedings to the Secretary-General of the United Nations, who shall transmit the information to the other States concerned and the international intergovernmental organizations concerned.

Article 8

1. The State Party in the territory of which the alleged offender is found shall, if it does not extradite him, be obliged, without exception whatsoever and whether or not the offence was committed in its territory, to submit the case to its competent authorities for the purpose of prosecution, through proceedings in accordance with the laws of that State. Those authorities shall take their decision in the same manner as in the case of any ordinary offence of a grave nature under the law of that State.

2. Any person regarding whom proceedings are being carried out in connection with any of the offences set forth in article 1 shall be guaranteed fair treatment at all stages of the proceedings, including enjoyment of all the rights and guarantees provided by the law of the State in the territory of which he is present.

Article 9

1. A request for the extradition of an alleged offender, pursuant to this Convention, shall not be granted if the requested State Party has substantial grounds for believing:

    (a) that the request for extradition for an offence set forth in article 1 has been made for the purpose of prosecuting or punishing a person on account of his race, religion, nationality, ethnic origin or political opinion; or

    (b) that the person's position may be prejudiced:

        (i) for any of the reasons mentioned in subparagraph (a) of this paragraph, or

        (ii) for the reason that communication with him by the appropriate authorities of the State entitled to exercise rights of protection cannot be effected.

2. With respect to the offences as defined in this Convention, the provisions of all extradition treaties and arrangements applicable between States Parties are modified as between States Parties to the extent that they are incompatible with this Convention.

Article 10

1. The offences set forth in article 1 shall be deemed to be included as extraditable offences in any extradition treaty existing between States Parties. States Parties undertake to include such offences as extraditable offences in every extradition treaty to be concluded between them.

2. If a State Party which makes extradition conditional on the existence of a treaty receives a request for extradition from another State Party with which it has no extradition treaty, the requested State may at its option consider this Convention as the legal basis for extradition in respect of the offences set forth in article 1. Extradition shall be subject to the other conditions provided by the law of the requested State.

3. States Parties which do not make extradition conditional on the existence of a treaty shall recognize the offences set forth in article I as extraditable offences between themselves subject to the conditions provided by the law of the requested State.

4. The offences set forth in article I shall be treated, for the purpose of extradition between States Parties, as if they had been committed not only in the place in which they occurred but also in the territories of the States required to establish their jurisdiction in accordance with paragraph I of article 5.

Article 11

1. States Parties shall afford one another the greatest measure of assistance in connexion with criminal proceedings brought in respect of the offences set forth in article I, including the supply of all evidence at their disposal necessary for the proceedings.

2. The provisions of paragraph I of this article shall not affect obligations concerning mutual judicial assistance embodied in any other treaty.

Article 12

In so far as the Geneva Conventions of 1949 for the protection of war victims or the Additional Protocols to those Conventions are applicable to a particular act of hostage-taking, and in so far as States Parties to this Convention are bound under those conventions to prosecute or hand over the hostage-taker, the present Convention shall not apply to an act of hostage-taking committed in the course of armed conflicts as defined in the Geneva Conventions of 1949 and the Protocols thereto, including armed conflicts mentioned in article I, paragraph 4, of Additional Protocol I of 1977, in which peoples are fighting against colonial domination and alien occupation and against racist regimes in the exercise of their right of self- determination, as enshrined in the Charter of the United Nations and the Declaration on Principles of International Law concerning Friendly Relations and Co-operation among States in accordance with the Charter of the United Nations.

Article 13

This Convention shall not apply where the offence is committed within a single State, the hostage and the alleged offender are nationals of that State and the alleged offender is found in the territory of that State.

Article 14

Nothing in this Convention shall be construed as justifying the violation of the territorial integrity or political independence of a State in contravention of the Charter of the United Nations.

Article 15

The provisions of this Convention shall not affect the application of the Treaties on Asylum, in force at the date of the adoption of this Convention, as between the States which are parties to those Treaties; but a State Party to this convention may not invoke those Treaties with respect to another State Party to this Convention which is not a party to those treaties.

Article 16

1. Any dispute between two or more States Parties concerning the interpretation or application of this Convention which is not settled by negotiation shall, at the request of one of them, be submitted to arbitration. If within six months from the date of the request for arbitration the parties are unable to agree on the organization of the arbitration, any one of those parties may refer the dispute to the International Court of Justice by request in conformity with the Statute of the Court.

2. Each State may at the time of signature or ratification of this Convention or accession thereto declare that it does not consider itself bound by paragraph I of this article. The other States

Parties shall not be bound by paragraph 1 of this article with respect to any State Party which has made such a reservation.

3. Any State Party which has made a reservation in accordance with paragraph 2 of this article may at any time withdraw that reservation by notification to the Secretary-General in the United Nations.

DOCUMENT 21

Convention on the Physical Protection of Nuclear Material 1980

1456 UNTS 246; 18 ILM 1422 (1979)

The Convention was concluded under the auspices of the International Atomic Energy Agency on 27 October 1979, although not opened for signature until 3 March 1980, and entered into force on 8 February 1987.

There are 110 parties, including all the major powers.

In recognition of the threat posed by the theft on nuclear material in transit (preamble), the International Atomic Energy Agency negotiated this Convention, which is restricted in scope to certain types of nuclear material (Article 1) used for peaceful (and non-military) purposes in international transport (Article 2), although, for most purposes, it extends to its domestic use, storage and transport (Article 2(2)).

The Convention identifies offences in relation to nuclear material and requires the Contracting States to criminalise these acts and to make them punishable by appropriate penalties (Article 7). Each Contracting State is to establish its jurisdiction when one of the Convention's offences is committed in its territory or on one of its ships or aircraft and when the offender is a national (Article 8(1)). Each Contracting State is required to report an offender to its prosecution authorities or to extradite him (Article 10) – the aut dedere aut judicare *principle. The Convention declares the specified offences to be extraditable offences under existing extradition treaties and to be included in future extradition treaties (Article 11(1)); if there is no extradition treaty, the Convention itself may be treated as such (Article 11(2)). There are fair treatment guarantees for proceedings under the Convention (Article 12). Parties are to afford one another the greatest measure of assistance in proceedings under the Convention (Article 11).*

Attempts to elaborate an International Convention for the Suppression of Acts of Nuclear Terrorism (and a Comprehensive Convention on International Terrorism) have been ongoing since 1996. The Nuclear Terrorism Convention was adopted on 4 April 2005 (Document 28).

See the other global terrorism Conventions (Documents 11–12, 15–17, 20, 22–26 and 28).

The States Parties to this Convention,

Recognising the right of all States to develop and apply nuclear energy for peaceful purposes and their legitimate interests in the potential benefits to be derived from the peaceful application of nuclear energy,

Convinced of the need for facilitating international co-operation in the peaceful application of nuclear energy,

Desiring to avert the potential dangers posed by the unlawful taking and use of nuclear material.

Convinced that offences relating to nuclear material are a matter of grave concern and that there is an urgent need to adopt appropriate and effective measures to ensure the prevention, detection and punishment of such offences,

Aware of the need for international co-operation to establish, in conformity with the national law of each State Party and with this Convention, effective measures for the physical protection of nuclear material,

Convinced that this Convention should facilitate the safe transfer of nuclear material.

Stressing also the importance of the physical protection of nuclear material in domestic use. storage and transport,

Recognising the importance of effective physical protection of nuclear material used for military purposes, and understanding that such material is and will continue to be accorded stringent physical protection.

Have agreed as follows:

Article 1

For the purposes of this Convention:

(a) "nuclear material" means plutonium except that with isotopic concentration exceeding 80% in plutonium-238; uranium-233; uranium enriched in the isotopes 235 or 233; uranium containing the mixture of isotopes as occurring in nature other than in the form of ore or ore-residue; any material containing one or more of the foregoing;

(b) "uranium enriched in the isotope 235 or 233" means uranium containing the isotopes 235 or 233 or both in an amount such that the abundance ratio of the sum of these isotopes to the isotope 238 is greater than the ratio of the isotope 235 to the isotope 238 occurring in nature;

(c) "international nuclear transport" means the carriage of a consignment of nuclear material by any means of transportation intended to go beyond the territory of the State where the shipment originates beginning with the departure from a facility of the shipper in that State and ending with the arrival at a facility of the receiver within the State of ultimate destination.

Article 2

1. This Convention shall apply to nuclear material used for peaceful purposes while in international nuclear transport.

2. With the exception of articles 3 and 4 and paragraph 3 of article 5, this Convention shall also apply to nuclear material used for peaceful purposes while in domestic use, storage and transport.

3. Apart from the commitments expressly undertaken by States Parties in the articles covered by paragraph 2 with respect to nuclear material used for peaceful purposes while in domestic use, storage and transport, nothing in this Convention shall be interpreted as affecting the sovereign rights of a State regarding the domestic use, storage and transport of such nuclear material.

Article 3

Each State Party shall take appropriate steps within the framework of its national law and consistent with international law to ensure as far as practicable that, during international nuclear transport, nuclear material within its territory, or on board a ship or aircraft under its jurisdiction insofar as such ship or aircraft is engaged in the transport to or from that State, is protected at the levels described in Annex 1.

Article 4

1. Each State Party shall not export or authorize the export of nuclear material unless the State Party has received assurances that such material will be protected during the international nuclear transport at the levels described in Annex 1.

2. Each State Party shall not import or authorize the import of nuclear material from a State not party to this Convention unless the State Party has received assurances that such material will during the international nuclear transport be protected at the levels described in Annex 1.

3. A State Party shall not allow the transit of its territory by land or internal waterways or through its airports or seaports of nuclear material between States that are not parties to this Convention unless the State Party has received assurances as far as practicable that this nuclear material will be protected during international nuclear transport at the levels described in Annex 1.

4. Each State Party shall apply within the framework of its national law the levels of physical protection described in Annex 1 to nuclear material being transported from a part of that State to another part of the same State through international waters or airspace.

5. The State Party responsible for receiving assurances that the nuclear material will be protected at the levels described in Annex 1 according to paragraphs 1 to 3 shall identify and inform in advance States which the nuclear material is expected to transit by land or internal waterways, or whose airports or seaports it is expected to enter.

6. The responsibility for obtaining assurances referred to in paragraph 1 may be transferred, by mutual agreement, to the State Party involved in the transport as the importing State.

7. Nothing in this article shall be interpreted as in any way affecting the territorial sovereignty and jurisdiction of a State, including that over its airspace and territorial sea.

Article 7

1. The intentional commission of:

   (a) an act without lawful authority which constitutes the receipt, possession, use, transfer, alteration, disposal or dispersal of nuclear material and which causes or is likely to cause death or serious injury to any person or substantial damage to property;

   (b) a theft or robbery of nuclear material;

   (c) an embezzlement or fraudulent obtaining of nuclear material;

   (d) an act constituting a demand for nuclear material by threat or use of force or by any other form of intimidation;

   (e) a threat:

       (i) to use nuclear material to cause death or serious injury to any person or substantial property damage, or

       (ii) to commit an offence described in sub-paragraph (b) in order to compel a natural or legal person, international organization or State to do or to refrain from doing any act;

   (f) an attempt to commit any offence described in paragraphs (a), (b) or (c); and

   (g) an act which constitutes participation in any offence described in paragraphs (a) to (f) shall be made a punishable offence by each State Party under its national law.

2. Each State Party shall make the offences described in this article punishable by appropriate penalties which take into account their grave nature.

Article 8

1. Each State Party shall take such measures as may be necessary to establish its jurisdiction over the offences set forth in article 7 in the following cases:

   (a) when the offence is committed in the territory of that State or on board a ship or aircraft registered in that State;

   (b) when the alleged offender is a national of that State.

2. Each State Party shall likewise take such measures as may be necessary to establish its jurisdiction over these offences in cases where the alleged offender is present in its territory and it does not extradite him pursuant to article 11 to any of the States mentioned in paragraph 1.

3. This Convention does not exclude any criminal jurisdiction exercised in accordance with national law.

4. In addition to the States Parties mentioned in paragraphs 1 and 2, each State Party may, consistent with international law, establish its jurisdiction over the offences set forth in article 7 when it is involved in international nuclear transport as the exporting or importing State.

Article 9

Upon being satisfied that the circumstances so warrant, the State Party in whose territory the alleged offender is present shall take appropriate measures, including detention, under its national law to ensure his presence for the purpose of prosecution or extradition. Measures taken according to this article shall be notified without delay to the States required to establish jurisdiction pursuant to article 8 and, where appropriate, all other States concerned.

Article 10

The State Party in whose territory the alleged offender is present shall, if it does not extradite him, submit, without exception whatsoever and without undue delay, the case to its competent authorities for the purpose of prosecution, through proceedings in accordance with the laws of that State.

Article 11

1. The offences in article 7 shall be deemed to be included as extraditable offences in any extradition treaty existing between States Parties. States Parties undertake to include those offences as extraditable offences in every future extradition treaty to be concluded between them.

2. If a State Party which makes extradition conditional on the existence of a treaty receives a request for extradition from another State Party with which it has no extradition treaty, it may at its option consider this Convention as the legal basis for extradition in respect of those offences. Extradition shall be subject to the other conditions provided by the law of the requested State.

3. States Parties which do not make extradition conditional on the existence of a treaty shall recognize those offences as extraditable offences between themselves subject to the conditions provided by the law of the requested State.

4. Each of the offences shall be treated, for the purpose of extradition between States Parties, as if it had been committed not only in the place in which it occurred but also in the territories of the States Parties required to establish their jurisdiction in accordance with paragraph 1 of article 8.

Article 12

Any person regarding whom proceedings are being carried out in connection with any of the offences set forth in article 7 shall be guaranteed fair treatment at all stages of the proceedings.

Article 13

1. States Parties shall afford one another the greatest measure of assistance in connection with criminal proceedings brought in respect of the offences set forth in article 7, including the supply of evidence at their disposal necessary for the proceedings. The law of the State requested shall apply in all cases.

2. The provisions of paragraph I shall not affect obligations under any other treaty, bilateral or multilateral, which governs or will govern, in whole or in part, mutual assistance in criminal matters.

Article 14

1. Each State Party shall inform the depositary of its laws and regulations which give effect to this Convention. The depositary shall communicate such information periodically to all States Parties.

2. The State Party where an alleged offender is prosecuted shall, wherever practicable, first communicate the final outcome of the proceedings to the States directly concerned. The State Party shall also communicate the final outcome to the depositary who shall inform all States.

3. Where an offence involves nuclear material used for peaceful purposes in domestic use, storage or transport, and both the alleged offender and the nuclear material remain in the territory of the State Party in which the offence was committed, nothing in this Convention shall be interpreted as requiring that State Party to provide information concerning criminal proceeding arising out of such an offence.

DOCUMENT 22

Convention for the Suppression of Unlawful Acts Against the Safety of Maritime Navigation 1988
1678 UNTS 221; 27 ILM 668 (1988)

The Convention was adopted under the auspices of the International Maritime Organization on 10 March 1988 and entered into force on 1 March 1992.

There are 112 parties, including all the major powers.

The increasing acts of violence against shipping on the high seas in the 1980s, particularly the hijacking of the Achille Lauro in October 1985, led to moves to draft a dedicated convention akin to the Hague and Montreal Conventions of 1970 and 1971 relating to aircraft (**Documents 12 and 15**). *The Convention applies to non-military vessels (Article 2(1)) on the high seas (Article 4(1)).*

The Convention identifies offences in relation to hijacking of ships (Article 3(1) and requires the Contracting States to make them punishable by appropriate penalties (Article 5). Each Contracting State is to establish its jurisdiction where one of the Convention's offences is committed on its ships, in its territory when the offender is a national (Article 61)). Additionally, the State may assert jurisdiction where the victim is a national or where the offence is designed to compel the State to do or abstain from doing some act (Article 6(2)). Each Contracting State is required to report an offender to its prosecution authorities or to extradite him (Article 10(1)) – the aut dedere aut judicare *principle. The Convention declares the specified offences to be extraditable offences under existing extradition treaties and to be included in future extradition treaties (Article 11(1)); if there is no extradition treaty, the Convention itself may be treated as such (Article 11(2)). There are fair treatment guarantees for proceedings under the Convention (Article 10(2)). Parties are to afford one another the greatest measure of assistance in proceedings under the Convention (Article 13(1)).*

See the Protocol for the Suppression of Unlawful Acts Against the Safety of Fixed Platforms Located on the Continental Shelf 1988 (**Document 23**).

See the other global terrorism conventions (**Documents 11–12, 15–17, 20–21, 24–26 and 28**).

The States Parties to this Convention,

Having in mind the purposes and principles of the Charter of the United Nations concerning the maintenance of international peace and security and the promotion of friendly relations and co-operation among States,

Recognising in particular that everyone has the right to life, liberty and security of person, as set out in the Universal Declaration of Human Rights and the International Covenant on Civil and Political Rights,

Deeply concerned about the world-wide escalation of acts of terrorism in all its forms, which endanger or take innocent human lives, jeopardize fundamental freedoms and seriously impair the dignity of human beings,

Considering that unlawful acts against the safety of maritime navigation jeopardize the safety of persons and property, seriously affect the operation of maritime services, and undermine the confidence of the peoples of the world in the safety of maritime navigation,

Considering that the occurrence of such acts is a matter of grave concern to the international community as a whole,

Being convinced of the urgent need to develop international co-operation between States in devising and adopting effective and practical measures for the prevention of all unlawful acts against the safety of maritime navigation, and the prosecution and punishment of their perpetrators,

Recalling resolution 40/61 of the General Assembly of the United Nations of 9 December 1985 which, *inter alia*, "urges all States unilaterally and in co-operation with other States, as well as relevant United Nations organs, to contribute to the progressive elimination of causes underlying international terrorism and to pay special attention to all situations, including colonialism, racism and situations involving mass and flagrant violations of human rights and fundamental freedoms and those involving alien occupation, that may give rise to international terrorism and may endanger international peace and security",

Recalling further that resolution 40/61 "unequivocally condemns, as criminal all acts, methods and practices of terrorism wherever and by whomever committed, including those which jeopardize friendly relations among States and their security",

Recalling also that by resolution 40/61, the International Maritime Organization was invited to "study the problem of terrorism aboard or against ships with a view to making recommendations on appropriate measures",

Having in mind resolution A.584(14) of 20 November 1985, of the Assembly of the International Maritime Organization, which called for development of measures to prevent unlawful acts which threaten the safety of ships and the security of their passengers and crews,

Noting that acts of the crew which are subject to normal shipboard discipline are outside the purview of this Convention,

Affirming the desirability of monitoring rules and standards relating to the prevention and control of unlawful acts against ships and persons on board ships, with a view to updating them as necessary, and, to this effect, taking note with satisfaction of the Measures to Prevent Unlawful Acts against Passengers and Crews on Board Ships, recommended by the Maritime Safety Committee of the International Maritime Organization,

Affirming further that matters not regulated by this Convention continue to be governed by the rules and principles of general international law,

Recognising the need for all States, in combating unlawful acts against the safety of maritime navigation, strictly to comply with rules and principles of general international law,

Have agreed as follows:

Article 1
For the purposes of this Convention, "ship" means a vessel of any type whatsoever not permanently attached to the sea-bed, including dynamically supported craft, submersibles, or any other floating craft.

Article 2
1. This Convention does not apply to:

    (a) a warship; or

    (b) a ship owned or operated by a State when being used as a naval auxiliary or for customs or police purposes; or

    (c) a ship which has been withdrawn from navigation or laid up.

2. Nothing in this Convention affects the immunities of warships and other government ships operated for non-commercial purposes.

Article 3
1. Any person commits an offence if that person unlawfully and intentionally:

    (a) seizes or exercises control over a ship by force or threat thereof or any other form of intimidation; or

    (b) performs an act of violence against a person on board a ship if that act is likely to endanger the safe navigation of that ship; or

    (c) destroys a ship or causes damage to a ship or to its cargo which is likely to endanger the safe navigation of that ship; or

    (d) places or causes to be placed on a ship, by any means whatsoever, a device or substance which is likely to destroy that ship, or cause damage to that ship or its cargo which endangers or is likely to endanger the safe navigation of that ship; or

    (e) destroys or seriously damages maritime navigational facilities or seriously interferes with their operation, if any such act is likely to endanger the safe navigation of a ship; or

    (f) communicates information which he knows to be false, thereby endangering the safe navigation of a ship; or

    (g) injures or kills any person, in connection with the commission or the attempted commission of any of the offences set forth in subparagraphs (a) to (f).

2. Any person also commits an offence if that person:

    (a) attempts to commit any of the offences set forth in paragraph 1; or

    (b) abets the commission of any of the offences set forth in paragraph 1 perpetrated by any person or is otherwise an accomplice of a person who commits such an offence; or

    (c) threatens, with or without a condition, as is provided for under national law, aimed at compelling a physical or juridical person to do or refrain from doing any act, to commit any of the of fences set forth in paragraph 1, subparagraphs (b), (c) and (e), if that threat is likely to endanger the safe navigation of the ship in question.

Article 4
1. This Convention applies if the ship is navigating of is scheduled to navigate into, through or from waters beyond the outer limit of the territorial sea of a single State, or the lateral limits of its territorial sea with adjacent States.

2. In cases where the Convention does not apply pursuant to paragraph 1, it nevertheless applies when the offender or the alleged offender is found in the territory of a State Party other than the State referred to in paragraph 1.

Article 5

Each State Party shall make the offences set forth in article 3 punishable by appropriate penalties which take into account the grave nature of those offences.

Article 6

1. Each State Party shall take such measures as may be necessary to establish its jurisdiction over the offences set forth in article 3 when the offence is committed:

    (a) against or on board a ship flying the flag of the State at the time the offence is committed; or

    (b) in the territory of that State, including its territorial sea; or

    (c) by a national of that State.

2. A State Party may also establish its jurisdiction over any such offence when:

    (a) it is committed by a stateless person whose habitual residence is in that State; or

    (b) during its commission a national of that State is seized, threatened, injured or killed; or

    (c) it is committed in an attempt to compel that State to do or abstain from doing any act.

3. Any State Party which has established jurisdiction mentioned in paragraph 2 shall notify the Secretary-General of the International Maritime Organization (hereinafter referred to as "the Secretary-General"). If such State Party subsequently rescinds that jurisdiction, it shall notify the Secretary-General.

4. Each State Party shall take such measures as may be necessary to establish its jurisdiction over the offences set forth in article 3 in cases where the alleged offender is present in its territory and it does not extradite him to any of the States Parties which have established their jurisdiction in accordance with paragraphs 1 and 2 of this article.

5. This Convention does not exclude any criminal jurisdiction exercised in accordance with national law.

Article 7

1. Upon being satisfied that the circumstances so warrant, any State Party in the territory of which the offender or the alleged offender is present shall, in accordance with its law, take him into custody or take other measures to ensure his presence for such time as is necessary to enable any criminal or extradition proceedings to be instituted.

2. Such State shall immediately make a preliminary inquiry into the facts, in accordance with its own legislation.

3. Any person regarding whom the measures referred to in paragraph 1 are being taken shall be entitled to:

    (a) communicate without delay with the nearest appropriate representative of the State of which he is a national or which is otherwise entitled to establish such communication or, if he is a stateless person, the State in the territory of which he has his habitual residence;

    (b) be visited by a representative of that State.

4. The rights referred to in paragraph 3 shall be exercised in conformity with the laws and regulations of the State in the territory of which the offender or the alleged offender is present, subject to the proviso that the said laws and regulations must enable full effect to be given to the purposes for which the rights accorded under paragraph 3 are intended.

5. When a State Party, pursuant to this article, has taken a person into custody, it shall immediately notify the States which have established jurisdiction in accordance with article 6, paragraph 1 and, if it considers it advisable, any other interested States, of the fact that such person is in custody and of the circumstances which warrant his detention. The State which makes the preliminary inquiry contemplated in paragraph 2 of this article shall promptly report its findings to the said States and shall indicate whether it intends to exercise jurisdiction.

Article 8

1. The master of a ship of a State Party (the "flag State") may deliver to the authorities of any other State Party (the "receiving State") any person who he has reasonable grounds to believe has committed one of the offences set forth in article 3.

2. The flag State shall ensure that the master of its ship is obliged, whenever practicable, and if possible before entering the territorial sea of the receiving State carrying on board any person whom the master intends to deliver in accordance with paragraph 1, to give notification to the authorities of the receiving State of his intention to deliver such person and the reasons therefor.

3. The receiving State shall accept the delivery, except where it has grounds to consider that the Convention is not applicable to the acts giving rise to the delivery, and shall proceed in accordance with the provisions of article 1. Any refusal to accept a delivery shall be accompanied by a statement of the reasons for refusal.

4. The flag State shall ensure that the master of its ship is obliged to furnish the authorities of the receiving State with the evidence in the master's possession which pertains to the alleged offence.

5. A receiving State which has accepted the delivery of a person in accordance with paragraph 3 may, in turn, request the flag State to accept delivery of that person. The flag State shall consider any such request, and if it accedes to the request it shall proceed in accordance with article 7. If the flag State declines a request, it shall furnish the receiving State with a statement of the reasons therefor.

Article 9

Nothing in this Convention shall affect in any way the rules of international law pertaining to the competence of States to exercise investigative or enforcement jurisdiction on board ships not flying their flag.

Article 10

1. The State Party in the territory of which the offender or the alleged offender is found shall, in cases to which article 6 applies, if it does not extradite him, be obliged, without exception whatsoever and whether or not the offence was committed in its territory, to submit the case without delay to its competent authorities for the purpose of prosecution, through proceedings in accordance with the laws of that State. Those authorities shall take their decision in the same manner as in the case of any other offence of a grave nature under the law of that State.

2. Any person regarding whom proceedings are being carried out in connection with any of the offences set forth in article 3 shall be guaranteed fair treatment at all stages of the proceedings, including enjoyment of all the rights and guarantees provided for such proceedings by the law of the State in the territory of which he is present.

Article 11

1. The offences set forth in article 3 shall be deemed to be included as extraditable offences in any extradition treaty existing between any of the States Parties. States Parties undertake to include such offences as extraditable offences in every extradition treaty to be concluded between them.

2. If a State Party which makes extradition conditional on the existence of a treaty receives a request for extradition from another State Party with which it has no extradition treaty, the requested State Party may, at its option, consider this Convention as a legal basis for extradition in respect of the offences set forth in article 3. Extradition shall be subject to the other conditions provided by the law of the requested State Party.

3. States Parties which do not make extradition conditional on the existence of a treaty shall recognize the offences set forth in article 3 as extraditable offences between themselves, subject to the conditions provided by the law of the requested State.

4. If necessary, the offences set forth in article 3 shall be treated, for the purposes of extradition between States Parties, as if they had been committed not only in the place in which they occurred but also in a place within the jurisdiction of the State Party requesting extradition.

5. A State Party which receives more than one request for extradition from States which have established jurisdiction in accordance with article 7 and which decides not to prosecute shall, in selecting the State to which the offender or alleged offender is to be extradited, pay due regard to the interests and responsibilities of the State Party whose flag the ship was flying at the time of the commission of the offence.

6. In considering a request for the extradition of an alleged offender pursuant to this Convention, the requested State shall pay due regard to whether his rights as set forth in article 7, paragraph 3, can be effected in the requesting State.

7. With respect to the offences as defined in this Convention, the provisions of all extradition treaties and arrangements applicable between States Parties are modified as between States Parties to the extent that they are incompatible with this Convention.

Article 12

1.   State Parties shall afford one another the greatest measure of assistance in connection with criminal proceedings brought in respect of the offences set forth in article 3, including assistance in obtaining evidence at their disposal necessary for the proceedings.

2. States Parties shall carry out their obligations under paragraph 1 in conformity with any treaties on mutual assistance that may exist between them. In the absence of such treaties, States Parties shall afford each other assistance in accordance with their national law.

Article 13

1. States Parties shall co-operate in the prevention of the offences set forth in article 3, particularly by:

    (a) taking all practicable measures to prevent preparations in their respective territories for the commission of those offences within or outside their territories;

    (b) exchanging information in accordance with their national law, and co-ordinating administrative and other measures taken as appropriate to prevent the commission of offences set forth in article 3.

2. When, due to the commission of an offence set forth in article 3, the passage of a ship has been delayed or interrupted, any State Party in whose territory the ship or passengers or crew are present shall be bound to exercise all possible efforts to avoid a ship, its passengers, crew or cargo being unduly detained or delayed.

Article 14

Any State Party having reason to believe that an offence set forth in article 3 will be committed shall, in accordance with its national law, furnish as promptly as possible any relevant information in its possession to those States which it believes would be the States having established jurisdiction in accordance with article 6.

Article 15

1. Each State Party shall, in accordance with its national law, provide to the Secretary-General, as promptly as possible, any relevant information in its possession concerning:

    (a) the circumstances of the offence;

(b) the action taken pursuant to article 13, paragraph 2;

(c) the measures taken in relation to the offender or the alleged offender and, in particular, the results of any extradition proceedings or other legal proceedings.

2. The State Party where the alleged offender is prosecuted shall, in accordance with its national law, communicate the final outcome of the proceedings to the Secretary-General.

3. The information transmitted in accordance with paragraphs 1 and 2 shall be communicated by the Secretary-General to all States Parties, to Members of the International Maritime Organization (hereinafter referred to as "the Organization"), to the other States concerned, and to the appropriate international intergovernmental organizations.

Article 16

1. Any dispute between two or more States Parties concerning the interpretation or application of this Convention which cannot be settled through negotiation within a reasonable time shall, at the request of one of them, be submitted to arbitration. If, within six months from the date of the request for arbitration, the parties are unable to agree on the organization of the arbitration any one of those parties may refer the dispute to the International Court of Justice by request in conformity with the Statute of the Court.

2. Each State may at the time of signature or ratification, acceptance or approval of this Convention or accession thereto, declare that it does not consider itself bound by any or all of the provisions of paragraph 1. The other States Parties shall not be bound by those provisions with respect to any State Party which has made such a reservation.

3. Any State which has made a reservation in accordance with paragraph 2 may, at any time, withdraw that reservation by notification to the Secretary-General.

DOCUMENT 23

Protocol for the Suppression of Unlawful Acts Against the Safety of Fixed Platforms Located on the Continental Shelf 1988

1678 UNTS 303; 27 ILM 685 (1988)

The Protocol was adopted under the auspices of the International Maritime Organization on 10 March 1988 and entered into force on 1 March 1992.

There are 104 parties, including all the major powers.

The Protocol was drafted and concluded at the same time as the Convention for the Suppression of Unlawful Acts against the Safety of Maritime Navigation (**Document 22**). *Essentially, it extends that Convention to fixed platforms on the continental shelf with only minor differences (Article 1). Thus, the proscribed acts (Article 2) and the extent of a Contracting State's jurisdiction (Article 3) are somewhat differently described.*

See the other global terrorism conventions (**Documents 11–12, 15–17, 20–21, 24–26 and 28**).

The States Parties to this Convention,

Being Parties to the Convention for the Suppression of Unlawful Acts Against the Safety of Maritime Navigation,

Recognising that the reasons for which the Convention was elaborated also apply to fixed platforms located on the continental shelf,

Taking account of the provisions of that Convention,

Affirming that matters not regulated by this Protocol continue to be governed by the rules and principles of general International law,

Have agreed as follows:

Article 1

1. The provisions of articles 5 and 7 and of articles 10 to 16 of the Convention for the Suppression of unlawful Acts against the Safety of Maritime Navigation (hereafter referred to as "the Convention") shall also apply *mutatis mutandis* to the offences set forth in article 2 of this Protocol where such offences are committed on board or against fixed platforms located on the continental shelf.

2. In cases where this Protocol does not apply pursuant to paragraph 1, it nevertheless applies when the offender or the alleged offender is found in the territory of a State Party other than the State in whose international waters or territorial sea the fixed platform is located.

3. For the purposes of this Protocol, "fixed platform" means an artificial island, installation or structure permanently attached to the sea-bed for the purpose of exploration or exploitation of resources or for other economic purposes.

Article 2

1. Any person commits an offence if that person unlawfully and intentionally:

    (a) seizes or exercises control over a fixed platform by force or threat thereof or any other form of intimidation; or

    (b) performs an act of violence against a person on board a fixed platform If that act is likely to endanger its safety; or

    (c) destroys a fixed platform or causes damage to it which is likely to endanger its safety; or

    (d) places or causes to be placed on a fixed platform, by any means whatsoever, a device or substance which is likely to destroy that fixed platform or likely to endanger its safety; or

    (e) injures or kills any person in connection with the commission or the attempted commission of any of the offences set forth in subparagraphs (a) to (d).

2. Any person also commits an offence if that person:

    (a) attempts to commit any of the offences set forth in paragraph 1; or

    (b) abets the commission of any such offences perpetrated by any person or is otherwise an accomplice of a person who commits such an offence; or

    (c) threatens, with or without a condition, as is provided for under national law, aimed at compelling a physical or juridical person to do or refrain from doing any act, to commit any of the offences set forth in paragraph 1, subparagraphs (b) and (c), If that threat is likely to endanger the safety of the fixed platform.

Article 3

1. Each State Party shall take such measures as may be necessary to establish its jurisdiction over the offences set forth in article 2 when the offence is committed:

    (a) against or on board a fixed platform while it is located on the continental shelf of that State; or

    (b) by a national of that State.

2. A State Party may also establish its jurisdiction over any such offence when:

    (a) it is committed by a stateless person whose habitual residence is in that State;

    (b) during its commission a national of that State is seized, threatened, injured or killed; or

(c) it is committed in an attempt to compel that State to do or abstain from doing any act.

3. Any State Party which has established jurisdiction mentioned in paragraph 2 shall notify the Secretary-General of the International Maritime Organisation (hereinafter referred to as "the Secretary-General"). If such State Party subsequently rescinds that Jurisdiction, it shall notify the Secretary-General.

4. Each State Party shall take such measures as may be necessary to establish its jurisdiction over the offences set forth in article 2 in cases where the alleged offender is present in its territory and it does not extradite him to any of the States Parties which have established their jurisdiction in accordance with paragraphs 1 and 2 of this article.

5. This Protocol does not exclude any criminal jurisdiction exercised in accordance with national law.

Article 4
Nothing in this Protocol shall affect in any way the rules of international law pertaining to fixed platforms located on the continental shelf.

DOCUMENT 24

Convention on the Marking of Plastic Explosives for the Purpose of Identification 1991
UN Doc S/22393 (1991); 30 ILM 721 (1991)

This Convention was adopted under the auspices of the International Civil Aviation Organization (ICAO) on 1 March 1991 and entered into force on 21 June 1998.

There are 111 parties, including all the major powers.

Following the destruction of Pan Am Flight 103 over Lockerbie in December 1988, the UN Security Council in Resolution 635 (1989) of 14 July 1989 called on ICAO to elaborate a regime for marking plastic explosives. This Convention is atypical of the global terrorism conventions (**Documents 11–12, 15–17, 20–23, 25–26 and 28**) *in that it identifies no specific offences to be criminalized and creates to explicit obligation to prosecute or extradite a suspected offender. It is concerned exclusively with measures to require the marking of plastic explosives. Nonetheless, extracts are included in the Deskbook because the Convention is generally regarded as one of the 13 global terrorism Conventions.*

The States Parties to this Convention,

Conscious of the implications of acts of terrorism for international security;

Expressing deep concern regarding terrorist acts aimed at destruction of aircraft, other means of transportation and other targets;

Concerned that plastic explosives have been used for such terrorist acts;

Considering that the marking of such explosives for the purpose of detection would contribute significantly to the prevention of such unlawful acts;

Recognising that for the purpose of deterring such unlawful acts there is an urgent need for an international instrument obliging States to adopt appropriate measures to ensure that plastic explosives are duly marked;

Considering United Nations Security Council Resolution 635 of 14 June 1989, and United Nations General Assembly Resolution 44/29 of 4 December 1989 urging the International Civil Aviation

Organization to intensify its work on devising an international regime for the marking of plastic or sheet explosives for the purpose of detection;

Bearing in mind Resolution A27–8 adopted unanimously by the 27th Session of the Assembly of the International Civil Aviation Organization which endorsed with the highest and overriding priority the preparation of a new international instrument regarding the marking of plastic or sheet explosives for detection;

Noting with satisfaction the role played by the Council of the International Civil Aviation Organization in the preparation of the Convention as well as its willingness to assume functions related to its implementation;

Have agreed as follows:

Article 1

For the purposes of this Convention:

1. "Explosives" mean explosive products, commonly known as "plastic explosives", including explosives in flexible or elastic sheet form, as described in the Technical Annex to this Convention.

2. "Detection agent" means a substance as described in the Technical Annex to this Convention which is introduced into an explosive to render it detectable.

3. "Marking" means introducing into an explosive a detection agent in accordance with the Technical Annex to this Convention.

4. "Manufacture" means any process, including reprocessing, that produces explosives.

5. "Duly authorized military devices" include, but are not restricted to, shells, bombs, projectiles, mines, missiles, rockets, shaped charges, grenades and perforators manufactured exclusively for military or police purposes according to the laws and regulations of the State Party concerned.

6. "Producer State" means any State in whose territory explosives are manufactured.

Article 2

Each State Party shall take the necessary and effective measures to prohibit and prevent the manufacture in its territory of unmarked explosives.

Article 3

1. Each State Party shall take the necessary and effective measures to prohibit and prevent the movement into or out of its territory of unmarked explosives.

2. The preceding paragraph shall not apply in respect of movements for purposes not inconsistent with the objectives of this Convention, by authorities of a State Party performing military or police functions, of unmarked explosives under the control of that State Party in accordance with paragraph 1 of Article IV.

Article 4

1. Each State Party shall take the necessary measures to exercise strict and effective control over the possession and transfer of possession of unmarked explosives which have been manufactured in or brought into its territory prior to the entry into force of this Convention in respect of that State, so as to prevent their diversion or use for purposes inconsistent with the objectives of this Convention.

2. Each State Party shall take the necessary measures to ensure that all stocks of those explosives referred to in paragraph 1 of this Article not held by its authorities performing military or police functions are destroyed or consumed for purposes not inconsistent with the objectives of this Convention, marked or rendered permanently ineffective, within a period of three years from the entry into force of this Convention in respect of that State.

3. Each State Party shall take the necessary measures to ensure that all stocks of those explosives referred to in paragraph I of this Article held by its authorities performing military or police functions and that are not incorporated as an integral part of duly authorized military devices are destroyed or consumed for purposes not inconsistent with the objectives of this Convention, marked or rendered permanently ineffective, within a period of fifteen years from the entry into force of this Convention in respect of that State.

4. Each State Party shall take the necessary measures to ensure the destruction, as soon as possible, in its territory of unmarked explosives which may be discovered therein and which are not referred to in the preceding paragraphs of this Article, other than stocks of unmarked explosives held by its authorities performing military or police functions and incorporated as an integral part of duly authorized military devices at the date of the entry into force of this Convention in respect of that State.

5. Each State Party shall take the necessary measures to exercise strict and effective control over the possession and transfer of possession of the explosives referred to in paragraph II of Part I of the Technical Annex to this Convention so as to prevent their diversion or use for purposes inconsistent with the objectives of this Convention.

6. Each State Party shall take the necessary measures to ensure the destruction, as soon as possible, in its territory of unmarked explosives manufactured since the coming into force of this Convention in respect of that State that are not incorporated as specified in paragraph II (d) of Part I of the Technical Annex to this Convention and of unmarked explosives which no longer fall within the scope of any other sub-paragraphs of the said paragraph II.

DOCUMENT 25

International Convention for the Suppression of Terrorist Bombings 1997
UN Doc A/RES/52/164 Annex; 37 ILM 249 (1997)

This Convention was adopted on 15 December 1997 as an annex to General Assembly Resolution 52/164 and entered into force on 23 May 2001.

There are 123 parties, including all the major powers.

The landmark General Assembly Declaration on Measures to Eliminate International Terrorism of 17 February 1995 (GA Res 49/60) began a process in the Assembly of addressing terrorism issues. The Declaration to Supplement the Declaration on Measures to Eliminate International Terrorism of 16 January 1997 (GA Res 51/210) established an Ad Hoc Committee charged, inter alia, *with elaborating an international convention for the suppression of terrorist bombings.*

The proscribed acts relating to terrorist bombings are identified and defined in fairly general terms in Article 2. The Convention requires the Contracting States to criminalise these acts (Article 4(a)) and make them punishable by appropriate penalties (Article 4(b)). It emphasises that these acts are to be under no circumstances justifiable in domestic law (Article 5). Each Contracting State is to establish its jurisdiction where one of the Convention's offences is committed in its territory or on its ships or aircraft or by one of its nationals (Article 6(1)). Additionally, the State may assert jurisdiction where the victim is a national, where the offence is committed against a State facility abroad or where the offence is designed to compel a State to do or abstain from doing some act (Article 6(2)). Each Contracting State is required to report an offender to its prosecution authorities or to extradite him (Article 8(1)) – the aut dedere aut judicare *principle. The Convention declares the proscribed acts to extraditable offences under existing extradition treaties and to be included in future extradition treaties (Article 9(1)); if there is no extradition treaty, the Convention itself may be treated as such (Article 9(2)). The Convention's offences are not to be regarded as political offences for the purpose of extradition (Article 11), although there may be no extradition where the purpose is to prosecute or punish a person on account of his race, religion, nationality, ethnic origin or political opinion (Article 12). There are fair treatment guarantees for proceedings under the Convention (Article 14). Parties are to afford one another the greatest measure of assistance in proceedings under the Convention (Article 10(1); see also Article 15).*

Attempts to elaborate a Comprehensive Convention on International Terrorism have been ongoing since 1996, as have negotiations towards an International Convention for the Suppression of Acts of Nuclear Terrorism. While the Nuclear Terrorism Convention was adopted in 2005 **(Document 28)** *and considerable progress has been made in the drafting of the Comprehensive Terrorism Convention, even the events of 11 September 2001 have not proved sufficient inspiration to overcome the remaining areas of disagreement, which in essence relate to whether the armed forces of States and national liberation movements are included in the Comprehensive Convention as capable of committing proscribed (terrorist) acts and whether the Comprehensive Convention prevails over the treaties in the sectoral régime. The Comprehensive Terrorism Convention is currently available in draft: UN Doc A/C.6/56/L.9 Annex I.*

See the other global terrorism conventions **(Documents 11–12, 15–17, 20–24 and 26)**.

The States Parties to this Convention,

Having in mind the purposes and principles of the Charter of the United Nations concerning the maintenance of international peace and security and the promotion of good-neighbourliness and friendly relations and cooperation among States,

Deeply concerned about the worldwide escalation of acts of terrorism in all its forms and manifestations,

Recalling the Declaration on the Occasion of the Fiftieth Anniversary of the United Nations of 24 October 1995,

Recalling also the Declaration on Measures to Eliminate International Terrorism, annexed to General Assembly resolution 49/60 of 9 December 1994, in which, *inter alia*, "the States Members of the United Nations solemnly reaffirm their unequivocal condemnation of all acts, methods and practices of terrorism as criminal and unjustifiable, wherever and by whomever committed, including those which jeopardize the friendly relations among States and peoples and threaten the territorial integrity and security of States",

Noting that the Declaration also encouraged States "to review urgently the scope of the existing international legal provisions on the prevention, repression and elimination of terrorism in all its forms and manifestations, with the aim of ensuring that there is a comprehensive legal framework covering all aspects of the matter",

Recalling General Assembly resolution 51/210 of 17 December 1996 and the Declaration to Supplement the 1994 Declaration on Measures to Eliminate International Terrorism annexed thereto,

Noting that terrorist attacks by means of explosives or other lethal devices have become increasingly widespread,

Noting also that existing multilateral legal provisions do not adequately address these attacks,

Being convinced of the urgent need to enhance international cooperation between States in devising and adopting effective and practical measures for the prevention of such acts of terrorism and for the prosecution and punishment of their perpetrators,

Considering that the occurrence of such acts is a matter of grave concern to the international community as a whole,

Noting that the activities of military forces of States are governed by rules of international law outside the framework of this Convention and that the exclusion of certain actions from the coverage of this Convention does not condone or make lawful otherwise unlawful acts, or preclude prosecution under other laws,

Have agreed as follows:

Article I

For the purposes of this Convention.

1. "State or government facility" includes any permanent or temporary facility or conveyance that is used or occupied by representatives of a State, members of Government, the legislature or the judiciary or by officials or employees of a State or any other public authority or entity or by employees or officials of an intergovernmental organization in connection with their official duties.

2. "Infrastructure facility" means any publicly or privately owned facility providing or distributing services for the benefit of the public, such as water, sewage, energy, fuel or communications.

3. "Explosive or other lethal device" means:

    (a) An explosive or incendiary weapon or device that is designed, or has the capability, to cause death, serious bodily injury or substantial material damage; or

    (b) A weapon or device that is designed, or has the capability, to cause death, serious bodily

4. "Military forces of a State" means the armed forces of a State which are organized, trained and equipped under its internal law for the primary purpose of national defence or security and persons acting in support of those armed forces who are under their formal command, control and responsibility.

5. "Place of public use means those parts of any building, land, street, waterway or other location that are accessible or open to members of the public, whether continuously, periodically or occasionally, and encompasses any commercial, business, cultural, historical, educational, religious, governmental, entertainment, recreational or similar place that is so accessible or open to the public.

6. "Public transportation system" means all facilities, conveyances and instrumentalities, whether publicly or privately owned, that are used in or for publicly available services for the transportation of persons or cargo.

Article 2

1. Any person commits an offence within the meaning of this Convention if that person unlawfully and intentionally delivers, places, discharges or detonates an explosive or other lethal device in, into or against a place of public use, a State or government facility, a public transportation system or an infrastructure facility:

    (a) With the intent to cause death or serious bodily injury; or

    (b) With the intent to cause extensive destruction of such a place, facility or system, where such destruction results in or is likely to result in major economic loss.

2. Any person also commits an offence if that person attempts to commit an offence as set forth in paragraph I of the present article.

3. Any person also commits an offence if that person:

(a) Participates as an accomplice in an offence as set forth in paragraph 1 or 2 of the present article; or

(b) Organizes or directs others to commit an offence as set forth in paragraph 1 or 2 of the present article; or

(c) In any other way contributes to the commission of one or more offences as set forth in paragraph 1 or 2 of the present article by a group of persons acting with a common purpose; such contribution shall be intentional and either be made with the aim of furthering the general criminal activity or purpose of the group or be made in the knowledge of the intention of the group to commit the offence or offences concerned.

Article 3

This Convention shall not apply where the offence is committed within a single State, the alleged offender and the victims are nationals of that State, the alleged offender is found in the territory of that State and no other State has a basis under article 6, paragraph 1 or paragraph 2, of this Convention to exercise jurisdiction, except that the provisions of articles 10 to 15 shall, as appropriate, apply in those cases.

Article 4

Each State Party shall adopt such measures as may be necessary:

(a) To establish as criminal offences under its domestic law the offences set forth in article 2 of this Convention;

(b) To make those offences punishable by appropriate penalties which take into account the grave nature of those offences.

Article 5

Each State Party shall adopt such measures as may be necessary, including, where appropriate, domestic legislation, to ensure that criminal acts within the scope of this Convention, in particular where they are intended or calculated to provoke a state of terror in the general public or in a group of persons or particular persons, are under no circumstances justifiable by considerations of a political, philosophical, ideological, racial, ethnic, religious or other similar nature and are punished by penalties consistent with their grave nature.

Article 6

1. Each State Party shall take such measures as may be necessary to establish its jurisdiction over the offences set forth in article 2 when:

   (a) The offence is committed in the territory of that State; or

   (b) The offence is committed on board a vessel flying the flag of that State or an aircraft which is registered under the laws of that State at the time the offence is committed; or

   (c) The offence is committed by a national of that State.

2. A State Party may also establish its jurisdiction over any such offence when:

   (a) The offence is committed against a national of that State; or

   (b) The offence is committed against a State or government facility of that State abroad, including an embassy or other diplomatic or consular premises of that State; or

   (c) The offence is committed by a stateless person who has his or her habitual residence in the territory of that State; or

   (d) The offence is committed in an attempt to compel that State to do or abstain from doing any act; or

   (e) The offence is committed on board an aircraft which is operated by the Government of that State.

3. Upon ratifying, accepting, approving or acceding to this Convention, each State Party shall notify the Secretary-General of the United Nations of the jurisdiction it has established under its domestic law in accordance with paragraph 2 of the present article. Should any change take place, the State Party concerned shall immediately notify the Secretary-General.

4. Each State Party shall likewise take such measures as may be necessary to establish its jurisdiction over the offences set forth in article 2 in cases where the alleged offender is present in its territory and it does not extradite that person to any of the States Parties which have established their jurisdiction in accordance with paragraph 1 or 2 of the present article.

5. This Convention does not exclude the exercise of any criminal jurisdiction established by a State Party in accordance with its domestic law.

Article 7

1. Upon receiving information that a person who has committed or who is alleged to have committed an offence as set forth in article 2 may be present in its territory, the State Party concerned shall take such measures as may be necessary under its domestic law to investigate the facts contained in the information.

2. Upon being satisfied that the circumstances so warrant, the State Party in whose territory the offender or alleged offender is present shall take the appropriate measures under its domestic law so as to ensure that person's presence for the purpose of prosecution or extradition.

3. Any person regarding whom the measures referred to in paragraph 2 of the present article are being taken shall be entitled to:

   (a) Communicate without delay with the nearest appropriate representative of the State of which that person is a national or which is otherwise entitled to protect that person's rights or, if that person is a stateless person, the State in the territory of which that person habitually resides;

   (b) Be visited by a representative of that State;

   (c) Be informed of that person's rights under subparagraphs (a) and (b).

4. The rights referred to in paragraph 3 of the present article shall be exercised in conformity with the laws and regulations of the State in the territory of which the offender or alleged offender is present, subject to the provision that the said laws and regulations must enable full effect to be given to the purposes for which the rights accorded under paragraph 3 are intended.

5. The provisions of paragraphs 3 and 4 of the present article shall be without prejudice to the right of any State Party having a claim to jurisdiction in accordance with article 6, subparagraph 1 (c) or 2 (c), to invite the International Committee of the Red Cross to communicate with and visit the alleged offender.

6. When a State Party, pursuant to the present article, has taken a person into custody, it shall immediately notify, directly or through the Secretary-General of the United Nations, the States Parties which have established jurisdiction in accordance with article 6, paragraphs 1 and 2, and, if it considers it advisable, any other interested States Parties, of the fact that that person is in custody and of the circumstances which warrant that person's detention. The State which makes the investigation contemplated in paragraph 1 of the present article shall promptly inform the said States Parties of its findings and shall indicate whether it intends to exercise jurisdiction.

Article 8

1. The State Party in the territory of which the alleged offender is present shall, in cases to which article 6 applies, if it does not extradite that person, be obliged, without exception whatsoever and whether or not the offence was committed in its territory, to submit the case without undue delay to its competent authorities for the purpose of prosecution, through proceedings in accordance with the laws of that State. Those authorities shall take their decision in the same manner as in the case of any other offence of a grave nature under the law of that State.

2. Whenever a State Party is permitted under its domestic law to extradite or otherwise surrender one of its nationals only upon the condition that the person will be returned to that State to serve the sentence imposed as a result of the trial or proceeding for which the extradition or surrender of the person was sought, and this State and the State seeking the extradition of the person agree with this option and other terms they may deem appropriate, such a conditional extradition or surrender shall be sufficient to discharge the obligation set forth in paragraph 1 of the present article.

Article 9

1. The offences set forth in article 2 shall be deemed to be included as extraditable offences in any extradition treaty existing between any of the States Parties before the entry into force of this Convention. States Parties undertake to include such offences as extraditable offences in every extradition treaty to be subsequently concluded between them.

2. When a State Party which makes extradition conditional on the existence of a treaty receives a request for extradition from another State Party with which it has no extradition treaty, the requested State Party may, at its option, consider this Convention as a legal basis for extradition in respect of the offences set forth in article 2. Extradition shall be subject to the other conditions provided by the law of the requested State.

3. States Parties which do not make extradition conditional on the existence of a treaty shall recognize the offences set forth in article 2 as extraditable offences between themselves, subject to the conditions provided by the law of the requested State.

4. If necessary, the offences set forth in article 2 shall be treated, for the purposes of extradition between States Parties, as if they had been committed not only in the place in which they occurred but also in the territory of the States that have established jurisdiction in accordance with article 6, paragraphs 1 and 2.

5. The provisions of all extradition treaties and arrangements between States Parties with regard to offences set forth in article 2 shall be deemed to be modified as between State Parties to the extent that they are incompatible with this Convention.

Article 10

1. States Parties shall afford one another the greatest measure of assistance in connection with investigations or criminal or extradition proceedings brought in respect of the offences set forth in article 2, including assistance in obtaining evidence at their disposal necessary for the proceedings.

2. States Parties shall carry out their obligations under paragraph 1 of the present article in conformity with any treaties or other arrangements on mutual legal assistance that may exist between them. In the absence of such treaties or arrangements, States Parties shall afford one another assistance in accordance with their domestic law.

Article 11

None of the offences set forth in article 2 shall be regarded, for the purposes of extradition or mutual legal assistance, as a political offence or as an offence connected with a political offence or as an offence inspired by political motives. Accordingly, a request for extradition or for mutual legal assistance based on such an offence may not be refused on the sole ground that it concerns a political offence or an offence connected with a political offence or an offence inspired by political motives.

Article 12

Nothing in this Convention shall be interpreted as imposing an obligation to extradite or to afford mutual legal assistance, if the requested State Party has substantial grounds for believing that the request for extradition for offences set forth in article 2 or for mutual legal assistance with respect to such offences has been made for the purpose of prosecuting or punishing a person on account of that person's race, religion, nationality, ethnic origin or political opinion or that compliance with the request would cause prejudice to that person's position for any of these reasons.

Article 13

1. A person who is being detained or is serving a sentence in the territory of one State Party whose presence in another State Party is requested for purposes of testimony, identification or otherwise providing assistance in obtaining evidence for the investigation or prosecution of offences under this Convention may be transferred if the following conditions are met:

   (a) The person freely gives his or her informed consent; and

   (b) The competent authorities of both States agree, subject to such conditions as those States may deem appropriate.

2. For the purposes of the present article:

   (a) The State to which the person is transferred shall have the authority and obligation to keep the person transferred in custody, unless otherwise requested or authorized by the State from which the person was transferred;

   (b) The State to which the person is transferred shall without delay implement its obligation to return the person to the custody of the State from which the person was transferred as agreed beforehand, or as otherwise agreed, by the competent authorities of both States;

   (c) The State to which the person is transferred shall not require the State from which the person was transferred to initiate extradition proceedings for the return of the person;

   (d) The person transferred shall receive credit for service of the sentence being served in the State from which he was transferred for time spent in the custody of the State to which he was transferred.

3. Unless the State Party from which a person is to be transferred in accordance with the present article so agrees, that person, whatever his or her nationality, shall not be prosecuted or detained or subjected to any other restriction of his or her personal liberty in the territory of the State to which that person is transferred in respect of acts or convictions anterior to his or her departure from the territory of the State from which such person was transferred.

Article 14

Any person who is taken into custody or regarding whom any other measures are taken or proceedings are carried out pursuant to this Convention shall be guaranteed fair treatment, including enjoyment of all rights and guarantees in conformity with the law of the State in the territory of which that person is present and applicable provisions of international law, including international law of human rights.

Article 15

States Parties shall cooperate in the prevention of the offences set forth in article 2, particularly:

(a) By taking all practicable measures, including, if necessary, adapting their domestic legislation, to prevent and counter preparations in their respective territories for the commission of those offences within or outside their territories, including measures to prohibit in their territories illegal activities of persons, groups and organizations that encourage, instigate, organize, knowingly finance or engage in the perpetration of offences as set forth in article 2;

(b) By exchanging accurate and verified information in accordance with their national law, and coordinating administrative and other measures taken as appropriate to prevent the commission of offences as set forth in article 2;

(c) Where appropriate, through research and development regarding methods of detection of explosives and other harmful substances that can cause death or bodily injury, consultations on the development of standards for marking explosives in order to identify their origin in post-blast investigations, exchange of information on preventive measures, cooperation and transfer of technology, equipment and related materials.

Article 16

The State Party where the alleged offender is prosecuted shall, in accordance with its domestic law or applicable procedures, communicate the final outcome of the proceedings to the Secretary-General of the United Nations, who shall transmit the information to the other States Parties.

Article 17

The States Parties shall carry out their obligations under this Convention in a manner consistent with the principles of sovereign equality and territorial integrity of States and that of non-intervention in the domestic affairs of other States.

Article 18

Nothing in this Convention entitles a State Party to undertake in the territory of another State Party the exercise of jurisdiction and performance of functions which are exclusively reserved for the authorities of that other State Party by its domestic law.

Article 19

1. Nothing in this Convention shall affect other rights, obligations and responsibilities of States and individuals under international law, in particular the purposes and principles of the Charter of the United Nations and international humanitarian law.

2. The activities of armed forces during an armed conflict, as those terms are understood under international humanitarian law, which are governed by that law, are not governed by this Convention, and the activities undertaken by military forces of a State in the exercise of their official duties, inasmuch as they are governed by other rules of international law, are not governed by this Convention.

Article 20

1. Any dispute between two or more States Parties concerning the interpretation or application of this Convention which cannot be settled through negotiation within a reasonable time shall, at the request of one of them, be submitted to arbitration. If, within six months from the date of the request for arbitration, the parties are unable to agree on the organization of the arbitration, any one of those parties may refer the dispute to the International Court of Justice, by application, in conformity with the Statute of the Court.

2. Each State may at the time of signature, ratification, acceptance or approval of this Convention or accession thereto declare that it does not consider itself bound by paragraph 1 of the present article. The other States Parties shall not be bound by paragraph 1 with respect to any State Party which has made such a reservation.

3. Any State which has made a reservation in accordance with paragraph 2 of the present article may at any time withdraw that reservation by notification to the Secretary-General of the United Nations.

DOCUMENT 26

International Convention for the Suppression of the Financing of Terrorism 1999
UN Doc A/54/615; 39 ILM 270 (2000)

This Convention was adopted as an annex to General Assembly Resolution 54/109 of 9 December 1999 and entered into force on 10 April 2002.

There are 117 parties, including all the major powers.

The landmark General Assembly Declaration on Measures to Eliminate International Terrorism of 17 February 1995 (GA Res 49/60) began a process in the Assembly of addressing terrorism issues. The Declaration to Supplement the Declaration on Measures to Eliminate International Terrorism of 16 January 1997 (GA Res 51/210) established an Ad Hoc Committee, which, by Resolution 53/108 of 8 December 1998, was charged, with elaborating an international convention for the suppression of terrorist financing.

The proscribed acts relating to terrorist financing are identified and defined in Article 2, that definition relating to terrorism as proscribed in the other global terrorism Conventions **(Documents 12, 15–17 and 20–25)** *(Article 2(1)(a) and Annex). The Convention requires the Contracting States to criminalise these acts (Article 4(a)) and make them punishable by appropriate penalties (Article 4(b)). It emphasises that these acts are to be under no circumstances justifiable in domestic law (Article 6). Each Contracting State is to establish its jurisdiction where one of the Convention's offences is committed in its territory or on its ships or aircraft or by one of its nationals (Article 7(1)). Additionally, the State may assert jurisdiction where the victim is a national, where the offence is committed against a State facility abroad or where the offence is designed to compel a State to do or abstain from doing some act (Article 7(2)). Each Contracting State is required to report an offender to its prosecution authorities or to extradite him (Article 10(1)) – the* aut dedere aut judicare *principle. The Convention declares the proscribed acts to extraditable offences under existing extradition treaties and to be included in future extradition treaties (Article 11(1)); if there is no extradition treaty, the Convention itself may be treated as such (Article 11(2)). The offences set out in Article 2 are not to be considered political offences (Article 13), although there may be no extradition where the purpose is to prosecute or punish a person on account of his race, religion, nationality, ethnic origin or political opinion (Article 14). There are fair treatment guarantees for proceedings under the Convention (Article 17). Parties are to afford one another the greatest measure of assistance in proceedings under the Convention (Article 12(1); see also Article 18).*

Attempts to elaborate a Comprehensive Convention on International Terrorism have been ongoing since 1996, as have negotiations towards an International Convention for the Suppression of Acts of Nuclear Terrorism. While the Nuclear Terrorism Convention was adopted in 2005 **(Document 28)** *and considerable progress has been made in the drafting of the Comprehensive Terrorism Convention even the events of 11 September 2001 have not proved sufficient inspiration to overcome the remaining areas of disagreement, which in essence relate to whether the armed forces of states and national liberation movements are included in the Comprehensive Convention as capable of committing proscribed (terrorist) acts and whether the Comprehensive Convention prevails over the treaties in the sectoral régime. The Comprehensive Nuclear Terrorism Convention is currently available in draft: UN Doc A/C.6/ 56/L.9 Annex I.*

See Security Council Resolution 1373 (2001) **(Document 27)**.

See the other global terrorism conventions **(Documents 11–12, 15–17 and 20–25)**.

The States Parties to this Convention,

Bearing in mind the purposes and principles of the Charter of the United Nations concerning the maintenance of international peace and security and the promotion of good-neighbourliness and friendly relations and cooperation among States,

Deeply concerned about the worldwide escalation of acts of terrorism in all its forms and manifestations,

Recalling the Declaration on the Occasion of the Fiftieth Anniversary of the United Nations, contained in General Assembly resolution 50/6 of 24 October 1995,

Recalling also all the relevant General Assembly resolutions on the matter, including resolution 49/60 of 9 December 1994 and the annex thereto on the Declaration on Measures to Eliminate International Terrorism, in which the States Members of the United Nations solemnly reaffirmed their unequivocal condemnation of all acts, methods and practices of terrorism as criminal and unjustifiable, wherever and by whomever committed, including those which jeopardize the friendly relations among States and peoples and threaten the territorial integrity and security of States,

Noting that the Declaration on Measures to Eliminate International Terrorism also encouraged States to review urgently the scope of the existing international legal provisions on the prevention, repression and elimination of terrorism in all its forms and manifestations, with the aim of ensuring that there is a comprehensive legal framework covering all aspects of the matter,

Recalling paragraph 3(f) of General Assembly resolution 51/210 of 17 December 1996, in which the Assembly called upon all States to take steps to prevent and counteract, through appropriate domestic measures, the financing of terrorists and terrorist organizations, whether such financing is direct or indirect through organizations which also have or claim to have charitable, social or cultural goals or which are also engaged in unlawful activities such as illicit arms trafficking, drug dealing and racketeering, including the exploitation of persons for purposes of funding terrorist activities, and in particular to consider, where appropriate, adopting regulatory measures to prevent and counteract movements of funds suspected to be intended for terrorist purposes without impeding in any way the freedom of legitimate capital movements and to intensify the exchange of information concerning international movements of such funds,

Recalling also General Assembly resolution 52/165 of 15 December 1997, in which the Assembly called upon States to consider, in particular, the implementation of the measures set out in paragraphs 3(a) to (f) of its resolution 51/210,

Recalling further General Assembly resolution 53/108 of 8 December 1998, in which the Assembly decided that the Ad Hoc Committee established by General Assembly resolution 51/210 of 17 December 1996 should elaborate a draft international convention for the suppression of terrorist financing to supplement related existing international instruments,

Considering that the financing of terrorism is a matter of grave concern to the international community as a whole,

Noting that the number and seriousness of acts of international terrorism depend on the financing that terrorists may obtain,

Noting also that existing multilateral legal instruments do not expressly address such financing,

Being convinced of the urgent need to enhance international cooperation among States in devising and adopting effective measures for the prevention of the financing of terrorism, as well as for its suppression through the prosecution and punishment of its perpetrators,

Have agreed as follows:

Article 1

For the purposes of this Convention:

1. "Funds" means assets of every kind, whether tangible or intangible, movable or immovable, however acquired, and legal documents or instruments in any form, including electronic or digital, evidencing title to, or interest in, such assets, including, but not limited to, bank credits, travellers cheques, bank cheques, money orders, shares, securities, bonds, drafts and letters of credit.

2. "State or government facility" means any permanent or temporary facility or conveyance that is used or occupied by representatives of a State, members of Government, the legislature or the judiciary or by officials or employees of a State or any other public authority or entity or by employees or officials of an intergovernmental organization in connection with their official duties.

3. "Proceeds" means any funds derived from or obtained, directly or indirectly, through the commission of an offence set forth in article 2.

Article 2

1. Any person commits an offence within the meaning of this Convention if that person by any means, directly or indirectly, unlawfully and wilfully, provides or collects funds with the intention that they should be used or in the knowledge that they are to be used, in full or in part, in order to carry out:

    (a) An act which constitutes an offence within the scope of and as defined in one of the treaties listed in the annex; or

    (b) Any other act intended to cause death or serious bodily injury to a civilian, or to any other person not taking an active part in the hostilities in a situation of armed conflict, when the purpose of such act, by its nature or context, is to intimidate a population, or to compel a Government or an international organization to do or to abstain from doing any act.

2. (a) On depositing its instrument of ratification, acceptance, approval or accession, a State Party which is not a party to a treaty listed in the annex may declare that, in the application of this Convention to the State Party, the treaty shall be deemed not to be included in the annex referred to in paragraph 1, subparagraph (a). The declaration shall cease to have effect as soon as the treaty enters into force for the State Party, which shall notify the depositary of this fact;

    (b) When a State Party ceases to be a party to a treaty listed in the annex, it may make a declaration as provided for in this article, with respect to that treaty.

3. For an act to constitute an offence set forth in paragraph 1, it shall not be necessary that the funds were actually used to carry out an offence referred to in paragraph 1, subparagraph (a) or (b).

4. Any person also commits an offence if that person attempts to commit an offence as set forth in paragraph 1 of this article.

5. Any person also commits an offence if that person:

    (a) Participates as an accomplice in an offence as set forth in paragraph 1 or 4 of this article;

    (b) Organizes or directs others to commit an offence as set forth in paragraph 1 or 4 of this article;

    (c) Contributes to the commission of one or more offences as set forth in paragraph 1 or 4 of this article by a group of persons acting with a common purpose. Such contribution shall be intentional and shall either:

        (i) Be made with the aim of furthering the criminal activity or criminal purpose of the group, where such activity or purpose involves the commission of an offence as set forth in paragraph 1 of this article; or

(ii) Be made in the knowledge of the intention of the group to commit an offence as set forth in paragraph 1 of this article.

Article 3

This Convention shall not apply where the offence is committed within a single State, the alleged offender is a national of that State and is present in the territory of that State and no other State has a basis under article 7, paragraph 1 or 2, to exercise jurisdiction, except that the provisions of articles 12 to 18 shall, as appropriate, apply in those cases.

Article 4

Each State Party shall adopt such measures as may be necessary:

(a) To establish as criminal offences under its domestic law the offences as set forth in article 2;

(b) To make those offences punishable by appropriate penalties which take into account the grave nature of the offences.

Article 5

1. Each State Party, in accordance with its domestic legal principles, shall take the necessary measures to enable a legal entity located in its territory or organized under its laws to be held liable when a person responsible for the management or control of that legal entity has, in that capacity, committed an offence as set forth in article 2. Such liability may be criminal, civil or administrative.

2. Such liability is incurred without prejudice to the criminal liability of individuals who have committed the offences.

3. Each State Party shall ensure, in particular, that legal entities liable in accordance with paragraph 1 above are subject to effective, proportionate and dissuasive criminal, civil or administrative sanctions. Such sanctions may include monetary sanctions.

Article 6

Each State Party shall adopt such measures as may be necessary, including, where appropriate, domestic legislation, to ensure that criminal acts within the scope of this Convention are under no circumstances justifiable by considerations of a political, philosophical, ideological, racial, ethnic, religious or other similar nature.

Article 7

1. Each State Party shall take such measures as may be necessary to establish its jurisdiction over the offences set forth in article 2 when:

(a) The offence is committed in the territory of that State;

(b) The offence is committed on board a vessel flying the flag of that State or an aircraft registered under the laws of that State at the time the offence is committed;

(c) The offence is committed by a national of that State.

2. A State Party may also establish its jurisdiction over any such offence when:

(a) The offence was directed towards or resulted in the carrying out of an offence referred to in article 2, paragraph 1, subparagraph (a) or (b), in the territory of or against a national of that State;

(b) The offence was directed towards or resulted in the carrying out of an offence referred to in article 2, paragraph 1, subparagraph (a) or (b), against a State or government facility of that State abroad, including diplomatic or consular premises of that State;

(c) The offence was directed towards or resulted in an offence referred to in article 2, paragraph 1, subparagraph (a) or (b), committed in an attempt to compel that State to do or abstain from doing any act;

(d) The offence is committed by a stateless person who has his or her habitual residence in the territory of that State;

(e) The offence is committed on board an aircraft which is operated by the Government of that State.

3. Upon ratifying, accepting, approving or acceding to this Convention, each State Party shall notify the Secretary-General of the United Nations of the jurisdiction it has established in accordance with paragraph 2. Should any change take place, the State Party concerned shall immediately notify the Secretary-General.

4. Each State Party shall likewise take such measures as may be necessary to establish its jurisdiction over the offences set forth in article 2 in cases where the alleged offender is present in its territory and it does not extradite that person to any of the States Parties that have established their jurisdiction in accordance with paragraphs 1 or 2.

5. When more than one State Party claims jurisdiction over the offences set forth in article 2, the relevant States Parties shall strive to coordinate their actions appropriately, in particular concerning the conditions for prosecution and the modalities for mutual legal assistance.

6. Without prejudice to the norms of general international law, this Convention does not exclude the exercise of any criminal jurisdiction established by a State Party in accordance with its domestic law.

Article 8

1. Each State Party shall take appropriate measures, in accordance with its domestic legal principles, for the identification, detection and freezing or seizure of any funds used or allocated for the purpose of committing the offences set forth in article 2 as well as the proceeds derived from such offences, for purposes of possible forfeiture.

2. Each State Party shall take appropriate measures, in accordance with its domestic legal principles, for the forfeiture of funds used or allocated for the purpose of committing the offences set forth in article 2 and the proceeds derived from such offences.

3. Each State Party concerned may give consideration to concluding agreements on the sharing with other States Parties, on a regular or case-by-case basis, of the funds derived from the forfeitures referred to in this article.

4. Each State Party shall consider establishing mechanisms whereby the funds derived from the forfeitures referred to in this article are utilized to compensate the victims of offences referred to in article 2, paragraph 1, subparagraph (a) or (b), or their families.

5. The provisions of this article shall be implemented without prejudice to the rights of third parties acting in good faith.

Article 9

1. Upon receiving information that a person who has committed or who is alleged to have committed an offence set forth in article 2 may be present in its territory, the State Party concerned shall take such measures as may be necessary under its domestic law to investigate the facts contained in the information.

2. Upon being satisfied that the circumstances so warrant, the State Party in whose territory the offender or alleged offender is present shall take the appropriate measures under its domestic law so as to ensure that person's presence for the purpose of prosecution or extradition.

3. Any person regarding whom the measures referred to in paragraph 2 are being taken shall be entitled:

(a) To communicate without delay with the nearest appropriate representative of the State of which that person is a national or which is otherwise entitled to protect that person's rights or, if that person is a stateless person, the State in the territory of which that person habitually resides;

(b) To be visited by a representative of that State;

(c) To be informed of that person's rights under subparagraphs (a) and (b).

4. The rights referred to in paragraph 3 shall be exercised in conformity with the laws and regulations of the State in the territory of which the offender or alleged offender is present, subject to the provision that the said laws and regulations must enable full effect to be given to the purposes for which the rights accorded under paragraph 3 are intended.

5. The provisions of paragraphs 3 and 4 shall be without prejudice to the right of any State Party having a claim to jurisdiction in accordance with article 7, paragraph 1, subparagraph (b), or paragraph 2, subparagraph (b), to invite the International Committee of the Red Cross to communicate with and visit the alleged offender.

6. When a State Party, pursuant to the present article, has taken a person into custody, it shall immediately notify, directly or through the Secretary-General of the United Nations, the States Parties which have established jurisdiction in accordance with article 7, paragraph 1 or 2, and, if it considers it advisable, any other interested States Parties, of the fact that such person is in custody and of the circumstances which warrant that person's detention. The State which makes the investigation contemplated in paragraph 1 shall promptly inform the said States Parties of its findings and shall indicate whether it intends to exercise jurisdiction.

Article 10

1. The State Party in the territory of which the alleged offender is present shall, in cases to which article 7 applies, if it does not extradite that person, be obliged, without exception whatsoever and whether or not the offence was committed in its territory, to submit the case without undue delay to its competent authorities for the purpose of prosecution, through proceedings in accordance with the laws of that State. Those authorities shall take their decision in the same manner as in the case of any other offence of a grave nature under the law of that State.

2. Whenever a State Party is permitted under its domestic law to extradite or otherwise surrender one of its nationals only upon the condition that the person will be returned to that State to serve the sentence imposed as a result of the trial or proceeding for which the extradition or surrender of the person was sought, and this State and the State seeking the extradition of the person agree with this option and other terms they may deem appropriate, such a conditional extradition or surrender shall be sufficient to discharge the obligation set forth in paragraph 1.

Article 11

1. The offences set forth in article 2 shall be deemed to be included as extraditable offences in any extradition treaty existing between any of the States Parties before the entry into force of this Convention. States Parties undertake to include such offences as extraditable offences in every extradition treaty to be subsequently concluded between them.

2. When a State Party which makes extradition conditional on the existence of a treaty receives a request for extradition from another State Party with which it has no extradition treaty, the requested State Party may, at its option, consider this Convention as a legal basis for extradition in respect of the offences set forth in article 2. Extradition shall be subject to the other conditions provided by the law of the requested State.

3. States Parties which do not make extradition conditional on the existence of a treaty shall recognize the offences set forth in article 2 as extraditable offences between themselves, subject to the conditions provided by the law of the requested State.

4. If necessary, the offences set forth in article 2 shall be treated, for the purposes of extradition between States Parties, as if they had been committed not only in the place in which they occurred but also in the territory of the States that have established jurisdiction in accordance with article 7, paragraphs 1 and 2.

5. The provisions of all extradition treaties and arrangements between States Parties with regard to offences set forth in article 2 shall be deemed to be modified as between States Parties to the extent that they are incompatible with this Convention.

Article 12

1. States Parties shall afford one another the greatest measure of assistance in connection with criminal investigations or criminal or extradition proceedings in respect of the offences set forth in article 2, including assistance in obtaining evidence in their possession necessary for the proceedings.

2. States Parties may not refuse a request for mutual legal assistance on the ground of bank secrecy.

3. The requesting Party shall not transmit or use information or evidence furnished by the requested Party for investigations, prosecutions or proceedings other than those stated in the request without the prior consent of the requested Party.

4. Each State Party may give consideration to establishing mechanisms to share with other States Parties information or evidence needed to establish criminal, civil or administrative liability pursuant to article 5.

5. States Parties shall carry out their obligations under paragraphs 1 and 2 in conformity with any treaties or other arrangements on mutual legal assistance or information exchange that may exist between them. In the absence of such treaties or arrangements, States Parties shall afford one another assistance in accordance with their domestic law.

Article 13

None of the offences set forth in article 2 shall be regarded, for the purposes of extradition or mutual legal assistance, as a fiscal offence. Accordingly, States Parties may not refuse a request for extradition or for mutual legal assistance on the sole ground that it concerns a fiscal offence.

Article 14

None of the offences set forth in article 2 shall be regarded for the purposes of extradition or mutual legal assistance as a political offence or as an offence connected with a political offence or as an offence inspired by political motives. Accordingly, a request for extradition or for mutual legal assistance based on such an offence may not be refused on the sole ground that it concerns a political offence or an offence connected with a political offence or an offence inspired by political motives.

Article 15

Nothing in this Convention shall be interpreted as imposing an obligation to extradite or to afford mutual legal assistance, if the requested State Party has substantial grounds for believing that the request for extradition for offences set forth in article 2 or for mutual legal assistance with respect to such offences has been made for the purpose of prosecuting or punishing a person on account of that person's race, religion, nationality, ethnic origin or political opinion or that compliance with the request would cause prejudice to that person's position for any of these reasons.

Article 16

1. A person who is being detained or is serving a sentence in the territory of one State Party whose presence in another State Party is requested for purposes of identification, testimony or otherwise providing assistance in obtaining evidence for the investigation or prosecution of offences set forth in article 2 may be transferred if the following conditions are met:

    (a) The person freely gives his or her informed consent;

    (b) The competent authorities of both States agree, subject to such conditions as those States may deem appropriate.

2. For the purposes of the present article:

   (a) The State to which the person is transferred shall have the authority and obligation to keep the person transferred in custody, unless otherwise requested or authorized by the State from which the person was transferred;

   (b) The State to which the person is transferred shall without delay implement its obligation to return the person to the custody of the State from which the person was transferred as agreed beforehand, or as otherwise agreed, by the competent authorities of both States;

   (c) The State to which the person is transferred shall not require the State from which the person was transferred to initiate extradition proceedings for the return of the person;

   (d) The person transferred shall receive credit for service of the sentence being served in the State from which he or she was transferred for time spent in the custody of the State to which he or she was transferred.

3. Unless the State Party from which a person is to be transferred in accordance with the present article so agrees, that person, whatever his or her nationality, shall not be prosecuted or detained or subjected to any other restriction of his or her personal liberty in the territory of the State to which that person is transferred in respect of acts or convictions anterior to his or her departure from the territory of the State from which such person was transferred.

Article 17

Any person who is taken into custody or regarding whom any other measures are taken or proceedings are carried out pursuant to this Convention shall be guaranteed fair treatment, including enjoyment of all rights and guarantees in conformity with the law of the State in the territory of which that person is present and applicable provisions of international law, including international human rights law.

Article 18

1. States Parties shall cooperate in the prevention of the offences set forth in article 2 by taking all practicable measures, inter alia, by adapting their domestic legislation, if necessary, to prevent and counter preparations in their respective territories for the commission of those offences within or outside their territories, including:

   (a) Measures to prohibit in their territories illegal activities of persons and organizations that knowingly encourage, instigate, organize or engage in the commission of offences set forth in article 2;

   (b) Measures requiring financial institutions and other professions involved in financial transactions to utilize the most efficient measures available for the identification of their usual or occasional customers, as well as customers in whose interest accounts are opened, and to pay special attention to unusual or suspicious transactions and report transactions suspected of stemming from a criminal activity. For this purpose, States Parties shall consider:

      (i) Adopting regulations prohibiting the opening of accounts, the holders or beneficiaries of which are unidentified or unidentifiable, and measures to ensure that such institutions verify the identity of the real owners of such transactions;

      (ii) With respect to the identification of legal entities, requiring financial institutions, when necessary, to take measures to verify the legal existence and the structure of the customer by obtaining, either from a public register or from the customer or both, proof of incorporation, including information concerning the customer's name, legal form, address, directors and provisions regulating the power to bind the entity;

      (iii) Adopting regulations imposing on financial institutions the obligation to report promptly to the competent authorities all complex, unusual large transactions and unusual patterns of transactions, which have no apparent economic or obviously lawful purpose, without fear of assuming criminal or civil liability for breach of any restriction on disclosure of information if they report their suspicions in good faith;

(iv) Requiring financial institutions to maintain, for at least five years, all necessary records on transactions, both domestic and international.

2. States Parties shall further cooperate in the prevention of offences set forth in article 2 by considering:

(a) Measures for the supervision, including, for example, the licensing, of all money-transmission agencies;

(b) Feasible measures to detect or monitor the physical cross-border transportation of cash and bearer negotiable instruments, subject to strict safeguards to ensure proper use of information and without impeding in any way the freedom of capital movements.

3. States Parties shall further cooperate in the prevention of the offences set forth in article 2 by exchanging accurate and verified information in accordance with their domestic law and coordinating administrative and other measures taken, as appropriate, to prevent the commission of offences set forth in article 2, in particular by:

(a) Establishing and maintaining channels of communication between their competent agencies and services to facilitate the secure and rapid exchange of information concerning all aspects of offences set forth in article 2;

(b) Cooperating with one another in conducting inquiries, with respect to the offences set forth in article 2, concerning:

(i) The identity, whereabouts and activities of persons in respect of whom reasonable suspicion exists that they are involved in such offences;

(ii) The movement of funds relating to the commission of such offences.

4. States Parties may exchange information through the International Criminal Police Organization (Interpol).

Article 19

The State Party where the alleged offender is prosecuted shall, in accordance with its domestic law or applicable procedures, communicate the final outcome of the proceedings to the Secretary-General of the United Nations, who shall transmit the information to the other States Parties.

Article 20

The States Parties shall carry out their obligations under this Convention in a manner consistent with the principles of sovereign equality and territorial integrity of States and that of non-intervention in the domestic affairs of other States.

Article 21

Nothing in this Convention shall affect other rights, obligations and responsibilities of States and individuals under international law, in particular the purposes of the Charter of the United Nations, international humanitarian law and other relevant conventions.

Article 22

Nothing in this Convention entitles a State Party to undertake in the territory of another State Party the exercise of jurisdiction or performance of functions which are exclusively reserved for the authorities of that other State Party by its domestic law.

Article 23

1. The annex may be amended by the addition of relevant treaties:

(a) That are open to the participation of all States;

(b)   That have entered into force;

(c)   That have been ratified, accepted, approved or acceded to by at least twenty-two States Parties to the present Convention.

2.   After the entry into force of this Convention, any State Party may propose such an amendment. Any proposal for an amendment shall be communicated to the depositary in written form. The depositary shall notify proposals that meet the requirements of paragraph 1 to all States Parties and seek their views on whether the proposed amendment should be adopted.

3.   The proposed amendment shall be deemed adopted unless one third of the States Parties object to it by a written notification not later than 180 days after its circulation.

4.   The adopted amendment to the annex shall enter into force 30 days after the deposit of the twenty-second instrument of ratification, acceptance or approval of such amendment for all those States Parties that have deposited such an instrument. For each State Party ratifying, accepting or approving the amendment after the deposit of the twenty-second instrument, the amendment shall enter into force on the thirtieth day after deposit by such State Party of its instrument of ratification, acceptance or approval.

Article 24

1.   Any dispute between two or more States Parties concerning the interpretation or application of this Convention which cannot be settled through negotiation within a reasonable time shall, at the request of one of them, be submitted to arbitration. If, within six months from the date of the request for arbitration, the parties are unable to agree on the organization of the arbitration, any one of those parties may refer the dispute to the International Court of Justice, by application, in conformity with the Statute of the Court.

2.   Each State may at the time of signature, ratification, acceptance or approval of this Convention or accession thereto declare that it does not consider itself bound by paragraph 1. The other States Parties shall not be bound by paragraph 1 with respect to any State Party which has made such a reservation.

3.   Any State which has made a reservation in accordance with paragraph 2 may at any time withdraw that reservation by notification to the Secretary-General of the United Nations.

ANNEX

1.   Convention for the Suppression of Unlawful Seizure of Aircraft, done at The Hague on 16 December 1970.

2.   Convention for the Suppression of Unlawful Acts against the Safety of Civil Aviation, done at Montreal on 23 September 1971.

3.   Convention on the Prevention and Punishment of Crimes against Internationally Protected Persons, including Diplomatic Agents, adopted by the General Assembly of the United Nations on 14 December 1973.

4.   International Convention against the Taking of Hostages, adopted by the General Assembly of the United Nations on 17 December 1979.

5.   Convention on the Physical Protection of Nuclear Material, adopted at Vienna on 3 March 1980.

6.   Protocol for the Suppression of Unlawful Acts of Violence at Airports Serving International Civil Aviation, supplementary to the Convention for the Suppression of Unlawful Acts against the Safety of Civil Aviation, done at Montreal on 24 February 1988.

7.   Convention for the Suppression of Unlawful Acts against the Safety of Maritime Navigation, done at Rome on 10 March 1988.

8. Protocol for the Suppression of Unlawful Acts against the Safety of Fixed Platforms located on the Continental Shelf, done at Rome on 10 March 1988.

9. International Convention for the Suppression of Terrorist Bombings, adopted by the General Assembly of the United Nations on 15 December 1997.

DOCUMENT 27

Security Council Resolution 1373 (2001)
UN Doc S/RES/1373 (2001); 40 ILM 1278 (2001)

In the immediate wake of the 9/11 atrocities, the Security Council unanimously adopted Resolution 1373 on 28 September 2001. In large part, it repeats the obligations on States under the International Convention for the Suppression of the Financing of Terrorism of 1999 **(Document 25)** *(see especially paras 1 and 2). It establishes a Counter-Terrorism Committee, of all 15 Security Council members, to monitor the implementation of the resolution (para 6)* **(see Document 79)**. *The resolution, being adopted under Chapter VII of the UN Charter, is binding on all 191 Member States by virtue of Article 25 of the Charter. Thus, while the obligations in the 1999 Convention are applicable among the Contracting States, the very similar obligations in Resolution 1373 are universally applicable.*

The Security Council,

Reaffirming its resolutions 1269 (1999) of 19 October 1999 and 1368 (2001) of 12 September 2001,

Reaffirming also its unequivocal condemnation of the terrorist attacks which took place in New York, Washington, DC, and Pennsylvania on 11 September 2001, and expressing its determination to prevent all such acts,

Reaffirming further that such acts, like any act of international terrorism, constitute a threat to international peace and security,

Reaffirming the inherent right of individual or collective self-defence as recognized by the Charter of the United Nations as reiterated in resolution 1368 (2001),

Reaffirming the need to combat by all means, in accordance with the Charter of the United Nations, threats to international peace and security caused by terrorist acts,

Deeply concerned by the increase, in various regions of the world, of acts of terrorism motivated by intolerance or extremism,

Calling on States to work together urgently to prevent and suppress terrorist acts, including through increased co-operation and full implementation of the relevant international conventions relating to terrorism,

Recognizing the need for States to complement international co-operation by taking additional measures to prevent and suppress, in their territories through all lawful means, the financing and preparation of any acts of terrorism,

Reaffirming the principle established by the General Assembly in its declaration of October 1970 (resolution 2625 (XXV)) and reiterated by the Security Council in its resolution 1189 (1998) of 13 August 1998, namely that every State has the duty to refrain from organizing, instigating, assisting or participating in terrorist acts in another State or acquiescing in organized activities within its territory directed towards the commission of such acts,

Acting under Chapter VII of the Charter of the United Nations,

1. Decides that all States shall:

    (a) Prevent and suppress the financing of terrorist acts;

    (b) Criminalize the wilful provision or collection, by any means, directly or indirectly, of funds by their nationals or in their territories with the intention that the funds should be used, or in the knowledge that they are to be used, in order to carry out terrorist acts;

    (c) Freeze without delay funds and other financial assets or economic resources of persons who commit, or attempt to commit, terrorist acts or participate in or facilitate the commission of terrorist acts; of entities owned or controlled directly or indirectly by such persons; and of persons and entities acting on behalf of, or at the direction of such persons and entities, including funds derived or generated from property owned or controlled directly or indirectly by such persons and associated persons and entities;

    (d) Prohibit their nationals or any persons and entities within their territories from making any funds, financial assets or economic resources or financial or other related services available, directly or indirectly, for the benefit of persons who commit or attempt to commit or facilitate or participate in the commission of terrorist acts, of entities owned or controlled, directly or indirectly, by such persons and of persons and entities acting on behalf of or at the direction of such persons;

2. Decides also that all States shall:

    (a) Refrain from providing any form of support, active or passive, to entities or persons involved in terrorist acts, including by suppressing recruitment of members of terrorist groups and eliminating the supply of weapons to terrorists;

    (b) Take the necessary steps to prevent the commission of terrorist acts, including by provision of early warning to other States by exchange of information;

    (c) Deny safe haven to those who finance, plan, support, or commit terrorist acts, or provide safe havens;

    (d) Prevent those who finance, plan, facilitate or commit terrorist acts from using their respective territories for those purposes against other States or their citizens;

    (e) Ensure that any person who participates in the financing, planning, preparation or perpetration of terrorist acts or in supporting terrorist acts is brought to justice and ensure that, in addition to any other measures against them, such terrorist acts are established as serious criminal offences in domestic laws and regulations and that the punishment duly reflects the seriousness of such terrorist acts;

    (f) Afford one another the greatest measure of assistance in connection with criminal investigations or criminal proceedings relating to the financing or support of terrorist acts, including assistance in obtaining evidence in their possession necessary for the proceedings;

    (g) Prevent the movement of terrorists or terrorist groups by effective border controls and controls on issuance of identity papers and travel documents, and through measures for preventing counterfeiting, forgery or fraudulent use of identity papers and travel documents;

3. Calls upon all States to:

    (a) Find ways of intensifying and accelerating the exchange of operational information, especially regarding actions or movements of terrorist persons or networks; forged or falsified travel documents; traffic in arms, explosives or sensitive materials; use of communications technologies by terrorist groups; and the threat posed by the possession of weapons of mass destruction by terrorist groups;

    (b) Exchange information in accordance with international and domestic law and co-operate on administrative and judicial matters to prevent the commission of terrorist acts;

    (c) Co-operate, particularly through bilateral and multilateral arrangements and agreements, to prevent and suppress terrorist attacks and take action against perpetrators of such acts;

(d) Become parties as soon as possible to the relevant international conventions and protocols relating to terrorism, including the International Convention for the Suppression of the Financing of Terrorism of 9 December 1999;

(e) Increase co-operation and fully implement the relevant international conventions and protocols relating to terrorism and Security Council resolutions 1269 (1999) and 1368 (2001);

(f) Take appropriate measures in conformity with the relevant provisions of national and international law, including international standards of human rights, before granting refugee status, for the purpose of ensuring that the asylum seeker has not planned, facilitated or participated in the commission of terrorist acts;

(g) Ensure, in conformity with international law, that refugee status is not abused by the perpetrators, organizers or facilitators of terrorist acts, and that claims of political motivation are not recognized as grounds for refusing requests for the extradition of alleged terrorists;

4. Notes with concern the close connection between international terrorism and transnational organized crime, illicit drugs, money-laundering, illegal arms-trafficking, and illegal movement of nuclear, chemical, biological and other potentially deadly materials, and in this regard emphasizes the need to enhance co-ordination of efforts on national, subregional, regional and international levels in order to strengthen a global response to this serious challenge and threat to international security;

5. Declares that acts, methods, and practices of terrorism are contrary to the purposes and principles of the United Nations and that knowingly financing, planning and inciting terrorist acts are also contrary to the purposes and principles of the United Nations;

6. Decides to establish, in accordance with rule 28 of its provisional rules of procedure, a Committee of the Security Council, consisting of all the members of the Council, to monitor implementation of this resolution, with the assistance of appropriate expertise, and calls upon all States to report to the Committee, no later than 90 days from the date of adoption of this resolution and thereafter according to a timetable to be proposed by the Committee, on the steps they have taken to implement this resolution;

7. Directs the Committee to delineate its tasks, submit a work programme within 30 days of the adoption of this resolution, and to consider the support it requires, in consultation with the Secretary-General;

8. Expresses its determination to take all necessary steps in order to ensure the full implementation of this resolution, in accordance with its responsibilities under the Charter;

9. Decides to remain seized of this matter.

DOCUMENT 28

International Convention for the Suppression of Acts of Nuclear Terrorism 2005
UN Doc A/59/766

This Convention was adopted as an annex to General Assembly Resolution 59/290 on 4 April 2005 and will be opened for signature between 14 September and 31 December 2005.

It is not yet in force.

The landmark General Assembly Declaration on Measures to Eliminate International Terrorism of 17 February 1995 (GA Res 49/60) began a process in the Assembly of addressing terrorism issues. The Declaration to Supplement the Declaration on Measures to

Eliminate International Terrorism of 16 January 1997 (GA Res 51/210) established an Ad Hoc Committee, which was charged with elaborating, inter alia, *an international Convention for the suppression of nuclear terrorism.*

The proscribed acts relating to nuclear terrorism are identified and defined in Article 2. The Convention requires the Contracting States to criminalise these acts (Article 5(a)) and make them punishable by appropriate penalties (Article 5(b)). It emphasises that these acts are to be under no circumstances justifiable in domestic law (Article 6). Each Contracting State is to establish its jurisdiction where one of the Convention's offences is committed in its territory or on its ships or aircraft or by one of its nationals (Article 9(1)). Additionally, the State may assert jurisdiction where the victim is a national, where the offence is committed against a State facility abroad or where the offence is designed to compel a State to do or abstain from doing some act (Article 9(2)). Each Contracting State is required to report an offender to its prosecution authorities or to extradite him (Article 11(1)) – the aut dedere aut judicare *principle. The Convention declares the proscribed acts to be extraditable offences under existing extradition treaties and to be included in future extradition treaties (Article 13(1)); if there is no extradition treaty, the Convention itself may be treated as such (Article 13(2)). The offences set out in Article 2 are not to be considered political offences (Article 15), although there may be no extradition or mutual assistance where the purpose is to prosecute or punish a person on account of his race, religion, nationality, ethnic origin or political opinion (Article 16). There are fair treatment guarantees for proceedings under the Convention (Article 12). Parties are to afford one another the greatest measure of assistance in proceedings under the Convention (Article 14; see also Articles 17 and 18).*

Attempts to elaborate a Comprehensive Convention on International Terrorism have been ongoing since 1996. While considerable progress has been made in the drafting of this instrument, even the events of 11 September 2001 have not proved sufficient inspiration to overcome the remaining areas of disagreement, which in essence relate to whether the armed forces of States and national liberation movements are included in the Comprehensive Convention as capable of committing proscribed (terrorist) acts and whether the Comprehensive Convention prevails over the treaties in the sectoral régime. The Comprehensive Convention is currently available in draft: UN Doc A/C.6/56/L.9 Annex I.

See the other global terrorism conventions **(Documents 11–12, 15–17, 20 and 22–25),** *especially the Convention on the Physical Protection of Nuclear Material 1979* **(Document 21)**.

The States Parties to this Convention,

Having in mind the purposes and principles of the Charter of the United Nations concerning the maintenance of international peace and security and the promotion of good-neighbourliness and friendly relations and cooperation among States,

Recalling the Declaration on the Occasion of the Fiftieth Anniversary of the United Nations of 24 October 1995,

Recognizing the right of all States to develop and apply nuclear energy for peaceful purposes and their legitimate interests in the potential benefits to be derived from the peaceful application of nuclear energy,

Bearing in mind the Convention on the Physical Protection of Nuclear Material of 1980,

Deeply concerned about the worldwide escalation of acts of terrorism in all its forms and manifestations,

Recalling also the Declaration on Measures to Eliminate International Terrorism, annexed to General Assembly resolution 49/60 of 9 December 1994, in which, *inter alia*, the States Members of the

United Nations solemnly reaffirm their unequivocal condemnation of all acts, methods and practices of terrorism as criminal and unjustifiable, wherever and by whomever committed, including those which jeopardize the friendly relations among States and peoples and threaten the territorial integrity and security of States,

Noting that the Declaration also encouraged States to review urgently the scope of the existing international legal provisions on the prevention, repression and elimination of terrorism in all its forms and manifestations, with the aim of ensuring that there is a comprehensive legal framework covering all aspects of the matter,

Recalling General Assembly resolution 51/210 of 17 December 1996 and the Declaration to Supplement the 1994 Declaration on Measures to Eliminate International Terrorism annexed thereto,

Recalling also that, pursuant to General Assembly resolution 51/210, an ad hoc committee was established to elaborate, *inter alia*, an international convention for the suppression of acts of nuclear terrorism to supplement related existing international instruments,

Noting that acts of nuclear terrorism may result in the gravest consequences and may pose a threat to international peace and security,

Noting also that existing multilateral legal provisions do not adequately address those attacks,

Being convinced of the urgent need to enhance international cooperation between States in devising and adopting effective and practical measures for the prevention of such acts of terrorism and for the prosecution and punishment of their perpetrators,

Noting that the activities of military forces of States are governed by rules of international law outside of the framework of this Convention and that the exclusion of certain actions from the coverage of this Convention does not condone or make lawful otherwise unlawful acts, or preclude prosecution under other laws,

Have agreed as follows:

Article 1

For the purposes of this Convention:

1. "Radioactive material" means nuclear material and other radioactive substances which contain nuclides which undergo spontaneous disintegration (a process accompanied by emission of one or more types of ionising radiation, such as alpha-, beta-, neutron particles and gamma rays) and which may, owing to their radiological or fissile properties, cause death, serious bodily injury or substantial damage to property or to the environment.

2. "Nuclear material" means plutonium, except that with isotopic concentration exceeding 80 per cent in plutonium–238; uranium–233; uranium enriched in the isotopes 235 or 233; uranium containing the mixture of isotopes as occurring in nature other than in the form of ore or ore residue; or any material containing one or more of the foregoing;

    Whereby "uranium enriched in the isotope 235 or 233" means uranium containing the isotope 235 or 233 or both in an amount such that the abundance ratio of the sum of these isotopes to the isotope 238 is greater than the ratio of the isotope 235 to the isotope 238 occurring in nature.

3. "Nuclear facility" means:

    (a) Any nuclear reactor, including reactors installed on vessels, vehicles, aircraft or space objects for use as an energy source in order to propel such vessels, vehicles, aircraft or space objects or for any other purpose;

    (b) Any plant or conveyance being used for the production, storage, processing or transport of radioactive material.

4. "Device" means:

    (a) Any nuclear explosive device; or

    (b) Any radioactive material dispersal or radiation-emitting device which may, owing to its radiological properties, cause death, serious bodily injury or substantial damage to property or the environment.

5. "State or government facility" includes any permanent or temporary facility or conveyance that is used or occupied by representatives of a State, members of Government, the legislature or the judiciary or by officials or employees of a State or any other public authority or entity or by employees or officials of an intergovernmental organization in connection with their official duties.

6. "Military forces of a State" means the armed forces of a State which are organized, trained and equipped under its internal law for the primary purpose of national defence or security and persons acting in support of those armed forces who are under their formal command, control and responsibility.

Article 2

1. Any person commits an offence within the meaning of this Convention if that person unlawfully and intentionally:

    (a) Possesses radioactive material or makes or possesses a device:

        (i)   With the intent to cause death or serious bodily injury; or

        (ii) With the intent to cause substantial damage to property or the environment;

    (b) Uses in any way radioactive material or a device, or uses or damages a nuclear facility in a manner which releases or risks the release of radioactive material:

        (i)   With the intent to cause death or serious bodily injury; or

        (ii) With the intent to cause substantial damage to property or the environment; or

        (iii) With the intent to compel a natural or legal person, an international organization or a State to do or refrain from doing an act.

2. Any person also commits an offence if that person:

    (a) Threatens, under circumstances which indicate the credibility of the threat, to commit an offence as set forth in subparagraph 1(b) of the present article; or

    (b) Demands unlawfully and intentionally radioactive material, a device or a nuclear facility by threat, under circumstances which indicate the credibility of the threat, or by use of force.

3. Any person also commits an offence if that person attempts to commit an offence as set forth in paragraph 1 of the present article.

4. Any person also commits an offence if that person:

    (a) Participates as an accomplice in an offence as set forth in paragraph 1, 2 or 3 of the present article; or

    (b) Organizes or directs others to commit an offence as set forth in paragraph 1, 2 or 3 of the present article; or

    (c) In any other way contributes to the commission of one or more offences as set forth in paragraph 1, 2 or 3 of the present article by a group of persons acting with a common purpose; such contribution shall be intentional and either be made with the aim of furthering the general criminal activity or purpose of the group or be made in the knowledge of the intention of the group to commit the offence or offences concerned.

Article 3

This Convention shall not apply where the offence is committed within a single State, the alleged offender and the victims are nationals of that State, the alleged offender is found in the territory of that State and no other State has a basis under article 9, paragraph 1 or paragraph 2, to exercise jurisdiction, except that the provisions of articles 7, 12, 14, 15, 16 and 17 shall, as appropriate, apply in those cases.

Article 4

1.   Nothing in this Convention shall affect other rights, obligations and responsibilities of States and individuals under international law, in particular the purposes and principles of the Charter of the United Nations and international humanitarian law.

2.   The activities of armed forces during an armed conflict, as those terms are understood under international humanitarian law, which are governed by that law are not governed by this Convention, and the activities undertaken by military forces of a State in the exercise of their official duties, inasmuch as they are governed by other rules of international law, are not governed by this Convention.

3.   The provisions of paragraph 2 of the present article shall not be interpreted as condoning or making lawful otherwise unlawful acts, or precluding prosecution under other laws.

4.   This Convention does not address, nor can it be interpreted as addressing, in any way, the issue of the legality of the use or threat of use of nuclear weapons by States.

Article 5

Each State Party shall adopt such measures as may be necessary:

(a)   To establish as criminal offences under its national law the offences set forth in article 2;

(b)   To make those offences punishable by appropriate penalties which take into account the grave nature of these offences.

Article 6

Each State Party shall adopt such measures as may be necessary, including, where appropriate, domestic legislation, to ensure that criminal acts within the scope of this Convention, in particular where they are intended or calculated to provoke a state of terror in the general public or in a group of persons or particular persons, are under no circumstances justifiable by considerations of a political, philosophical, ideological, racial, ethnic, religious or other similar nature and are punished by penalties consistent with their grave nature.

Article 7

1.   States Parties shall cooperate by:

(a)   Taking all practicable measures, including, if necessary, adapting their national law, to prevent and counter preparations in their respective territories for the commission within or outside their territories of the offences set forth in article 2, including measures to prohibit in their territories illegal activities of persons, groups and organizations that encourage, instigate, organize, knowingly finance or knowingly provide technical assistance or information or engage in the perpetration of those offences;

(b)   Exchanging accurate and verified information in accordance with their national law and in the manner of and subject to the conditions specified herein, and coordinating administrative and other measures taken as appropriate to detect, prevent, suppress and investigate the offences set forth in article 2 and also in order to institute criminal proceedings against persons alleged to have committed those crimes. In particular, a State Party shall take appropriate measures in order to inform without delay the other States referred to in article 9 in respect of the commission of the offences set forth in article 2 as well as preparations to commit such offences about which it has learned, and also to inform, where appropriate, international organizations.

2. States Parties shall take appropriate measures consistent with their national law to protect the confidentiality of any information which they receive in confidence by virtue of the provisions of this Convention from another State Party or through participation in an activity carried out for the implementation of this Convention. If States Parties provide information to international organizations in confidence, steps shall be taken to ensure that the confidentiality of such information is protected.

3. States Parties shall not be required by this Convention to provide any information which they are not permitted to communicate pursuant to national law or which would jeopardize the security of the State concerned or the physical protection of nuclear material.

4. States Parties shall inform the Secretary-General of the United Nations of their competent authorities and liaison points responsible for sending and receiving the information referred to in the present article. The Secretary-General of the United Nations shall communicate such information regarding competent authorities and liaison points to all States Parties and the International Atomic Energy Agency. Such authorities and liaison points must be accessible on a continuous basis.

Article 8

For purposes of preventing offences under this Convention, States Parties shall make every effort to adopt appropriate measures to ensure the protection of radioactive material, taking into account relevant recommendations and functions of the International Atomic Energy Agency.

Article 9

1. Each State Party shall take such measures as may be necessary to establish its jurisdiction over the offences set forth in article 2 when:

    (a) The offence is committed in the territory of that State; or

    (b) The offence is committed on board a vessel flying the flag of that State or an aircraft which is registered under the laws of that State at the time the offence is committed; or

    (c) The offence is committed by a national of that State.

2. A State Party may also establish its jurisdiction over any such offence when:

    (a) The offence is committed against a national of that State; or

    (b) The offence is committed against a State or government facility of that State abroad, including an embassy or other diplomatic or consular premises of that State; or

    (c) The offence is committed by a stateless person who has his or her habitual residence in the territory of that State; or

    (d) The offence is committed in an attempt to compel that State to do or abstain from doing any act; or

    (e) The offence is committed on board an aircraft which is operated by the Government of that State.

3. Upon ratifying, accepting, approving or acceding to this Convention, each State Party shall notify the Secretary-General of the United Nations of the jurisdiction it has established under its national law in accordance with paragraph 2 of the present article. Should any change take place, the State Party concerned shall immediately notify the Secretary-General.

4. Each State Party shall likewise take such measures as may be necessary to establish its jurisdiction over the offences set forth in article 2 in cases where the alleged offender is present in its territory and it does not extradite that person to any of the States Parties which have established their jurisdiction in accordance with paragraph 1 or 2 of the present article.

5. This Convention does not exclude the exercise of any criminal jurisdiction established by a State Party in accordance with its national law.

Article 10

1. Upon receiving information that an offence set forth in article 2 has been committed or is being committed in the territory of a State Party or that a person who has committed or who is alleged to have committed such an offence may be present in its territory, the State Party concerned shall take such measures as may be necessary under its national law to investigate the facts contained in the information.

2. Upon being satisfied that the circumstances so warrant, the State Party in whose territory the offender or alleged offender is present shall take the appropriate measures under its national law so as to ensure that person's presence for the purpose of prosecution or extradition.

3. Any person regarding whom the measures referred to in paragraph 2 of the present article are being taken shall be entitled to:

   (a) Communicate without delay with the nearest appropriate representative of the State of which that person is a national or which is otherwise entitled to protect that person's rights or, if that person is a stateless person, the State in the territory of which that person habitually resides;

   (b) Be visited by a representative of that State;

   (c) Be informed of that person's rights under subparagraphs (a) and (b).

4. The rights referred to in paragraph 3 of the present article shall be exercised in conformity with the laws and regulations of the State in the territory of which the offender or alleged offender is present, subject to the provision that the said laws and regulations must enable full effect to be given to the purposes for which the rights accorded under paragraph 3 are intended.

5. The provisions of paragraphs 3 and 4 of the present article shall be without prejudice to the right of any State Party having a claim to jurisdiction in accordance with article 9, subparagraph 1(c) or 2(c), to invite the International Committee of the Red Cross to communicate with and visit the alleged offender.

6. When a State Party, pursuant to the present article, has taken a person into custody, it shall immediately notify, directly or through the Secretary-General of the United Nations, the States Parties which have established jurisdiction in accordance with article 9, paragraphs 1 and 2 and, if it considers it advisable, any other interested States Parties, of the fact that that person is in custody and of the circumstances which warrant that person's detention. The State which makes the investigation contemplated in paragraph 1 of the present article shall promptly inform the said States Parties of its findings and shall indicate whether it intends to exercise jurisdiction.

Article 11

1. The State Party in the territory of which the alleged offender is present shall, in cases to which article 9 applies, if it does not extradite that person, be obliged, without exception whatsoever and whether or not the offence was committed in its territory, to submit the case without undue delay to its competent authorities for the purpose of prosecution, through proceedings in accordance with the laws of that State. Those authorities shall take their decision in the same manner as in the case of any other offence of a grave nature under the law of that State.

2. Whenever a State Party is permitted under its national law to extradite or otherwise surrender one of its nationals only upon the condition that the person will be returned to that State to serve the sentence imposed as a result of the trial or proceeding for which the extradition or surrender of the person was sought, and this State and the State seeking the extradition of the person agree with this option and other terms they may deem appropriate, such a conditional extradition or surrender shall be sufficient to discharge the obligation set forth in paragraph 1 of the present article.

Article 12

Any person who is taken into custody or regarding whom any other measures are taken or proceedings are carried out pursuant to this Convention shall be guaranteed fair treatment, including enjoyment of all rights and guarantees in conformity with the law of the State in the territory of which that person is present and applicable provisions of international law, including international law of human rights.

Article 13

1. The offences set forth in article 2 shall be deemed to be included as extraditable offences in any extradition treaty existing between any of the States Parties before the entry into force of this Convention. States Parties undertake to include such offences as extraditable offences in every extradition treaty to be subsequently concluded between them.

2. When a State Party which makes extradition conditional on the existence of a treaty receives a request for extradition from another State Party with which it has no extradition treaty, the requested State Party may, at its option, consider this Convention as a legal basis for extradition in respect of the offences set forth in article 2. Extradition shall be subject to the other conditions provided by the law of the requested State.

3. States Parties which do not make extradition conditional on the existence of a treaty shall recognize the offences set forth in article 2 as extraditable offences between themselves, subject to the conditions provided by the law of the requested State.

4. If necessary, the offences set forth in article 2 shall be treated, for the purposes of extradition between States Parties, as if they had been committed not only in the place in which they occurred but also in the territory of the States that have established jurisdiction in accordance with article 9, paragraphs 1 and 2.

5. The provisions of all extradition treaties and arrangements between States Parties with regard to offences set forth in article 2 shall be deemed to be modified as between States Parties to the extent that they are incompatible with this Convention.

Article 14

1. States Parties shall afford one another the greatest measure of assistance in connection with investigations or criminal or extradition proceedings brought in respect of the offences set forth in article 2, including assistance in obtaining evidence at their disposal necessary for the proceedings.

2. States Parties shall carry out their obligations under paragraph 1 of the present article in conformity with any treaties or other arrangements on mutual legal assistance that may exist between them. In the absence of such treaties or arrangements, States Parties shall afford one another assistance in accordance with their national law.

Article 15

None of the offences set forth in article 2 shall be regarded, for the purposes of extradition or mutual legal assistance, as a political offence or as an offence connected with a political offence or as an offence inspired by political motives. Accordingly, a request for extradition or for mutual legal assistance based on such an offence may not be refused on the sole ground that it concerns a political offence or an offence connected with a political offence or an offence inspired by political motives.

Article 16

Nothing in this Convention shall be interpreted as imposing an obligation to extradite or to afford mutual legal assistance if the requested State Party has substantial grounds for believing that the request for extradition for offences set forth in article 2 or for mutual legal assistance with respect to such offences has been made for the purpose of prosecuting or punishing a person on account of that person's race, religion, nationality, ethnic origin or political opinion or that compliance with the request would cause prejudice to that person's position for any of these reasons.

Article 17

1. A person who is being detained or is serving a sentence in the territory of one State Party whose presence in another State Party is requested for purposes of testimony, identification or otherwise providing assistance in obtaining evidence for the investigation or prosecution of offences under this Convention may be transferred if the following conditions are met:

    (a) The person freely gives his or her informed consent; and

    (b) The competent authorities of both States agree, subject to such conditions as those States may deem appropriate.

2. For the purposes of the present article:

    (a) The State to which the person is transferred shall have the authority and obligation to keep the person transferred in custody, unless otherwise requested or authorized by the State from which the person was transferred;

    (b) The State to which the person is transferred shall without delay implement its obligation to return the person to the custody of the State from which the person was transferred as agreed beforehand, or as otherwise agreed, by the competent authorities of both States;

    (c) The State to which the person is transferred shall not require the State from which the person was transferred to initiate extradition proceedings for the return of the person;

    (d) The person transferred shall receive credit for service of the sentence being served in the State from which he was transferred for time spent in the custody of the State to which he was transferred.

3. Unless the State Party from which a person is to be transferred in accordance with the present article so agrees, that person, whatever his or her nationality, shall not be prosecuted or detained or subjected to any other restriction of his or her personal liberty in the territory of the State to which that person is transferred in respect of acts or convictions anterior to his or her departure from the territory of the State from which such person was transferred.

Article 18

1. Upon seizing or otherwise taking control of radioactive material, devices or nuclear facilities, following the commission of an offence set forth in article 2, the State Party in possession of it shall:

    (a) Take steps to render harmless the radioactive material, device or nuclear facility;

    (b) Ensure that any nuclear material is held in accordance with applicable International Atomic Energy Agency safeguards; and

    (c) Have regard to physical protection recommendations and health and safety standards published by the International Atomic Energy Agency.

2. Upon the completion of any proceedings connected with an offence set forth in article 2, or sooner if required by international law, any radioactive material, device or nuclear facility shall be returned, after consultations (in particular, regarding modalities of return and storage) with the States Parties concerned to the State Party to which it belongs, to the State Party of which the natural or legal person owning such radioactive material, device or facility is a national or resident, or to the State Party from whose territory it was stolen or otherwise unlawfully obtained.

3.1 Where a State Party is prohibited by national or international law from returning or accepting such radioactive material, device or nuclear facility or where the States Parties concerned so agree, subject to paragraph 3.2 of the present article, the State Party in possession of the radioactive material, devices or nuclear facilities shall continue to take the steps described in paragraph 1 of the present article; such radioactive material, devices or nuclear facilities shall be used only for peaceful purposes.

3.2 Where it is not lawful for the State Party in possession of the radioactive material, devices or nuclear facilities to possess them, that State shall ensure that they are as soon as possible placed in the possession of a State for which such possession is lawful and which, where appropriate, has provided assurances consistent with the requirements of paragraph 1 of the present article in consultation with that State, for the purpose of rendering it harmless; such radioactive material, devices or nuclear facilities shall be used only for peaceful purposes.

4. If the radioactive material, devices or nuclear facilities referred to in paragraphs 1 and 2 of the present article do not belong to any of the States Parties or to a national or resident of a State Party or was not stolen or otherwise unlawfully obtained from the territory of a State Party, or if no State is willing to receive such item pursuant to paragraph 3 of the present article, a separate decision concerning its disposition shall, subject to paragraph 3.2 of the present article, be taken after consultations between the States concerned and any relevant international organizations.

5. For the purposes of paragraphs 1, 2, 3 and 4 of the present article, the State Party in possession of the radioactive material, device or nuclear facility may request the assistance and cooperation of other States Parties, in particular the States Parties concerned, and any relevant international organizations, in particular the International Atomic Energy Agency. States Parties and the relevant international organizations are encouraged to provide assistance pursuant to this paragraph to the maximum extent possible.

6. The States Parties involved in the disposition or retention of the radioactive material, device or nuclear facility pursuant to the present article shall inform the Director General of the International Atomic Energy Agency of the manner in which such an item was disposed of or retained. The Director General of the International Atomic Energy Agency shall transmit the information to the other States Parties.

7. In the event of any dissemination in connection with an offence set forth in article 2, nothing in the present article shall affect in any way the rules of international law governing liability for nuclear damage, or other rules of international law.

Article 19
The State Party where the alleged offender is prosecuted shall, in accordance with its national law or applicable procedures, communicate the final outcome of the proceedings to the Secretary-General of the United Nations, who shall transmit the information to the other States Parties.

Article 20
States Parties shall conduct consultations with one another directly or through the Secretary-General of the United Nations, with the assistance of international organizations as necessary, to ensure effective implementation of this Convention.

Article 21
The States Parties shall carry out their obligations under this Convention in a manner consistent with the principles of sovereign equality and territorial integrity of States and that of non-intervention in the domestic affairs of other States.

Article 22
Nothing in this Convention entitles a State Party to undertake in the territory of another State Party the exercise of jurisdiction and performance of functions which are exclusively reserved for the authorities of that other State Party by its national law.

Article 23

1. Any dispute between two or more States Parties concerning the interpretation or application of this Convention which cannot be settled through negotiation within a reasonable time shall, at the request of one of them, be submitted to arbitration. If, within six months from the date of the request for arbitration, the parties are unable to agree on the organization of the arbitration, any one of those parties may refer the dispute to the International Court of Justice, by application, in conformity with the Statute of the Court.

2. Each State may, at the time of signature, ratification, acceptance or approval of this Convention or accession thereto, declare that it does not consider itself bound by paragraph 1 of the present article. The other States Parties shall not be bound by paragraph 1 with respect to any State Party which has made such a reservation.

3. Any State which has made a reservation in accordance with paragraph 2 of the present article may at any time withdraw that reservation by notification to the Secretary-General of the United Nations.

MISCELLANEOUS CRIMES

DOCUMENT 29

Treaty of Versailles 1919
225 CTS 188

The Treaty was adopted and signed on 28 June 1919 and entered into force on 10 January 1920.

There were 20 original signatories to the Treaty, including France, Italy, the UK and the USA, although the USA did not ratify the treaty.

The Treaty of Versailles was drafted during the Paris Peace Conference of 12 January 1919 to 20 January 1920 following the First World War. The Paris Conference met in various locations around the city and adopted a total of five treaties, each named after a Paris suburb. In addition to the Treaty of Versailles with Germany, the principal instrument, treaties were adopted at Saint-Germain-en-Laye on 10 September 1919 with Austria (226 CTS 8), Sèvres on 27 November 1919 with Bulgaria (28 LNTS 226), Trianon on 4 June 1920 with Hungary (6 LNTS 188) and Neuilly-sur-Seine on 10 August 1920 with Turkey (226 CTS 382).

The Treaty of Versailles is divided into 16 parts. Part VII, entitled 'Penalties', consists of four articles (227–30) that evince an early attempt to establish individual responsibility for war crimes and to create tribunals for their adjudication. In the event, Kaiser Wilhelm II successfully escaped prosecution through Dutch sanctuary and only nine alleged German war criminals were tried – and they before a Leipzig court and not a military tribunal as envisaged by Article 228.

Article 227

The Allied and Associated Powers publicly arraign William II of Hohenzollern, formerly German Emperor, for a supreme offence against international morality and the sanctity of treaties.

A special tribunal will be constituted to try the accused, thereby assuring him the guarantees essential to the right of defence. It will be composed of five judges, one appointed by each of the following Powers: namely, the United States of America, Great Britain, France, Italy and Japan.

In its decision the tribunal will be guided by the highest motives of international policy, with a view to vindicating the solemn obligations of international undertakings and the validity of international morality. It will be its duty to fix the punishment which it considers should be imposed.

The Allied and Associated Powers will address a request to the Government of the Netherlands for the surrender to them of the ex-Emperor in order that he may be put on trial.

Article 228

The German Government recognises the right of the Allied and Associated Powers to bring before military tribunals persons accused of having committed acts in violation of the laws and customs of war. Such persons shall, if found guilty, be sentenced to punishments laid down by law. This provision will apply notwithstanding any proceedings or prosecution before a tribunal in Germany or in the territory of her allies.

The German Government shall hand over to the Allied and Associated Powers, or to such one of them as shall so request, all persons accused of having committed an act in violation of the laws and customs of war, who are specified either by name or by the rank, office or employment which they held under the German authorities.

Article 229

Persons guilty of criminal acts against the nationals of one of the Allied and Associated Powers will be brought before the military tribunals of that Power.

Persons guilty of criminal acts against the nationals of more than one of the Allied and Associated Powers will be brought before military tribunals composed of members of the military tribunals of the Powers concerned.

In every case the accused will be entitled to name his own counsel.

Article 230

The German Government undertakes to furnish all documents and information of every kind, the production of which may be considered necessary to ensure the full knowledge of the incriminating acts, the discovery of offenders and the just appreciation of responsibility.

DOCUMENT 30

Treaty of Peace with Italy 1947
42 UNTS 3; 42 AJIL (Supp) 47 (1948)

The Convention was adopted on 10 February 1947 and entered into force on 15 September 1947.

There are 21 parties to the Treaty, including France, the UK, the USA and the USSR.

The Paris Peace Conference convened from 29 July to 15 October 1947 to consider the terms of peace to be established between the Allies and the defeated European powers. In addition to the Treaty with Italy, treaties of peace were also concluded with Bulgaria (41 UNTS 21), Finland (48 UNTS 203), Hungary (41 UNTS 133) and Romania (42 UNTS 3).

The Treaty of Peace with Italy is divided into 11 parts. Part III, entitled 'War Criminals', has a single article (45) and is a clear example of an attempt to extend responsibility for war crimes and crimes against humanity to a range of individuals beyond those dealt with at the Nuremberg Tribunal **(see Documents 47–48)** *and under Control Council Law No 10* **(Document 49).** *Identical provisions appear in the Treaties of Peace with Bulgaria (Article 5), Finland (Article 9), Hungary (Article 6) and Romania (Article 6).*

Article 45

1. Italy shall take all necessary steps to ensure the apprehension and surrender for trial of:

    (a) Persons accused of having committed, ordered or abetted war crimes and crimes against peace or humanity;

    (b) Nationals of any Allied or Associated Power accused of having violated their national law by treason or collaboration with the enemy during the war.

2. At the request of the United Nations Government concerned, Italy shall likewise make available as witnesses persons within its jurisdiction, whose evidence is required for the trial of the

persons referred to in paragraph 1 of this Article.3. Any disagreement concerning the application of the provisions of paragraphs 1 and 2 of this Article shall be referred by any of the Governments concerned to the Ambassadors in Rome of the Soviet Union, of the United Kingdom, of the United States of America, and of France, who will reach agreement with regard to the difficulty.

DOCUMENT 31

Principles of International Law Recognized in the Charter of the Nuremberg Tribunal and in the Judgment of the Tribunal 1950

1950 ILC Yb, Vol II, 374; UN Doc A/CN.4/SER.A/1950/Add 1; 44 AJIL (Supp) 15 (1950)

In Resolution 177 (II) of 21 November 1947, the General Assembly instructed the International Law Commission to 'formulate the principles of international law recognized in the Charter of the Nuremberg Tribunal [Document 48] and in the judgment of the Tribunal'. The Commission determined that, as the General Assembly had affirmed the principles, it should not evaluate the principles qua *principles of international law, but merely formulate them: see Commentary in 1950 ILC Yb, Vol II, 374–78.*

The seven Nuremberg Principles, as they are popularly known, have informed much of the development of international criminal law. They are, eg, incorporated into the two Draft Codes of Crimes Against the Peace and Security of Mankind (Documents 32–33) *and are core to the Statutes of the International Criminal Tribunals for the Former Yugoslavia* (Document 51) *and Rwanda* (Document 52) *and of the International Criminal Court* (Document 53). *Principle I reaffirms individual responsibility for any crime under international law, including responsibility for complicity (Principle VII) and irrespective of whether the crime is also a crime under internal law (Principle II). Political status and superior orders afford no impunity (Principles III and IV). Principle VI identifies and defines those crimes that are punishable under international law: crimes against peace, war crimes and crimes against humanity. A person charged with any of these offences is entitled to 'a fair trial on the facts and law' (Principle V).*

Principle I
Any person who commits an act which constitutes a crime under international law is responsible therefor and liable to punishment.

Principle II
The fact that internal law does not impose a penalty for an act which constitutes a crime under international law does not relieve the person who committed the act from responsibility under international law.

Principle III
The fact that a person who committed an act which constitutes a crime under international law acted as Head of State or responsible Government official does not relieve him from responsibility under international law.

Principle IV

The fact that a person acted pursuant to order of his Government or of a superior does not relieve him from responsibility under international law, provided a moral choice was in fact possible to him.

Principle V

Any person charged with a crime under international law has the right to a fair trial on the facts and law.

Principle VI

The crimes hereinafter set out are punishable as crimes under; international law:

(a) **Crimes against peace:**

    (i) Planning, preparation, initiation or waging of a war of aggression or a war in violation international treaties, agreements or assurances;

    (ii) Participation in a common plan or conspiracy for the accomplishment of any of the acts mentioned under (i).

(b) **War crimes:**

Violations of the laws or customs of war which include, but are not limited to, murder, ill-treatment or deportation to slave-labor or for any other purpose of civilian population of or in occupied territory, murder or ill-treatment of prisoners of war, of persons on the seas, killing of hostages, plunder of public or private property, wanton destruction of cities, towns, or villages, or devastation not justified by military necessity.

(c) **Crimes against humanity:**

Murder, extermination, enslavement, deportation and other inhuman acts done against any civilian population, or persecutions on political, racial or religious grounds, when such acts are done or such persecutions are carried on in execution of or in connection with any crime against peace or any war crime.

Principle VII

Complicity in the commission of a crime against peace, a war crime, or a crime against humanity as set forth in Principles VI is a crime under international law.

DOCUMENT 32

Draft Code of Offences Against the Peace and Security of Mankind 1954

1954 ILC Yb, Vol II, 149; UN Doc A/2693 (1954)

This Draft Code was adopted by the International Law Commission at its sixth session in 1954.

In Resolution 177 (II) of 21 November 1947, in the same resolution as it instructed a formulation of the Nuremberg Principles (Document 31), *the General Assembly invited the International Law Commission to 'prepare a draft code of offences against the peace and security of mankind'.*

The Draft Code contains four short articles. The first article reaffirms individual responsibility for all offences against the peace and security of mankind, as defined in Article 2.

As in the Nuremberg Principles, political status and superior orders afford no impunity (Articles 3–4). A revised and expanded Draft Code was adopted in 1996 **(Document 33)**.

See the International Law Commission commentary: 1954 ILC Yb, Vol II, 151–56.

Article I

Offences against the peace and security of mankind, as defined in this Code, are crimes under international law, for which the responsible individuals shall be punished.

Article 2

The following acts are offences against the peace and security of mankind:

(1) Any act of aggression, including the employment by the authorities of a State of armed force against another State for any purpose other than national or collective self-defence or in pursuance of a decision or recommendation of a competent organ of the United Nations.

(2) Any threat by the authorities of a State to resort to an act of aggression against another State.

(3) The preparation by the authorities of a State of the employment of armed force against another State for any purpose other than national or collective self-defence or in pursuance of a decision or recommendation of a competent organ of the United Nations.

(4) The organization, or the encouragement of the organization, by the authorities of a State, of armed bands within its territory or any other territory for incursions into the territory of another State, or the toleration of the organization of such bands in its own territory, or the toleration of the use by such armed bands of its territory as a base of operations or as a point of departure for incursions into the territory of another State, as well as direct participation in or support of such incursions.

(5) The undertaking or encouragement by the authorities of a State of activities calculated to foment civil strife in another State, or the toleration by the authorities of a State of organized activities calculated to foment civil strife in another State.

(6) The undertaking or encouragement by the authorities of a State of terrorist activities in another State, or the toleration by the authorities of a State of organized activities calculated to carry out terrorist acts in another State.

(7) Acts by the authorities of a State in violation of its obligations under a treaty which is designed to ensure international peace and security by means of restrictions or limitations on armaments, or on military training, or on fortifications, or of other restrictions of the same character.

(8) The annexation by the authorities of a State of territory belonging to another State, by means of acts contrary to international law.

(9) The intervention by the authorities of a State in the internal or external affairs of another State, by means of coercive measures of an economic or political character in order to force its will and thereby obtain advantages of any kind.

(10) Acts by the authorities of a State or by private individuals committed with intent to destroy, in whole or in part, a national, ethnic, racial or religious group as such, including:

(i) Killing members of the group;

(ii) Causing serious bodily or mental harm to members of the group;

(iii) Deliberately inflicting on the group conditions of life calculated to bring about its physical destruction in whole or in part;

(iv) Imposing measures intended to prevent births within the group;

(v) Forcibly transferring children of the group to another group.

(11) Inhuman acts such as murder, extermination, enslavement deportation or persecutions, committed against any civilian population on social, political, racial, religious or cultural grounds by the authorities of a State or by private individuals acting at the instigation or with toleration of such authorities.

(12) Acts in violation of the laws or customs of war.

(13) Acts which constitute:

    (i) Conspiracy to commit any of the offences defined in the preceding paragraphs of this article; or

    (ii) Direct incitement to commit any of the offences defined in the preceding paragraphs of this article; or

    (iii) Complicity in the commission of any of the offences defined in the preceding paragraphs of this article; or

    (iv) Attempts to commit any of the offences defined in the preceding paragraphs of this article.

Article 3

The fact that a person acted as Head of State or as responsible government official does not relieve him of responsibility for committing any of the offences defined in this Code.

Article 4

The fact that a person charged with an offence defined in this Code acted pursuant to an order of his Government or of a superior does not relieve him of responsibility in international law if, in the circumstances at the time, it was possible for him not to comply with that order.

DOCUMENT 33

Draft Code of Crimes Against the Peace and Security of Mankind 1996

1996 ILC Yb, Vol II, 15; UN Doc A/48/10 (1996)

The Draft Code was adopted by the International Law Commission on 26 July 1996.

In Resolution 36/106 of 10 December 1981, the General Assembly invited the International Law Commission to resume its work with a view to elaborating the draft Code of Offences against the Peace and Security of Mankind. A revised Draft Code was provisionally agreed in 1991 (1991 ILC Yb, Vol II, 94), the finalised version being adopted in 1996. The ILC suggested that the Draft Code might be included in an international convention or a General Assembly resolution or incorporated into the Statute of the International Criminal Court. The Draft Code clearly impacted on the Statute of the ICC of 1998 (Document 53).

The 1996 Draft Code of Crimes against the Peace and Security of Mankind is much longer and more specific than its 1954 counterpart (Document 32). Its 20 articles are divided into two parts. Part I contains general provisions, including individual responsibility for international crimes (Article 2), the irrelevance to criminal responsibility of the political status of the individual (Article 7) or of superior orders (Article 5). It requires a fair trial (Article 11); and adds the obligation to establish jurisdiction over the Draft Code's offences (Article 8) and to extradite or prosecute any individual alleged to have committed any of these offences (Article 9). The obligation to extradite or prosecute (the aut dedere aut judicare principle) has become an integral competent of international criminal law, particularly the terrorism conventions (see C. Terrorism, above, and the documents therein). Part II of the Draft Code defines crimes against the peace and security of mankind: aggression (Article 16), genocide (Article 17), crimes against humanity (Article 18), crimes against United Nations and associated personnel (Article 19), and war crimes (Article 20).

See the International Law Commission Commentary: 1996 ILC Yb, Vol II, 15–56.

Part I: General Principles

Article 1 Scope and application of the present Code

1. The present Code applies to the crimes against the peace and security of mankind set out in Part II.

2. Crimes against the peace and security of mankind are crimes under international law and punishable as such, whether or not they are punishable under national law.

Article 2 Individual responsibility

1. A crime against the peace and security of mankind entails individual responsibility.

2. An individual shall be responsible for the crime of aggression in accordance with article 16.

3. An individual shall be responsible for a crime set out in articles 17, 18, 19 or 20 if that individual:

    (a) intentionally commits such a crime;

    (b) orders the commission of such a crime which in fact occurs or is attempted;

    (c) fails to prevent or repress the commission of such a crime in the circumstances set out in article 6;

    (d) knowingly aids, abets or otherwise assists, directly and substantially, in the commission of such a crime, including providing the means for its commission;

    (e) directly participates in planning or conspiring to commit such a crime which in fact occurs;

    (f) directly and publicly incites another individual to commit such a crime which in fact occurs;

    (g) attempts to commit such a crime by taking action commencing the execution of a crime which does not in fact occur because of circumstances independent of his intentions.

Article 3 Punishment

An individual who is responsible for a crime against the peace and security of mankind shall be liable to punishment. The punishment shall be commensurate with the character and gravity of the crime.

Article 4 Responsibility of States

The fact that the present Code provides for the responsibility of individuals for crimes against the peace and security of mankind is without prejudice to any question of the responsibility of States under international law.

Article 5 Order of a Government or a superior

The fact that an individual charged with a crime against the peace and security of mankind acted pursuant to an order of a Government or a superior does not relieve him of criminal responsibility, but may be considered in mitigation of punishment if justice so requires.

Article 6 Responsibility of the superior

The fact that a crime against the peace and security of mankind was committed by a subordinate does not relieve his superiors of criminal responsibility, if they knew or had reason to know, in the circumstances at the time, that the subordinate was committing or was going to commit such a crime and if they did not take all necessary measures within their power to prevent or repress the crime.

Article 7 Official position and responsibility

The official position of an individual who commits a crime against the peace and security of mankind, even if he acted as head of State or Government, does not relieve him of criminal responsibility or mitigate punishment.

Article 8 Establishment of jurisdiction

Without prejudice to the jurisdiction of an international criminal court, each State Party shall take such measures as may be necessary to establish its jurisdiction over the crimes set out in articles 17, 18, 19 and 20, irrespective of where or by whom those crimes were committed. Jurisdiction over the crime set out in article 16 shall rest with an international criminal court. However, a State referred to in article 16 is not precluded from trying its nationals for the crime set out in that article.

Article 9 Obligation to extradite or prosecute

Without prejudice to the jurisdiction of an international criminal court, the State Party in the territory of which an individual alleged to have committed a crime set out in articles 17, 18, 19 or 20 is found shall extradite or prosecute that individual.

Article 10 Extradition of alleged offenders

1. To the extent that the crimes set out in articles 17, 18, 19 and 20 are not extraditable offences in any extradition treaty existing between States Parties, they shall be deemed to be included as such therein. States Parties undertake to include those crimes as extraditable offences in every extradition treaty to be concluded between them.

2. If a State Party which makes extradition conditional on the existence of a treaty receives a request for extradition from another State Party with which it has no extradition treaty, it may at its option consider the present Code as the legal basis for extradition in respect of those crimes. Extradition shall be subject to the conditions provided in the law of the requested State.

3. State Parties which do not make extradition conditional on the existence of a treaty shall recognize those crimes as extraditable offences between themselves subject to the conditions provided in the law of the requested State.

4. Each of those crimes shall be treated, for the purpose of extradition between States Parties, as if it had been committed not only in the place in which it occurred but also in the territory of any other State Party.

Article 11 Judicial guarantees

1. An individual charged with a crime against the peace and security of mankind shall be presumed innocent until proved guilty and shall be entitled without discrimination to the minimum guarantees due to all human beings with regard to the law and the facts and shall have the rights:

    (a) in the determination of any charge against him, to have a fair and public hearing by a competent, independent and impartial tribunal duly established by law;

    (b) to be informed promptly and in detail in a language which he understands of the nature and cause of the charge against him;

    (c) to have adequate time and facilities for the preparation of his defence and to communicate with counsel of his own choosing;

    (d) to be tried without undue delay;

    (e) to be tried in his presence, and to defend himself in person or through legal assistance of his own choosing; to be informed, if he does not have legal assistance, of this right; and to have legal assistance assigned to him and without payment by him if he does not have sufficient means to pay for it;

(f) to examine, or have examined, the witnesses against him and to obtain the attendance and examination of witnesses on his behalf under the same conditions as witnesses against him;

(g) to have the free assistance of an interpreter if he cannot understand or speak the language used in court;

(h) not to be compelled to testify against himself or to confess guilt.

2. An individual convicted of a crime shall have the right to his conviction and sentence being reviewed according to law.

Article 12 *Non bis in idem*

1. No one shall be tried for a crime against the peace and security of mankind of which he has already been finally convicted or acquitted by an international criminal court.

2. An individual may not be tried again for a crime of which he has been finally convicted or acquitted by a national court except in the following cases:

(a) by an international criminal court, if:

    (i) the act which was the subject of the judgment in the national court was characterized by that court as an ordinary crime and not as a crime against the peace and security of mankind; or

    (ii) the national court proceedings were not impartial or independent or were designed to shield the accused from international criminal responsibility or the case was not diligently prosecuted;

(b) by a national court of another State, if:

    (i) the act which was the subject of the previous judgment took place in the territory of that State; or

    (ii) that State was the main victim of the crime.

3. In the case of a subsequent conviction under the present Code, the court, in passing sentence, shall take into account the extent to which any penalty imposed by a national court on the same person for the same act has already been served.

Article 13 **Non-retroactivity**

1. No one shall be convicted under the present Code for acts committed before its entry into force.

2. Nothing in this article precludes the trial of anyone for any act which, at the time when it was committed, was criminal in accordance with international law or national law.

Article 14 **Defences**

The competent court shall determine the admissibility of defences in accordance with the general principles of law, in the light of the character of each crime.

Article 15 **Extenuating circumstances**

In passing sentence, the court shall, where appropriate, take into account extenuating circumstances in accordance with the general principles of law.

Part II: Crimes against the Peace and Security of Mankind

Article 16 **Crime of aggression**

An individual who, as leader or organizer, actively participates in or orders the planning, preparation, initiation or waging of aggression committed by a State shall be responsible for a crime of aggression.

Article 17 Crime of genocide

A crime of genocide means any of the following acts committed with intent to destroy, in whole or in part, a national, ethnic, racial or religious group, as such:

(a) killing members of the group;

(b) causing serious bodily or mental harm to members of the group;

(c) deliberately inflicting on the group conditions of life calculated to bring about its physical destruction in whole or in part;

(d) imposing measures intended to prevent births within the group;

(e) forcibly transferring children of the group to another group.

Article 18 Crimes against humanity

A crime against humanity means any of the following acts, when committed in a systematic manner or on a large scale and instigated or directed by a Government or by any organization or group:

(a) murder;

(b) extermination;

(c) torture;

(d) enslavement;

(e) persecution on political, racial, religious or ethnic grounds;

(f) institutionalized discrimination on racial, ethnic or religious grounds involving the violation of fundamental human rights and freedoms and resulting in seriously disadvantaging a part of the population;

(g) arbitrary deportation or forcible transfer of population;

(h) arbitrary imprisonment;

(i) forced disappearance of persons;

(j) rape, enforced prostitution and other forms of sexual abuse;

(k) other inhumane acts which severely damage physical or mental integrity, health or human dignity, such as mutilation and severe bodily harm.

Article 19 Crimes against United Nations and associated personnel

1. The following crimes constitute crimes against the peace and security of mankind when committed intentionally and in a systematic manner or on a large scale against United Nations and associated personnel involved in a United Nations operation with a view to preventing or impeding that operation from fulfilling its mandate:

    (a) murder, kidnapping or other attack upon the person or liberty of any such personnel;

    (b) violent attack upon the official premises, the private accommodation or the means of transportation of any such personnel likely to endanger his or her person or liberty.

2. This article shall not apply to a United Nations operation authorized by the Security Council as an enforcement action under Chapter VII of the Charter of the United Nations in which any of the personnel are engaged as combatants against organized armed forces and to which the law of international armed conflict applies.

Article 20 War crimes

Any of the following war crimes constitutes a crime against the peace and security of mankind when committed in a systematic manner or on a large scale:

(a) any of the following acts committed in violation of international humanitarian law:

    (i) wilful killing;

    (ii)   torture or inhuman treatment, including biological experiments;

    (iii) wilfully causing great suffering or serious injury to body or health;

    (iv) extensive destruction and appropriation of property, not justified by military necessity and carried out unlawfully and wantonly;

    (v)   compelling a prisoner of war or other protected person to serve in the forces of a hostile Power;

    (vi) wilfully depriving a prisoner of war or other protected person of the rights of fair and regular trial;

    (vii) unlawful deportation or transfer or unlawful confinement of protected persons;

    (viii) taking of hostages;

(b) any of the following acts committed wilfully in violation of international humanitarian law and causing death or serious injury to body or health:

    (i)   making the civilian population or individual civilians the object of attack;

    (ii) launching an indiscriminate attack affecting the civilian population or civilian objects in the knowledge that such attack will cause excessive loss of life, injury to civilians or damage to civilian objects;

    (iii) launching an attack against works or installations containing dangerous forces in the knowledge that such attack will cause excessive loss of life, injury to civilians or damage to civilian objects;

    (iv) making a person the object of attack in the knowledge that he is hors de combat;

    (v)   the perfidious use of the distinctive emblem of the red cross, red crescent or red lion and sun or of other recognized protective signs;

(c) any of the following acts committed wilfully in violation of international humanitarian law:

    (i)   the transfer by the Occupying Power of parts of its own civilian population into the territory it occupies;

    (ii) unjustifiable delay in the repatriation of prisoners of war or civilians;

(d) outrages upon personal dignity in violation of international humanitarian law, in particular humiliating and degrading treatment, rape, enforced prostitution and any form of indecent assault;

(e) any of the following acts committed in violation of the laws or customs of war:

    (i)   employment of poisonous weapons or other weapons calculated to cause unnecessary suffering;

    (ii) wanton destruction of cities, towns or villages, or devastation not justified by military necessity;

    (iii) attack, or bombardment, by whatever means, of undefended towns, villages, dwellings or buildings or of demilitarized zones;

    (iv) seizure of, destruction of or wilful damage done to institutions dedicated to religion, charity and education, the arts and sciences, historic monuments and works of art and science;

    (v)   plunder of public or private property;

(f) any of the following acts committed in violation of international humanitarian law applicable in armed conflict not of an international character:

    (i)   violence to the life, health and physical or mental well-being of persons, in particular murder as well as cruel treatment such as torture, mutilation or any form of corporal punishment;

    (ii) collective punishments;

    (iii) taking of hostages;

    (iv) acts of terrorism;

(v) outrages upon personal dignity, in particular humiliating and degrading treatment, rape, enforced prostitution and any form of indecent assault;

(vi) pillage;

(vii) the passing of sentences and the carrying out of executions without previous judgment pronounced by a regularly constituted court, affording all the judicial guarantees which are generally recognized as indispensable;

(g) in the case of armed conflict, using methods or means of warfare not justified by military necessity with the intent to cause widespread, long-term and severe damage to the natural environment and thereby gravely prejudice the health or survival of the population and such damage occurs.

DOCUMENT 34

Single Convention on Narcotic Drugs 1961 (as amended by the Protocol of 1972)

520 UNTS 151; Protocol 976 UNTS 3; 10 ILM 261 (1972)

This Convention was adopted at New York on 30 March 1961 and entered into force on 13 December 1964. The Protocol amending the Convention was adopted at Geneva on 25 March 1972 and entered into force on 8 August 1975.

There are 149 parties to the Single Convention, including Afghanistan, China, Colombia, France, Germany, the UK and the USA; and there are 121 parties to the 1972 Protocol.

The first international instrument to regulate narcotic drugs was the Convention for Limiting the Manufacture and Regulating the Distribution of Narcotic Drugs of 13 July 1931 (139 LNTS 301) which, along with other instruments, was codified in the Protocol amending the Agreements, Conventions and Protocols on Narcotic Drugs of 11 December 1946 (12 UNTS 179). There are three major drug control treaties currently in force: this Convention and its 1972 Protocol; the Convention on Psychotropic Substances of 21 February 1971 (1019 UNTS 175); and the UN Convention against Illicit Traffic in Narcotic Drugs and Psychotropic Substances of 20 December 1988 (Document 35).

The Single Convention requires each State party to make a range of offences punishable under its law (Article 36(1)(a); see also Article 34). There is an obligation to prosecute serious offences placed on the State in whose territory the offence occurs and on the State in which the offender is found if extradition is not possible (Article 36(a)(iv)). The Convention's offences are deemed to be included in existing extradition treaties and are to be included in future treaties (Article 36(2)(b)(i)); and, in the absence of an extradition treaty, the Convention itself can be used as such (Article 36(2)(b)(ii)). The Single Convention contains extensive duties on States to co-operate (Article 35).

The Parties,

Concerned with the health and welfare of mankind,

Recognising that the medical use of narcotic drugs continues to be indispensable for the relief of pain and suffering and that adequate provision must be made to ensure the availability of narcotic drugs for such purposes,

Recognising that addiction to narcotic drugs constitutes a serious evil for the individual and is fraught with social and economic danger to mankind,

Conscious of their duty to prevent and combat this evil,

Considering that effective measures against abuse of narcotic drugs require coordinated and universal action,

Understanding that such universal action calls for international cooperation guided by the same principles and aimed at common objectives,

Acknowledging the competence of the United Nations in the field of narcotics control and desirous that the international organs concerned should be within the framework of that Organization,

Desiring to conclude a generally acceptable international convention replacing existing treaties on narcotic drugs, limiting such drugs to medical and scientific use, and providing for continuous international cooperation and control for the achievement of such aims and objectives,

Hereby agree as follows:

Article 4 General obligations

1. The Parties shall take such legislative and administrative measures as may be necessary:

    (a) To give effect to and carry out the provisions of this Convention within their own territories;

    (b) To cooperate with other States in the execution of the provisions of this Convention; and

    (c) Subject to the provisions of this Convention, to limit exclusively to medical and scientific purposes the production, manufacture, export, import, distribution of, trade in, use and possession of drugs.

Article 33 Possession of drugs

The Parties shall not permit the possession of drugs except under legal authority.

Article 34 Measures of supervision and inspection

The Parties shall require:

(a) That all persons who obtain licences as provided in accordance with this Convention, or who have managerial or supervisory positions in a State enterprise established in accordance with this Convention, shall have adequate qualifications for the effective and faithful execution of the provisions of such laws and regulations as are enacted in pursuance thereof; and

(b) That governmental authorities, manufacturers, traders, scientists, scientific institutions and hospitals keep such records as will show the quantities of each drug manufactured and of each individual acquisition and disposal of drugs. Such records shall respectively be preserved for a period of not less than two years. Where counterfoil books ... of official prescriptions are used, such books including the counterfoils shall also be kept for a period of not less than two years.

Article 35 Action against the illicit traffic

Having due regard to their constitutional, legal and administrative systems, the Parties shall:

(a) Make arrangements at the national level for co-ordination of preventive and repressive action against the illicit traffic; to this end they may usefully designate an appropriate agency responsible for such co-ordination;

(b) Assist each other in the campaign against the illicit traffic in narcotic drugs;

(c) Co-operate closely with each other and with the competent international organizations of which they are members with a view to maintaining a coordinated campaign against the illicit traffic;

(d) Ensure that international co-operation between the appropriate agencies be conducted in an expeditious manner;

(e) Ensure that where legal papers are transmitted internationally for the purposes of a prosecution, the transmittal be effected in an expeditious manner to the bodies designated by the Parties; this requirement shall be without prejudice to the right of a Party to require that legal papers be sent to it through the diplomatic channel;

(f) Furnish, if they deem it appropriate, to the Board and the Commission through the Secretary-General, in addition to information . . . , information relating to illicit drug activity within their borders, including information on illicit cultivation, production, manufacture and use of, and on illicit trafficking in, drugs; and

(g) Furnish the information referred to in the preceding paragraph as far as possible in such manner and by such dates as the Board may request; if requested by a Party, the Board may offer its advice to it in furnishing the information and in endeavouring to reduce the illicit drug activity within the borders of that Party.

Article 36 Penal provisions

1. (a) Subject to its constitutional limitations, each Party shall adopt such measures as will ensure that cultivation, production, manufacture, extraction, preparation, possession, offering, offering for sale, distribution, purchase, sale, delivery on any terms whatsoever, brokerage, dispatch, dispatch in transit, transport, importation and exportation of drugs contrary to the provisions of this Convention, and any other action which in the opinion of such Party may be contrary to the provisions of this Convention, shall be punishable offences when committed intentionally, and that serious offences shall be liable to adequate punishment particularly by imprisonment or other penalties of deprivation of liberty.

   (b) Notwithstanding the preceding sub-paragraph, when abusers of drugs have committed such offences, the Parties may provide, either as an alternative to conviction or punishment or in addition to conviction or punishment, that such abusers shall undergo measures of treatment, education, after-care, rehabilitation and social reintegration . . .

2. Subject to the constitutional limitations of a Party, its legal system and domestic law:

   (a) (i) Each of the offences enumerated in paragraph 1, if committed in different countries, shall be considered as a distinct offence;

   (ii) Intentional participation in, conspiracy to commit and attempts to commit, any of such offences, and preparatory acts and financial operations in connexion with the offences referred to in this article, shall be punishable offences as provided in paragraph 1;

   (iii) Foreign convictions for such offences shall be taken into account for the purpose of establishing recidivism; and

   (iv) Serious offences heretofore referred to committed either by nationals or by foreigners shall be prosecuted by the Party in whose territory the offence was committed, or by the Party in whose territory the offender is found if extradition is not acceptable in conformity with the law of the Party to which application is made, and if such offender has not already been prosecuted and judgment given.

   (b) (i) Each of the offences enumerated in paragraphs 1 and 2(a)(ii) of this article shall be deemed to be included as an extraditable offence in any extradition treaty existing between Parties. Parties undertake to include such offences as extraditable offences in every extradition treaty to be concluded between them.

   (ii) If a Party which makes extradition conditional on the existence of a treaty receives a request for extradition from another Party with which it has no extradition treaty, it may at its option consider this Convention as the legal basis for extradition in respect of the offences enumerated in paragraphs 1 and 2(a)(ii) of this article. Extradition shall be subject to the other conditions provided by the law of the requested Party.

   (iii) Parties which do not make extradition conditional on the existence of a treaty shall recognize the offences enumerated in paragraphs 1 and 2(a)(ii) of this article as extraditable offences between themselves, subject to the conditions provided by the law of the requested Party.

(iv) Extradition shall be granted in conformity with the law of the Party to which application is made, and, notwithstanding sub-paragraphs (b)(i), (ii) and (iii) of this paragraph, the Party shall have the right to refuse to grant the extradition in cases where the competent authorities consider that the offence is not sufficiently serious.

3. The provisions of this Article shall be subject to the provisions of the criminal law of the Party concerned on questions of jurisdiction.

4. Nothing contained in this Article shall affect the principle that the offences to which it refers shall be defined, prosecuted and punished in conformity with the domestic law of a Party.

Article 37 Seizure and confiscation

Any drugs, substances and equipment used in or intended for the commission of any of the offences, referred to in Article 36, shall be liable to seizure and confiscation.

DOCUMENT 35

UN Convention Against Illicit Traffic in Narcotic Drugs and Psychotropic Substances 1988
UN Doc E/CONF.82/15; 28 ILM 497 (1989)

This Convention was adopted on 20 December by the United Nations Conference for the Adoption of a Convention Against Illicit Traffic in Narcotic Drugs and Psychotropic Substances, held at Vienna, and entered into force on 11 November 1990.

There are 170 parties to the Convention, including Afghanistan, China, Colombia, France, Germany, Russia, the UK and the USA.

The first international instrument to regulate narcotic drugs was the Convention for Limiting the Manufacture and Regulating the Distribution of Narcotic Drugs of 13 July 1931 (139 LNTS 301) which, along with other instruments, was codified in the Protocol amending the Agreements, Conventions and Protocols on Narcotic Drugs of 11 December 1946 (12 UNTS 179). There are three major drug control treaties currently in force: the Single Convention on Narcotic Drugs 1962 with its 1972 Protocol (Document 34); the Convention on Psychotropic Substances of 21 February 1971 (1019 UNTS 175); and this Convention.

The Convention provides that the detailed offences set out in Article 3(1) are to be criminalised in the domestic law of each State party (Article 3(2)) and subject to suitable sanctions (Article 3(4)(a)). Each State party is to exercise jurisdiction over offences committed in its territory or on its ships and aircraft (Article 4(1)(a)). Additionally, a party may exercise jurisdiction over offences committed by its nationals, on board vessels visited under Article 17 and committed abroad with the intention of being committed in its territory (Article 4(1)(b)). If a party does not prosecute an offender, it is obliged to extradite him (Article 4(2)) – the aut dedere aut judicare principle. The offences under the Convention are not to be considered political offences for the purpose of extradition (Article 3(10)). The Convention's offences are deemed to be included in existing extradition treaties and are to be included in future treaties (Article 6(2)); and, in the absence of an extradition treaty, the Convention itself can be used as such (Article 6(3)). The Convention contains extensive duties on States to co-operate (Articles 5–7 and 9).

Article 2 Scope of the Convention

1. The purpose of this Convention is to promote co-operation among the Parties so that they may address more effectively the various aspects of illicit traffic in narcotic drugs and psychotropic substances having an international dimension. In carrying out their obligations under the Convention, the Parties shall take necessary measures, including legislative and administrative measures, in conformity with the fundamental provisions of their respective domestic legislative systems.

2. The Parties shall carry out their obligations under this Convention in a manner consistent with the principles of sovereign equality and territorial integrity of States and that of non-intervention in the domestic affairs of other States.

3. A Party shall not undertake in the territory of another Party the exercise of jurisdiction and performance of functions which are exclusively reserved for the authorities of that other Party by its domestic law.

Article 3 Offences and sanctions

1. Each Party shall adopt such measures as may be necessary to establish as criminal offences under its domestic law, when committed intentionally:

    (a) (i) The production, manufacture, extraction, preparation, offering, offering for sale, distribution, sale, delivery on any terms whatsoever, brokerage, dispatch, dispatch in transit, transport, importation or exportation of any narcotic drug or any psychotropic substance contrary to the provisions of the 1961 Convention, the 1961 Convention as amended or the 1971 Convention;

    (ii) The cultivation of opium poppy, coca bush or cannabis plant for the purpose of the production of narcotic drugs contrary to the provisions of the 1961 Convention and the 1961 Convention as amended;

    (iii) The possession or purchase of any narcotic drug or psychotropic substance for the purpose of any of the activities enumerated in (i) above;

    (iv) The manufacture, transport or distribution of equipment, materials or of substances listed in Table I and Table II, knowing that they are to be used in or for the illicit cultivation, production or manufacture of narcotic drugs or psychotropic substances;

    (v) The organization, management or financing of any of the offences enumerated in (i), (ii), (iii) or (iv) above;

    (b) (i) The conversion or transfer of property, knowing that such property is derived from any offence or offences established in accordance with subparagraph (a) of this paragraph, or from an act of participation in such offence or offences, for the purpose of concealing or disguising the illicit origin of the property or of assisting any person who is involved in the commission of such an offence or offences to evade the legal consequences of his actions;

    (ii) The concealment or disguise of the true nature, source, location, disposition, movement, rights with respect to, or ownership of property, knowing that such property is derived from an offence or offences established in accordance with subparagraph (a) of this paragraph or from an act of participation in such an offence or offences;

    (c) Subject to its constitutional principles and the basic concepts of its legal system:

    (i) The acquisition, possession or use of property, knowing, at the time of receipt, that such property was derived from an offence or offences established in accordance with subparagraph (a) of this paragraph or from an act of participation in such offence or offences;

    (ii) The possession of equipment or materials or substances listed in Table I and Table II, knowing that they are being or are to be used in or for the illicit cultivation, production or manufacture of narcotic drugs or psychotropic substances;

    (iii) Publicly inciting or inducing others, by any means, to commit any of the offences established in accordance with this article or to use narcotic drugs or psychotropic substances illicitly;

    (iv) Participation in, association or conspiracy to commit, attempt to commit and aiding, abetting, facilitating and counselling the commission of any of the offences established in accordance with this article.

2.   Subject to its constitutional principles and the basic concepts of its legal system, each Party shall adopt such measures as may be necessary to establish as a criminal offence under its domestic law, when committed intentionally, the possession, purchase or cultivation of narcotic drugs or psychotropic substances for personal consumption contrary to the provisions of the 1961 Convention, the 1961 Convention as amended or the 1971 Convention.

3.   Knowledge, intent or purpose required as an element of an offence set forth in paragraph 1 of this article may be inferred from objective factual circumstances.

4.   (a) Each Party shall make the commission of the offences established in accordance with paragraph 1 of this article liable to sanctions which take into account the grave nature of these offences, such as imprisonment or other forms of deprivation of liberty, pecuniary sanctions and confiscation.

    (b) The Parties may provide, in addition to conviction or punishment, for an offence established in accordance with paragraph 1 of this article, that the offender shall undergo measures such as treatment, education, aftercare, rehabilitation or social reintegration.

    (c) Notwithstanding the preceding subparagraphs, in appropriate cases of a minor nature, the Parties may provide, as alternatives to conviction or punishment, measures such as education, rehabilitation or social reintegration, as well as, when the offender is a drug abuser, treatment and aftercare.

    (d) The Parties may provide, either as an alternative to conviction or punishment, or in addition to conviction or punishment of an offence established in accordance with paragraph 2 of this article, measures for the treatment, education, aftercare, rehabilitation or social reintegration of the offender.

5.   The Parties shall ensure that their courts and other competent authorities having jurisdiction can take into account factual circumstances which make the commission of the offences established in accordance with paragraph 1 of this article particularly serious, such as:

    (a) The involvement in the offence of an organized criminal group to which the offender belongs;

    (b) The involvement of the offender in other international organized criminal activities;

    (c) The involvement of the offender in other illegal activities facilitated by commission of the offence;

    (d) The use of violence or arms by the offender;

    (e) The fact that the offender holds a public office and that the offence is connected with the office in question;

    (f) The victimization or use of minors;

    (g) The fact that the offence is committed in a penal institution or in an educational institution or social service facility or in their immediate vicinity or in other places to which school children and students resort for educational, sports and social activities;

    (h) Prior conviction, particularly for similar offences, whether foreign or domestic, to the extent permitted under the domestic law of a Party.

6. The Parties shall endeavour to ensure that any discretionary legal powers under their domestic law relating to the prosecution of persons for offences established in accordance with this article are exercised to maximize the effectiveness of law enforcement measures in respect of those offences and with due regard to the need to deter the commission of such offences.

7. The Parties shall ensure that their courts or other competent authorities bear in mind the serious nature of the offences enumerated in paragraph 1 of this article and the circumstances enumerated in paragraph 5 of this article when considering the eventuality of early release or parole of persons convicted of such offences.

8. Each Party shall, where appropriate, establish under its domestic law a long statute of limitations period in which to commence proceedings for any offence established in accordance with paragraph 1 of this article, and a longer period where the alleged offender has evaded the administration of justice.

9. Each Party shall take appropriate measures, consistent with its legal system, to ensure that a person charged with or convicted of an offence established in accordance with paragraph 1 of this article, who is found within its territory, is present at the necessary criminal proceedings.

10. For the purpose of co-operation among the Parties under this Convention, including, in particular, co-operation under articles 5, 6, 7 and 9, offences established in accordance with this article shall not be considered as fiscal offences or as political offences or regarded as politically motivated, without prejudice to the constitutional limitations and the fundamental domestic law of the Parties.

11. Nothing contained in this article shall affect the principle that the description of the offences to which it refers and of legal defences thereto is reserved to the domestic law of a Party and that such offences shall be prosecuted and punished in conformity with that law.

Article 4 Jurisdiction

1. Each Party:

   (a) Shall take such measures as may be necessary to establish its jurisdiction over the offences it has established in accordance with article 3, paragraph 1, when:

   (i) The offence is committed in its territory;

   (ii) The offence is committed on board a vessel flying its flag or an aircraft which is registered under its laws at the time the offence is committed;

   (b) May take such measures as may be necessary to establish its jurisdiction over the offences it has established in accordance with article 3, paragraph 1, when:

   (i) The offence is committed by one of its nationals or by a person who has his habitual residence in its territory;

   (ii) The offence is committed on board a vessel concerning which that Party has been authorized to take appropriate action pursuant to article 17, provided that such jurisdiction shall be exercised only on the basis of agreements or arrangements referred to in paragraphs 4 and 9 of that article;

   (iii) The offence is one of those established in accordance with article 3, paragraph 1, subparagraph (c)(iv), and is committed outside its territory with a view to the commission, within its territory, of an offence established in accordance with article 3, paragraph 1.

2. Each Party:

   (a) Shall also take such measures as may be necessary to establish its jurisdiction over the offences it has established in accordance with article 3, paragraph 1, when the alleged offender is present in its territory and it does not extradite him to another Party on the ground:

   (i) That the offence has been committed in its territory or on board a vessel flying its flag or an aircraft which was registered under its law at the time the offence was committed; or

    (ii)   That the offence has been committed by one of its nationals;

  (b) May also take such measures as may be necessary to establish its jurisdiction over the offences it has established in accordance with article 3, paragraph 1, when the alleged offender is present in its territory and it does not extradite him to another Party.

3.   This Convention does not exclude the exercise of any criminal jurisdiction established by a Party in accordance with its domestic law.

Article 6 Extradition

1.   This article shall apply to the offences established by the Parties in accordance with article 3, paragraph 1.

2.   Each of the offences to which this article applies shall be deemed to be included as an extraditable offence in any extradition treaty existing between Parties. The Parties undertake to include such offences as extraditable offences in every extradition treaty to be concluded between them.

3.   If a Party which makes extradition conditional on the existence of a treaty receives a request for extradition from another Party with which it has no extradition treaty, it may consider this Convention as the legal basis for extradition in respect of any offence to which this article applies. The Parties which require detailed legislation in order to use this Convention as a legal basis for extradition shall consider enacting such legislation as may be necessary.

4.   The Parties which do not make extradition conditional on the existence of a treaty shall recognize offences to which this article applies as extraditable offences between themselves.

5.   Extradition shall be subject to the conditions provided for by the law of the requested Party or by applicable extradition treaties, including the grounds upon which the requested Party may refuse extradition.

6.   In considering requests received pursuant to this article, the requested State may refuse to comply with such requests where there are substantial grounds leading its judicial or other competent authorities to believe that compliance would facilitate the prosecution or punishment of any person on account of his race, religion, nationality or political opinions, or would cause prejudice for any of those reasons to any person affected by the request.

7.   The Parties shall endeavour to expedite extradition procedures and to simplify evidentiary requirements relating thereto in respect of any offence to which this article applies.

8.   Subject to the provisions of its domestic law and its extradition treaties, the requested Party may, upon being satisfied that the circumstances so warrant and are urgent, and at the request of the requesting Party, take a person whose extradition is sought and who is present in its territory into custody or take other appropriate measures to ensure his presence at extradition proceedings.

9.   Without prejudice to the exercise of any criminal jurisdiction established in accordance with its domestic law, a Party in whose territory an alleged offender is found shall:

  (a) If it does not extradite him in respect of an offence established in accordance with article 3, paragraph 1, on the grounds set forth in article 4, paragraph 2, subparagraph (a), submit the case to its competent authorities for the purpose of prosecution, unless otherwise agreed with the requesting Party;

  (b) If it does not extradite him in respect of such an offence and has established its jurisdiction in relation to that offence in accordance with article 4, paragraph 2, subparagraph (b), submit the case to its competent authorities for the purpose of prosecution, unless otherwise requested by the requesting Party for the purposes of preserving its legitimate jurisdiction.

10. If extradition, sought for purposes of enforcing a sentence, is refused because the person sought is a national of the requested Party, the requested Party shall, if its law so permits and in conformity with the requirements of such law, upon application of the requesting Party, consider the enforcement of the sentence which has been imposed under the law of the requesting Party, or the remainder thereof.

11. The Parties shall seek to conclude bilateral and multilateral agreements to carry out or to enhance the effectiveness of extradition.

12. The Parties may consider entering into bilateral or multilateral agreements, whether *ad hoc* or general, on the transfer to their country of persons sentenced to imprisonment and other forms of deprivation of liberty for offences to which this article applies, in order that they may complete their sentences there.

Article 17 Illicit traffic by sea

1. The Parties shall co-operate to the fullest extent possible to suppress illicit traffic by sea, in conformity with the international law of the sea.

2. A Party which has reasonable grounds to suspect that a vessel flying its flag or not displaying a flag or marks of registry is engaged in illicit traffic may request the assistance of other Parties in suppressing its use for that purpose. The Parties so requested shall render such assistance within the means available to them.

3. A Party which has reasonable grounds to suspect that a vessel exercising freedom of navigation in accordance with international law and flying the flag or displaying marks of registry of another Party is engaged in illicit traffic may so notify the flag State, request confirmation of registry and, if confirmed, request authorization from the flag State to take appropriate measures in regard to that vessel.

4. In accordance with paragraph 3 or in accordance with treaties in force between them or in accordance with any agreement or arrangement otherwise reached between those Parties, the flag State may authorize the requesting State to, *inter alia*:

   (a) Board the vessel;

   (b) Search the vessel;

   (c) If evidence of involvement in illicit traffic is found, take appropriate action with respect to the vessel, persons and cargo on board.

5. Where action is taken pursuant to this article, the Parties concerned shall take due account of the need not to endanger the safety of life at sea, the security of the vessel and the cargo or to prejudice the commercial and legal interests of the flag State or any other interested State.

6. The flag State may, consistent with its obligations in paragraph 1 of this article, subject its authorization to conditions to be mutually agreed between it and the requesting Party, including conditions relating to responsibility.

7. For the purposes of paragraphs 3 and 4 of this article, a Party shall respond expeditiously to a request from another Party to determine whether a vessel that is flying its flag is entitled to do so, and to requests for authorization made pursuant to paragraph 3. At the time of becoming a Party to this Convention, each Party shall designate an authority or, when necessary, authorities to receive and respond to such requests. Such designation shall be notified through the Secretary-General to all other Parties within one month of the designation.

8. A Party which has taken any action in accordance with this article shall promptly inform the flag State concerned of the results of that action.

9. The Parties shall consider entering into bilateral or regional agreements or arrangements to carry out, or to enhance the effectiveness of, the provisions of this article.

10. Action pursuant to paragraph 4 of this article shall be carried out only by warships or military aircraft, or other ships or aircraft clearly marked and identifiable as being on government service and authorized to that effect.

11. Any action taken in accordance with this article shall take due account of the need not to interfere with or affect the rights and obligations and the exercise of jurisdiction of coastal States in accordance with the international law of the sea.

DOCUMENT 36

UN Convention on the Law of the Sea 1982
1833 UNTS 3; 21 ILM 1293 (1982)

This Convention was drafted by the Third UN Conference on the Law of the Sea and adopted at Montego Bay, Jamaica, on 16 November 1973; it entered into force on 16 November 1994.

There are 145 parties, including all the major powers, but not the USA.

By Resolution 2750C (XXV) of 17 December 1970, the UN General Assembly decided to convene the Third UN Conference on the Law of the Sea, charged with elaborating a régime for deep-sea mining and revising the four Geneva Conventions on the law of the sea of 29 April 1958: the Convention on the Territorial Sea and Contiguous Zone (516 UNTS 205), Convention on the High Seas (450 UNTS 82), Convention on Fishing and the Conservation of the Living Resources of the High Seas (559 UNTS 285) and Convention on the Continental Shelf (499 UNTS 311). UNCLOS III first met in 1973 and concluded in late 1982 with the adoption of the UN Convention on the Law of the Sea.

As regards those provisions bearing upon international criminal law, the Convention provides that States parties may only exercise criminal jurisdiction over foreign vessels in their territorial sea in limited circumstances (Article 27). On the high seas, and with limited exceptions, vessels are subject to the exclusive jurisdiction of the flag State (Article 92(1)). In cases of collisions on the high seas involving penal or disciplinary measures, jurisdiction is vested in the flag State and the State of nationality of the wrongdoer (Article 97)(1)), nullifying the effect of the judgment in the Lotus *case (1927) PCIJ, Series A, No 10. The Convention codifies the long-standing legal rules on piracy: it defines the crime (Article 101) and permits any State to seize a pirate vessel on the high seas and prosecute the pirates (Article 105). Piracy, one of the oldest international crimes, is therefore subject to universal jurisdiction. See the Princeton Principles on Universal Jurisdiction 2001* **(Document 78)**. *Additionally, the Convention proscribes the transport of slaves (Article 99; see* **Document 7**), *the illicit traffic in narcotic drugs and psychotropic substances (Article 108; see* **Documents 34–35**) *and unauthorised broadcasting (Article 109). In respect of unauthorised broadcasting, jurisdiction is vested in the flag State, the national State of the offender and any State which can receive the broadcast or suffers interference from the broadcast (Article 109(3)). The right of visit on the high seas is conferred on all States in respect of,* inter alia, *piracy, slave trading and unauthorised broadcasting (Article 110(1)).*

The States Parties to this Convention,

Prompted by the desire to settle, in a spirit of mutual understanding and cooperation, all issues relating to the law of the sea and aware of the historic significance of this Convention as an important contribution to the maintenance of peace, justice and progress for all peoples of the world,

Noting that developments since the United Nations Conferences on the Law of the Sea held at Geneva in 1958 and 1960 have accentuated the need for a new and generally acceptable Convention on the law of the sea,

Conscious that the problems of ocean space are closely interrelated and need to be considered as a whole,

Recognizing the desirability of establishing through this Convention, with due regard for the sovereignty of all States, a legal order for the seas and oceans which will facilitate international communication, and will promote the peaceful uses of the seas and oceans, the equitable and efficient utilization of their resources, the conservation of their living resources, and the study, protection and preservation of the marine environment,

Bearing in mind that the achievement of these goals will contribute to the realization of a just and equitable international economic order which takes into account the interests and needs of mankind as a whole and, in particular, the special interests and needs of developing countries, whether coastal or land-locked,

Desiring by this Convention to develop the principles embodied in resolution 2749 (XXV) of 17 December 1970 in which the General Assembly of the United Nations solemnly declared *inter alia* that the area of the seabed and ocean floor and the subsoil thereof, beyond the limits of national jurisdiction, as well as its resources, are the common heritage of mankind, the exploration and exploitation of which shall be carried out for the benefit of mankind as a whole, irrespective of the geographical location of States,

Believing that the codification and progressive development of the law of the sea achieved in this Convention will contribute to the strengthening of peace, security, cooperation and friendly relations among all nations in conformity with the principles of justice and equal rights and will promote the economic and social advancement of all peoples of the world, in accordance with the Purposes and Principles of the United Nations as set forth in the Charter,

Affirming that matters not regulated by this Convention continue to be governed by the rules and principles of general international law,

Have agreed as follows:

Article 27 Criminal jurisdiction on board a foreign ship

1. The criminal jurisdiction of the coastal State should not be exercised on board a foreign ship passing through the territorial sea to arrest any person or to conduct any investigation in connection with any crime committed on board the ship during its passage, save only in the following cases:

    (a) if the consequences of the crime extend to the coastal State;

    (b) if the crime is of a kind to disturb the peace of the country or the good order of the territorial sea;

    (c) if the assistance of the local authorities has been requested by the master of the ship or by a diplomatic agent or consular officer of the flag State; or

    (d) if such measures are necessary for the suppression of illicit traffic in narcotic drugs or psychotropic substances.

2. The above provisions do not affect the right of the coastal State to take any steps authorized by its laws for the purpose of an arrest or investigation on board a foreign ship passing through the territorial sea after leaving internal waters.

3. In the cases provided for in paragraphs 1 and 2, the coastal State shall, if the master so requests, notify a diplomatic agent or consular officer of the flag State before taking any steps, and shall facilitate contact between such agent or officer and the ship's crew. In cases of emergency this notification may be communicated while the measures are being taken.

4. In considering whether or in what manner an arrest should be made, the local authorities shall have due regard to the interests of navigation.

5. Except as provided in Part XII or with respect to violations of laws and regulations adopted in accordance with Part V, the coastal State may not take any steps on board a foreign ship passing through the territorial sea to arrest any person or to conduct any investigation in connection with any crime committed before the ship entered the territorial sea, if the ship, proceeding from a foreign port, is only passing through the territorial sea without entering internal waters.

Article 92 Status of ships

1. Ships shall sail under the flag of one State only and, save in exceptional cases expressly provided for in international treaties or in this Convention, shall be subject to its exclusive jurisdiction on the high seas. A ship may not change its flag during a voyage or while in a port of call, save in the case of a real transfer of ownership or change of registry.

2. A ship which sails under the flags of two or more States, using them according to convenience, may not claim any of the nationalities in question with respect to any other State, and may be assimilated to a ship without nationality.

Article 97 Penal jurisdiction in matters of collision or any other incident of navigation

1. In the event of a collision or any other incident of navigation concerning a ship on the high seas, involving the penal or disciplinary responsibility of the master or of any other person in the service of the ship, no penal or disciplinary proceedings may be instituted against such person except before the judicial or administrative authorities either of the flag State or of the State of which such person is a national.

2. In disciplinary matters, the State which has issued a master's certificate or a certificate of competence or licence shall alone be competent, after due legal process, to pronounce the withdrawal of such certificates, even if the holder is not a national of the State which issued them.

3. No arrest or detention of the ship, even as a measure of investigation, shall be ordered by any authorities other than those of the flag State.

Article 99 Prohibition of the transport of slaves

Every State shall take effective measures to prevent and punish the transport of slaves in ships authorised to fly its flag and to prevent the unlawful use of its flag for that purpose. Any slave taking refuge on board any ship, whatever its flag, shall *ipso facto* be free.

Article 100 Duty to co-operate in the repression of piracy

All States shall co-operate to the fullest possible extent in the repression of piracy on the high seas or in any other place outside the jurisdiction of any State.

Article 101 Definition of piracy

Piracy consists of any of the following acts:

(a) any illegal acts of violence or detention, or any act of depredation, committed for private ends by the crew or the passengers of a private ship or a private aircraft, and directed:

    (i) on the high seas, against another ship or aircraft, or against persons or property on board such ship or aircraft;

    (ii) against a ship, aircraft, persons or property in a place outside the jurisdiction of any State;

(b) any act of voluntary participation in the operation of a ship or of an aircraft with knowledge of facts making it a pirate ship or aircraft;

(c) any act of inciting or of intentionally facilitating an act described in subparagraph (a) or (b).

Article 102 Piracy by a warship, government ship or government aircraft whose crew has mutinied

The acts of piracy, as defined in article 101, committed by a warship, government ship or government aircraft whose crew has mutinied and taken control of the ship or aircraft are assimilated to acts committed by a private ship or aircraft.

Article 103 Definition of a pirate ship or aircraft

A ship or aircraft is considered a pirate ship or aircraft if it is intended by the persons in dominant control to be used for the purpose of committing one of the acts referred to in article 101. The same applies if the ship or aircraft has been used to commit any such act, so long as it remains under the control of the persons guilty of that act.

Article 104 Retention or loss of the nationality of a pirate ship or aircraft

A ship or aircraft may retain its nationality although it has become a pirate ship or aircraft. The retention or loss of nationality is determined by the law of the State from which such nationality was derived.

Article 105 Seizure of a pirate ship or aircraft

On the high seas, or in any other place outside the jurisdiction of any State, every State may seize a pirate ship or aircraft, or a ship or aircraft taken by piracy and under the control of pirates, and arrest the persons and seize the property on board. The courts of the State which carried out the seizure may decide upon the penalties to be imposed, and may also determine the action to be taken with regard to the ships, aircraft or property, subject to the rights of third parties acting in good faith.

Article 106 Liability for seizure without adequate grounds

Where the seizure of a ship or aircraft on suspicion of piracy has been effected without adequate grounds, the State making the seizure shall be liable to the State the nationality of which is possessed by the ship or aircraft for any loss or damage caused by the seizure.

Article 107 Ships and aircraft which are entitled to seize on account of piracy

A seizure on account of piracy may be carried out only by warships or military aircraft, or other ships or aircraft clearly marked and identifiable as being on government service and authorized to that effect.

Article 108 Illicit traffic in narcotic drugs or psychotropic substances

1. All States shall cooperate in the suppression of illicit traffic in narcotic drugs and psychotropic substances engaged in by ships on the high seas contrary to international conventions.

2. Any State which has reasonable grounds for believing that a ship flying its flag is engaged in illicit traffic in narcotic drugs or psychotropic substances may request the cooperation of other States to suppress such traffic.

Article 109 Unauthorized broadcasting from the high seas

1. All States shall cooperate in the suppression of unauthorized broadcasting from the high seas.

2. For the purposes of this Convention, "unauthorized broadcasting" means the transmission of sound radio or television broadcasts from a ship or installation on the high seas intended for reception by the general public contrary to international regulations, but excluding the transmission of distress calls.

3. Any person engaged in unauthorized broadcasting may be prosecuted before the court of:

    (a) the flag State of the ship;

    (b) the State of registry of the installation;

    (c) the State of which the person is a national;

    (d) any State where the transmissions can be received; or

    (e) any State where authorized radio communication is suffering interference.

4. On the high seas, a State having jurisdiction in accordance with paragraph 3 may, in conformity with article 110, arrest any person or ship engaged in unauthorized broadcasting and seize the broadcasting apparatus.

Article 110 Right of visit

1. Except where acts of interference derive from powers conferred by treaty, a warship which encounters on the high seas a foreign ship, other than a ship entitled to complete immunity in accordance with articles 95 and 96, is not justified in boarding it unless there is reasonable ground for suspecting that:

    (a) the ship is engaged in piracy;

    (b) the ship is engaged in the slave trade;

    (c) the ship is engaged in unauthorized broadcasting and the flag State of the warship has jurisdiction under article 109;

    (d) the ship is without nationality; or

    (e) though flying a foreign flag or refusing to show its flag, the ship is, in reality, of the same nationality as the warship.

2. In the cases provided for in paragraph 1, the warship may proceed to verify the ship's right to fly its flag. To this end, it may send a boat under the command of an officer to the suspected ship. If suspicion remains after the documents have been checked, it may proceed to a further examination on board the ship, which must be carried out with all possible consideration.

3. If the suspicions prove to be unfounded, and provided that the ship boarded has not committed any act justifying them, it shall be compensated for any loss or damage that may have been sustained.

4. These provisions apply *mutatis mutandis* to military aircraft.

5. These provisions also apply to any other duly authorized ships or aircraft clearly marked and identifiable as being on government service.

DOCUMENT 37

International Convention Against the Recruitment, Use, Financing and Training of Mercenaries 1989
2163 UNTS 75; 29 ILM 89 (1990)

The Convention was adopted on 4 December 1989 as an annex to General Assembly Resolution 44/34 and entered into force on 20 October 2001.

There are only 26 parties to the Convention. None of the permanent members of the UN Security Council is a party.

While the use of mercenaries dates back to Roman times, international concern about their use, particularly in suppressing national liberation movements and supporting drug trafficking, emerged in the 1970s. The first international instrument to address mercenaries was Protocol I Additional to the Geneva Conventions of 1977 (Article 47; **Document 5***).*

The Convention provides an extensive definition of a mercenary (Article 1), thereafter making it an offence to act as a mercenary (Article 3(1)) or to recruit, use, finance or train a mercenary (Article 2; see also Article 4). Each State party is required to take steps necessary to assert jurisdiction over offences committed in its territory or on its ships or aircraft or by its nationals (Article 9(1)). If an offender is found within its territory, a party is required to either extradite or report that individual for prosecution (Article 12) – the aut dedere aut judicare principle. As between the parties, the Convention's offences are deemed to be included in existing extradition treaties and are to be included in future extradition treaties (Article 15(1));

and the Convention itself may be used as the basis of extradition in the absence of an extradition treaty (Article 15(2)). The Convention provides for fair treatment in any proceedings (Article 11). There are duties on the parties to afford one another the greatest measure of assistance in any proceedings under the Convention (Article 13(1)).

The States Parties to the present Convention,

Reaffirming the purposes and principles enshrined in the Charter of the United Nations and in the Declaration on the Principles of International Law concerning Friendly Relations and Co-operation among States in accordance with the Charter of the United Nations,

Being aware of the recruitment, use, financing and training of mercenaries for activities which violate principles of international law such as those of sovereign equality, political independence, territorial integrity of States and self-determination of peoples,

Affirming that the recruitment, use, financing and training of mercenaries should be considered as offences of grave concern to all States and that any person committing any of these offences should either be prosecuted or extradited,

Convinced of the necessity to develop and enhance international co-operation among States for the prevention, prosecution and punishment of such offences,

Expressing concern at new unlawful international activities linking drug traffickers and mercenaries in the perpetration of violent actions which undermine the constitutional order of States,

Also convinced that the adoption of a convention against the recruitment, use, financing and training of mercenaries would contribute to the eradication of these nefarious activities and thereby to the observance of the purposes and principles enshrined in the Charter of the United Nations,

Cognizant that matters not regulated by such a convention continue to be governed by the rules and principles of international law,

Have agreed as follows:

Article I

For the purposes of the present Convention,

1. A mercenary is any person who:

    (a) Is specially recruited locally or abroad in order to fight in an armed conflict;

    (b) Is motivated to take part in the hostilities essentially by the desire for private gain and, in fact, is promised, by or on behalf of a party to the conflict, material compensation substantially in excess of that promised or paid to combatants of similar rank and functions in the armed forces of that party;

    (c) Is neither a national of a party to the conflict nor a resident of territory controlled by a party to the conflict;

    (d) Is not a member of the armed forces of a party to the conflict; and

    (e) Has not been sent by a State which is not a party to the conflict on official duty as a member of its armed forces.

2. A mercenary is also any person who, in any other situation:

    (a) Is specially recruited locally or abroad for the purpose of participating in a concerted act of violence aimed at:

        (i)   Overthrowing a Government or otherwise undermining the constitutional order of a State; or

        (ii) Undermining the territorial integrity of a State;

    (b) Is motivated to take part therein essentially by the desire for significant private gain and is prompted by the promise or payment of material compensation;

(c) Is neither a national nor a resident of the State against which such an act is directed;

(d) Has not been sent by a State on official duty; and

(e) Is not a member of the armed forces of the State on whose territory the act is undertaken.

Article 2

Any person who recruits, uses, finances or trains mercenaries, as defined in article 1 of the present Convention, commits an offence for the purposes of the Convention.

Article 3

1. A mercenary, as defined in article 1 of the present Convention, who participates directly in hostilities or in a concerted act of violence, as the case may be, commits an offence for the purposes of the Convention.

2. Nothing in this article limits the scope of application of article 4 of the present Convention.

Article 4

An offence is committed by any person who:

(a) Attempts to commit one of the offences set forth in the present Convention;

(b) Is the accomplice of a person who commits or attempts to commit any of the offences set forth in the present Convention.

Article 5

1. States Parties shall not recruit, use, finance or train mercenaries and shall prohibit such activities in accordance with the provisions of the present Convention.

2. States Parties shall not recruit, use, finance or train mercenaries for the purpose of opposing the legitimate exercise of the inalienable right of peoples to self-determination, as recognized by international law, and shall take, in conformity with international law, the appropriate measures to prevent the recruitment, use, financing or training of mercenaries for that purpose.

3. They shall make the offences set forth in the present Convention punishable by appropriate penalties which take into account the grave nature of those offences.

Article 6

States Parties shall co-operate in the prevention of the offences set forth in the present Convention, particularly by:

(a) Taking all practicable measures to prevent preparations in their respective territories for the commission of those offences within or outside their territories, including the prohibition of illegal activities of persons, groups and organizations that encourage, instigate, organize or engage in the perpetration of such offences;

(b) Co-ordinating the taking of administrative and other measures as appropriate to prevent the commission of those offences.

Article 7

States Parties shall co-operate in taking the necessary measures for the implementation of the present Convention.

Article 8

Any State Party having reason to believe that one of the offences set forth in the present Convention has been, is being or will be committed shall, in accordance with its national law, communicate the relevant information, as soon as it comes to its knowledge, directly or through the Secretary-General of the United Nations, to the States Parties affected.

Article 9

1. Each State Party shall take such measures as may be necessary to establish its jurisdiction over any of the offences set forth in the present Convention which are committed:

    (a) In its territory or on board a ship or aircraft registered in that State;

    (b) By any of its nationals or, if that State considers it appropriate, by those stateless persons who have their habitual residence in that territory.

2. Each State Party shall likewise take such measures as may be necessary to establish its jurisdiction over the offences set forth in articles 2, 3 and 4 of the present Convention in cases where the alleged offender is present in its territory and it does not extradite him to any of the States mentioned in paragraph 1 of this article.

3. The present Convention does not exclude any criminal jurisdiction exercised in accordance with national law.

Article 10

1. Upon being satisfied that the circumstances so warrant, any State Party in whose territory the alleged offender is present shall, in accordance with its laws, take him into custody or take such other measures to ensure his presence for such time as is necessary to enable any criminal or extradition proceedings to be instituted. The State Party shall immediately make a preliminary inquiry into the facts.

2. When a State Party, pursuant to this article, has taken a person into custody or has taken such other measures referred to in paragraph 1 of this article, it shall notify without delay either directly or through the Secretary-General of the United Nations:

    (a) The State Party where the offence was committed;

    (b) The State Party against which the offence has been directed or attempted;

    (c) The State Party of which the natural or juridical person against whom the offence has been directed or attempted is a national;

    (d) The State Party of which the alleged offender is a national or, if he is a stateless person, in whose territory he has his habitual residence;

    (e) Any other interested State Party which it considers it appropriate to notify.

3. Any person regarding whom the measures referred to in paragraph 1 of this article are being taken shall be entitled:

    (a) To communicate without delay with the nearest appropriate representative of the State of which he is a national or which is otherwise entitled to protect his rights or, if he is a stateless person, the State in whose territory he has his habitual residence;

    (b) To be visited by a representative of that State.

4. The provisions of paragraph 3 of this article shall be without prejudice to the right of any State Party having a claim to jurisdiction in accordance with article 9, paragraph 1 (b), to invite the International Committee of the Red Cross to communicate with and visit the alleged offender.

5. The State which makes the preliminary inquiry contemplated in paragraph 1 of this article shall promptly report its findings to the States referred to in paragraph 2 of this article and indicate whether it intends to exercise jurisdiction.

Article 11

Any person regarding whom proceedings are being carried out in connection with any of the offences set forth in the present Convention shall be guaranteed at all stages of the proceedings fair treatment and all the rights and guarantees provided for in the law of the State in question. Applicable norms of international law should be taken into account.

Article 12

The State Party in whose territory the alleged offender is found shall, if it does not extradite him, be obliged, without exception whatsoever and whether or not the offence was committed in its territory, to submit the case to its competent authorities for the purpose of prosecution, through proceedings in accordance with the laws of that State. Those authorities shall take their decision in the same manner as in the case of any other offence of a grave nature under the law of that State.

Article 13

1. States Parties shall afford one another the greatest measure of assistance in connection with criminal proceedings brought in respect of the offences set forth in the present Convention, including the supply of all evidence at their disposal necessary for the proceedings. The law of the State whose assistance is requested shall apply in all cases.

2. The provisions of paragraph 1 of this article shall not affect obligations concerning mutual judicial assistance embodied in any other treaty.

Article 14

The State Party where the alleged offender is prosecuted shall in accordance with its laws communicate the final outcome of the proceedings to the Secretary-General of the United Nations, who shall transmit the information to the other States concerned.

Article 15

1. The offences set forth in articles 2, 3 and 4 of the present Convention shall be deemed to be included as extraditable offences in any extradition treaty existing between States Parties. States Parties undertake to include such offences as extraditable offences in every extradition treaty to be concluded between them.

2. If a State Party which makes extradition conditional on the existence of a treaty receives a request for extradition from another State Party with which it has no extradition treaty, it may at its option consider the present Convention as the legal basis for extradition in respect of those offences. Extradition shall be subject to the other conditions provided by the law of the requested State.

3. States Parties which do not make extradition conditional on the existence of a treaty shall recognize those offences as extraditable offences between themselves, subject to the conditions provided by the law of the requested State.

4. The offences shall be treated, for the purpose of extradition between States Parties, as if they had been committed not only in the place in which they occurred but also in the territories of the States required to establish their jurisdiction in accordance with article 9 of the present Convention.

Article 16

The present Convention shall be applied without prejudice to:

(a) The rules relating to the international responsibility of States;

(b) The law of armed conflict and international humanitarian law, including the provisions relating to the status of combatant or of prisoner of war.

Article 17

1. Any dispute between two or more States Parties concerning the interpretation or application of the present Convention which is not settled by negotiation shall, at the request of one of them, be submitted to arbitration. If, within six months from the date of the request for arbitration, the parties are unable to agree on the organization of the arbitration, any one of those parties may refer the dispute to the International Court of Justice by a request in conformity with the Statute of the Court.

2. Each State may, at the time of signature or ratification of the present Convention or accession thereto, declare that it does not consider itself bound by paragraph I of this article. The other States Parties shall not be bound by paragraph I of this article with respect to any State Party which has made such a reservation.

3. Any State Party which has made a reservation in accordance with paragraph 2 of this article may at any time withdraw that reservation by notification to the Secretary-General of the United Nations.

DOCUMENT 38

Convention on the Safety of United Nations and Associated Personnel 1994
2051 UNTS 363; 34 ILM 482 (1995)

The Convention was adopted on 9 December 1994 as an annex to General Assembly Resolution 49/59 and entered into force on 15 January 1999.

There are 74 parties to the Convention, including France, Germany, Russia and the UK; China and the USA are not parties.

The exposure of UN personnel, particularly those involved in peacekeeping operations (and there have been 59 such operations since 1948), to danger prompted the elaboration of a convention dedicated to their protection. The Convention protects UN and associated personnel, which term is broadly defined in Article 1 to include persons engaged by the UN and the Specialised Agencies and, with appropriate UN approval, persons engaged by other intergovernmental and non-governmental organisations. The Convention establishes rules that UN and associated personnel must follow (Articles 3 and 6) and rules that host and transit States must follow (Articles 7–8).

The Convention specifically lists acts considered crimes against UN and associated personnel (Article 9(1)) and requires each State party to criminalise these acts in its domestic law (Article 9(2)). Each party is to assert jurisdiction over these crimes committed in its territory or on it ships or aircraft or by its nationals (Article 10(1)). Additionally, a party may extend its jurisdiction to crimes committed against its nationals or committed to compel the State to do or abstain from doing some act (Article 10(2)). If an offender is found within its territory, a party is required to either extradite or report that individual for prosecution (Article 14) – the aut dedere aut judicare principle. As between the parties, the Convention's offences are deemed to be included in existing extradition treaties and are to be included in future extradition treaties (Article 15(1)); and the Convention itself may be used as the basis of extradition in the absence of an extradition treaty (Article 15(2)). The Convention provides for fair treatment in any proceedings (Article 17). There are duties on the parties to afford one another the greatest measure of assistance in any proceedings under the Convention (Article 16; see also Article 12).

The States Parties to this Convention,

Deeply concerned over the growing number of deaths and injuries resulting from deliberate attacks against United Nations and associated personnel,

Bearing in mind that attacks against, or other mistreatment of, personnel who act on behalf of the United Nations are unjustifiable and unacceptable, by whomsoever committed,

Recognizing that United Nations operations are conducted in the common interest of the international community and in accordance with the principles and purposes of the Charter of the United Nations,

Acknowledging the important contribution that United Nations and associated personnel make in respect of United Nations efforts in the fields of preventive diplomacy, peacemaking, peace-keeping, peace-building and humanitarian and other operations,

Conscious of the existing arrangements for ensuring the safety of United Nations and associated personnel, including the steps taken by the principal organs of the United Nations, in this regard,

Recognizing none the less that existing measures of protection for United Nations and associated personnel are inadequate,

Acknowledging that the effectiveness and safety of United Nations operations are enhanced where such operations are conducted with the consent and cooperation of the host State,

Appealing to all States in which United Nations and associated personnel are deployed and to all others on whom such personnel may rely, to provide comprehensive support aimed at facilitating the conduct and fulfilling the mandate of United Nations operations,

Convinced that there is an urgent need to adopt appropriate and effective measures for the prevention of attacks committed against United Nations and associated personnel and for the punishment of those who have committed such attacks,

Have agreed as follows:

Article 1 Definitions

For the purposes of this Convention:

(a) "United Nations personnel" means:

    (i) Persons engaged or deployed by the Secretary-General of the United Nations as members of the military, police or civilian components of a United Nations operation;

    (ii) Other officials and experts on mission of the United Nations or its specialized agencies or the International Atomic Energy Agency who are present in an official capacity in the area where a United Nations operation is being conducted;

(b) "Associated personnel" means:

    (i) Persons assigned by a Government or an intergovernmental organization with the agreement of the competent organ of the United Nations;

    (ii) Persons engaged by the Secretary-General of the United Nations or by a specialized agency or by the International Atomic Energy Agency;

    (iii) Persons deployed by a humanitarian non-governmental organization or agency under an agreement with the Secretary-General of the United Nations or with a specialized agency or with the International Atomic Energy Agency, to carry out activities in support of the fulfilment of the mandate of a United Nations operation;

(c) "United Nations operation" means an operation established by the competent organ of the United Nations in accordance with the Charter of the United Nations and conducted under United Nations authority and control:

    (i) Where the operation is for the purpose of maintaining or restoring international peace and security; or

    (ii) Where the Security Council or the General Assembly has declared, for the purposes of this Convention, that there exists an exceptional risk to the safety of the personnel participating in the operation;

(d) "Host State" means a State in whose territory a United Nations operation is conducted;

(e) "Transit State" means a State, other than the host State, in whose territory United Nations and associated personnel or their equipment are in transit or temporarily present in connection with a United Nations operation.

Article 2 Scope of application

1. This Convention applies in respect of United Nations and associated personnel and United Nations operations, as defined in article 1.

2. This Convention shall not apply to a United Nations operation authorized by the Security Council as an enforcement action under Chapter VII of the Charter of the United Nations in which any of the personnel are engaged as combatants against organized armed forces and to which the law of international armed conflict applies.

Article 3 Identification

1. The military and police components of a United Nations operation and their vehicles, vessels and aircraft shall bear distinctive identification. Other personnel, vehicles, vessels and aircraft involved in the United Nations operation shall be appropriately identified unless otherwise decided by the Secretary-General of the United Nations.

2. All United Nations and associated personnel shall carry appropriate identification documents.

Article 4 Agreements on the status of the operation

The host State and the United Nations shall conclude as soon as possible an agreement on the status of the United Nations operation and all personnel engaged in the operation including, *inter alia*, provisions on privileges and immunities for military and police components of the operation.

Article 5 Transit

A transit State shall facilitate the unimpeded transit of United Nations and associated personnel and their equipment to and from the host State.

Article 6 Respect for laws and regulations

1. Without prejudice to such privileges and immunities as they may enjoy or to the requirements of their duties, United Nations and associated personnel shall:

   (a) Respect the laws and regulations of the host State and the transit State; and

   (b) Refrain from any action or activity incompatible with the impartial and international nature of their duties.

2. The Secretary-General of the United Nations shall take all appropriate measures to ensure the observance of these obligations.

Article 7 Duty to ensure the safety and security of United Nations and associated personnel

1. United Nations and associated personnel, their equipment and premises shall not be made the object of attack or of any action that prevents them from discharging their mandate.

2. States Parties shall take all appropriate measures to ensure the safety and security of United Nations and associated personnel. In particular, States Parties shall take all appropriate steps to protect United Nations and associated personnel who are deployed in their territory from the crimes set out in article 9.

3. States Parties shall cooperate with the United Nations and other States Parties, as appropriate, in the implementation of this Convention, particularly in any case where the host State is unable itself to take the required measures.

Article 8 Duty to release or return United Nations and associated personnel captured or detained

Except as otherwise provided in an applicable status-of-forces agreement, if United Nations or associated personnel are captured or detained in the course of the performance of their duties and their identification has been established, they shall not be subjected to interrogation and they shall be promptly released and returned to United Nations or other appropriate authorities. Pending their release such personnel shall be treated in accordance with universally recognized standards of human rights and the principles and spirit of the Geneva Conventions of 1949.

Article 9 Crimes against United Nations and associated personnel

1.   The intentional commission of:

   (a) A murder, kidnapping or other attack upon the person or liberty of any United Nations or associated personnel;

   (b) A violent attack upon the official premises, the private accommodation or the means of transportation of any United Nations or associated personnel likely to endanger his or her person or liberty;

   (c) A threat to commit any such attack with the objective of compelling a physical or juridical person to do or to refrain from doing any act;

   (d) An attempt to commit any such attack; and

   (e) An act constituting participation as an accomplice in any such attack, or in an attempt to commit such attack, or in organizing or ordering others to commit such attack, shall be made by each State Party a crime under its national law.

2   Each State Party shall make the crimes set out in paragraph 1 punishable by appropriate penalties which shall take into account their grave nature.

Article 10 Establishment of jurisdiction

1.   Each State Party shall take such measures as may be necessary to establish its jurisdiction over the crimes set out in article 9 in the following cases:

   (a) When the crime is committed in the territory of that State or on board a ship or aircraft registered in that State;

   (b) When the alleged offender is a national of that State.

2.   A State Party may also establish its jurisdiction over any such crime when it is committed:

   (a) By a stateless person whose habitual residence is in that State; or

   (b) With respect to a national of that State; or

   (c) In an attempt to compel that State to do or to abstain from doing any act.

3.   Any State Party which has established jurisdiction as mentioned in paragraph 2 shall notify the Secretary-General of the United Nations. If such State Party subsequently rescinds that jurisdiction, it shall notify the Secretary-General of the United Nations.

4.   Each State Party shall take such measures as may be necessary to establish its jurisdiction over the crimes set out in article 9 in cases where the alleged offender is present in its territory and it does not extradite such person pursuant to article 15 to any of the States Parties which have established their jurisdiction in accordance with paragraph 1 or 2.

5.   This Convention does not exclude any criminal jurisdiction exercised in accordance with national law.

Article 11 Prevention of crimes against United Nations and associated personnel

States Parties shall cooperate in the prevention of the crimes set out in article 9, particularly by:

(a) Taking all practicable measures to prevent preparations in their respective territories for the commission of those crimes within or outside their territories; and

(b) Exchanging information in accordance with their national law and coordinating the taking of administrative and other measures as appropriate to prevent the commission of those crimes.

Article 12 Communication of information

1. Under the conditions provided for in its national law, the State Party in whose territory a crime set out in article 9 has been committed shall, if it has reason to believe that an alleged offender has fled from its territory, communicate to the Secretary-General of the United Nations and, directly or through the Secretary-General, to the State or States concerned all the pertinent facts regarding the crime committed and all available information regarding the identity of the alleged offender.

2. Whenever a crime set out in article 9 has been committed, any State Party which has information concerning the victim and circumstances of the crime shall endeavour to transmit such information, under the conditions provided for in its national law, fully and promptly to the Secretary-General of the United Nations and the State or States concerned.

Article 13 Measures to ensure prosecution or extradition

1. Where the circumstances so warrant, the State Party in whose territory the alleged offender is present shall take the appropriate measures under its national law to ensure that person's presence for the purpose of prosecution or extradition.

2. Measures taken in accordance with paragraph 1 shall be notified, in conformity with national law and without delay, to the Secretary-General of the United Nations and, either directly or through the Secretary-General, to:

   (a) The State where the crime was committed;

   (b) The State or States of which the alleged offender is a national or, if such person is a stateless person, in whose territory that person has his or her habitual residence;

   (c) The State or States of which the victim is a national; and

   (d) Other interested States.

Article 14 Prosecution of alleged offenders

The State Party in whose territory the alleged offender is present shall, if it does not extradite that person, submit, without exception whatsoever and without undue delay, the case to its competent authorities for the purpose of prosecution, through proceedings in accordance with the law of that State. Those authorities shall take their decision in the same manner as in the case of an ordinary offence of a grave nature under the law of that State.

Article 15 Extradition of alleged offenders

1. To the extent that the crimes set out in article 9 are not extraditable offences in any extradition treaty existing between States Parties, they shall be deemed to be included as such therein. States Parties undertake to include those crimes as extraditable offences in every extradition treaty to be concluded between them.

2. If a State Party which makes extradition conditional on the existence of a treaty receives a request for extradition from another State Party with which it has no extradition treaty, it may at its option consider this Convention as the legal basis for extradition in respect of those crimes. Extradition shall be subject to the conditions provided in the law of the requested State.

3. States Parties which do not make extradition conditional on the existence of a treaty shall recognize those crimes as extraditable offences between themselves subject to the conditions provided in the law of the requested State.

4. Each of those crimes shall be treated, for the purposes of extradition between States Parties, as if it had been committed not only in the place in which it occurred but also in the territories of the States Parties which have established their jurisdiction in accordance with paragraph 1 or 2 of article 10.

Article 16 Mutual assistance in criminal matters

1. States Parties shall afford one another the greatest measure of assistance in connection with criminal proceedings brought in respect of the crimes set out in article 9, including assistance in obtaining evidence at their disposal necessary for the proceedings. The law of the requested State shall apply in all cases.

2. The provisions of paragraph 1 shall not affect obligations concerning mutual assistance embodied in any other treaty.

Article 17 Fair treatment

1. Any person regarding whom investigations or proceedings are being carried out in connection with any of the crimes set out in article 9 shall be guaranteed fair treatment, a fair trial and full protection of his or her rights at all stages of the investigations or proceedings.

2. Any alleged offender shall be entitled:

   (a) To communicate without delay with the nearest appropriate representative of the State or States of which such person is a national or which is otherwise entitled to protect that person's rights or, if such person is a stateless person, of the State which, at that person's request, is willing to protect that person's rights; and

   (b) To be visited by a representative of that State or those States.

Article 18 Notification of outcome of proceedings

The State Party where an alleged offender is prosecuted shall communicate the final outcome of the proceedings to the Secretary-General of the United Nations, who shall transmit the information to other States Parties.

Article 19 Dissemination

The States Parties undertake to disseminate this Convention as widely as possible and, in particular, to include the study thereof, as well as relevant provisions of international humanitarian law, in their programmes of military instruction.

Article 20 Savings clauses

Nothing in this Convention shall affect:

(a) The applicability of international humanitarian law and universally recognized standards of human rights as contained in international instruments in relation to the protection of United Nations operations and United Nations and associated personnel or the responsibility of such personnel to respect such law and standards;

(b) The rights and obligations of States, consistent with the Charter of the United Nations, regarding the consent to entry of persons into their territories;

(c) The obligation of United Nations and associated personnel to act in accordance with the terms of the mandate of a United Nations operation;

(d) The right of States which voluntarily contribute personnel to a United Nations operation to withdraw their personnel from participation in such operation; or

(e) The entitlement to appropriate compensation payable in the event of death, disability, injury or illness attributable to peace-keeping service by persons voluntarily contributed by States to United Nations operations.

Article 21 Right of self-defence

Nothing in this Convention shall be construed so as to derogate from the right to act in self-defence.

Article 22 Dispute settlement

1. Any dispute between two or more States Parties concerning the interpretation or application of this Convention which is not settled by negotiation shall, at the request of one of them, be submitted to arbitration. If within six months from the date of the request for arbitration the parties are unable to agree on the organization of the arbitration, any one of those parties may refer the dispute to the International Court of Justice by application in conformity with the Statute of the Court.

2. Each State Party may at the time of signature, ratification, acceptance or approval of this Convention or accession thereto declare that it does not consider itself bound by all or part of paragraph 1. The other States Parties shall not be bound by paragraph 1 or the relevant part thereof with respect to any State Party which has made such a reservation.

3. Any State Party which has made a reservation in accordance with paragraph 2 may at any time withdraw that reservation by notification to the Secretary-General of the United Nations.

DOCUMENT 39

European Convention on the Protection of the Environment through Criminal Law 1998
ETS No 172; 38 ILM 259 (1999)

The Convention was adopted under the auspices of the Council of Europe on 4 November 1998 and has not entered into force.

Only one State (Estonia) has ratified the Convention. There are 13 signatories.

The Convention was drafted by a group of governmental experts under the authority of the European Committee of Crime Problems, a committee within the Council of Europe. The Convention is noteworthy as the first international instrument designed to address environmental protection through the medium of the criminal law, while accepting that criminal law is the solution of last resort (see Explanatory Report: www.conventions. coe.int/Treaty/en/Reports/Html/172.htm).

States parties to the Convention are required to adopt measures to attach criminal liability in respect of individuals and corporations (Article 9) to violations listed in the Convention that have serious consequences, whether they are committed intentionally (Article 2) or negligently (Article 3). See Article 4 on other criminal offences. States are likewise required to establish their jurisdiction over these offences (Article 5(1)) and to punish these offences by appropriate penalties (Article 6; see also Article 7 on confiscation and Article 8 on reinstatement). The Convention requires that a State party in which an offender is found either to prosecute or to extradite that individual (Article 5(2)), although there are no provisions facilitating extradition. There are duties of co-operation among the parties in investigating and prosecuting environmental crimes (Articles 10 and 12).

Cf European Convention on Civil Liability for Damage resulting from Activities Dangerous to the Environment of 21 June 1993 (ETS No 150).

The member States of the Council of Europe and the other States signatory hereto,

Considering that the aim of the Council of Europe is to achieve a greater unity between its members;

Convinced of the need to pursue a common criminal policy aimed at the protection of the environment;

Considering that unregulated industrial development may give rise to a degree of pollution which poses risks to the environment;

Considering that the life and health of human beings, the environmental media and fauna and flora must be protected by all possible means;

Considering that the uncontrolled use of technology and the excessive exploitation of natural resources entail serious environmental hazards which must be overcome by appropriate and concerted measures;

Recognising that, whilst the prevention of the impairment of the environment must be achieved primarily through other measures, criminal law has an important part to play in protecting the environment;

Recalling that environmental violations having serious consequences must be established as criminal offences subject to appropriate sanctions;

Wishing to take effective measures to ensure that the perpetrators of such acts do not escape prosecution and punishment and desirous of fostering international co-operation to this end;

Convinced that imposing criminal or administrative sanctions on legal persons can play an effective role in the prevention of environmental violations and noting the growing international trend in this regard;

Mindful of the existing international conventions which already contain provisions aiming at the protection of the environment through criminal law;

Having regard to the conclusions of the 7th and 17th Conferences of European Ministers of Justice held in Basle in 1972 and in Istanbul in 1990, and to Recommendation 1192 (1992) of the Parliamentary Assembly,

Have agreed as follows:

Article 1 Definitions
For the purposes of this Convention:

(a) "unlawful" means infringing a law, an administrative regulation or a decision taken by a competent authority, aiming at the protection of the environment;

(b) "water" means all kinds of groundwater and surface water including the water of lakes, rivers, oceans and seas.

Article 2 Intentional offences
1. Each Party shall adopt such appropriate measures as may be necessary to establish as criminal offences under its domestic law:

   (a) the discharge, emission or introduction of a quantity of substances or ionising radiation into air, soil or water which:

      (i) causes death or serious injury to any person, or

      (ii) creates a significant risk of causing death or serious injury to any person;

   (b) the unlawful discharge, emission or introduction of a quantity of substances or ionising radiation into air, soil or water which causes or is likely to cause their lasting deterioration or death or serious injury to any person or substantial damage to protected monuments, other protected objects, property, animals or plants;

(c) the unlawful disposal, treatment, storage, transport, export or import of hazardous waste which causes or is likely to cause death or serious injury to any person or substantial damage to the quality of air, soil, water, animals or plants;

(d) the unlawful operation of a plant in which a dangerous activity is carried out and which causes or is likely to cause death or serious injury to any person or substantial damage to the quality of air, soil, water, animals or plants;

(e) the unlawful manufacture, treatment, storage, use, transport, export or import of nuclear materials or other hazardous radioactive substances which causes or is likely to cause death or serious injury to any person or substantial damage to the quality of air, soil, water, animals or plants, when committed intentionally.

2. Each Party shall adopt such appropriate measures as may be necessary to establish as criminal offences under its domestic law aiding or abetting the commission of any of the offences established in accordance with paragraph 1 of this article.

Article 3 Negligent offences

1. Each Party shall adopt such appropriate measures as may be necessary to establish as criminal offences under its domestic law, when committed with negligence, the offences enumerated in Article 2. paragraph 1(a) to (e).

2. Any State may, at the time of signature or when depositing its instrument of ratification, acceptance, approval or accession, by a declaration addressed to the Secretary General of the Council of Europe, declare that paragraph 1 of this article, in part or in whole, shall only apply to offences which were committed with gross negligence.

3. Any State may, at the time of signature or when depositing its instrument of ratification, acceptance, approval or accession, by a declaration addressed to the Secretary General of the Council of Europe, declare that paragraph 1 of this article, in part or in whole, shall not apply to:

–   subparagraph 1(a)(ii) of Article 2,

–   subparagraph 1(b) of Article 2, insofar as the offence relates to protect monuments, to other protected objects or to property.

Article 4 Other criminal offences or administrative offences

Insofar as these are not covered by the provisions of Articles 2 and 3, each Party shall adopt such appropriate measures as may be necessary to establish as criminal offences or administrative offences, liable to sanctions or other measures under its domestic law, when committed intentionally or with negligence:

(a) the unlawful discharge, emission or introduction of a quantity of substances or ionising radiation into air, soil or water;

(b) the unlawful causing of noise;

(c) the unlawful disposal, treatment, storage, transport, export or import of waste;

(d) the unlawful operation of a plant;

(e) the unlawful manufacture, treatment, use, transport, export or import of nuclear materials, other radioactive substances or hazardous chemicals;

(f) the unlawful causing of changes detrimental to natural components of a national park, nature reserve, water conservation area or other protected areas;

(g) the unlawful possession, taking, damaging, killing or trading of or in protected wild flora and fauna species.

Article 5 Jurisdiction

1. Each Party shall adopt such appropriate measures as may be necessary to establish jurisdiction over a criminal offence established in accordance with this Convention when the offence is committed:

    (a) in its territory; or

    (b) on board a ship or an aircraft registered in it or flying its flag; or

    (c) by one of its nationals if the offence is punishable under criminal law where it was committed or if the place where it was committed does not fall under any territorial jurisdiction.

2   Each Party shall adopt such appropriate measures as may be necessary to establish jurisdiction over a criminal offence established in accordance with this Convention, in cases where an alleged offender is present in its territory and it does not extradite him to another Party after a request for extradition.

3. This Convention does not exclude any criminal jurisdiction exercised by a Party in accordance with its domestic law.

4. Each Party may, at the time of signature or when depositing its instrument of ratification, acceptance, approval or accession, by a declaration addressed to the Secretary General of the Council of Europe, declare that paragraphs 1 c and 2 of this article, in part or in whole, shall not apply.

Article 6 Sanctions for environmental offences

Each Party shall adopt, in accordance with the relevant international instruments, such appropriate measures as may be necessary to enable it to make the offences established in accordance with Articles 2 and 3 punishable by criminal sanctions which take into account the serious nature of these offences. The sanctions available shall include imprisonment and pecuniary sanctions and may include reinstatement of the environment.

Article 7 Confiscation measures

1. Each Party shall adopt such appropriate measures as may be necessary to enable it to confiscate instrumentalities and proceeds, or property the value of which corresponds to such proceeds, in respect of offences enumerated in Articles 2 and 3.

2. Each Party may, at the time of signature or when depositing its instrument of ratification, acceptance, approval or accession, by a declaration addressed to the Secretary General of the Council of Europe, declare that it will not apply paragraph 1 of this Article either in respect of offences specified in such declaration or in respect of certain categories of instrumentalities or of proceeds, or property the value of which corresponds to such proceeds.

Article 8 Reinstatement of the environment

Each Party may, at any time, in a declaration addressed to the Secretary General of the Council of Europe, declare that it will provide for reinstatement of the environment according to the following provisions of this article:

(a) the competent authority may order the reinstatement of the environment in relation to an offence established in accordance with this Convention. Such an order may be made subject to certain conditions;

(b) where an order for the reinstatement of the environment has not been complied with, the competent authority may, in accordance with domestic law, make it executable at the expense of the person subject to the order or that person may be liable to other criminal sanctions instead of or in addition to it.

Article 9 Corporate liability

1. Each Party shall adopt such appropriate measures as may be necessary to enable it to impose criminal or administrative sanctions or measures on legal persons on whose behalf an offence referred to in Articles 2 or 3 has been committed by their organs or by members thereof or by another representative.

2. Corporate liability under paragraph 1 of this article shall not exclude criminal proceedings against a natural person.

3. Any State may, at the time of signature or when depositing its instrument of ratification, acceptance, approval or accession, by a declaration addressed to the Secretary General of the Council of Europe, declare that it reserves the right not to apply paragraph 1 of this article or any part thereof or that it applies only to offences specified in such declaration.

Article 10 Co-operation between authorities

1. Each Party shall adopt such appropriate measures as may be necessary to ensure that the authorities responsible for environmental protection co-operate with the authorities responsible for investigating and prosecuting criminal offences:

    (a) by informing the latter authorities, on their own initiative, where there are reasonable grounds to believe that an offence under Article 2 has been committed;

    (b) by providing, upon request, all necessary information to the latter authorities, in accordance with domestic law.

2. Any State may, at the time of signature or when depositing its instrument of ratification, acceptance, approval or accession, by a declaration addressed to the Secretary General of the Council of Europe, declare that it reserves the right not to apply paragraph 1(a) of this article or that it applies only to offences specified in such declaration.

Article 11 Rights for groups to participate in proceedings

Each Party may, at any time, in a declaration addressed to the Secretary General of the Council of Europe, declare that it will, in accordance with domestic law, grant any group, foundation or association which, according to its statutes, aims at the protection of the environment, the right to participate in criminal proceedings concerning offences established in accordance with this Convention.

Article 12 International co-operation

1. The Parties shall afford each other, in accordance with the provisions of relevant international instruments on international co-operation in criminal matters and with their domestic law, the widest measure of co-operation in investigations and judicial proceedings relating to criminal offences established in accordance with this Convention.

2. The Parties may afford each other assistance in investigations and proceedings relating to those acts defined in Article 4 of this Convention which are not covered by paragraph 1 of this article.

DOCUMENT 40

UN Convention Against Transnational Organized Crime 2000
UN Doc A/55/383; 40 ILM 353 (2001)

The Convention was adopted on 15 November 2000 as an annex to General Assembly Resolution 55/25 and entered into force 29 September 2003.

There are 99 parties to the Convention, including China, France and Russia; Germany, the UK and the USA have signed but have not ratified the Convention.

Transnational organised crime first attracted active UN interest in the early 1990s, when the General Assembly adopted Resolution 49/159 which expressed concern at 'the rapid growth and geographical extension of organised crime in its various forms' and endorsed the call by the Naples Political Declaration and Global Action Plan Against Organized Transnational Crime of November 1994 (UN Doc A/49/748) for a global action plan to combat such crime. By Resolution 53/111 of 9 December 1998, the General Assembly established an Ad Hoc Committee, open to all States, to elaborate the international convention against transnational organised crime and three additional international legal protocols **(Documents 41–43).**

The Convention requires each party to criminalise the offences specified in Articles 5, 6, and 23, punishable by sanctions that recognise their gravity (Article 11(1)). Each party is to assert jurisdiction over these crimes committed in its territory or on it ships or aircraft (Article 15(1)). Additionally, a party may extend its jurisdiction to crimes committed by or against its nationals or committed abroad with the intention of being committed within its territory (Article 15(2)). The Convention, through Article 11 (see also Article 34), restricts the discretion as to the prosecution of any offender; and there is a duty to prosecute where a request for extradition is declined on the sole ground that the offender is one of its nationals (Article 16(10)). As to extradition, the Convention's offences are deemed to be included in existing extradition treaties and are to be included in future extradition treaties (Article 16(3)); and the Convention itself may be used as the basis of extradition in the absence of an extradition treaty (Article 15(4)). The Convention's offences are not to be regarded as fiscal offences for the purpose of extradition (Article 16(15)), though there may be no extradition where the purpose is to prosecute or punish a person on account of his race, religion, nationality, ethnic origin or political opinion (Article 16(14)). The Convention provides for fair treatment in any proceedings (Article 11(3)). The Convention contains extensive obligations of co-operation among the parties in the prevention, investigation, prosecution and punishment of the proscribed offences (see eg Articles 27–30).

Article 1 Statement of purpose

The purpose of this Convention is to promote cooperation to prevent and combat transnational organized crime more effectively.

Article 2 Use of terms

For the purposes of this Convention:

(a) "Organized criminal group" shall mean a structured group of three or more persons, existing for a period of time and acting in concert with the aim of committing one or more serious crimes or offences established in accordance with this Convention, in order to obtain, directly or indirectly, a financial or other material benefit;

(b) "Serious crime" shall mean conduct constituting an offence punishable by a maximum deprivation of liberty of at least four years or a more serious penalty;

(c) "Structured group" shall mean a group that is not randomly formed for the immediate commission of an offence and that does not need to have formally defined roles for its members, continuity of its membership or a developed structure;

(d) "Property" shall mean assets of every kind, whether corporeal or incorporeal, movable or immovable, tangible or intangible, and legal documents or instruments evidencing title to, or interest in, such assets;

(e) "Proceeds of crime" shall mean any property derived from or obtained, directly or indirectly, through the commission of an offence;

(f) "Freezing" or "seizure" shall mean temporarily prohibiting the transfer, conversion, disposition or movement of property or temporarily assuming custody or control of property on the basis of an order issued by a court or other competent authority;

(g) "Confiscation", which includes forfeiture where applicable, shall mean the permanent deprivation of property by order of a court or other competent authority;

(h) "Predicate offence" shall mean any offence as a result of which proceeds have been generated that may become the subject of an offence as defined in article 6 of this Convention;

(i) "Controlled delivery" shall mean the technique of allowing illicit or suspect consignments to pass out of, through or into the territory of one or more States, with the knowledge and under the supervision of their competent authorities, with a view to the investigation of an offence and the identification of persons involved in the commission of the offence;

(j) "Regional economic integration organization" shall mean an organization constituted by sovereign States of a given region, to which its member States have transferred competence in respect of matters governed by this Convention and which has been duly authorized, in accordance with its internal procedures, to sign, ratify, accept, approve or accede to it; references to "States Parties" under this Convention shall apply to such organizations within the limits of their competence.

Article 3 Scope of application

1. This Convention shall apply, except as otherwise stated herein, to the prevention, investigation and prosecution of:

    (a) The offences established in accordance with articles 5, 6, 8 and 23 of this Convention; and

    (b) Serious crime as defined in article 2 of this Convention; where the offence is transnational in nature and involves an organized criminal group.

2. For the purpose of paragraph 1 of this article, an offence is transnational in nature if:

    (a) It is committed in more than one State;

    (b) It is committed in one State but a substantial part of its preparation, planning, direction or control takes place in another State;

    (c) It is committed in one State but involves an organized criminal group that engages in criminal activities in more than one State; or

    (d) It is committed in one State but has substantial effects in another State.

Article 4 Protection of sovereignty

1. States Parties shall carry out their obligations under this Convention in a manner consistent with the principles of sovereign equality and territorial integrity of States and that of non-intervention in the domestic affairs of other States.

2. Nothing in this Convention entitles a State Party to undertake in the territory of another State the exercise of jurisdiction and performance of functions that are reserved exclusively for the authorities of that other State by its domestic law.

Article 5 Criminalization of participation in an organized criminal group

1. Each State Party shall adopt such legislative and other measures as may be necessary to establish as criminal offences, when committed intentionally:

    (a) Either or both of the following as criminal offences distinct from those involving the attempt or completion of the criminal activity:

        (i) Agreeing with one or more other persons to commit a serious crime for a purpose relating directly or indirectly to the obtaining of a financial or other material benefit and, where required by domestic law, involving an act undertaken by one of the participants in furtherance of the agreement or involving an organized criminal group;

    (ii)   Conduct by a person who, with knowledge of either the aim and general criminal activity of an organized criminal group or its intention to commit the crimes in question, takes an active part in:

        (a)   Criminal activities of the organized criminal group;

        (b)   Other activities of the organized criminal group in the knowledge that his or her participation will contribute to the achievement of the above-described criminal aim;

  (b) Organizing, directing, aiding, abetting, facilitating or counselling the commission of serious crime involving an organized criminal group.

2.   The knowledge, intent, aim, purpose or agreement referred to in paragraph 1 of this article may be inferred from objective factual circumstances.

3.   States Parties whose domestic law requires involvement of an organized criminal group for purposes of the offences established in accordance with paragraph 1(a)(i) of this article shall ensure that their domestic law covers all serious crimes involving organized criminal groups. Such States Parties, as well as States Parties whose domestic law requires an act in furtherance of the agreement for purposes of the offences established in accordance with paragraph 1(a)(i) of this article, shall so inform the Secretary-General of the United Nations at the time of their signature or of deposit of their instrument of ratification, acceptance or approval of or accession to this Convention.

Article 6 Criminalization of the laundering of proceeds of crime

1.   Each State Party shall adopt, in accordance with fundamental principles of its domestic law, such legislative and other measures as may be necessary to establish as criminal offences, when committed intentionally:

  (a) (i)   The conversion or transfer of property, knowing that such property is the proceeds of crime, for the purpose of concealing or disguising the illicit origin of the property or of helping any person who is involved in the commission of the predicate offence to evade the legal consequences of his or her action;

      (ii) The concealment or disguise of the true nature, source, location, disposition, movement or ownership of or rights with respect to property, knowing that such property is the proceeds of crime;

  (b) Subject to the basic concepts of its legal system:

      (i)   The acquisition, possession or use of property, knowing, at the time of receipt, that such property is the proceeds of crime;

      (ii) Participation in, association with or conspiracy to commit, attempts to commit and aiding, abetting, facilitating and counselling the commission of any of the offences established in accordance with this article.

2.   For purposes of implementing or applying paragraph 1 of this article:

  (a) Each State Party shall seek to apply paragraph 1 of this article to the widest range of predicate offences;

  (b) Each State Party shall include as predicate offences all serious crime as defined in article 2 of this Convention and the offences established in accordance with articles 5, 8 and 23 of this Convention. In the case of States Parties whose legislation sets out a list of specific predicate offences, they shall, at a minimum, include in such list a comprehensive range of offences associated with organized criminal groups;

  (c) For the purposes of subparagraph (b), predicate offences shall include offences committed both within and outside the jurisdiction of the State Party in question. However, offences committed outside the jurisdiction of a State Party shall constitute predicate offences only when the relevant conduct is a criminal offence under the domestic law of the State where it is committed and would be a criminal offence under the domestic law of the State Party implementing or applying this article had it been committed there;

(d) Each State Party shall furnish copies of its laws that give effect to this article and of any subsequent changes to such laws or a f to the Secretary-General of the United Nations;

(e) If required by fundamental principles of the domestic law of a State Party, it may be provided that the offences set forth in paragraph 1 of this article do not apply to the persons who committed the predicate offence;

(f) Knowledge, intent or purpose required as an element of an offence set forth in paragraph 1 of this article may be inferred from objective factual circumstances.

Article 8 Criminalization of corruption

1. Each State Party shall adopt such legislative and other measures as may be necessary to establish as criminal offences, when committed intentionally:

   (a) The promise, offering or giving to a public official, directly or indirectly, of an undue advantage, for the official himself or herself or another person or entity, in order that the official act or refrain from acting in the exercise of his or her official duties;

   (b) The solicitation or acceptance by a public official, directly or indirectly, of an undue advantage, for the official himself or herself or another person or entity, in order that the official act or refrain from acting in the exercise of his or her official duties.

2. Each State Party shall consider adopting such legislative and other measures as may be necessary to establish as criminal offences conduct referred to in paragraph 1 of this article involving a foreign public official or international civil servant. Likewise, each State Party shall consider establishing as criminal offences other forms of corruption.

3. Each State Party shall also adopt such measures as may be necessary to establish as a criminal offence participation as an accomplice in an offence established in accordance with this article.

4. For the purposes of paragraph 1 of this article and article 9 of this Convention, "public official" shall mean a public official or a person who provides a public service as defined in the domestic law and as applied in the criminal law of the State Party in which the person in question performs that function.

Article 10 Liability of legal persons

1. Each State Party shall adopt such measures as may be necessary, consistent with its legal principles, to establish the liability of legal persons for participation in serious crimes involving an organized criminal group and for the offences established in accordance with articles 5, 6, 8 and 23 of this Convention.

2. Subject to the legal principles of the State Party, the liability of legal persons may be criminal, civil or administrative.

3. Such liability shall be without prejudice to the criminal liability of the natural persons who have committed the offences.

4. Each State Party shall, in particular, ensure that legal persons held liable in accordance with this article are subject to effective, proportionate and dissuasive criminal or non-criminal sanctions, including monetary sanctions.

Article 11 Prosecution, adjudication and sanctions

1. Each State Party shall make the commission of an offence established in accordance with articles 5, 6, 8 and 23 of this Convention liable to sanctions that take into account the gravity of that offence.

2. Each State Party shall endeavour to ensure that any discretionary legal powers under its domestic law relating to the prosecution of persons for offences covered by this Convention are exercised to maximize the effectiveness of law enforcement measures in respect of those offences and with due regard to the need to deter the commission of such offences.

3. In the case of offences established in accordance with articles 5, 6, 8 and 23 of this Convention, each State Party shall take appropriate measures, in accordance with its domestic law and with due regard to the rights of the defence, to seek to ensure that conditions imposed in connection with decisions on release pending trial or appeal take into consideration the need to ensure the presence of the defendant at subsequent criminal proceedings.

4. Each State Party shall ensure that its courts or other competent authorities bear in mind the grave nature of the offences covered by this Convention when considering the eventuality of early release or parole of persons convicted of such offences.

5. Each State Party shall, where appropriate, establish under its domestic law a long statute of limitations period in which to commence proceedings for any offence covered by this Convention and a longer period where the alleged offender has evaded the administration of justice.

6. Nothing contained in this Convention shall affect the principle that the description of the offences established in accordance with this Convention and of the applicable legal defences or other legal principles controlling the lawfulness of conduct is reserved to the domestic law of a State Party and that such offences shall be prosecuted and punished in accordance with that law.

Article 15 Jurisdiction

1. Each State Party shall adopt such measures as may be necessary to establish its jurisdiction over the offences established in accordance with articles 5, 6, 8 and 23 of this Convention when:

   (a) The offence is committed in the territory of that State Party; or

   (b) The offence is committed on board a vessel that is flying the flag of that State Party or an aircraft that is registered under the laws of that State Party at the time that the offence is committed.

2. Subject to article 4 of this Convention, a State Party may also establish its jurisdiction over any such offence when:

   (a) The offence is committed against a national of that State Party;

   (b) The offence is committed by a national of that State Party or a stateless person who has his or her habitual residence in its territory; or

   (c) The offence is:

   (i) One of those established in accordance with article 5, paragraph 1, of this Convention and is committed outside its territory with a view to the commission of a serious crime within its territory;

   (ii) One of those established in accordance with article 6, paragraph 1(b)(ii), of this Convention and is committed outside its territory with a view to the commission of an offence established in accordance with article 6, paragraph 1(a)(i) or (ii) or (b)(i), of this Convention within its territory.

3. For the purposes of article 16, paragraph 10, of this Convention, each State Party shall adopt such measures as may be necessary to establish its jurisdiction over the offences covered by this Convention when the alleged offender is present in its territory and it does not extradite such person solely on the ground that he or she is one of its nationals.

4. Each State Party may also adopt such measures as may be necessary to establish its jurisdiction over the offences covered by this Convention when the alleged offender is present in its territory and it does not extradite him or her.

5. If a State Party exercising its jurisdiction under paragraph 1 or 2 of this article has been notified, or has otherwise learned, that one or more other States Parties are conducting an investigation, prosecution or judicial proceeding in respect of the same conduct, the competent authorities of those States Parties shall, as appropriate, consult one another with a view to coordinating their actions.

6. Without prejudice to norms of general international law, this Convention does not exclude the exercise of any criminal jurisdiction established by a State Party in accordance with its domestic law.

Article 16 Extradition

1. This article shall apply to the offences covered by this Convention or in cases where an offence referred to in article 3, paragraph 1(a) or (b), involves an organized criminal group and the person who is the subject of the request for extradition is located in the territory of the requested State Party, provided that the offence for which extradition is sought is punishable under the domestic law of both the requesting State Party and the requested State Party.

2. If the request for extradition includes several separate serious crimes, some of which are not covered by this article, the requested State Party may apply this article also in respect of the latter offences.

3. Each of the offences to which this article applies shall be deemed to be included as an extraditable offence in any extradition treaty existing between States Parties. States Parties undertake to include such offences as extraditable offences in every extradition treaty to be concluded between them.

4. If a State Party that makes extradition conditional on the existence of a treaty receives a request for extradition from another State Party with which it has no extradition treaty, it may consider this Convention the legal basis for extradition in respect of any offence to which this article applies.

5. States Parties that make extradition conditional on the existence of a treaty shall:

    (a) At the time of deposit of their instrument of ratification, acceptance, approval of or accession to this Convention, inform the Secretary-General of the United Nations whether they will take this Convention as the legal basis for cooperation on extradition with other States Parties to this Convention; and

    (b) If they do not take this Convention as the legal basis for cooperation on extradition, seek, where appropriate, to conclude treaties on extradition with other States Parties to this Convention in order to implement this article.

6. States Parties that do not make extradition conditional on the existence of a treaty shall recognize offences to which this article applies as extraditable offences between themselves.

7. Extradition shall be subject to the conditions provided for by the domestic law of the requested State Party or by applicable extradition treaties, including, *inter alia*, conditions in relation to the minimum penalty requirement for extradition and the grounds upon which the requested State Party may refuse extradition.

8. States Parties shall, subject to their domestic law, endeavour to expedite extradition procedures and to simplify evidentiary requirements relating thereto in respect of any offence to which this article applies.

9. Subject to the provisions of its domestic law and its extradition treaties, the requested State Party may, upon being satisfied that the circumstances so warrant and are urgent and at the request of the requesting State Party, take a person whose extradition is sought and who is present in its territory into custody or take other appropriate measures to ensure his or her presence at extradition proceedings.

10. A State Party in whose territory an alleged offender is found, if it does not extradite such person in respect of an offence to which this article applies solely on the ground that he or she

is one of its nationals, shall, at the request of the State Party seeking extradition, be obliged to submit the case without undue delay to its competent authorities for the purpose of prosecution. Those authorities shall take their decision and conduct their proceedings in the same manner as in the case of any other offence of a grave nature under the domestic law of that State Party. The States Parties concerned shall cooperate with each other, in particular on procedural and evidentiary aspects, to ensure the efficiency of such prosecution.

11. Whenever a State Party is permitted under its domestic law to extradite or otherwise surrender one of its nationals only upon the condition that the person will be returned to that State Party to serve the sentence imposed as a result of the trial or proceedings for which the extradition or surrender of the person was sought and that State Party and the State Party seeking the extradition of the person agree with this option and other terms that they may deem appropriate, such conditional extradition or surrender shall be sufficient to discharge the obligation set forth in paragraph 10 of this article.

12. If extradition, sought for purposes of enforcing a sentence, is refused because the person sought is a national of the requested State Party, the requested Party shall, if its domestic law so permits and in conformity with the requirements of such law, upon application of the requesting Party, consider the enforcement of the sentence that has been imposed under the domestic law of the requesting Party or the remainder thereof.

13. Any person regarding whom proceedings are being carried out in connection with any of the offences to which this article applies shall be guaranteed fair treatment at all stages of the proceedings, including enjoyment of all the rights and guarantees provided by the domestic law of the State Party in the territory of which that person is present.

14. Nothing in this Convention shall be interpreted as imposing an obligation to extradite if the requested State Party has substantial grounds for believing that the request has been made for the purpose of prosecuting or punishing a person on account of that person's sex, race, religion, nationality, ethnic origin or political opinions or that compliance with the request would cause prejudice to that person's position for any one of these reasons.

15. States Parties may not refuse a request for extradition on the sole ground that the offence is also considered to involve fiscal matters.

16. Before refusing extradition, the requested State Party shall, where appropriate, consult with the requesting State Party to provide it with ample opportunity to present its opinions and to provide information relevant to its allegation.

17. States Parties shall seek to conclude bilateral and multilateral agreements or arrangements to carry out or to enhance the effectiveness of extradition.

Article 23 Criminalization of obstruction of justice

Each State Party shall adopt such legislative and other measures as may be necessary to establish as criminal offences, when committed intentionally:

(a) The use of physical force, threats or intimidation or the promise, offering or giving of an undue advantage to induce false testimony or to interfere in the giving of testimony or the production of evidence in a proceeding in relation to the commission of offences covered by this Convention;

(b) The use of physical force, threats or intimidation to interfere with the exercise of official duties by a justice or law enforcement official in relation to the commission of offences covered by this Convention.

Nothing in this subparagraph shall prejudice the right of States Parties to have legislation that protects other categories of public officials.

Article 24 Protection of witnesses

1. Each State Party shall take appropriate measures within its means to provide effective protection from potential retaliation or intimidation for witnesses in criminal proceedings who

give testimony concerning offences covered by this Convention and, as appropriate, for their relatives and other persons close to them.

2. The measures envisaged in paragraph 1 of this article may include, *inter alia*, without prejudice to the rights of the defendant, including the right to due process:

    (a) Establishing procedures for the physical protection of such persons, such as, to the extent necessary and feasible, relocating them and permitting, where appropriate, non-disclosure or limitations on the disclosure of information concerning the identity and whereabouts of such persons;

    (b) Providing evidentiary rules to permit witness testimony to be given in a manner that ensures the safety of the witness, such as permitting testimony to be given through the use of communications technology such as video links or other adequate means.

3. States Parties shall consider entering into agreements or arrangements with other States for the relocation of persons referred to in paragraph 1 of this article.

4. The provisions of this article shall also apply to victims insofar as they are witnesses.

Article 25 Assistance to and protection of victims

1. Each State Party shall take appropriate measures within its means to provide assistance and protection to victims of offences covered by this Convention, in particular in cases of threat of retaliation or intimidation.

2. Each State Party shall establish appropriate procedures to provide access to compensation and restitution for victims of offences covered by this Convention.

3. Each State Party shall, subject to its domestic law, enable views and concerns of victims to be presented and considered at appropriate stages of criminal proceedings against offenders in a manner not prejudicial to the rights of the defence.

Article 26 Measures to enhance cooperation with law enforcement authorities

1. Each State Party shall take appropriate measures to encourage persons who participate or who have participated in organized criminal groups:

    (a) To supply information useful to competent authorities for investigative and evidentiary purposes on such matters as:

        (i)   The identity, nature, composition, structure, location or activities of organized criminal groups;

        (ii) Links, including international links, with other organized criminal groups;

        (iii) Offences that organized criminal groups have committed or may commit;

    (b) To provide factual, concrete help to competent authorities that may contribute to depriving organized criminal groups of their resources or of the proceeds of crime.

2. Each State Party shall consider providing for the possibility, in appropriate cases, of mitigating punishment of an accused person who provides substantial cooperation in the investigation or prosecution of an offence covered by this Convention.

3. Each State Party shall consider providing for the possibility, in accordance with fundamental principles of its domestic law, of granting immunity from prosecution to a person who provides substantial cooperation in the investigation or prosecution of an offence covered by this Convention.

4. Protection of such persons shall be as provided for in article 24 of this Convention.

5. Where a person referred to in paragraph 1 of this article located in one State Party can provide substantial cooperation to the competent authorities of another State Party, the States Parties concerned may consider entering into agreements or arrangements, in accordance with their domestic law, concerning the potential provision by the other State Party of the treatment set forth in paragraphs 2 and 3 of this article.

Article 27 Law enforcement cooperation

1. States Parties shall cooperate closely with one another, consistent with their respective domestic legal and administrative systems, to enhance the effectiveness of law enforcement action to combat the offences covered by this Convention. Each State Party shall, in particular, adopt effective measures:

   (a) To enhance and, where necessary, to establish channels of communication between their competent authorities, agencies and services in order to facilitate the secure and rapid exchange of information concerning all aspects of the offences covered by this Convention, including, if the States Parties concerned deem it appropriate, links with other criminal activities;

   (b) To cooperate with other States Parties in conducting inquiries with respect to offences covered by this Convention concerning:

      (i) The identity, whereabouts and activities of persons suspected of involvement in such offences or the location of other persons concerned;

      (ii) The movement of proceeds of crime or property derived from the commission of such offences;

      (iii) The movement of property, equipment or other instrumentalities used or intended for use in the commission of such offences;

   (c) To provide, when appropriate, necessary items or quantities of substances for analytical or investigative purposes;

   (d) To facilitate effective coordination between their competent authorities, agencies and services and to promote the exchange of personnel and other experts, including, subject to bilateral agreements or arrangements between the States Parties concerned, the posting of liaison officers;

   (e) To exchange information with other States Parties on specific means and methods used by organized criminal groups, including, where applicable, routes and conveyances and the use of false identities, altered or false documents or other means of concealing their activities;

   (f) To exchange information and coordinate administrative and other measures taken as appropriate for the purpose of early identification of the offences covered by this Convention.

2. With a view to giving effect to this Convention, States Parties shall consider entering into bilateral or multilateral agreements or arrangements on direct cooperation between their law enforcement agencies and, where such agreements or arrangements already exist, amending them. In the absence of such agreements or arrangements between the States Parties concerned, the Parties may consider this Convention as the basis for mutual law enforcement cooperation in respect of the offences covered by this Convention. Whenever appropriate, States Parties shall make full use of agreements or arrangements, including international or regional organizations, to enhance the cooperation between their law enforcement agencies.

3. States Parties shall endeavour to cooperate within their means to respond to transnational organized crime committed through the use of modern technology.

Article 34 Implementation of the Convention

1. Each State Party shall take the necessary measures, including legislative and administrative measures, in accordance with fundamental principles of its domestic law, to ensure the implementation of its obligations under this Convention.

2. The offences established in accordance with articles 5, 6, 8 and 23 of this Convention shall be established in the domestic law of each State Party independently of the transnational nature or the involvement of an organized criminal group as described in article 3, paragraph 1, of this Convention, except to the extent that article 5 of this Convention would require the involvement of an organized criminal group.

3. Each State Party may adopt more strict or severe measures than those provided for by this Convention for preventing and combating transnational organized crime.

DOCUMENT 41

Protocol to Prevent, Suppress and Punish Trafficking in Persons, especially Women and Children 2000
UN Doc A/55/383; 40 ILM 377 (2001)

This Protocol was adopted on 15 November 2000 as an annex to General Assembly Resolution 55/25 and entered into force on 25 December 2003.

There are 79 parties to the Protocol, including France and Russia. Among the non-parties are China, Germany, Japan, the UK and the USA.

Trafficking of women and children has been the subject of a number of international instruments, beginning in 1904: the International Agreements for the Suppression of White Slave Traffic of 1904 and 1910 (1 LNTS 1 and 1 LNTS 83), amended by a Protocol of 3 December 1948 (30 UNTS 23), the International Convention for the Suppression of Trafficking of Women and Children of 30 September 1921 (9 LNTS 415) and the Convention for the Suppression of the Traffic in Women of Full Age of 11 October 1933 (150 LNTS 431), these last two being amended by the Protocol of 12 November 1947 (53 UNTS 13). See also the Convention for the Suppression of Traffic in Persons and of the Exploitation and Prostitution of Others of 2 December 1949 (96 UNTS 271) and the Convention on the Elimination of All Forms of Discrimination Against Women of 18 December 1979 (1249 UNTS 13).

The Protocol to the UN Convention Against Transnational Organized Crime (**Document 40**), *open only to States which are parties to the Convention, is intended to prevent trafficking, to assist victims, and to promote international cooperation (Article 2). It requires each State party to criminalise the acts set out in Article 3 (Article 5(1)) and to establish its jurisdiction over these offences (Article 5(2)). Thereafter, it relies on the Convention Against Transnational Organized Crime for measures of implementation, enforcement and co-operation (Article 1).*

Article 1 Relation with the United Nations Convention against Transnational Organized Crime

1.   This Protocol supplements the United Nations Convention against Transnational Organized Crime. It shall be interpreted together with the Convention.

2.   The provisions of the Convention shall apply, *mutatis mutandis*, to this Protocol unless otherwise provided herein.

3.   The offences established in accordance with article 5 of this Protocol shall be regarded as offences established in accordance with the Convention.

Article 2 Statement of purpose

The purposes of this Protocol are:

(a)   To prevent and combat trafficking in persons, paying particular attention to women and children;

(b)   To protect and assist the victims of such trafficking, with full respect for their human rights; and

(c)   To promote cooperation among States Parties in order to meet those objectives.

Article 3 Use of terms

For the purposes of this Protocol:

(a) "Trafficking in persons" shall mean the recruitment, transportation, transfer, harbouring or receipt of persons, by means of the threat or use of force or other forms of coercion, of abduction, of fraud, of deception, of the abuse of power or of a position of vulnerability or of the giving or receiving of payments or benefits to achieve the consent of a person having control over another person, for the purpose of exploitation. Exploitation shall include, at a minimum, the exploitation of the prostitution of others or other forms of sexual exploitation, forced labour or services, slavery or practices similar to slavery, servitude or the removal of organs;

(b) The consent of a victim of trafficking in persons to the intended exploitation set forth in subparagraph (a) of this article shall be irrelevant where any of the means set forth in subparagraph (a) have been used;

(c) The recruitment, transportation, transfer, harbouring or receipt of a child for the purpose of exploitation shall be considered "trafficking in persons" even if this does not involve any of the means set forth in subparagraph (a) of this article;

(d) "Child" shall mean any person under eighteen years of age.

Article 4 Scope of application

This Protocol shall apply, except as otherwise stated herein, to the prevention, investigation and prosecution of the offences established in accordance with article 5 of this Protocol, where those offences are transnational in nature and involve an organized criminal group, as well as to the protection of victims of such offences.

Article 5 Criminalization

1. Each State Party shall adopt such legislative and other measures as may be necessary to establish as criminal offences the conduct set forth in article 3 of this Protocol, when committed intentionally.

2. Each State Party shall also adopt such legislative and other measures as may be necessary to establish as criminal offences:

   (a) Subject to the basic concepts of its legal system, attempting to commit an offence established in accordance with paragraph 1 of this article;

   (b) Participating as an accomplice in an offence established in accordance with paragraph 1 of this article; and

   (c) Organizing or directing other persons to commit an offence established in accordance with paragraph 1 of this article.

DOCUMENT 42

Protocol Against the Smuggling of Migrants by Land, Sea and Air 2000
UN Doc A/55/383; 40 ILM 384 (2001)

This Protocol was adopted on 15 November 2000 as an annex to General Assembly Resolution 55/25 and entered into force on 28 January 2004.

There are 67 parties to the Protocol, including France and Russia. Among the non-parties are China, Germany, Japan, the UK and the USA.

The link between organised crime and the smuggling of migrants was recognised in the Naples Political Declaration and Global Action Plan Against Organized Transnational Crime of November 1994 (UN Doc A/49/748). By Resolution 53/111 of 9 December 1998, the General Assembly established an Ad Hoc Committee, open to all States, to elaborate the international convention against transnational organised crime and three additional international legal protocols, one of which was to suppress the smuggling of migrants **(see Documents 40–41 and 43).**

This Protocol to the UN Convention Against Transnational Organized Crime **(Document 40)***, open only to parties to the Convention, is intended to prevent the smuggling of migrants, to protect migrants and to promote international co-operation (Article 2). It requires each State party to criminalise the acts set out in Article 6(1), as defined by Article 3. Thereafter, it relies on the Convention Against Transnational Organized Crime for measures of implementation, enforcement and co-operation (Article 1).*

Article 1 Relation with the United Nations Convention Against Transnational Organized Crime

1. This Protocol supplements the United Nations Convention against Transnational Organized Crime. It shall be interpreted together with the Convention.

2. The provisions of the Convention shall apply, *mutatis mutandis*, to this Protocol unless otherwise provided herein.

3. The offences established in accordance with article 6 of this Protocol shall be regarded as offences established in accordance with the Convention.

Article 2 Statement of purpose

The purpose of this Protocol is to prevent and combat the smuggling of migrants, as well as to promote cooperation among States Parties to that end, while protecting the rights of smuggled migrants.

Article 3 Use of terms

For the purposes of this Protocol:

(a) "Smuggling of migrants" shall mean the procurement, in order to obtain, directly or indirectly, a financial or other material benefit, of the illegal entry of a person into a State Party of which the person is not a national or a permanent resident;

(b) "Illegal entry" shall mean crossing borders without complying with the necessary requirements for legal entry into the receiving State;

(c) "Fraudulent travel or identity document" shall mean any travel or identity document:

   (i) That has been falsely made or altered in some material way by anyone other than a person or agency lawfully authorized to make or issue the travel or identity document on behalf of a State; or

   (ii) That has been improperly issued or obtained through misrepresentation, corruption or duress or in any other unlawful manner; or

   (iii) That is being used by a person other than the rightful holder;

(d) "Vessel" shall mean any type of water craft, including nondisplacement craft and seaplanes, used or capable of being used as a means of transportation on water, except a warship, naval auxiliary or other vessel owned or operated by a Government and used, for the time being, only on government non-commercial service.

Article 4 Scope of application

This Protocol shall apply, except as otherwise stated herein, to the prevention, investigation and prosecution of the offences established in accordance with article 6 of this Protocol, where the offences are transnational in nature and involve an organized criminal group, as well as to the protection of the rights of persons who have been the object of such offences.

Article 5 Criminal liability of migrants

Migrants shall not become liable to criminal prosecution under this Protocol for the fact of having been the object of conduct set forth in article 6 of this Protocol.

Article 6 Criminalization

1. Each State Party shall adopt such legislative and other measures as may be necessary to establish as criminal offences, when committed intentionally and in order to obtain, directly or indirectly, a financial or other material benefit:

   (a) The smuggling of migrants;

   (b) When committed for the purpose of enabling the smuggling of migrants:

      (i) Producing a fraudulent travel or identity document;

      (ii) Procuring, providing or possessing such a document;

   (c) Enabling a person who is not a national or a permanent resident to remain in the State concerned without complying with the necessary requirements for legally remaining in the State by the means mentioned in subparagraph (b) of this paragraph or any other illegal means.

2. Each State Party shall also adopt such legislative and other measures as may be necessary to establish as criminal offences:

   (a) Subject to the basic concepts of its legal system, attempting to commit an offence established in accordance with paragraph 1 of this article;

   (b) Participating as an accomplice in an offence established in accordance with paragraph 1(a), (b)(i) or (c) of this article and, subject to the basic concepts of its legal system, participating as an accomplice in an offence established in accordance with paragraph 1(b)(ii) of this article;

   (c) Organizing or directing other persons to commit an offence established in accordance with paragraph 1 of this article.

3. Each State Party shall adopt such legislative and other measures as may be necessary to establish as aggravating circumstances to the offences established in accordance with paragraph 1(a), (b)(i) and (c) of this article and, subject to the basic concepts of its legal system, to the offences established in accordance with paragraph 2(b) and (c) of this article, circumstances:

   (a) That endanger, or are likely to endanger, the lives or safety of the migrants concerned; or

   (b) That entail inhuman or degrading treatment, including for exploitation, of such migrants.

4. Nothing in this Protocol shall prevent a State Party from taking measures against a person whose conduct constitutes an offence under its domestic law.

DOCUMENT 43

Protocol Against the Illicit Manufacturing of and Trafficking in Firearms, Their Parts and Components and Ammunition 2001
UN Doc A/55/383/Add 2

This Protocol was adopted on 31 May 2001 as an annex to General Assembly Resolution 55/255; it entered into force on 3 July 2005 .

There are 32 parties to the Protocol; none of the major powers is a party.

The link between organised crime and the illicit manufacturing of and trafficking in firearms is not as obvious as the link between organised crime and trafficking in people and smuggling of migrants. However, the link was recognised in the Naples Political Declaration and Global Action Plan Against Organized Transnational Crime of November 1994 (UN Doc A/49/748). By Resolution 53/111 of 9 December 1998, the General Assembly established an Ad Hoc Committee, open to all States, to elaborate the international convention against transnational organised crime and three additional international legal protocols, one of which was to suppress the illicit manufacturing of and trafficking in firearms **(see Documents 40–42)**.

This Protocol to the UN Convention Against Transnational Organized Crime **(Document 40)**, *open only to parties to the Convention, is intended to eradicate the illicit manufacturing of and trafficking in firearms and to promote international cooperation (Article 2). It requires each State party to criminalise the acts set out in Article 5, as defined by Article 3. Thereafter, it relies on the Convention Against Transnational Organized Crime for measures of implementation, enforcement and co-operation (Article 1).*

Article 1 Relation with the United Nations Convention Against Transnational Organized Crime

1. This Protocol supplements the United Nations Convention against Transnational Organized Crime. It shall be interpreted together with the Convention.

2. The provisions of the Convention shall apply, *mutatis mutandis*, to this Protocol unless otherwise provided herein.

3. The offences established in accordance with article 5 of this Protocol shall be regarded as offences established in accordance with the Convention.

Article 2 Statement of purpose

The purpose of this Protocol is to promote, facilitate and strengthen cooperation among States Parties in order to prevent, combat and eradicate the illicit manufacturing of and trafficking in firearms, their parts and components and ammunition.

Article 3 Use of terms

For the purposes of this Protocol:

(a) "Firearm" shall mean any portable barrelled weapon that expels, is designed to expel or may be readily converted to expel a shot, bullet or projectile by the action of an explosive, excluding antique firearms or their replicas. Antique firearms and their replicas shall be defined in accordance with domestic law. In no case, however, shall antique firearms include firearms manufactured after 1899;

(b) "Parts and components" shall mean any element or replacement element specifically designed for a firearm and essential to its operation, including a barrel, frame or receiver, slide or cylinder, bolt or breech block, and any device designed or adapted to diminish the sound caused by firing a firearm;

(c) "Ammunition" shall mean the complete round or its components, including cartridge cases, primers, propellant powder, bullets or projectiles, that are used in a firearm, provided that those components are themselves subject to authorization in the respective State Party;

(d) "Illicit manufacturing" shall mean the manufacturing or assembly of firearms, their parts and components or ammunition:

   (i) From parts and components illicitly trafficked;

   (ii) Without a licence or authorization from a competent authority of the State Party where the manufacture or assembly takes place; or

   (iii) Without marking the firearms at the time of manufacture, in accordance with article 8 of this Protocol;

Licensing or authorization of the manufacture of parts and components shall be in accordance with domestic law;

(e) "Illicit trafficking" shall mean the import, export, acquisition, sale, delivery, movement or transfer of firearms, their parts and components and ammunition from or across the territory of one State Party to that of another State Party if any one of the States Parties concerned does not authorize it in accordance with the terms of this Protocol or if the firearms are not marked in accordance with article 8 of this Protocol;

(f) "Tracing" shall mean the systematic tracking of firearms and, where possible, their parts and components and ammunition from manufacturer to purchaser for the purpose of assisting the competent authorities of States Parties in detecting, investigating and analysing illicit manufacturing and illicit trafficking.

Article 4 Scope of application

1. This Protocol shall apply, except as otherwise stated herein, to the prevention of illicit manufacturing of and trafficking in firearms, their parts and components and ammunition and to the investigation and prosecution of offences established in accordance with article 5 of this Protocol where those offences are transnational in nature and involve an organized criminal group.

2. This Protocol shall not apply to state-to-state transactions or to state transfers in cases where the application of the Protocol would prejudice the right of a State Party to take action in the interest of national security consistent with the Charter of the United Nations.

Article 5 Criminalization

1. Each State Party shall adopt such legislative and other measures as may be necessary to establish as criminal offences the following conduct, when committed intentionally:

   (a) Illicit manufacturing of firearms, their parts and components and ammunition;

   (b) Illicit trafficking in firearms, their parts and components and ammunition;

   (c) Falsifying or illicitly obliterating, removing or altering the marking(s) on firearms required by article 8 of this Protocol.

2. Each State Party shall also adopt such legislative and other measures as may be necessary to establish as criminal offences the following conduct:

   (a) Subject to the basic concepts of its legal system, attempting to commit or participating as an accomplice in an offence established in accordance with paragraph 1 of this article; and

   (b) Organizing, directing, aiding, abetting, facilitating or counselling the commission of an offence established in accordance with paragraph 1 of this article.

DOCUMENT 44

European Convention on Cybercrime 2001
ETS No 185; 41 ILM 282 (2002)

The Convention was adopted under the auspices of the Council of Europe on 23 November 2001 and entered into force on 21 July 2004.

There are nine parties, although none of the major powers is a party.

In 1997, a group of Council of Europe experts began four years of work to establish a convention to address crimes committed via the Internet, particularly copyright infringements, computer-related fraud, child pornography and breaches of network security. The resulting Convention represents the first international instrument relating to cybercrime. The central premise of the Convention is that 'an effective fight against cybercrime requires increased, rapid and well-functioning international co-operation in criminal matters' (preamble).

Chapter II of the Convention addresses the acts to be criminalised in the domestic law of each State party, divided into four classes: offences against confidentiality and data integrity (Articles 2–6), computer-related offences of forgery and fraud (Articles 7–8), computer-related offences of child pornography (Article 9), offences related to copyright infringement (Article 10). The essence of the Convention being co-operation, there is only an implicit obligation on each State party to prosecute the proscribed acts; there is no explicit obligation, absent prosecution, to extradite. As to extradition, the Convention's offences are deemed to be included in existing extradition treaties and are to be included in future extradition treaties (Article 24(2)); and the Convention itself may be used as the basis of extradition in the absence of an extradition treaty (Article 24(3)). However, where a request for extradition is refused on the sole ground of the nationality of the offender, there is a duty to prosecute (Article 24(5)) The Convention contains extensive obligations of co-operation among the parties in the prevention, investigation, prosecution and punishment of the proscribed offences (see eg Articles 14 and 25). In any proceedings under the Convention, human rights are to be protected (Article 15).

See the Additional Protocol to the Convention on Cybercrime concerning the Criminalisation of Acts or a Racist and Xenophobic Nature through Computer Systems 2003 **(Document 45)**.

The member States of the Council of Europe and the other States signatory hereto,

Considering that the aim of the Council of Europe is to achieve a greater unity between its members;

Recognising the value of fostering co-operation with the other States parties to this Convention;

Convinced of the need to pursue, as a matter of priority, a common criminal policy aimed at the protection of society against cybercrime, *inter alia*, by adopting appropriate legislation and fostering international co-operation;

Conscious of the profound changes brought about by the digitalisation, convergence and continuing globalisation of computer networks;

Concerned at the risk that computer networks and electronic information may also be used for committing criminal offences and that evidence relating to such offences may be stored and transferred by these networks;

Recognising the need for co-operation between States and private industry in combating cybercrime and the need to protect legitimate interests in the use and development of information technologies;

Believing that an effective fight against cybercrime requires increased, rapid and well-functioning international co-operation in criminal matters;

Convinced that the present Convention is necessary to deter actions directed against the confidentiality, integrity and availability of computer systems, networks and computer data, as well as the misuse of such systems, networks and data, by providing for the criminalisation of such conduct, as described in this Convention, and the adoption of powers sufficient for effectively combating such criminal offences, by facilitating the detection, investigation and prosecution of such criminal offences at both the domestic and international level, and by providing arrangements for fast and reliable international co-operation;

Mindful of the need to ensure a proper balance between the interests of law enforcement and respect for fundamental human rights, as enshrined in the 1950 Council of Europe Convention for the Protection of Human Rights and Fundamental Freedoms, the 1966 United Nations International Covenant on Civil and Political Rights, as well as other applicable international human rights treaties, which reaffirm the right of everyone to hold opinions without interference, as well as the right to freedom of expression, including the freedom to seek, receive, and impart information and ideas of all kinds, regardless of frontiers, and the rights concerning the respect for privacy;

Mindful also of the protection of personal data, as conferred e.g. by the 1981 Council of Europe Convention for the Protection of Individuals with Regard to Automatic Processing of Personal Data;

Considering the 1989 United Nations Convention on the Rights of the Child and the 1999 International Labour Organization Worst Forms of Child Labour Convention;

Taking into account the existing Council of Europe conventions on co-operation in the penal field as well as similar treaties which exist between Council of Europe member States and other States and stressing that the present Convention is intended to supplement those conventions in order to make criminal investigations and proceedings concerning criminal offences related to computer systems and data more effective and to enable the collection of evidence in electronic form of a criminal offence;

Welcoming recent developments which further advance international understanding and co-operation in combating cybercrimes, including actions of the United Nations, the OECD, the European Union and the G8;

Recalling Recommendation No R (85) 10 concerning the practical application of the European Convention on Mutual Assistance in Criminal Matters in respect of letters rogatory for the interception of telecommunications, Recommendation No R (88) 2 on piracy in the field of copyright and neighbouring rights, Recommendation No R (87) 15 regulating the use of personal data in the police sector, Recommendation No R (95) 4 on the protection of personal data in the area of telecommunication services, with particular reference to telephone services as well as Recommendation No R (89) 9 on computer-related crime providing guidelines for national legislatures concerning the definition of certain computer crimes and Recommendation No R (95) 13 concerning problems of criminal procedural law connected with Information Technology;

Having regard to Resolution No 1 adopted by the European Ministers of Justice at their 21st Conference (Prague, June 1997), which recommended the Committee of Ministers to support the work carried out by the European Committee on Crime Problems (CDPC) on cybercrime in order to bring domestic criminal law provisions closer to each other and enable the use of effective means of investigation concerning such offences, as well as to Resolution No 3, adopted at the 23rd Conference of the European Ministers of Justice (London, June 2000), which encouraged the negotiating parties to pursue their efforts with a view to finding appropriate solutions so as to enable the largest possible number of States to become parties to the Convention and acknowledged the need for a swift and efficient system of international co-operation, which duly takes into account the specific requirements of the fight against cybercrime;

Having also regard to the Action Plan adopted by the Heads of State and Government of the Council of Europe, on the occasion of their Second Summit (Strasbourg, 10–11 October 1997), to seek common responses to the development of the new information technologies, based on the standards and values of the Council of Europe;

Have agreed as follows:

Article 1 Definitions

For the purposes of this Convention:

(a) "computer system" means any device or a group of inter-connected or related devices, one or more of which, pursuant to a program, performs automatic processing of data;

(b) "computer data" means any representation of facts, information or concepts in a form suitable for processing in a computer system, including a program suitable to cause a computer system to perform a function;

(c) "service provider" means:

  (i) any public or private entity that provides to users of its service the ability to communicate by means of a computer system, and

  (ii) any other entity that processes or stores computer data on behalf of such communication service or users of such service;

(d) "traffic data" means any computer data relating to a communication by means of a computer system, generated by a computer system that formed a part in the chain of communication, indicating the communication's origin, destination, route, time, date, size, duration, or type of underlying service.

Article 2 Illegal access

Each Party shall adopt such legislative and other measures as may be necessary to establish as criminal offences under its domestic law, when committed intentionally, the access to the whole or any part of a computer system without right. A Party may require that the offence be committed by infringing security measures, with the intent of obtaining computer data or other dishonest intent, or in relation to a computer system that is connected to another computer system.

Article 3 Illegal interception

Each Party shall adopt such legislative and other measures as may be necessary to establish as criminal offences under its domestic law, when committed intentionally, the interception without right, made by technical means, of non-public transmissions of computer data to, from or within a computer system, including electromagnetic emissions from a computer system carrying such computer data. A Party may require that the offence be committed with dishonest intent, or in relation to a computer system that is connected to another computer system.

Article 4 Data interference

1. Each Party shall adopt such legislative and other measures as may be necessary to establish as criminal offences under its domestic law, when committed intentionally, the damaging, deletion, deterioration, alteration or suppression of computer data without right.

2. A Party may reserve the right to require that the conduct described in paragraph 1 result in serious harm.

Article 5 System interference

Each Party shall adopt such legislative and other measures as may be necessary to establish as criminal offences under its domestic law, when committed intentionally, the serious hindering without right of the functioning of a computer system by inputting, transmitting, damaging, deleting, deteriorating, altering or suppressing computer data.

Article 6 Misuse of devices

1. Each Party shall adopt such legislative and other measures as may be necessary to establish as criminal offences under its domestic law, when committed intentionally and without right:

   (a) the production, sale, procurement for use, import, distribution or otherwise making available of:

      (i) a device, including a computer program, designed or adapted primarily for the purpose of committing any of the offences established in accordance with Articles 2–5;

      (ii) a computer password, access code, or similar data by which the whole or any part of a computer system is capable of being accessed with intent that it be used for the purpose of committing any of the offences established in Articles 2–5; and

   (b) the possession of an item referred to in paragraphs (a)(1) or (2) above, with intent that it be used for the purpose of committing any of the offences established in Articles 2–5. A Party may require by law that a number of such items be possessed before criminal liability attaches.

2. This article shall not be interpreted as imposing criminal liability where the production, sale, procurement for use, import, distribution or otherwise making available or possession referred to in paragraph 1 of this Article is not for the purpose of committing an offence established in accordance with articles 2 through 5 of this Convention, such as for the authorised testing or protection of a computer system.

3. Each Party may reserve the right not to apply paragraph 1 of this Article, provided that the reservation does not concern the sale, distribution or otherwise making available of the items referred to in paragraph 1(a)(2).

Article 7 Computer-related forgery

Each Party shall adopt such legislative and other measures as may be necessary to establish as criminal offences under its domestic law, when committed intentionally and without right, the input, alteration, deletion, or suppression of computer data, resulting in inauthentic data with the intent that it be considered or acted upon for legal purposes as if it were authentic, regardless whether or not the data is directly readable and intelligible. A Party may require an intent to defraud, or similar dishonest intent, before criminal liability attaches.

Article 8 Computer-related fraud

Each Party shall adopt such legislative and other measures as may be necessary to establish as criminal offences under its domestic law, when committed intentionally and without right, the causing of a loss of property to another by:

(a) any input, alteration, deletion or suppression of computer data,

(b) any interference with the functioning of a computer system, with fraudulent or dishonest intent of procuring, without right, an economic benefit for oneself or for another.

Article 9 Offences related to child pornography

1. Each Party shall adopt such legislative and other measures as may be necessary to establish as criminal offences under its domestic law, when committed intentionally and without right, the following conduct:

   (a) producing child pornography for the purpose of its distribution through a computer system;

   (b) offering or making available child pornography through a computer system;

   (c) distributing or transmitting child pornography through a computer system;

   (d) procuring child pornography through a computer system for oneself or for another;

(e) possessing child pornography in a computer system or on a computer-data storage medium.

2. For the purpose of paragraph 1 above "child pornography" shall include pornographic material that visually depicts:

   (a) a minor engaged in sexually explicit conduct;

   (b) a person appearing to be a minor engaged in sexually explicit conduct;

   (c) realistic images representing a minor engaged in sexually explicit conduct.

3. For the purpose of paragraph 2 above, the term "minor" shall include all persons under 18 years of age. A Party may, however, require a lower age-limit, which shall be not less than 16 years.

4. Each Party may reserve the right not to apply, in whole or in part, paragraph 1(d) and 1(e), and 2(b) and 2(c).

Article 10 Offences related to infringements of copyright and related rights

1. Each Party shall adopt such legislative and other measures as may be necessary to establish as criminal offences under its domestic law the infringement of copyright, as defined under the law of that Party pursuant to the obligations it has undertaken under the Paris Act of 24 July 1971 of the Bern Convention for the Protection of Literary and Artistic Works, the Agreement on Trade-Related Aspects of Intellectual Property Rights and the WIPO Copyright Treaty, with the exception of any moral rights conferred by such Conventions, where such acts are committed wilfully, on a commercial scale and by means of a computer system.

2. Each Party shall adopt such legislative and other measures as may be necessary to establish as criminal offences under its domestic law the infringement of related rights, as defined under the law of that Party, pursuant to the obligations it has undertaken under the International Convention for the Protection of Performers, Producers of Phonograms and Broadcasting Organisations done in Rome (Rome Convention), the Agreement on Trade-Related Aspects of Intellectual Property Rights and the WIPO Performances and Phonograms Treaty, with the exception of any moral rights conferred by such Conventions, where such acts are committed wilfully, on a commercial scale and by means of a computer system.

3. A Party may reserve the right not to impose criminal liability under paragraphs 1 and 2 of this article in limited circumstances, provided that other effective remedies are available and that such reservation does not derogate from the Party's international obligations set forth in the international instruments referred to in paragraphs 1 and 2 of this article.

Article 11 Attempt and aiding or abetting

1. Each Party shall adopt such legislative and other measures as may be necessary to establish as criminal offences under its domestic law, when committed intentionally, aiding or abetting the commission of any of the offences established in accordance with Articles 2–10 of the present Convention with intent that such offence be committed.

2. Each Party shall adopt such legislative and other measures as may be necessary to establish as criminal offences under its domestic law, when committed intentionally, an attempt to commit any of the offences established in accordance with Articles 3 through 5, 7, 8, 9.1(a) and 9.1(c) of this Convention.

3. Each Party may reserve the right not to apply, in whole or in part, paragraph 2 of this article.

Article 12 Corporate liability

1. Each Party shall adopt such legislative and other measures as may be necessary to ensure that a legal person can be held liable for a criminal offence established in accordance with this Convention, committed for its benefit by any natural person, acting either individually or as

part of an organ of the legal person, who has a leading position within the legal person, based on:

(a) a power of representation of the legal person;

(b) an authority to take decisions on behalf of the legal person;

(c) an authority to exercise control within the legal person.

2. Apart from the cases already provided for in paragraph 1, each Party shall take the measures necessary to ensure that a legal person can be held liable where the lack of supervision or control by a natural person referred to in paragraph 1 has made possible the commission of a criminal offence established in accordance with this Convention for the benefit of that legal person by a natural person acting under its authority.

3. Subject to the legal principles of the Party, the liability of a legal person may be criminal, civil or administrative.

4. Such liability shall be without prejudice to the criminal liability of the natural persons who have committed the offence.

Article 13 Sanctions and measures

1. Each Party shall adopt such legislative and other measures as may be necessary to ensure that the criminal offences established in accordance with Articles 2–11 are punishable by effective, proportionate and dissuasive sanctions, which include deprivation of liberty.

2. Each Party shall ensure that legal persons held liable in accordance with Article 12 shall be subject to effective, proportionate and dissuasive criminal or non-criminal sanctions or measures, including monetary sanctions.

Article 14 Scope of procedural provisions

1. Each Party shall adopt such legislative and other measures as may be necessary to establish the powers and procedures provided for in this Section for the purpose of specific criminal investigations or proceedings.

2. Except as specifically otherwise provided in Article 21, each Party shall apply the powers and procedures referred to in paragraph 1 to:

(a) the criminal offences established in accordance with articles 2–11 of this Convention;

(b) other criminal offences committed by means of a computer system; and

(c) the collection of evidence in electronic form of a criminal offence.

3. (a) Each Party may reserve the right to apply the measures referred to in Article 20 only to offences or categories of offences specified in the reservation, provided that the range of such offences or categories of offences is not more restricted than the range of offences to which it applies the measures referred to in Article 21. a. Each Party shall consider restricting such a reservation to enable the broadest application of the measure referred to in Article 20.

(b) Where a Party, due to limitations in its legislation in force at the time of the adoption of the present Convention, is not able to apply the measures referred to in Articles 20 and 21 to communications being transmitted within a computer system of a service provider, which system

(i) is being operated for the benefit of a closed group of users, and

(ii) does not employ public communications networks and is not connected with another computer system, whether public or private, that Party may reserve the right not to apply these measures to such communications. Each Party shall consider restricting such a reservation to enable the broadest application of the measures referred to in Articles 20 and 21.

Article 15 Conditions and safeguards

1. Each Party shall ensure that the establishment, implementation and application of the powers and procedures provided for in this Section are subject to conditions and safeguards provided for under its domestic law, which shall provide for the adequate protection of human rights and liberties, including rights arising pursuant to obligations it has undertaken under the 1950 Council of Europe Convention for the Protection of Human Rights and Fundamental Freedoms, the 1966 United Nations International Covenant on Civil and Political Rights, and other applicable international human rights instruments, and which shall incorporate the principle of proportionality.

2. Such conditions and safeguards shall, as appropriate in view of the nature of the power or procedure concerned, *inter alia*, include judicial or other independent supervision, grounds justifying application, and limitation on the scope and the duration of such power or procedure.

3. To the extent that it is consistent with the public interest, in particular the sound administration of justice, a Party shall consider the impact of the powers and procedures in this Section upon the rights, responsibilities and legitimate interests of third parties.

Article 22 Jurisdiction

1. Each Party shall adopt such legislative and other measures as may be necessary to establish jurisdiction over any offence established in accordance with Articles 2–11 of this Convention, when the offence is committed:

    (a) in its territory; or

    (b) on board a ship flying the flag of that Party; or

    (c) on board an aircraft registered under the laws of that Party; or

    (d) by one of its nationals, if the offence is punishable under criminal law where it was committed or if the offence is committed outside the territorial jurisdiction of any State.

2. Each Party may reserve the right not to apply or to apply only in specific cases or conditions the jurisdiction rules laid down in paragraphs 1(b)–(d) of this article or any part thereof.

3. Each Party shall adopt such measures as may be necessary to establish jurisdiction over the offences referred to in Article 24, paragraph 1 of this Convention, in cases where an alleged offender is present in its territory and it does not extradite him/her to another Party, solely on the basis of his/her nationality, after a request for extradition.

4. This Convention does not exclude any criminal jurisdiction exercised in accordance with domestic law.

5. When more than one Party claims jurisdiction over an alleged offence established in accordance with this Convention, the Parties involved shall, where appropriate, consult with a view to determining the most appropriate jurisdiction for prosecution.

Article 23 General principles relating to international co-operation

The Parties shall co-operate with each other, in accordance with the provisions of this chapter, and through application of relevant international instruments on international co-operation in criminal matters, arrangements agreed on the basis of uniform or reciprocal legislation, and domestic laws, to the widest extent possible for the purposes of investigations or proceedings concerning criminal offences related to computer systems and data, or for the collection of evidence in electronic form of a criminal offence.

Article 24 Extradition

1. (a) This article applies to extradition between Parties for the criminal offences established in accordance with Articles 2–11 of this Convention, provided that they are punishable under the laws of both Parties concerned by deprivation of liberty for a maximum period of at least one year, or by a more severe penalty.

(b) Where a different minimum penalty is to be applied under an arrangement agreed on the basis of uniform or reciprocal legislation or an extradition treaty, including the European Convention on Extradition (ETS No 24), applicable between two or more parties, the minimum penalty provided for under such arrangement or treaty shall apply.

2. The criminal offences described in paragraph 1 of this Article shall be deemed to be included as extraditable offences in any extradition treaty existing between or among the Parties. The Parties undertake to include such offences as extraditable offences in any extradition treaty to be concluded between or among them.

3. If a Party that makes extradition conditional on the existence of a treaty receives a request for extradition from another Party with which it does not have an extradition treaty, it may consider this Convention as the legal basis for extradition with respect to any criminal offence referred to in paragraph 1 of this article.

4. Parties that do not make extradition conditional on the existence of a treaty shall recognise the criminal offences referred to in paragraph 1 of this article as extraditable offences between themselves.

5. Extradition shall be subject to the conditions provided for by the law of the requested Party or by applicable extradition treaties, including the grounds on which the requested Party may refuse extradition.

6. If extradition for a criminal offence referred to in paragraph 1 of this article is refused solely on the basis of the nationality of the person sought, or because the requested Party deems that it has jurisdiction over the offence, the requested Party shall submit the case at the request of the requesting Party to its competent authorities for the purpose of prosecution and shall report the final outcome to the requesting Party in due course. Those authorities shall take their decision and conduct their investigations and proceedings in the same manner as in the case of any other offence of a comparable nature under the law of that Party.

7. (a) Each Party shall, at the time of signature or when depositing its instrument of ratification, acceptance, approval or accession, communicate to the Secretary General of the Council of Europe the name and addresses of each authority responsible for the making to or receipt of a request for extradition or provisional arrest in the absence of a treaty.

(b) The Secretary General of the Council of Europe shall set up and keep updated a register of authorities so designated by the Parties. Each Party shall ensure that the details held on the register are correct at all times.

Article 25 General principles relating to mutual assistance

1. The Parties shall afford one another mutual assistance to the widest extent possible for the purpose of investigations or proceedings concerning criminal offences related to computer systems and data, or for the collection of evidence in electronic form of a criminal offence.

2. Each Party shall also adopt such legislative and other measures as may be necessary to carry out the obligations set forth in Articles 27–35.

3. Each Party may, in urgent circumstances, make requests for mutual assistance or communications related thereto by expedited means of communications, including fax or e-mail, to the extent that such means provide appropriate levels of security and authentication (including the use of encryption, where necessary), with formal confirmation to follow, where required by the requested Party. The requested Party shall accept and respond to the request by any such expedited means of communication.

4. Except as otherwise specifically provided in Articles in this Chapter, mutual assistance shall be subject to the conditions provided for by the law of the requested Party or by applicable mutual assistance treaties, including the grounds on which the requested Party may refuse co-operation. The requested Party shall not exercise the right to refuse mutual assistance in relation to the offences referred to in Articles 2 to 11 solely on the ground that the request concerns an offence which it considers a fiscal offence.

5. Where, in accordance with the provisions of this chapter, the requested Party is permitted to make mutual assistance conditional upon the existence of dual criminality, that condition shall be deemed fulfilled, irrespective of whether its laws place the offence within the same category of offence or denominates the offence by the same terminology as the requesting Party, if the conduct underlying the offence for which assistance is sought is a criminal offence under its laws.

DOCUMENT 45

Additional Protocol to the Convention on Cybercrime concerning the Criminalisation of Acts of a Racist and Xenophobic Nature through Computer Systems 2003
CETS No 189

This Protocol was adopted on 28 January 2003 and is not in force.

There are only two parties to the Protocol.

During the drafting of the European Convention on Cybercrime of 2003 (**Document 44**), *it was recognised that an additional protocol was necessary to address racist and xenophobic acts disseminated through computer systems. This Protocol requires each State party to criminalise a range of acts of a racist or xenophobic nature (Articles 3–7). Thereafter, it relies on the European Convention on Cybercrime for measures of implementation, enforcement and co-operation (Article 8).*

The member States of the Council of Europe and the other States Parties to the Convention on Cybercrime, opened for signature in Budapest on 23 November 2001, signatory hereto;

Considering that the aim of the Council of Europe is to achieve a greater unity between its members;

Recalling that all human beings are born free and equal in dignity and rights;

Stressing the need to secure a full and effective implementation of all human rights without any discrimination or distinction, as enshrined in European and other international instruments;

Convinced that acts of a racist and xenophobic nature constitute a violation of human rights and a threat to the rule of law and democratic stability;

Considering that national and international law need to provide adequate legal responses to propaganda of a racist and xenophobic nature committed through computer systems;

Aware of the fact that propaganda to such acts is often subject to criminalisation in national legislation;

Having regard to the Convention on Cybercrime, which provides for modern and flexible means of international co-operation and convinced of the need to harmonise substantive law provisions concerning the fight against racist and xenophobic propaganda;

Aware that computer systems offer an unprecedented means of facilitating freedom of expression and communication around the globe;

Recognising that freedom of expression constitutes one of the essential foundations of a democratic society, and is one of the basic conditions for its progress and for the development of every human being;

Concerned, however, by the risk of misuse or abuse of such computer systems to disseminate racist and xenophobic propaganda;

Mindful of the need to ensure a proper balance between freedom of expression and an effective fight against acts of a racist and xenophobic nature;

Recognising that this Protocol is not intended to affect established principles relating to freedom of expression in national legal systems;

Taking into account the relevant international legal instruments in this field, and in particular the Convention for the Protection of Human Rights and Fundamental Freedoms and its Protocol No 12 concerning the general prohibition of discrimination, the existing Council of Europe conventions on co-operation in the penal field, in particular the Convention on Cybercrime, the United Nations International Convention on the Elimination of All Forms of Racial Discrimination of 21 December 1965, the European Union Joint Action of 15 July 1996 adopted by the Council on the basis of Article K.3 of the Treaty on European Union, concerning action to combat racism and xenophobia;

Welcoming the recent developments which further advance international understanding and co-operation in combating cybercrime and racism and xenophobia;

Having regard to the Action Plan adopted by the Heads of State and Government of the Council of Europe on the occasion of their Second Summit (Strasbourg, 10–11 October 1997) to seek common responses to the developments of the new technologies based on the standards and values of the Council of Europe;

Have agreed as follows:

Article 1 Purpose
The purpose of this Protocol is to supplement, as between the Parties to the Protocol, the provisions of the Convention on Cybercrime, opened for signature in Budapest on 23 November 2001 (hereinafter referred to as "the Convention"), as regards the criminalisation of acts of a racist and xenophobic nature committed through computer systems.

Article 2 Definition
1.   For the purposes of this Protocol:

   "racist and xenophobic material" means any written material, any image or any other representation of ideas or theories, which advocates, promotes or incites hatred, discrimination or violence, against any individual or group of individuals, based on race, colour, descent or national or ethnic origin, as well as religion if used as a pretext for any of these factors.

2.   The terms and expressions used in this Protocol shall be interpreted in the same manner as they are interpreted under the Convention.

Article 3 Dissemination of racist and xenophobic material through computer systems
1.   Each Party shall adopt such legislative and other measures as may be necessary to establish as criminal offences under its domestic law, when committed intentionally and without right, the following conduct: distributing, or otherwise making available, racist and xenophobic material to the public through a computer system.

2.   A Party may reserve the right not to attach criminal liability to conduct as defined by paragraph 1 of this article, where the material, as defined in Article 2, paragraph 1, advocates, promotes or incites discrimination that is not associated with hatred or violence, provided that other effective remedies are available.

3.   Notwithstanding paragraph 2 of this article, a Party may reserve the right not to apply paragraph 1 to those cases of discrimination for which, due to established principles in its national legal system concerning freedom of expression, it cannot provide for effective remedies as referred to in the said paragraph 2.

Article 4 Racist and xenophobic motivated threat

Each Party shall adopt such legislative and other measures as may be necessary to establish as criminal offences under its domestic law, when committed intentionally and without right, the following conduct: threatening, through a computer system, with the commission of a serious criminal offence as defined under its domestic law, (i) persons for the reason that they belong to a group, distinguished by race, colour, descent or national or ethnic origin, as well as religion, if used as a pretext for any of these factors, or (ii) a group of persons which is distinguished by any of these characteristics.

Article 5 Racist and xenophobic motivated insult

1. Each Party shall adopt such legislative and other measures as may be necessary to establish as criminal offences under its domestic law, when committed intentionally and without right, the following conduct: insulting publicly, through a computer system, (i) persons for the reason that they belong to a group distinguished by race, colour, descent or national or ethnic origin, as well as religion, if used as a pretext for any of these factors; or (ii) a group of persons which is distinguished by any of these characteristics.

2. A Party may either:

    (a) require that the offence referred to in paragraph 1 of this article has the effect that the person or group of persons referred to in paragraph 1 is exposed to hatred, contempt or ridicule; or

    (b) reserve the right not to apply, in whole or in part, paragraph 1 of this article.

Article 6 Denial, gross minimisation, approval or justification of genocide or crimes against humanity

1. Each Party shall adopt such legislative measures as may be necessary to establish the following conduct as criminal offences under its domestic law, when committed intentionally and without right: distributing or otherwise making available, through a computer system to the public, material which denies, grossly minimises, approves or justifies acts constituting genocide or crimes against humanity, as defined by international law and recognised as such by final and binding decisions of the International Military Tribunal, established by the London Agreement of 8 August 1945, or of any other international court established by relevant international instruments and whose jurisdiction is recognised by that Party.

2. A Party may either:

    (a) require that the denial or the gross minimisation referred to in paragraph 1 of this article is committed with the intent to incite hatred, discrimination or violence against any individual or group of individuals, based on race, colour, descent or national or ethnic origin, as well as religion if used as a pretext for any of these factors, or otherwise;

    (b) reserve the right not to apply, in whole or in part, paragraph 1 of this article.

Article 7 Aiding and abetting

Each Party shall adopt such legislative and other measures as may be necessary to establish as criminal offences under its domestic law, when committed intentionally and without right, aiding or abetting the commission of any of the offences established in accordance with this Protocol, with intent that such offence be committed.

Article 8 Relations between the Convention and this Protocol

1. Articles 1, 12, 13, 22, 41, 44, 45 and 46 of the Convention shall apply, *mutatis mutandis*, to this Protocol.

2. The Parties shall extend the scope of application of the measures defined in Articles 14 to 21 and Articles 23 to 35 of the Convention, to Articles 2 to 7 of this Protocol.

DOCUMENT 46

UN Convention Against Corruption 2003
UN Doc A/58/422; 43 ILM 37 (2004)

This Convention was adopted on 31 October 2003 as an annex to General Assembly Resolution 58/4. It is not in force.

There are nine parties. None of the major powers is a party.

In Resolution 55/61 of 4 December 2000, the General Assembly recognised that it was desirable to adopt a convention dedicated to the eradication of corruption, separate from the Convention Against Transnational Organized Crime of 2000 **(Document 40)**, *and to that end established an Ad Hoc Committee to elaborate the Convention. The aim of the Convention is to combat corruption, to improve integrity and accountability and to promote international co-operation (Article 2).*

The Convention requires each State party to criminalise the offences specified in Articles 15–27, punishable by sanctions that recognise their gravity (Article 30(1)). Each party is to assert jurisdiction over these crimes committed in its territory or on it ships or aircraft (Article 42(1)). Additionally, a party may extend its jurisdiction to crimes committed by or against its nationals or committed abroad with the intention of being committed within its territory (Article 42(2)). The Convention, through Article 30(3), restricts the discretion as to the prosecution of any offender; and there is a duty to prosecute where a request for extradition is declined on the sole ground that the offender is one of its nationals (Article 44(11)). As to extradition, the Convention's offences are deemed to be included in existing extradition treaties and are to be included in future extradition treaties (Article 44(4)); and the Convention itself may be used as the basis of extradition in the absence of an extradition treaty (Article 44(5)). The Convention's offences are not to be regarded as fiscal offences for the purpose of extradition (Article 44(16)), although there may be no extradition where the purpose is to prosecute or punish a person on account of his race, religion, nationality, ethnic origin or political opinion (Article 44(15). The Convention provides for fair treatment in any proceedings (Article 44(14); see also Article 30(9)). The Convention contains extensive obligations of cooperation among the parties in the prevention, investigation, prosecution and punishment of the proscribed offences (see eg Article 43).

The States Parties to this Convention,

Concerned about the seriousness of problems and threats posed by corruption to the stability and security of societies, undermining the institutions and values of democracy, ethical values and justice and jeopardizing sustainable development and the rule of law,

Concerned also about the links between corruption and other forms of crime, in particular organized crime and economic crime, including money-laundering,

Concerned further about cases of corruption that involve vast quantities of assets, which may constitute a substantial proportion of the resources of States, and that threaten the political stability and sustainable development of those States,

Convinced that corruption is no longer a local matter but a transnational phenomenon that affects all societies and economies, making international cooperation to prevent and control it essential,

Convinced also that a comprehensive and multidisciplinary approach is required to prevent and combat corruption effectively,

Convinced further that the availability of technical assistance can play an important role in enhancing the ability of States, including by strengthening capacity and by institution-building, to prevent and combat corruption effectively,

Convinced that the illicit acquisition of personal wealth can be particularly damaging to democratic institutions, national economies and the rule of law,

Determined to prevent, detect and deter in a more effective manner international transfers of illicitly acquired assets and to strengthen international cooperation in asset recovery,

Acknowledging the fundamental principles of due process of law in criminal proceedings and in civil or administrative proceedings to adjudicate property rights,

Bearing in mind that the prevention and eradication of corruption is a responsibility of all States and that they must cooperate with one another, with the support and involvement of individuals and groups outside the public sector, such as civil society, non-governmental organizations and community-based organizations, if their efforts in this area are to be effective,

Bearing also in mind the principles of proper management of public affairs and public property, fairness, responsibility and equality before the law and the need to safeguard integrity and to foster a culture of rejection of corruption,

Commending the work of the Commission on Crime Prevention and Criminal Justice and the United Nations Office on Drugs and Crime in preventing and combating corruption,

Recalling the work carried out by other international and regional organizations in this field, including the activities of the African Union, the Council of Europe, the Customs Cooperation Council (also known as the World Customs Organization), the European Union, the League of Arab States, the Organisation for Economic Cooperation and Development and the Organization of American States,

Taking note with appreciation of multilateral instruments to prevent and combat corruption, including, *inter alia*, the Inter-American Convention against Corruption, adopted by the Organization of American States on 29 March 1996, the Convention on the Fight against Corruption involving Officials of the European Communities or Officials of Member States of the European Union, adopted by the Council of the European Union on 26 May 1997, the Convention on Combating Bribery of Foreign Public Officials in International Business Transactions, adopted by the Organisation for Economic Cooperation and Development on 21 November 1997, the Criminal Law Convention on Corruption, adopted by the Committee of Ministers of the Council of Europe on 27 January 1999, the Civil Law Convention on Corruption, adopted by the Committee of Ministers of the Council of Europe on 4 November 1999, and the African Union Convention on Preventing and Combating Corruption, adopted by the Heads of State and Government of the African Union on 12 July 2003,

Welcoming the entry into force on 29 September 2003 of the United Nations Convention against Transnational Organized Crime,

Have agreed as follows:

Article 1 Statement of purpose

The purposes of this Convention are:

(a) To promote and strengthen measures to prevent and combat corruption more efficiently and effectively;

(b) To promote, facilitate and support international cooperation and technical assistance in the prevention of and fight against corruption, including in asset recovery;

(c) To promote integrity, accountability and proper management of public affairs and public property.

Article 2 Use of terms

For the purposes of this Convention:

(a) "Public official" shall mean:

    (i) any person holding a legislative, executive, administrative or judicial office of a State Party, whether appointed or elected, whether permanent or temporary, whether paid or unpaid, irrespective of that person's seniority;

    (ii) any other person who performs a public function, including for a public agency or public enterprise, or provides a public service, as defined in the domestic law of the State Party and as applied in the pertinent area of law of that State Party;

    (iii) any other person defined as a "public official" in the domestic law of a State Party. However, for the purpose of some specific measures contained in chapter II of this Convention, "public official" may mean any person who performs a public function or provides a public service as defined in the domestic law of the State Party and as applied in the pertinent area of law of that State Party;

(b) "Foreign public official" shall mean any person holding a legislative, executive, administrative or judicial office of a foreign country, whether appointed or elected; and any person exercising a public function for a foreign country, including for a public agency or public enterprise;

(c) "Official of a public international organization" shall mean an international civil servant or any person who is authorized by such an organization to act on behalf of that organization;

(d) "Property" shall mean assets of every kind, whether corporeal or incorporeal, movable or immovable, tangible or intangible, and legal documents or instruments evidencing title to or interest in such assets;

(e) "Proceeds of crime" shall mean any property derived from or obtained, directly or indirectly, through the commission of an offence;

(f) "Freezing" or "seizure" shall mean temporarily prohibiting the transfer, conversion, disposition or movement of property or temporarily assuming custody or control of property on the basis of an order issued by a court or other competent authority;

(g) "Confiscation", which includes forfeiture where applicable, shall mean the permanent deprivation of property by order of a court or other competent authority;

(h) "Predicate offence" shall mean any offence as a result of which proceeds have been generated that may become the subject of an offence as defined in article 23 of this Convention;

(i) "Controlled delivery" shall mean the technique of allowing illicit or suspect consignments to pass out of, through or into the territory of one or more States, with the knowledge and under the supervision of their competent authorities, with a view to the investigation of an offence and the identification of persons involved in the commission of the offence.

Article 3 Scope of application

1. This Convention shall apply, in accordance with its terms, to the prevention, investigation and prosecution of corruption and to the freezing, seizure, confiscation and return of the proceeds of offences established in accordance with this Convention.

2. For the purposes of implementing this Convention, it shall not be necessary, except as otherwise stated herein, for the offences set forth in it to result in damage or harm to state property.

Article 4 Protection of sovereignty

1. States Parties shall carry out their obligations under this Convention in a manner consistent with the principles of sovereign equality and territorial integrity of States and that of non-intervention in the domestic affairs of other States.

2. Nothing in this Convention shall entitle a State Party to undertake in the territory of another State the exercise of jurisdiction and performance of functions that are reserved exclusively for the authorities of that other State by its domestic law.

Article 15 Bribery of national public officials

Each State Party shall adopt such legislative and other measures as may be necessary to establish as criminal offences, when committed intentionally:

(a) The promise, offering or giving, to a public official, directly or indirectly, of an undue advantage, for the official himself or herself or another person or entity, in order that the official act or refrain from acting in the exercise of his or her official duties;

(b) The solicitation or acceptance by a public official, directly or indirectly, of an undue advantage, for the official himself or herself or another person or entity, in order that the official act or refrain from acting in the exercise of his or her official duties.

Article 16 Bribery of foreign public officials and officials of public international organizations

1. Each State Party shall adopt such legislative and other measures as may be necessary to establish as a criminal offence, when committed intentionally, the promise, offering or giving to a foreign public official or an official of a public international organization, directly or indirectly, of an undue advantage, for the official himself or herself or another person or entity, in order that the official act or refrain from acting in the exercise of his or her official duties, in order to obtain or retain business or other undue advantage in relation to the conduct of international business.

2. Each State Party shall consider adopting such legislative and other measures as may be necessary to establish as a criminal offence, when committed intentionally, the solicitation or acceptance by a foreign public official or an official of a public international organization, directly or indirectly, of an undue advantage, for the official himself or herself or another person or entity, in order that the official act or refrain from acting in the exercise of his or her official duties.

Article 17 Embezzlement, misappropriation or other diversion of property by a public official

Each State Party shall adopt such legislative and other measures as may be necessary to establish as criminal offences, when committed intentionally, the embezzlement, misappropriation or other diversion by a public official for his or her benefit or for the benefit of another person or entity, of any property, public or private funds or securities or any other thing of value entrusted to the public official by virtue of his or her position.

Article 18 Trading in influence

Each State Party shall consider adopting such legislative and other measures as may be necessary to establish as criminal offences, when committed intentionally:

(a) The promise, offering or giving to a public official or any other person, directly or indirectly, of an undue advantage in order that the public official or the person abuse his or her real or supposed influence with a view to obtaining from an administration or public authority of the State Party an undue advantage for the original instigator of the act or for any other person;

(b) The solicitation or acceptance by a public official or any other person, directly or indirectly, of an undue advantage for himself or herself or for another person in order that the public official or the person abuse his or her real or supposed influence with a view to obtaining from an administration or public authority of the State Party an undue advantage.

Article 19 Abuse of functions

Each State Party shall consider adopting such legislative and other measures as may be necessary to establish as a criminal offence, when committed intentionally, the abuse of functions or position, that is, the performance of or failure to perform an act, in violation of laws, by a public official in the discharge of his or her functions, for the purpose of obtaining an undue advantage for himself or herself or for another person or entity.

Article 20 Illicit enrichment

Subject to its constitution and the fundamental principles of its legal system, each State Party shall consider adopting such legislative and other measures as may be necessary to establish as a criminal offence, when committed intentionally, illicit enrichment, that is, a significant increase in the assets of a public official that he or she cannot reasonably explain in relation to his or her lawful income.

Article 21 Bribery in the private sector

Each State Party shall consider adopting such legislative and other measures as may be necessary to establish as criminal offences, when committed intentionally in the course of economic, financial or commercial activities:

(a) The promise, offering or giving, directly or indirectly, of an undue advantage to any person who directs or works, in any capacity, for a private sector entity, for the person himself or herself or for another person, in order that he or she, in breach of his or her duties, act or refrain from acting;

(b) The solicitation or acceptance, directly or indirectly, of an undue advantage by any person who directs or works, in any capacity, for a private sector entity, for the person himself or herself or for another person, in order that he or she, in breach of his or her duties, act or refrain from acting.

Article 22 Embezzlement of property in the private sector

Each State Party shall consider adopting such legislative and other measures as may be necessary to establish as a criminal offence, when committed intentionally in the course of economic, financial or commercial activities, embezzlement by a person who directs or works, in any capacity, in a private sector entity of any property, private funds or securities or any other thing of value entrusted to him or her by virtue of his or her position.

Article 23 Laundering of proceeds of crime

1. Each State Party shall adopt, in accordance with fundamental principles of its domestic law, such legislative and other measures as may be necessary to establish as criminal offences, when committed intentionally:

   (a) (i) The conversion or transfer of property, knowing that such property is the proceeds of crime, for the purpose of concealing or disguising the illicit origin of the property or of helping any person who is involved in the commission of the predicate offence to evade the legal consequences of his or her action;

   (ii) The concealment or disguise of the true nature, source, location, disposition, movement or ownership of or rights with respect to property, knowing that such property is the proceeds of crime;

   (b) Subject to the basic concepts of its legal system:

   (i) The acquisition, possession or use of property, knowing, at the time of receipt, that such property is the proceeds of crime;

   (ii) Participation in, association with or conspiracy to commit, attempts to commit and aiding, abetting, facilitating and counselling the commission of any of the offences established in accordance with this article.

2. For purposes of implementing or applying paragraph 1 of this article:

   (a) Each State Party shall seek to apply paragraph 1 of this article to the widest range of predicate offences;

(b) Each State Party shall include as predicate offences at a minimum a comprehensive range of criminal offences established in accordance with this Convention;

(c) For the purposes of subparagraph (b) above, predicate offences shall include offences committed both within and outside the jurisdiction of the State Party in question. However, offences committed outside the jurisdiction of a State Party shall constitute predicate offences only when the relevant conduct is a criminal offence under the domestic law of the State where it is committed and would be a criminal offence under the domestic law of the State Party implementing or applying this article had it been committed there;

(d) Each State Party shall furnish copies of its laws that give effect to this article and of any subsequent changes to such laws or a description thereof to the Secretary-General of the United Nations;

(e) If required by fundamental principles of the domestic law of a State Party, it may be provided that the offences set forth in paragraph 1 of this article do not apply to the persons who committed the predicate offence.

Article 24 Concealment

Without prejudice to the provisions of article 23 of this Convention, each State Party shall consider adopting such legislative and other measures as may be necessary to establish as a criminal offence, when committed intentionally after the commission of any of the offences established in accordance with this Convention without having participated in such offences, the concealment or continued retention of property when the person involved knows that such property is the result of any of the offences established in accordance with this Convention.

Article 25 Obstruction of justice

Each State Party shall adopt such legislative and other measures as may be necessary to establish as criminal offences, when committed intentionally:

(a) The use of physical force, threats or intimidation or the promise, offering or giving of an undue advantage to induce false testimony or to interfere in the giving of testimony or the production of evidence in a proceeding in relation to the commission of offences established in accordance with this Convention;

(b) The use of physical force, threats or intimidation to interfere with the exercise of official duties by a justice or law enforcement official in relation to the commission of offences established in accordance with this Convention. Nothing in this subparagraph shall prejudice the right of States Parties to have legislation that protects other categories of public official.

Article 26 Liability of legal persons

1. Each State Party shall adopt such measures as may be necessary, consistent with its legal principles, to establish the liability of legal persons for participation in the offences established in accordance with this Convention.

2. Subject to the legal principles of the State Party, the liability of legal persons may be criminal, civil or administrative.

3. Such liability shall be without prejudice to the criminal liability of the natural persons who have committed the offences.

4. Each State Party shall, in particular, ensure that legal persons held liable in accordance with this article are subject to effective, proportionate and dissuasive criminal or non-criminal sanctions, including monetary sanctions.

Article 27 Participation and attempt

1. Each State Party shall adopt such legislative and other measures as may be necessary to establish as a criminal offence, in accordance with its domestic law, participation in any capacity

such as an accomplice, assistant or instigator in an offence established in accordance with this Convention.

2. Each State Party may adopt such legislative and other measures as may be necessary to establish as a criminal offence, in accordance with its domestic law, any attempt to commit an offence established in accordance with this Convention.

3. Each State Party may adopt such legislative and other measures as may be necessary to establish as a criminal offence, in accordance with its domestic law, the preparation for an offence established in accordance with this Convention.

Article 28 Knowledge, intent and purpose as elements of an offence

Knowledge, intent or purpose required as an element of an offence established in accordance with this Convention may be inferred from objective factual circumstances.

Article 29 Statute of limitations

Each State Party shall, where appropriate, establish under its domestic law a long statute of limitations period in which to commence proceedings for any offence established in accordance with this Convention and establish a longer statute of limitations period or provide for the suspension of the statute of limitations where the alleged offender has evaded the administration of justice.

Article 30 Prosecution, adjudication and sanctions

1. Each State Party shall make the commission of an offence established in accordance with this Convention liable to sanctions that take into account the gravity of that offence.

2. Each State Party shall take such measures as may be necessary to establish or maintain, in accordance with its legal system and constitutional principles, an appropriate balance between any immunities or jurisdictional privileges accorded to its public officials for the performance of their functions and the possibility, when necessary, of effectively investigating, prosecuting and adjudicating offences established in accordance with this Convention.

3. Each State Party shall endeavour to ensure that any discretionary legal powers under its domestic law relating to the prosecution of persons for offences established in accordance with this Convention are exercised to maximize the effectiveness of law enforcement measures in respect of those offences and with due regard to the need to deter the commission of such offences.

4. In the case of offences established in accordance with this Convention, each State Party shall take appropriate measures, in accordance with its domestic law and with due regard to the rights of the defence, to seek to ensure that conditions imposed in connection with decisions on release pending trial or appeal take into consideration the need to ensure the presence of the defendant at subsequent criminal proceedings.

5. Each State Party shall take into account the gravity of the offences concerned when considering the eventuality of early release or parole of persons convicted of such offences.

6. Each State Party, to the extent consistent with the fundamental principles of its legal system, shall consider establishing procedures through which a public official accused of an offence established in accordance with this Convention may, where appropriate, be removed, suspended or reassigned by the appropriate authority, bearing in mind respect for the principle of the presumption of innocence.

7. Where warranted by the gravity of the offence, each State Party, to the extent consistent with the fundamental principles of its legal system, shall consider establishing procedures for the disqualification, by court order or any other appropriate means, for a period of time determined by its domestic law, of persons convicted of offences established in accordance with this Convention from:

   (a) Holding public office; and

   (b) Holding office in an enterprise owned in whole or in part by the State.

8. Paragraph 1 of this article shall be without prejudice to the exercise of disciplinary powers by the competent authorities against civil servants.

9. Nothing contained in this Convention shall affect the principle that the description of the offences established in accordance with this Convention and of the applicable legal defences or other legal principles controlling the lawfulness of conduct is reserved to the domestic law of a State Party and that such offences shall be prosecuted and punished in accordance with that law.

10. States Parties shall endeavour to promote the reintegration into society of persons convicted of offences established in accordance with this Convention.

Article 42 Jurisdiction

1. Each State Party shall adopt such measures as may be necessary to establish its jurisdiction over the offences established in accordance with this Convention when:

    (a) The offence is committed in the territory of that State Party; or

    (b) The offence is committed on board a vessel that is flying the flag of that State Party or an aircraft that is registered under the laws of that State Party at the time that the offence is committed.

2. Subject to article 4 of this Convention, a State Party may also establish its jurisdiction over any such offence when:

    (a) The offence is committed against a national of that State Party; or

    (b) The offence is committed by a national of that State Party or a stateless person who has his or her habitual residence in its territory; or

    (c) The offence is one of those established in accordance with article 23, paragraph 1 (b) (ii), of this Convention and is committed outside its territory with a view to the commission of an offence established in accordance with article 23, paragraph 1 (a) (i) or (ii) or (b) (i), of this Convention within its territory; or

    (d) The offence is committed against the State Party.

3. For the purposes of article 44 of this Convention, each State Party shall take such measures as may be necessary to establish its jurisdiction over the offences established in accordance with this Convention when the alleged offender is present in its territory and it does not extradite such person solely on the ground that he or she is one of its nationals.

4. Each State Party may also take such measures as may be necessary to establish its jurisdiction over the offences established in accordance with this Convention when the alleged offender is present in its territory and it does not extradite him or her.

5. If a State Party exercising its jurisdiction under paragraph 1 or 2 of this article has been notified, or has otherwise learned, that any other States Parties are conducting an investigation, prosecution or judicial proceeding in respect of the same conduct, the competent authorities of those States Parties shall, as appropriate, consult one another with a view to coordinating their actions.

6. Without prejudice to norms of general international law, this Convention shall not exclude the exercise of any criminal jurisdiction established by a State Party in accordance with its domestic law.

Article 43 International cooperation

1. States Parties shall cooperate in criminal matters in accordance with articles 44 to 50 of this Convention. Where appropriate and consistent with their domestic legal system, States Parties shall consider assisting each other in investigations of and proceedings in civil and administrative matters relating to corruption.

2. In matters of international cooperation, whenever dual criminality is considered a requirement, it shall be deemed fulfilled irrespective of whether the laws of the requested State Party place

the offence within the same category of offence or denominate the offence by the same terminology as the requesting State Party, if the conduct underlying the offence for which assistance is sought is a criminal offence under the laws of both States Parties.

Article 44 Extradition

1. This article shall apply to the offences established in accordance with this Convention where the person who is the subject of the request for extradition is present in the territory of the requested State Party, provided that the offence for which extradition is sought is punishable under the domestic law of both the requesting State Party and the requested State Party.

2. Notwithstanding the provisions of paragraph 1 of this article, a State Party whose law so permits may grant the extradition of a person for any of the offences covered by this Convention that are not punishable under its own domestic law.

3. If the request for extradition includes several separate offences, at least one of which is extraditable under this article and some of which are not extraditable by reason of their period of imprisonment but are related to offences established in accordance with this Convention, the requested State Party may apply this article also in respect of those offences.

4. Each of the offences to which this article applies shall be deemed to be included as an extraditable offence in any extradition treaty existing between States Parties. States Parties undertake to include such offences as extraditable offences in every extradition treaty to be concluded between them. A State Party whose law so permits, in case it uses this Convention as the basis for extradition, shall not consider any of the offences established in accordance with this Convention to be a political offence.

5. If a State Party that makes extradition conditional on the existence of a treaty receives a request for extradition from another State Party with which it has no extradition treaty, it may consider this Convention the legal basis for extradition in respect of any offence to which this article applies.

6. A State Party that makes extradition conditional on the existence of a treaty shall:

    (a) At the time of deposit of its instrument of ratification, acceptance or approval of or accession to this Convention, inform the Secretary-General of the United Nations whether it will take this Convention as the legal basis for cooperation on extradition with other States Parties to this Convention; and

    (b) If it does not take this Convention as the legal basis for cooperation on extradition, seek, where appropriate, to conclude treaties on extradition with other States Parties to this Convention in order to implement this article.

7. States Parties that do not make extradition conditional on the existence of a treaty shall recognize offences to which this article applies as extraditable offences between themselves.

8. Extradition shall be subject to the conditions provided for by the domestic law of the requested State Party or by applicable extradition treaties, including, *inter alia*, conditions in relation to the minimum penalty requirement for extradition and the grounds upon which the requested State Party may refuse extradition.

9. States Parties shall, subject to their domestic law, endeavour to expedite extradition procedures and to simplify evidentiary requirements relating thereto in respect of any offence to which this article applies.

10. Subject to the provisions of its domestic law and its extradition treaties, the requested State Party may, upon being satisfied that the circumstances so warrant and are urgent and at the request of the requesting State Party, take a person whose extradition is sought and who is present in its territory into custody or take other appropriate measures to ensure his or her presence at extradition proceedings.

11. A State Party in whose territory an alleged offender is found, if it does not extradite such person in respect of an offence to which this article applies solely on the ground that he or she

is one of its nationals, shall, at the request of the State Party seeking extradition, be obliged to submit the case without undue delay to its competent authorities for the purpose of prosecution. Those authorities shall take their decision and conduct their proceedings in the same manner as in the case of any other offence of a grave nature under the domestic law of that State Party. The States Parties concerned shall cooperate with each other, in particular on procedural and evidentiary aspects, to ensure the efficiency of such prosecution.

12. Whenever a State Party is permitted under its domestic law to extradite or otherwise surrender one of its nationals only upon the condition that the person will be returned to that State Party to serve the sentence imposed as a result of the trial or proceedings for which the extradition or surrender of the person was sought and that State Party and the State Party seeking the extradition of the person agree with this option and other terms that they may deem appropriate, such conditional extradition or surrender shall be sufficient to discharge the obligation set forth in paragraph 11 of this article.

13. If extradition, sought for purposes of enforcing a sentence, is refused because the person sought is a national of the requested State Party, the requested State Party shall, if its domestic law so permits and in conformity with the requirements of such law, upon application of the requesting State Party, consider the enforcement of the sentence imposed under the domestic law of the requesting State Party or the remainder thereof.

14. Any person regarding whom proceedings are being carried out in connection with any of the offences to which this article applies shall be guaranteed fair treatment at all stages of the proceedings, including enjoyment of all the rights and guarantees provided by the domestic law of the State Party in the territory of which that person is present.

15. Nothing in this Convention shall be interpreted as imposing an obligation to extradite if the requested State Party has substantial grounds for believing that the request has been made for the purpose of prosecuting or punishing a person on account of that person's sex, race, religion, nationality, ethnic origin or political opinions or that compliance with the request would cause prejudice to that person's position for any one of these reasons.

16. States Parties may not refuse a request for extradition on the sole ground that the offence is also considered to involve fiscal matters.

17. Before refusing extradition, the requested State Party shall, where appropriate, consult with the requesting State Party to provide it with ample opportunity to present its opinions and to provide information relevant to its allegation.

18. States Parties shall seek to conclude bilateral and multilateral agreements or arrangements to carry out or to enhance the effectiveness of extradition.

Article 65 Implementation of the Convention

1. Each State Party shall take the necessary measures, including legislative and administrative measures, in accordance with fundamental principles of its domestic law, to ensure the implementation of its obligations under this Convention.

2. Each State Party may adopt more strict or severe measures than those provided for by this Convention for preventing and combating corruption.

PART II

PROCEDURAL INTERNATIONAL CRIMINAL LAW

TRIBUNALS

I. INTERNATIONAL

DOCUMENT 47

London Agreement for the Prosecution and Punishment of the Major War Criminals of the European Axis 1945
82 UNTS 279

The treaty was signed on 8 August 1945 and came into effect on the same day.

There were four parties to the agreement, namely France, the UK, the Union of Socialist Soviet Republics, and the USA.

The agreement established the International Military Tribunal for the prosecution of war criminals in Nuremberg, Germany. The Charter for the International Military Tribunal (**Document 48**) *was annexed to the agreement.*

Whereas the United Nations have from time to time made declarations of their intention that War Criminals shall be brought to justice;

And whereas the Moscow Declaration of the 30th October 1943 on German atrocities in Occupied Europe stated that those German Officers and men and members of the Nazi Party who have been responsible for or have taken a consenting part in atrocities and crimes will be sent back to the countries in which their abominable deeds were done in order that they may be judged and punished according to the laws of these liberated countries and of the free Governments that will be created therein;

And whereas this Declaration was stated to be without prejudice to the case of major criminals whose offenses have no particular geographical location and who will be punished by the joint decision of the Governments of the Allies;

Now therefore the Government of the United States of America, the Provisional Government of the French Republic, the Government of the United Kingdom of Great Britain and Northern Ireland and the Government of the Union of Soviet Socialist Republics (hereinafter called "the Signatories") acting in the interests of all the United Nations and by their representatives duly authorized thereto have concluded this Agreement.

Article 1
There shall be established after consultation with the Control Council for Germany an International Military Tribunal for the trial of war criminals whose offenses have no particular geographical location whether they be accused individually or in their capacity as members of the organizations or groups or in both capacities.

Article 2
The constitution, jurisdiction and functions of the International Military Tribunal shall be those set in the Charter annexed to this Agreement, which Charter shall form an integral part of this Agreement.

Article 3

Each of the Signatories shall take the necessary steps to make available for the investigation of the charges and trial the major war criminals detained by them who are to be tried by the International Military Tribunal. The Signatories shall also use their best endeavors to make available for investigation of the charges against and the trial before the International Military Tribunal such of the major war criminals as are not in the territories of any of the Signatories.

Article 4

Nothing in this Agreement shall prejudice the provisions established by the Moscow Declaration concerning the return of war criminals to the countries where they committed their crimes.

Article 5

Any Government of the United Nations may adhere to this Agreement by notice given through the diplomatic channel to the Government of the United Kingdom, who shall inform the other signatory and adhering Governments of each such adherence.

Article 6

Nothing in this Agreement shall prejudice the jurisdiction or the powers of any national or occupation court established or to be established in any allied territory or in Germany for the trial of war criminals.

Article 7

This Agreement shall come into force on the day of signature and shall remain in force for the period of one year and shall continue thereafter, subject to the right of any Signatory to give, through the diplomatic channel, one month's notice of intention to terminate it. Such termination shall not prejudice any proceedings already taken or any findings already made in pursuance of this Agreement.

DOCUMENT 48

Charter of the (Nuremberg) International Military Tribunal 1945
82 UNTS 279

The charter was annexed to the London Agreement for the Prosecution and Punishment of the Major War Criminals of the European Axis 1945 **(Document 47)** *which established the Nuremberg International Military Tribunal (IMT) and which was signed by France, the UK, the USSR and the USA. The charter came into effect on 8 August 1945.*

The IMT was established as a mechanism for the prosecution of major war criminals of the European Axis countries (Article 1). The jurisdiction of the IMT covered crimes against peace, war crimes and crimes against humanity for which there was to be individual criminal responsibility (Article 6). The charter was the first international instrument to establish a number of key principles of international criminal law, including individual criminal responsibility (Article 6), the non-applicability of official status as a bar to prosecution (Article 7) and the non-availability of the defence of superior orders (Article 8). More controversially, the charter also provided for trials in absentia (Article 12).

The IMT consisted of four judges, one appointed by each of the signatory States (Article 2). Prosecutions were led by one or more of the four chief prosecutors who were also appointed by each of the signatory States (Articles 14–15). The charter set out the procedure for the IMT, which was based on the Anglo-American adversarial system of criminal justice with minor qualifications in order to reflect the inquisitorial systems familiar to France and the Soviet Union (Articles 17–25). This allowed the IMT to play a more active role in the prosecutions than might otherwise have been the case in a truly adversarial system.

The IMT met in Berlin from 14 November 1945 to 1 October 1946. Twenty-four individuals were brought to trial before the IMT. The trial resulted in the prosecution of 19 defendants. Three defendants were acquitted and, of the remaining two defendants, one committed suicide and one was declared unfit to stand trial. Of the 19 defendants found guilty, 12 were sentenced to death, three were sentenced to life imprisonment and four were given lesser prison sentences. Lower-ranking defendants were tried through a system of national tribunals under the terms of Control Council Law No 10 (1945) **(Document 49)**.

See Trial of the Major War Criminals before the International Military Tribunal *(42 volumes, 1947–49).*

Article 1

In pursuance of the Agreement signed on the 8th day of August 1945 by the Government of the United States of America, the Provisional Government of the French Republic, the Government of the United Kingdom of Great Britain and Northern Ireland and the Government of the Union of Soviet Socialist Republics, there shall be established an International Military Tribunal (hereinafter called "the Tribunal") for the just and prompt trial and punishment of the major war criminals of the European Axis.

Article 2

The Tribunal shall consist of four members, each with an alternate. One member and one alternate shall be appointed by each of the Signatories. The alternates shall, so far as they are able, be present at all sessions of the Tribunal. In case of illness of any member of the Tribunal or his incapacity for some other reason to fulfill his functions, his alternate shall take his place.

Article 3

Neither the Tribunal, its members nor their alternates can be challenged by the prosecution, or by the Defendants or their Counsel. Each Signatory may replace its members of the Tribunal or his alternate for reasons of health or for other good reasons, except that no replacement may take place during a Trial, other than by an alternate.

Article 4

(a) The presence of all four members of the Tribunal or the alternate for any absent member shall be necessary to constitute the quorum.

(b) The members of the Tribunal shall, before any trial begins, agree among themselves upon the selection from their number of a President, and the President shall hold office during the trial, or as may otherwise be agreed by a vote of not less than three members. The principle of rotation of presidency for successive trials is agreed. If, however, a session of the Tribunal takes place on the territory of one of the four Signatories, the representative of that Signatory on the Tribunal shall preside.

(c) Save as aforesaid the Tribunal shall take decisions by a majority vote and in case the votes are evenly divided, the vote of the President shall be decisive: provided always that convictions and sentences shall only be imposed by affirmative votes of at least three members of the Tribunal.

Article 5

In case of need and depending on the number of the matters to be tried, other Tribunals may be set up; and the establishment, functions, and procedure of each Tribunal shall be identical, and shall be governed by this Charter.

Article 6

The Tribunal established by the Agreement referred to m Article 1 hereof for the trial and punishment of the major war criminals of the European Axis countries shall have the power to try and punish persons who, acting in the interests of the European Axis countries, whether as individuals or as members of organizations, committed any of the following crimes.

The following acts, or any of them, are crimes coming within the jurisdiction of the Tribunal for which there shall be individual responsibility:

(a) Crimes against Peace: namely, planning, preparation, initiation or waging of a war of aggression, or a war in violation of international treaties, agreements or assurances, or participation in a common plan or conspiracy for the accomplishment of any of the foregoing;

(b) War Crimes: namely, violations of the laws or customs of war. Such violations shall include, but not be limited to, murder, ill-treatment or deportation to slave labor or for any other purpose of civilian population of or in occupied territory, murder or ill-treatment of prisoners of war or persons on the seas, killing of hostages, plunder of public or private property, wanton destruction of cities, towns or villages, or devastation not justified by military necessity;

(c) Crimes against Humanity: namely, murder, extermination, enslavement, deportation, and other inhumane acts committed against any civilian population, before or during the war; or persecutions on political, racial or religious grounds in execution of or in connection with any crime within the jurisdiction of the Tribunal, whether or not in violation of the domestic law of the country where perpetrated.

Leaders, organizers, instigators and accomplices participating in the formulation or execution of a common plan or conspiracy to commit any of the foregoing crimes are responsible for all acts performed by any persons in execution of such plan.

Article 7

The official position of defendants, whether as Heads of State or responsible officials in Government Departments, shall not be considered as freeing them from responsibility or mitigating punishment.

Article 8

The fact that the Defendant acted pursuant to order of his Government or of a superior shall not free him from responsibility, but may be considered in mitigation of punishment if the Tribunal determines that justice so requires.

Article 9

At the trial of any individual member of any group or organization the Tribunal may declare (in connection with any act of which the individual may be convicted) that the group or organization of which the individual was a member was a criminal organization.

After the receipt of the Indictment the Tribunal shall give such notice as it thinks fit that the prosecution intends to ask the Tribunal to make such declaration and any member of the organization will be entitled to apply to the Tribunal for leave to be heard by the Tribunal upon the question of the criminal character of the organization. The Tribunal shall have power to allow or reject the application. If the application is allowed, the Tribunal may direct in what manner the applicants shall be represented and heard.

Article 10

In cases where a group or organization is declared criminal by the Tribunal, the competent national authority of any Signatory shall have the right to bring individuals to trial for membership therein before national, military or occupation courts. In any such case the criminal nature of the group or organization is considered proved and shall not be questioned.

Article 11

Any person convicted by the Tribunal may be charged before a national, military or occupation court, referred to in Article 10 of this Charter, with a crime other than of membership in a criminal group or organization and such court may, after convicting him, impose upon him punishment independent of and additional to the punishment imposed by the Tribunal for participation in the criminal activities of such group or organization.

Article 12

The Tribunal shall have the right to take proceedings against a person charged with crimes set out in Article 6 of this Charter in his absence, if he has not been found or if the Tribunal, for any reason, finds it necessary, in the interests of justice, to conduct the hearing in his absence.

Article 13

The Tribunal shall draw up rules for its procedure. These rules shall not be inconsistent with the provisions of this Charter.

Article 14

Each Signatory shall appoint a Chief Prosecutor for the investigation of the charges against and the prosecution of major war criminals.

The Chief Prosecutors shall act as a committee for the following purposes:

(a) to agree upon a plan of the individual work of each of the Chief Prosecutors and his staff,

(b) to settle the final designation of major war criminals to be tried by the Tribunal,

(c) to approve the Indictment and the documents to be submitted therewith,

(d) to lodge the Indictment and the accompany documents with the Tribunal,

(e) to draw up and recommend to the Tribunal for its approval draft rules of procedure, contemplated by Article 13 of this Charter. The Tribunal shall have the power to accept, with or without amendments, or to reject, the rules so recommended.

The Committee shall act in all the above matters by a majority vote and shall appoint a Chairman as may be convenient and in accordance with the principle of rotation: provided that if there is an equal division of vote concerning the designation of a Defendant to be tried by the Tribunal, or the crimes with which he shall be charged, that proposal will be adopted which was made by the party which proposed that the particular Defendant be tried, or the particular charges be preferred against him.

Article 15

The Chief Prosecutors shall individually, and acting in collaboration with one another, also undertake the following duties:

(a) investigation, collection and production before or at the Trial of all necessary evidence,

(b) the preparation of the Indictment for approval by the Committee in accordance with paragraph (c) of Article 14 hereof,

(c) the preliminary examination of all necessary witnesses and of all Defendants,

(d) to act as prosecutor at the Trial,

(e) to appoint representatives to carry out such duties as may be assigned them,

(f) to undertake such other matters as may appear necessary to them for the purposes of the preparation for and conduct of the Trial.

It is understood that no witness or Defendant detained by the Signatory shall be taken out of the possession of that Signatory without its assent.

Article 16

In order to ensure fair trial for the Defendants, the following procedure shall be followed:

(a) The Indictment shall include full particulars specifying in detail the charges against the Defendants. A copy of the Indictment and of all the documents lodged with the Indictment, translated into a language which he understands, shall be furnished to the Defendant at reasonable time before the Trial.

(b) During any preliminary examination or trial of a Defendant he will have the right to give any explanation relevant to the charges made against him.

(c) A preliminary examination of a Defendant and his Trial shall be conducted in, or translated into, a language which the Defendant understands.

(d) A Defendant shall have the right to conduct his own defense before the Tribunal or to have the assistance of Counsel.

(e) A Defendant shall have the right through himself or through his Counsel to present evidence at the Trial in support of his defense, and to cross-examine any witness called by the Prosecution.

Article 17

The Tribunal shall have the power:

(a) to summon witnesses to the Trial and to require their attendance and testimony and to put questions to them

(b) to interrogate any Defendant,

(c) to require the production of documents and other evidentiary material,

(d) to administer oaths to witnesses,

(e) to appoint officers for the carrying out of any task designated by the Tribunal including the power to have evidence taken on commission.

Article 18

The Tribunal shall:

(a) confine the Trial strictly to an expeditious hearing of the cases raised by the charges,

(b) take strict measures to prevent any action which will cause unreasonable delay, and rule out irrelevant issues and statements of any kind whatsoever,

(c) deal summarily with any contumacy, imposing appropriate punishment, including exclusion of any Defendant or his Counsel from some or all further proceedings, but without prejudice to the determination of the charges.

Article 19

The Tribunal shall not be bound by technical rules of evidence. It shall adopt and apply to the greatest possible extent expeditious and nontechnical procedure, and shall admit any evidence which it deems to be of probative value.

Article 20

The Tribunal may require to be informed of the nature of any evidence before it is entered so that it may rule upon the relevance thereof.

Article 21

The Tribunal shall not require proof of facts of common knowledge but shall take judicial notice thereof. It shall also take judicial notice of official governmental documents and reports of the United Nations, including the acts and documents of the committees set up in the various allied countries for the investigation of war crimes, and of records and findings of military or other Tribunals of any of the United Nations.

Article 22

The permanent seat of the Tribunal shall be in Berlin. The first meetings of the members of the Tribunal and of the Chief Prosecutors shall be held at Berlin in a place to be designated by the Control Council for Germany. The first trial shall be held at Nuremberg, and any subsequent trials shall be held at such places as the Tribunal may decide.

Article 23

One or more of the Chief Prosecutors may take part in the prosecution at each Trial. The function of any Chief Prosecutor may be discharged by him personally, or by any person or persons authorized by him.

The function of Counsel for a Defendant may be discharged at the Defendant's request by any Counsel professionally qualified to conduct cases before the Courts of his own country, or by any other person who may be specially authorized thereto by the Tribunal.

Article 24

The proceedings at the Trial shall take the following course:

(a) The Indictment shall be read in court.

(b) The Tribunal shall ask each Defendant whether he pleads "guilty" or "not guilty."

(c) The prosecution shall make an opening statement.

(d) The Tribunal shall ask the prosecution and the defense what evidence (if any) they wish to submit to the Tribunal, and the Tribunal shall rule upon the admissibility of any such evidence.

(e) The witnesses for the Prosecution shall be examined and after that the witnesses for the Defense. Thereafter such rebutting evidence as may be held by the Tribunal to be admissible shall be called by either the Prosecution or the Defense.

(f) The Tribunal may put any question to any witness and to any defendant, at any time.

(g) The Prosecution and the Defense shall interrogate and may cross examine any witnesses and any Defendant who gives testimony.

(h) The Defense shall address the court.

(i) The Prosecution shall address the court.

(j) Each Defendant may make a statement to the Tribunal.

(k) The Tribunal shall deliver judgment and pronounce sentence.

Article 25

All official documents shall be produced, and all court proceedings conducted, in English, French and Russian, and in the language of the Defendant. So much of the record and of the proceedings may also be translated into the language of any country in which the Tribunal is sitting, as the Tribunal considers desirable in the interests of the justice and public opinion.

Article 26

The judgment of the Tribunal as to the guilt or the innocence of any Defendant shall give the reasons on which it is based, and shall be final and not subject to review.

Article 27

The Tribunal shall have the right to impose upon a Defendant, on conviction, death or such other punishment as shall be determined by it to be just.

Article 28

In addition to any punishment imposed by it, the Tribunal shall have the right to deprive the convicted person of any stolen property and order its delivery to the Control Council for Germany.

Article 29

In case of guilt, sentences shall be carried out in accordance with the orders of the Control Council for Germany, which may at any time reduce or otherwise alter the sentences, but may not increase the severity thereof. If the Control Council for Germany, after any Defendant has been convicted and sentenced, discovers fresh evidence which, in its opinion, would found a fresh charge against him, the Council shall report accordingly to the Committee established under Article 14 hereof, for such action as they may consider proper, having regard to the interests of justice.

Article 30

The expenses of the Tribunal and of the Trials, shall be charged by the Signatories against the funds allotted for maintenance of the Control Council of Germany.

DOCUMENT 49

Control Council Law No 10 1945
Punishment of Persons Guilty of War Crimes, Crimes Against Peace and Crimes Against Humanity
3 Official Gazette: Control Council for Germany 50–55 (1946); 36 ILR 31

The Nuremberg International Military Tribunal (IMT) **(Documents 47–48)** *was created by the allied powers to deal with major war criminals. Control Council Law No 10 put in place the mechanism used for dealing with war criminals other than those identified as major war criminals. The law was enacted on 20 December 1945 by the Control Council for Germany, a body created by the Soviet Union, the USA and the UK in the Potsdam Agreement of 2 August 1945. The Control Council, which included France as a member as well as the three signatory States to the Potsdam Agreement, was charged with administering post-war Germany as a whole, but provided for each State to controll a zone of occupation within Germany.*

The law envisaged the arrest and detention of suspected war criminals by each occupying authority within its zone of occupation. Arrested individuals were to be tried by an appropriate tribunal, which could include, where authorised, a German court (Article III). The law also provided for the transfer of suspects between zones and between countries in order that prosecutions might take place 'in the country or zone in which the crime was committed' (Article IV). The crimes covered by the law were limited to crimes against peace, war crimes, crimes against humanity and membership in categories of a criminal group or organisation declared criminal by the IMT, all as defined in the law (Article II). It is interesting to note that, while the charter of the IMT requires crimes against humanity to be committed 'before or during the war' **(Document 48,** Article 6*), no such restriction applies in relation to the definition of crimes against humanity in Control Council Law No 10.*

See Trials of the War Criminals before the Nuremberg Military Tribunals under Control Council Law No 10 *(15 volumes, 1949–50)*; Taylor, Final Report to the Secretary of the Army on the Nuremberg War Crimes Trials Under Control Council Law No 10 *(1997).*

In order to give effect to the terms of the Moscow Declaration of 30 October 1943 and the London Agreement of 8 August 1945, and the Charter issued pursuant thereto and in order to establish a uniform legal basis in Germany for the prosecution of war criminals and other similar offenders, other than those dealt with by the International Military Tribunal, the Control Council enacts as follows:

Article I

The Moscow Declaration of 30 October 1943 "Concerning Responsibility of Hitlerites for Committed Atrocities" and the London Agreement of 8 August 1945 "Concerning Prosecution and Punishment of Major War Criminals of European Axis" are made integral parts of this Law. Adherence to the provisions of the London Agreement by any of the United Nations, as provided for in Article V of that Agreement, shall not entitle such Nation to participate or interfere in the operation of this Law within the Control Council area of authority in Germany.

Article II

1. Each of the following acts is recognized as a crime:

    (a) Crimes against Peace. Initiation of invasions of other countries and wars of aggression in violation of international laws and treaties, including but not limited to planning, preparation, initiation or waging a war of aggression, or a war of violation of international treaties, agreements or assurances, or participation in a common plan or conspiracy for the accomplishment of any of the foregoing.

    (b) War Crimes. Atrocities or offenses against persons or property constituting violations of the laws or customs of war, including but not limited to, murder, ill treatment or deportation to slave labour or for any other purpose, of civilian population from occupied territory, murder or ill treatment of prisoners of war or persons on the seas, killing of hostages, plunder of public or private property, wanton destruction of cities, towns or villages, or devastation not justified by military necessity.

    (c) Crimes against Humanity. Atrocities and offenses, including but not limited to murder, extermination, enslavement, deportation, imprisonment, torture, rape, or other inhumane acts committed against any civilian population, or persecutions on political, racial or religious grounds whether or not in violation of the domestic laws of the country where perpetrated.

    (d) Membership in categories of a criminal group or organization declared criminal by the International Military Tribunal.

2. Any person without regard to nationality or the capacity in which he acted, is deemed to have committed a crime as defined in paragraph 1 of this Article, if he was (a) a principal or (b) was an accessory to the commission of any such crime or ordered or abetted the same or (c) took a consenting part therein or (d) was connected with plans or enterprises involving its commission or (e) was a member of any organization or group connected with the commission of any such crime or (f) with reference to paragraph 1(a) if he held a high political, civil or military (including General Staff) position in Germany or in one of its Allies, co-belligerents or satellites or held high position in the financial, industrial or economic life of any such country.

3. Any persons found guilty of any of the crimes above mentioned may upon conviction be punished as shall be determined by the tribunal to be just. Such punishment may consist of one or more of the following:

    (a) Death.

    (b) Imprisonment for life or a term of years, with or without hard labor.

    (c) Fine, and imprisonment with or without hard labour, in lieu thereof.

    (d) Forfeiture of property.

    (e) Restitution of property wrongfully acquired.

    (f) Deprivation of some or all civil rights.

    Any property declared to be forfeited or the restitution of which is ordered by the Tribunal shall be delivered to the Control Council for Germany, which shall decide on its disposal.

4. (a) The official position of any person, whether as Head of State or as a responsible official in a Government Department, does not free him from responsibility for a crime or entitle him to mitigation of punishment.

    (b) The fact that any person acted pursuant to the order of his Government or of a superior does not free him from responsibility for a crime, but may be considered in mitigation.

5. In any trial or prosecution for a crime herein referred to, the accused shall not be entitled to the benefits of any statute of limitation in respect to the period from 30 January 1933 to 1 July 1945, nor shall any immunity, pardon or amnesty granted under the Nazi regime be admitted as a bar to trial or punishment.

Article III

1. Each occupying authority, within its Zone of Occupation:

    (a) shall have the right to cause persons within such Zone suspected of having committed a crime, including those charged with crime by one of the United Nations, to be arrested and shall take under control the property, real and personal, owned or controlled by the said persons, pending decisions as to its eventual disposition.

    (b) shall report to the Legal Directorate the name of all suspected criminals, the reasons for and the places of their detention, if they are detained, and the names and location of witnesses.

    (c) shall take appropriate measures to see that witnesses and evidence will be available when required.

    (d) shall have the right to cause all persons so arrested and charged, and not delivered to another authority as herein provided, or released, to be brought to trial before an appropriate tribunal. Such tribunal may, in the case of crimes committed by persons of German citizenship or nationality against other persons of German citizenship or nationality, or stateless persons, be a German Court, if authorized by the occupying authorities.

2. The tribunal by which persons charged with offenses hereunder shall be tried and the rules and procedure thereof shall be determined or designated by each Zone Commander for his respective Zone. Nothing herein is intended to, or shall impair or limit the Jurisdiction or power of any court or tribunal now or hereafter established in any Zone by the Commander thereof, or of the International Military Tribunal established by the London Agreement of 8 August 1945.

3. Persons wanted for trial by an International Military Tribunal will not be tried without the consent of the Committee of Chief Prosecutors. Each Zone Commander will deliver such persons who are within his Zone to that committee upon request and will make witnesses and evidence available to it.

4. Persons known to be wanted for trial in another Zone or outside Germany will not be tried prior to decision under Article IV unless the fact of their apprehension has been reported in

accordance with Section 1 (b) of this Article, three months have elapsed thereafter, and no request for delivery of the type contemplated by Article IV has been received by the Zone Commander concerned.

5. The execution of death sentences may be deferred but not to exceed one month after the sentence has become final when the Zone Commander concerned has reason to believe that the testimony of those under sentence would be of value in the investigation and trial of crimes within or without his zone.

6. Each Zone Commander will cause such effect to be given to the judgments of courts of competent jurisdiction, with respect to the property taken under his control pursuant thereto, as he may deem proper in the interest of justice.

Article IV

1. When any person in a Zone in Germany is alleged to have committed a crime, as defined in Article II, in a country other than Germany or in another Zone, the government of that nation or the Commander of the latter Zone, as the case may be, may request the Commander of the Zone in which the person is located for his arrest and delivery for trial to the country or Zone in which the crime was committed. Such request for delivery shall be granted by the Commander receiving it unless he believes such person is wanted for trial or as a witness by an International Military Tribunal, or in Germany, or in a nation other than the one making the request, or the Commander is not satisfied that delivery should be made, in any of which cases he shall have the right to forward the said request to the Legal Directorate of the Allied Control Authority. A similar procedure shall apply to witnesses, material exhibits and other forms of evidence.

2. The Legal Directorate shall consider all requests referred to it, and shall determine the same in accordance with the following principles, its determination to be communicated to the Zone Commander.

    (a) A person wanted for trial or as a witness by an International Military Tribunal shall not be delivered for trial or required to give evidence outside Germany, as the case may be, except upon approval by the Committee of Chief Prosecutors acting under the London Agreement of 8 August 1945.

    (b) A person wanted for trial by several authorities (other than an International Military Tribunal) shall be disposed of in accordance with the following priorities:

        (i)   If wanted for trial in the Zone in which he is, he should not be delivered unless arrangements are made for his return after trial elsewhere;

        (ii) If wanted for trial in a Zone other than that in which he is, he should be delivered to that Zone in preference to delivery outside Germany unless arrangements are made for his return to that Zone after trial elsewhere;

        (iii) If wanted for trial outside Germany by two or more of the United Nations, of one of which he is a citizen, that one should have priority;

        (iv) If wanted for trial outside Germany by several countries, not all of which are United Nations, United Nations should have priority;

        (v)   If wanted for trial outside Germany by two or more of the United Nations, then, subject to Article IV 2(b)(iii) above, that which has the most serious charges against him, which are moreover supported by evidence, should have priority.

Article V

The delivery, under Article IV of this law, of persons for trial shall be made on demands of the Governments or Zone Commanders in such a manner that the delivery of criminals to one jurisdiction will not become the means of defeating or unnecessarily delaying the carrying out of justice in another place. If within six months the delivered person has not been convicted by the Court of the Zone or country to which he has been delivered, then such person shall be returned upon demand of the Commander of the Zone where the person was located prior to delivery.

DOCUMENT 50

Charter of the (Tokyo) International Military Tribunal for the Far East 1946
14 State Dept Bull 391, 890; TIAS No 1589

On 26 July 1945, the Soviet Union, the USA and the UK issued the Potsdam Declaration announcing the intention of these States to prosecute major Japanese war criminals. In January 1946, the Supreme Commander for the Allied Powers, who was also the US Supreme Commander-in-Chief in Japan, proclaimed the Charter of the International Military Tribunal for the Far East (IMTFE), closely modelled on the Nuremberg Charter (**Document 48**).

The jurisdiction of the IMTFE covered crimes against peace, war crimes and crimes against humanity committed before and during the war (Article 5). The IMTFE consisted of 11 judges appointed by the Supreme Commander for the Allied Powers from amongst the signatory countries to the Japanese Instrument of Surrender, as well as India and the Philippines (Article 2). The Supreme Commander for the Allied Powers also appointed the IMTFE's chief of counsel (Article 8). The procedure of the IMTFE was based primarily on the adversarial system of criminal justice but, as with the Nuremberg International Military Tribunal, some aspects of the inquisitorial system were present (Articles 11–15).

The IMTFE met in Tokyo from 3 May 1946 until 12 November 1948. Twenty-eight individuals were brought to trial before the IMTFE. The trial resulted in the prosecution of 25 defendants. Of the other three defendants, two died of natural causes and one was declared unfit to stand trial, having had a breakdown on the first day of the trial. Of the 25 defendants found guilty, seven were sentenced to death, 16 were given life imprisonment and two were given lesser prison sentences. Other suspected war criminals were tried in the countries in which the alleged offences took place.

See Trial of the Japanese Major War Criminals *(1948) 15 ILR 356; Pritchard and Zaide,* The Tokyo War Crimes Trials: The Complete Transcripts of the Proceedings of the International Military Tribunal for the Far East *(22 volumes, 1981).*

Article I Tribunal Established
The International Military Tribunal for the Far East is hereby established for the just and prompt trial and punishment of the major war criminals in the Far East. The permanent seat of the Tribunal is in Tokyo.

Article 2 Members
The Tribunal shall consist of not less than six members nor more than eleven members, appointed by the Supreme Commander for the Allied Powers from the names submitted by the Signatories to the Instrument of Surrender, India, and the Commonwealth of the Philippines.

Article 3 Officers and Secretariat
(a) President. The Supreme Commander for the Allied Powers shall appoint a Member to be President of the Tribunal.

(b) Secretariat.

    (i) The Secretariat of the Tribunal shall be composed of a General Secretary to be appointed by the Supreme Commander for the Allied Powers and such assistant secretaries, clerks, interpreters, and other personnel as may be necessary.

(ii) The General Secretary shall organize and direct the work of the Secretariat.

(iii) The Secretariat shall receive all documents addressed to the Tribunal, maintain the records of the Tribunal, provide assistance to the work of the Tribunal.

Article 4 Convening and Quorum, Voting and Absence

(a) Convening and Quorum. When as many as six members of the Tribunal are present, they may convene the Tribunal in formal session. The presence of a majority of all members shall be necessary to constitute a quorum.

(b) Voting. All decisions and judgments of this Tribunal, including convictions and sentences, shall be by a majority vote of those Members of the Tribunal present. In case the votes are evenly divided, the vote of the President shall be decisive.

(c) Absence. If a member at any time is absent and afterwards is able to be present, he shall take part in all subsequent proceedings; unless he declares in open court that he is disqualified by reason of insufficient familiarity with the proceedings which took place in his absence.

Article 5 Jurisdiction Over Persons and Offenses

The Tribunal shall have the power to try and punish Far Eastern war criminals who as individuals or as members of organizations are charged with offenses which include Crimes against Peace.

The following acts, or any of them, are crimes coming within the jurisdiction of the Tribunal for which there shall be individual responsibility:

(a) Crimes against Peace: Namely, the planning, preparation, initiation or waging of a declared or undeclared war of aggression, or a war in violation of international law, treaties, agreements or assurances, or participation in a common plan or conspiracy for the accomplishment of any of the foregoing;

(b) Conventional War Crimes: Namely, violations of the laws or customs of war;

(c) Crimes against Humanity: Namely, murder, extermination, enslavement, deportation, and other inhumane acts committed against any civilian population, before or during the war, or persecutions on political or racial grounds in execution of or in connection with any crime within the jurisdiction of the Tribunal, whether or not in violation of the domestic law of the country where perpetrated. Leaders, organizers, instigators and accomplices participating in the formulation or execution of a common plan or conspiracy to commit any of the foregoing crimes are responsible for all acts performed by any person in execution of such plan.

Article 6 Responsibility of Accused

Neither the official position, at any time, of an accused, nor the fact that an accused acted pursuant to order of his government or of a superior shall, of itself, be sufficient to free such accused from responsibility for any crime with which he is charged, but such circumstances may be considered in mitigation of punishment if the Tribunal determines that justice so requires.

Article 7 Rules of Procedure

The Tribunal may draft and amend rules of procedure consistent with the fundamental provisions of this Charter.

Article 8 Counsel

(a) Chief of Counsel. The Chief of Counsel designated by the Supreme Commander for the Allied Powers is responsible for the investigation and prosecution of charges against war criminals within the jurisdiction of this Tribunal, and will render such legal assistance to the Supreme Commander as is appropriate.

(b) Associate Counsel. Any United Nation with which Japan has been at war may appoint an Associate Counsel to assist the Chief of Counsel.

Article 9 Procedure for Fair Trial

In order to insure fair trial for the accused the following procedure shall be followed:

(a) Indictment. The indictment shall consist of a plain, concise, and adequate statement of each offense charged. Each accused shall be furnished, in adequate time for defense, a copy of the indictment, including any amendment, and of this Charter, in a language understood by the accused.

(b) Language. The trial and related proceedings shall be conducted in English and in the language of the accused. Translations of documents and other papers shall be provided as needed and requested.

(c) Counsel for Accused. Each accused shall have the right to be represented by counsel of his own selection, subject to the disapproval of such counsel at any time by the Tribunal. The accused shall file with the General Secretary of the Tribunal the name of his counsel. If an accused is not represented by counsel and in open court requests the appointment of counsel, the Tribunal shall designate counsel for him. In the absence of such request the Tribunal may appoint counsel for an accused if in its judgment such appointment is necessary to provide for a fair trial.

(d) Evidence for Defense. An accused shall have the right, through himself or through his counsel (but not through both), to conduct his defense, including the right to examine any witness, subject to such reasonable restrictions as the Tribunal may determine.

(e) Production of Evidence for the Defense. An accused may apply in writing to the Tribunal for the production of witnesses or of documents. The application shall state where the witness or document is thought to be located. It shall also state the facts proposed to be proved by the witness or the document and the relevancy of such facts to the defense. If the Tribunal grants the application the Tribunal shall be given such aid in obtaining production of the evidence as the circumstances require.

Article 10 Applications and Motions before Trial

All motions, applications, or other requests addressed to the Tribunal prior to the commencement of trial shall be made in writing and filed with the General Secretary of the Tribunal for action by the Tribunal.

Article 11 Powers

The Tribunal shall have the power:

(a) To summon witnesses to the trial, to require them to attend and testify, and to question them,

(b) To interrogate each accused and to permit comment on his refusal to answer any question,

(c) To require the production of documents and other evidentiary material,

(d) To require of each witness an oath, affirmation, or such declaration as is customary in the country of the witness, and to administer oaths,

(e) To appoint officers for the carrying out of any task designated by the Tribunal, including the power to have evidence taken on commission.

Article 12 Conduct of Trial

The Tribunal shall:

(a) Confine the trial strictly to an expeditious hearing of the issues raised by the charges;

(b) Take strict measures to prevent any action which would cause any unreasonable delay and rule out irrelevant issues and statements of any kind whatsoever;

(c) Provide for the maintenance of order at the trial and deal summarily with any contumacy, imposing appropriate punishment, including exclusion of any accused or his counsel from some or all further proceedings, but without prejudice to the determination of the charges;

(d) Determine the mental and physical capacity of any accused to proceed to trial.

Article 13 Evidence

(a) Admissibility. The Tribunal shall not be bound by technical rules of evidence. It shall adopt and apply to the greatest possible extent expeditious and non-technical procedure, and shall admit any evidence which it deems to have probative value. All purported admissions or statements of the accused are admissible.

(b) Relevance. The Tribunal may require to be informed of the nature of any evidence before it is offered in order to rule upon the relevance.

(c) Specific Evidence Admissible. In particular, and without limiting in any way the scope of the foregoing general rules, the following evidence may be admitted:

(i) A document, regardless of its security classification and without proof of its issuance or signature, which appears to the Tribunal to have been signed or issued by any officer, department, agency or member of the armed forces of any government.

(ii) A report which appears to the Tribunal to have been signed or issued by the International Red Cross or a member thereof, or by a doctor of medicine or any medical service personnel, or by an investigator or intelligence officer, or by any other person who appears to the Tribunal to have personal knowledge of the matters contained in the report.

(iii) An affidavit, deposition or other signed statement.

(iv) A diary, letter or other document, including sworn or unsworn statements which appear to the Tribunal to contain information relating to the charge.

(v) A copy of a document or other secondary evidence of its contents, if the original is not immediately available.

(d) Judicial Notice. The Tribunal shall neither require proof, of facts of common knowledge, nor of the authenticity of official government documents and reports of any nation nor of the proceedings, records, and findings of military or other agencies of any of the United Nations.

(e) Records, Exhibits and Documents. The transcript of the proceedings, and exhibits and documents submitted to the Tribunal, will be filed with the General Secretary of the Tribunal and will constitute part of the Record.

Article 14 Place of Trial

The first trial will be held at Tokyo and any subsequent trials will be held at such places as the Tribunal decided.

Article 15 Course of Trial Proceedings

The proceedings the Trial will take the following course:

(a) The indictment will be read in court unless the reading is waived by all accused.

(b) The Tribunal will ask each accused whether he pleads "guilty" or "not guilty."

(c) The prosecution and each accused (by counsel only, if represented) may make a concise opening statement.

(d) The prosecution and defense may offer evidence and the admissibility of the same shall be determined by the Tribunal.

(e) The prosecution and each accused (by counsel only, if represented) may examine each witness and each accused who gives testimony.

(f) Accused (by counsel only, if represented) may address the Tribunal.

(g) The prosecution may address the Tribunal.

(h) The Tribunal will deliver judgment and pronounce sentence.

Article 16 Penalty

The Tribunal shall have the power to impose upon an accused, on conviction, death or such other punishment as shall be determined by it to be just.

Article 17 Judgment and Review

The judgment will be announced in open court and will give the reasons on which it is based. The record of the trial will be transmitted directly to the Supreme Commander for the Allied Powers for his action thereon. A sentence will be carried out in accordance with the order of the Supreme Commander for the Allied Powers, who may at any time reduce or otherwise alter the sentence except to increase its severity.

DOCUMENT 51

Statute of the International Criminal Tribunal for the Former Yugoslavia 1993 (as amended in 1998, 2000, 2002 and 2003)

UN Doc S/RES/827 (1993); 32 ILM 1203 (1993)

The Ad Hoc International Tribunal for the Prosecution of Persons Responsible for Serious Violations of International Humanitarian Law Committed in the Territory of the Former Yugoslavia was established by the United Nations Security Council acting under Chapter VII of the UN Charter on 25 May 1993 (SC Resolution 827 (1993)). The Security Council adopted the statute of the tribunal in the same resolution. The statute has been subsequently amended by the Security Council in Resolutions 1166 (1998), 1329 (2000), 1411(2002), 1431 (2002) and 1481 (2003).

The tribunal was created to prosecute serious violations of international humanitarian law committed on the territory of the former Yugoslavia since 1991 (Article 1). It has jurisdiction over natural persons (Article 6) in relation to grave breaches of the Geneva Conventions of 1949 (Article 2), war crimes (Article 3), the crime of genocide (Article 4) and crimes against humanity (Article 5). The statute provides for the individual criminal responsibility of persons responsible for the planning, instigation, ordering or committing of such crimes (Article 7). The tribunal has concurrent jurisdiction with national courts, but has primacy over them (Article 9).

The tribunal has its seat at The Hague in the Netherlands. It consists of three trial chambers together with the prosecutor and a registry (Article 11). There are 16 permanent judges and up to a maximum at any one time of 9 ad litem judges (Articles 12–13). The appeal chamber, which is shared with the International Criminal Tribunal for Rwanda, consists of seven permanent judges. Each appeal is heard by five permanent judges (Article 12(3)). The Rules of Procedure and Evidence of the tribunal were adopted by the court in accordance with Article 15 of the statute on 11 February 1994 and came into force on 14 March 1994. The tribunal has amended these rules on a number of occasions. The administration and servicing of the tribunal is undertaken by the registry (Article 17).

Responsibility for the investigation and prosecution of crimes before the tribunal lies with the prosecutor who is appointed by the Security Council and who is entitled to such staff as he or she may require (Article 16). He or she has the power to initiate prosecutions and to prepare indictments (Article 18). Indictments are reviewed by the judge of the trial chamber to whom the indictment has been transferred and that person shall confirm the indictment if satisfied that a prima facie *case has been established by the prosecutor (Article 19). The trial chamber has responsibility for ensuring that the trial is fair and expeditious and conducted in accordance with the rules of procedure and evidence (Article 20). The rights of the accused are specified in Article 21. The rules of evidence are to include provisions on the protection of witnesses (Article 22).*

Judgments of the tribunal are to be by majority (Article 23) and the penalties of the tribunal are limited to imprisonment (Article 24). Appeals may be heard on the basis of an error on a question of law invalidating the decision or an error of fact which has occasioned a miscarriage of justice (Article 25).

One hundred and fifty-nine individuals have been indicted before the ICTY. One hundred and eight individuals have appeared in proceedings before the tribunal. Fifty-one accused are currently in proceedings before the tribunal, including Slobodan Milosevic, the former Serbian President. The ICTY has a staff of 1,238 and has an annual budget of $271,854,600. The tribunal is due to complete its trial proceedings by the end of 2008 and to complete all of its work by the end of 2010 (SC Resolution 1503).

See also www.un.org/icty.

Having been established by the Security Council acting under Chapter VII of the Charter of the United Nations, the International Tribunal for the Prosecution of Persons Responsible for Serious Violations of International Humanitarian Law Committed in the Territory of the Former Yugoslavia since 1991 (hereinafter referred to as "the International Tribunal") shall function in accordance with the provisions of the present Statute.

Article 1 Competence of the International Tribunal

The International Tribunal shall have the power to prosecute persons responsible for serious violations of international humanitarian law committed in the territory of the former Yugoslavia since 1991 in accordance with the provisions of the present Statute.

Article 2 Grave breaches of the Geneva Conventions of 1949

The International Tribunal shall have the power to prosecute persons committing or ordering to be committed grave breaches of the Geneva Conventions of 12 August 1949, namely the following acts against persons or property protected under the provisions of the relevant Geneva Convention:

(a) wilful killing;

(b) torture or inhuman treatment, including biological experiments;

(c) wilfully causing great suffering or serious injury to body or health;

(d) extensive destruction and appropriation of property, not justified by military necessity and carried out unlawfully and wantonly;

(e) compelling a prisoner of war or a civilian to serve in the forces of a hostile power;

(f) wilfully depriving a prisoner of war or a civilian of the rights of fair and regular trial;

(g) unlawful deportation or transfer or unlawful confinement of a civilian;

(h) taking civilians as hostages.

Article 3 Violations of the laws or customs of war

The International Tribunal shall have the power to prosecute persons violating the laws or customs of war. Such violations shall include, but not be limited to:

(a) employment of poisonous weapons or other weapons calculated to cause unnecessary suffering;

(b) wanton destruction of cities, towns or villages, or devastation not justified by military necessity;

(c) attack, or bombardment, by whatever means, of undefended towns, villages, dwellings, or buildings;

(d) seizure of, destruction or wilful damage done to institutions dedicated to religion, charity and education, the arts and sciences, historic monuments and works of art and science;

(e) plunder of public or private property.

Article 4 Genocide

1. The International Tribunal shall have the power to prosecute persons committing genocide as defined in paragraph 2 of this article or of committing any of the other acts enumerated in paragraph 3 of this article.

2. Genocide means any of the following acts committed with intent to destroy, in whole or in part, a national, ethnical, racial or religious group, as such:

(a) killing members of the group;

(b) causing serious bodily or mental harm to members of the group;

(c) deliberately inflicting on the group conditions of life calculated to bring about its physical destruction in whole or in part;

(d) imposing measures intended to prevent births within the group;

(e) forcibly transferring children of the group to another group.

3. The following acts shall be punishable:

(a) genocide;

(b) conspiracy to commit genocide;

(c) direct and public incitement to commit genocide;

(d) attempt to commit genocide;

(e) complicity in genocide.

Article 5 Crimes against humanity

The International Tribunal shall have the power to prosecute persons responsible for the following crimes when committed in armed conflict, whether international or internal in character, and directed against any civilian population:

(a) murder;

(b) extermination;

(c) enslavement;

(d) deportation;

(e) imprisonment;

(f) torture;

(g) rape;

(h) persecutions on political, racial and religious grounds;

(i) other inhumane acts.

Article 6 Personal jurisdiction

The International Tribunal shall have jurisdiction over natural persons pursuant to the provisions of the present Statute.

Article 7 Individual criminal responsibility

1. A person who planned, instigated, ordered, committed or otherwise aided and abetted in the planning, preparation or execution of a crime referred to in articles 2 to 5 of the present Statute, shall be individually responsible for the crime.

2. The official position of any accused person, whether as Head of State or Government or as a responsible Government official, shall not relieve such person of criminal responsibility nor mitigate punishment.

3. The fact that any of the acts referred to in articles 2 to 5 of the present Statute was committed by a subordinate does not relieve his superior of criminal responsibility if he knew or had reason to know that the subordinate was about to commit such acts or had done so and the superior failed to take the necessary and reasonable measures to prevent such acts or to punish the perpetrators thereof.

4. The fact that an accused person acted pursuant to an order of a Government or of a superior shall not relieve him of criminal responsibility, but may be considered in mitigation of punishment if the International Tribunal determines that justice so requires.

Article 8 Territorial and temporal jurisdiction

The territorial jurisdiction of the International Tribunal shall extend to the territory of the former Socialist Federal Republic of Yugoslavia, including its land surface, airspace and territorial waters. The temporal jurisdiction of the International Tribunal shall extend to a period beginning on 1 January 1991.

Article 9 Concurrent jurisdiction

1. The International Tribunal and national courts shall have concurrent jurisdiction to prosecute persons for serious violations of international humanitarian law committed in the territory of the former Yugoslavia since 1 January 1991.

2. The International Tribunal shall have primacy over national courts. At any stage of the procedure, the International Tribunal may formally request national courts to defer to the competence of the International Tribunal in accordance with the present Statute and the Rules of Procedure and Evidence of the International Tribunal.

Article 10 *Non-bis-in-idem*

1. No person shall be tried before a national court for acts constituting serious violations of international humanitarian law under the present Statute, for which he or she has already been tried by the International Tribunal.

2. A person who has been tried by a national court for acts constituting serious violations of international humanitarian law may be subsequently tried by the International Tribunal only if:

    (a) the act for which he or she was tried was characterized as an ordinary crime; or

    (b) the national court proceedings were not impartial or independent, were designed to shield the accused from international criminal responsibility, or the case was not diligently prosecuted.

3. In considering the penalty to be imposed on a person convicted of a crime under the present Statute, the International Tribunal shall take into account the extent to which any penalty imposed by a national court on the same person for the same act has already been served.

Article 11 Organization of the International Tribunal

The International Tribunal shall consist of the following organs:

(a) The Chambers, comprising three Trial Chambers and an Appeals Chamber;

(b) The Prosecutor, and

(c) A Registry, servicing both the Chambers and the Prosecutor.

Article 12 Composition of the Chambers

1. The Chambers shall be composed of sixteen independent judges, no two of whom may be nationals of the same State, and a maximum at any one time of nine *ad litem* independent judges appointed in accordance with article ter, paragraph 2, of the Statute, no two of whom may be nationals of the same State.

2. Three permanent and a maximum at any one time of six *ad litem* judges shall be members of each Trial Chamber. Each Trial Chamber to which *ad litem* judges are assigned may be divided into sections of three judges each, composed of both permanent and *ad litem* judges. A section of the Trial Chamber shall have the same powers and responsibilities as a Trial Chamber under the Statute and shall render judgment in accordance with the same rules.

3. Seven of the permanent judges shall be members of the Appeals Chamber. The Appeals Chamber shall, for each appeal, be composed of five of its members.

4. A person who for the purposes of membership of the Chambers of the International Tribunal could be regarded as a national of more than one State shall be deemed to be a national of the State in which that person ordinarily exercises civil and political rights.

Article 13 Qualifications of judges

The permanent and *ad litem* judges shall be persons of high moral character, impartiality and integrity who possess the qualifications required in their respective countries for appointment to the highest judicial offices. In the overall composition of the Chambers and sections of the Trial Chambers, due account shall be taken of the experience of the judges in criminal law, international law, including international humanitarian law and human rights law.

Article 13 *bis* Election of permanent judges

1. Fourteen of the permanent judges of the International Tribunal shall be elected by the General Assembly from a list submitted by the Security Council, in the following manner:

    (a) The Secretary-General shall invite nominations for judges of the International Tribunal from States Members of the United Nations and non-member States maintaining permanent observer missions at United Nations Headquarters;

    (b) Within sixty days of the date of the invitation of the Secretary-General, each State may nominate up to two candidates meeting the qualifications set out in article 13 of the Statute, no two of whom shall be of the same nationality and neither of whom shall be of the same nationality as any judge who is a member of the Appeals Chamber and who was elected or appointed a permanent judge of the International Criminal Tribunal for the Prosecution of Persons Responsible for Genocide and Other Serious Violations of International Humanitarian Law Committed in the Territory of Rwanda and Rwandan Citizens Responsible for Genocide and Other Such Violations Committed in the Territory of Neighbouring States, between 1 January 1994 and 31 December 1994 (hereinafter referred to as "The International Tribunal for Rwanda") in accordance with article 12 *bis* of the Statute of that Tribunal;

    (c) The Secretary-General shall forward the nominations received to the Security Council. From the nominations received the Security Council shall establish a list of not less than twenty-eight and not more than forty-two candidates, taking due account of the adequate representation of the principal legal systems of the world;

    (d) The President of the Security Council shall transmit the list of candidates to the President of the General Assembly. From that list the General Assembly shall elect fourteen permanent judges of the International Tribunal. The candidates who receive an absolute majority of the votes of the States Members of the United Nations and of the non-member States maintaining permanent observer missions at United Nations Headquarters, shall be declared elected. Should two candidates of the same nationality obtain the required majority vote, the one who received the higher number of votes shall be considered elected.

2. In the event of a vacancy in the Chambers amongst the permanent judges elected or appointed in accordance with this article, after consultation with the Presidents of the Security Council and of the General Assembly, the Secretary-General shall appoint a person meeting the qualifications of article 13 of the Statute, for the remainder of the term of office concerned.

3.   The permanent judges elected in accordance with this article shall be elected for a term of four years. The terms and conditions of service shall be those of the judges of the International Court of Justice. They shall be eligible for re-election.

Article 13 *ter* Election and appointment of *ad litem* judges

1.   The *ad litem* judges of the International Tribunal shall be elected by the General Assembly from a list submitted by the Security Council, in the following manner:

(a)   The Secretary-General shall invite nominations for *ad litem* judges of the International Tribunal from States Members of the United Nations and non-member States maintaining permanent observer missions at United Nations Headquarters.

(b)   Within sixty days of the date of the invitation of the Secretary-General, each State may nominate up to four candidates meeting the qualifications set out in article 13 of the Statute, taking into account the importance of a fair representation of female and male candidates.

(c)   The Secretary-General shall forward the nominations received to the Security Council. From the nominations received the Security Council shall establish a list of not less than fifty-four candidates, taking due account of the adequate representation of the principal legal systems of the world and bearing in mind the importance of equitable geographical distribution.

(d)   The President of the Security Council shall transmit the list of candidates to the President of the General Assembly. From that list the General Assembly shall elect the twenty-seven *ad litem* judges of the International Tribunal. The candidates who receive an absolute majority of the votes of the States Members of the United Nations and of the non-member States maintaining permanent observer missions at United Nations Headquarters shall be declared elected.

(e)   The *ad litem* judges shall be elected for a term of four years. They shall not be eligible for re-election.

2.   During their term, *ad litem* judges will be appointed by the Secretary-General, upon request of the President of the International Tribunal, to serve in the Trial Chambers for one or more trials, for a cumulative period of up to, but not including, three years. When requesting the appointment of any particular *ad litem* judge, the President of the International Tribunal shall bear in mind the criteria set out in article 13 of the Statute regarding the composition of the Chambers and sections of the Trial Chambers, the considerations set out in paragraphs 1 (b) and (c) above and the number of votes the *ad litem* judge received in the General Assembly.

Article 13 *quater* Status of *ad litem* judges

1.   During the period in which they are appointed to serve in the International Tribunal, *ad litem* judges shall:

(a)   Benefit from the same terms and conditions of service mutatis mutandis as the permanent judges of the International Tribunal;

(b)   Enjoy, subject to paragraph 2 below, the same powers as the permanent judges of the International Tribunal;

(c)   Enjoy the privileges and immunities, exemptions and facilities of a judge of the International Tribunal;

(d)   Enjoy the power to adjudicate in pre-trial proceedings in cases other than those that they have been appointed to try.

2.   During the period in which they are appointed to serve in the International Tribunal, *ad litem* judges shall not:

(a)   Be eligible for election as, or to vote in the election of, the President of the Tribunal or the Presiding Judge of a Trial Chamber pursuant to article 14 of the Statute;

(b) Have power:
  (i) To adopt rules of procedure and evidence pursuant to article 15 of the Statute. They shall, however, be consulted before the adoption of those rules;
  (ii) To review an indictment pursuant to article 19 of the Statute;
  (iii) To consult with the President in relation to the assignment of judges pursuant to article 14 of the Statute or in relation to a pardon or commutation of sentence pursuant to article 28 of the Statute.

Article 14 Officers and members of the Chambers

1. The permanent judges of the International Tribunal shall elect a President from amongst their number.

2. The President of the International Tribunal shall be a member of the Appeals Chamber and shall preside over its proceedings.

3. After consultation with the permanent judges of the International Tribunal, the President shall assign four of the permanent judges elected or appointed in accordance with Article 13 *bis* of the Statute to the Appeals Chamber and nine to the Trial Chambers.

4. Two of the permanent judges of the International Tribunal for Rwanda elected or appointed in accordance with article 12 *bis* of the Statute of that Tribunal shall be assigned by the President of that Tribunal, in consultation with the President of the International Tribunal, to be members of the Appeals Chamber and permanent judges of the International Tribunal.

5. After consultation with the permanent judges of the International Tribunal, the President shall assign such *ad litem* judges as may from time to time be appointed to serve in the International Tribunal to the Trial Chambers.

6. A judge shall serve only in the Chamber to which he or she was assigned.

7. The permanent judges of each Trial Chamber shall elect a Presiding Judge from amongst their number, who shall oversee the work of the Trial Chamber as a whole.

Article 15 Rules of procedure and evidence

The judges of the International Tribunal shall adopt rules of procedure and evidence for the conduct of the pre-trial phase of the proceedings, trials and appeals, the admission of evidence, the protection of victims and witnesses and other appropriate matters.

Article 16 The Prosecutor

1. The Prosecutor shall be responsible for the investigation and prosecution of persons responsible for serious violations of international humanitarian law committed in the territory of the former Yugoslavia since 1 January 1991.

2. The Prosecutor shall act independently as a separate organ of the International Tribunal. He or she shall not seek or receive instructions from any Government or from any other source.

3. The Office of the Prosecutor shall be composed of a Prosecutor and such other qualified staff as may be required.

4. The Prosecutor shall be appointed by the Security Council on nomination by the Secretary-General. He or she shall be of high moral character and possess the highest level of competence and experience in the conduct of investigations and prosecutions of criminal cases. The Prosecutor shall serve for a four-year term and be eligible for reappointment. The terms and conditions of service of the Prosecutor shall be those of an Under-Secretary-General of the United Nations.

5. The staff of the Office of the Prosecutor shall be appointed by the Secretary-General on the recommendation of the Prosecutor.

Article 17 The Registry

1. The Registry shall be responsible for the administration and servicing of the International Tribunal.

2. The Registry shall consist of a Registrar and such other staff as may be required.

3. The Registrar shall be appointed by the Secretary-General after consultation with the President of the International Tribunal. He or she shall serve for a four-year term and be eligible for reappointment. The terms and conditions of service of the Registrar shall be those of an Assistant Secretary-General of the United Nations.

4. The staff of the Registry shall be appointed by the Secretary-General on the recommendation of the Registrar.

Article 18 Investigation and preparation of indictment

1. The Prosecutor shall initiate investigations *ex-officio* or on the basis of information obtained from any source, particularly from Governments, United Nations organs, intergovernmental and non-governmental organizations. The Prosecutor shall assess the information received or obtained and decide whether there is sufficient basis to proceed.

2. The Prosecutor shall have the power to question suspects, victims and witnesses, to collect evidence and to conduct on-site investigations. In carrying out these tasks, the Prosecutor may, as appropriate, seek the assistance of the State authorities concerned.

3. If questioned, the suspect shall be entitled to be assisted by counsel of his own choice, including the right to have legal assistance assigned to him without payment by him in any such case if he does not have sufficient means to pay for it, as well as to necessary translation into and from a language he speaks and understands.

4. Upon a determination that a *prima facie* case exists, the Prosecutor shall prepare an indictment containing a concise statement of the facts and the crime or crimes with which the accused is charged under the Statute. The indictment shall be transmitted to a judge of the Trial Chamber.

Article 19 Review of the indictment

1. The judge of the Trial Chamber to whom the indictment has been transmitted shall review it. If satisfied that a *prima facie* case has been established by the Prosecutor, he shall confirm the indictment. If not so satisfied, the indictment shall be dismissed.

2. Upon confirmation of an indictment, the judge may, at the request of the Prosecutor, issue such orders and warrants for the arrest, detention, surrender or transfer of persons, and any other orders as may be required for the conduct of the trial.

Article 20 Commencement and conduct of trial proceedings

1. The Trial Chambers shall ensure that a trial is fair and expeditious and that proceedings are conducted in accordance with the rules of procedure and evidence, with full respect for the rights of the accused and due regard for the protection of victims and witnesses.

2. A person against whom an indictment has been confirmed shall, pursuant to an order or an arrest warrant of the International Tribunal, be taken into custody, immediately informed of the charges against him and transferred to the International Tribunal.

3. The Trial Chamber shall read the indictment, satisfy itself that the rights of the accused are respected, confirm that the accused understands the indictment, and instruct the accused to enter a plea. The Trial Chamber shall then set the date for trial.

4. The hearings shall be public unless the Trial Chamber decides to close the proceedings in accordance with its rules of procedure and evidence.

Article 21 Rights of the accused

1. All persons shall be equal before the International Tribunal.

2. In the determination of charges against him, the accused shall be entitled to a fair and public hearing, subject to article 22 of the Statute.

3. The accused shall be presumed innocent until proved guilty according to the provisions of the present Statute.

4. In the determination of any charge against the accused pursuant to the present Statute, the accused shall be entitled to the following minimum guarantees, in full equality:

    (a) to be informed promptly and in detail in a language which he understands of the nature and cause of the charge against him;

    (b) to have adequate time and facilities for the preparation of his defence and to communicate with counsel of his own choosing;

    (c) to be tried without undue delay;

    (d) to be tried in his presence, and to defend himself in person or through legal assistance of his own choosing; to be informed, if he does not have legal assistance, of this right; and to have legal assistance assigned to him, in any case where the interests of justice so require, and without payment by him in any such case if he does not have sufficient means to pay for it;

    (e) to examine, or have examined, the witnesses against him and to obtain the attendance and examination of witnesses on his behalf under the same conditions as witnesses against him;

    (f) to have the free assistance of an interpreter if he cannot understand or speak the language used in the International Tribunal;

    (g) not to be compelled to testify against himself or to confess guilt.

Article 22 Protection of victims and witnesses

The International Tribunal shall provide in its rules of procedure and evidence for the protection of victims and witnesses. Such protection measures shall include, but shall not be limited to, the conduct of in camera proceedings and the protection of the victim's identity.

Article 23 Judgment

1. The Trial Chambers shall pronounce judgments and impose sentences and penalties on persons convicted of serious violations of international humanitarian law.

2. The judgment shall be rendered by a majority of the judges of the Trial Chamber, and shall be delivered by the Trial Chamber in public. It shall be accompanied by a reasoned opinion in writing, to which separate or dissenting opinions may be appended.

Article 24 Penalties

1. The penalty imposed by the Trial Chamber shall be limited to imprisonment. In determining the terms of imprisonment, the Trial Chambers shall have recourse to the general practice regarding prison sentences in the courts of the former Yugoslavia.

2. In imposing the sentences, the Trial Chambers should take into account such factors as the gravity of the offence and the individual circumstances of the convicted person.

3. In addition to imprisonment, the Trial Chambers may order the return of any property and proceeds acquired by criminal conduct, including by means of duress, to their rightful owners.

Article 25 Appellate proceedings

1. The Appeals Chamber shall hear appeals from persons convicted by the Trial Chambers or from the Prosecutor on the following grounds:

    (a) an error on a question of law invalidating the decision; or

    (b) an error of fact which has occasioned a miscarriage of justice.

2.　The Appeals Chamber may affirm, reverse or revise the decisions taken by the Trial Chambers.

Article 26 Review proceedings

Where a new fact has been discovered which was not known at the time of the proceedings before the Trial Chambers or the Appeals Chamber and which could have been a decisive factor in reaching the decision, the convicted person or the Prosecutor may submit to the International Tribunal an application for review of the judgment.

Article 27 Enforcement of sentences

Imprisonment shall be served in a State designated by the International Tribunal from a list of States which have indicated to the Security Council their willingness to accept convicted persons. Such imprisonment shall be in accordance with the applicable law of the State concerned, subject to the supervision of the International Tribunal.

Article 28 Pardon or commutation of sentences

If, pursuant to the applicable law of the State in which the convicted person is imprisoned, he or she is eligible for pardon or commutation of sentence, the State concerned shall notify the International Tribunal accordingly. The President of the International Tribunal, in consultation with the judges, shall decide the matter on the basis of the interests of justice and the general principles of law.

Article 29 Cooperation and judicial assistance

1.　States shall cooperate with the International Tribunal in the investigation and prosecution of persons accused of committing serious violations of international humanitarian law.

2.　States shall comply without undue delay with any request for assistance or an order issued by a Trial Chamber, including, but not limited to:

　(a)　the identification and location of persons;

　(b)　the taking of testimony and the production of evidence;

　(c)　the service of documents;

　(d)　the arrest or detention of persons;

　(e)　the surrender or the transfer of the accused to the International Tribunal.

Article 30 The status, privileges and immunities of the International Tribunal

1.　The Convention on the Privileges and Immunities of the United Nations of 13 February 1946 shall apply to the International Tribunal, the judges, the Prosecutor and his staff, and the Registrar and his staff.

2.　The judges, the Prosecutor and the Registrar shall enjoy the privileges and immunities, exemptions and facilities accorded to diplomatic envoys, in accordance with international law.

3.　The staff of the Prosecutor and of the Registrar shall enjoy the privileges and immunities accorded to officials of the United Nations under articles V and VII of the Convention referred to in paragraph 1 of this article.

4.　Other persons, including the accused, required at the seat of the International Tribunal shall be accorded such treatment as is necessary for the proper functioning of the International Tribunal.

Article 31 Seat of the International Tribunal

The International Tribunal shall have its seat at The Hague.

Article 32 Expenses of the International Tribunal

The expenses of the International Tribunal shall be borne by the regular budget of the United Nations in accordance with Article 17 of the Charter of the United Nations.

Article 33 Working languages
The working languages of the International Tribunal shall be English and French.

Article 34 Annual report
The President of the International Tribunal shall submit an annual report of the International Tribunal to the Security Council and to the General Assembly.

DOCUMENT 52

Statute of the International Criminal Tribunal for Rwanda 1994 (as amended in 1998, 2000, 2002 and 2003)

UN Doc S/RES/955 (1994); 33 ILM 1598 (1994)

The Ad Hoc International Criminal Tribunal for the Prosecution of Persons Responsible for Genocide and Other Serious Violations of International Humanitarian Law Committed in the Territory of Rwanda and Rwandan Citizens responsible for Genocide and Other Serious Violations Committed in the Territory of Neighbouring States, between 1 January 1994 and 31 December 1994 was established by the United Nations Security Council acting under Chapter VII of the UN Charter on 8 November 1994 (SC Resolution 955). The Security Council adopted the statute of the tribunal in the same resolution. The statute has been subsequently amended by the Security Council in Resolutions 1165 (1998), 1329 (2000), 1411 (2002), 1431 (2002), 1503 (2003), and 1512 (2003).

The tribunal was created to prosecute the crime of genocide and other serious violations of international humanitarian law committed on the territory of Rwanda and on the territory of neighbouring States by the citizens of Rwanda during the calendar year 1994 (Article 1). It has jurisdiction over natural persons (Article 5) in relation to the crime of genocide (Article 2), crimes against humanity (Article 3) and breaches of Article 3 common to the Geneva Conventions and of Additional Protocol II (Article 4). The statute provides for the individual criminal responsibility of persons responsible for the planning, instigation, ordering or committing of such crimes (Article 6). The tribunal has concurrent jurisdiction with national courts but has primacy over them (Article 8).

The tribunal has its seat at Arusha in Tanzania (see SC Resolution 977). It consists of three trial chambers together with the prosecutor and a registry (Article 10). There are 16 permanent judges and up to a maximum at any one time of four ad litem judges (Articles 11 and 12). The appeal chamber, which is shared with the International Criminal Tribunal for the Former Yugoslavia, consists of seven permanent judges. Each appeal is heard by five permanent judges (Article 11(3)). The rules of procedure and evidence of the tribunal were adopted by the court in accordance with Article 15 of the statute on 29 June 1995 and came into force on the same day. The tribunal has amended these rules on a number of occasions. The administration and servicing of the tribunal is undertaken by the registry (Article 16).

Responsibility for the investigation and prosecution of crimes before the tribunal lies with the prosecutor who is appointed by the Security Council and who is entitled to such staff as he or she may require (Article 15). He or she has the power to initiate prosecutions and to prepare indictments (Article 17). Indictments are reviewed by the judge of the trial chamber to whom the indictment has been transferred and that person shall confirm the indictment if satisfied that a prima facie case has been established by the prosecutor (Article 18). The trial chamber has responsibility of ensuring that the trial is fair and expeditious and conducted in accordance with the rules of procedure and evidence (Article 19). The rights of the accused are specified in Article 20. The rules of evidence are to include provisions on the protection of witnesses (Article 21).

Judgments of the tribunal shall be by majority (Article 22) and the penalties of the tribunal are limited to imprisonment (Article 23). Appeals may be heard on the basis of an error on a question of law invalidating the decision or an error of fact which has occasioned a miscarriage of justice (Article 24).

Sixty-nine individuals have been indicted before the tribunal. Twenty-three cases have been completed leading to the imprisonment of 20 individuals. Twenty-five individuals are currently on trial and 18 others are detained awaiting trial. The tribunal is due to complete its trial proceedings by the end of 2008 and to complete all of its work by the end of 2010 (SC Resolution 1503).

See also www.ictr.org.

Article I Competence of the International Tribunal for Rwanda

The International Tribunal for Rwanda shall have the power to prosecute persons responsible for serious violations of international humanitarian law committed in the territory of Rwanda and Rwandan citizens responsible for such violations committed in the territory of neighbouring States between 1 January 1994 and 31 December 1994, in accordance with the provisions of the present Statute.

Article 2 Genocide

1. The International Tribunal for Rwanda shall have the power to prosecute persons committing genocide as defined in paragraph 2 of this Article or of committing any of the other acts enumerated in paragraph 3 of this Article.

2. Genocide means any of the following acts committed with intent to destroy, in whole or in part, a national, ethnical, racial or religious group, as such:

    (a) Killing members of the group;

    (b) Causing serious bodily or mental harm to members of the group;

    (c) Deliberately inflicting on the group conditions of life calculated to bring about its physical destruction in whole or in part;

    (d) Imposing measures intended to prevent births within the group;

    (e) Forcibly transferring children of the group to another group.

3. The following acts shall be punishable:

    (a) Genocide;

    (b) Conspiracy to commit genocide;

    (c) Direct and public incitement to commit genocide;

    (d) Attempt to commit genocide;

    (e) Complicity in genocide.

Article 3 Crimes against Humanity

The International Tribunal for Rwanda shall have the power to prosecute persons responsible for the following crimes when committed as part of a widespread or systematic attack against any civilian population on national, political, ethnic, racial or religious grounds:

(a) Murder;

(b) Extermination;

(c) Enslavement;

(d) Deportation;

(e) Imprisonment;

(f) Torture;

(g) Rape;

(h) Persecutions on political, racial and religious grounds;

(i) Other inhumane acts.

Article 4 Violations of Article 3 Common to the Geneva Conventions and Additional Protocol II

The International Tribunal for Rwanda shall have the power to prosecute persons committing or ordering to be committed serious violations of Article 3 common to the Geneva Conventions of 12 August 1949 for the Protection of War Victims, and of Additional Protocol II thereto of 8 June 1977. These violations shall include, but shall not be limited to:

(a) Violence to life, health and physical or mental well-being of persons, in particular murder as well as cruel treatment such as torture, mutilation or any form of corporal punishment;

(b) Collective punishments;

(c) Taking of hostages;

(d) Acts of terrorism;

(e) Outrages upon personal dignity, in particular humiliating and degrading treatment, rape, enforced prostitution and any form of indecent assault;

(f) Pillage;

(g) The passing of sentences and the carrying out of executions without previous judgment pronounced by a regularly constituted court, affording all the judicial guarantees which are recognized as indispensable by civilised peoples;

(h) Threats to commit any of the foregoing acts.

Article 5 Personal Jurisdiction

The International Tribunal for Rwanda shall have jurisdiction over natural persons pursuant to the provisions of the present Statute.

Article 6 Individual Criminal Responsibility

1. A person who planned, instigated, ordered, committed or otherwise aided and abetted in the planning, preparation or execution of a crime referred to in Articles 2 to 4 of the present Statute, shall be individually responsible for the crime.

2. The official position of any accused person, whether as Head of State or Government or as a responsible Government official, shall not relieve such person of criminal responsibility nor mitigate punishment.

3. The fact that any of the acts referred to in Articles 2 to 4 of the present Statute was committed by a subordinate does not relieve his or her superior of criminal responsibility if he or she knew or had reason to know that the subordinate was about to commit such acts or had done so

and the superior failed to take the necessary and reasonable measures to prevent such acts or to punish the perpetrators thereof.

4. The fact that an accused person acted pursuant to an order of a government or of a superior shall not relieve him or her of criminal responsibility, but may be considered in mitigation of punishment if the International Tribunal for Rwanda determines that justice so requires.

Article 7 Territorial and Temporal Jurisdiction

The territorial jurisdiction of the International Tribunal for Rwanda shall extend to the territory of Rwanda including its land surface and airspace as well as to the territory of neighbouring States in respect of serious violations of international humanitarian law committed by Rwandan citizens. The temporal jurisdiction of the International Tribunal for Rwanda shall extend to a period beginning on 1 January 1994 and ending on 31 December 1994.

Article 8 Concurrent Jurisdiction

1. The International Tribunal for Rwanda and national courts shall have concurrent jurisdiction to prosecute persons for serious violations of international humanitarian law committed in the territory of Rwanda and Rwandan citizens for such violations committed in the territory of the neighbouring States, between 1 January 1994 and 31 December 1994.

2. The International Tribunal for Rwanda shall have the primacy over the national courts of all States. At any stage of the procedure, the International Tribunal for Rwanda may formally request national courts to defer to its competence in accordance with the present Statute and the Rules of Procedure and Evidence of the International Tribunal for Rwanda.

Article 9 *Non Bis in Idem*

1. No person shall be tried before a national court for acts constituting serious violations of international humanitarian law under the present Statute, for which he or she has already been tried by the International Tribunal for Rwanda.

2. A person who has been tried before a national court for acts constituting serious violations of international humanitarian law may be subsequently tried by the International Tribunal for Rwanda only if:

    (a) The act for which he or she was tried was characterised as an ordinary crime; or

    (b) The national court proceedings were not impartial or independent, were designed to shield the accused from international criminal responsibility, or the case was not diligently prosecuted.

3. In considering the penalty to be imposed on a person convicted of a crime under the present Statute, the International Tribunal for Rwanda shall take into account the extent to which any penalty imposed by a national court on the same person for the same act has already been served.

Article 10 Organisation of the International Tribunal for Rwanda

The International Tribunal for Rwanda shall consist of the following organs:

(a) The Chambers, comprising three Trial Chambers and an Appeals Chamber;

(b) The Prosecutor;

(c) A Registry.

Article 11 Composition of the Chambers

1. The Chambers shall be composed of 16 permanent independent judges, no two of whom may be nationals of the same State, and a maximum at any one time of four *ad litem* independent judges appointed in accordance with article 12 *ter*, paragraph 2, of the present Statute, no two of whom may be nationals of the same State.

2. Three permanent judges and a maximum at any one time of four *ad litem* judges shall be members of each Trial Chamber. Each Trial Chamber to which *ad litem* judges are assigned may be divided into sections of three judges each, composed of both permanent and *ad litem* judges. A section of a Trial Chamber shall have the same powers and responsibilities as a Trial Chamber under the present Statute and shall render judgment in accordance with the same rules.

3. Seven of the permanent judges shall be members of the Appeals Chamber. The Appeals Chamber shall, for each appeal, be composed of five of its members.

4. A person who for the purposes of membership of the Chambers of the International Tribunal for Rwanda could be regarded as a national of more than one State shall be deemed to be a national of the State in which that person ordinarily exercises civil and political rights.

Article 12 Qualification and Election of Judges

The permanent and *ad litem* judges shall be persons of high moral character, impartiality and integrity who possess the qualifications required in their respective countries for appointment to the highest judicial offices. In the overall composition of the Chambers and sections of the Trial Chambers, due account shall be taken of the experience of the judges in criminal law, international law, including international humanitarian law and human rights law.

Article 12 *bis* Election of Permanent Judges

1. Eleven of the permanent judges of the International Tribunal for Rwanda shall be elected by the General Assembly from a list submitted by the Security Council, in the following manner:

   (a) The Secretary-General shall invite nominations for permanent judges of the International Tribunal for Rwanda from States Members of the United Nations and non-member States maintaining permanent observer missions at United Nations Headquarters;

   (b) Within sixty days of the date of the invitation of the Secretary-General, each State may nominate up to two candidates meeting the qualifications set out in article 12 of the present Statute, no two of whom shall be of the same nationality and neither of whom shall be of the same nationality as any judge who is a member of the Appeals Chamber and who was elected or appointed a permanent judge of the International Tribunal for the Prosecution of Persons Responsible for Serious Violations of International Humanitarian Law Committed in the Territory of the Former Yugoslavia since 1991 (hereinafter referred to as 'the International Tribunal for the Former Yugoslavia') in accordance with article 13 *bis* of the Statute of that Tribunal;

   (c) The Secretary-General shall forward the nominations received to the Security Council. From the nominations received the Security Council shall establish a list of not less than twenty-two and not more than thirty-three candidates, taking due account of the adequate representation on the International Tribunal for Rwanda of the principal legal systems of the world;

   (d) The President of the Security Council shall transmit the list of candidates to the President of the General Assembly. From that list the General Assembly shall elect eleven permanent judges of the International Tribunal for Rwanda. The candidates who receive an absolute majority of the votes of the States Members of the United Nations and of the non-member States maintaining permanent observer missions at United Nations Headquarters, shall be declared elected. Should two candidates of the same nationality obtain the required majority vote, the one who received the higher number of votes shall be considered elected.

2. In the event of a vacancy in the Chambers amongst the permanent judges elected or appointed in accordance with this article, after consultation with the Presidents of the Security Council and of the General Assembly, the Secretary-General shall appoint a person meeting the qualifications of article 12 of the present Statute, for the remainder of the term of office concerned.

3. The permanent judges elected in accordance with this article shall be elected for a term of four years. The terms and conditions of service shall be those of the permanent judges of the International Tribunal for the Former Yugoslavia. They shall be eligible for re-election.

Article 12 ter: Election and Appointment of *Ad Litem* Judges

1. The *ad litem* judges of the International Tribunal for Rwanda shall be elected by the General Assembly from a list submitted by the Security Council, in the following manner:

   (a) The Secretary-General shall invite nominations for *ad litem* judges of the International Tribunal for Rwanda from States Members of the United Nations and non-member States maintaining permanent observer missions at United Nations Headquarters;

   (b) Within sixty days of the date of the invitation of the Secretary-General, each State may nominate up to four candidates meeting the qualifications set out in article 12 of the present Statute, taking into account the importance of a fair representation of female and male candidates;

   (c) The Secretary-General shall forward the nominations received to the Security Council. From the nominations received the Security Council shall establish a list of not less than thirty-six candidates, taking due account of the adequate representation of the principal legal systems of the world and bearing in mind the importance of equitable geographical distribution;

   (d) The President of the Security Council shall transmit the list of candidates to the President of the General Assembly. From that list the General Assembly shall elect the eighteen *ad litem* judges of the International Tribunal for Rwanda. The candidates who receive an absolute majority of the votes of the States Members of the United Nations and of the non-member States maintaining permanent observer missions at United Nations Headquarters shall be declared elected;

   (e) The *ad litem* judges shall be elected for a term of four years. They shall not be eligible for re-election.

2. During their term, *ad litem* judges will be appointed by the Secretary-General, upon request of the President of the International Tribunal for Rwanda, to serve in the Trial Chambers for one or more trials, for a cumulative period of up to, but not including, three years. When requesting the appointment of any particular *ad litem* judge, the President of the International Tribunal for Rwanda shall bear in mind the criteria set out in article 12 of the present Statute regarding the composition of the Chambers and sections of the Trial Chambers, the considerations set out in paragraphs 1 (b) and (c) above and the number of votes the *ad litem* judge received in the General Assembly.

Article 12 Quarter: Status of *Ad Litem* Judges

1. During the period in which they are appointed to serve in the International Tribunal for Rwanda, *ad litem* judges shall:

   (a) Benefit from the same terms and conditions of service *mutatis mutandis* as the permanent judges of the International Tribunal for Rwanda;

   (b) Enjoy, subject to paragraph 2 below, the same powers as the permanent judges of the International Tribunal for Rwanda;

   (c) Enjoy the privileges and immunities, exemptions and facilities of a judge of the International Tribunal for Rwanda.

2. During the period in which they are appointed to serve in the International Tribunal for Rwanda, *ad litem* judges shall not:

   (a) Be eligible for election as, or to vote in the election of, the President of the International Tribunal for Rwanda or the Presiding Judge of a Trial Chamber pursuant to article 13 of the present Statute;

(b) Have power:

    (i) To adopt rules of procedure and evidence pursuant to article 14 of the present Statute. They shall, however, be consulted before the adoption of those rules;

    (ii) To review an indictment pursuant to article 18 of the present Statute;

    (iii) To consult with the President of the International Tribunal for Rwanda in relation to the assignment of judges pursuant to article 13 of the present Statute or in relation to a pardon or commutation of sentence pursuant to article 27 of the present Statute;

    (iv) To adjudicate in pre-trial proceedings.

Article 13 Officers and Members of the Chambers

1. The permanent judges of the International Tribunal for Rwanda shall elect a President from amongst their number.

2. The President of the International Tribunal for Rwanda shall be a member of one of its Trial Chambers.

3. After consultation with the permanent judges of the International Tribunal for Rwanda, the President shall assign two of the permanent judges elected or appointed in accordance with article 12 bis of the present Statute to be members of the Appeals Chamber of the International Tribunal for the Former Yugoslavia and eight to the Trial Chambers of the International Tribunal for Rwanda.

4. The members of the Appeals Chamber of the International Tribunal for the Former Yugoslavia shall also serve as the members of the Appeals Chamber of the International Tribunal for Rwanda.

5. After consultation with the permanent judges of the International Tribunal for Rwanda, the President shall assign such ad litem judges as may from time to time be appointed to serve in the International Tribunal for Rwanda to the Trial Chambers.

6. A judge shall serve only in the Chamber to which he or she was assigned.

7. The permanent judges of each Trial Chamber shall elect a Presiding Judge from amongst their number, who shall oversee the work of that Trial Chamber as a whole.

Article 14 Rules of Procedure and Evidence

The Judges of the International Tribunal for Rwanda shall adopt, for the purpose of proceedings before the International Tribunal for Rwanda, the Rules of Procedure and Evidence for the conduct of the pre-trial phase of the proceedings, trials and appeals, the admission of evidence, the protection of victims and witnesses and other appropriate matters of the International Tribunal for the Former Yugoslavia with such changes as they deem necessary.

Article 15 The Prosecutor

1. The Prosecutor shall be responsible for the investigation and prosecution of persons responsible for serious violations of international humanitarian law committed in the territory of Rwanda and Rwandan citizens responsible for such violations committed in the territory of neighbouring States, between 1 January 1994 and 31 December 1994.

2. The Prosecutor shall act independently as a separate organ of the International Tribunal for Rwanda. He or she shall not seek or receive instructions from any government or from any other source.

3. The Prosecutor of the International Tribunal for the Former Yugoslavia shall also serve as the Prosecutor of the International Tribunal for Rwanda. He or she shall have additional staff, including an additional Deputy Prosecutor, to assist with prosecutions before the International Tribunal for Rwanda. Such staff shall be appointed by the Secretary-General on the recommendation of the Prosecutor.

Article 16 The Registry

1. The Registry shall be responsible for the administration and servicing of the International Tribunal for Rwanda.

2. The Registry shall consist of a Registrar and such other staff as may be required.

3. The Registrar shall be appointed by the Secretary-General after consultation with the President of the International Tribunal for Rwanda. He or she shall serve for a four-year term and be eligible for re-appointment. The terms and conditions of service of the Registrar shall be those of an Assistant Secretary-General of the United Nations.

4. The Staff of the Registry shall be appointed by the Secretary-General on the recommendation of the Registrar.

Article 17 Investigation and Preparation of Indictment

1. The Prosecutor shall initiate investigations ex-officio or on the basis of information obtained from any source, particularly from governments, United Nations organs, intergovernmental and non-governmental organizations. The Prosecutor shall assess the information received or obtained and decide whether there is sufficient basis to proceed.

2. The Prosecutor shall have the power to question suspects, victims and witnesses, to collect evidence and to conduct on-site investigations. In carrying out these tasks, the Prosecutor may, as appropriate, seek the assistance of the State authorities concerned.

3. If questioned, the suspect shall be entitled to be assisted by Counsel of his or her own choice, including the right to have legal assistance assigned to the suspect without payment by him or her in any such case if he or she does not have sufficient means to pay for it, as well as necessary translation into and from a language he or she speaks and understands.

4. Upon a determination that a *prima facie* case exists, the Prosecutor shall prepare an indictment containing a concise statement of the facts and the crime or crimes with which the accused is charged under the Statute. The indictment shall be transmitted to a judge of the Trial Chamber.

Article 18 Review of the Indictment

1. The judge of the Trial Chamber to whom the indictment has been transmitted shall review it. If satisfied that a *prima facie* case has been established by the Prosecutor, he or she shall confirm the indictment. If not so satisfied, the indictment shall be dismissed.

2. Upon confirmation of an indictment, the judge may, at the request of the Prosecutor, issue such orders and warrants for the arrest, detention, surrender or transfer of persons, and any other orders as may be required for the conduct of the trial.

Article 19 Commencement and Conduct of Trial Proceedings

1. The Trial Chambers shall ensure that a trial is fair and expeditious and that proceedings are conducted in accordance with the Rules of Procedure and Evidence, with full respect for the rights of the accused and due regard for the protection of victims and witnesses.

2. A person against whom an indictment has been confirmed shall, pursuant to an order or an arrest warrant of the International Tribunal for Rwanda, be taken into custody, immediately informed of the charges against him or her and transferred to the International Tribunal for Rwanda.

3. The Trial Chamber shall read the indictment, satisfy itself that the rights of the accused are respected, confirm that the accused understands the indictment, and instruct the accused to enter a plea. The Trial Chamber shall then set the date for trial.

4. The hearings shall be public unless the Trial Chamber decides to close the proceedings in accordance with its Rules of Procedure and Evidence.

Article 20 Rights of the Accused

1. All persons shall be equal before the International Tribunal for Rwanda.

2. In the determination of charges against him or her, the accused shall be entitled to a fair and public hearing, subject to Article 21 of the Statute.

3. The accused shall be presumed innocent until proven guilty according to the provisions of the present Statute.

4. In the determination of any charge against the accused pursuant to the present Statute, the accused shall be entitled to the following minimum guarantees, in full equality:

    (a) To be informed promptly and in detail in a language which he or she understands of the nature and cause of the charge against him or her;

    (b) To have adequate time and facilities for the preparation of his or her defence and to communicate with counsel of his or her own choosing;

    (c) To be tried without undue delay;

    (d) To be tried in his or her presence, and to defend himself or herself in person or through legal assistance of his or her own choosing; to be informed, if he or she does not have legal assistance, of this right; and to have legal assistance assigned to him or her, in any case where the interest of justice so require, and without payment by him or her in any such case if he or she does not have sufficient means to pay for it;

    (e) To examine, or have examined, the witnesses against him or her and to obtain the attendance and examination of witnesses on his or her behalf under the same conditions as witnesses against him or her;

    (f) To have the free assistance of an interpreter if he or she cannot understand or speak the language used in the International Tribunal for Rwanda;

    (g) Not to be compelled to testify against himself or herself or to confess guilt.

Article 21 Protection of Victims and Witnesses

The International Tribunal for Rwanda shall provide in its Rules of Procedure and Evidence for the protection of victims and witnesses. Such protection measures shall include, but shall not be limited to, the conduct of in camera proceedings and the protection of the victim's identity.

Article 22 Judgment

1. The Trial Chambers shall pronounce judgments and impose sentences and penalties on persons convicted of serious violations of international humanitarian law.

2. The judgment shall be rendered by a majority of the judges of the Trial Chamber, and shall be delivered by the Trial Chamber in public. It shall be accompanied by a reasoned opinion in writing, to which separate or dissenting opinions may be appended.

Article 23 Penalties

1. The penalty imposed by the Trial Chamber shall be limited to imprisonment. In determining the terms of imprisonment, the Trial Chambers shall have recourse to the general practice regarding prison sentences in the courts of Rwanda.

2. In imposing the sentences, the Trial Chambers should take into account such factors as the gravity of the offence and the individual circumstances of the convicted person.

3. In addition to imprisonment, the Trial Chambers may order the return of any property and proceeds acquired by criminal conduct, including by means of duress, to their rightful owners.

Article 24 Appellate Proceedings

1. The Appeals Chamber shall hear appeals from persons convicted by the Trial Chambers or from the Prosecutor on the following grounds:

    (a) An error on a question of law invalidating the decision; or

    (b) An error of fact which has occasioned a miscarriage of justice.

2. The Appeals Chamber may affirm, reverse or revise the decisions taken by the Trial Chambers.

Article 25 Review Proceedings

Where a new fact has been discovered which was not known at the time of the proceedings before the Trial Chambers or the Appeals Chamber and which could have been a decisive factor in reaching the decision, the convicted person or the Prosecutor may submit to the International Tribunal for Rwanda an application for review of the judgment.

Article 26 Enforcement of Sentences

Imprisonment shall be served in Rwanda or any of the States on a list of States which have indicated to the Security Council their willingness to accept convicted persons, as designated by the International Tribunal for Rwanda. Such imprisonment shall be in accordance with the applicable law of the State concerned, subject to the supervision of the International Tribunal for Rwanda.

Article 27 Pardon or Commutation of Sentences

If, pursuant to the applicable law of the State in which the convicted person is imprisoned, he or she is eligible for pardon or commutation of sentence, the State concerned shall notify the International Tribunal for Rwanda accordingly. There shall only be pardon or commutation of sentence if the President of the International Tribunal for Rwanda, in consultation with the judges, so decides on the basis of the interests of justice and the general principles of law.

Article 28 Cooperation and Judicial Assistance

1. States shall cooperate with the International Tribunal for Rwanda in the investigation and prosecution of persons accused of committing serious violations of international humanitarian law.

2. States shall comply without undue delay with any request for assistance or an order issued by a Trial Chamber, including but not limited to:

    (a) The identification and location of persons;

    (b) The taking of testimony and the production of evidence;

    (c) The service of documents;

    (d) The arrest or detention of persons;

    (e) The surrender or the transfer of the accused to the International Tribunal for Rwanda.

Article 29 The Status, Privileges and Immunities of the International Tribunal for Rwanda

1. The Convention on the Privileges and Immunities of the United Nations of 13 February 1946 shall apply to the International Tribunal for Rwanda, the judges, the Prosecutor and his or her staff, and the Registrar and his or her staff.

2. The judges, the Prosecutor and the Registrar shall enjoy the privileges and immunities, exemptions and facilities accorded to diplomatic envoys, in accordance with international law.

3. The staff of the Prosecutor and of the Registrar shall enjoy the privileges and immunities accorded to officials of the United Nations under Articles V and VII of the Convention referred to in paragraph 1 of this article.

4. Other persons, including the accused, required at the seat or meeting place of the International Tribunal for Rwanda shall be accorded such treatment as is necessary for the proper functioning of the International Tribunal for Rwanda.

Article 30 Expenses of the International Tribunal for Rwanda
The expenses of the International Tribunal for Rwanda shall be expenses of the Organisation in accordance with Article 17 of the Charter of the United Nations.

Article 31 Working Languages
The working languages of the International Tribunal for Rwanda shall be English and French.

Article 32 Annual Report
The President of the International Tribunal for Rwanda shall submit an annual report of the International Tribunal for Rwanda to the Security Council and to the General Assembly.

DOCUMENT 53

Rome Statute of the International Criminal Court 1998
2187 UNTS 3; 37 ILM 999 (1998)

The statute was adopted on 17 July 1998 at Rome at the conclusion of the United Nations Conference of Plenipotentiaries on the Establishment of an International Criminal Court (ICC) and entered into effect on 1 July 2002.

There are 139 parties. Among the notable non-parties are China, Egypt, Iran, Russia and the USA (which famously 'unsigned' the statute on 6 May 2002).

While the first suggestions for an international criminal court date back to 1872, work towards the creation of such a court began in earnest shortly after the end of the Second World War when the International Law Commission (ILC) considered two aspects of international criminal law: the preparation of a draft code of offences against the peace and security of mankind and the drafting of a statute for the establishment of an international criminal court. The work of the ILC on these subjects produced the Draft Code of Offences Against the Peace and Security of Mankind in 1954 **(Document 32)**, *work on an international criminal court having by then been deferred pending the adoption of the 1954 Draft Code and an agreed definition of aggression.*

The work of the ILC on offences against the peace and security of mankind resumed in 1982 and produced a further Draft Code of Crimes Against the Peace and Security of Mankind 1996 **(Document 33)**. *However, development of the draft code was overtaken by new moves to establish the ICC which were revived in 1989 after a proposal from Trinidad and Tobago in order to deal with the problem of drug trafficking. The matter was referred to the ILC in 1993 and the ILC's final draft was completed in 1994. The General Assembly then set up the Preparatory Committee for the Establishment of an International Criminal Court which met six times between 1996 and 1998 and worked on the ILC's draft. The final draft was submitted to the Rome Conference which met from 15 June to 17 July 1998 and adopted the Rome Statute of* *the International Criminal Court 1998. The ICC came into existence on 1 July 2002 and is located in The Hague, Netherlands.*

Although originally conceived as covering a wide range of international crimes, the jurisdiction of the ICC is, in fact, limited to the most serious crimes of concern to the international community (Article 5) including the crime of genocide (Article 6), crimes against humanity (Article 7), war crimes (Article 8) and the crime of aggression. However, the crime of aggression has yet to be defined (Article 5). The ICC has jurisdiction only over crimes committed after the entry into force of the Statute on 1 July 2002 (Article 11). The ICC can exercise jurisdiction over crimes committed on the territory of a State party, including on board a ship or aircraft registered to a State party, and in respect of crimes committed by a national of a State party (Article 12). Alleged crimes may be referred to the prosecutor by a State party in terms of Article 14 or by the United Nations Security Council. Alternatively, prosecutions may be initiated by the prosecutor ex proprio motu in terms of Article 15 (Article 13). The Security Council may request the court to defer an investigation or prosecution for a period of 12 months, which term may be renewed (Article 16).

The jurisdiction of the ICC is 'complementary to national criminal jurisdictions' (Article 1). This basic principle of complementarity is given substance by Article 17 which deals with issues of admissibility. That article requires the ICC to declare a case inadmissible where it is being investigated and prosecuted by a State which has jurisdiction over it or where a decision has been made by a State not to prosecute in such a case as long as the ICC is satisfied that the State was able and willing to carry out an investigation or prosecution (Article 17(1)(a)–(b)). Furthermore, a case cannot be admitted where the accused has already been tried for the conduct in question and where the alleged misconduct is not of sufficient gravity. In determining the question of lack of willingness to investigate or prosecute and in relation to the veracity of a previous prosecution, the ICC may consider the question of whether the national proceedings were undertaken to shield the accused from the jurisdiction of the ICC, whether there has been unjustified delay in the proceedings or whether the proceedings have been independent and impartial (Article 17(2)). (See also Article 20(3) for the purposes of completed trials.)

Article 9 provides for the adoption of Elements of Crime. This document was adopted on 30 June 2000 **(Document 54)**. *According to Article 21 of the Statute, the ICC is to apply in the first place, the Statute, Elements of Crime and its Rules of Procedure and Evidence* **(Document 55)**. *Thereafter, it may apply applicable treaties and the principles and rules of international law before considering general principles of law. Part 3 of the Statute deals with general principles of criminal law including, inter alia, principles of nullen crimen sine lege (Article 22); non-retroactivity (Article 24); individual criminal responsibility (Article 25); irrelevance of official capacity (Article 27); command responsibility (Article 28); and superior orders (Article 33).*

The ICC comprises the presidency, an appeals division, a trial division and a pre-trial division, the office of the prosecutor and the registry (Article 34). The ICC has 18 judges, elected by the Assembly of State Parties for a non-renewable term of nine years (Article 36). The president of the ICC and the first and second vice-presidents are elected by the judges (Article 38). The appeal division comprises the president of the ICC and four other judges who sit together on all appeals. The trial division and pre-trial division consist of no less than six judges each who sit in chambers (Article 39). The office of the prosecutor is an independent, separate organ of the ICC, headed by the prosecutor and one or more deputy prosecutors, elected for a term of nine years (Article 42). Matters relating to the registry and the staff of the ICC are dealt with in Articles 43–52 of the Statute. The Statute also provides for the establishment of an Assembly of State Parties comprising one representative from each of the States parties to supervise the work of the ICC (Article 112).

The Statute contains extensive provisions dealing with matters such as investigation and prosecution (Articles 53–61); the trial (Articles 62–76); penalties, which do not include the death penalty (Articles 77–80); appeal and revision (Articles 81–85); international co-operation and judicial assistance (Articles 86–102); enforcement (Articles 103–11); and finance (Articles 113–18).

See Official Records of the United Nations Conference of Plenipotentiaries on the Establishment of an International Criminal Court (3 volumes, 2002: UN Doc A/CONF. 183/13).

See also www.un.org/law/icc/; www.icc-cpi.int.

The States Parties to this Statute,

Conscious that all peoples are united by common bonds, their cultures pieced together in a shared heritage, and concerned that this delicate mosaic may be shattered at any time,

Mindful that during this century millions of children, women and men have been victims of unimaginable atrocities that deeply shock the conscience of humanity,

Recognizing that such grave crimes threaten the peace, security and well-being of the world,

Affirming that the most serious crimes of concern to the international community as a whole must not go unpunished and that their effective prosecution must be ensured by taking measures at the national level and by enhancing international cooperation,

Determined to put an end to impunity for the perpetrators of these crimes and thus to contribute to the prevention of such crimes,

Recalling that it is the duty of every State to exercise its criminal jurisdiction over those responsible for international crimes,

Reaffirming the Purposes and Principles of the Charter of the United Nations, and in particular that all States shall refrain from the threat or use of force against the territorial integrity or political independence of any State, or in any other manner inconsistent with the Purposes of the United Nations,

Emphasizing in this connection that nothing in this Statute shall be taken as authorizing any State Party to intervene in an armed conflict or in the internal affairs of any State,

Determined to these ends and for the sake of present and future generations, to establish an independent permanent International Criminal Court in relationship with the United Nations system, with jurisdiction over the most serious crimes of concern to the international community as a whole,

Emphasizing that the International Criminal Court established under this Statute shall be complementary to national criminal jurisdictions,

Resolved to guarantee lasting respect for and the enforcement of international justice,

Have agreed as follows:

Part I Establishment of the court

Article I The Court

An International Criminal Court ("the Court") is hereby established. It shall be a permanent institution and shall have the power to exercise its jurisdiction over persons for the most serious crimes of international concern, as referred to in this Statute, and shall be complementary to national criminal jurisdictions. The jurisdiction and functioning of the Court shall be governed by the provisions of this Statute.

Article 2 Relationship of the Court with the United Nations

The Court shall be brought into relationship with the United Nations through an agreement to be approved by the Assembly of States Parties to this Statute and thereafter concluded by the President of the Court on its behalf.

Article 3 Seat of the Court

1. The seat of the Court shall be established at The Hague in the Netherlands ("the host State").
2. The Court shall enter into a headquarters agreement with the host State, to be approved by the Assembly of States Parties and thereafter concluded by the President of the Court on its behalf.
3. The Court may sit elsewhere, whenever it considers it desirable, as provided in this Statute.

Article 4 Legal status and powers of the Court

1. The Court shall have international legal personality. It shall also have such legal capacity as may be necessary for the exercise of its functions and the fulfilment of its purposes.
2. The Court may exercise its functions and powers, as provided in this Statute, on the territory of any State Party and, by special agreement, on the territory of any other State.

Part 2 Jurisdiction, admissibility and applicable law

Article 5 Crimes within the jurisdiction of the Court

1. The jurisdiction of the Court shall be limited to the most serious crimes of concern to the international community as a whole. The Court has jurisdiction in accordance with this Statute with respect to the following crimes:
   (a) The crime of genocide;
   (b) Crimes against humanity;
   (c) War crimes;
   (d) The crime of aggression.
2. The Court shall exercise jurisdiction over the crime of aggression once a provision is adopted in accordance with articles 121 and 123 defining the crime and setting out the conditions under which the Court shall exercise jurisdiction with respect to this crime. Such a provision shall be consistent with the relevant provisions of the Charter of the United Nations.

Article 6 Genocide

For the purpose of this Statute, "genocide" means any of the following acts committed with intent to destroy, in whole or in part, a national, ethnical, racial or religious group, as such:

(a) Killing members of the group;
(b) Causing serious bodily or mental harm to members of the group;
(c) Deliberately inflicting on the group conditions of life calculated to bring about its physical destruction in whole or in part;
(d) Imposing measures intended to prevent births within the group;
(e) Forcibly transferring children of the group to another group.

Article 7 Crimes against humanity

1. For the purpose of this Statute, "crime against humanity" means any of the following acts when committed as part of a widespread or systematic attack directed against any civilian population, with knowledge of the attack:
   (a) Murder;
   (b) Extermination;

   (c) Enslavement;

   (d) Deportation or forcible transfer of population;

   (e) Imprisonment or other severe deprivation of physical liberty in violation of fundamental rules of international law;

   (f) Torture;

   (g) Rape, sexual slavery, enforced prostitution, forced pregnancy, enforced sterilization, or any other form of sexual violence of comparable gravity;

   (h) Persecution against any identifiable group or collectivity on political, racial, national, ethnic, cultural, religious, gender as defined in paragraph 3, or other grounds that are universally recognized as impermissible under international law, in connection with any act referred to in this paragraph or any crime within the jurisdiction of the Court;

   (i) Enforced disappearance of persons;

   (j) The crime of apartheid;

   (k) Other inhumane acts of a similar character intentionally causing great suffering, or serious injury to body or to mental or physical health.

2. For the purpose of paragraph 1:

   (a) "Attack directed against any civilian population" means a course of conduct involving the multiple commission of acts referred to in paragraph 1 against any civilian population, pursuant to or in furtherance of a State or organizational policy to commit such attack;

   (b) "Extermination" includes the intentional infliction of conditions of life, *inter alia* the deprivation of access to food and medicine, calculated to bring about the destruction of part of a population;

   (c) "Enslavement" means the exercise of any or all of the powers attaching to the right of ownership over a person and includes the exercise of such power in the course of trafficking in persons, in particular women and children;

   (d) "Deportation or forcible transfer of population" means forced displacement of the persons concerned by expulsion or other coercive acts from the area in which they are lawfully present, without grounds permitted under international law;

   (e) "Torture" means the intentional infliction of severe pain or suffering, whether physical or mental, upon a person in the custody or under the control of the accused; except that torture shall not include pain or suffering arising only from, inherent in or incidental to, lawful sanctions;

   (f) "Forced pregnancy" means the unlawful confinement of a woman forcibly made pregnant, with the intent of affecting the ethnic composition of any population or carrying out other grave violations of international law. This definition shall not in any way be interpreted as affecting national laws relating to pregnancy;

   (g) "Persecution" means the intentional and severe deprivation of fundamental rights contrary to international law by reason of the identity of the group or collectivity;

   (h) "The crime of apartheid" means inhumane acts of a character similar to those referred to in paragraph 1, committed in the context of an institutionalized regime of systematic oppression and domination by one racial group over any other racial group or groups and committed with the intention of maintaining that regime;

   (i) "Enforced disappearance of persons" means the arrest, detention or abduction of persons by, or with the authorization, support or acquiescence of, a State or a political organization, followed by a refusal to acknowledge that deprivation of freedom or to give information on the fate or whereabouts of those persons, with the intention of removing them from the protection of the law for a prolonged period of time.

3. For the purpose of this Statute, it is understood that the term "gender" refers to the two sexes, male and female, within the context of society. The term "gender" does not indicate any meaning different from the above.

Article 8 War crimes

1. The Court shall have jurisdiction in respect of war crimes in particular when committed as part of a plan or policy or as part of a large-scale commission of such crimes.

2. For the purpose of this Statute, "war crimes" means:

    (a) Grave breaches of the Geneva Conventions of 12 August 1949, namely, any of the following acts against persons or property protected under the provisions of the relevant Geneva Convention:

        (i)   Wilful killing;

        (ii)   Torture or inhuman treatment, including biological experiments;

        (iii) Wilfully causing great suffering, or serious injury to body or health;

        (iv)   Extensive destruction and appropriation of property, not justified by military necessity and carried out unlawfully and wantonly;

        (v)   Compelling a prisoner of war or other protected person to serve in the forces of a hostile Power;

        (vi)   Wilfully depriving a prisoner of war or other protected person of the rights of fair and regular trial;

        (vii) Unlawful deportation or transfer or unlawful confinement;

        (viii) Taking of hostages.

    (b) Other serious violations of the laws and customs applicable in international armed conflict, within the established framework of international law, namely, any of the following acts:

        (i)   Intentionally directing attacks against the civilian population as such or against individual civilians not taking direct part in hostilities;

        (ii)   Intentionally directing attacks against civilian objects, that is, objects which are not military objectives;

        (iii) Intentionally directing attacks against personnel, installations, material, units or vehicles involved in a humanitarian assistance or peacekeeping mission in accordance with the Charter of the United Nations, as long as they are entitled to the protection given to civilians or civilian objects under the international law of armed conflict;

        (iv)   Intentionally launching an attack in the knowledge that such attack will cause incidental loss of life or injury to civilians or damage to civilian objects or widespread, long-term and severe damage to the natural environment which would be clearly excessive in relation to the concrete and direct overall military advantage anticipated;

        (v)   Attacking or bombarding, by whatever means, towns, villages, dwellings or buildings which are undefended and which are not military objectives;

        (vi)   Killing or wounding a combatant who, having laid down his arms or having no longer means of defence, has surrendered at discretion;

        (vii) Making improper use of a flag of truce, of the flag or of the military insignia and uniform of the enemy or of the United Nations, as well as of the distinctive emblems of the Geneva Conventions, resulting in death or serious personal injury;

        (viii) The transfer, directly or indirectly, by the Occupying Power of parts of its own civilian population into the territory it occupies, or the deportation or transfer of all or parts of the population of the occupied territory within or outside this territory;

(ix)   Intentionally directing attacks against buildings dedicated to religion, education, art, science or charitable purposes, historic monuments, hospitals and places where the sick and wounded are collected, provided they are not military objectives;

(x)   Subjecting persons who are in the power of an adverse party to physical mutilation or to medical or scientific experiments of any kind which are neither justified by the medical, dental or hospital treatment of the person concerned nor carried out in his or her interest, and which cause death to or seriously endanger the health of such person or persons;

(xi)   Killing or wounding treacherously individuals belonging to the hostile nation or army;

(xii)   Declaring that no quarter will be given;

(xiii) Destroying or seizing the enemy's property unless such destruction or seizure be imperatively demanded by the necessities of war;

(xiv)   Declaring abolished, suspended or inadmissible in a court of law the rights and actions of the nationals of the hostile party;

(xv)   Compelling the nationals of the hostile party to take part in the operations of war directed against their own country, even if they were in the belligerent's service before the commencement of the war;

(xvi)   Pillaging a town or place, even when taken by assault;

(xvii) Employing poison or poisoned weapons;

(xviii) Employing asphyxiating, poisonous or other gases, and all analogous liquids, materials or devices;

(xix)   Employing bullets which expand or flatten easily in the human body, such as bullets with a hard envelope which does not entirely cover the core or is pierced with incisions;

(xx)   Employing weapons, projectiles and material and methods of warfare which are of a nature to cause superfluous injury or unnecessary suffering or which are inherently indiscriminate in violation of the international law of armed conflict, provided that such weapons, projectiles and material and methods of warfare are the subject of a comprehensive prohibition and are included in an annex to this Statute, by an amendment in accordance with the relevant provisions set forth in articles 121 and 123;

(xxi)   Committing outrages upon personal dignity, in particular humiliating and degrading treatment;

(xxii) Committing rape, sexual slavery, enforced prostitution, forced pregnancy, as defined in article 7, paragraph 2(f), enforced sterilization, or any other form of sexual violence also constituting a grave breach of the Geneva Conventions;

(xxiii) Utilizing the presence of a civilian or other protected person to render certain points, areas or military forces immune from military operations;

(xxiv) Intentionally directing attacks against buildings, material, medical units and transport, and personnel using the distinctive emblems of the Geneva Conventions in conformity with international law;

(xxv)   Intentionally using starvation of civilians as a method of warfare by depriving them of objects indispensable to their survival, including wilfully impeding relief supplies as provided for under the Geneva Conventions;

(xxvi) Conscripting or enlisting children under the age of fifteen years into the national armed forces or using them to participate actively in hostilities.

(c) In the case of an armed conflict not of an international character, serious violations of article 3 common to the four Geneva Conventions of 12 August 1949, namely, any of the following acts committed against persons taking no active part in the hostilities, including members of armed forces who have laid down their arms and those placed *hors de combat* by sickness, wounds, detention or any other cause:

(i) Violence to life and person, in particular murder of all kinds, mutilation, cruel treatment and torture;

(ii) Committing outrages upon personal dignity, in particular humiliating and degrading treatment;

(iii) Taking of hostages;

(iv) The passing of sentences and the carrying out of executions without previous judgment pronounced by a regularly constituted court, affording all judicial guarantees which are generally recognized as indispensable.

(d) Paragraph 2(c) applies to armed conflicts not of an international character and thus does not apply to situations of internal disturbances and tensions, such as riots, isolated and sporadic acts of violence or other acts of a similar nature.

(e) Other serious violations of the laws and customs applicable in armed conflicts not of an international character, within the established framework of international law, namely, any of the following acts:

(i) Intentionally directing attacks against the civilian population as such or against individual civilians not taking direct part in hostilities;

(ii) Intentionally directing attacks against buildings, material, medical units and transport, and personnel using the distinctive emblems of the Geneva Conventions in conformity with international law;

(iii) Intentionally directing attacks against personnel, installations, material, units or vehicles involved in a humanitarian assistance or peacekeeping mission in accordance with the Charter of the United Nations, as long as they are entitled to the protection given to civilians or civilian objects under the international law of armed conflict;

(iv) Intentionally directing attacks against buildings dedicated to religion, education, art, science or charitable purposes, historic monuments, hospitals and places where the sick and wounded are collected, provided they are not military objectives;

(v) Pillaging a town or place, even when taken by assault;

(vi) Committing rape, sexual slavery, enforced prostitution, forced pregnancy, as defined in article 7, paragraph 2(f), enforced sterilization, and any other form of sexual violence also constituting a serious violation of article 3 common to the four Geneva Conventions;

(vii) Conscripting or enlisting children under the age of fifteen years into armed forces or groups or using them to participate actively in hostilities;

(viii) Ordering the displacement of the civilian population for reasons related to the conflict, unless the security of the civilians involved or imperative military reasons so demand;

(ix) Killing or wounding treacherously a combatant adversary;

(x) Declaring that no quarter will be given;

(xi) Subjecting persons who are in the power of another party to the conflict to physical mutilation or to medical or scientific experiments of any kind which are neither justified by the medical, dental or hospital treatment of the person concerned nor carried out in his or her interest, and which cause death to or seriously endanger the health of such person or persons;

(xii) Destroying or seizing the property of an adversary unless such destruction or seizure be imperatively demanded by the necessities of the conflict;

(f) Paragraph 2(e) applies to armed conflicts not of an international character and thus does not apply to situations of internal disturbances and tensions, such as riots, isolated and sporadic acts of violence or other acts of a similar nature. It applies to armed conflicts that take place in the territory of a State when there is protracted armed conflict between governmental authorities and organized armed groups or between such groups.

3. Nothing in paragraph 2(c) and (e) shall affect the responsibility of a Government to maintain or re-establish law and order in the State or to defend the unity and territorial integrity of the State, by all legitimate means.

Article 9 Elements of Crimes

1. Elements of Crimes shall assist the Court in the interpretation and application of articles 6, 7 and 8. They shall be adopted by a two-thirds majority of the members of the Assembly of States Parties.

2. Amendments to the Elements of Crimes may be proposed by:

    (a) Any State Party;

    (b) The judges acting by an absolute majority;

    (c) The Prosecutor.

Such amendments shall be adopted by a two-thirds majority of the members of the Assembly of States Parties.

3. The Elements of Crimes and amendments thereto shall be consistent with this Statute.

Article 10

Nothing in this Part shall be interpreted as limiting or prejudicing in any way existing or developing rules of international law for purposes other than this Statute.

Article 11 Jurisdiction *ratione temporis*

1. The Court has jurisdiction only with respect to crimes committed after the entry into force of this Statute.

2. If a State becomes a Party to this Statute after its entry into force, the Court may exercise its jurisdiction only with respect to crimes committed after the entry into force of this Statute for that State, unless that State has made a declaration under article 12, paragraph 3.

Article 12 Preconditions to the exercise of jurisdiction

1. A State which becomes a Party to this Statute thereby accepts the jurisdiction of the Court with respect to the crimes referred to in article 5.

2. In the case of article 13, paragraph (a) or (c), the Court may exercise its jurisdiction if one or more of the following States are Parties to this Statute or have accepted the jurisdiction of the Court in accordance with paragraph 3:

    (a) The State on the territory of which the conduct in question occurred or, if the crime was committed on board a vessel or aircraft, the State of registration of that vessel or aircraft;

    (b) The State of which the person accused of the crime is a national.

3. If the acceptance of a State which is not a Party to this Statute is required under paragraph 2, that State may, by declaration lodged with the Registrar, accept the exercise of jurisdiction by the Court with respect to the crime in question. The accepting State shall cooperate with the Court without any delay or exception in accordance with Part 9.

Article 13 Exercise of jurisdiction

The Court may exercise its jurisdiction with respect to a crime referred to in article 5 in accordance with the provisions of this Statute if:

(a) A situation in which one or more of such crimes appears to have been committed is referred to the Prosecutor by a State Party in accordance with article 14;

(b) A situation in which one or more of such crimes appears to have been committed is referred to the Prosecutor by the Security Council acting under Chapter VII of the Charter of the United Nations; or

(c) The Prosecutor has initiated an investigation in respect of such a crime in accordance with article 15.

Article 14 Referral of a situation by a State Party

1. A State Party may refer to the Prosecutor a situation in which one or more crimes within the jurisdiction of the Court appear to have been committed requesting the Prosecutor to investigate the situation for the purpose of determining whether one or more specific persons should be charged with the commission of such crimes.

2. As far as possible, a referral shall specify the relevant circumstances and be accompanied by such supporting documentation as is available to the State referring the situation.

Article 15 Prosecutor

1. The Prosecutor may initiate investigations *proprio motu* on the basis of information on crimes within the jurisdiction of the Court.

2. The Prosecutor shall analyse the seriousness of the information received. For this purpose, he or she may seek additional information from States, organs of the United Nations, intergovernmental or non-governmental organizations, or other reliable sources that he or she deems appropriate, and may receive written or oral testimony at the seat of the Court.

3. If the Prosecutor concludes that there is a reasonable basis to proceed with an investigation, he or she shall submit to the Pre-Trial Chamber a request for authorization of an investigation, together with any supporting material collected. Victims may make representations to the Pre-Trial Chamber, in accordance with the Rules of Procedure and Evidence.

4. If the Pre-Trial Chamber, upon examination of the request and the supporting material, considers that there is a reasonable basis to proceed with an investigation, and that the case appears to fall within the jurisdiction of the Court, it shall authorize the commencement of the investigation, without prejudice to subsequent determinations by the Court with regard to the jurisdiction and admissibility of a case.

5. The refusal of the Pre-Trial Chamber to authorize the investigation shall not preclude the presentation of a subsequent request by the Prosecutor based on new facts or evidence regarding the same situation.

6. If, after the preliminary examination referred to in paragraphs 1 and 2, the Prosecutor concludes that the information provided does not constitute a reasonable basis for an investigation, he or she shall inform those who provided the information. This shall not preclude the Prosecutor from considering further information submitted to him or her regarding the same situation in the light of new facts or evidence.

Article 16 Referral of investigation or prosecution

No investigation or prosecution may be commenced or proceeded with under this Statute for a period of 12 months after the Security Council, in a resolution adopted under Chapter VII of the Charter of the United Nations, has requested the Court to that effect; that request may be renewed by the Council under the same conditions.

Article 17 Issues of admissibility

1. Having regard to paragraph 10 of the Preamble and article 1, the Court shall determine that a case is inadmissible where:

(a) The case is being investigated or prosecuted by a State which has jurisdiction over it, unless the State is unwilling or unable genuinely to carry out the investigation or prosecution;

(b) The case has been investigated by a State which has jurisdiction over it and the State has decided not to prosecute the person concerned, unless the decision resulted from the unwillingness or inability of the State genuinely to prosecute;

(c) The person concerned has already been tried for conduct which is the subject of the complaint, and a trial by the Court is not permitted under article 20, paragraph 3;

(d) The case is not of sufficient gravity to justify further action by the Court.

2. In order to determine unwillingness in a particular case, the Court shall consider, having regard to the principles of due process recognized by international law, whether one or more of the following exist, as applicable:

(a) The proceedings were or are being undertaken or the national decision was made for the purpose of shielding the person concerned from criminal responsibility for crimes within the jurisdiction of the Court referred to in article 5;

(b) There has been an unjustified delay in the proceedings which in the circumstances is inconsistent with an intent to bring the person concerned to justice;

(c) The proceedings were not or are not being conducted independently or impartially, and they were or are being conducted in a manner which, in the circumstances, is inconsistent with an intent to bring the person concerned to justice.

3. In order to determine inability in a particular case, the Court shall consider whether, due to a total or substantial collapse or unavailability of its national judicial system, the State is unable to obtain the accused or the necessary evidence and testimony or otherwise unable to carry out its proceedings.

Article 18 Preliminary rulings regarding admissibility

1. When a situation has been referred to the Court pursuant to article 13(a) and the Prosecutor has determined that there would be a reasonable basis to commence an investigation, or the Prosecutor initiates an investigation pursuant to articles 13(c) and 15, the Prosecutor shall notify all States Parties and those States which, taking into account the information available, would normally exercise jurisdiction over the crimes concerned. The Prosecutor may notify such States on a confidential basis and, where the Prosecutor believes it necessary to protect persons, prevent destruction of evidence or prevent the absconding of persons, may limit the scope of the information provided to States.

2. Within one month of receipt of that notification, a State may inform the Court that it is investigating or has investigated its nationals or others within its jurisdiction with respect to criminal acts which may constitute crimes referred to in article 5 and which relate to the information provided in the notification to States. At the request of that State, the Prosecutor shall defer to the State's investigation of those persons unless the Pre-Trial Chamber, on the application of the Prosecutor, decides to authorize the investigation.

3. The Prosecutor's deferral to a State's investigation shall be open to review by the Prosecutor six months after the date of deferral or at any time when there has been a significant change of circumstances based on the State's unwillingness or inability genuinely to carry out the investigation.

4. The State concerned or the Prosecutor may appeal to the Appeals Chamber against a ruling of the Pre-Trial Chamber, in accordance with article 82. The appeal may be heard on an expedited basis.

5. When the Prosecutor has deferred an investigation in accordance with paragraph 2, the Prosecutor may request that the State concerned periodically inform the Prosecutor of the progress of its investigations and any subsequent prosecutions. States Parties shall respond to such requests without undue delay.

6. Pending a ruling by the Pre-Trial Chamber, or at any time when the Prosecutor has deferred an investigation under this article, the Prosecutor may, on an exceptional basis, seek authority from

the Pre-Trial Chamber to pursue necessary investigative steps for the purpose of preserving evidence where there is a unique opportunity to obtain important evidence or there is a significant risk that such evidence may not be subsequently available.

7. A State which has challenged a ruling of the Pre-Trial Chamber under this article may challenge the admissibility of a case under article 19 on the grounds of additional significant facts or significant change of circumstances.

Article 19 Challenges to the jurisdiction of the Court or the admissibility of a case

1. The Court shall satisfy itself that it has jurisdiction in any case brought before it. The Court may, on its own motion, determine the admissibility of a case in accordance with article 17.

2. Challenges to the admissibility of a case on the grounds referred to in article 17 or challenges to the jurisdiction of the Court may be made by:

    (a) An accused or a person for whom a warrant of arrest or a summons to appear has been issued under article 58;

    (b) A State which has jurisdiction over a case, on the ground that it is investigating or prosecuting the case or has investigated or prosecuted; or

    (c) A State from which acceptance of jurisdiction is required under article 12.

3. The Prosecutor may seek a ruling from the Court regarding a question of jurisdiction or admissibility. In proceedings with respect to jurisdiction or admissibility, those who have referred the situation under article 13, as well as victims, may also submit observations to the Court.

4. The admissibility of a case or the jurisdiction of the Court may be challenged only once by any person or State referred to in paragraph 2. The challenge shall take place prior to or at the commencement of the trial. In exceptional circumstances, the Court may grant leave for a challenge to be brought more than once or at a time later than the commencement of the trial. Challenges to the admissibility of a case, at the commencement of a trial, or subsequently with the leave of the Court, may be based only on article 17, paragraph 1(c).

5. A State referred to in paragraph 2(b) and (c) shall make a challenge at the earliest opportunity.

6. Prior to the confirmation of the charges, challenges to the admissibility of a case or challenges to the jurisdiction of the Court shall be referred to the Pre-Trial Chamber. After confirmation of the charges, they shall be referred to the Trial Chamber. Decisions with respect to jurisdiction or admissibility may be appealed to the Appeals Chamber in accordance with article 82.

7. If a challenge is made by a State referred to in paragraph 2 (b) or (c), the Prosecutor shall suspend the investigation until such time as the Court makes a determination in accordance with article 17.

8. Pending a ruling by the Court, the Prosecutor may seek authority from the Court:

    (a) To pursue necessary investigative steps of the kind referred to in article 18, paragraph 6;

    (b) To take a statement or testimony from a witness or complete the collection and examination of evidence which had begun prior to the making of the challenge; and

    (c) In cooperation with the relevant States, to prevent the absconding of persons in respect of whom the Prosecutor has already requested a warrant of arrest under article 58.

9. The making of a challenge shall not affect the validity of any act performed by the Prosecutor or any order or warrant issued by the Court prior to the making of the challenge.

10. If the Court has decided that a case is inadmissible under article 17, the Prosecutor may submit a request for a review of the decision when he or she is fully satisfied that new facts have arisen which negate the basis on which the case had previously been found inadmissible under article 17.

11. If the Prosecutor, having regard to the matters referred to in article 17, defers an investigation, the Prosecutor may request that the relevant State make available to the Prosecutor information on the proceedings. That information shall, at the request of the State concerned, be confidential. If the Prosecutor thereafter decides to proceed with an investigation, he or she shall notify the State to which deferral of the proceedings has taken place.

Article 20 *Ne bis in idem*

1. Except as provided in this Statute, no person shall be tried before the Court with respect to conduct which formed the basis of crimes for which the person has been convicted or acquitted by the Court.

2. No person shall be tried by another court for a crime referred to in article 5 for which that person has already been convicted or acquitted by the Court.

3. No person who has been tried by another court for conduct also proscribed under article 6, 7 or 8 shall be tried by the Court with respect to the same conduct unless the proceedings in the other court:

   (a) Were for the purpose of shielding the person concerned from criminal responsibility for crimes within the jurisdiction of the Court; or

   (b) Otherwise were not conducted independently or impartially in accordance with the norms of due process recognized by international law and were conducted in a manner which, in the circumstances, was inconsistent with an intent to bring the person concerned to justice.

Article 21 Applicable law

1. The Court shall apply:

   (a) In the first place, this Statute, Elements of Crimes and its Rules of Procedure and Evidence;

   (b) In the second place, where appropriate, applicable treaties and the principles and rules of international law, including the established principles of the international law of armed conflict;

   (c) Failing that, general principles of law derived by the Court from national laws of legal systems of the world including, as appropriate, the national laws of States that would normally exercise jurisdiction over the crime, provided that those principles are not inconsistent with this Statute and with international law and internationally recognized norms and standards.

2. The Court may apply principles and rules of law as interpreted in its previous decisions.

3. The application and interpretation of law pursuant to this article must be consistent with internationally recognized human rights, and be without any adverse distinction founded on grounds such as gender as defined in article 7, paragraph 3, age, race, colour, language, religion or belief, political or other opinion, national, ethnic or social origin, wealth, birth or other status.

Part 3 General principles of criminal law

Article 22 *Nullum crimen sine lege*

1. A person shall not be criminally responsible under this Statute unless the conduct in question constitutes, at the time it takes place, a crime within the jurisdiction of the Court.

2. The definition of a crime shall be strictly construed and shall not be extended by analogy. In case of ambiguity, the definition shall be interpreted in favour of the person being investigated, prosecuted or convicted.

3. This article shall not affect the characterization of any conduct as criminal under international law independently of this Statute.

Article 23 *Nulla poena sine lege*

A person convicted by the Court may be punished only in accordance with this Statute.

Article 24 **Non-retroactivity** *ratione personae*

1. No person shall be criminally responsible under this Statute for conduct prior to the entry into force of the Statute.

2. In the event of a change in the law applicable to a given case prior to a final judgment, the law more favourable to the person being investigated, prosecuted or convicted shall apply.

Article 25 **Individual criminal responsibility**

1. The Court shall have jurisdiction over natural persons pursuant to this Statute.

2. A person who commits a crime within the jurisdiction of the Court shall be individually responsible and liable for punishment in accordance with this Statute.

3. In accordance with this Statute, a person shall be criminally responsible and liable for punishment for a crime within the jurisdiction of the Court if that person:

    (a) Commits such a crime, whether as an individual, jointly with another or through another person, regardless of whether that other person is criminally responsible;

    (b) Orders, solicits or induces the commission of such a crime which in fact occurs or is attempted;

    (c) For the purpose of facilitating the commission of such a crime, aids, abets or otherwise assists in its commission or its attempted commission, including providing the means for its commission;

    (d) In any other way contributes to the commission or attempted commission of such a crime by a group of persons acting with a common purpose. Such contribution shall be intentional and shall either:

        (i) Be made with the aim of furthering the criminal activity or criminal purpose of the group, where such activity or purpose involves the commission of a crime within the jurisdiction of the Court; or

        (ii) Be made in the knowledge of the intention of the group to commit the crime;

    (e) In respect of the crime of genocide, directly and publicly incites others to commit genocide;

    (f) Attempts to commit such a crime by taking action that commences its execution by means of a substantial step, but the crime does not occur because of circumstances independent of the person's intentions. However, a person who abandons the effort to commit the crime or otherwise prevents the completion of the crime shall not be liable for punishment under this Statute for the attempt to commit that crime if that person completely and voluntarily gave up the criminal purpose.

4. No provision in this Statute relating to individual criminal responsibility shall affect the responsibility of States under international law.

Article 26 **Exclusion of jurisdiction over persons under eighteen**

The Court shall have no jurisdiction over any person who was under the age of 18 at the time of the alleged commission of a crime.

Article 27 **Irrelevance of official capacity**

1. This Statute shall apply equally to all persons without any distinction based on official capacity. In particular, official capacity as a Head of State or Government, a member of a Government or parliament, an elected representative or a government official shall in no case exempt a person

from criminal responsibility under this Statute, nor shall it, in and of itself, constitute a ground for reduction of sentence.

2. Immunities or special procedural rules which may attach to the official capacity of a person, whether under national or international law, shall not bar the Court from exercising its jurisdiction over such a person.

Article 28 Responsibility of commanders and other superiors

In addition to other grounds of criminal responsibility under this Statute for crimes within the jurisdiction of the Court:

(a) A military commander or person effectively acting as a military commander shall be criminally responsible for crimes within the jurisdiction of the Court committed by forces under his or her effective command and control, or effective authority and control as the case may be, as a result of his or her failure to exercise control properly over such forces, where:

(i) That military commander or person either knew or, owing to the circumstances at the time, should have known that the forces were committing or about to commit such crimes; and

(ii) That military commander or person failed to take all necessary and reasonable measures within his or her power to prevent or repress their commission or to submit the matter to the competent authorities for investigation and prosecution.

(b) With respect to superior and subordinate relationships not described in paragraph (a), a superior shall be criminally responsible for crimes within the jurisdiction of the Court committed by subordinates under his or her effective authority and control, as a result of his or her failure to exercise control properly over such subordinates, where:

(i) The superior either knew, or consciously disregarded information which clearly indicated, that the subordinates were committing or about to commit such crimes;

(ii) The crimes concerned activities that were within the effective responsibility and control of the superior; and

(iii) The superior failed to take all necessary and reasonable measures within his or her power to prevent or repress their commission or to submit the matter to the competent authorities for investigation and prosecution.

Article 29 Non-applicability of statute of limitations

The crimes within the jurisdiction of the Court shall not be subject to any statute of limitations.

Article 30 Mental element

1. Unless otherwise provided, a person shall be criminally responsible and liable for punishment for a crime within the jurisdiction of the Court only if the material elements are committed with intent and knowledge.

2. For the purposes of this article, a person has intent where:

(a) In relation to conduct, that person means to engage in the conduct;

(b) In relation to a consequence, that person means to cause that consequence or is aware that it will occur in the ordinary course of events.

3. For the purposes of this article, "knowledge" means awareness that a circumstance exists or a consequence will occur in the ordinary course of events. "Know" and "knowingly" shall be construed accordingly.

Article 31 Grounds for excluding criminal responsibility

1. In addition to other grounds for excluding criminal responsibility provided for in this Statute, a person shall not be criminally responsible if, at the time of that person's conduct:

    (a) The person suffers from a mental disease or defect that destroys that person's capacity to appreciate the unlawfulness or nature of his or her conduct, or capacity to control his or her conduct to conform to the requirements of law;

    (b) The person is in a state of intoxication that destroys that person's capacity to appreciate the unlawfulness or nature of his or her conduct, or capacity to control his or her conduct to conform to the requirements of law, unless the person has become voluntarily intoxicated under such circumstances that the person knew, or disregarded the risk, that, as a result of the intoxication, he or she was likely to engage in conduct constituting a crime within the jurisdiction of the Court;

    (c) The person acts reasonably to defend himself or herself or another person or, in the case of war crimes, property which is essential for the survival of the person or another person or property which is essential for accomplishing a military mission, against an imminent and unlawful use of force in a manner proportionate to the degree of danger to the person or the other person or property protected. The fact that the person was involved in a defensive operation conducted by forces shall not in itself constitute a ground for excluding criminal responsibility under this subparagraph;

    (d) The conduct which is alleged to constitute a crime within the jurisdiction of the Court has been caused by duress resulting from a threat of imminent death or of continuing or imminent serious bodily harm against that person or another person, and the person acts necessarily and reasonably to avoid this threat, provided that the person does not intend to cause a greater harm than the one sought to be avoided. Such a threat may either be:

    (i) Made by other persons; or

    (ii) Constituted by other circumstances beyond that person's control.

2. The Court shall determine the applicability of the grounds for excluding criminal responsibility provided for in this Statute to the case before it.

3. At trial, the Court may consider a ground for excluding criminal responsibility other than those referred to in paragraph 1 where such a ground is derived from applicable law as set forth in article 21. The procedures relating to the consideration of such a ground shall be provided for in the Rules of Procedure and Evidence.

Article 32 Mistake of fact or mistake of law

1. A mistake of fact shall be a ground for excluding criminal responsibility only if it negates the mental element required by the crime.

2. A mistake of law as to whether a particular type of conduct is a crime within the jurisdiction of the Court shall not be a ground for excluding criminal responsibility. A mistake of law may, however, be a ground for excluding criminal responsibility if it negates the mental element required by such a crime, or as provided for in article 33.

Article 33 Superior orders and prescription of law

1. The fact that a crime within the jurisdiction of the Court has been committed by a person pursuant to an order of a Government or of a superior, whether military or civilian, shall not relieve that person of criminal responsibility unless:

    (a) The person was under a legal obligation to obey orders of the Government or the superior in question;

(b) The person did not know that the order was unlawful; and

(c) The order was not manifestly unlawful.

2. For the purposes of this article, orders to commit genocide or crimes against humanity are manifestly unlawful.

Part 4 Composition and administration of the court

Article 34 Organs of the Court

The Court shall be composed of the following organs:

(a) The Presidency;

(b) An Appeals Division, a Trial Division and a Pre-Trial Division;

(c) The Office of the Prosecutor;

(d) The Registry.

Article 35 Service of judges

1. All judges shall be elected as full-time members of the Court and shall be available to serve on that basis from the commencement of their terms of office.

2. The judges composing the Presidency shall serve on a full-time basis as soon as they are elected.

3. The Presidency may, on the basis of the workload of the Court and in consultation with its members, decide from time to time to what extent the remaining judges shall be required to serve on a full-time basis. Any such arrangement shall be without prejudice to the provisions of article 40.

4. The financial arrangements for judges not required to serve on a full-time basis shall be made in accordance with article 49.

Article 36 Qualifications, nomination and election of judges

1. Subject to the provisions of paragraph 2, there shall be 18 judges of the Court.

2. (a) The Presidency, acting on behalf of the Court, may propose an increase in the number of judges specified in paragraph 1, indicating the reasons why this is considered necessary and appropriate. The Registrar shall promptly circulate any such proposal to all States Parties.

  (b) Any such proposal shall then be considered at a meeting of the Assembly of States Parties to be convened in accordance with article 112. The proposal shall be considered adopted if approved at the meeting by a vote of two thirds of the members of the Assembly of States Parties and shall enter into force at such time as decided by the Assembly of States Parties.

  (c) (i) Once a proposal for an increase in the number of judges has been adopted under subparagraph (b), the election of the additional judges shall take place at the next session of the Assembly of States Parties in accordance with paragraphs 3 to 8, and article 37, paragraph 2;

    (ii) Once a proposal for an increase in the number of judges has been adopted and brought into effect under subparagraphs (b) and (c)(i), it shall be open to the Presidency at any time thereafter, if the workload of the Court justifies it, to propose a reduction in the number of judges, provided that the number of judges shall not be reduced below that specified in paragraph 1. The proposal shall be dealt with in accordance with the procedure laid down in subparagraphs (a) and (b). In the event that the proposal is adopted, the number of judges shall be progressively decreased as the terms of office of serving judges expire, until the necessary number has been reached.

3. (a) The judges shall be chosen from among persons of high moral character, impartiality and integrity who possess the qualifications required in their respective States for appointment to the highest judicial offices.

   (b) Every candidate for election to the Court shall:

       (i) Have established competence in criminal law and procedure, and the necessary relevant experience, whether as judge, prosecutor, advocate or in other similar capacity, in criminal proceedings; or

       (ii) Have established competence in relevant areas of international law such as international humanitarian law and the law of human rights, and extensive experience in a professional legal capacity which is of relevance to the judicial work of the Court;

   (c) Every candidate for election to the Court shall have an excellent knowledge of and be fluent in at least one of the working languages of the Court.

4. (a) Nominations of candidates for election to the Court may be made by any State Party to this Statute, and shall be made either:

       (i) By the procedure for the nomination of candidates for appointment to the highest judicial offices in the State in question; or

       (ii) By the procedure provided for the nomination of candidates for the International Court of Justice in the Statute of that Court. Nominations shall be accompanied by a statement in the necessary detail specifying how the candidate fulfils the requirements of paragraph 3.

   (b) Each State Party may put forward one candidate for any given election who need not necessarily be a national of that State Party but shall in any case be a national of a State Party.

   (c) The Assembly of States Parties may decide to establish, if appropriate, an Advisory Committee on nominations. In that event, the Committee's composition and mandate shall be established by the Assembly of States Parties.

5. For the purposes of the election, there shall be two lists of candidates: List A containing the names of candidates with the qualifications specified in paragraph 3(b)(i); and List B containing the names of candidates with the qualifications specified in paragraph 3(b)(ii). A candidate with sufficient qualifications for both lists may choose on which list to appear. At the first election to the Court, at least nine judges shall be elected from list A and at least five judges from list B. Subsequent elections shall be so organized as to maintain the equivalent proportion on the Court of judges qualified on the two lists.

6. (a) The judges shall be elected by secret ballot at a meeting of the Assembly of States Parties convened for that purpose under article 112. Subject to paragraph 7, the persons elected to the Court shall be the 18 candidates who obtain the highest number of votes and a two-thirds majority of the States Parties present and voting.

   (b) In the event that a sufficient number of judges is not elected on the first ballot, successive ballots shall be held in accordance with the procedures laid down in subparagraph (a) until the remaining places have been filled.

7. No two judges may be nationals of the same State. A person who, for the purposes of membership of the Court, could be regarded as a national of more than one State shall be deemed to be a national of the State in which that person ordinarily exercises civil and political rights.

8. (a) The States Parties shall, in the selection of judges, take into account the need, within the membership of the Court, for:

       (i) The representation of the principal legal systems of the world;

       (ii) Equitable geographical representation; and

       (iii) A fair representation of female and male judges.

(b) States Parties shall also take into account the need to include judges with legal expertise on specific issues, including, but not limited to, violence against women or children.

9. (a) Subject to subparagraph (b), judges shall hold office for a term of nine years and, subject to subparagraph (c) and to article 37, paragraph 2, shall not be eligible for re-election.

(b) At the first election, one third of the judges elected shall be selected by lot to serve for a term of three years; one third of the judges elected shall be selected by lot to serve for a term of six years; and the remainder shall serve for a term of nine years.

(c) A judge who is selected to serve for a term of three years under subparagraph (b) shall be eligible for re-election for a full term.

10. Notwithstanding paragraph 9, a judge assigned to a Trial or Appeals Chamber in accordance with article 39 shall continue in office to complete any trial or appeal the hearing of which has already commenced before that Chamber.

Article 37 Judicial vacancies

1. In the event of a vacancy, an election shall be held in accordance with article 36 to fill the vacancy.

2. A judge elected to fill a vacancy shall serve for the remainder of the predecessor's term and, if that period is three years or less, shall be eligible for re-election for a full term under article 36.

Article 38 The Presidency

1. The President and the First and Second Vice-Presidents shall be elected by an absolute majority of the judges. They shall each serve for a term of three years or until the end of their respective terms of office as judges, whichever expires earlier. They shall be eligible for re-election once.

2. The First Vice-President shall act in place of the President in the event that the President is unavailable or disqualified. The Second Vice-President shall act in place of the President in the event that both the President and the First Vice-President are unavailable or disqualified.

3. The President, together with the First and Second Vice-Presidents, shall constitute the Presidency, which shall be responsible for:

(a) The proper administration of the Court, with the exception of the Office of the Prosecutor; and

(b) The other functions conferred upon it in accordance with this Statute.

4. In discharging its responsibility under paragraph 3 (a), the Presidency shall coordinate with and seek the concurrence of the Prosecutor on all matters of mutual concern.

Article 39 Chambers

1. As soon as possible after the election of the judges, the Court shall organize itself into the divisions specified in article 34, paragraph (b). The Appeals Division shall be composed of the President and four other judges, the Trial Division of not less than six judges and the Pre-Trial Division of not less than six judges. The assignment of judges to divisions shall be based on the nature of the functions to be performed by each division and the qualifications and experience of the judges elected to the Court, in such a way that each division shall contain an appropriate combination of expertise in criminal law and procedure and in international law. The Trial and Pre-Trial Divisions shall be composed predominantly of judges with criminal trial experience.

2. (a) The judicial functions of the Court shall be carried out in each division by Chambers.

(b) (i) The Appeals Chamber shall be composed of all the judges of the Appeals Division;

(ii) The functions of the Trial Chamber shall be carried out by three judges of the Trial Division;

(iii) The functions of the Pre-Trial Chamber shall be carried out either by three judges of the Pre-Trial Division or by a single judge of that division in accordance with this Statute and the Rules of Procedure and Evidence;

(c) Nothing in this paragraph shall preclude the simultaneous constitution of more than one Trial Chamber or Pre-Trial Chamber when the efficient management of the Court's workload so requires.

3. (a) Judges assigned to the Trial and Pre-Trial Divisions shall serve in those divisions for a period of three years, and thereafter until the completion of any case the hearing of which has already commenced in the division concerned.

(b) Judges assigned to the Appeals Division shall serve in that division for their entire term of office.

4. Judges assigned to the Appeals Division shall serve only in that division. Nothing in this article shall, however, preclude the temporary attachment of judges from the Trial Division to the Pre-Trial Division or vice versa, if the Presidency considers that the efficient management of the Court's workload so requires, provided that under no circumstances shall a judge who has participated in the pre-trial phase of a case be eligible to sit on the Trial Chamber hearing that case.

Article 40 Independence of the judges

1. The judges shall be independent in the performance of their functions.

2. Judges shall not engage in any activity which is likely to interfere with their judicial functions or to affect confidence in their independence.

3. Judges required to serve on a full-time basis at the seat of the Court shall not engage in any other occupation of a professional nature.

4. Any question regarding the application of paragraphs 2 and 3 shall be decided by an absolute majority of the judges. Where any such question concerns an individual judge, that judge shall not take part in the decision.

Article 41 Excusing and disqualification of judges

1. The Presidency may, at the request of a judge, excuse that judge from the exercise of a function under this Statute, in accordance with the Rules of Procedure and Evidence.

2. (a) A judge shall not participate in any case in which his or her impartiality might reasonably be doubted on any ground. A judge shall be disqualified from a case in accordance with this paragraph if, *inter alia*, that judge has previously been involved in any capacity in that case before the Court or in a related criminal case at the national level involving the person being investigated or prosecuted. A judge shall also be disqualified on such other grounds as may be provided for in the Rules of Procedure and Evidence.

(b) The Prosecutor or the person being investigated or prosecuted may request the disqualification of a judge under this paragraph.

(c) Any question as to the disqualification of a judge shall be decided by an absolute majority of the judges. The challenged judge shall be entitled to present his or her comments on the matter, but shall not take part in the decision.

Article 42 The Office of the Prosecutor

1. The Office of the Prosecutor shall act independently as a separate organ of the Court. It shall be responsible for receiving referrals and any substantiated information on crimes within the jurisdiction of the Court, for examining them and for conducting investigations and prosecutions before the Court. A member of the Office shall not seek or act on instructions from any external source.

2. The Office shall be headed by the Prosecutor. The Prosecutor shall have full authority over the management and administration of the Office, including the staff, facilities and other resources thereof. The Prosecutor shall be assisted by one or more Deputy Prosecutors, who shall be entitled to carry out any of the acts required of the Prosecutor under this Statute. The

Prosecutor and the Deputy Prosecutors shall be of different nationalities. They shall serve on a full-time basis.

3. The Prosecutor and the Deputy Prosecutors shall be persons of high moral character, be highly competent in and have extensive practical experience in the prosecution or trial of criminal cases. They shall have an excellent knowledge of and be fluent in at least one of the working languages of the Court.

4. The Prosecutor shall be elected by secret ballot by an absolute majority of the members of the Assembly of States Parties. The Deputy Prosecutors shall be elected in the same way from a list of candidates provided by the Prosecutor. The Prosecutor shall nominate three candidates for each position of Deputy Prosecutor to be filled. Unless a shorter term is decided upon at the time of their election, the Prosecutor and the Deputy Prosecutors shall hold office for a term of nine years and shall not be eligible for re-election.

5. Neither the Prosecutor nor a Deputy Prosecutor shall engage in any activity which is likely to interfere with his or her prosecutorial functions or to affect confidence in his or her independence. They shall not engage in any other occupation of a professional nature.

6. The Presidency may excuse the Prosecutor or a Deputy Prosecutor, at his or her request, from acting in a particular case.

7. Neither the Prosecutor nor a Deputy Prosecutor shall participate in any matter in which their impartiality might reasonably be doubted on any ground. They shall be disqualified from a case in accordance with this paragraph if, *inter alia*, they have previously been involved in any capacity in that case before the Court or in a related criminal case at the national level involving the person being investigated or prosecuted.

8. Any question as to the disqualification of the Prosecutor or a Deputy Prosecutor shall be decided by the Appeals Chamber.

   (a) The person being investigated or prosecuted may at any time request the disqualification of the Prosecutor or a Deputy Prosecutor on the grounds set out in this article;

   (b) The Prosecutor or the Deputy Prosecutor, as appropriate, shall be entitled to present his or her comments on the matter;

9. The Prosecutor shall appoint advisers with legal expertise on specific issues, including, but not limited to, sexual and gender violence and violence against children.

Article 43 The Registry

1. The Registry shall be responsible for the non-judicial aspects of the administration and servicing of the Court, without prejudice to the functions and powers of the Prosecutor in accordance with article 42.

2. The Registry shall be headed by the Registrar, who shall be the principal administrative officer of the Court. The Registrar shall exercise his or her functions under the authority of the President of the Court.

3. The Registrar and the Deputy Registrar shall be persons of high moral character, be highly competent and have an excellent knowledge of and be fluent in at least one of the working languages of the Court.

4. The judges shall elect the Registrar by an absolute majority by secret ballot, taking into account any recommendation by the Assembly of States Parties. If the need arises and upon the recommendation of the Registrar, the judges shall elect, in the same manner, a Deputy Registrar.

5. The Registrar shall hold office for a term of five years, shall be eligible for re-election once and shall serve on a full-time basis. The Deputy Registrar shall hold office for a term of five years or such shorter term as may be decided upon by an absolute majority of the judges, and may be elected on the basis that the Deputy Registrar shall be called upon to serve as required.

6. The Registrar shall set up a Victims and Witnesses Unit within the Registry. This Unit shall provide, in consultation with the Office of the Prosecutor, protective measures and security arrangements, counselling and other appropriate assistance for witnesses, victims who appear before the Court, and others who are at risk on account of testimony given by such witnesses. The Unit shall include staff with expertise in trauma, including trauma related to crimes of sexual violence.

Article 44 Staff

1. The Prosecutor and the Registrar shall appoint such qualified staff as may be required to their respective offices. In the case of the Prosecutor, this shall include the appointment of investigators.

2. In the employment of staff, the Prosecutor and the Registrar shall ensure the highest standards of efficiency, competency and integrity, and shall have regard, *mutatis mutandis*, to the criteria set forth in article 36, paragraph 8.

3. The Registrar, with the agreement of the Presidency and the Prosecutor, shall propose Staff Regulations which include the terms and conditions upon which the staff of the Court shall be appointed, remunerated and dismissed. The Staff Regulations shall be approved by the Assembly of States Parties.

4. The Court may, in exceptional circumstances, employ the expertise of gratis personnel offered by States Parties, intergovernmental organizations or non-governmental organizations to assist with the work of any of the organs of the Court. The Prosecutor may accept any such offer on behalf of the Office of the Prosecutor. Such gratis personnel shall be employed in accordance with guidelines to be established by the Assembly of States Parties.

Article 45 Solemn undertaking

Before taking up their respective duties under this Statute, the judges, the Prosecutor, the Deputy Prosecutors, the Registrar and the Deputy Registrar shall each make a solemn undertaking in open court to exercise his or her respective functions impartially and conscientiously.

Article 46 Removal from office

1. A judge, the Prosecutor, a Deputy Prosecutor, the Registrar or the Deputy Registrar shall be removed from office if a decision to this effect is made in accordance with paragraph 2, in cases where that person:

    (a) Is found to have committed serious misconduct or a serious breach of his or her duties under this Statute, as provided for in the Rules of Procedure and Evidence; or

    (b) Is unable to exercise the functions required by this Statute.

2. A decision as to the removal from office of a judge, the Prosecutor or a Deputy Prosecutor under paragraph 1 shall be made by the Assembly of States Parties, by secret ballot:

    (a) In the case of a judge, by a two-thirds majority of the States Parties upon a recommendation adopted by a two-thirds majority of the other judges;

    (b) In the case of the Prosecutor, by an absolute majority of the States Parties;

    (c) In the case of a Deputy Prosecutor, by an absolute majority of the States Parties upon the recommendation of the Prosecutor.

3. A decision as to the removal from office of the Registrar or Deputy Registrar shall be made by an absolute majority of the judges.

4. A judge, Prosecutor, Deputy Prosecutor, Registrar or Deputy Registrar whose conduct or ability to exercise the functions of the office as required by this Statute is challenged under this article shall have full opportunity to present and receive evidence and to make submissions in accordance with the Rules of Procedure and Evidence. The person in question shall not otherwise participate in the consideration of the matter.

Article 47 Disciplinary measures

A judge, Prosecutor, Deputy Prosecutor, Registrar or Deputy Registrar who has committed misconduct of a less serious nature than that set out in article 46, paragraph 1, shall be subject to disciplinary measures, in accordance with the Rules of Procedure and Evidence.

Article 48 Privileges and immunities

1. The Court shall enjoy in the territory of each State Party such privileges and immunities as are necessary for the fulfilment of its purposes.

2. The judges, the Prosecutor, the Deputy Prosecutors and the Registrar shall, when engaged on or with respect to the business of the Court, enjoy the same privileges and immunities as are accorded to heads of diplomatic missions and shall, after the expiry of their terms of office, continue to be accorded immunity from legal process of every kind in respect of words spoken or written and acts performed by them in their official capacity.

3. The Deputy Registrar, the staff of the Office of the Prosecutor and the staff of the Registry shall enjoy the privileges and immunities and facilities necessary for the performance of their functions, in accordance with the agreement on the privileges and immunities of the Court.

4. Counsel, experts, witnesses or any other person required to be present at the seat of the Court shall be accorded such treatment as is necessary for the proper functioning of the Court, in accordance with the agreement on the privileges and immunities of the Court.

5. The privileges and immunities of:

    (a) A judge or the Prosecutor may be waived by an absolute majority of the judges;

    (b) The Registrar may be waived by the Presidency;

    (c) The Deputy Prosecutors and staff of the Office of the Prosecutor may be waived by the Prosecutor;

    (d) The Deputy Registrar and staff of the Registry may be waived by the Registrar.

Article 49 Salaries, allowances and expenses

The judges, the Prosecutor, the Deputy Prosecutors, the Registrar and the Deputy Registrar shall receive such salaries, allowances and expenses as may be decided upon by the Assembly of States Parties. These salaries and allowances shall not be reduced during their terms of office.

Article 50 Official and working languages

1. The official languages of the Court shall be Arabic, Chinese, English, French, Russian and Spanish. The judgments of the Court, as well as other decisions resolving fundamental issues before the Court, shall be published in the official languages. The Presidency shall, in accordance with the criteria established by the Rules of Procedure and Evidence, determine which decisions may be considered as resolving fundamental issues for the purposes of this paragraph.

2. The working languages of the Court shall be English and French. The Rules of Procedure and Evidence shall determine the cases in which other official languages may be used as working languages.

3. At the request of any party to a proceeding or a State allowed to intervene in a proceeding, the Court shall authorize a language other than English or French to be used by such a party or State, provided that the Court considers such authorization to be adequately justified.

Article 51 Rules of Procedure and Evidence

1. The Rules of Procedure and Evidence shall enter into force upon adoption by a two-thirds majority of the members of the Assembly of States Parties.

2. Amendments to the Rules of Procedure and Evidence may be proposed by:

    (a) Any State Party;

(b) The judges acting by an absolute majority; or

(c) The Prosecutor.

Such amendments shall enter into force upon adoption by a two-thirds majority of the members of the Assembly of States Parties.

3. After the adoption of the Rules of Procedure and Evidence, in urgent cases where the Rules do not provide for a specific situation before the Court, the judges may, by a two-thirds majority, draw up provisional Rules to be applied until adopted, amended or rejected at the next ordinary or special session of the Assembly of States Parties.

4. The Rules of Procedure and Evidence, amendments thereto and any provisional Rule shall be consistent with this Statute. Amendments to the Rules of Procedure and Evidence as well as provisional Rules shall not be applied retroactively to the detriment of the person who is being investigated or prosecuted or who has been convicted.

5. In the event of conflict between the Statute and the Rules of Procedure and Evidence, the Statute shall prevail.

Article 52 Regulations of the Court

1. The judges shall, in accordance with this Statute and the Rules of Procedure and Evidence, adopt, by an absolute majority, the Regulations of the Court necessary for its routine functioning.

2. The Prosecutor and the Registrar shall be consulted in the elaboration of the Regulations and any amendments thereto.

3. The Regulations and any amendments thereto shall take effect upon adoption unless otherwise decided by the judges. Immediately upon adoption, they shall be circulated to States Parties for comments. If within six months there are no objections from a majority of States Parties, they shall remain in force.

Part 5 Investigation and prosecution

Article 53 Initiation of an investigation

1. The Prosecutor shall, having evaluated the information made available to him or her, initiate an investigation unless he or she determines that there is no reasonable basis to proceed under this Statute. In deciding whether to initiate an investigation, the Prosecutor shall consider whether:

(a) The information available to the Prosecutor provides a reasonable basis to believe that a crime within the jurisdiction of the Court has been or is being committed;

(b) The case is or would be admissible under article 17; and

(c) Taking into account the gravity of the crime and the interests of victims, there are nonetheless substantial reasons to believe that an investigation would not serve the interests of justice.

If the Prosecutor determines that there is no reasonable basis to proceed and his or her determination is based solely on subparagraph (c) above, he or she shall inform the Pre-Trial Chamber.

2. If, upon investigation, the Prosecutor concludes that there is not a sufficient basis for a prosecution because:

(a) There is not a sufficient legal or factual basis to seek a warrant or summons under article 58;

(b) The case is inadmissible under article 17; or

(c) A prosecution is not in the interests of justice, taking into account all the circumstances, including the gravity of the crime, the interests of victims and the age or infirmity of the alleged perpetrator, and his or her role in the alleged crime;

the Prosecutor shall inform the Pre-Trial Chamber and the State making a referral under article 14 or the Security Council in a case under article 13, paragraph (b), of his or her conclusion and the reasons for the conclusion.

3. (a) At the request of the State making a referral under article 14 or the Security Council under article 13, paragraph (b), the Pre-Trial Chamber may review a decision of the Prosecutor under paragraph 1 or 2 not to proceed and may request the Prosecutor to reconsider that decision.

    (b) In addition, the Pre-Trial Chamber may, on its own initiative, review a decision of the Prosecutor not to proceed if it is based solely on paragraph 1 (c) or 2 (c). In such a case, the decision of the Prosecutor shall be effective only if confirmed by the Pre-Trial Chamber.

4. The Prosecutor may, at any time, reconsider a decision whether to initiate an investigation or prosecution based on new facts or information.

Article 54 Duties and powers of the Prosecutor with respect to investigations

1. The Prosecutor shall:

    (a) In order to establish the truth, extend the investigation to cover all facts and evidence relevant to an assessment of whether there is criminal responsibility under this Statute, and, in doing so, investigate incriminating and exonerating circumstances equally;

    (b) Take appropriate measures to ensure the effective investigation and prosecution of crimes within the jurisdiction of the Court, and in doing so, respect the interests and personal circumstances of victims and witnesses, including age, gender as defined in article 7, paragraph 3, and health, and take into account the nature of the crime, in particular where it involves sexual violence, gender violence or violence against children; and

    (c) Fully respect the rights of persons arising under this Statute.

2. The Prosecutor may conduct investigations on the territory of a State:

    (a) In accordance with the provisions of Part 9; or

    (b) As authorized by the Pre-Trial Chamber under article 57, paragraph 3(d).

3. The Prosecutor may:

    (a) Collect and examine evidence;

    (b) Request the presence of and question persons being investigated, victims and witnesses;

    (c) Seek the cooperation of any State or intergovernmental organization or arrangement in accordance with its respective competence and/or mandate;

    (d) Enter into such arrangements or agreements, not inconsistent with this Statute, as may be necessary to facilitate the cooperation of a State, intergovernmental organization or person;

    (e) Agree not to disclose, at any stage of the proceedings, documents or information that the Prosecutor obtains on the condition of confidentiality and solely for the purpose of generating new evidence, unless the provider of the information consents; and

    (f) Take necessary measures, or request that necessary measures be taken, to ensure the confidentiality of information, the protection of any person or the preservation of evidence.

Article 55 Rights of persons during an investigation

1. In respect of an investigation under this Statute, a person:

    (a) Shall not be compelled to incriminate himself or herself or to confess guilt;

    (b) Shall not be subjected to any form of coercion, duress or threat, to torture or to any other form of cruel, inhuman or degrading treatment or punishment;

    (c) Shall, if questioned in a language other than a language the person fully understands and speaks, have, free of any cost, the assistance of a competent interpreter and such translations as are necessary to meet the requirements of fairness; and

(d) Shall not be subjected to arbitrary arrest or detention, and shall not be deprived of his or her liberty except on such grounds and in accordance with such procedures as are established in this Statute.

2. Where there are grounds to believe that a person has committed a crime within the jurisdiction of the Court and that person is about to be questioned either by the Prosecutor, or by national authorities pursuant to a request made under Part 9, that person shall also have the following rights of which he or she shall be informed prior to being questioned:

(a) To be informed, prior to being questioned, that there are grounds to believe that he or she has committed a crime within the jurisdiction of the Court;

(b) To remain silent, without such silence being a consideration in the determination of guilt or innocence;

(c) To have legal assistance of the person's choosing, or, if the person does not have legal assistance, to have legal assistance assigned to him or her, in any case where the interests of justice so require, and without payment by the person in any such case if the person does not have sufficient means to pay for it; and

(d) To be questioned in the presence of counsel unless the person has voluntarily waived his or her right to counsel.

Article 56 Role of the Pre-Trial Chamber in relation to a unique investigative opportunity

1. (a) Where the Prosecutor considers an investigation to present a unique opportunity to take testimony or a statement from a witness or to examine, collect or test evidence, which may not be available subsequently for the purposes of a trial, the Prosecutor shall so inform the Pre-Trial Chamber.

(b) In that case, the Pre-Trial Chamber may, upon request of the Prosecutor, take such measures as may be necessary to ensure the efficiency and integrity of the proceedings and, in particular, to protect the rights of the defence.

(c) Unless the Pre-Trial Chamber orders otherwise, the Prosecutor shall provide the relevant information to the person who has been arrested or appeared in response to a summons in connection with the investigation referred to in subparagraph (a), in order that he or she may be heard on the matter.

2. The measures referred to in paragraph 1 (b) may include:

(a) Making recommendations or orders regarding procedures to be followed;

(b) Directing that a record be made of the proceedings;

(c) Appointing an expert to assist;

(d) Authorizing counsel for a person who has been arrested, or appeared before the Court in response to a summons, to participate, or where there has not yet been such an arrest or appearance or counsel has not been designated, appointing another counsel to attend and represent the interests of the defence;

(e) Naming one of its members or, if necessary, another available judge of the Pre-Trial or Trial Division to observe and make recommendations or orders regarding the collection and preservation of evidence and the questioning of persons;

(f) Taking such other action as may be necessary to collect or preserve evidence.

3. (a) Where the Prosecutor has not sought measures pursuant to this article but the Pre-Trial Chamber considers that such measures are required to preserve evidence that it deems would be essential for the defence at trial, it shall consult with the Prosecutor as to whether there is good reason for the Prosecutor's failure to request the measures. If upon consultation, the Pre-Trial Chamber concludes that the Prosecutor's failure to request such measures is unjustified, the Pre-Trial Chamber may take such measures on its own initiative.

(b) A decision of the Pre-Trial Chamber to act on its own initiative under this paragraph may be appealed by the Prosecutor. The appeal shall be heard on an expedited basis.

4. The admissibility of evidence preserved or collected for trial pursuant to this article, or the record thereof, shall be governed at trial by article 69, and given such weight as determined by the Trial Chamber.

Article 57 Functions and powers of the Pre-Trial Chamber

1. Unless otherwise provided in this Statute, the Pre-Trial Chamber shall exercise its functions in accordance with the provisions of this article.

2. (a) Orders or rulings of the Pre-Trial Chamber issued under articles 15, 18, 19, 54, paragraph 2, 61, paragraph 7, and 72 must be concurred in by a majority of its judges.

   (b) In all other cases, a single judge of the Pre-Trial Chamber may exercise the functions provided for in this Statute, unless otherwise provided for in the Rules of Procedure and Evidence or by a majority of the Pre-Trial Chamber.

3. In addition to its other functions under this Statute, the Pre-Trial Chamber may:

   (a) At the request of the Prosecutor, issue such orders and warrants as may be required for the purposes of an investigation;

   (b) Upon the request of a person who has been arrested or has appeared pursuant to a summons under article 58, issue such orders, including measures such as those described in article 56, or seek such cooperation pursuant to Part 9 as may be necessary to assist the person in the preparation of his or her defence;

   (c) Where necessary, provide for the protection and privacy of victims and witnesses, the preservation of evidence, the protection of persons who have been arrested or appeared in response to a summons, and the protection of national security information;

   (d) Authorize the Prosecutor to take specific investigative steps within the territory of a State Party without having secured the cooperation of that State under Part 9 if, whenever possible having regard to the views of the State concerned, the Pre-Trial Chamber has determined in that case that the State is clearly unable to execute a request for cooperation due to the unavailability of any authority or any component of its judicial system competent to execute the request for cooperation under Part 9.

   (e) Where a warrant of arrest or a summons has been issued under article 58, and having due regard to the strength of the evidence and the rights of the parties concerned, as provided for in this Statute and the Rules of Procedure and Evidence, seek the cooperation of States pursuant to article 93, paragraph 1 (k), to take protective measures for the purpose of forfeiture, in particular for the ultimate benefit of victims.

Article 58 Issuance by the Pre-Trial Chamber of a warrant of arrest or a summons to appear

1. At any time after the initiation of an investigation, the Pre-Trial Chamber shall, on the application of the Prosecutor, issue a warrant of arrest of a person if, having examined the application and the evidence or other information submitted by the Prosecutor, it is satisfied that:

   (a) There are reasonable grounds to believe that the person has committed a crime within the jurisdiction of the Court; and

   (b) The arrest of the person appears necessary:

      (i) To ensure the person's appearance at trial,

      (ii) To ensure that the person does not obstruct or endanger the investigation or the court proceedings, or

      (iii) Where applicable, to prevent the person from continuing with the commission of that crime or a related crime which is within the jurisdiction of the Court and which arises out of the same circumstances.

2.   The application of the Prosecutor shall contain:

   (a) The name of the person and any other relevant identifying information;

   (b) A specific reference to the crimes within the jurisdiction of the Court which the person is alleged to have committed;

   (c) A concise statement of the facts which are alleged to constitute those crimes;

   (d) A summary of the evidence and any other information which establish reasonable grounds to believe that the person committed those crimes; and

   (e) The reason why the Prosecutor believes that the arrest of the person is necessary.

3.   The warrant of arrest shall contain:

   (a) The name of the person and any other relevant identifying information;

   (b) A specific reference to the crimes within the jurisdiction of the Court for which the person's arrest is sought; and

   (c) A concise statement of the facts which are alleged to constitute those crimes.

4.   The warrant of arrest shall remain in effect until otherwise ordered by the Court.

5.   On the basis of the warrant of arrest, the Court may request the provisional arrest or the arrest and surrender of the person under Part 9.

6.   The Prosecutor may request the Pre-Trial Chamber to amend the warrant of arrest by modifying or adding to the crimes specified therein. The Pre-Trial Chamber shall so amend the warrant if it is satisfied that there are reasonable grounds to believe that the person committed the modified or additional crimes.

7.   As an alternative to seeking a warrant of arrest, the Prosecutor may submit an application requesting that the Pre-Trial Chamber issue a summons for the person to appear. If the Pre-Trial Chamber is satisfied that there are reasonable grounds to believe that the person committed the crime alleged and that a summons is sufficient to ensure the person's appearance, it shall issue the summons, with or without conditions restricting liberty (other than detention) if provided for by national law, for the person to appear. The summons shall contain:

   (a) The name of the person and any other relevant identifying information;

   (b) The specified date on which the person is to appear;

   (c) A specific reference to the crimes within the jurisdiction of the Court which the person is alleged to have committed; and

   (d) A concise statement of the facts which are alleged to constitute the crime.

   The summons shall be served on the person.

Article 59 Arrest proceedings in the custodial State

1.   A State Party which has received a request for provisional arrest or for arrest and surrender shall immediately take steps to arrest the person in question in accordance with its laws and the provisions of Part 9.

2.   A person arrested shall be brought promptly before the competent judicial authority in the custodial State which shall determine, in accordance with the law of that State, that:

   (a) The warrant applies to that person;

   (b) The person has been arrested in accordance with the proper process; and

   (c) The person's rights have been respected.

3.   The person arrested shall have the right to apply to the competent authority in the custodial State for interim release pending surrender.

4.   In reaching a decision on any such application, the competent authority in the custodial State shall consider whether, given the gravity of the alleged crimes, there are urgent and exceptional circumstances to justify interim release and whether necessary safeguards exist to ensure that

the custodial State can fulfil its duty to surrender the person to the Court. It shall not be open to the competent authority of the custodial State to consider whether the warrant of arrest was properly issued in accordance with article 58, paragraph 1(a) and (b).

5. The Pre-Trial Chamber shall be notified of any request for interim release and shall make recommendations to the competent authority in the custodial State. The competent authority in the custodial State shall give full consideration to such recommendations, including any recommendations on measures to prevent the escape of the person, before rendering its decision.

6. If the person is granted interim release, the Pre-Trial Chamber may request periodic reports on the status of the interim release.

7. Once ordered to be surrendered by the custodial State, the person shall be delivered to the Court as soon as possible.

Article 60 Initial proceedings before the Court

1. Upon the surrender of the person to the Court, or the person's appearance before the Court voluntarily or pursuant to a summons, the Pre-Trial Chamber shall satisfy itself that the person has been informed of the crimes which he or she is alleged to have committed, and of his or her rights under this Statute, including the right to apply for interim release pending trial.

2. A person subject to a warrant of arrest may apply for interim release pending trial. If the Pre-Trial Chamber is satisfied that the conditions set forth in article 58, paragraph 1, are met, the person shall continue to be detained. If it is not so satisfied, the Pre-Trial Chamber shall release the person, with or without conditions.

3. The Pre-Trial Chamber shall periodically review its ruling on the release or detention of the person, and may do so at any time on the request of the Prosecutor or the person. Upon such review, it may modify its ruling as to detention, release or conditions of release, if it is satisfied that changed circumstances so require.

4. The Pre-Trial Chamber shall ensure that a person is not detained for an unreasonable period prior to trial due to inexcusable delay by the Prosecutor. If such delay occurs, the Court shall consider releasing the person, with or without conditions.

5. If necessary, the Pre-Trial Chamber may issue a warrant of arrest to secure the presence of a person who has been released.

Article 61 Confirmation of the charges before trial

1. Subject to the provisions of paragraph 2, within a reasonable time after the person's surrender or voluntary appearance before the Court, the Pre-Trial Chamber shall hold a hearing to confirm the charges on which the Prosecutor intends to seek trial. The hearing shall be held in the presence of the Prosecutor and the person charged, as well as his or her counsel.

2. The Pre-Trial Chamber may, upon request of the Prosecutor or on its own motion, hold a hearing in the absence of the person charged to confirm the charges on which the Prosecutor intends to seek trial when the person has:

   (a) Waived his or her right to be present; or

   (b) Fled or cannot be found and all reasonable steps have been taken to secure his or her appearance before the Court and to inform the person of the charges and that a hearing to confirm those charges will be held.

   In that case, the person shall be represented by counsel where the Pre-Trial Chamber determines that it is in the interests of justice.

3. Within a reasonable time before the hearing, the person shall:

   (a) Be provided with a copy of the document containing the charges on which the Prosecutor intends to bring the person to trial; and

   (b) Be informed of the evidence on which the Prosecutor intends to rely at the hearing.

The Pre-Trial Chamber may issue orders regarding the disclosure of information for the purposes of the hearing.

4. Before the hearing, the Prosecutor may continue the investigation and may amend or withdraw any charges. The person shall be given reasonable notice before the hearing of any amendment to or withdrawal of charges. In case of a withdrawal of charges, the Prosecutor shall notify the Pre-Trial Chamber of the reasons for the withdrawal.

5. At the hearing, the Prosecutor shall support each charge with sufficient evidence to establish substantial grounds to believe that the person committed the crime charged. The Prosecutor may rely on documentary or summary evidence and need not call the witnesses expected to testify at the trial.

6. At the hearing, the person may:

   (a) Object to the charges;

   (b) Challenge the evidence presented by the Prosecutor; and

   (c) Present evidence.

7. The Pre-Trial Chamber shall, on the basis of the hearing, determine whether there is sufficient evidence to establish substantial grounds to believe that the person committed each of the crimes charged. Based on its determination, the Pre-Trial Chamber shall:

   (a) Confirm those charges in relation to which it has determined that there is sufficient evidence, and commit the person to a Trial Chamber for trial on the charges as confirmed;

   (b) Decline to confirm those charges in relation to which it has determined that there is insufficient evidence;

   (c) Adjourn the hearing and request the Prosecutor to consider:

      (i) Providing further evidence or conducting further investigation with respect to a particular charge; or

      (ii) Amending a charge because the evidence submitted appears to establish a different crime within the jurisdiction of the Court.

8. Where the Pre-Trial Chamber declines to confirm a charge, the Prosecutor shall not be precluded from subsequently requesting its confirmation if the request is supported by additional evidence.

9. After the charges are confirmed and before the trial has begun, the Prosecutor may, with the permission of the Pre-Trial Chamber and after notice to the accused, amend the charges. If the Prosecutor seeks to add additional charges or to substitute more serious charges, a hearing under this article to confirm those charges must be held. After commencement of the trial, the Prosecutor may, with the permission of the Trial Chamber, withdraw the charges.

10. Any warrant previously issued shall cease to have effect with respect to any charges which have not been confirmed by the Pre-Trial Chamber or which have been withdrawn by the Prosecutor.

11. Once the charges have been confirmed in accordance with this article, the Presidency shall constitute a Trial Chamber which, subject to paragraph 9 and to article 64, paragraph 4, shall be responsible for the conduct of subsequent proceedings and may exercise any function of the Pre-Trial Chamber that is relevant and capable of application in those proceedings.

Part 6 The trial

Article 62 Place of trial

Unless otherwise decided, the place of the trial shall be the seat of the Court.

Article 63 Trial in the presence of the accused

1. The accused shall be present during the trial.

2. If the accused, being present before the Court, continues to disrupt the trial, the Trial Chamber may remove the accused and shall make provision for him or her to observe the trial and instruct counsel from outside the courtroom, through the use of communications technology, if required. Such measures shall be taken only in exceptional circumstances after other reasonable alternatives have proved inadequate, and only for such duration as is strictly required.

Article 64 Functions and powers of the Trial Chamber

1. The functions and powers of the Trial Chamber set out in this article shall be exercised in accordance with this Statute and the Rules of Procedure and Evidence.

2. The Trial Chamber shall ensure that a trial is fair and expeditious and is conducted with full respect for the rights of the accused and due regard for the protection of victims and witnesses.

3. Upon assignment of a case for trial in accordance with this Statute, the Trial Chamber assigned to deal with the case shall:

    (a) Confer with the parties and adopt such procedures as are necessary to facilitate the fair and expeditious conduct of the proceedings;

    (b) Determine the language or languages to be used at trial; and

    (c) Subject to any other relevant provisions of this Statute, provide for disclosure of documents or information not previously disclosed, sufficiently in advance of the commencement of the trial to enable adequate preparation for trial.

4. The Trial Chamber may, if necessary for its effective and fair functioning, refer preliminary issues to the Pre-Trial Chamber or, if necessary, to another available judge of the Pre-Trial Division.

5. Upon notice to the parties, the Trial Chamber may, as appropriate, direct that there be joinder or severance in respect of charges against more than one accused.

6. In performing its functions prior to trial or during the course of a trial, the Trial Chamber may, as necessary:

    (a) Exercise any functions of the Pre-Trial Chamber referred to in article 61, paragraph 11;

    (b) Require the attendance and testimony of witnesses and production of documents and other evidence by obtaining, if necessary, the assistance of States as provided in this Statute;

    (c) Provide for the protection of confidential information;

    (d) Order the production of evidence in addition to that already collected prior to the trial or presented during the trial by the parties;

    (e) Provide for the protection of the accused, witnesses and victims; and

    (f) Rule on any other relevant matters.

7. The trial shall be held in public. The Trial Chamber may, however, determine that special circumstances require that certain proceedings be in closed session for the purposes set forth in article 68, or to protect confidential or sensitive information to be given in evidence.

8. (a) At the commencement of the trial, the Trial Chamber shall have read to the accused the charges previously confirmed by the Pre-Trial Chamber. The Trial Chamber shall satisfy itself that the accused understands the nature of the charges. It shall afford him or her the opportunity to make an admission of guilt in accordance with article 65 or to plead not guilty.

    (b) At the trial, the presiding judge may give directions for the conduct of proceedings, including to ensure that they are conducted in a fair and impartial manner. Subject to any directions of the presiding judge, the parties may submit evidence in accordance with the provisions of this Statute.

9. The Trial Chamber shall have, *inter alia*, the power on application of a party or on its own motion to:

   (a) Rule on the admissibility or relevance of evidence; and

   (b) Take all necessary steps to maintain order in the course of a hearing.

10. The Trial Chamber shall ensure that a complete record of the trial, which accurately reflects the proceedings, is made and that it is maintained and preserved by the Registrar.

Article 65 Proceedings on an admission of guilt

1. Where the accused makes an admission of guilt pursuant to article 64, paragraph 8(a), the Trial Chamber shall determine whether:

   (a) The accused understands the nature and consequences of the admission of guilt;

   (b) The admission is voluntarily made by the accused after sufficient consultation with defence counsel; and

   (c) The admission of guilt is supported by the facts of the case that are contained in:

   (i)   The charges brought by the Prosecutor and admitted by the accused;

   (ii) Any materials presented by the Prosecutor which supplement the charges and which the accused accepts; and

   (iii) Any other evidence, such as the testimony of witnesses, presented by the Prosecutor or the accused.

2. Where the Trial Chamber is satisfied that the matters referred to in paragraph 1 are established, it shall consider the admission of guilt, together with any additional evidence presented, as establishing all the essential facts that are required to prove the crime to which the admission of guilt relates, and may convict the accused of that crime.

3. Where the Trial Chamber is not satisfied that the matters referred to in paragraph 1 are established, it shall consider the admission of guilt as not having been made, in which case it shall order that the trial be continued under the ordinary trial procedures provided by this Statute and may remit the case to another Trial Chamber.

4. Where the Trial Chamber is of the opinion that a more complete presentation of the facts of the case is required in the interests of justice, in particular the interests of the victims, the Trial Chamber may:

   (a) Request the Prosecutor to present additional evidence, including the testimony of witnesses; or

   (b) Order that the trial be continued under the ordinary trial procedures provided by this Statute, in which case it shall consider the admission of guilt as not having been made and may remit the case to another Trial Chamber.

5. Any discussions between the Prosecutor and the defence regarding modification of the charges, the admission of guilt or the penalty to be imposed shall not be binding on the Court.

Article 66 Presumption of innocence

1. Everyone shall be presumed innocent until proved guilty before the Court in accordance with the applicable law.

2. The onus is on the Prosecutor to prove the guilt of the accused.

3. In order to convict the accused, the Court must be convinced of the guilt of the accused beyond reasonable doubt.

Article 67 Rights of the accused

1. In the determination of any charge, the accused shall be entitled to a public hearing, having regard to the provisions of this Statute, to a fair hearing conducted impartially, and to the following minimum guarantees, in full equality:

    (a) To be informed promptly and in detail of the nature, cause and content of the charge, in a language which the accused fully understands and speaks;

    (b) To have adequate time and facilities for the preparation of the defence and to communicate freely with counsel of the accused's choosing in confidence;

    (c) To be tried without undue delay;

    (d) Subject to article 63, paragraph 2, to be present at the trial, to conduct the defence in person or through legal assistance of the accused's choosing, to be informed, if the accused does not have legal assistance, of this right and to have legal assistance assigned by the Court in any case where the interests of justice so require, and without payment if the accused lacks sufficient means to pay for it;

    (e) To examine, or have examined, the witnesses against him or her and to obtain the attendance and examination of witnesses on his or her behalf under the same conditions as witnesses against him or her. The accused shall also be entitled to raise defences and to present other evidence admissible under this Statute;

    (f) To have, free of any cost, the assistance of a competent interpreter and such translations as are necessary to meet the requirements of fairness, if any of the proceedings of or documents presented to the Court are not in a language which the accused fully understands and speaks;

    (g) Not to be compelled to testify or to confess guilt and to remain silent, without such silence being a consideration in the determination of guilt or innocence;

    (h) To make an unsworn oral or written statement in his or her defence; and

    (i) Not to have imposed on him or her any reversal of the burden of proof or any onus of rebuttal.

2. In addition to any other disclosure provided for in this Statute, the Prosecutor shall, as soon as practicable, disclose to the defence evidence in the Prosecutor's possession or control which he or she believes shows or tends to show the innocence of the accused, or to mitigate the guilt of the accused, or which may affect the credibility of prosecution evidence. In case of doubt as to the application of this paragraph, the Court shall decide.

Article 68
Protection of the victims and witnesses and their participation in the proceedings

1. The Court shall take appropriate measures to protect the safety, physical and psychological well-being, dignity and privacy of victims and witnesses. In so doing, the Court shall have regard to all relevant factors, including age, gender as defined in article 7, paragraph 3, and health, and the nature of the crime, in particular, but not limited to, where the crime involves sexual or gender violence or violence against children. The Prosecutor shall take such measures particularly during the investigation and prosecution of such crimes. These measures shall not be prejudicial to or inconsistent with the rights of the accused and a fair and impartial trial.

2. As an exception to the principle of public hearings provided for in article 67, the Chambers of the Court may, to protect victims and witnesses or an accused, conduct any part of the proceedings *in camera* or allow the presentation of evidence by electronic or other special means. In particular, such measures shall be implemented in the case of a victim of sexual violence or a child who is a victim or a witness, unless otherwise ordered by the Court, having regard to all the circumstances, particularly the views of the victim or witness.

3. Where the personal interests of the victims are affected, the Court shall permit their views and concerns to be presented and considered at stages of the proceedings determined to be appropriate by the Court and in a manner which is not prejudicial to or inconsistent with the rights of the accused and a fair and impartial trial. Such views and concerns may be presented by the legal representatives of the victims where the Court considers it appropriate, in accordance with the Rules of Procedure and Evidence.

4. The Victims and Witnesses Unit may advise the Prosecutor and the Court on appropriate protective measures, security arrangements, counselling and assistance as referred to in article 43, paragraph 6.

5. Where the disclosure of evidence or information pursuant to this Statute may lead to the grave endangerment of the security of a witness or his or her family, the Prosecutor may, for the purposes of any proceedings conducted prior to the commencement of the trial, withhold such evidence or information and instead submit a summary thereof. Such measures shall be exercised in a manner which is not prejudicial to or inconsistent with the rights of the accused and a fair and impartial trial.

6. A State may make an application for necessary measures to be taken in respect of the protection of its servants or agents and the protection of confidential or sensitive information.

Article 69 Evidence

1. Before testifying, each witness shall, in accordance with the Rules of Procedure and Evidence, give an undertaking as to the truthfulness of the evidence to be given by that witness.

2. The testimony of a witness at trial shall be given in person, except to the extent provided by the measures set forth in article 68 or in the Rules of Procedure and Evidence. The Court may also permit the giving of *viva voce* (oral) or recorded testimony of a witness by means of video or audio technology, as well as the introduction of documents or written transcripts, subject to this Statute and in accordance with the Rules of Procedure and Evidence. These measures shall not be prejudicial to or inconsistent with the rights of the accused.

3. The parties may submit evidence relevant to the case, in accordance with article 64. The Court shall have the authority to request the submission of all evidence that it considers necessary for the determination of the truth.

4. The Court may rule on the relevance or admissibility of any evidence, taking into account, *inter alia*, the probative value of the evidence and any prejudice that such evidence may cause to a fair trial or to a fair evaluation of the testimony of a witness, in accordance with the Rules of Procedure and Evidence.

5. The Court shall respect and observe privileges on confidentiality as provided for in the Rules of Procedure and Evidence.

6. The Court shall not require proof of facts of common knowledge but may take judicial notice of them.

7. Evidence obtained by means of a violation of this Statute or internationally recognized human rights shall not be admissible if:

    (a) The violation casts substantial doubt on the reliability of the evidence; or

    (b) The admission of the evidence would be antithetical to and would seriously damage the integrity of the proceedings.

8. When deciding on the relevance or admissibility of evidence collected by a State, the Court shall not rule on the application of the State's national law.

Article 70 Offences against the administration of justice

1. The Court shall have jurisdiction over the following offences against its administration of justice when committed intentionally:

    (a) Giving false testimony when under an obligation pursuant to article 69, paragraph 1, to tell the truth;

(b) Presenting evidence that the party knows is false or forged;

(c) Corruptly influencing a witness, obstructing or interfering with the attendance or testimony of a witness, retaliating against a witness for giving testimony or destroying, tampering with or interfering with the collection of evidence;

(d) Impeding, intimidating or corruptly influencing an official of the Court for the purpose of forcing or persuading the official not to perform, or to perform improperly, his or her duties;

(e) Retaliating against an official of the Court on account of duties performed by that or another official;

(f) Soliciting or accepting a bribe as an official of the Court in connection with his or her official duties.

2. The principles and procedures governing the Court's exercise of jurisdiction over offences under this article shall be those provided for in the Rules of Procedure and Evidence. The conditions for providing international cooperation to the Court with respect to its proceedings under this article shall be governed by the domestic laws of the requested State.

3. In the event of conviction, the Court may impose a term of imprisonment not exceeding five years, or a fine in accordance with the Rules of Procedure and Evidence, or both.

4. (a) Each State Party shall extend its criminal laws penalizing offences against the integrity of its own investigative or judicial process to offences against the administration of justice referred to in this article, committed on its territory, or by one of its nationals;

(b) Upon request by the Court, whenever it deems it proper, the State Party shall submit the case to its competent authorities for the purpose of prosecution. Those authorities shall treat such cases with diligence and devote sufficient resources to enable them to be conducted effectively.

Article 71 Sanctions for misconduct before the Court

1. The Court may sanction persons present before it who commit misconduct, including disruption of its proceedings or deliberate refusal to comply with its directions, by administrative measures other than imprisonment, such as temporary or permanent removal from the courtroom, a fine or other similar measures provided for in the Rules of Procedure and Evidence.

2. The procedures governing the imposition of the measures set forth in paragraph 1 shall be those provided for in the Rules of Procedure and Evidence.

Article 72 Protection of national security information

1. This article applies in any case where the disclosure of the information or documents of a State would, in the opinion of that State, prejudice its national security interests. Such cases include those falling within the scope of article 56, paragraphs 2 and 3, article 61, paragraph 3, article 64, paragraph 3, article 67, paragraph 2, article 68, paragraph 6, article 87, paragraph 6 and article 93, as well as cases arising at any other stage of the proceedings where such disclosure may be at issue.

2. This article shall also apply when a person who has been requested to give information or evidence has refused to do so or has referred the matter to the State on the ground that disclosure would prejudice the national security interests of a State and the State concerned confirms that it is of the opinion that disclosure would prejudice its national security interests.

3. Nothing in this article shall prejudice the requirements of confidentiality applicable under article 54, paragraph 3(e) and (f), or the application of article 73.

4. If a State learns that information or documents of the State are being, or are likely to be, disclosed at any stage of the proceedings, and it is of the opinion that disclosure would

prejudice its national security interests, that State shall have the right to intervene in order to obtain resolution of the issue in accordance with this article.

5. If, in the opinion of a State, disclosure of information would prejudice its national security interests, all reasonable steps will be taken by the State, acting in conjunction with the Prosecutor, the defence or the Pre-Trial Chamber or Trial Chamber, as the case may be, to seek to resolve the matter by cooperative means. Such steps may include:

    (a) Modification or clarification of the request;

    (b) A determination by the Court regarding the relevance of the information or evidence sought, or a determination as to whether the evidence, though relevant, could be or has been obtained from a source other than the requested State;

    (c) Obtaining the information or evidence from a different source or in a different form; or

    (d) Agreement on conditions under which the assistance could be provided including, among other things, providing summaries or redactions, limitations on disclosure, use of *in camera* or *ex parte* proceedings, or other protective measures permissible under the Statute and the Rules of Procedure and Evidence.

6. Once all reasonable steps have been taken to resolve the matter through cooperative means, and if the State considers that there are no means or conditions under which the information or documents could be provided or disclosed without prejudice to its national security interests, it shall so notify the Prosecutor or the Court of the specific reasons for its decision, unless a specific description of the reasons would itself necessarily result in such prejudice to the State's national security interests.

7. Thereafter, if the Court determines that the evidence is relevant and necessary for the establishment of the guilt or innocence of the accused, the Court may undertake the following actions:

    (a) Where disclosure of the information or document is sought pursuant to a request for cooperation under Part 9 or the circumstances described in paragraph 2, and the State has invoked the ground for refusal referred to in article 93, paragraph 4:

        (i)   The Court may, before making any conclusion referred to in subparagraph 7(a)(ii), request further consultations for the purpose of considering the State's representations, which may include, as appropriate, hearings *in camera* and *ex parte*;

        (ii) If the Court concludes that, by invoking the ground for refusal under article 93, paragraph 4, in the circumstances of the case, the requested State is not acting in accordance with its obligations under this Statute, the Court may refer the matter in accordance with article 87, paragraph 7, specifying the reasons for its conclusion; and

        (iii) The Court may make such inference in the trial of the accused as to the existence or non-existence of a fact, as may be appropriate in the circumstances; or

    (b) In all other circumstances:

        (i)   Order disclosure; or

        (ii) To the extent it does not order disclosure, make such inference in the trial of the accused as to the existence or non-existence of a fact, as may be appropriate in the circumstances.

Article 73 Third-party information or documents

If a State Party is requested by the Court to provide a document or information in its custody, possession or control, which was disclosed to it in confidence by a State, intergovernmental organization or international organization, it shall seek the consent of the originator to disclose that document or information. If the originator is a State Party, it shall either consent to disclosure of the information or document or undertake to resolve the issue of disclosure with the Court, subject to the provisions of article 72. If the originator is not a State Party and refuses to consent to disclosure, the requested State shall inform the Court that it is unable to provide the document or information because of a pre-existing obligation of confidentiality to the originator.

Article 74 Requirements for the decision

1. All the judges of the Trial Chamber shall be present at each stage of the trial and throughout their deliberations. The Presidency may, on a case-by-case basis, designate, as available, one or more alternate judges to be present at each stage of the trial and to replace a member of the Trial Chamber if that member is unable to continue attending.

2. The Trial Chamber's decision shall be based on its evaluation of the evidence and the entire proceedings. The decision shall not exceed the facts and circumstances described in the charges and any amendments to the charges. The Court may base its decision only on evidence submitted and discussed before it at the trial.

3. The judges shall attempt to achieve unanimity in their decision, failing which the decision shall be taken by a majority of the judges.

4. The deliberations of the Trial Chamber shall remain secret.

5. The decision shall be in writing and shall contain a full and reasoned statement of the Trial Chamber's findings on the evidence and conclusions. The Trial Chamber shall issue one decision. When there is no unanimity, the Trial Chamber's decision shall contain the views of the majority and the minority. The decision or a summary thereof shall be delivered in open court.

Article 75 Reparations to victims

1. The Court shall establish principles relating to reparations to, or in respect of, victims, including restitution, compensation and rehabilitation. On this basis, in its decision the Court may, either upon request or on its own motion in exceptional circumstances, determine the scope and extent of any damage, loss and injury to, or in respect of, victims and will state the principles on which it is acting.

2. The Court may make an order directly against a convicted person specifying appropriate reparations to, or in respect of, victims, including restitution, compensation and rehabilitation. Where appropriate, the Court may order that the award for reparations be made through the Trust Fund provided for in article 79.

3. Before making an order under this article, the Court may invite and shall take account of representations from or on behalf of the convicted person, victims, other interested persons or interested States.

4. In exercising its power under this article, the Court may, after a person is convicted of a crime within the jurisdiction of the Court, determine whether, in order to give effect to an order which it may make under this article, it is necessary to seek measures under article 93, paragraph 1.

5. A State Party shall give effect to a decision under this article as if the provisions of article 109 were applicable to this article.

6. Nothing in this article shall be interpreted as prejudicing the rights of victims under national or international law.

Article 76 Sentencing

1. In the event of a conviction, the Trial Chamber shall consider the appropriate sentence to be imposed and shall take into account the evidence presented and submissions made during the trial that are relevant to the sentence.

2. Except where article 65 applies and before the completion of the trial, the Trial Chamber may on its own motion and shall, at the request of the Prosecutor or the accused, hold a further hearing to hear any additional evidence or submissions relevant to the sentence, in accordance with the Rules of Procedure and Evidence.

3. Where paragraph 2 applies, any representations under article 75 shall be heard during the further hearing referred to in paragraph 2 and, if necessary, during any additional hearing.

4. The sentence shall be pronounced in public and, wherever possible, in the presence of the accused.

Part 7 Penalties

Article 77 Applicable penalties

1. Subject to article 110, the Court may impose one of the following penalties on a person convicted of a crime referred to in article 5 of this Statute:

   (a) Imprisonment for a specified number of years, which may not exceed a maximum of 30 years; or

   (b) A term of life imprisonment when justified by the extreme gravity of the crime and the individual circumstances of the convicted person.

2. In addition to imprisonment, the Court may order:

   (a) A fine under the criteria provided for in the Rules of Procedure and Evidence;

   (b) A forfeiture of proceeds, property and assets derived directly or indirectly from that crime, without prejudice to the rights of bona fide third parties.

Article 78 Determination of the sentence

1. In determining the sentence, the Court shall, in accordance with the Rules of Procedure and Evidence, take into account such factors as the gravity of the crime and the individual circumstances of the convicted person.

2. In imposing a sentence of imprisonment, the Court shall deduct the time, if any, previously spent in detention in accordance with an order of the Court. The Court may deduct any time otherwise spent in detention in connection with conduct underlying the crime.

3. When a person has been convicted of more than one crime, the Court shall pronounce a sentence for each crime and a joint sentence specifying the total period of imprisonment. This period shall be no less than the highest individual sentence pronounced and shall not exceed 30 years imprisonment or a sentence of life imprisonment in conformity with article 77, paragraph 1 (b).

Article 79 Trust Fund

1. A Trust Fund shall be established by decision of the Assembly of States Parties for the benefit of victims of crimes within the jurisdiction of the Court, and of the families of such victims.

2. The Court may order money and other property collected through fines or forfeiture to be transferred, by order of the Court, to the Trust Fund.

3. The Trust Fund shall be managed according to criteria to be determined by the Assembly of States Parties.

Article 80 Non-prejudice to national application of penalties and national laws

Nothing in this Part affects the application by States of penalties prescribed by their national law, nor the law of States which do not provide for penalties prescribed in this Part.

Part 8 Appeal and revision

Article 81 Appeal against decision of acquittal or conviction or against sentence

1. A decision under article 74 may be appealed in accordance with the Rules of Procedure and Evidence as follows:

   (a) The Prosecutor may make an appeal on any of the following grounds:

      (i) Procedural error,

      (ii) Error of fact, or

      (iii) Error of law;

  (b) The convicted person, or the Prosecutor on that person's behalf, may make an appeal on any of the following grounds:

      (i) Procedural error,

      (ii) Error of fact,

      (iii) Error of law, or

      (iv) Any other ground that affects the fairness or reliability of the proceedings or decision.

2. (a) A sentence may be appealed, in accordance with the Rules of Procedure and Evidence, by the Prosecutor or the convicted person on the ground of disproportion between the crime and the sentence;

  (b) If on an appeal against sentence the Court considers that there are grounds on which the conviction might be set aside, wholly or in part, it may invite the Prosecutor and the convicted person to submit grounds under article 81, paragraph 1(a) or (b), and may render a decision on conviction in accordance with article 83;

  (c) The same procedure applies when the Court, on an appeal against conviction only, considers that there are grounds to reduce the sentence under paragraph 2(a).

3. (a) Unless the Trial Chamber orders otherwise, a convicted person shall remain in custody pending an appeal;

  (b) When a convicted person's time in custody exceeds the sentence of imprisonment imposed, that person shall be released, except that if the Prosecutor is also appealing, the release may be subject to the conditions under subparagraph (c) below;

  (c) In case of an acquittal, the accused shall be released immediately, subject to the following:

      (i) Under exceptional circumstances, and having regard, *inter alia*, to the concrete risk of flight, the seriousness of the offence charged and the probability of success on appeal, the Trial Chamber, at the request of the Prosecutor, may maintain the detention of the person pending appeal;

      (ii) A decision by the Trial Chamber under subparagraph (c)(i) may be appealed in accordance with the Rules of Procedure and Evidence.

4. Subject to the provisions of paragraph 3(a) and (b), execution of the decision or sentence shall be suspended during the period allowed for appeal and for the duration of the appeal proceedings.

Article 82 Appeal against other decisions

1. Either party may appeal any of the following decisions in accordance with the Rules of Procedure and Evidence:

  (a) A decision with respect to jurisdiction or admissibility;

  (b) A decision granting or denying release of the person being investigated or prosecuted;

  (c) A decision of the Pre-Trial Chamber to act on its own initiative under article 56, paragraph 3;

  (d) A decision that involves an issue that would significantly affect the fair and expeditious conduct of the proceedings or the outcome of the trial, and for which, in the opinion of the Pre-Trial or Trial Chamber, an immediate resolution by the Appeals Chamber may materially advance the proceedings.

2. A decision of the Pre-Trial Chamber under article 57, paragraph 3(d), may be appealed against by the State concerned or by the Prosecutor, with the leave of the Pre-Trial Chamber. The appeal shall be heard on an expedited basis.

3. An appeal shall not of itself have suspensive effect unless the Appeals Chamber so orders, upon request, in accordance with the Rules of Procedure and Evidence.

4.　A legal representative of the victims, the convicted person or a bona fide owner of property adversely affected by an order under article 75 may appeal against the order for reparations, as provided in the Rules of Procedure and Evidence.

Article 83 Proceedings on appeal

1.　For the purposes of proceedings under article 81 and this article, the Appeals Chamber shall have all the powers of the Trial Chamber.

2.　If the Appeals Chamber finds that the proceedings appealed from were unfair in a way that affected the reliability of the decision or sentence, or that the decision or sentence appealed from was materially affected by error of fact or law or procedural error, it may:

(a)　Reverse or amend the decision or sentence; or

(b)　Order a new trial before a different Trial Chamber.

For these purposes, the Appeals Chamber may remand a factual issue to the original Trial Chamber for it to determine the issue and to report back accordingly, or may itself call evidence to determine the issue. When the decision or sentence has been appealed only by the person convicted, or the Prosecutor on that person's behalf, it cannot be amended to his or her detriment.

3.　If in an appeal against sentence the Appeals Chamber finds that the sentence is disproportionate to the crime, it may vary the sentence in accordance with Part 7.

4.　The judgment of the Appeals Chamber shall be taken by a majority of the judges and shall be delivered in open court. The judgment shall state the reasons on which it is based. When there is no unanimity, the judgment of the Appeals Chamber shall contain the views of the majority and the minority, but a judge may deliver a separate or dissenting opinion on a question of law.

5.　The Appeals Chamber may deliver its judgment in the absence of the person acquitted or convicted.

Article 84 Revision of conviction or sentence

1.　The convicted person or, after death, spouses, children, parents or one person alive at the time of the accused's death who has been given express written instructions from the accused to bring such a claim, or the Prosecutor on the person's behalf, may apply to the Appeals Chamber to revise the final judgment of conviction or sentence on the grounds that:

(a)　New evidence has been discovered that:

(i)　Was not available at the time of trial, and such unavailability was not wholly or partially attributable to the party making application; and

(ii)　Is sufficiently important that had it been proved at trial it would have been likely to have resulted in a different verdict;

(b)　It has been newly discovered that decisive evidence, taken into account at trial and upon which the conviction depends, was false, forged or falsified;

(c)　One or more of the judges who participated in conviction or confirmation of the charges has committed, in that case, an act of serious misconduct or serious breach of duty of sufficient gravity to justify the removal of that judge or those judges from office under article 46.

2.　The Appeals Chamber shall reject the application if it considers it to be unfounded. If it determines that the application is meritorious, it may, as appropriate:

(a)　Reconvene the original Trial Chamber;

(b)　Constitute a new Trial Chamber; or

(c)　Retain jurisdiction over the matter,

with a view to, after hearing the parties in the manner set forth in the Rules of Procedure and Evidence, arriving at a determination on whether the judgment should be revised.

Article 85 Compensation to an arrested or convicted person

1. Anyone who has been the victim of unlawful arrest or detention shall have an enforceable right to compensation.

2. When a person has by a final decision been convicted of a criminal offence, and when subsequently his or her conviction has been reversed on the ground that a new or newly discovered fact shows conclusively that there has been a miscarriage of justice, the person who has suffered punishment as a result of such conviction shall be compensated according to law, unless it is proved that the non-disclosure of the unknown fact in time is wholly or partly attributable to him or her.

3. In exceptional circumstances, where the Court finds conclusive facts showing that there has been a grave and manifest miscarriage of justice, it may in its discretion award compensation, according to the criteria provided in the Rules of Procedure and Evidence, to a person who has been released from detention following a final decision of acquittal or a termination of the proceedings for that reason.

Part 9 International cooperation and judicial assistance

Article 86 General obligation to cooperate

States Parties shall, in accordance with the provisions of this Statute, cooperate fully with the Court in its investigation and prosecution of crimes within the jurisdiction of the Court.

Article 87 Requests for cooperation: general provisions

1. (a) The Court shall have the authority to make requests to States Parties for cooperation. The requests shall be transmitted through the diplomatic channel or any other appropriate channel as may be designated by each State Party upon ratification, acceptance, approval or accession.

    Subsequent changes to the designation shall be made by each State Party in accordance with the Rules of Procedure and Evidence.

    (b) When appropriate, without prejudice to the provisions of subparagraph (a), requests may also be transmitted through the International Criminal Police Organization or any appropriate regional organization.

2. Requests for cooperation and any documents supporting the request shall either be in or be accompanied by a translation into an official language of the requested State or one of the working languages of the Court, in accordance with the choice made by that State upon ratification, acceptance, approval or accession. Subsequent changes to this choice shall be made in accordance with the Rules of Procedure and Evidence.

3. The requested State shall keep confidential a request for cooperation and any documents supporting the request, except to the extent that the disclosure is necessary for execution of the request.

4. In relation to any request for assistance presented under this Part, the Court may take such measures, including measures related to the protection of information, as may be necessary to ensure the safety or physical or psychological well-being of any victims, potential witnesses and their families. The Court may request that any information that is made available under this Part shall be provided and handled in a manner that protects the safety and physical or psychological well-being of any victims, potential witnesses and their families.

5. (a) The Court may invite any State not party to this Statute to provide assistance under this Part on the basis of an ad hoc arrangement, an agreement with such State or any other appropriate basis.

    (b) Where a State not party to this Statute, which has entered into an ad hoc arrangement or an agreement with the Court, fails to cooperate with requests pursuant to any such arrangement or agreement, the Court may so inform the Assembly of States Parties or, where the Security Council referred the matter to the Court, the Security Council.

6. The Court may ask any intergovernmental organization to provide information or documents. The Court may also ask for other forms of cooperation and assistance which may be agreed upon with such an organization and which are in accordance with its competence or mandate.

7. Where a State Party fails to comply with a request to cooperate by the Court contrary to the provisions of this Statute, thereby preventing the Court from exercising its functions and powers under this Statute, the Court may make a finding to that effect and refer the matter to the Assembly of States Parties or, where the Security Council referred the matter to the Court, to the Security Council.

Article 88 Availability of procedures under national law

States Parties shall ensure that there are procedures available under their national law for all of the forms of cooperation which are specified under this Part.

Article 89 Surrender of persons to the Court

1. The Court may transmit a request for the arrest and surrender of a person, together with the material supporting the request outlined in article 91, to any State on the territory of which that person may be found and shall request the cooperation of that State in the arrest and surrender of such a person. States Parties shall, in accordance with the provisions of this Part and the procedure under their national law, comply with requests for arrest and surrender.

2. Where the person sought for surrender brings a challenge before a national court on the basis of the principle of *ne bis in idem* as provided in article 20, the requested State shall immediately consult with the Court to determine if there has been a relevant ruling on admissibility. If the case is admissible, the requested State shall proceed with the execution of the request. If an admissibility ruling is pending, the requested State may postpone the execution of the request for surrender of the person until the Court makes a determination on admissibility.

3. (a) A State Party shall authorize, in accordance with its national procedural law, transportation through its territory of a person being surrendered to the Court by another State, except where transit through that State would impede or delay the surrender.

   (b) A request by the Court for transit shall be transmitted in accordance with article 87. The request for transit shall contain:

   (i) A description of the person being transported;

   (ii) A brief statement of the facts of the case and their legal characterization; and

   (iii) The warrant for arrest and surrender;

   (c) A person being transported shall be detained in custody during the period of transit;

   (d) No authorization is required if the person is transported by air and no landing is scheduled on the territory of the transit State;

   (e) If an unscheduled landing occurs on the territory of the transit State, that State may require a request for transit from the Court as provided for in subparagraph (b). The transit State shall detain the person being transported until the request for transit is received and the transit is effected, provided that detention for purposes of this subparagraph may not be extended beyond 96 hours from the unscheduled landing unless the request is received within that time.

4. If the person sought is being proceeded against or is serving a sentence in the requested State for a crime different from that for which surrender to the Court is sought, the requested State, after making its decision to grant the request, shall consult with the Court.

Article 90 Competing requests

1. A State Party which receives a request from the Court for the surrender of a person under article 89 shall, if it also receives a request from any other State for the extradition of the same person for the same conduct which forms the basis of the crime for which the Court seeks the person's surrender, notify the Court and the requesting State of that fact.

2. Where the requesting State is a State Party, the requested State shall give priority to the request from the Court if:

    (a) The Court has, pursuant to article 18 or 19, made a determination that the case in respect of which surrender is sought is admissible and that determination takes into account the investigation or prosecution conducted by the requesting State in respect of its request for extradition; or

    (b) The Court makes the determination described in subparagraph (a) pursuant to the requested State's notification under paragraph 1.

3. Where a determination under paragraph 2 (a) has not been made, the requested State may, at its discretion, pending the determination of the Court under paragraph 2 (b), proceed to deal with the request for extradition from the requesting State but shall not extradite the person until the Court has determined that the case is inadmissible. The Court's determination shall be made on an expedited basis.

4. If the requesting State is a State not Party to this Statute the requested State, if it is not under an international obligation to extradite the person to the requesting State, shall give priority to the request for surrender from the Court, if the Court has determined that the case is admissible.

5. Where a case under paragraph 4 has not been determined to be admissible by the Court, the requested State may, at its discretion, proceed to deal with the request for extradition from the requesting State.

6. In cases where paragraph 4 applies except that the requested State is under an existing international obligation to extradite the person to the requesting State not Party to this Statute, the requested State shall determine whether to surrender the person to the Court or extradite the person to the requesting State. In making its decision, the requested State shall consider all the relevant factors, including but not limited to:

    (a) The respective dates of the requests;

    (b) The interests of the requesting State including, where relevant, whether the crime was committed in its territory and the nationality of the victims and of the person sought; and

    (c) The possibility of subsequent surrender between the Court and the requesting State.

7. Where a State Party which receives a request from the Court for the surrender of a person also receives a request from any State for the extradition of the same person for conduct other than that which constitutes the crime for which the Court seeks the person's surrender:

    (a) The requested State shall, if it is not under an existing international obligation to extradite the person to the requesting State, give priority to the request from the Court;

    (b) The requested State shall, if it is under an existing international obligation to extradite the person to the requesting State, determine whether to surrender the person to the Court or to extradite the person to the requesting State. In making its decision, the requested State shall consider all the relevant factors, including but not limited to those set out in paragraph 6, but shall give special consideration to the relative nature and gravity of the conduct in question.

8. Where pursuant to a notification under this article, the Court has determined a case to be inadmissible, and subsequently extradition to the requesting State is refused, the requested State shall notify the Court of this decision.

Article 91 Contents of request for arrest and surrender

1. A request for arrest and surrender shall be made in writing. In urgent cases, a request may be made by any medium capable of delivering a written record, provided that the request shall be confirmed through the channel provided for in article 87, paragraph 1(a).

2. In the case of a request for the arrest and surrender of a person for whom a warrant of arrest has been issued by the Pre-Trial Chamber under article 58, the request shall contain or be supported by:

    (a) Information describing the person sought, sufficient to identify the person, and information as to that person's probable location;

    (b) A copy of the warrant of arrest; and

    (c) Such documents, statements or information as may be necessary to meet the requirements for the surrender process in the requested State, except that those requirements should not be more burdensome than those applicable to requests for extradition pursuant to treaties or arrangements between the requested State and other States and should, if possible, be less burdensome, taking into account the distinct nature of the Court.

3. In the case of a request for the arrest and surrender of a person already convicted, the request shall contain or be supported by:

    (a) A copy of any warrant of arrest for that person;

    (b) A copy of the judgment of conviction;

    (c) Information to demonstrate that the person sought is the one referred to in the judgment of conviction; and

    (d) If the person sought has been sentenced, a copy of the sentence imposed and, in the case of a sentence for imprisonment, a statement of any time already served and the time remaining to be served.

4. Upon the request of the Court, a State Party shall consult with the Court, either generally or with respect to a specific matter, regarding any requirements under its national law that may apply under paragraph 2 (c). During the consultations, the State Party shall advise the Court of the specific requirements of its national law.

Article 92 Provisional arrest

1. In urgent cases, the Court may request the provisional arrest of the person sought, pending presentation of the request for surrender and the documents supporting the request as specified in article 91.

2. The request for provisional arrest shall be made by any medium capable of delivering a written record and shall contain:

    (a) Information describing the person sought, sufficient to identify the person, and information as to that person's probable location;

    (b) A concise statement of the crimes for which the person's arrest is sought and of the facts which are alleged to constitute those crimes, including, where possible, the date and location of the crime;

    (c) A statement of the existence of a warrant of arrest or a judgment of conviction against the person sought; and

    (d) A statement that a request for surrender of the person sought will follow.

3. A person who is provisionally arrested may be released from custody if the requested State has not received the request for surrender and the documents supporting the request as specified in article 91 within the time limits specified in the Rules of Procedure and Evidence. However, the person may consent to surrender before the expiration of this period if permitted by the law of the requested State. In such a case, the requested State shall proceed to surrender the person to the Court as soon as possible.

4. The fact that the person sought has been released from custody pursuant to paragraph 3 shall not prejudice the subsequent arrest and surrender of that person if the request for surrender and the documents supporting the request are delivered at a later date.

Article 93 Other forms of cooperation

1. States Parties shall, in accordance with the provisions of this Part and under procedures of national law, comply with requests by the Court to provide the following assistance in relation to investigations or prosecutions:

    (a) The identification and whereabouts of persons or the location of items;

    (b) The taking of evidence, including testimony under oath, and the production of evidence, including expert opinions and reports necessary to the Court;

    (c) The questioning of any person being investigated or prosecuted;

    (d) The service of documents, including judicial documents;

    (e) Facilitating the voluntary appearance of persons as witnesses or experts before the Court;

    (f) The temporary transfer of persons as provided in paragraph 7;

    (g) The examination of places or sites, including the exhumation and examination of grave sites;

    (h) The execution of searches and seizures;

    (i) The provision of records and documents, including official records and documents;

    (j) The protection of victims and witnesses and the preservation of evidence;

    (k) The identification, tracing and freezing or seizure of proceeds, property and assets and instrumentalities of crimes for the purpose of eventual forfeiture, without prejudice to the rights of *bona fide* third parties; and

    (l) Any other type of assistance which is not prohibited by the law of the requested State, with a view to facilitating the investigation and prosecution of crimes within the jurisdiction of the Court.

2. The Court shall have the authority to provide an assurance to a witness or an expert appearing before the Court that he or she will not be prosecuted, detained or subjected to any restriction of personal freedom by the Court in respect of any act or omission that preceded the departure of that person from the requested State.

3. Where execution of a particular measure of assistance detailed in a request presented under paragraph 1, is prohibited in the requested State on the basis of an existing fundamental legal principle of general application, the requested State shall promptly consult with the Court to try to resolve the matter. In the consultations, consideration should be given to whether the assistance can be rendered in another manner or subject to conditions. If after consultations the matter cannot be resolved, the Court shall modify the request as necessary.

4. In accordance with article 72, a State Party may deny a request for assistance, in whole or in part, only if the request concerns the production of any documents or disclosure of evidence which relates to its national security.

5. Before denying a request for assistance under paragraph 1(l), the requested State shall consider whether the assistance can be provided subject to specified conditions, or whether the assistance can be provided at a later date or in an alternative manner, provided that if the Court or the Prosecutor accepts the assistance subject to conditions, the Court or the Prosecutor shall abide by them.

6. If a request for assistance is denied, the requested State Party shall promptly inform the Court or the Prosecutor of the reasons for such denial.

7. (a) The Court may request the temporary transfer of a person in custody for purposes of identification or for obtaining testimony or other assistance. The person may be transferred if the following conditions are fulfilled:

    (i)   The person freely gives his or her informed consent to the transfer; and

    (ii) The requested State agrees to the transfer, subject to such conditions as that State and the Court may agree.

(b) The person being transferred shall remain in custody. When the purposes of the transfer have been fulfilled, the Court shall return the person without delay to the requested State.

8. (a) The Court shall ensure the confidentiality of documents and information, except as required for the investigation and proceedings described in the request.

(b) The requested State may, when necessary, transmit documents or information to the Prosecutor on a confidential basis. The Prosecutor may then use them solely for the purpose of generating new evidence.

(c) The requested State may, on its own motion or at the request of the Prosecutor, subsequently consent to the disclosure of such documents or information. They may then be used as evidence pursuant to the provisions of Parts 5 and 6 and in accordance with the Rules of Procedure and Evidence.

9. (a) (i) In the event that a State Party receives competing requests, other than for surrender or extradition, from the Court and from another State pursuant to an international obligation, the State Party shall endeavour, in consultation with the Court and the other State, to meet both requests, if necessary by postponing or attaching conditions to one or the other request.

(ii) Failing that, competing requests shall be resolved in accordance with the principles established in article 90.

(b) Where, however, the request from the Court concerns information, property or persons which are subject to the control of a third State or an international organization by virtue of an international agreement, the requested States shall so inform the Court and the Court shall direct its request to the third State or international organization.

10. (a) The Court may, upon request, cooperate with and provide assistance to a State Party conducting an investigation into or trial in respect of conduct which constitutes a crime within the jurisdiction of the Court or which constitutes a serious crime under the national law of the requesting State.

(b) (i) The assistance provided under subparagraph (a) shall include, *inter alia*:

   a. The transmission of statements, documents or other types of evidence obtained in the course of an investigation or a trial conducted by the Court; and

   b. The questioning of any person detained by order of the Court;

(ii) In the case of assistance under subparagraph (b)(i)a.:

   a. If the documents or other types of evidence have been obtained with the assistance of a State, such transmission shall require the consent of that State;

   b. If the statements, documents or other types of evidence have been provided by a witness or expert, such transmission shall be subject to the provisions of article 68.

(c) The Court may, under the conditions set out in this paragraph, grant a request for assistance under this paragraph from a State which is not a Party to this Statute.

Article 94 Postponement of execution of a request in respect of ongoing investigation or prosecution

1. If the immediate execution of a request would interfere with an ongoing investigation or prosecution of a case different from that to which the request relates, the requested State may postpone the execution of the request for a period of time agreed upon with the Court. However, the postponement shall be no longer than is necessary to complete the relevant investigation or prosecution in the requested State. Before making a decision to postpone, the requested State should consider whether the assistance may be immediately provided subject to certain conditions.

2. If a decision to postpone is taken pursuant to paragraph 1, the Prosecutor may, however, seek measures to preserve evidence, pursuant to article 93, paragraph 1 (j).

Article 95 Postponement of execution of a request in respect of an admissibility challenge

Where there is an admissibility challenge under consideration by the Court pursuant to article 18 or 19, the requested State may postpone the execution of a request under this Part pending a determination by the Court, unless the Court has specifically ordered that the Prosecutor may pursue the collection of such evidence pursuant to article 18 or 19.

Article 96 Contents of request for other forms of assistance under article 93

1. A request for other forms of assistance referred to in article 93 shall be made in writing. In urgent cases, a request may be made by any medium capable of delivering a written record, provided that the request shall be confirmed through the channel provided for in article 87, paragraph 1(a).

2. The request shall, as applicable, contain or be supported by the following:

    (a) A concise statement of the purpose of the request and the assistance sought, including the legal basis and the grounds for the request;

    (b) As much detailed information as possible about the location or identification of any person or place that must be found or identified in order for the assistance sought to be provided;

    (c) A concise statement of the essential facts underlying the request;

    (d) The reasons for and details of any procedure or requirement to be followed;

    (e) Such information as may be required under the law of the requested State in order to execute the request; and

    (f) Any other information relevant in order for the assistance sought to be provided.

3. Upon the request of the Court, a State Party shall consult with the Court, either generally or with respect to a specific matter, regarding any requirements under its national law that may apply under paragraph 2(e). During the consultations, the State Party shall advise the Court of the specific requirements of its national law.

4. The provisions of this article shall, where applicable, also apply in respect of a request for assistance made to the Court.

Article 97 Consultations

Where a State Party receives a request under this Part in relation to which it identifies problems which may impede or prevent the execution of the request, that State shall consult with the Court without delay in order to resolve the matter. Such problems may include, *inter alia*:

(a) Insufficient information to execute the request;

(b) In the case of a request for surrender, the fact that despite best efforts, the person sought cannot be located or that the investigation conducted has determined that the person in the requested State is clearly not the person named in the warrant; or

(c) The fact that execution of the request in its current form would require the requested State to breach a pre-existing treaty obligation undertaken with respect to another State.

Article 98 Cooperation with respect to waiver of immunity and consent to surrender

1. The Court may not proceed with a request for surrender or assistance which would require the requested State to act inconsistently with its obligations under international law with respect to the State or diplomatic immunity of a person or property of a third State, unless the Court can first obtain the cooperation of that third State for the waiver of the immunity.

2. The Court may not proceed with a request for surrender which would require the requested State to act inconsistently with its obligations under international agreements pursuant to which the consent of a sending State is required to surrender a person of that State to the Court, unless the Court can first obtain the cooperation of the sending State for the giving of consent for the surrender.

Article 99 Execution of requests under articles 93 and 96

1. Requests for assistance shall be executed in accordance with the relevant procedure under the law of the requested State and, unless prohibited by such law, in the manner specified in the request, including following any procedure outlined therein or permitting persons specified in the request to be present at and assist in the execution process.

2. In the case of an urgent request, the documents or evidence produced in response shall, at the request of the Court, be sent urgently.

3. Replies from the requested State shall be transmitted in their original language and form.

4. Without prejudice to other articles in this Part, where it is necessary for the successful execution of a request which can be executed without any compulsory measures, including specifically the interview of or taking evidence from a person on a voluntary basis, including doing so without the presence of the authorities of the requested State Party if it is essential for the request to be executed, and the examination without modification of a public site or other public place, the Prosecutor may execute such request directly on the territory of a State as follows:

    (a) When the State Party requested is a State on the territory of which the crime is alleged to have been committed, and there has been a determination of admissibility pursuant to article 18 or 19, the Prosecutor may directly execute such request following all possible consultations with the requested State Party;

    (b) In other cases, the Prosecutor may execute such request following consultations with the requested State Party and subject to any reasonable conditions or concerns raised by that State Party. Where the requested State Party identifies problems with the execution of a request pursuant to this subparagraph it shall, without delay, consult with the Court to resolve the matter.

5. Provisions allowing a person heard or examined by the Court under article 72 to invoke restrictions designed to prevent disclosure of confidential information connected with national security shall also apply to the execution of requests for assistance under this article.

Article 100 Costs

1. The ordinary costs for execution of requests in the territory of the requested State shall be borne by that State, except for the following, which shall be borne by the Court:

    (a) Costs associated with the travel and security of witnesses and experts or the transfer under article 93 of persons in custody;

    (b) Costs of translation, interpretation and transcription;

    (c) Travel and subsistence costs of the judges, the Prosecutor, the Deputy Prosecutors, the Registrar, the Deputy Registrar and staff of any organ of the Court;

    (d) Costs of any expert opinion or report requested by the Court;

    (e) Costs associated with the transport of a person being surrendered to the Court by a custodial State; and

    (f) Following consultations, any extraordinary costs that may result from the execution of a request.

2. The provisions of paragraph 1 shall, as appropriate, apply to requests from States Parties to the Court. In that case, the Court shall bear the ordinary costs of execution.

Article 101 Rule of speciality

1. A person surrendered to the Court under this Statute shall not be proceeded against, punished or detained for any conduct committed prior to surrender, other than the conduct or course of conduct which forms the basis of the crimes for which that person has been surrendered.

2. The Court may request a waiver of the requirements of paragraph 1 from the State which surrendered the person to the Court and, if necessary, the Court shall provide additional information in accordance with article 91. States Parties shall have the authority to provide a waiver to the Court and should endeavour to do so.

Article 102 Use of terms

For the purposes of this Statute:

(a) "surrender" means the delivering up of a person by a State to the Court, pursuant to this Statute.

(b) "extradition" means the delivering up of a person by one State to another as provided by treaty, convention or national legislation.

Part 10 Enforcement

Article 103 Role of States in enforcement of sentences of imprisonment

1. (a) A sentence of imprisonment shall be served in a State designated by the Court from a list of States which have indicated to the Court their willingness to accept sentenced persons.

   (b) At the time of declaring its willingness to accept sentenced persons, a State may attach conditions to its acceptance as agreed by the Court and in accordance with this Part.

   (c) A State designated in a particular case shall promptly inform the Court whether it accepts the Court's designation.

2. (a) The State of enforcement shall notify the Court of any circumstances, including the exercise of any conditions agreed under paragraph 1, which could materially affect the terms or extent of the imprisonment. The Court shall be given at least 45 days' notice of any such known or foreseeable circumstances. During this period, the State of enforcement shall take no action that might prejudice its obligations under article 110.

   (b) Where the Court cannot agree to the circumstances referred to in subparagraph (a), it shall notify the State of enforcement and proceed in accordance with article 104, paragraph 1.

3. In exercising its discretion to make a designation under paragraph 1, the Court shall take into account the following:

   (a) The principle that States Parties should share the responsibility for enforcing sentences of imprisonment, in accordance with principles of equitable distribution, as provided in the Rules of Procedure and Evidence;

   (b) The application of widely accepted international treaty standards governing the treatment of prisoners;

   (c) The views of the sentenced person;

   (d) The nationality of the sentenced person;

   (e) Such other factors regarding the circumstances of the crime or the person sentenced, or the effective enforcement of the sentence, as may be appropriate in designating the State of enforcement.

4. If no State is designated under paragraph 1, the sentence of imprisonment shall be served in a prison facility made available by the host State, in accordance with the conditions set out in the headquarters agreement referred to in article 3, paragraph 2. In such a case, the costs arising out of the enforcement of a sentence of imprisonment shall be borne by the Court.

Article 104 Change in designation of State of enforcement

1. The Court may, at any time, decide to transfer a sentenced person to a prison of another State.

2. A sentenced person may, at any time, apply to the Court to be transferred from the State of enforcement.

Article 105 Enforcement of the sentence

1. Subject to conditions which a State may have specified in accordance with article 103, paragraph 1(b), the sentence of imprisonment shall be binding on the States Parties, which shall in no case modify it.

2. The Court alone shall have the right to decide any application for appeal and revision. The State of enforcement shall not impede the making of any such application by a sentenced person.

Article 106 Supervision of enforcement of sentences and conditions of imprisonment

1. The enforcement of a sentence of imprisonment shall be subject to the supervision of the Court and shall be consistent with widely accepted international treaty standards governing treatment of prisoners.

2. The conditions of imprisonment shall be governed by the law of the State of enforcement and shall be consistent with widely accepted international treaty standards governing treatment of prisoners; in no case shall such conditions be more or less favourable than those available to prisoners convicted of similar offences in the State of enforcement.

3. Communications between a sentenced person and the Court shall be unimpeded and confidential.

Article 107 Transfer of the person upon completion of sentence

1. Following completion of the sentence, a person who is not a national of the State of enforcement may, in accordance with the law of the State of enforcement, be transferred to a State which is obliged to receive him or her, or to another State which agrees to receive him or her, taking into account any wishes of the person to be transferred to that State, unless the State of enforcement authorizes the person to remain in its territory.

2. If no State bears the costs arising out of transferring the person to another State pursuant to paragraph 1, such costs shall be borne by the Court.

3. Subject to the provisions of article 108, the State of enforcement may also, in accordance with its national law, extradite or otherwise surrender the person to a State which has requested the extradition or surrender of the person for purposes of trial or enforcement of a sentence.

Article 108 Limitation on the prosecution or punishment of other offences

1. A sentenced person in the custody of the State of enforcement shall not be subject to prosecution or punishment or to extradition to a third State for any conduct engaged in prior to that person's delivery to the State of enforcement, unless such prosecution, punishment or extradition has been approved by the Court at the request of the State of enforcement.

2. The Court shall decide the matter after having heard the views of the sentenced person.

3. Paragraph 1 shall cease to apply if the sentenced person remains voluntarily for more than 30 days in the territory of the State of enforcement after having served the full sentence imposed by the Court, or returns to the territory of that State after having left it.

Article 109 Enforcement of fines and forfeiture measures

1. States Parties shall give effect to fines or forfeitures ordered by the Court under Part 7, without prejudice to the rights of bona fide third parties, and in accordance with the procedure of their national law.

2. If a State Party is unable to give effect to an order for forfeiture, it shall take measures to recover the value of the proceeds, property or assets ordered by the Court to be forfeited, without prejudice to the rights of bona fide third parties.

3. Property, or the proceeds of the sale of real property or, where appropriate, the sale of other property, which is obtained by a State Party as a result of its enforcement of a judgment of the Court shall be transferred to the Court.

Article 110 Review by the Court concerning reduction of sentence

1. The State of enforcement shall not release the person before expiry of the sentence pronounced by the Court.

2. The Court alone shall have the right to decide any reduction of sentence, and shall rule on the matter after having heard the person.

3. When the person has served two thirds of the sentence, or 25 years in the case of life imprisonment, the Court shall review the sentence to determine whether it should be reduced. Such a review shall not be conducted before that time.

4. In its review under paragraph 3, the Court may reduce the sentence if it finds that one or more of the following factors are present:

    (a) The early and continuing willingness of the person to cooperate with the Court in its investigations and prosecutions;

    (b) The voluntary assistance of the person in enabling the enforcement of the judgments and orders of the Court in other cases, and in particular providing assistance in locating assets subject to orders of fine, forfeiture or reparation which may be used for the benefit of victims; or

    (c) Other factors establishing a clear and significant change of circumstances sufficient to justify the reduction of sentence, as provided in the Rules of Procedure and Evidence.

5. If the Court determines in its initial review under paragraph 3 that it is not appropriate to reduce the sentence, it shall thereafter review the question of reduction of sentence at such intervals and applying such criteria as provided for in the Rules of Procedure and Evidence.

Article 111 Escape

If a convicted person escapes from custody and flees the State of enforcement, that State may, after consultation with the Court, request the person's surrender from the State in which the person is located pursuant to existing bilateral or multilateral arrangements, or may request that the Court seek the person's surrender, in accordance with Part 9. It may direct that the person be delivered to the State in which he or she was serving the sentence or to another State designated by the Court.

Part 11 Assembly of states parties

Article 112 Assembly of States Parties

1. An Assembly of States Parties to this Statute is hereby established. Each State Party shall have one representative in the Assembly who may be accompanied by alternates and advisers. Other States which have signed this Statute or the Final Act may be observers in the Assembly.

2. The Assembly shall:

    (a) Consider and adopt, as appropriate, recommendations of the Preparatory Commission;

    (b) Provide management oversight to the Presidency, the Prosecutor and the Registrar regarding the administration of the Court;

    (c) Consider the reports and activities of the Bureau established under paragraph 3 and take appropriate action in regard thereto;

    (d) Consider and decide the budget for the Court;

(e) Decide whether to alter, in accordance with article 36, the number of judges;

(f) Consider pursuant to article 87, paragraphs 5 and 7, any question relating to non-cooperation;

(g) Perform any other function consistent with this Statute or the Rules of Procedure and Evidence.

3. (a) The Assembly shall have a Bureau consisting of a President, two Vice-Presidents and 18 members elected by the Assembly for three-year terms.

(b) The Bureau shall have a representative character, taking into account, in particular, equitable geographical distribution and the adequate representation of the principal legal systems of the world.

(c) The Bureau shall meet as often as necessary, but at least once a year. It shall assist the Assembly in the discharge of its responsibilities.

4. The Assembly may establish such subsidiary bodies as may be necessary, including an independent oversight mechanism for inspection, evaluation and investigation of the Court, in order to enhance its efficiency and economy.

5. The President of the Court, the Prosecutor and the Registrar or their representatives may participate, as appropriate, in meetings of the Assembly and of the Bureau.

6. The Assembly shall meet at the seat of the Court or at the Headquarters of the United Nations once a year and, when circumstances so require, hold special sessions. Except as otherwise specified in this Statute, special sessions shall be convened by the Bureau on its own initiative or at the request of one third of the States Parties.

7. Each State Party shall have one vote. Every effort shall be made to reach decisions by consensus in the Assembly and in the Bureau. If consensus cannot be reached, except as otherwise provided in the Statute:

(a) Decisions on matters of substance must be approved by a two-thirds majority of those present and voting provided that an absolute majority of States Parties constitutes the quorum for voting;

(b) Decisions on matters of procedure shall be taken by a simple majority of States Parties present and voting.

8. A State Party which is in arrears in the payment of its financial contributions towards the costs of the Court shall have no vote in the Assembly and in the Bureau if the amount of its arrears equals or exceeds the amount of the contributions due from it for the preceding two full years. The Assembly may, nevertheless, permit such a State Party to vote in the Assembly and in the Bureau if it is satisfied that the failure to pay is due to conditions beyond the control of the State Party.

9. The Assembly shall adopt its own rules of procedure.

10. The official and working languages of the Assembly shall be those of the General Assembly of the United Nations.

Part 12 Financing

Article 113 Financial Regulations
Except as otherwise specifically provided, all financial matters related to the Court and the meetings of the Assembly of States Parties, including its Bureau and subsidiary bodies, shall be governed by this Statute and the Financial Regulations and Rules adopted by the Assembly of States Parties.

Article 114 Payment of expenses
Expenses of the Court and the Assembly of States Parties, including its Bureau and subsidiary bodies, shall be paid from the funds of the Court.

Article 115 Funds of the Court and of the Assembly of States Parties

The expenses of the Court and the Assembly of States Parties, including its Bureau and subsidiary bodies, as provided for in the budget decided by the Assembly of States Parties, shall be provided by the following sources:

(a) Assessed contributions made by States Parties;

(b) Funds provided by the United Nations, subject to the approval of the General Assembly, in particular in relation to the expenses incurred due to referrals by the Security Council.

Article 116 Voluntary contributions

Without prejudice to article 115, the Court may receive and utilize, as additional funds, voluntary contributions from Governments, international organizations, individuals, corporations and other entities, in accordance with relevant criteria adopted by the Assembly of States Parties.

Article 117 Assessment of contributions

The contributions of States Parties shall be assessed in accordance with an agreed scale of assessment, based on the scale adopted by the United Nations for its regular budget and adjusted in accordance with the principles on which that scale is based.

Article 118 Annual audit

The records, books and accounts of the Court, including its annual financial statements, shall be audited annually by an independent auditor.

Part 13 Final clauses

Article 119 Settlement of disputes

1. Any dispute concerning the judicial functions of the Court shall be settled by the decision of the Court.

2. Any other dispute between two or more States Parties relating to the interpretation or application of this Statute which is not settled through negotiations within three months of their commencement shall be referred to the Assembly of States Parties. The Assembly may itself seek to settle the dispute or may make recommendations on further means of settlement of the dispute, including referral to the International Court of Justice in conformity with the Statute of that Court.

Article 120 Reservations

No reservations may be made to this Statute.

Article 121 Amendments

1. After the expiry of seven years from the entry into force of this Statute, any State Party may propose amendments thereto. The text of any proposed amendment shall be submitted to the Secretary-General of the United Nations, who shall promptly circulate it to all States Parties.

2. No sooner than three months from the date of notification, the Assembly of States Parties, at its next meeting, shall, by a majority of those present and voting, decide whether to take up the proposal. The Assembly may deal with the proposal directly or convene a Review Conference if the issue involved so warrants.

3. The adoption of an amendment at a meeting of the Assembly of States Parties or at a Review Conference on which consensus cannot be reached shall require a two-thirds majority of States Parties.

4. Except as provided in paragraph 5, an amendment shall enter into force for all States Parties one year after instruments of ratification or acceptance have been deposited with the Secretary-General of the United Nations by seven-eighths of them.

5. Any amendment to articles 5, 6, 7 and 8 of this Statute shall enter into force for those States Parties which have accepted the amendment one year after the deposit of their instruments of ratification or acceptance. In respect of a State Party which has not accepted the amendment, the Court shall not exercise its jurisdiction regarding a crime covered by the amendment when committed by that State Party's nationals or on its territory.

6. If an amendment has been accepted by seven-eighths of States Parties in accordance with paragraph 4, any State Party which has not accepted the amendment may withdraw from this Statute with immediate effect, notwithstanding article 127, paragraph 1, but subject to article 127, paragraph 2, by giving notice no later than one year after the entry into force of such amendment.

7. The Secretary-General of the United Nations shall circulate to all States Parties any amendment adopted at a meeting of the Assembly of States Parties or at a Review Conference.

Article 122 Amendments to provisions of an institutional nature

1. Amendments to provisions of this Statute which are of an exclusively institutional nature, namely, article 35, article 36, paragraphs 8 and 9, article 37, article 38, article 39, paragraphs 1 (first two sentences), 2 and 4, article 42, paragraphs 4 to 9, article 43, paragraphs 2 and 3, and articles 44, 46, 47 and 49, may be proposed at any time, notwithstanding article 121, paragraph 1, by any State Party. The text of any proposed amendment shall be submitted to the Secretary-General of the United Nations or such other person designated by the Assembly of States Parties who shall promptly circulate it to all States Parties and to others participating in the Assembly.

2. Amendments under this article on which consensus cannot be reached shall be adopted by the Assembly of States Parties or by a Review Conference, by a two-thirds majority of States Parties. Such amendments shall enter into force for all States Parties six months after their adoption by the Assembly or, as the case may be, by the Conference.

Article 123 Review of the Statute

1. Seven years after the entry into force of this Statute the Secretary-General of the United Nations shall convene a Review Conference to consider any amendments to this Statute. Such review may include, but is not limited to, the list of crimes contained in article 5. The Conference shall be open to those participating in the Assembly of States Parties and on the same conditions.

2. At any time thereafter, at the request of a State Party and for the purposes set out in paragraph 1, the Secretary-General of the United Nations shall, upon approval by a majority of States Parties, convene a Review Conference.

3. The provisions of article 121, paragraphs 3 to 7, shall apply to the adoption and entry into force of any amendment to the Statute considered at a Review Conference.

Article 124 Transitional Provision

Notwithstanding article 12, paragraphs 1 and 2, a State, on becoming a party to this Statute, may declare that, for a period of seven years after the entry into force of this Statute for the State concerned, it does not accept the jurisdiction of the Court with respect to the category of crimes referred to in article 8 when a crime is alleged to have been committed by its nationals or on its territory. A declaration under this article may be withdrawn at any time. The provisions of this article shall be reviewed at the Review Conference convened in accordance with article 123, paragraph 1.

Article 125 Signature, ratification, acceptance, approval or accession

1. This Statute shall be open for signature by all States in Rome, at the headquarters of the Food and Agriculture Organization of the United Nations, on 17 July 1998. Thereafter, it shall remain open for signature in Rome at the Ministry of Foreign Affairs of Italy until 17 October 1998.

After that date, the Statute shall remain open for signature in New York, at United Nations Headquarters, until 31 December 2000.

2. This Statute is subject to ratification, acceptance or approval by signatory States. Instruments of ratification, acceptance or approval shall be deposited with the Secretary-General of the United Nations.

3. This Statute shall be open to accession by all States. Instruments of accession shall be deposited with the Secretary-General of the United Nations.

Article 126 Entry into force

1. This Statute shall enter into force on the first day of the month after the 60th day following the date of the deposit of the 60th instrument of ratification, acceptance, approval or accession with the Secretary-General of the United Nations.

2. For each State ratifying, accepting, approving or acceding to this Statute after the deposit of the 60th instrument of ratification, acceptance, approval or accession, the Statute shall enter into force on the first day of the month after the 60th day following the deposit by such State of its instrument of ratification, acceptance, approval or accession.

Article 127 Withdrawal

1. A State Party may, by written notification addressed to the Secretary-General of the United Nations, withdraw from this Statute. The withdrawal shall take effect one year after the date of receipt of the notification, unless the notification specifies a later date.

2. A State shall not be discharged, by reason of its withdrawal, from the obligations arising from this Statute while it was a Party to the Statute, including any financial obligations which may have accrued. Its withdrawal shall not affect any cooperation with the Court in connection with criminal investigations and proceedings in relation to which the withdrawing State had a duty to cooperate and which were commenced prior to the date on which the withdrawal became effective, nor shall it prejudice in any way the continued consideration of any matter which was already under consideration by the Court prior to the date on which the withdrawal became effective.

Article 128 Authentic texts

The original of this Statute, of which the Arabic, Chinese, English, French, Russian and Spanish texts are equally authentic, shall be deposited with the Secretary-General of the United Nations, who shall send certified copies thereof to all States.

DOCUMENT 54

Rules of Procedure and Evidence of the International Criminal Court 2002
PCNICC/2000/1/Add 1

Resolution F of the Final Act of the United Nations Diplomatic Conference of Plenipotentiaries on the Establishment of an International Criminal Court established the Preparatory Commission for the International Criminal Court (PCNICC) to 'prepare proposals for practical arrangements for the establishment and coming into operation of the Court', including draft texts of, inter alia, Rules of Procedure and Evidence and Elements of Crime (Document 55). *Both of these draft texts were to be finalised before 30 June 2000. The draft rules were considered by the PCNICC at its first to fifth sessions and the final text was adopted in time on 30 June 2000. The rules entered into force upon adoption at the first session of the Assembly of States Parties in New York from 3–10 September 2002.*

According to Article 21 of the statute of the International Criminal Court **(Document 53)**, *the Rules of Procedure and Evidence constitute part of the applicable law of the International Criminal Court (ICC). However, they are subordinate to the provisions of the Statute itself (ICC Statute, Article 51(5)).*

The 225 rules cover a broad range of issues such as the composition and administration of the ICC (Chapter 2). This chapter includes rules relating to the administration of the victims and witnesses unit (Rules 16–19) and counsel for the defence (Rules 20–22). Chapter 3 concerns jurisdiction and admissibility. Chapter 4 includes provisions relating to various stages of the proceedings including rules on evidence (Rules 63–75) covering issues such as admissibility, compellability, the use of video and audio technology, privileged communications and self-incrimination as well as specific principles of evidence in cases of sexual violence, disclosure (Rules 76–84), and victims and witnesses (Rules 85–99). Chapter 5 of the rules is concerned with investigation and prosecution, Chapter 6 with trial procedure, Chapter 7 with penalties and Chapter 8 with appeals. Chapters 9–12 of the rules deal with offences and misconduct against the ICC, compensation to an arrested or convicted person, international co-operation and judicial assistance and enforcement respectively.

See also www.un.org/law/icc/prepcomm/report/prepreportdocs.htm.

Chapter I General provisions

Rule I Use of terms
In the present document:

"article" refers to articles of the Rome Statute;

"Chamber" refers to a Chamber of the Court;

"Part" refers to the Parts of the Rome Statute;

"Presiding Judge" refers to the Presiding Judge of a Chamber;

"the President" refers to the President of the Court;

"the Regulations" refers to the Regulations of the Court;

"the Rules" refers to the Rules of Procedure and Evidence.

Rule 2 Authentic texts
The Rules have been adopted in the official languages of the Court established by article 50, paragraph 1.

1.   All texts are equally authentic.

Rule 3 Amendments
1.   Amendments to the rules that are proposed in accordance with article 51, paragraph 2, shall be forwarded to the President of the Bureau of the Assembly of States Parties.
2.   The President of the Bureau of the Assembly of States Parties shall ensure that all proposed amendments are translated into the official languages of the Court and are transmitted to the States Parties.
3.   The procedure described in sub-rules 1 and 2 shall also apply to the provisional rules referred to in article 51, paragraph 3.

Chapter 2 Composition and administration of the Court
Section I General provisions relating to the composition and administration of the Court

Rule 4 Plenary sessions

1. The judges shall meet in plenary session not later than two months after their election. At that first session, after having made their solemn undertaking, in conformity with rule 5, the judges shall:

    (a) Elect the President and Vice-Presidents;

    (b) Assign judges to divisions.

2. The judges shall meet subsequently in plenary session at least once a year to exercise their functions under the Statute, the Rules and the Regulations and, if necessary, in special plenary sessions convened by the President on his or her own motion or at the request of one half of the judges.

3. The quorum for each plenary session shall be two-thirds of the judges.

4. Unless otherwise provided in the Statute or the Rules, the decisions of the plenary sessions shall be taken by the majority of the judges present. In the event of an equality of votes, the President, or the judge acting in the place of the President, shall have a casting vote.

5. The Regulations shall be adopted as soon as possible in plenary sessions.

Rule 5 Solemn undertaking under article 45

1. As provided in article 45, before exercising their functions under the Statute, the following solemn undertakings shall be made:

    (a) In the case of a judge: "I solemnly undertake that I will perform my duties and exercise my powers as a judge of the International Criminal Court honourably, faithfully, impartially and conscientiously, and that I will respect the confidentiality of investigations and prosecutions and the secrecy of deliberations.";

    (b) In the case of the Prosecutor, a Deputy Prosecutor, the Registrar and the Deputy Registrar of the Court: "I solemnly undertake that I will perform my duties and exercise my powers as (title) of the International Criminal Court honourably, faithfully, impartially and conscientiously, and that I will respect the confidentiality of investigations and prosecutions."

2. The undertaking, signed by the person making it and witnessed by the President or a Vice-President of the Bureau of the Assembly of States Parties, shall be filed with the Registry and kept in the records of the Court.

Rule 6 Solemn undertaking by the staff of the Office of the Prosecutor, the Registry, interpreters and translators

1. Upon commencing employment, every staff member of the Office of the Prosecutor and the Registry shall make the following undertaking: "I solemnly undertake that I will perform my duties and exercise my powers as (title) of the International Criminal Court honourably, faithfully, impartially and conscientiously, and that I will respect the confidentiality of investigations and prosecutions." The undertaking, signed by the person making it and witnessed, as appropriate, by the Prosecutor, the Deputy Prosecutor, the Registrar or the Deputy Registrar, shall be filed with the Registry and kept in the records of the Court.

2. Before performing any duties, an interpreter or a translator shall make the following undertaking: "I solemnly declare that I will perform my duties faithfully, impartially and with full respect for the duty of confidentiality." The undertaking, signed by the person making it and witnessed by the President of the Court or his or her representative, shall be filed with the Registry and kept in the records of the Court.

Rule 7 Single judge under article 39, paragraph 2(b)(iii)

1. Whenever the Pre-Trial Chamber designates a judge as a single judge in accordance with article 39, paragraph 2(b)(iii), it shall do so on the basis of objective pre-established criteria.

2. The designated judge shall make the appropriate decisions on those questions on which decision by the full Chamber is not expressly provided for in the Statute or the Rules.

3. The Pre-Trial Chamber, on its own motion or, if appropriate, at the request of a party, may decide that the functions of the single judge be exercised by the full Chamber.

Rule 8 Code of Professional Conduct

1. The Presidency, on the basis of a proposal made by the Registrar, shall draw up a draft Code of Professional Conduct for counsel, after having consulted the Prosecutor. In the preparation of the proposal, the Registrar shall conduct the consultations in accordance with rule 20, sub-rule 3.13.

2. The draft Code shall then be transmitted to the Assembly of States Parties, for the purpose of adoption, according to article 112, paragraph 7.

3. The Code shall contain procedures for its amendment.

Section II The Office of the Prosecutor

Rule 9 Operation of the Office of the Prosecutor

In discharging his or her responsibility for the management and administration of the Office of the Prosecutor, the Prosecutor shall put in place regulations to govern the operation of the Office. In preparing or amending these regulations, the Prosecutor shall consult with the Registrar on any matters that may affect the operation of the Registry.

Rule 10 Retention of information and evidence

The Prosecutor shall be responsible for the retention, storage and security of information and physical evidence obtained in the course of the investigations by his or her Office.

Rule 11 Delegation of the Prosecutor's functions

Except for the inherent powers of the Prosecutor set forth in the Statute, *inter alia,* those described in articles 15 and 53, the Prosecutor or a Deputy Prosecutor may authorize staff members of the Office of the Prosecutor, other than those referred to in article 44, paragraph 4, to represent him or her in the exercise of his or her functions.

Section III The Registry
Subsection 1 General provisions relating to the Registry

Rule 12 Qualifications and election of the Registrar and the Deputy Registrar

1. As soon as it is elected, the Presidency shall establish a list of candidates who satisfy the criteria laid down in article 43, paragraph 3, and shall transmit the list to the Assembly of States Parties with a request for any recommendations.

2. Upon receipt of any recommendations from the Assembly of States Parties, the President shall, without delay, transmit the list together with the recommendations to the plenary session.

3. As provided for in article 43, paragraph 4, the Court, meeting in plenary session, shall, as soon as possible, elect the Registrar by an absolute majority, taking into account any recommendations by the Assembly of States Parties. In the event that no candidate obtains an absolute majority on the first ballot, successive ballots shall be held until one candidate obtains an absolute majority.

4. If the need for a Deputy Registrar arises, the Registrar may make a recommendation to the President to that effect. The President shall convene a plenary session to decide on the matter. If

the Court, meeting in plenary session, decides by an absolute majority that a Deputy Registrar is to be elected, the Registrar shall submit a list of candidates to the Court.

5. The Deputy Registrar shall be elected by the Court, meeting in plenary session, in the same manner as the Registrar.

Rule 13 Functions of the Registrar

1. Without prejudice to the authority of the Office of the Prosecutor under the Statute to receive, obtain and provide information and to establish channels of communication for this purpose, the Registrar shall serve as the channel of communication of the Court.

2. The Registrar shall also be responsible for the internal security of the Court in consultation with the Presidency and the Prosecutor, as well as the host State.

Rule 14 Operation of the Registry

1. In discharging his or her responsibility for the organization and management of the Registry, the Registrar shall put in place regulations to govern the operation of the Registry. In preparing or amending these regulations, the Registrar shall consult with the Prosecutor on any matters which may affect the operation of the Office of the Prosecutor. The regulations shall be approved by the Presidency.

2. The regulations shall provide for defence counsel to have access to appropriate and reasonable administrative assistance from the Registry.

Rule 15 Records

1. The Registrar shall keep a database containing all the particulars of each case brought before the Court, subject to any order of a judge or Chamber providing for the non-disclosure of any document or information, and to the protection of sensitive personal data. Information on the database shall be available to the public in the working languages of the Court.

2. The Registrar shall also maintain the other records of the Court.

Subsection 2 Victims and Witnesses Unit

Rule 16 Responsibilities of the Registrar relating to victims and witnesses

1. In relation to victims, the Registrar shall be responsible for the performance of the following functions in accordance with the Statute and these Rules:

   (a) Providing notice or notification to victims or their legal representatives;

   (b) Assisting them in obtaining legal advice and organizing their legal representation, and providing their legal representatives with adequate support, assistance and information, including such facilities as may be necessary for the direct performance of their duty, for the purpose of protecting their rights during all stages of the proceedings in accordance with rules 89 to 91;

   (c) Assisting them in participating in the different phases of the proceedings in accordance with rules 89 to 91;

   (d) Taking gender-sensitive measures to facilitate the participation of victims of sexual violence at all stages of the proceedings.

2. In relation to victims, witnesses and others who are at risk on account of testimony given by such witnesses, the Registrar shall be responsible for the performance of the following functions in accordance with the Statute and these Rules:

   (a) Informing them of their rights under the Statute and the Rules, and of the existence, functions and availability of the Victims and Witnesses Unit;

   (b) Ensuring that they are aware, in a timely manner, of the relevant decisions of the Court that may have an impact on their interests, subject to provisions on confidentiality.

3. For the fulfilment of his or her functions, the Registrar may keep a special register for victims who have expressed their intention to participate in relation to a specific case.

4. Agreements on relocation and provision of support services on the territory of a State of traumatized or threatened victims, witnesses and others who are at risk on account of testimony given by such witnesses may be negotiated with the States by the Registrar on behalf of the Court. Such agreements may remain confidential.

Rule 17 Functions of the Unit

1. The Victims and Witnesses Unit shall exercise its functions in accordance with article 43, paragraph 6.

2. The Victims and Witnesses Unit shall, *inter alia,* perform the following functions, in accordance with the Statute and the Rules, and in consultation with the Chamber, the Prosecutor and the defence, as appropriate:

    (a) With respect to all witnesses, victims who appear before the Court, and others who are at risk on account of testimony given by such witnesses, in accordance with their particular needs and circumstances:

        (i)   Providing them with adequate protective and security measures and formulating long- and short-term plans for their protection;

        (ii) Recommending to the organs of the Court the adoption of protection measures and also advising relevant States of such measures;

        (iii) Assisting them in obtaining medical, psychological and other appropriate assistance;

        (iv) Making available to the Court and the parties training in issues of trauma, sexual violence, security and confidentiality;

        (v)   Recommending, in consultation with the Office of the Prosecutor, the elaboration of a code of conduct, emphasizing the vital nature of security and confidentiality for investigators of the Court and of the defence and all intergovernmental and non-governmental organizations acting at the request of the Court, as appropriate;

        (vi) Cooperating with States, where necessary, in providing any of the measures stipulated in this rule;

    (b) With respect to witnesses:

        (i)   Advising them where to obtain legal advice for the purpose of protecting their rights, in particular in relation to their testimony;

        (ii) Assisting them when they are called to testify before the Court;

        (iii) Taking gender-sensitive measures to facilitate the testimony of victims of sexual violence at all stages of the proceedings.

3. In performing its functions, the Unit shall give due regard to the particular needs of children, elderly persons and persons with disabilities. In order to facilitate the participation and protection of children as witnesses, the Unit may assign, as appropriate, and with the agreement of the parents or the legal guardian, a child-support person to assist a child through all stages of the proceedings.

Rule 18 Responsibilities of the Unit

For the efficient and effective performance of its work, the Victims and Witnesses Unit shall:

(a) Ensure that the staff in the Unit maintain confidentiality at all times;

(b) While recognizing the specific interests of the Office of the Prosecutor, the defence and the witnesses, respect the interests of the witness, including, where necessary, by maintaining an appropriate separation of the services provided to the prosecution and defence witnesses, and act impartially when cooperating with all parties and in accordance with the rulings and decisions of the Chambers;

(c) Have administrative and technical assistance available for witnesses, victims who appear before the Court, and others who are at risk on account of testimony given by such witnesses, during all stages of the proceedings and thereafter, as reasonably appropriate;

(d) Ensure training of its staff with respect to victims' and witnesses' security, integrity and dignity, including matters related to gender and cultural sensitivity;

(e) Where appropriate, cooperate with intergovernmental and non-governmental organizations.

Rule 19 Expertise in the Unit

In addition to the staff mentioned in article 43, paragraph 6, and subject to article 44, the Victims and Witnesses Unit may include, as appropriate, persons with expertise, *inter alia,* in the following areas:

(a) Witness protection and security;

(b) Legal and administrative matters, including areas of humanitarian and criminal law;

(c) Logistics administration;

(d) Psychology in criminal proceedings;

(e) Gender and cultural diversity;

(f) Children, in particular traumatized children;

(g) Elderly persons, in particular in connection with armed conflict and exile trauma;

(h) Persons with disabilities;

(i) Social work and counselling;

(j) Health care;

(k) Interpretation and translation.

Subsection 3 Counsel for the defence

Rule 20 Responsibilities of the Registrar relating to the rights of the defence

1. In accordance with article 43, paragraph 1, the Registrar shall organize the staff of the Registry in a manner that promotes the rights of the defence, consistent with the principle of fair trial as defined in the Statute. For that purpose, the Registrar shall, *inter alia:*

    (a) Facilitate the protection of confidentiality, as defined in article 67, paragraph 1(b); 18

    (b) Provide support, assistance, and information to all defence counsel appearing before the Court and, as appropriate, support for professional investigators necessary for the efficient and effective conduct of the defence;

    (c) Assist arrested persons, persons to whom article 55, paragraph 2, applies and the accused in obtaining legal advice and the assistance of legal counsel;

    (d) Advise the Prosecutor and the Chambers, as necessary, on relevant defence-related issues;

    (e) Provide the defence with such facilities as may be necessary for the direct performance of the duty of the defence;

    (f) Facilitate the dissemination of information and case law of the Court to defence counsel and, as appropriate, cooperate with national defence and bar associations or any independent representative body of counsel and legal associations referred to in sub-rule 3 to promote the specialization and training of lawyers in the law of the Statute and the Rules.

2. The Registrar shall carry out the functions stipulated in sub-rule 1, including the financial administration of the Registry, in such a manner as to ensure the professional independence of defence counsel.

3. For purposes such as the management of legal assistance in accordance with rule 21 and the development of a Code of Professional Conduct in accordance with rule 8, the Registrar shall consult, as appropriate, with any independent representative body of counsel or legal

associations, including any such body the establishment of which may be facilitated by the Assembly of States Parties.

Rule 21 Assignment of legal assistance

1. Subject to article 55, paragraph 2 (c), and article 67, paragraph 1 (d), criteria and procedures for assignment of legal assistance shall be established in the Regulations, based on a proposal by the Registrar, following consultations with any independent representative body of counsel or legal associations, as referred to in Rule 20, sub-rule 3.

2. The Registrar shall create and maintain a list of counsel who meet the criteria set forth in rule 22 and the Regulations. The person shall freely choose his or her counsel from this list or other counsel who meets the required criteria and is willing to be included in the list.

3. A person may seek from the Presidency a review of a decision to refuse a request for assignment of counsel. The decision of the Presidency shall be final. If a request is refused, a further request may be made by a person to the Registrar, upon showing a change in circumstances.

4. A person choosing to represent himself or herself shall so notify the Registrar in writing at the first opportunity.

5. Where a person claims to have insufficient means to pay for legal assistance and this is subsequently found not to be so, the Chamber dealing with the case at that time may make an order of contribution to recover the cost of providing counsel.

Rule 22 Appointment and qualifications of Counsel for the defence

1. A counsel for the defence shall have established competence in international or criminal law and procedure, as well as the necessary relevant experience, whether as judge, prosecutor, advocate or in other similar capacity, in criminal proceedings. A counsel for the defence shall have an excellent knowledge of and be fluent in at least one of the working languages of the Court. Counsel for the defence may be assisted by other persons, including professors of law, with relevant expertise.

2. Counsel for the defence engaged by a person exercising his or her right under the Statute to retain legal counsel of his or her choosing shall file a power of attorney with the Registrar at the earliest opportunity.

3. In the performance of their duties, Counsel for the defence shall be subject to the Statute, the Rules, the Regulations, the Code of Professional Conduct for Counsel adopted in accordance with rule 8 and any other document adopted by the Court that may be relevant to the performance of their duties.

Section IV Situations that may affect the functioning of the Court
Subsection I Removal from office and disciplinary measures

Rule 23 General principle

A judge, the Prosecutor, a Deputy Prosecutor, the Registrar and a Deputy Registrar shall be removed from office or shall be subject to disciplinary measures in such cases and with such guarantees as are established in the Statute and the Rules.

Rule 24 Definition of serious misconduct and serious breach of duty

1. For the purposes of article 46, paragraph 1 (a), "serious misconduct" shall be constituted by conduct that:

    (a) If it occurs in the course of official duties, is incompatible with official functions, and causes or is likely to cause serious harm to the proper administration of justice before the Court or the proper internal functioning of the Court, such as:

        (i) Disclosing facts or information that he or she has acquired in the course of his or her duties or on a matter which is *sub judice,* where such disclosure is seriously prejudicial to the judicial proceedings or to any person;

     (ii)   Concealing information or circumstances of a nature sufficiently serious to have precluded him or her from holding office;

     (iii) Abuse of judicial office in order to obtain unwarranted favourable treatment from any authorities, officials or professionals; or

  (b) If it occurs outside the course of official duties, is of a grave nature that causes or is likely to cause serious harm to the standing of the Court.

2.   For the purposes of article 46, paragraph 1(a), a "serious breach of duty" occurs where a person has been grossly negligent in the performance of his or her duties or has knowingly acted in contravention of those duties. This may include, *inter alia,* situations where the person:

  (a) Fails to comply with the duty to request to be excused, knowing that there are grounds for doing so;

  (b) Repeatedly causes unwarranted delay in the initiation, prosecution or trial of cases, or in the exercise of judicial powers.

Rule 25 Definition of misconduct of a less serious nature

1.   For the purposes of article 47, "misconduct of a less serious nature" shall be constituted by conduct that:

  (a) If it occurs in the course of official duties, causes or is likely to cause harm to the proper administration of justice before the Court or the proper internal functioning of the Court, such as:

     (i)   Interfering in the exercise of the functions of a person referred to in article 47;

     (ii)   Repeatedly failing to comply with or ignoring requests made by the Presiding Judge or by the Presidency in the exercise of their lawful authority;

     (iii) Failing to enforce the disciplinary measures to which the Registrar or a Deputy Registrar and other officers of the Court are subject when a judge knows or should know of a serious breach of duty on their part; or

  (b) If it occurs outside the course of official duties, causes or is likely to cause harm to the standing of the Court.

2   Nothing in this rule precludes the possibility of the conduct set out in sub-rule 1(a) constituting "serious misconduct" or "serious breach of duty" for the purposes of article 46, paragraph 1(a).

Rule 26 Receipt of complaints

1.   For the purposes of article 46, paragraph 1, and article 47, any complaint concerning any conduct defined under rules 24 and 25 shall include the grounds on which it is based, the identity of the complainant and, if available, any relevant evidence. The complaint shall remain confidential.

2.   All complaints shall be transmitted to the Presidency, which may also initiate proceedings on its own motion, and which shall, pursuant to the Regulations, set aside anonymous or manifestly unfounded complaints and transmit the other complaints to the competent organ. The Presidency shall be assisted in this task by one or more judges, appointed on the basis of automatic rotation, in accordance with the Regulations.

Rule 27 Common provisions on the rights of the defence

1.   In any case in which removal from office under article 46 or disciplinary measures under article 47 is under consideration, the person concerned shall be so informed in a written statement.

2.   The person concerned shall be afforded full opportunity to present and receive evidence, to make written submissions and to supply answers to any questions put to him or her.

3.   The person may be represented by counsel during the process established under this rule .

Rule 28 Suspension from duty

Where an allegation against a person who is the subject of a complaint is of a sufficiently serious nature, the person may be suspended from duty pending the final decision of the competent organ.

Rule 29 Procedure in the event of a request for removal from office

1. In the case of a judge, the Registrar or a Deputy Registrar, the question of removal from office shall be put to a vote at a plenary session.

2. The Presidency shall advise the President of the Bureau of the Assembly of States Parties in writing of any recommendation adopted in the case of a judge, and any decision adopted in the case of the Registrar or a Deputy Registrar.

3. The Prosecutor shall advise the President of the Bureau of the Assembly of States Parties in writing of any recommendation he or she makes in the case of a Deputy Prosecutor.

4. Where the conduct is found not to amount to serious misconduct or a serious breach of duty, it may be decided in accordance with article 47 that the person concerned has engaged in misconduct of a less serious nature and a disciplinary measure imposed.

Rule 30 Procedure in the event of a request for disciplinary measures

1. In the case of a judge, the Registrar or a Deputy Registrar, any decision to impose a disciplinary measure shall be taken by the Presidency.

2. In the case of the Prosecutor, any decision to impose a disciplinary measure shall be taken by an absolute majority of the Bureau of the Assembly of States Parties.

3. In the case of a Deputy Prosecutor:

   (a) Any decision to give a reprimand shall be taken by the Prosecutor;

   (b) Any decision to impose a pecuniary sanction shall be taken by an absolute majority of the Bureau of the Assembly of States Parties upon the recommendation of the Prosecutor.

4. Reprimands shall be recorded in writing and shall be transmitted to the President of the Bureau of the Assembly of States Parties.

Rule 31 Removal from office

Once removal from office has been pronounced, it shall take effect immediately. The person concerned shall cease to form part of the Court, including for unfinished cases in which he or she was taking part.

Rule 32 Disciplinary measures

The disciplinary measures that may be imposed are:

(a) A reprimand; or

(b) A pecuniary sanction that may not exceed six months of the salary paid by the Court to the person concerned.

Subsection 2 Excusing, disqualification, death and resignation

Rule 33 Excusing of a judge, the Prosecutor or a Deputy Prosecutor

1. A judge, the Prosecutor or a Deputy Prosecutor seeking to be excused from his or her functions shall make a request in writing to the Presidency, setting out the grounds upon which he or she should be excused.

2. The Presidency shall treat the request as confidential and shall not make public the reasons for its decision without the consent of the person concerned.

Rule 34 Disqualification of a judge, the Prosecutor or a Deputy Prosecutor

1. In addition to the grounds set out in article 41, paragraph 2, and article 42, paragraph 7, the grounds for disqualification of a judge, the Prosecutor or a Deputy Prosecutor shall include, *inter alia,* the following:

    (a) Personal interest in the case, including a spousal, parental or other close family, personal or professional relationship, or a subordinate relationship, with any of the parties;

    (b) Involvement, in his or her private capacity, in any legal proceedings initiated prior to his or her involvement in the case, or initiated by him or her subsequently, in which the person being investigated or prosecuted was or is an opposing party;

    (c) Performance of functions, prior to taking office, during which he or she could be expected to have formed an opinion on the case in question, on the parties or on their legal representatives that, objectively, could adversely affect the required impartiality of the person concerned;

    (d) Expression of opinions, through the communications media, in writing or in public actions, that, objectively, could adversely affect the required impartiality of the person concerned.

2. Subject to the provisions set out in article 41, paragraph 2, and article 42, paragraph 8, a request for disqualification shall be made in writing as soon as there is knowledge of the grounds on which it is based. The request shall state the grounds and attach any relevant evidence, and shall be transmitted to the person concerned, who shall be entitled to present written submissions.

3. Any question relating to the disqualification of the Prosecutor or a Deputy Prosecutor shall be decided by a majority of the judges of the Appeals Chamber.

Rule 35 Duty of a judge, the Prosecutor or a Deputy Prosecutor to request to be excused

Where a judge, the Prosecutor or a Deputy Prosecutor has reason to believe that a ground for disqualification exists in relation to him or her, he or she shall make a request to be excused and shall not wait for a request for disqualification to be made in accordance with article 41, paragraph 2, or article 42, paragraph 7, and Rule 34. The request shall be made and the Presidency shall deal with it in accordance with Rule 33.

Rule 36 Death of a judge, the Prosecutor, a Deputy Prosecutor, the Registrar or a Deputy Registrar

The Presidency shall inform, in writing, the President of the Bureau of the Assembly of States Parties of the death of a judge, the Prosecutor, a Deputy Prosecutor, the Registrar or a Deputy Registrar.

Rule 37 Resignation of a judge, the Prosecutor, a Deputy Prosecutor, the Registrar or a Deputy Registrar

1. A judge, the Prosecutor, a Deputy Prosecutor, the Registrar or a Deputy Registrar shall communicate to the Presidency, in writing, his or her decision to resign. The Presidency shall inform, in writing, the President of the Bureau of the Assembly of States Parties.

2. A judge, the Prosecutor, a Deputy Prosecutor, the Registrar or a Deputy Registrar shall endeavour to give notice of the date on which his or her resignation will take effect at least six months in advance. Before the resignation of a judge takes effect, he or she shall make every effort to discharge his or her outstanding responsibilities.

Subsection 3 Replacements and alternate judges

Rule 38 Replacements

1. A judge may be replaced for objective and justified reasons, *inter alia:*

    (a) Resignation;

(b) Accepted excuse;

(c) Disqualification;

(d) Removal from office;

(e) Death.

2. Replacement shall take place in accordance with the pre-established procedure in the Statute, the Rules and the Regulations.

Rule 39 Alternate judges

Where an alternate judge has been assigned by the Presidency to a Trial Chamber pursuant to article 74, paragraph 1, he or she shall sit through all proceedings and deliberations of the case, but may not take any part therein and shall not exercise any of the functions of the members of the Trial Chamber hearing the case, unless and until he or she is required to replace a member of the Trial Chamber if that member is unable to continue attending. Alternate judges shall be designated in accordance with a procedure pre-established by the Court.

Section V Publication, languages and translation

Rule 40 Publication of decisions in official languages of the Court

1. For the purposes of article 50, paragraph 1, the following decisions shall be considered as resolving fundamental issues:

(a) All decisions of the Appeals Division;

(b) All decisions of the Court on its jurisdiction or on the admissibility of a case pursuant to articles 17, 18, 19 and 20;

(c) All decisions of a Trial Chamber on guilt or innocence, sentencing and reparations to victims pursuant to articles 74, 75 and 76;

(d) All decisions of a Pre-Trial Chamber pursuant to article 57, paragraph 3(d).

2. Decisions on confirmation of charges under article 61, paragraph 7, and on offences against the administration of justice under article 70, paragraph 3, shall be published in all the official languages of the Court when the Presidency determines that they resolve fundamental issues.

3. The Presidency may decide to publish other decisions in all the official languages when such decisions concern major issues relating to the interpretation or the implementation of the Statute or concern a major issue of general interest.

Rule 41 Working languages of the Court

1. For the purposes of article 50, paragraph 2, the Presidency shall authorize the use of an official language of the Court as a working language when:

(a) That language is understood and spoken by the majority of those involved in a case before the Court and any of the participants in the proceedings so requests; or

(b) The Prosecutor and the defence so request.

2. The Presidency may authorize the use of an official language of the Court as a working language if it considers that it would facilitate the efficiency of the proceedings.

Rule 42 Translation and interpretation services

The Court shall arrange for the translation and interpretation services necessary to ensure the implementation of its obligations under the Statute and the Rules.

Rule 43 Procedure applicable to the publication of documents of the Court

The Court shall ensure that all documents subject to publication in accordance with the Statute and the Rules respect the duty to protect the confidentiality of the proceedings and the security of victims and witnesses.

Chapter 3 Jurisdiction and admissibility
Section I Declarations and referrals relating to articles 11, 12, 13 and 14

Rule 44 Declaration provided for in article 12, paragraph 3

1. The Registrar, at the request of the Prosecutor, may inquire of a State that is not a Party to the Statute or that has become a Party to the Statute after its entry into force, on a confidential basis, whether it intends to make the declaration provided for in article 12, paragraph 3.

2. When a State lodges, or declares to the Registrar its intent to lodge, a declaration with the Registrar pursuant to article 12, paragraph 3, or when the Registrar acts pursuant to sub-Rule 1, the Registrar shall inform the State concerned that the declaration under article 12, paragraph 3, has as a consequence the acceptance of jurisdiction with respect to the crimes referred to in article 5 of relevance to the situation and the provisions of Part 9, and any Rules thereunder concerning States Parties, shall apply.

Rule 45 Referral of a situation to the Prosecutor

A referral of a situation to the Prosecutor shall be in writing.

Section II Initiation of investigations under article 15

Rule 46 Information provided to the Prosecutor under article 15, paragraphs 1 and 2

Where information is submitted under article 15, paragraph 1, or where oral or written testimony is received pursuant to article 15, paragraph 2, at the seat of the Court, the Prosecutor shall protect the confidentiality of such information and testimony or take any other necessary measures, pursuant to his or her duties under the Statute.

Rule 47 Testimony under article 15, paragraph 2

1. The provisions of rules 111 and 112 shall apply, *mutatis mutandis,* to testimony received by the Prosecutor pursuant to article 15, paragraph 2.

2. When the Prosecutor considers that there is a serious risk that it might not be possible for the testimony to be taken subsequently, he or she may request the Pre-Trial Chamber to take such measures as may be necessary to ensure the efficiency and integrity of the proceedings and, in particular, to appoint a counsel or a judge from the Pre-Trial Chamber to be present during the taking of the testimony in order to protect the rights of the defence. If the testimony is subsequently presented in the proceedings, its admissibility shall be governed by article 69, paragraph 4, and given such weight as determined by the relevant Chamber.

Rule 48 Determination of reasonable basis to proceed with an investigation under article 15, paragraph 3

In determining whether there is a reasonable basis to proceed with an investigation under article 15, paragraph 3, the Prosecutor shall consider the factors set out in article 53, paragraph 1(a) to (c).

Rule 49 Decision and notice under article 15, paragraph 6

1. Where a decision under article 15, paragraph 6, is taken, the Prosecutor shall promptly ensure that notice is provided, including reasons for his or her decision, in a manner that prevents any danger to the safety, well-being and privacy of those who provided information to him or her under article 15, paragraphs 1 and 2, or the integrity of investigations or proceedings.

2. The notice shall also advise of the possibility of submitting further information regarding the same situation in the light of new facts and evidence.

Rule 50 Procedure for authorization by the Pre-Trial Chamber of the commencement of the investigation

1. When the Prosecutor intends to seek authorization from the Pre-Trial Chamber to initiate an investigation pursuant to article 15, paragraph 3, the Prosecutor shall inform victims, known to him or her or to the Victims and Witnesses Unit, or their legal representatives, unless the Prosecutor decides that doing so would pose a danger to the integrity of the investigation or the life or well-being of victims and witnesses. The Prosecutor may also give notice by general means in order to reach groups of victims if he or she determines in the particular circumstances of the case that such notice could not pose a danger to the integrity and effective conduct of the investigation or to the security and well-being of victims and witnesses. In performing these functions, the Prosecutor may seek the assistance of the Victims and Witnesses Unit as appropriate.

2. A request for authorization by the Prosecutor shall be in writing.

3. Following information given in accordance with sub-rule 1, victims may make representations in writing to the Pre-Trial Chamber within such time limit as set forth in the Regulations.

4. The Pre-Trial Chamber, in deciding on the procedure to be followed, may request additional information from the Prosecutor and from any of the victims who have made representations, and, if it considers it appropriate, may hold a hearing.

5. The Pre-Trial Chamber shall issue its decision, including its reasons, as to whether to authorize the commencement of the investigation in accordance with article 15, paragraph 4, with respect to all or any part of the request by the Prosecutor. The Chamber shall give notice of the decision to victims who have made representations.

6. The above procedure shall also apply to a new request to the Pre-Trial Chamber pursuant to article 15, paragraph 5.

Section III Challenges and preliminary rulings under articles 17, 18 and 19

Rule 51 Information provided under article 17

In considering the matters referred to in article 17, paragraph 2, and in the context of the circumstances of the case, the Court may consider, *inter alia,* information that the State referred to in article 17, paragraph 1, may choose to bring to the attention of the Court showing that its courts meet internationally recognized norms and standards for the independent and impartial prosecution of similar conduct, or that the State has confirmed in writing to the Prosecutor that the case is being investigated or prosecuted.

Rule 52 Notification provided for in article 18, paragraph 1

1. Subject to the limitations provided for in article 18, paragraph 1, the notification shall contain information about the acts that may constitute crimes referred to in article 5, relevant for the purposes of article 18, paragraph 2.

2. A State may request additional information from the Prosecutor to assist it in the application of article 18, paragraph 2. Such a request shall not affect the one-month time limit provided for in article 18, paragraph 2, and shall be responded to by the Prosecutor on an expedited basis.

Rule 53 Deferral provided for in article 18, paragraph 2

When a State requests a deferral pursuant to article 18, paragraph 2, that State shall make this request in writing and provide information concerning its investigation, taking into account article 18, paragraph 2. The Prosecutor may request additional information from that State.

Rule 54 Application by the Prosecutor under article 18, paragraph 2

1. An application submitted by the Prosecutor to the Pre-Trial Chamber in accordance with article 18, paragraph 2, shall be in writing and shall contain the basis for the application. The

information provided by the State under Rule 53 shall be communicated by the Prosecutor to the Pre-Trial Chamber.

2. The Prosecutor shall inform that State in writing when he or she makes an application to the Pre-Trial Chamber under article 18, paragraph 2, and shall include in the notice a summary of the basis of the application.

Rule 55 Proceedings concerning article 18, paragraph 2

1. The Pre-Trial Chamber shall decide on the procedure to be followed and may take appropriate measures for the proper conduct of the proceedings. It may hold a hearing.

2. The Pre-Trial Chamber shall examine the Prosecutor's application and any observations submitted by a State that requested a deferral in accordance with article 18, paragraph 2, and shall consider the factors in article 17 in deciding whether to authorize an investigation.

3. The decision and the basis for the decision of the Pre-Trial Chamber shall be communicated as soon as possible to the Prosecutor and to the State that requested a deferral of an investigation.

Rule 56 Application by the Prosecutor following review under article 18, paragraph 3

1. Following a review by the Prosecutor as set forth in article 18, paragraph 3, the Prosecutor may apply to the Pre-Trial Chamber for authorization in accordance with article 18, paragraph 2. The application to the Pre-Trial Chamber shall be in writing and shall contain the basis for the application.

2. Any further information provided by the State under article 18, paragraph 5, shall be communicated by the Prosecutor to the Pre-Trial Chamber.

3. The proceedings shall be conducted in accordance with Rule s 54, sub-rule 2, and 55.

Rule 57 Provisional measures under article 18, paragraph 6

An application to the Pre-Trial Chamber by the Prosecutor in the circumstances provided for in article 18, paragraph 6, shall be considered ex parte and in camera. The Pre-Trial Chamber shall Rule on the application on an expedited basis.

Rule 58 Proceedings under article 19

1. A request or application made under article 19 shall be in writing and contain the basis for it.

2. When a Chamber receives a request or application raising a challenge or question concerning its jurisdiction or the admissibility of a case in accordance with article 19, paragraph 2 or 3, or is acting on its own motion as provided for in article 19, paragraph 1, it shall decide on the procedure to be followed and may take appropriate measures for the proper conduct of the proceedings. It may hold a hearing. It may join the challenge or question to a confirmation or a trial proceeding as long as this does not cause undue delay, and in this circumstance shall hear and decide on the challenge or question first.

3. The Court shall transmit a request or application received under sub-rule 2 to the Prosecutor and to the person referred to in article 19, paragraph 2, who has been surrendered to the Court or who has appeared voluntarily or pursuant to a summons, and shall allow them to submit written observations to the request or application within a period of time determined by the Chamber.

4. The Court shall Rule on any challenge or question of jurisdiction first and then on any challenge or question of admissibility.

Rule 59 Participation in proceedings under article 19, paragraph 3

1. For the purpose of article 19, paragraph 3, the Registrar shall inform the following of any question or challenge of jurisdiction or admissibility which has arisen pursuant to article 19, paragraphs 1, 2 and 3:

   (a) Those who have referred a situation pursuant to article 13;

   (b) The victims who have already communicated with the Court in relation to that case or their legal representatives.

2. The Registrar shall provide those referred to in sub-rule 1, in a manner consistent with the duty of the Court regarding the confidentiality of information, the protection of any person and the preservation of evidence, with a summary of the grounds on which the jurisdiction of the Court or the admissibility of the case has been challenged.

3. Those receiving the information, as provided for in sub-rule 1, may make representation in writing to the competent Chamber within such time limit as it considers appropriate.

Rule 60 Competent organ to receive challenges

If a challenge to the jurisdiction of the Court or to the admissibility of a case is made after a confirmation of the charges but before the constitution or designation of the Trial Chamber, it shall be addressed to the Presidency, which shall refer it to the Trial Chamber as soon as the latter is constituted or designated in accordance with Rule 130.

Rule 61 Provisional measures under article 19, paragraph 8

When the Prosecutor makes application to the competent Chamber in the circumstances provided for in article 19, paragraph 8, rule 57 shall apply.

Rule 62 Proceedings under article 19, paragraph 10

1. If the Prosecutor makes a request under article 19, paragraph 10, he or she shall make the request to the Chamber that made the latest ruling on admissibility. The provisions of rules 58, 59 and 61 shall be applicable.

2. The State or States whose challenge to admissibility under article 19, paragraph 2, provoked the decision of inadmissibility provided for in article 19, paragraph 10, shall be notified of the request of the Prosecutor and shall be given a time limit within which to make representations.

Chapter 4 Provisions relating to various stages of the proceedings
Section I Evidence

Rule 63 General provisions relating to evidence

1. The rules of evidence set forth in this chapter, together with article 69, shall apply in proceedings before all Chambers.

2. A Chamber shall have the authority, in accordance with the discretion described in article 64, paragraph 9, to assess freely all evidence submitted in order to determine its relevance or admissibility in accordance with article 69.

3. A Chamber shall rule on an application of a party or on its own motion, made under article 64, subparagraph 9 (a), concerning admissibility when it is based on the grounds set out in article 69, paragraph 7.

4. Without prejudice to article 66, paragraph 3, a Chamber shall not impose a legal requirement that corroboration is required in order to prove any crime within the jurisdiction of the Court, in particular, crimes of sexual violence.

5. The Chambers shall not apply national laws governing evidence, other than in accordance with article 21.

Rule 64 Procedure relating to the relevance or admissibility of evidence

1. An issue relating to relevance or admissibility must be raised at the time when the evidence is submitted to a Chamber. Exceptionally, when those issues were not known at the time when the evidence was submitted, it may be raised immediately after the issue has become known. The Chamber may request that the issue be raised in writing. The written motion shall be communicated by the Court to all those who participate in the proceedings, unless otherwise decided by the Court.

2. A Chamber shall give reasons for any rulings it makes on evidentiary matters. These reasons shall be placed in the record of the proceedings if they have not already been incorporated into the record during the course of the proceedings in accordance with article 64, paragraph 10, and rule 137, sub-rule 1.

3. Evidence ruled irrelevant or inadmissible shall not be considered by the Chamber.

Rule 65 Compellability of witnesses

1. A witness who appears before the Court is compellable by the Court to provide testimony, unless otherwise provided for in the Statute and the rules, in particular rules 73, 74 and 75.

2. Rule 171 applies to a witness appearing before the Court who is compellable to provide testimony under sub-Rule 1.

Rule 66 Solemn undertaking

1. Except as described in sub-rule 2, every witness shall, in accordance with article 69, paragraph 1, make the following solemn undertaking before testifying: "I solemnly declare that I will speak the truth, the whole truth and nothing but the truth."

2. A person under the age of 18 or a person whose judgment has been impaired and who, in the opinion of the Chamber, does not understand the nature of a solemn undertaking may be allowed to testify without this solemn undertaking if the Chamber considers that the person is able to describe matters of which he or she has knowledge and that the person understands the meaning of the duty to speak the truth.

3. Before testifying, the witness shall be informed of the offence defined in article 70, paragraph 1 (a).

Rule 67 Live testimony by means of audio or video-link technology

1. In accordance with article 69, paragraph 2, a Chamber may allow a witness to give *viva voce* (oral) testimony before the Chamber by means of audio or video technology, provided that such technology permits the witness to be examined by the Prosecutor, the defence, and by the Chamber itself, at the time that the witness so testifies.

2. The examination of a witness under this rule shall be conducted in accordance with the relevant rules of this chapter.

3. The Chamber, with the assistance of the Registry, shall ensure that the venue chosen for the conduct of the audio or video-link testimony is conducive to the giving of truthful and open testimony and to the safety, physical and psychological well-being, dignity and privacy of the witness.

Rule 68 Prior recorded testimony

When the Pre-Trial Chamber has not taken measures under article 56, the Trial Chamber may, in accordance with article 69, paragraph 2, allow the introduction of previously recorded audio or video testimony of a witness, or the transcript or other documented evidence of such testimony, provided that:

(a) If the witness who gave the previously recorded testimony is not present before the Trial Chamber, both the Prosecutor and the defence had the opportunity to examine the witness during the recording; or

(b) If the witness who gave the previously recorded testimony is present before the Trial Chamber, he or she does not object to the submission of the previously recorded testimony and the Prosecutor, the defence and the Chamber have the opportunity to examine the witness during the proceedings.

Rule 69 Agreements as to evidence

The Prosecutor and the defence may agree that an alleged fact, which is contained in the charges, the contents of a document, the expected testimony of a witness or other evidence is not contested and, accordingly, a Chamber may consider such alleged fact as being proven, unless the Chamber is of the opinion that a more complete presentation of the alleged facts is required in the interests of justice, in particular the interests of the victims.

Rule 70 Principles of evidence in cases of sexual violence

In cases of sexual violence, the Court shall be guided by and, where appropriate, apply the following principles:

(a) Consent cannot be inferred by reason of any words or conduct of a victim where force, threat of force, coercion or taking advantage of a coercive environment undermined the victim's ability to give voluntary and genuine consent;

(b) Consent cannot be inferred by reason of any words or conduct of a victim where the victim is incapable of giving genuine consent;

(c) Consent cannot be inferred by reason of the silence of, or lack of resistance by, a victim to the alleged sexual violence;

(d) Credibility, character or predisposition to sexual availability of a victim or witness cannot be inferred by reason of the sexual nature of the prior or subsequent conduct of a victim or witness.

Rule 71 Evidence of other sexual conduct

In the light of the definition and nature of the crimes within the jurisdiction of the Court, and subject to article 69, paragraph 4, a Chamber shall not admit evidence of the prior or subsequent sexual conduct of a victim or witness.

Rule 72 In camera procedure to consider relevance or admissibility of evidence

1. Where there is an intention to introduce or elicit, including by means of the questioning of a victim or witness, evidence that the victim consented to an alleged crime of sexual violence, or evidence of the words, conduct, silence or lack of resistance of a victim or witness as referred to in principles (a) through (d) of rule 70, notification shall be provided to the Court which shall describe the substance of the evidence intended to be introduced or elicited and the relevance of the evidence to the issues in the case.

2. In deciding whether the evidence referred to in sub-rule 1 is relevant or admissible, a Chamber shall hear in camera the views of the Prosecutor, the defence, the witness and the victim or his or her legal representative, if any, and shall take into account whether that evidence has a sufficient degree of probative value to an issue in the case and the prejudice that such evidence may cause, in accordance with article 69, paragraph 4. For this purpose, the Chamber shall have regard to article 21, paragraph 3, and articles 67 and 68, and shall be guided by principles (a) to (d) of Rule 70, especially with respect to the proposed questioning of a victim.

3. Where the Chamber determines that the evidence referred to in sub-rule 2 is admissible in the proceedings, the Chamber shall state on the record the specific purpose for which the evidence is admissible. In evaluating the evidence during the proceedings, the Chamber shall apply principles (a) to (d) of Rule 70.

Rule 73 Privileged communications and information

1. Without prejudice to article 67, paragraph 1 (b), communications made in the context of the professional relationship between a person and his or her legal counsel shall be regarded as privileged, and consequently not subject to disclosure, unless:

   (a) The person consents in writing to such disclosure; or

   (b) The person voluntarily disclosed the content of the communication to a third party, and that third party then gives evidence of that disclosure.

2. Having regard to rule 63, sub-rule 5, communications made in the context of a class of professional or other confidential relationships shall be regarded as privileged, and consequently not subject to disclosure, under the same terms as in sub-rules 1(a) and 1(b) if a Chamber decides in respect of that class that:

   (a) Communications occurring within that class of relationship are made in the course of a confidential relationship producing a reasonable expectation of privacy and non-disclosure;

   (b) Confidentiality is essential to the nature and type of relationship between the person and the confidant; and

   (c) Recognition of the privilege would further the objectives of the Statute and the rules.

3. In making a decision under sub-rule 2, the Court shall give particular regard to recognizing as privileged those communications made in the context of the professional relationship between a person and his or her medical doctor, psychiatrist, psychologist or counsellor, in particular those related to or involving victims, or between a person and a member of a religious clergy; and in the latter case, the Court shall recognize as privileged those communications made in the context of a sacred confession where it is an integral part of the practice of that religion.

4. The Court shall regard as privileged, and consequently not subject to disclosure, including by way of testimony of any present or past official or employee of the International Committee of the Red Cross (ICRC), any information, documents or other evidence which it came into the possession of in the course, or as a consequence, of the performance by ICRC of its functions under the Statutes of the International Red Cross and Red Crescent Movement, unless:

   (a) After consultations undertaken pursuant to sub-rule 6, ICRC does not object in writing to such disclosure, or otherwise has waived this privilege; or

   (b) Such information, documents or other evidence is contained in public statements and documents of ICRC.

5. Nothing in sub-rule 4 shall affect the admissibility of the same evidence obtained from a source other than ICRC and its officials or employees when such evidence has also been acquired by this source independently of ICRC and its officials or employees.

6. If the Court determines that ICRC information, documents or other evidence are of great importance for a particular case, consultations shall be held between the Court and ICRC in order to seek to resolve the matter by cooperative means, bearing in mind the circumstances of the case, the relevance of the evidence sought, whether the evidence could be obtained from a source other than ICRC, the interests of justice and of victims, and the performance of the Court's and ICRC's functions.

Rule 74 Self-incrimination by a witness

1. Unless a witness has been notified pursuant to rule 190, the Chamber shall notify a witness of the provisions of this rule before his or her testimony.

2. Where the Court determines that an assurance with respect to self-incrimination should be provided to a particular witness, it shall provide the assurances under sub-rule 3, paragraph (c), before the witness attends, directly or pursuant to a request under article 93, paragraph (1)(e).

3. (a) A witness may object to making any statement that might tend to incriminate him or her.

   (b) Where the witness has attended after receiving an assurance under sub-rule 2, the Court may require the witness to answer the question or questions.

   (c) In the case of other witnesses, the Chamber may require the witness to answer the question or questions, after assuring the witness that the evidence provided in response to the questions:

      (i) Will be kept confidential and will not be disclosed to the public or any State; and

      (ii) Will not be used either directly or indirectly against that person in any subsequent prosecution by the Court, except under articles 70 and 71.

4. Before giving such an assurance, the Chamber shall seek the views of the Prosecutor, *ex parte*, to determine if the assurance should be given to this particular witness.

5. In determining whether to require the witness to answer, the Chamber shall consider:

   (a) The importance of the anticipated evidence;

   (b) Whether the witness would be providing unique evidence;

   (c) The nature of the possible incrimination, if known; and

   (d) The sufficiency of the protections for the witness, in the particular circumstances.

6. If the Chamber determines that it would not be appropriate to provide an assurance to this witness, it shall not require the witness to answer the question. If the Chamber determines not to require the witness to answer, it may still continue the questioning of the witness on other matters.

7. In order to give effect to the assurance, the Chamber shall:

   (a) Order that the evidence of the witness be given in camera;

   (b) Order that the identity of the witness and the content of the evidence given shall not be disclosed, in any manner, and provide that the breach of any such order will be subject to sanction under article 71;

   (c) Specifically advise the Prosecutor, the accused, the defence counsel, the legal representative of the victim and any Court staff present of the consequences of a breach of the order under subparagraph (b);

   (d) Order the sealing of any record of the proceedings; and

   (e) Use protective measures with respect to any decision of the Court to ensure that the identity of the witness and the content of the evidence given are not disclosed.

8. Where the Prosecutor is aware that the testimony of any witness may raise issues with respect to self-incrimination, he or she shall request an in camera hearing and advise the Chamber of this, in advance of the testimony of the witness. The Chamber may impose the measures outlined in sub-rule 7 for all or a part of the testimony of that witness.

9. The accused, the defence counsel or the witness may advise the Prosecutor or the Chamber that the testimony of a witness will raise issues of self-incrimination before the witness testifies and the Chamber may take the measures outlined in sub-rule 7.

10. If an issue of self-incrimination arises in the course of the proceedings, the Chamber shall suspend the taking of the testimony and provide the witness with an opportunity to obtain legal advice if he or she so requests for the purpose of the application of the rule.

Rule 75 Incrimination by family members

1. A witness appearing before the Court, who is a spouse, child or parent of an accused person, shall not be required by a Chamber to make any statement that might tend to incriminate that accused person. However, the witness may choose to make such a statement.

2. In evaluating the testimony of a witness, a Chamber may take into account that the witness, referred to in sub-rule 1, objected to reply to a question which was intended to contradict a

previous statement made by the witness, or the witness was selective in choosing which questions to answer.

Section II Disclosure

Rule 76 Pre-trial disclosure relating to prosecution witnesses

1. The Prosecutor shall provide the defence with the names of witnesses whom the Prosecutor intends to call to testify and copies of any prior statements made by those witnesses. This shall be done sufficiently in advance to enable the adequate preparation of the defence.

2. The Prosecutor shall subsequently advise the defence of the names of any additional prosecution witnesses and provide copies of their statements when the decision is made to call those witnesses.

3. The statements of prosecution witnesses shall be made available in original and in a language which the accused fully understands and speaks.

4. This rule is subject to the protection and privacy of victims and witnesses and the protection of confidential information as provided for in the Statute and rules 81 and 82.

Rule 77 Inspection of material in possession or control of the Prosecutor

The Prosecutor shall, subject to the restrictions on disclosure as provided for in the Statute and in rules 81 and 82, permit the defence to inspect any books, documents, photographs and other tangible objects in the possession or control of the Prosecutor, which are material to the preparation of the defence or are intended for use by the Prosecutor as evidence for the purposes of the confirmation hearing or at trial, as the case may be, or were obtained from or belonged to the person.

Rule 78 Inspection of material in possession or control of the defence

The defence shall permit the Prosecutor to inspect any books, documents, photographs and other tangible objects in the possession or control of the defence, which are intended for use by the defence as evidence for the purposes of the confirmation hearing or at trial.

Rule 79 Disclosure by the defence

1. The defence shall notify the Prosecutor of its intent to:

   (a) Raise the existence of an alibi, in which case the notification shall specify the place or places at which the accused claims to have been present at the time of the alleged crime and the names of witnesses and any other evidence upon which the accused intends to rely to establish the alibi; or

   (b) Raise a ground for excluding criminal responsibility provided for in article 31, paragraph 1, in which case the notification shall specify the names of witnesses and any other evidence upon which the accused intends to rely to establish the ground.

2. With due regard to time limits set forth in other rules, notification under sub-rule 1 shall be given sufficiently in advance to enable the Prosecutor to prepare adequately and to respond. The Chamber dealing with the matter may grant the Prosecutor an adjournment to address the issue raised by the defence.

3. Failure of the defence to provide notice under this rule shall not limit its right to raise matters dealt with in sub-rule 1 and to present evidence.

4. This rule does not prevent a Chamber from ordering disclosure of any other evidence.

Rule 80 Procedures for raising a ground for excluding criminal responsibility under article 31, paragraph 3

1. The defence shall give notice to both the Trial Chamber and the Prosecutor if it intends to raise a ground for excluding criminal responsibility under article 31, paragraph 3. This shall be done

sufficiently in advance of the commencement of the trial to enable the Prosecutor to prepare adequately for trial.

2. Following notice given under sub-rule 1, the Trial Chamber shall hear both the Prosecutor and the defence before deciding whether the defence can raise a ground for excluding criminal responsibility.

3. If the defence is permitted to raise the ground, the Trial Chamber may grant the Prosecutor an adjournment to address that ground.

Rule 81 Restrictions on disclosure

1. Reports, memoranda or other internal documents prepared by a party, its assistants or representatives in connection with the investigation or preparation of the case are not subject to disclosure.

2. Where material or information is in the possession or control of the Prosecutor which must be disclosed in accordance with the Statute, but disclosure may prejudice further or ongoing investigations, the Prosecutor may apply to the Chamber dealing with the matter for a ruling as to whether the material or information must be disclosed to the defence. The matter shall be heard on an ex parte basis by the Chamber. However, the Prosecutor may not introduce such material or information into evidence during the confirmation hearing or the trial without adequate prior disclosure to the accused.

3. Where steps have been taken to ensure the confidentiality of information, in accordance with articles 54, 57, 64, 72 and 93, and, in accordance with article 68, to protect the safety of witnesses and victims and members of their families, such information shall not be disclosed, except in accordance with those articles. When the disclosure of such information may create a risk to the safety of the witness, the Court shall take measures to inform the witness in advance.

4. The Chamber dealing with the matter shall, on its own motion or at the request of the Prosecutor, the accused or any State, take the necessary steps to ensure the confidentiality of information, in accordance with articles 54, 72 and 93, and, in accordance with article 68, to protect the safety of witnesses and victims and members of their families, including by authorizing the non-disclosure of their identity prior to the commencement of the trial.

5. Where material or information is in the possession or control of the Prosecutor which is withheld under article 68, paragraph 5, such material and information may not be subsequently introduced into evidence during the confirmation hearing or the trial without adequate prior disclosure to the accused.

6. Where material or information is in the possession or control of the defence which is subject to disclosure, it may be withheld in circumstances similar to those which would allow the Prosecutor to rely on article 68, paragraph 5, and a summary thereof submitted instead. Such material and information may not be subsequently introduced into evidence during the confirmation hearing or the trial without adequate prior disclosure to the Prosecutor.

Rule 82 Restrictions on disclosure of material and information protected under article 54, paragraph 3(e)

1. Where material or information is in the possession or control of the Prosecutor which is protected under article 54, paragraph 3(e), the Prosecutor may not subsequently introduce such material or information into evidence without the prior consent of the provider of the material or information and adequate prior disclosure to the accused.

2. If the Prosecutor introduces material or information protected under article 54, paragraph 3(e), into evidence, a Chamber may not order the production of additional evidence received from the provider of the initial material or information, nor may a Chamber for the purpose of obtaining such additional evidence itself summon the provider or a representative of the provider as a witness or order their attendance.

3. If the Prosecutor calls a witness to introduce in evidence any material or information which has been protected under article 54, paragraph 3(e), a Chamber may not compel that witness to answer any question relating to the material or information or its origin, if the witness declines to answer on grounds of confidentiality.

4. The right of the accused to challenge evidence which has been protected under article 54, paragraph 3 (e), shall remain unaffected subject only to the limitations contained in sub-rules 2 and 3.

5. A Chamber dealing with the matter may order, upon application by the defence, that, in the interests of justice, material or information in the possession of the accused, which has been provided to the accused under the same conditions as set forth in article 54, paragraph 3(e), and which is to be introduced into evidence, shall be subject *mutatis mutandis* to sub-rules 1, 2 and 3.

Rule 83 Ruling on exculpatory evidence under article 67, paragraph 2

The Prosecutor may request as soon as practicable a hearing on an *ex parte* basis before the Chamber dealing with the matter for the purpose of obtaining a ruling under article 67, paragraph 2.

Rule 84 Disclosure and additional evidence for trial

In order to enable the parties to prepare for trial and to facilitate the fair and expeditious conduct of the proceedings, the Trial Chamber shall, in accordance with article 64, paragraphs 3(c) and 6(d), and article 67, paragraph (2), and subject to article 68, paragraph 5, make any necessary orders for the disclosure of documents or information not previously disclosed and for the production of additional evidence. To avoid delay and to ensure that the trial commences on the set date, any such orders shall include strict time limits which shall be kept under review by the Trial Chamber.

Section III Victims and witnesses
Subsection 1 Definition and general principle relating to victims

Rule 85 Definition of victims

For the purposes of the Statute and the rules of Procedure and Evidence:

(a) "Victims" means natural persons who have suffered harm as a result of the commission of any crime within the jurisdiction of the Court;

(b) Victims may include organizations or institutions that have sustained direct harm to any of their property which is dedicated to religion, education, art or science or charitable purposes, and to their historic monuments, hospitals and other places and objects for humanitarian purposes.

Rule 86 General principle

A Chamber in making any direction or order, and other organs of the Court in performing their functions under the Statute or the rules, shall take into account the needs of all victims and witnesses in accordance with article 68, in particular, children, elderly persons, persons with disabilities and victims of sexual or gender violence.

Subsection 2 Protection of victims and witnesses

Rule 87 Protective measures

1. Upon the motion of the Prosecutor or the defence or upon the request of a witness or a victim or his or her legal representative, if any, or on its own motion, and after having consulted with the Victims and Witnesses Unit, as appropriate, a Chamber may order measures to protect a victim, a witness or another person at risk on account of testimony given by a witness pursuant to article 68, paragraphs 1 and 2. The Chamber shall seek to obtain, whenever possible, the consent of the person in respect of whom the protective measure is sought prior to ordering the protective measure.

2. A motion or request under sub-rule 1 shall be governed by Rule 134, provided that:

   (a) Such a motion or request shall not be submitted *ex parte*;

   (b) A request by a witness or by a victim or his or her legal representative, if any, shall be served on both the Prosecutor and the defence, each of whom shall have the opportunity to respond;

   (c) A motion or request affecting a particular witness or a particular victim shall be served on that witness or victim or his or her legal representative, if any, in addition to the other party, each of whom shall have the opportunity to respond;

   (d) When the Chamber proceeds on its own motion, notice and opportunity to respond shall be given to the Prosecutor and the defence, and to any witness or any victim or his or her legal representative, if any, who would be affected by such protective measure; and

   (e) A motion or request may be filed under seal, and, if so filed, shall remain sealed until otherwise ordered by a Chamber. Responses to motions or requests filed under seal shall also be filed under seal.

3. A Chamber may, on a motion or request under sub-rule 1, hold a hearing, which shall be conducted in camera, to determine whether to order measures to prevent the release to the public or press and information agencies, of the identity or the location of a victim, a witness or other person at risk on account of testimony given by a witness by ordering, *inter alia*:

   (a) That the name of the victim, witness or other person at risk on account of testimony given by a witness or any information which could lead to his or her identification, be expunged from the public records of the Chamber;

   (b) That the Prosecutor, the defence or any other participant in the proceedings be prohibited from disclosing such information to a third party;

   (c) That testimony be presented by electronic or other special means, including the use of technical means enabling the alteration of pictures or voice, the use of audio-visual technology, in particular videoconferencing and closed-circuit television, and the exclusive use of the sound media;

   (d) That a pseudonym be used for a victim, a witness or other person at risk on account of testimony given by a witness; or

   (e) That a Chamber conduct part of its proceedings in camera.

Rule 88 Special measures

1. Upon the motion of the Prosecutor or the defence, or upon the request of a witness or a victim or his or her legal representative, if any, or on its own motion, and after having consulted with the Victims and Witnesses Unit, as appropriate, a Chamber may, taking into account the views of the victim or witness, order special measures such as, but not limited to, measures to facilitate the testimony of a traumatized victim or witness, a child, an elderly person or a victim of sexual violence, pursuant to article 68, paragraphs 1 and 2. The Chamber shall seek to obtain, whenever possible, the consent of the person in respect of whom the special measure is sought prior to ordering that measure.

2. A Chamber may hold a hearing on a motion or a request under sub-rule 1, if necessary in camera or ex parte, to determine whether to order any such special measure, including but not limited to an order that a counsel, a legal representative, a psychologist or a family member be permitted to attend during the testimony of the victim or the witness.

3. For *inter partes* motions or requests filed under this rule, the provisions of rule 87, sub-rules 2(b) to (d), shall apply *mutatis mutandis*.

4. A motion or request filed under this rule may be filed under seal, and if so filed shall remain sealed until otherwise ordered by a Chamber. Any responses to *inter partes* motions or requests filed under seal shall also be filed under seal.

5. Taking into consideration that violations of the privacy of a witness or victim may create risk to his or her security, a Chamber shall be vigilant in controlling the manner of questioning a witness or victim so as to avoid any harassment or intimidation, paying particular attention to attacks on victims of crimes of sexual violence.

Subsection 3 Participation of victims in the proceedings

Rule 89 Application for participation of victims in the proceedings

1. In order to present their views and concerns, victims shall make written application to the Registrar, who shall transmit the application to the relevant Chamber. Subject to the provisions of the Statute, in particular article 68, paragraph 1, the Registrar shall provide a copy of the application to the Prosecutor and the defence, who shall be entitled to reply within a time limit to be set by the Chamber. Subject to the provisions of sub-rule 2, the Chamber shall then specify the proceedings and manner in which participation is considered appropriate, which may include making opening and closing statements.

2. The Chamber, on its own initiative or on the application of the Prosecutor or the defence, may reject the application if it considers that the person is not a victim or that the criteria set forth in article 68, paragraph 3, are not otherwise fulfilled. A victim whose application has been rejected may file a new application later in the proceedings.

3. An application referred to in this rule may also be made by a person acting with the consent of the victim, or a person acting on behalf of a victim, in the case of a victim who is a child or, when necessary, a victim who is disabled.

4. Where there are a number of applications, the Chamber may consider the applications in such a manner as to ensure the effectiveness of the proceedings and may issue one decision.

Rule 90 Legal representatives of victims

1. A victim shall be free to choose a legal representative.

2. Where there are a number of victims, the Chamber may, for the purposes of ensuring the effectiveness of the proceedings, request the victims or particular groups of victims, if necessary with the assistance of the Registry, to choose a common legal representative or representatives. In facilitating the coordination of victim representation, the Registry may provide assistance, *inter alia,* by referring the victims to a list of counsel, maintained by the Registry, or suggesting one or more common legal representatives.

3. If the victims are unable to choose a common legal representative or representatives within a time limit that the Chamber may decide, the Chamber may request the Registrar to choose one or more common legal representatives.

4. The Chamber and the Registry shall take all reasonable steps to ensure that in the selection of common legal representatives, the distinct interests of the victims, particularly as provided in article 68, paragraph 1, are represented and that any conflict of interest is avoided.

5. A victim or group of victims who lack the necessary means to pay for a common legal representative chosen by the Court may receive assistance from the Registry, including, as appropriate, financial assistance.

6. A legal representative of a victim or victims shall have the qualifications set forth in rule 22, sub-rule 1.

Rule 91 Participation of legal representatives in the proceedings

1. A Chamber may modify a previous ruling under Rule 89.

2. A legal representative of a victim shall be entitled to attend and participate in the proceedings in accordance with the terms of the ruling of the Chamber and any modification thereof given under rules 89 and 90. This shall include participation in hearings unless, in the circumstances of the case, the Chamber concerned is of the view that the representative's intervention should be

confined to written observations or submissions. The Prosecutor and the defence shall be allowed to reply to any oral or written observation by the legal representative for victims.

3. (a) When a legal representative attends and participates in accordance with this rule, and wishes to question a witness, including questioning under rules 67 and 68, an expert or the accused, the legal representative must make application to the Chamber. The Chamber may require the legal representative to provide a written note of the questions and in that case the questions shall be communicated to the Prosecutor and, if appropriate, the defence, who shall be allowed to make observations within a time limit set by the Chamber.

    (b) The Chamber shall then issue a ruling on the request, taking into account the stage of the proceedings, the rights of the accused, the interests of witnesses, the need for a fair, impartial and expeditious trial and in order to give effect to article 68, paragraph 3. The ruling may include directions on the manner and order of the questions and the production of documents in accordance with the powers of the Chamber under article 64. The Chamber may, if it considers it appropriate, put the question to the witness, expert or accused on behalf of the victim's legal representative.

4. For a hearing limited to reparations under article 75, the restrictions on questioning by the legal representative set forth in sub-rule 2 shall not apply. In that case, the legal representative may, with the permission of the Chamber concerned, question witnesses, experts and the person concerned.

Rule 92 Notification to victims and their legal representatives

1. This Rule on notification to victims and their legal representatives shall apply to all proceedings before the Court, except in proceedings provided for in Part 2.

2. In order to allow victims to apply for participation in the proceedings in accordance with rule 89, the Court shall notify victims concerning the decision of the Prosecutor not to initiate an investigation or not to prosecute pursuant to article 53. Such a notification shall be given to victims or their legal representatives who have already participated in the proceedings or, as far as possible, to those who have communicated with the Court in respect of the situation or case in question. The Chamber may order the measures outlined in sub-rule 8 if it considers it appropriate in the particular circumstances.

3. In order to allow victims to apply for participation in the proceedings in accordance with rule 89, the Court shall notify victims regarding its decision to hold a hearing to confirm charges pursuant to article 61. Such a notification shall be given to victims or their legal representatives who have already participated in the proceedings or, as far as possible, to those who have communicated with the Court in respect of the case in question.

4. When a notification for participation as provided for in sub-rules 2 and 3 has been given, any subsequent notification as referred to in sub-rules 5 and 6 shall only be provided to victims or their legal representatives who may participate in the proceedings in accordance with a ruling of the Chamber pursuant to rule 89 and any modification thereof.

5. In a manner consistent with the ruling made under rules 89 to 91, victims or their legal representatives participating in proceedings shall, in respect of those proceedings, be notified by the Registrar in a timely manner of:

    (a) Proceedings before the Court, including the date of hearings and any postponements thereof, and the date of delivery of the decision;

    (b) Requests, submissions, motions and other documents relating to such requests, submissions or motions.

6. Where victims or their legal representatives have participated in a certain stage of the proceedings, the Registrar shall notify them as soon as possible of the decisions of the Court in those proceedings.

7. Notifications as referred to in sub-rules 5 and 6 shall be in writing or, where written notification is not possible, in any other form as appropriate. The Registry shall keep a record of all notifications. Where necessary, the Registrar may seek the cooperation of States Parties in accordance with article 93, paragraph 1(d) and (l).

8. For notification as referred to in sub-rule 3 and otherwise at the request of a Chamber, the Registrar shall take necessary measures to give adequate publicity to the proceedings. In doing so, the Registrar may seek, in accordance with Part 9, the cooperation of relevant States Parties, and seek the assistance of intergovernmental organizations.

Rule 93 Views of victims or their legal representatives

A Chamber may seek the views of victims or their legal representatives participating pursuant to rules 89 to 91 on any issue, *inter alia,* in relation to issues referred to in rules 107, 109, 125, 128, 136, 139 and 191. In addition, a Chamber may seek the views of other victims, as appropriate.

Subsection 4 Reparations to victims

Rule 94 Procedure upon request

1. A victim's request for reparations under article 75 shall be made in writing and filed with the Registrar. It shall contain the following particulars:

    (a) The identity and address of the claimant;

    (b) A description of the injury, loss or harm;

    (c) The location and date of the incident and, to the extent possible, the identity of the person or persons the victim believes to be responsible for the injury, loss or harm;

    (d) Where restitution of assets, property or other tangible items is sought, a description of them;

    (e) Claims for compensation;

    (f) Claims for rehabilitation and other forms of remedy;

    (g) To the extent possible, any relevant supporting documentation, including names and addresses of witnesses.

2. At commencement of the trial and subject to any protective measures, the Court shall ask the Registrar to provide notification of the request to the person or persons named in the request or identified in the charges and, to the extent possible, to any interested persons or any interested States. Those notified shall file with the Registry any representation made under article 75, paragraph 3.

Rule 95 Procedure on the motion of the Court

1. In cases where the Court intends to proceed on its own motion pursuant to article 75, paragraph 1, it shall ask the Registrar to provide notification of its intention to the person or persons against whom the Court is considering making a determination, and, to the extent possible, to victims, interested persons and interested States. Those notified shall file with the Registry any representation made under article 75, paragraph 3.

2. If, as a result of notification under sub-rule 1:

    (a) A victim makes a request for reparations, that request will be determined as if it had been brought under rule 94;

    (b) A victim requests that the Court does not make an order for reparations, the Court shall not proceed to make an individual order in respect of that victim.

Rule 96 Publication of reparation proceedings

1. Without prejudice to any other Rules on notification of proceedings, the Registrar shall, insofar as practicable, notify the victims or their legal representatives and the person or persons

concerned. The Registrar shall also, having regard to any information provided by the Prosecutor, take all the necessary measures to give adequate publicity of the reparation proceedings before the Court, to the extent possible, to other victims, interested persons and interested States.

2. In taking the measures described in sub-rule 1, the Court may seek, in accordance with Part 9, the cooperation of relevant States Parties, and seek the assistance of intergovernmental organizations in order to give publicity, as widely as possible and by all possible means, to the reparation proceedings before the Court.

Rule 97 Assessment of reparations

1. Taking into account the scope and extent of any damage, loss or injury, the Court may award reparations on an individualized basis or, where it deems it appropriate, on a collective basis or both.

2. At the request of victims or their legal representatives, or at the request of the convicted person, or on its own motion, the Court may appoint appropriate experts to assist it in determining the scope, extent of any damage, loss and injury to, or in respect of victims and to suggest various options concerning the appropriate types and modalities of reparations. The Court shall invite, as appropriate, victims or their legal representatives, the convicted person as well as interested persons and interested States to make observations on the reports of the experts.

3. In all cases, the Court shall respect the rights of victims and the convicted person.

Rule 98 Trust Fund

1. Individual awards for reparations shall be made directly against a convicted person.

2. The Court may order that an award for reparations against a convicted person be deposited with the Trust Fund where at the time of making the order it is impossible or impracticable to make individual awards directly to each victim. The award for reparations thus deposited in the Trust Fund shall be separated from other resources of the Trust Fund and shall be forwarded to each victim as soon as possible.

3. The Court may order that an award for reparations against a convicted person be made through the Trust Fund where the number of the victims and the scope, forms and modalities of reparations makes a collective award more appropriate.

4. Following consultations with interested States and the Trust Fund, the Court may order that an award for reparations be made through the Trust Fund to an intergovernmental, international or national organization approved by the Trust Fund.

5. Other resources of the Trust Fund may be used for the benefit of victims subject to the provisions of article 79.

Rule 99 Cooperation and protective measures for the purpose of forfeiture under articles 57, paragraph 3 (e), and 75, paragraph 4

1. The Pre-Trial Chamber, pursuant to article 57, paragraph 3 (e), or the Trial Chamber, pursuant to article 75, paragraph 4, may, on its own motion or on the application of the Prosecutor or at the request of the victims or their legal representatives who have made a request for reparations or who have given a written undertaking to do so, determine whether measures should be requested.

2. Notice is not required unless the Court determines, in the particular circumstances of the case, that notification could not jeopardize the effectiveness of the measures requested. In the latter case, the Registrar shall provide notification of the proceedings to the person against whom a request is made and so far as is possible to any interested persons or interested States.

3. If an order is made without prior notification, the relevant Chamber shall request the Registrar, as soon as is consistent with the effectiveness of the measures requested, to notify those against

whom a request is made and, to the extent possible, to any interested persons or any interested States and invite them to make observations as to whether the order should be revoked or otherwise modified.

4.　The Court may make orders as to the timing and conduct of any proceedings necessary to determine these issues.

Section IV Miscellaneous provisions

Rule 100 Place of the proceedings

1.　In a particular case, where the Court considers that it would be in the interests of justice, it may decide to sit in a State other than the host State.

2.　An application or recommendation changing the place where the Court sits may be filed at any time after the initiation of an investigation, either by the Prosecutor, the defence or by a majority of the judges of the Court. Such an application or recommendation shall be addressed to the Presidency. It shall be made in writing and specify in which State the Court would sit. The Presidency shall satisfy itself of the views of the relevant Chamber.

3.　The Presidency shall consult the State where the Court intends to sit. If that State agrees that the Court can sit in that State, then the decision to sit in a State other than the host State shall be taken by the judges, in plenary session, by a two-thirds majority.

Rule 101 Time limits

1.　In making any order setting time limits regarding the conduct of any proceedings, the Court shall have regard to the need to facilitate fair and expeditious proceedings, bearing in mind in particular the rights of the defence and the victims.

2.　Taking into account the rights of the accused, in particular under article 67, paragraph (1)(c), all those participating in the proceedings to whom any order is directed shall endeavour to act as expeditiously as possible, within the time limit ordered by the Court.

Rule 102 Communications other than in writing

Where a person is unable, due to a disability or illiteracy, to make a written request, application, observation or other communication to the Court, the person may make such request, application, observation or communication in audio, video or other electronic form.

Rule 103 Amicus curiae and other forms of submission

1.　At any stage of the proceedings, a Chamber may, if it considers it desirable for the proper determination of the case, invite or grant leave to a State, organization or person to submit, in writing or orally, any observation on any issue that the Chamber deems appropriate.

2.　The Prosecutor and the defence shall have the opportunity to respond to the observations submitted under sub-rule 1.

3.　A written observation submitted under sub-rule 1 shall be filed with the Registrar, who shall provide copies to the Prosecutor and the defence. The Chamber shall determine what time limits shall apply to the filing of such observations.

Chapter 5 Investigation and prosecution
Section I Decision of the Prosecutor regarding the initiation
of an investigation under article 53, paragraphs 1 and 2

Rule 104 Evaluation of information by the Prosecutor

1.　In acting pursuant to article 53, paragraph 1, the Prosecutor shall, in evaluating the information made available to him or her, analyse the seriousness of the information received.

2. For the purposes of sub-rule 1, the Prosecutor may seek additional information from States, organs of the United Nations, intergovernmental and non-governmental organizations, or other reliable sources that he or she deems appropriate, and may receive written or oral testimony at the seat of the Court. The procedure set out in rule 47 shall apply to the receiving of such testimony.

Rule 105 Notification of a decision by the Prosecutor not to initiate an investigation

1. When the Prosecutor decides not to initiate an investigation under article 53, paragraph 1, he or she shall promptly inform in writing the State or States that referred a situation under article 14, or the Security Council in respect of a situation covered by article 13, paragraph (b).

2. When the Prosecutor decides not to submit to the Pre-Trial Chamber a request for authorization of an investigation, rule 49 shall apply.

3. The notification referred to in sub-rule 1 shall contain the conclusion of the Prosecutor and, having regard to article 68, paragraph 1, the reasons for the conclusion.

4. In case the Prosecutor decides not to investigate solely on the basis of article 53, paragraph 1 (c), he or she shall inform in writing the Pre-Trial Chamber promptly after making that decision.

5. The notification shall contain the conclusion of the Prosecutor and the reasons for the conclusion.

Rule 106 Notification of a decision by the Prosecutor not to prosecute

1. When the Prosecutor decides that there is not a sufficient basis for prosecution under article 53, paragraph 2, he or she shall promptly inform in writing the Pre-Trial Chamber, together with the State or States that referred a situation under article 14, or the Security Council in respect of a situation covered by article 13, paragraph (b).

2. The notifications referred to in sub-rule 1 shall contain the conclusion of the Prosecutor and, having regard to article 68, paragraph 1, the reasons for the conclusion.

Section II Procedure under article 53, paragraph 3

Rule 107 Request for review under article 53, paragraph 3(a)

1. A request under article 53, paragraph 3, for a review of a decision by the Prosecutor not to initiate an investigation or not to prosecute shall be made in writing, and be supported with reasons, within 90 days following the notification given under rule 105 or 106.

2. The Pre-Trial Chamber may request the Prosecutor to transmit the information or documents in his or her possession, or summaries thereof, that the Chamber considers necessary for the conduct of the review.

3. The Pre-Trial Chamber shall take such measures as are necessary under articles 54, 72 and 93 to protect the information and documents referred to in sub-rule 2 and, under article 68, paragraph 5, to protect the safety of witnesses and victims and members of their families.

4. When a State or the Security Council makes a request referred to in sub-rule 1, the Pre-Trial Chamber may seek further observations from them.

5. Where an issue of jurisdiction or admissibility of the case is raised, rule 59 shall apply.

Rule 108 Decision of the Pre-Trial Chamber under article 53, paragraph 3(a)

1. A decision of the Pre-Trial Chamber under article 53, paragraph 3(a), must be concurred in by a majority of its judges and shall contain reasons. It shall be communicated to all those who participated in the review.

2. Where the Pre-Trial Chamber requests the Prosecutor to review, in whole or in part, his or her decision not to initiate an investigation or not to prosecute, the Prosecutor shall reconsider that decision as soon as possible.

3. Once the Prosecutor has taken a final decision, he or she shall notify the Pre-Trial Chamber in writing. This notification shall contain the conclusion of the Prosecutor and the reasons for the conclusion. It shall be communicated to all those who participated in the review.

Rule 109 Review by the Pre-Trial Chamber under article 53, paragraph 3(b)

1. Within 180 days following a notification given under Rule 105 or 106, the Pre-Trial Chamber may on its own initiative decide to review a decision of the Prosecutor taken solely under article 53, paragraph 1(c) or 2(c). The Pre-Trial Chamber shall inform the Prosecutor of its intention to review his or her decision and shall establish a time limit within which the Prosecutor may submit observations and other material.

2. In cases where a request has been submitted to the Pre-Trial Chamber by a State or by the Security Council, they shall also be informed and may submit observations in accordance with Rule 107.

Rule 110 Decision by the Pre-Trial Chamber under article 53, paragraph 3(b)

1. A decision by the Pre-Trial Chamber to confirm or not to confirm a decision taken by the Prosecutor solely under article 53, paragraph 1(c) or 2(c), must be concurred in by a majority of its judges and shall contain reasons. It shall be communicated to all those who participated in the review.

2. When the Pre-Trial Chamber does not confirm the decision by the Prosecutor referred to in sub-rule 1, he or she shall proceed with the investigation or prosecution.

Section III Collection of evidence

Rule 111 Record of questioning in general

1. A record shall be made of formal statements made by any person who is questioned in connection with an investigation or with proceedings. The record shall be signed by the person who records and conducts the questioning and by the person who is questioned and his or her counsel, if present, and, where applicable, the Prosecutor or the judge who is present. The record shall note the date, time and place of, and all persons present during the questioning. It shall also be noted when someone has not signed the record as well as the reasons therefor.

2. When the Prosecutor or national authorities question a person, due regard shall be given to article 55. When a person is informed of his or her rights under article 55, paragraph 2, the fact that this information has been provided shall be noted in the record.

Rule 112 Recording of questioning in particular cases

1. Whenever the Prosecutor questions a person to whom article 55, paragraph 2, applies, or for whom a warrant of arrest or a summons to appear has been issued under article 58, paragraph 7, the questioning shall be audio-or video-recorded, in accordance with the following procedure:

    (a) The person questioned shall be informed, in a language he or she fully understands and speaks, that the questioning is to be audio-or video-recorded, and that the person concerned may object if he or she so wishes. The fact that this information has been provided and the response given by the person concerned shall be noted in the record. The person may, before replying, speak in private with his or her counsel, if present. If the person questioned refuses to be audio-or video-recorded, the procedure in rule 111 shall be followed;

    (b) A waiver of the right to be questioned in the presence of counsel shall be recorded in writing and, if possible, be audio-or video-recorded;

(c) In the event of an interruption in the course of questioning, the fact and the time of the interruption shall be recorded before the audio-or video-recording ends as well as the time of resumption of the questioning;

(d) At the conclusion of the questioning, the person questioned shall be offered the opportunity to clarify anything he or she has said and to add anything he or she may wish. The time of conclusion of the questioning shall be noted;

(e) The tape shall be transcribed as soon as practicable after the conclusion of the questioning and a copy of the transcript supplied to the person questioned together with a copy of the recorded tape or, if multiple recording apparatus was used, one of the original recorded tapes;

(f) The original tape or one of the original tapes shall be sealed in the presence of the person questioned and his or her counsel, if present, under the signature of the Prosecutor and the person questioned and the counsel, if present.

2. The Prosecutor shall make every reasonable effort to record the questioning in accordance with sub-rule 1. As an exception, a person may be questioned without the questioning being audio-or video-recorded where the circumstances prevent such recording taking place. In this case, the reasons for not recording the questioning shall be stated in writing and the procedure in rule 111 shall be followed.

3. When, pursuant to sub-rule 1(a) or 2, the questioning is not audio-or video-recorded, the person questioned shall be provided with a copy of his or her statement.

4. The Prosecutor may choose to follow the procedure in this rule when questioning other persons than those mentioned in sub-rule 1, in particular where the use of such procedures could assist in reducing any subsequent traumatization of a victim of sexual or gender violence, a child or a person with disabilities in providing their evidence. The Prosecutor may make an application to the relevant Chamber.

5. The Pre-Trial Chamber may, in pursuance of article 56, paragraph 2, order that the procedure in this rule be applied to the questioning of any person.

Rule 113 Collection of information regarding the state of health of the person concerned

1. The Pre-Trial Chamber may, on its own initiative or at the request of the Prosecutor, the person concerned or his or her counsel, order that a person having the rights in article 55, paragraph 2, be given a medical, psychological or psychiatric examination. In making its determination, the Pre-Trial Chamber shall consider the nature and purpose of the examination and whether the person consents to the examination.

2. The Pre-Trial Chamber shall appoint one or more experts from the list of experts approved by the Registrar, or an expert approved by the Pre-Trial Chamber at the request of a party.

Rule 114 Unique investigative opportunity under article 56

1. Upon being advised by the Prosecutor in accordance with article 56, paragraph 1(a), the Pre-Trial Chamber shall hold consultations without delay with the Prosecutor and, subject to the provisions of article 56, paragraph 1(c), with the person who has been arrested or who has appeared before the Court pursuant to summons and his or her counsel, in order to determine the measures to be taken and the modalities of their implementation, which may include measures to ensure that the right to communicate under article 67, paragraph 1(b), is protected.

2. A decision of the Pre-Trial Chamber to take measures pursuant to article 56, paragraph 3, must be concurred in by a majority of its judges after consultations with the Prosecutor. During the consultations, the Prosecutor may advise the Pre-Trial Chamber that intended measures could jeopardize the proper conduct of the investigation.

Rule 115 Collection of evidence in the territory of a State Party under article 57, paragraph 3(d)

1. Where the Prosecutor considers that article 57, paragraph 3(d), applies, the Prosecutor may submit a written request to the Pre-Trial Chamber for authorization to take certain measures in the territory of the State Party in question. After a submission of such a request, the Pre-Trial Chamber shall, whenever possible, inform and invite views from the State Party concerned.

2. In arriving at its determination as to whether the request is well founded, the Pre-Trial Chamber shall take into account any views expressed by the State Party concerned. The Pre-Trial Chamber may, on its own initiative or at the request of the Prosecutor or the State Party concerned, decide to hold a hearing.

3. An authorization under article 57, paragraph 3(d), shall be issued in the form of an order and shall state the reasons, based on the criteria set forth in that paragraph. The order may specify procedures to be followed in carrying out such collection of evidence.

Rule 116 Collection of evidence at the request of the defence under article 57, paragraph 3(b)

1. The Pre-Trial Chamber shall issue an order or seek cooperation under article 57, paragraph 3(b), where it is satisfied:

   (a) That such an order would facilitate the collection of evidence that may be material to the proper determination of the issues being adjudicated, or to the proper preparation of the person's defence; and

   (b) In a case of cooperation under Part 9, that sufficient information to comply with article 96, paragraph 2, has been provided.

2. Before taking a decision whether to issue an order or seek cooperation under article 57, paragraph 3(b), the Pre-Trial Chamber may seek the views of the Prosecutor.

Section IV Procedures in respect of restriction and deprivation of liberty

Rule 117 Detention in the custodial State

1. The Court shall take measures to ensure that it is informed of the arrest of a person in response to a request made by the Court under article 89 or 92. Once so informed, the Court shall ensure that the person receives a copy of the arrest warrant issued by the Pre-Trial Chamber under article 58 and any relevant provisions of the Statute. The documents shall be made available in a language that the person fully understands and speaks.

2. At any time after arrest, the person may make a request to the Pre-Trial Chamber for the appointment of counsel to assist with proceedings before the Court and the Pre-Trial Chamber shall take a decision on such request.

3. A challenge as to whether the warrant of arrest was properly issued in accordance with article 58, paragraph 1(a) and (b), shall be made in writing to the Pre-Trial Chamber. The application shall set out the basis for the challenge. After having obtained the views of the Prosecutor, the Pre-Trial Chamber shall decide on the application without delay.

4. When the competent authority of the custodial State notifies the Pre-Trial Chamber that a request for release has been made by the person arrested, in accordance with article 59, paragraph 5, the Pre-Trial Chamber shall provide its recommendations within any time limit set by the custodial State.

5. When the Pre-Trial Chamber is informed that the person has been granted interim release by the competent authority of the custodial State, the Pre-Trial Chamber shall inform the custodial State how and when it would like to receive periodic reports on the status of the interim release.

Rule 118 Pre-trial detention at the seat of the Court

1. If the person surrendered to the Court makes an initial request for interim release pending trial, either upon first appearance in accordance with rule 121 or subsequently, the Pre-Trial Chamber shall decide upon the request without delay, after seeking the views of the Prosecutor.

2. The Pre-Trial Chamber shall review its ruling on the release or detention of a person in accordance with article 60, paragraph 3, at least every 120 days and may do so at any time on the request of the person or the Prosecutor.

3. After the first appearance, a request for interim release must be made in writing. The Prosecutor shall be given notice of such a request. The Pre-Trial Chamber shall decide after having received observations in writing of the Prosecutor and the detained person. The Pre-Trial Chamber may decide to hold a hearing, at the request of the Prosecutor or the detained person or on its own initiative. A hearing must be held at least once every year.

Rule 119 Conditional release

1. The Pre-Trial Chamber may set one or more conditions restricting liberty, including the following:

    (a) The person must not travel beyond territorial limits set by the Pre-Trial Chamber without the explicit agreement of the Chamber;

    (b) The person must not go to certain places or associate with certain persons as specified by the Pre-Trial Chamber;

    (c) The person must not contact directly or indirectly victims or witnesses;

    (d) The person must not engage in certain professional activities;

    (e) The person must reside at a particular address as specified by the Pre-Trial Chamber;

    (f) The person must respond when summoned by an authority or qualified person designated by the Pre-Trial Chamber;

    (g) The person must post bond or provide real or personal security or surety, for which the amount and the schedule and mode of payment shall be determined by the Pre-Trial Chamber;

    (h) The person must supply the Registrar with all identity documents, particularly his or her passport.

2. At the request of the person concerned or the Prosecutor or on its own initiative, the Pre-Trial Chamber may at any time decide to amend the conditions set pursuant to sub-rule 1.

3. Before imposing or amending any conditions restricting liberty, the Pre-Trial Chamber shall seek the views of the Prosecutor, the person concerned, any relevant State and victims that have communicated with the Court in that case and whom the Chamber considers could be at risk as a result of a release or conditions imposed.

4. If the Pre-Trial Chamber is convinced that the person concerned has failed to comply with one or more of the obligations imposed, it may, on such basis, at the request of the Prosecutor or on its own initiative, issue a warrant of arrest in respect of the person.

5. When the Pre-Trial Chamber issues a summons to appear pursuant to article 58, paragraph 7, and intends to set conditions restricting liberty, it shall ascertain the relevant provisions of the national law of the State receiving the summons. In a manner that is in keeping with the national law of the State receiving the summons, the Pre-Trial Chamber shall proceed in accordance with sub-rules 1, 2 and 3. If the Pre-Trial Chamber receives information that the person concerned has failed to comply with conditions imposed, it shall proceed in accordance with sub-rule 4.

Rule 120 Instruments of restraint

Personal instruments of restraint shall not be used except as a precaution against escape, for the protection of the person in the custody of the Court and others or for other security reasons, and shall be removed when the person appears before a Chamber.

Section V Proceedings with regard to the confirmation of charges under article 61

Rule 121 Proceedings before the confirmation hearing

1. A person subject to a warrant of arrest or a summons to appear under article 58 shall appear before the Pre-Trial Chamber, in the presence of the Prosecutor, promptly upon arriving at the Court. Subject to the provisions of articles 60 and 61, the person shall enjoy the rights set forth in article 67. At this first appearance, the Pre-Trial Chamber shall set the date on which it intends to hold a hearing to confirm the charges. It shall ensure that this date, and any postponements under sub-rule 7, are made public.

2. In accordance with article 61, paragraph 3, the Pre-Trial Chamber shall take the necessary decisions regarding disclosure between the Prosecutor and the person in respect of whom a warrant of arrest or a summons to appear has been issued. During disclosure:

    (a) The person concerned may be assisted or represented by the counsel of his or her choice or by a counsel assigned to him or her;

    (b) The Pre-Trial Chamber shall hold status conferences to ensure that disclosure takes place under satisfactory conditions. For each case, a judge of the Pre-Trial Chamber shall be appointed to organize such status conferences, on his or her own motion, or at the request of the Prosecutor or the person;

    (c) All evidence disclosed between the Prosecutor and the person for the purposes of the confirmation hearing shall be communicated to the Pre-Trial Chamber.

3. The Prosecutor shall provide to the Pre-Trial Chamber and the person, no later than 30 days before the date of the confirmation hearing, a detailed description of the charges together with a list of the evidence which he or she intends to present at the hearing.

4. Where the Prosecutor intends to amend the charges pursuant to article 61, paragraph 4, he or she shall notify the Pre-Trial Chamber and the person no later than 15 days before the date of the hearing of the amended charges together with a list of evidence that the Prosecutor intends to bring in support of those charges at the hearing.

5. Where the Prosecutor intends to present new evidence at the hearing, he or she shall provide the Pre-Trial Chamber and the person with a list of that evidence no later than 15 days before the date of the hearing.

6. If the person intends to present evidence under article 61, paragraph 6, he or she shall provide a list of that evidence to the Pre-Trial Chamber no later than 15 days before the date of the hearing. The Pre-Trial Chamber shall transmit the list to the Prosecutor without delay. The person shall provide a list of evidence that he or she intends to present in response to any amended charges or a new list of evidence provided by the Prosecutor.

7. The Prosecutor or the person may ask the Pre-Trial Chamber to postpone the date of the confirmation hearing. The Pre-Trial Chamber may also, on its own motion, decide to postpone the hearing.

8. The Pre-Trial Chamber shall not take into consideration charges and evidence presented after the time limit, or any extension thereof, has expired.

9. The Prosecutor and the person may lodge written submissions with the Pre-Trial Chamber, on points of fact and on law, including grounds for excluding criminal responsibility set forth in article 31, paragraph 1, no later than three days before the date of the hearing. A copy of these submissions shall be transmitted immediately to the Prosecutor or the person, as the case may be.

10. The Registry shall create and maintain a full and accurate record of all proceedings before the Pre-Trial Chamber, including all documents transmitted to the Chamber pursuant to this rule. Subject to any restrictions concerning confidentiality and the protection of national security information, the record may be consulted by the Prosecutor, the person and victims or their legal representatives participating in the proceedings pursuant to rules 89 to 91.

Rule 122 Proceedings at the confirmation hearing in the presence of the person charged

1. The Presiding Judge of the Pre-Trial Chamber shall ask the officer of the Registry assisting the Chamber to read out the charges as presented by the Prosecutor. The Presiding Judge shall determine how the hearing is to be conducted and, in particular, may establish the order and the conditions under which he or she intends the evidence contained in the record of the proceedings to be presented.

2. If a question or challenge concerning jurisdiction or admissibility arises, rule 58 applies.

3. Before hearing the matter on the merits, the Presiding Judge of the Pre-Trial Chamber shall ask the Prosecutor and the person whether they intend to raise objections or make observations concerning an issue related to the proper conduct of the proceedings prior to the confirmation hearing.

4. At no subsequent point may the objections and observations made under sub-rule 3 be raised or made again in the confirmation or trial proceedings.

5. If objections or observations referred to in sub-rule 3 are presented, the Presiding Judge of the Pre-Trial Chamber shall invite those referred to in sub-rule 3 to present their arguments, in the order which he or she shall establish. The person shall have the right to reply.

6. If the objections raised or observations made are those referred to in sub-rule 3, the Pre-Trial Chamber shall decide whether to join the issue raised with the examination of the charges and the evidence, or to separate them, in which case it shall adjourn the confirmation hearing and render a decision on the issues raised.

7. During the hearing on the merits, the Prosecutor and the person shall present their arguments in accordance with article 61, paragraphs 5 and 6.

8. The Pre-Trial Chamber shall permit the Prosecutor and the person, in that order, to make final observations.

9. Subject to the provisions of article 61, article 69 shall apply *mutatis mutandis* at the confirmation hearing.

Rule 123 Measures to ensure the presence of the person concerned at the confirmation hearing

1. When a warrant of arrest or summons to appear in accordance with article 58, paragraph 7, has been issued for a person by the Pre-Trial Chamber and the person is arrested or served with the summons, the Pre-Trial Chamber shall ensure that the person is notified of the provisions of article 61, paragraph 2.

2. The Pre-Trial Chamber may hold consultations with the Prosecutor, at the request of the latter or on its own initiative, in order to determine whether there is cause to hold a hearing on confirmation of charges under the conditions set forth in article 61, paragraph 2 (b). When the person concerned has a counsel known to the Court, the consultations shall be held in the presence of the counsel unless the Pre-Trial Chamber decides otherwise.

3. The Pre-Trial Chamber shall ensure that a warrant of arrest for the person concerned has been issued and, if the warrant of arrest has not been executed within a reasonable period of time after the issuance of the warrant, that all reasonable measures have been taken to locate and arrest the person.

Rule 124 Waiver of the right to be present at the confirmation hearing

1. If the person concerned is available to the Court but wishes to waive the right to be present at the hearing on confirmation of charges, he or she shall submit a written request to the Pre-Trial Chamber, which may then hold consultations with the Prosecutor and the person concerned, assisted or represented by his or her counsel.

2. A confirmation hearing pursuant to article 61, paragraph 2(a), shall only be held when the Pre-Trial Chamber is satisfied that the person concerned understands the right to be present at the hearing and the consequences of waiving this right.

3. The Pre-Trial Chamber may authorize and make provision for the person to observe the hearing from outside the courtroom through the use of communications technology, if required.

4. The waiving of the right to be present at the hearing does not prevent the Pre-Trial Chamber from receiving written observations on issues before the Chamber from the person concerned.

Rule 125 Decision to hold the confirmation hearing in the absence of the person concerned

1. After holding consultations under rules 123 and 124, the Pre-Trial Chamber shall decide whether there is cause to hold a hearing on confirmation of charges in the absence of the person concerned, and in that case, whether the person may be represented by counsel. The Pre-Trial Chamber shall, when appropriate, set a date for the hearing and make the date public.

2. The decision of the Pre-Trial Chamber shall be notified to the Prosecutor and, if possible, to the person concerned or his or her counsel.

3. If the Pre-Trial Chamber decides not to hold a hearing on confirmation of charges in the absence of the person concerned, and the person is not available to the Court, the confirmation of charges may not take place until the person is available to the Court. The Pre-Trial Chamber may review its decision at any time, at the request of the Prosecutor or on its own initiative.

4. If the Pre-Trial Chamber decides not to hold a hearing on confirmation of charges in the absence of the person concerned, and the person is available to the Court, it shall order the person to appear.

Rule 126 Confirmation hearing in the absence of the person concerned

1. The provisions of rules 121 and 122 shall apply *mutatis mutandis* to the preparation for and holding of a hearing on confirmation of charges in the absence of the person concerned.

2. If the Pre-Trial Chamber has determined that the person concerned shall be represented by counsel, the counsel shall have the opportunity to exercise the rights of that person.

3. When the person who has fled is subsequently arrested and the Court has confirmed the charges upon which the Prosecutor intends to pursue the trial, the person charged shall be committed to the Trial Chamber established under article 61, paragraph 11. The person charged may request in writing that the Trial Chamber refer issues to the Pre-Trial Chamber that are necessary for the Chamber's effective and fair functioning in accordance with article 64, paragraph 4.

Section VI Closure of the pre-trial phase

Rule 127 Procedure in the event of different decisions on multiple charges

If the Pre-Trial Chamber is ready to confirm some of the charges but adjourns the hearing on other charges under article 61, paragraph 7(c), it may decide that the committal of the person concerned to the Trial Chamber on the charges that it is ready to confirm shall be deferred pending the continuation of the hearing. The Pre-Trial Chamber may then establish a time limit within which the Prosecutor may proceed in accordance with article 61, paragraph 7(c)(i) or (ii).

Rule 128 Amendment of the charges

1. If the Prosecutor seeks to amend charges already confirmed before the trial has begun, in accordance with article 61, the Prosecutor shall make a written request to the Pre-Trial Chamber, and that Chamber shall so notify the accused.

2. Before deciding whether to authorize the amendment, the Pre-Trial Chamber may request the accused and the Prosecutor to submit written observations on certain issues of fact or law.

3. If the Pre-Trial Chamber determines that the amendments proposed by the Prosecutor constitute additional or more serious charges, it shall proceed, as appropriate, in accordance with rules 121 and 122 or rules 123 to 126.

Rule 129 Notification of the decision on the confirmation of charges

The decision of the Pre-Trial Chamber on the confirmation of charges and the committal of the accused to the Trial Chamber shall be notified, if possible, to the Prosecutor, the person concerned and his or her counsel. Such decision and the record of the proceedings of the Pre-Trial Chamber shall be transmitted to the Presidency.

Rule 130 Constitution of the Trial Chamber

When the Presidency constitutes a Trial Chamber and refers the case to it, the Presidency shall transmit the decision of the Pre-Trial Chamber and the record of the proceedings to the Trial Chamber. The Presidency may also refer the case to a previously constituted Trial Chamber.

Chapter 6 Trial procedure

Rule 131 Record of the proceedings transmitted by the Pre-Trial Chamber

1. The Registrar shall maintain the record of the proceedings transmitted by the Pre-Trial Chamber, pursuant to rule 121, sub-rule 10.

2. Subject to any restrictions concerning confidentiality and the protection of national security information, the record may be consulted by the Prosecutor, the defence, the representatives of States when they participate in the proceedings, and the victims or their legal representatives participating in the proceedings pursuant to rules 89 to 91.

Rule 132 Status conferences

1. Promptly after it is constituted, the Trial Chamber shall hold a status conference in order to set the date of the trial. The Trial Chamber, on its own motion, or at the request of the Prosecutor or the defence, may postpone the date of the trial. The Trial Chamber shall notify the trial date to all those participating in the proceedings. The Trial Chamber shall ensure that this date and any postponements are made public.

2. In order to facilitate the fair and expeditious conduct of the proceedings, the Trial Chamber may confer with the parties by holding status conferences as necessary.

Rule 133 Motions challenging admissibility or jurisdiction

Challenges to the jurisdiction of the Court or the admissibility of the case at the commencement of the trial, or subsequently with the leave of the Court, shall be dealt with by the Presiding Judge and the Trial Chamber in accordance with rule 58.

Rule 134 Motions relating to the trial proceedings

1. Prior to the commencement of the trial, the Trial Chamber on its own motion, or at the request of the Prosecutor or the defence, may rule on any issue concerning the conduct of the proceedings. Any request from the Prosecutor or the defence shall be in writing and, unless the request is for an *ex parte* procedure, served on the other party. For all requests other than those submitted for an *ex parte* procedure, the other party shall have the opportunity to file a response.

2. At the commencement of the trial, the Trial Chamber shall ask the Prosecutor and the defence whether they have any objections or observations concerning the conduct of the proceedings which have arisen since the confirmation hearings. Such objections or observations may not be raised or made again on a subsequent occasion in the trial proceedings, without leave of the Trial Chamber in this proceeding.

3. After the commencement of the trial, the Trial Chamber, on its own motion, or at the request of the Prosecutor or the defence, may rule on issues that arise during the course of the trial.

Rule 135 Medical examination of the accused

1. The Trial Chamber may, for the purpose of discharging its obligations under article 64, paragraph 8 (a), or for any other reasons, or at the request of a party, order a medical, psychiatric or psychological examination of the accused, under the conditions set forth in rule 113.

2. The Trial Chamber shall place its reasons for any such order on the record.

3. The Trial Chamber shall appoint one or more experts from the list of experts approved by the Registrar, or an expert approved by the Trial Chamber at the request of a party.

4. Where the Trial Chamber is satisfied that the accused is unfit to stand trial, it shall order that the trial be adjourned. The Trial Chamber may, on its own motion or at the request of the prosecution or the defence, review the case of the accused. In any event, the case shall be reviewed every 120 days unless there are reasons to do otherwise. If necessary, the Trial Chamber may order further examinations of the accused. When the Trial Chamber is satisfied that the accused has become fit to stand trial, it shall proceed in accordance with rule 132.

Rule 136 Joint and separate trials

1. Persons accused jointly shall be tried together unless the Trial Chamber, on its own motion or at the request of the Prosecutor or the defence, orders that separate trials are necessary, in order to avoid serious prejudice to the accused, to protect the interests of justice or because a person jointly accused has made an admission of guilt and can be proceeded against in accordance with article 65, paragraph 2.

2. In joint trials, each accused shall be accorded the same rights as if such accused were being tried separately.

Rule 137 Record of the trial proceedings

1. In accordance with article 64, paragraph 10, the Registrar shall take measures to make, and preserve, a full and accurate record of all proceedings, including transcripts, audio-and video-recordings and other means of capturing sound or image.

2. A Trial Chamber may order the disclosure of all or part of the record of closed proceedings when the reasons for ordering its non-disclosure no longer exist.

3. The Trial Chamber may authorize persons other than the Registrar to take photographs, audio- and video-recordings and other means of capturing the sound or image of the trial.

Rule 138 Custody of evidence

The Registrar shall retain and preserve, as necessary, all the evidence and other materials offered during the hearing, subject to any order of the Trial Chamber.

Rule 139 Decision on admission of guilt

1. After having proceeded in accordance with article 65, paragraph 1, the Trial Chamber, in order to decide whether to proceed in accordance with article 65, paragraph 4, may invite the views of the Prosecutor and the defence.

2. The Trial Chamber shall then make its decision on the admission of guilt and shall give reasons for this decision, which shall be placed on the record.

Rule 140 Directions for the conduct of the proceedings and testimony

1. If the Presiding Judge does not give directions under article 64, paragraph 8, the Prosecutor and the defence shall agree on the order and manner in which the evidence shall be submitted to the Trial Chamber. If no agreement can be reached, the Presiding Judge shall issue directions.

2. In all cases, subject to article 64, paragraphs 8 (b) and 9, article 69, paragraph 4, and rule 88, sub-rule 5, a witness may be questioned as follows:

   (a) A party that submits evidence in accordance with article 69, paragraph 3, by way of a witness, has the right to question that witness;

   (b) The prosecution and the defence have the right to question that witness about relevant matters related to the witness's testimony and its reliability, the credibility of the witness and other relevant matters;

   (c) The Trial Chamber has the right to question a witness before or after a witness is questioned by a participant referred to in sub-rules 2(a) or (b);

   (d) The defence shall have the right to be the last to examine a witness.

3. Unless otherwise ordered by the Trial Chamber, a witness other than an expert, or an investigator if he or she has not yet testified, shall not be present when the testimony of another witness is given. However, a witness who has heard the testimony of another witness shall not for that reason alone be disqualified from testifying. When a witness testifies after hearing the testimony of others, this fact shall be noted in the record and considered by the Trial Chamber when evaluating the evidence.

Rule 141 Closure of evidence and closing statements

1. The Presiding Judge shall declare when the submission of evidence is closed.

2. The Presiding Judge shall invite the Prosecutor and the defence to make their closing statements. The defence shall always have the opportunity to speak last.

Rule 142 Deliberations

1. After the closing statements, the Trial Chamber shall retire to deliberate, in camera. The Trial Chamber shall inform all those who participated in the proceedings of the date on which the Trial Chamber will pronounce its decision. The pronouncement shall be made within a reasonable period of time after the Trial Chamber has retired to deliberate.

2. When there is more than one charge, the Trial Chamber shall decide separately on each charge. When there is more than one accused, the Trial Chamber shall decide separately on the charges against each accused.

Rule 143 Additional hearings on matters related to sentence or reparations

Pursuant to article 76, paragraphs 2 and 3, for the purpose of holding a further hearing on matters related to sentence and, if applicable, reparations, the Presiding Judge shall set the date of the further hearing. This hearing can be postponed, in exceptional circumstances, by the Trial Chamber, on its own motion or at the request of the Prosecutor, the defence or the legal representatives of the victims participating in the proceedings pursuant to rules 89 to 91 and, in respect of reparations hearings, those victims who have made a request under rule 94.

Rule 144 Delivery of the decisions of the Trial Chamber

1. Decisions of the Trial Chamber concerning admissibility of a case, the jurisdiction of the Court, criminal responsibility of the accused, sentence and reparations shall be pronounced in public and, wherever possible, in the presence of the accused, the Prosecutor, the victims or the legal representatives of the victims participating in the proceedings pursuant to rules 89 to 91, and the representatives of the States which have participated in the proceedings.

2. Copies of all the above-mentioned decisions shall be provided as soon as possible to:

   (a) All those who participated in the proceedings, in a working language of the Court;

   (b) The accused, in a language he or she fully understands or speaks, if necessary to meet the requirements of fairness under article 67, paragraph 1 (f).

Chapter 7 Penalties

Rule 145 Determination of sentence

1. In its determination of the sentence pursuant to article 78, paragraph 1, the Court shall:

    (a) Bear in mind that the totality of any sentence of imprisonment and fine, as the case may be, imposed under article 77 must reflect the culpability of the convicted person;

    (b) Balance all the relevant factors, including any mitigating and aggravating factors and consider the circumstances both of the convicted person and of the crime;

    (c) In addition to the factors mentioned in article 78, paragraph 1, give consideration, *inter alia*, to the extent of the damage caused, in particular the harm caused to the victims and their families, the nature of the unlawful behaviour and the means employed to execute the crime; the degree of participation of the convicted person; the degree of intent; the circumstances of manner, time and location; and the age, education, social and economic condition of the convicted person.

2. In addition to the factors mentioned above, the Court shall take into account, as appropriate:

    (a) Mitigating circumstances such as:

        (i) The circumstances falling short of constituting grounds for exclusion of criminal responsibility, such as substantially diminished mental capacity or duress;

        (ii) The convicted person's conduct after the act, including any efforts by the person to compensate the victims and any cooperation with the Court;

    (b) As aggravating circumstances:

        (i)   Any relevant prior criminal convictions for crimes under the jurisdiction of the Court or of a similar nature;

        (ii) Abuse of power or official capacity;

        (iii) Commission of the crime where the victim is particularly defenceless;

        (iv) Commission of the crime with particular cruelty or where there were multiple victims;

        (v)   Commission of the crime for any motive involving discrimination on any of the grounds referred to in article 21, paragraph 3;

        (vi) Other circumstances which, although not enumerated above, by virtue of their nature are similar to those mentioned.

3. Life imprisonment may be imposed when justified by the extreme gravity of the crime and the individual circumstances of the convicted person, as evidenced by the existence of one or more aggravating circumstances.

Rule 146 Imposition of fines under article 77

1. In determining whether to order a fine under article 77, paragraph 2(a), and in fixing the amount of the fine, the Court shall determine whether imprisonment is a sufficient penalty. The Court shall give due consideration to the financial capacity of the convicted person, including any orders for forfeiture in accordance with article 77, paragraph 2(b), and, as appropriate, any orders for reparation in accordance with article 75. The Court shall take into account, in addition to the factors referred to in rule 145, whether and to what degree the crime was motivated by personal financial gain.

2. A fine imposed under article 77, paragraph 2(a), shall be set at an appropriate level. To this end, the Court shall, in addition to the factors referred to above, in particular take into consideration the damage and injuries caused as well as the proportionate gains derived from the crime by the perpetrator. Under no circumstances may the total amount exceed 75 per cent of the value of the convicted person's identifiable assets, liquid or realizable, and property, after deduction of an appropriate amount that would satisfy the financial needs of the convicted person and his or her dependants.

3.   In imposing a fine, the Court shall allow the convicted person a reasonable period in which to pay the fine. The Court may provide for payment of a lump sum or by way of instalments during that period.

4.   In imposing a fine, the Court may, as an option, calculate it according to a system of daily fines. In such cases, the minimum duration shall be 30 days and the maximum duration five years. The Court shall decide the total amount in accordance with sub-rules 1 and 2. It shall determine the amount of daily payment in the light of the individual circumstances of the convicted person, including the financial needs of his or her dependants.

5.   If the convicted person does not pay the fine imposed in accordance with the conditions set above, appropriate measures may be taken by the Court pursuant to rules 217 to 222 and in accordance with article 109. Where, in cases of continued wilful non-payment, the Presidency, on its own motion or at the request of the Prosecutor, is satisfied that all available enforcement measures have been exhausted, it may as a last resort extend the term of imprisonment for a period not to exceed a quarter of such term or five years, whichever is less. In the determination of such period of extension, the Presidency shall take into account the amount of the fine, imposed and paid. Any such extension shall not apply in the case of life imprisonment. The extension may not lead to a total period of imprisonment in excess of 30 years.

6.   In order to determine whether to order an extension and the period involved, the Presidency shall sit in camera for the purpose of obtaining the views of the sentenced person and the Prosecutor. The sentenced person shall have the right to be assisted by counsel.

7.   In imposing a fine, the Court shall warn the convicted person that failure to pay the fine in accordance with the conditions set out above may result in an extension of the period of imprisonment as described in this rule.

Rule 147 Orders of forfeiture

1.   In accordance with article 76, paragraphs 2 and 3, and rules 63, sub-rule 1, and 143, at any hearing to consider an order of forfeiture, Chamber shall hear evidence as to the identification and location of specific proceeds, property or assets which have been derived directly or indirectly from the crime.

2.   If before or during the hearing, a Chamber becomes aware of any bona fide third party who appears to have an interest in relevant proceeds, property or assets, it shall give notice to that third party.

3.   The Prosecutor, the convicted person and any bona fide third party with an interest in the relevant proceeds, property or assets may submit evidence relevant to the issue.

4.   After considering any evidence submitted, a Chamber may issue an order of forfeiture in relation to specific proceeds, property or assets if it is satisfied that these have been derived directly or indirectly from the crime.

Rule 148 Orders to transfer fines or forfeitures to the Trust Fund

Before making an order pursuant to article 79, paragraph 2, a Chamber may request the representatives of the Fund to submit written or oral observations to it.

Chapter 8 Appeal and revision
Section I General provisions

Rule 149 Rules governing proceedings in the Appeals Chamber

Parts 5 and 6 and rules governing proceedings and the submission of evidence in the Pre-Trial and Trial Chambers shall apply *mutatis mutandis* to proceedings in the Appeals Chamber.

Section II Appeals against convictions, acquittals, sentences and reparation orders

Rule 150 Appeal

1. Subject to sub-rule 2, an appeal against a decision of conviction or acquittal under article 74, a sentence under article 76 or a reparation order under article 75 may be filed not later than 30 days from the date on which the party filing the appeal is notified of the decision, the sentence or the reparation order.

2. The Appeals Chamber may extend the time limit set out in sub-rule 1, for good cause, upon the application of the party seeking to file the appeal.

3. The appeal shall be filed with the Registrar.

4. If an appeal is not filed as set out in sub-rules 1 to 3, the decision, the sentence or the reparation order of the Trial Chamber shall become final.

Rule 151 Procedure for the appeal

1. Upon the filing of an appeal under rule 150, the Registrar shall transmit the trial record to the Appeals Chamber.

2. The Registrar shall notify all parties who participated in the proceedings before the Trial Chamber that an appeal has been filed.

Rule 152 Discontinuance of the appeal

1. Any party who has filed an appeal may discontinue the appeal at any time before judgment has been delivered. In such case, the party shall file with the Registrar a written notice of discontinuance of appeal. The Registrar shall inform the other parties that such a notice has been filed.

2. If the Prosecutor has filed an appeal on behalf of a convicted person in accordance with article 81, paragraph 1(b), before filing any notice of discontinuance, the Prosecutor shall inform the convicted person that he or she intends to discontinue the appeal in order to give him or her the opportunity to continue the appeal proceedings.

Rule 153 Judgment on appeals against reparation orders

1. The Appeals Chamber may confirm, reverse or amend a reparation order made under article 75.

2. The judgment of the Appeals Chamber shall be delivered in accordance with article 83, paragraphs 4 and 5.

Section III Appeals against other decisions

Rule 154 Appeals that do not require the leave of the Court

1. An appeal may be filed under article 81, paragraph 3 (c) (ii), or article 82, paragraph 1 (a) or (b), not later than five days from the date upon which the party filing the appeal is notified of the decision.

2. An appeal may be filed under article 82, paragraph 1 (c), not later than two days from the date upon which the party filing the appeal is notified of the decision.

3. Rule 150, sub-rules 3 and 4, shall apply to appeals filed under sub-rules 1 and 2 of this rule.

Rule 155 Appeals that require leave of the Court

1. When a party wishes to appeal a decision under article 82, paragraph 1(d), or article 82, paragraph 2, that party shall, within five days of being notified of that decision, make a written application to the Chamber that gave the decision, setting out the reasons for the request for leave to appeal.

2. The Chamber shall render a decision and shall notify all parties who participated in the proceedings that gave rise to the decision referred to in sub-rule 1.

Rule 156 Procedure for the appeal

1. As soon as an appeal has been filed under rule 154 or as soon as leave to appeal has been granted under rule 155, the Registrar shall transmit to the Appeals Chamber the record of the proceedings of the Chamber that made the decision that is the subject of the appeal.

2. The Registrar shall give notice of the appeal to all parties who participated in the proceedings before the Chamber that gave the decision that is the subject of the appeal, unless they have already been notified by the Chamber under rule 155, sub-rule 2.

3. The appeal proceedings shall be in writing unless the Appeals Chamber decides to convene a hearing.

4. The appeal shall be heard as expeditiously as possible.

5. When filing the appeal, the party appealing may request that the appeal have suspensive effect in accordance with article 82, paragraph 3.

Rule 157 Discontinuance of the appeal

Any party who has filed an appeal under rule 154 or who has obtained the leave of a Chamber to appeal a decision under rule 155 may discontinue the appeal at any time before judgment has been delivered. In such case, the party shall file with the Registrar a written notice of discontinuance of appeal. The Registrar shall inform the other parties that such a notice has been filed.

Rule 158 Judgment on the appeal

1. An Appeals Chamber which considers an appeal referred to in this section may confirm, reverse or amend the decision appealed.

2. The judgment of the Appeals Chamber shall be delivered in accordance with article 83, paragraph 4.

Section IV Revision of conviction or sentence

Rule 159 Application for revision

1. An application for revision provided for in article 84, paragraph 1, shall be in writing and shall set out the grounds on which the revision is sought. It shall as far as possible be accompanied by supporting material.

2. The determination on whether the application is meritorious shall be taken by a majority of the judges of the Appeals Chamber and shall be supported by reasons in writing.

3. Notification of the decision shall be sent to the applicant and, as far as possible, to all the parties who participated in the proceedings related to the initial decision.

Rule 160 Transfer for the purpose of revision

1. For the conduct of the hearing provided for in rule 161, the relevant Chamber shall issue its order sufficiently in advance to enable the transfer of the sentenced person to the seat of the Court, as appropriate.

2. The determination of the Court shall be communicated without delay to the State of enforcement.

3. The provisions of rule 206, sub-rule 3, shall be applicable.

Rule 161 Determination on revision

1. On a date which it shall determine and shall communicate to the applicant and to all those having received notification under rule 159, sub-rule 3, the relevant Chamber shall hold a hearing to determine whether the conviction or sentence should be revised.

2. For the conduct of the hearing, the relevant Chamber shall exercise, *mutatis mutandis,* all the powers of the Trial Chamber pursuant to Part 6 and the rules governing proceedings and the submission of evidence in the Pre-Trial and Trial Chambers.

3. The determination on revision shall be governed by the applicable provisions of article 83, paragraph 4.

Chapter 9 Offences and misconduct against the Court
Section I Offences against the administration of justice under article 70

Rule 162 Exercise of jurisdiction

1. Before deciding whether to exercise jurisdiction, the Court may consult with States Parties that may have jurisdiction over the offence.

2. In making a decision whether or not to exercise jurisdiction, the Court may consider, in particular:

   (a) The availability and effectiveness of prosecution in a State Party;

   (b) The seriousness of an offence;

   (c) The possible joinder of charges under article 70 with charges under articles 5 to 8;

   (d) The need to expedite proceedings;

   (e) Links with an ongoing investigation or a trial before the Court; and

   (f) Evidentiary considerations.

3. The Court shall give favourable consideration to a request from the host State for a waiver of the power of the Court to exercise jurisdiction in cases where the host State considers such a waiver to be of particular importance.

4. If the Court decides not to exercise its jurisdiction, it may request a State Party to exercise jurisdiction pursuant to article 70, paragraph 4.

Rule 163 Application of the Statute and the Rules

1. Unless otherwise provided in sub-rules 2 and 3, rule 162 and rules 164 to 169, the Statute and the Rules shall apply *mutatis mutandis* to the Court's investigation, prosecution and punishment of offences defined in article 70.

2. The provisions of Part 2, and any rules thereunder, shall not apply, with the exception of article 21.

3. The provisions of Part 10, and any rules thereunder, shall not apply, with the exception of articles 103, 107, 109 and 111.

Rule 164 Periods of limitation

1. If the Court exercises jurisdiction in accordance with rule 162, it shall apply the periods of limitation set forth in this rule.

2. Offences defined in article 70 shall be subject to a period of limitation of five years from the date on which the offence was committed, provided that during this period no investigation or prosecution has been initiated. The period of limitation shall be interrupted if an investigation or prosecution has been initiated during this period, either before the Court or by a State Party with jurisdiction over the case pursuant to article 70, paragraph 4(a).

3. Enforcement of sanctions imposed with respect to offences defined in article 70 shall be subject to a period of limitation of 10 years from the date on which the sanction has become final. The period of limitation shall be interrupted with the detention of the convicted person or while the person concerned is outside the territory of the States Parties.

Rule 165 Investigation, prosecution and trial

1. The Prosecutor may initiate and conduct investigations with respect to the offences defined in article 70 on his or her own initiative, on the basis of information communicated by a Chamber or any reliable source.

2. Articles 53 and 59, and any rules thereunder, shall not apply.

3. For purposes of article 61, the Pre-Trial Chamber may make any of the determinations set forth in that article on the basis of written submissions, without a hearing, unless the interests of justice otherwise require.

4. A Trial Chamber may, as appropriate and taking into account the rights of the defence, direct that there be joinder of charges under article 70 with charges under articles 5 to 8.

Rule 166 Sanctions under article 70

1. If the Court imposes sanctions with respect to article 70, this rule shall apply.

2. Article 77, and any rules thereunder, shall not apply, with the exception of an order of forfeiture under article 77, paragraph 2(b), which may be ordered in addition to imprisonment or a fine or both.

3. Each offence may be separately fined and those fines may be cumulative. Under no circumstances may the total amount exceed 50 per cent of the value of the convicted person's identifiable assets, liquid or realizable, and property, after deduction of an appropriate amount that would satisfy the financial needs of the convicted person and his or her dependants.

4. In imposing a fine the Court shall allow the convicted person a reasonable period in which to pay the fine. The Court may provide for payment of a lump sum or by way of instalments during that period.

5. If the convicted person does not pay a fine imposed in accordance with the conditions set forth in sub-rule 4, appropriate measures may be taken by the Court pursuant to rules 217 to 222 and in accordance with article 109. Where, in cases of continued wilful non-payment, the Court, on its own motion or at the request of the Prosecutor, is satisfied that all available enforcement measures have been exhausted, it may as a last resort impose a term of imprisonment in accordance with article 70, paragraph 3. In the determination of such term of imprisonment, the Court shall take into account the amount of fine paid.

Rule 167 International cooperation and judicial assistance

1. With regard to offences under article 70, the Court may request a State to provide any form of international cooperation or judicial assistance corresponding to those forms set forth in Part 9. In any such request, the Court shall indicate that the basis for the request is an investigation or prosecution of offences under article 70.

2. The conditions for providing international cooperation or judicial assistance to the Court with respect to offences under article 70 shall be those set forth in article 70, paragraph 2.

Rule 168 *Ne bis in idem*

In respect of offences under article 70, no person shall be tried before the Court with respect to conduct which formed the basis of an offence for which the person has already been convicted or acquitted by the Court or another court.

Rule 169 Immediate arrest

In the case of an alleged offence under article 70 committed in the presence of a Chamber, the Prosecutor may orally request that Chamber to order the immediate arrest of the person concerned.

Section II Misconduct before the Court under article 71

Rule 170 Disruption of proceedings

Having regard to article 63, paragraph 2, the Presiding Judge of the Chamber dealing with the matter may, after giving a warning:

(a) Order a person disrupting the proceedings of the Court to leave or be removed from the courtroom; or,

(b) In case of repeated misconduct, order the interdiction of that person from attending the proceedings.

Rule 171 Refusal to comply with a direction by the Court

1. When the misconduct consists of deliberate refusal to comply with an oral or written direction by the Court, not covered by rule 170, and that direction is accompanied by a warning of sanctions in case of breach, the Presiding Judge of the Chamber dealing with the matter may order the interdiction of that person from the proceedings for a period not exceeding 30 days or, if the misconduct is of a more serious nature, impose a fine.

2. If the person committing misconduct as described in sub-rule 1 is an official of the Court, or a defence counsel, or a legal representative of victims, the Presiding Judge of the Chamber dealing with the matter may also order the interdiction of that person from exercising his or her functions before the Court for a period not exceeding 30 days.

3. If the Presiding Judge in cases under sub-rules 1 and 2 considers that a longer period of interdiction is appropriate, the Presiding Judge shall refer the matter to the Presidency, which may hold a hearing to determine whether to order a longer or permanent period of interdiction.

4. A fine imposed under sub-rule 1 shall not exceed 2,000 euros, or the equivalent amount in any currency, provided that in cases of continuing misconduct, a new fine may be imposed on each day that the misconduct continues, and such fines shall be cumulative.

5. The person concerned shall be given an opportunity to be heard before a sanction for misconduct, as described in this rule, is imposed.

Rule 172 Conduct covered by both articles 70 and 71

If conduct covered by article 71 also constitutes one of the offences defined in article 70, the Court shall proceed in accordance with article 70 and rules 162 to 169.

Chapter 10 Compensation to an arrested or convicted person

Rule 173 Request for compensation

1. Anyone seeking compensation on any of the grounds indicated in article 85 shall submit a request, in writing, to the Presidency, which shall designate a Chamber composed of three judges to consider the request. These judges shall not have participated in any earlier judgment of the Court regarding the person making the request.

2. The request for compensation shall be submitted not later than six months from the date the person making the request was notified of the decision of the Court concerning:

    (a) The unlawfulness of the arrest or detention under article 85, paragraph 1;

    (b) The reversal of the conviction under article 85, paragraph 2;

    (c) The existence of a grave and manifest miscarriage of justice under article 85, paragraph 3.

3. The request shall contain the grounds and the amount of compensation requested.

4. The person requesting compensation shall be entitled to legal assistance.

Rule 174 Procedure for seeking compensation

1.   A request for compensation and any other written observation by the person filing the request shall be transmitted to the Prosecutor, who shall have an opportunity to respond in writing. Any observations by the Prosecutor shall be notified to the person filing the request.

2.   The Chamber designated under rule 173, sub-rule 1, may either hold a hearing or determine the matter on the basis of the request and any written observations by the Prosecutor and the person filing the request. A hearing shall be held if the Prosecutor or the person seeking compensation so requests.

3.   The decision shall be taken by the majority of the judges. The decision shall be notified to the Prosecutor and to the person filing the request.

Rule 175 Amount of compensation

In establishing the amount of any compensation in conformity with article 85, paragraph 3, the Chamber designated under rule 173, sub-rule 1, shall take into consideration the consequences of the grave and manifest miscarriage of justice on the personal, family, social and professional situation of the person filing the request.

Chapter 11 International cooperation and judicial assistance
Section I Requests for cooperation under article 87

Rule 176 Organs of the Court responsible for the transmission and receipt of any communications relating to international cooperation and judicial assistance

1.   Upon and subsequent to the establishment of the Court, the Registrar shall obtain from the Secretary-General of the United Nations any communication made by States pursuant to article 87, paragraphs 1(a) and 2.

2.   The Registrar shall transmit the requests for cooperation made by the Chambers and shall receive the responses, information and documents from requested States. The Office of the Prosecutor shall transmit the requests for cooperation made by the Prosecutor and shall receive the responses, information and documents from requested States.

3.   The Registrar shall be the recipient of any communication from States concerning subsequent changes in the designation of the national channels charged with receiving requests for cooperation, as well as of any change in the language in which requests for cooperation should be made, and shall, upon request, make such information available to States Parties as may be appropriate.

4.   The provisions of sub-rule 2 are applicable *mutatis mutandis* where the Court requests information, documents or other forms of cooperation and assistance from an intergovernmental organization.

5.   The Registrar shall transmit any communications referred to in sub-rules 1 and 3 and rule 177, sub-rule 2, as appropriate, to the Presidency or the Office of the Prosecutor, or both.

Rule 177 Channels of communication

1.   Communications concerning the national authority charged with receiving requests for cooperation made upon ratification, acceptance, approval or accession shall provide all relevant information about such authorities.

2.   When an intergovernmental organization is asked to assist the Court under article 87, paragraph 6, the Registrar shall, when necessary, ascertain its designated channel of communication and obtain all relevant information relating thereto.

Rule 178 Language chosen by States Parties under article 87, paragraph 2

1. When a requested State Party has more than one official language, it may indicate upon ratification, acceptance, approval or accession that requests for cooperation and any supporting documents can be drafted in any one of its official languages.

2. When the requested State Party has not chosen a language for communication with the Court upon ratification, acceptance, accession or approval, the request for cooperation shall either be in or be accompanied by a translation into one of the working languages of the Court pursuant to article 87, paragraph 2.

Rule 179 Language of requests directed to States not party to the Statute

When a State not party to the Statute has agreed to provide assistance to the Court under article 87, paragraph 5, and has not made a choice of language for such requests, the requests for cooperation shall either be in or be accompanied by a translation into one of the working languages of the Court.

Rule 180 Changes in the channels of communication or the languages of requests for cooperation

1. Changes concerning the channel of communication or the language a State has chosen under article 87, paragraph 2, shall be communicated in writing to the Registrar at the earliest opportunity.

2. Such changes shall take effect in respect of requests for cooperation made by the Court at a time agreed between the Court and the State or, in the absence of such an agreement, 45 days after the Court has received the communication and, in all cases, without prejudice to current requests or requests in progress.

Section II Surrender, transit and competing requests under articles 89 and 90

Rule 181 Challenge to admissibility of a case before a national court

When a situation described in article 89, paragraph 2, arises, and without prejudice to the provisions of article 19 and of rules 58 to 62 on procedures applicable to challenges to the jurisdiction of the Court or the admissibility of a case, the Chamber dealing with the case, if the admissibility ruling is still pending, shall take steps to obtain from the requested State all the relevant information about the *ne bis in idem* challenge brought by the person.

Rule 182 Request for transit under article 89, paragraph 3 (e)

1. In situations described in article 89, paragraph 3(e), the Court may transmit the request for transit by any medium capable of delivering a written record.

2. When the time limit provided for in article 89, paragraph 3(e), has expired and the person concerned has been released, such a release is without prejudice to a subsequent arrest of the person in accordance with the provisions of article 89 or article 92.

Rule 183 Possible temporary surrender

Following the consultations referred to in article 89, paragraph 4, the requested State may temporarily surrender the person sought in accordance with conditions determined between the requested State and the Court. In such case the person shall be kept in custody during his or her presence before the Court and shall be transferred to the requested State once his or her presence before the Court is no longer required, at the latest when the proceedings have been completed.

Rule 184 Arrangements for surrender

1. The requested State shall immediately inform the Registrar when the person sought by the Court is available for surrender.

2.   The person shall be surrendered to the Court by the date and in the manner agreed upon between the authorities of the requested State and the Registrar.

3.   If circumstances prevent the surrender of the person by the date agreed, the authorities of the requested State and the Registrar shall agree upon a new date and manner by which the person shall be surrendered.

4.   The Registrar shall maintain contact with the authorities of the host State in relation to the arrangements for the surrender of the person to the Court.

Rule 185 Release of a person from the custody of the Court other than upon completion of sentence

1.   Subject to sub-rule 2, where a person surrendered to the Court is released from the custody of the Court because the Court does not have jurisdiction, the case is inadmissible under article 17, paragraph 1(b), (c) or (d), the charges have not been confirmed under article 61, the person has been acquitted at trial or on appeal, or for any other reason, the Court shall, as soon as possible, make such arrangements as it considers appropriate for the transfer of the person, taking into account the views of the person, to a State which is obliged to receive him or her, to another State which agrees to receive him or her, or to a State which has requested his or her extradition with the consent of the original surrendering State. In this case, the host State shall facilitate the transfer in accordance with the agreement referred to in article 3, paragraph 2, and the related arrangements.

2.   Where the Court has determined that the case is inadmissible under article 17, paragraph 1(a), the Court shall make arrangements, as appropriate, for the transfer of the person to a State whose investigation or prosecution has formed the basis of the successful challenge to admissibility, unless the State that originally surrendered the person requests his or her return.

Rule 186 Competing requests in the context of a challenge to the admissibility of the case

In situations described in article 90, paragraph 8, the requested State shall provide the notification of its decision to the Prosecutor in order to enable him or her to act in accordance with article 19, paragraph 10.

Section III Documents for arrest and surrender under articles 91 and 92

Rule 187 Translation of documents accompanying request for surrender

For the purposes of article 67, paragraph 1(a), and in accordance with rule 117, sub-rule 1, the request under article 91 shall be accompanied, as appropriate, by a translation of the warrant of arrest or of the judgment of conviction and by a translation of the text of any relevant provisions of the Statute, in a language that the person fully understands and speaks.

Rule 188 Time limit for submission of documents after provisional arrest

For the purposes of article 92, paragraph 3, the time limit for receipt by the requested State of the request for surrender and the documents supporting the request shall be 60 days from the date of the provisional arrest.

Rule 189 Transmission of documents supporting the request

When a person has consented to surrender in accordance with the provisions of article 92, paragraph 3, and the requested State proceeds to surrender the person to the Court, the Court shall not be required to provide the documents described in article 91 unless the requested State indicates otherwise.

Section IV Cooperation under article 93

Rule 190 Instruction on self-incrimination accompanying request for witness

When making a request under article 93, paragraph 1 (e), with respect to a witness, the Court shall annex an instruction, concerning rule 74 relating to self-incrimination, to be provided to the witness in question, in a language that the person fully understands and speaks.

Rule 191 Assurance provided by the Court under article 93, paragraph 2

The Chamber dealing with the case, on its own motion or at the request of the Prosecutor, defence or witness or expert concerned, may decide, after taking into account the views of the Prosecutor and the witness or expert concerned, to provide the assurance described in article 93, paragraph 2.

Rule 192 Transfer of a person in custody

1. Transfer of a person in custody to the Court in accordance with article 93, paragraph 7, shall be arranged by the national authorities concerned in liaison with the Registrar and the authorities of the host State.

2. The Registrar shall ensure the proper conduct of the transfer, including the supervision of the person while in the custody of the Court.

3. The person in custody before the Court shall have the right to raise matters concerning the conditions of his or her detention with the relevant Chamber.

4. In accordance with article 93, paragraph 7(b), when the purposes of the transfer have been fulfilled, the Registrar shall arrange for the return of the person in custody to the requested State.

Rule 193 Temporary transfer of the person from the State of enforcement

1. The Chamber that is considering the case may order the temporary transfer from the State of enforcement to the seat of the Court of any person sentenced by the Court whose testimony or other assistance is necessary to the Court. The provisions of article 93, paragraph 7, shall not apply.

2. The Registrar shall ensure the proper conduct of the transfer, in liaison with the authorities of the State of enforcement and the authorities of the host State. When the purposes of the transfer have been fulfilled, the Court shall return the sentenced person to the State of enforcement.

3. The person shall be kept in custody during his or her presence before the Court. The entire period of detention spent at the seat of the Court shall be deducted from the sentence remaining to be served.

Rule 194 Cooperation requested from the Court

1. In accordance with article 93, paragraph 10, and consistent with article 96, *mutatis mutandis*, a State may transmit to the Court a request for cooperation or assistance to the Court, either in or accompanied by a translation into one of the working languages of the Court.

2. Requests described in sub-rule 1 are to be sent to the Registrar, which shall transmit them, as appropriate, either to the Prosecutor or to the Chamber concerned.

3. If protective measures within the meaning of article 68 have been adopted, the Prosecutor or Chamber, as appropriate, shall consider the views of the Chamber which ordered the measures as well as those of the relevant victim or witness, before deciding on the request.

4. If the request relates to documents or evidence as described in article 93, paragraph 10(b)(ii), the Prosecutor or Chamber, as appropriate, shall obtain the written consent of the relevant State before proceeding with the request.

5. When the Court decides to grant the request for cooperation or assistance from a State, the request shall be executed, insofar as possible, following any procedure outlined therein by the requesting State and permitting persons specified in the request to be present.

Section V Cooperation under article 98

Rule 195 Provision of information

1. When a requested State notifies the Court that a request for surrender or assistance raises a problem of execution in respect of article 98, the requested State shall provide any information relevant to assist the Court in the application of article 98. Any concerned third State or sending State may provide additional information to assist the Court.

2. The Court may not proceed with a request for the surrender of a person without the consent of a sending State if, under article 98, paragraph 2, such a request would be inconsistent with obligations under an international agreement pursuant to which the consent of a sending State is required prior to the surrender of a person of that State to the Court.

Section VI Rule of speciality under article 101

Rule 196 Provision of views on article 101, paragraph 1

A person surrendered to the Court may provide views on a perceived violation of the provisions of article 101, paragraph 1.

Rule 197 Extension of the surrender

When the Court has requested a waiver of the requirements of article 101, paragraph 1, the requested State may ask the Court to obtain and provide the views of the person surrendered to the Court.

Chapter 12 Enforcement
Section I Role of States in enforcement of sentences of imprisonment and change in designation of State of enforcement under articles 103 and 104

Rule 198 Communications between the Court and States

Unless the context otherwise requires, article 87 and rules 176 to 180 shall apply, as appropriate, to communications between the Court and a State on matters relating to enforcement of sentences.

Rule 199 Organ responsible under Part 10

Unless provided otherwise in the Rules, the functions of the Court under Part 10 shall be exercised by the Presidency.

Rule 200 List of States of enforcement

1. A list of States that have indicated their willingness to accept sentenced persons shall be established and maintained by the Registrar.

2. The Presidency shall not include a State on the list provided for in article 103, paragraph 1(a), if it does not agree with the conditions that such a State attaches to its acceptance. The Presidency may request any additional information from that State prior to taking a decision.

3. A State that has attached conditions of acceptance may at any time withdraw such conditions. Any amendments or additions to such conditions shall be subject to confirmation by the Presidency.

4. A State may at any time inform the Registrar of its withdrawal from the list. Such withdrawal shall not affect the enforcement of the sentences in respect of persons that the State has already accepted.

5. The Court may enter bilateral arrangements with States with a view to establishing a framework for the acceptance of prisoners sentenced by the Court. Such arrangements shall be consistent with the Statute.

Rule 201 Principles of equitable distribution

Principles of equitable distribution for purposes of article 103, paragraph 3, shall include:

(a) The principle of equitable geographical distribution;

(b) The need to afford each State on the list an opportunity to receive sentenced persons;

(c) The number of sentenced persons already received by that State and other States of enforcement;

(d) Any other relevant factors.

Rule 202 Timing of delivery of the sentenced person to the State of enforcement

The delivery of a sentenced person from the Court to the designated State of enforcement shall not take place unless the decision on the conviction and the decision on the sentence have become final.

Rule 203 Views of the sentenced person

1. The Presidency shall give notice in writing to the sentenced person that it is addressing the designation of a State of enforcement. The sentenced person shall, within such time limit as the Presidency shall prescribe, submit in writing his or her views on the question to the Presidency.

2. The Presidency may allow the sentenced person to make oral presentations.

3. The Presidency shall allow the sentenced person:

(a) To be assisted, as appropriate, by a competent interpreter and to benefit from any translation necessary for the presentation of his or her views;

(b) To be granted adequate time and facilities necessary to prepare for the presentation of his or her views.

Rule 204 Information relating to designation

When the Presidency notifies the designated State of its decision, it shall also transmit the following information and documents:

(a) The name, nationality, date and place of birth of the sentenced person;

(b) A copy of the final judgment of conviction and of the sentence imposed;

(c) The length and commencement date of the sentence and the time remaining to be served;

(d) After having heard the views of the sentenced person, any necessary information concerning the state of his or her health, including any medical treatment that he or she is receiving.

Rule 205 Rejection of designation in a particular case

Where a State in a particular case rejects the designation by the Presidency, the Presidency may designate another State.

Rule 206 Delivery of the sentenced person to the State of enforcement

1. The Registrar shall inform the Prosecutor and the sentenced person of the State designated to enforce the sentence.

2. The sentenced person shall be delivered to the State of enforcement as soon as possible after the designated State of enforcement accepts.

3. The Registrar shall ensure the proper conduct of the delivery of the person in consultation with the authorities of the State of enforcement and the host State.

Rule 207 Transit

1. No authorization is required if the sentenced person is transported by air and no landing is scheduled on the territory of the transit State. If an unscheduled landing occurs on the territory of the transit State, that State shall, to the extent possible under the procedure of national law, detain the sentenced person in custody until a request for transit as provided in sub-rule 2 or a request under article 89, paragraph 1, or article 92 is received.

2. To the extent possible under the procedure of national law, a State Party shall authorize the transit of a sentenced person through its territory and the provisions of article 89, paragraph 3(b) and (c), and articles 105 and 108 and any rules relating thereto shall, as appropriate, apply. A copy of the final judgment of conviction and of the sentence imposed shall be attached to such request for transit.

Rule 208 Costs

1. The ordinary costs for the enforcement of the sentence in the territory of the State of enforcement shall be borne by that State.

2. Other costs, including those for the transport of the sentenced person and those referred to in article 100, paragraph 1(c), (d) and (e), shall be borne by the Court.

Rule 209 Change in designation of State of enforcement

1. The Presidency, acting on its own motion or at the request of the sentenced person or the Prosecutor, may at any time act in accordance with article 104, paragraph 1.

2. The request of the sentenced person or of the Prosecutor shall be made in writing and shall set out the grounds upon which the transfer is sought.

Rule 210 Procedure for change in the designation of a State of enforcement

1. Before deciding to change the designation of a State of enforcement, the Presidency may:

    (a) Request views from the State of enforcement;

    (b) Consider written or oral presentations of the sentenced person and the Prosecutor;

    (c) Consider written or oral expert opinion concerning, *inter alia,* the sentenced person;

    (d) Obtain any other relevant information from any reliable sources.

2. The provisions of rule 203, sub-rule 3, shall apply, as appropriate.

3. If the Presidency refuses to change the designation of the State of enforcement, it shall, as soon as possible, inform the sentenced person, the Prosecutor and the Registrar of its decision and of the reasons therefor. It shall also inform the State of enforcement.

**Section II Enforcement, supervision and transfer under
articles 105, 106 and 107**

**Rule 211 Supervision of enforcement of sentences and conditions
of imprisonment**

1. In order to supervise the enforcement of sentences of imprisonment, the Presidency:

    (a) Shall, in consultation with the State of enforcement, ensure that in establishing appropriate arrangements for the exercise by any sentenced person of his or her right to communicate with the Court about the conditions of imprisonment, the provisions of article 106, paragraph 3, shall be respected;

    (b) May, when necessary, request any information, report or expert opinion from the State of enforcement or from any reliable sources;

(c) May, where appropriate, delegate a judge of the Court or a member of the staff of the Court who will be responsible, after notifying the State of enforcement, for meeting the sentenced person and hearing his or her views, without the presence of national authorities;

(d) May, where appropriate, give the State of enforcement an opportunity to comment on the views expressed by the sentenced person under sub-rule 1 (c).

2. When a sentenced person is eligible for a prison programme or benefit available under the domestic law of the State of enforcement which may entail some activity outside the prison facility, the State of enforcement shall communicate that fact to the Presidency, together with any relevant information or observation, to enable the Court to exercise its supervisory function.

Rule 212 Information on location of the person for enforcement of fines, forfeitures or reparation measures

For the purpose of enforcement of fines and forfeiture measures and of reparation measures ordered by the Court, the Presidency may, at any time or at least 30 days before the scheduled completion of the sentence served by the sentenced person, request the State of enforcement to transmit to it the relevant information concerning the intention of that State to authorize the person to remain in its territory or the location where it intends to transfer the person.

Rule 213 Procedure for article 107, paragraph 3

With respect to article 107, paragraph 3, the procedure set out in rules 214 and 215 shall apply, as appropriate.

Section III Limitation on the prosecution or punishment of other offences under article 108

Rule 214 Request to prosecute or enforce a sentence for prior conduct

1. For the application of article 108, when the State of enforcement wishes to prosecute or enforce a sentence against the sentenced person for any conduct engaged in prior to that person's transfer, it shall notify its intention to the Presidency and transmit to it the following documents:

   (a) A statement of the facts of the case and their legal characterization;

   (b) A copy of any applicable legal provisions, including those concerning the statute of limitation and the applicable penalties;

   (c) A copy of any sentence, warrant of arrest or other document having the same force, or of any other legal writ which the State intends to enforce;

   (d) A protocol containing views of the sentenced person obtained after the person has been informed sufficiently about the proceedings.

2. In the event of a request for extradition made by another State, the State of enforcement shall transmit the entire request to the Presidency with a protocol containing the views of the sentenced person obtained after informing the person sufficiently about the extradition request.

3. The Presidency may in all cases request any document or additional information from the State of enforcement or the State requesting extradition.

4. If the person was surrendered to the Court by a State other than the State of enforcement or the State seeking extradition, the Presidency shall consult with the State that surrendered the person and take into account any views expressed by that State.

5. Any information or documents transmitted to the Presidency under sub-rules 1 to 4 shall be transmitted to the Prosecutor, who may comment.

6. The Presidency may decide to conduct a hearing.

Rule 215 Decision on request to prosecute or enforce a sentence

1. The Presidency shall make a determination as soon as possible. This determination shall be notified to all those who have participated in the proceedings.

2. If the request submitted under sub-rules 1 or 2 of rule 214 concerns the enforcement of a sentence, the sentenced person may serve that sentence in the State designated by the Court to enforce the sentence pronounced by it or be extradited to a third State only after having served the full sentence pronounced by the Court, subject to the provisions of article 110.

3. The Presidency may authorize the temporary extradition of the sentenced person to a third State for prosecution only if it has obtained assurances which it deems to be sufficient that the sentenced person will be kept in custody in the third State and transferred back to the State responsible for enforcement of the sentence pronounced by the Court, after the prosecution.

Rule 216 Information on enforcement

The Presidency shall request the State of enforcement to inform it of any important event concerning the sentenced person, and of any prosecution of that person for events subsequent to his or her transfer.

Section IV Enforcement of fines, forfeiture measures and reparation orders

Rule 217 Cooperation and measures for enforcement of fines, forfeiture or reparation orders

For the enforcement of fines, forfeiture or reparation orders, the Presidency shall, as appropriate, seek cooperation and measures for enforcement in accordance with Part 9, as well as transmit copies of relevant orders to any State with which the sentenced person appears to have direct connection by reason of either nationality, domicile or habitual residence or by virtue of the location of the sentenced person's assets and property or with which the victim has such connection. The Presidency shall, as appropriate, inform the State of any third-party claims or of the fact that no claim was presented by a person who received notification of any proceedings conducted pursuant to article 75.

Rule 218 Orders for forfeiture and reparations

1. In order to enable States to give effect to an order for forfeiture, the order shall specify:

    (a) The identity of the person against whom the order has been issued;

    (b) The proceeds, property and assets that have been ordered by the Court to be forfeited; and

    (c) That if the State Party is unable to give effect to the order for forfeiture in relation to the specified proceeds, property or assets, it shall take measures to recover the value of the same.

2. In the request for cooperation and measures for enforcement, the Court shall also provide available information as to the location of the proceeds, property and assets that are covered by the order for forfeiture.

3. In order to enable States to give effect to an order for reparations, the order shall specify:

    (a) The identity of the person against whom the order has been issued;

    (b) In respect of reparations of a financial nature, the identity of the victims to whom individual reparations have been granted, and, where the award for reparations shall be deposited with the Trust Fund, the particulars of the Trust Fund for the deposit of the award; and

    (c) The scope and nature of the reparations ordered by the Court, including, where applicable, the property and assets for which restitution has been ordered.

4. Where the Court awards reparations on an individual basis, a copy of the reparation order shall be transmitted to the victim concerned.

Rule 219 Non-modification of orders for reparation

The Presidency shall, when transmitting copies of orders for reparations to States Parties under rule 217, inform them that, in giving effect to an order for reparations, the national authorities shall not modify the reparations specified by the Court, the scope or the extent of any damage, loss or injury determined by the Court or the principles stated in the order, and shall facilitate the enforcement of such order.

Rule 220 Non-modification of judgments in which fines were imposed

When transmitting copies of judgments in which fines were imposed to States Parties for the purpose of enforcement in accordance with article 109 and rule 217, the Presidency shall inform them that in enforcing the fines imposed, national authorities shall not modify them.

Rule 221 Decision on disposition or allocation of property or assets

1. The Presidency shall, after having consulted, as appropriate, with the Prosecutor, the sentenced person, the victims or their legal representatives, the national authorities of the State of enforcement or any relevant third party, or representatives of the Trust Fund provided for in article 79, decide on all matters related to the disposition or allocation of property or assets realized through enforcement of an order of the Court.

2. In all cases, when the Presidency decides on the disposition or allocation of property or assets belonging to the sentenced person, it shall give priority to the enforcement of measures concerning reparations to victims.

Rule 222 Assistance for service or any other measure

The Presidency shall assist the State in the enforcement of fines, forfeiture or reparation orders, as requested, with the service of any relevant notification on the sentenced person or any other relevant persons, or the carrying out of any other measures necessary for the enforcement of the order under the procedure of the national law of the enforcement State.

Section V Review concerning reduction of sentence under article 110

Rule 223 Criteria for review concerning reduction of sentence

In reviewing the question of reduction of sentence pursuant to article 110, paragraphs 3 and 5, the three judges of the Appeals Chamber shall take into account the criteria listed in article 110, paragraph 4(a) and (b), and the following criteria:

(a) The conduct of the sentenced person while in detention, which shows a genuine dissociation from his or her crime;

(b) The prospect of the resocialization and successful resettlement of the sentenced person;

(c) Whether the early release of the sentenced person would give rise to significant social instability;

(d) Any significant action taken by the sentenced person for the benefit of the victims as well as any impact on the victims and their families as a result of the early release;

(e) Individual circumstances of the sentenced person, including a worsening state of physical or mental health or advanced age.

Rule 224 Procedure for review concerning reduction of sentence

1. For the application of article 110, paragraph 3, three judges of the Appeals Chamber appointed by that Chamber shall conduct a hearing, unless they decide otherwise in a particular case, for exceptional reasons. The hearing shall be conducted with the sentenced person, who may be assisted by his or her counsel, with interpretation, as may be required. Those three judges shall invite the Prosecutor, the State of enforcement of any penalty under article 77 or any reparation order pursuant to article 75 and, to the extent possible, the victims or their legal representatives who participated in the proceedings, to participate in the hearing or to submit written observations. Under exceptional circumstances, this hearing may be conducted by way of a videoconference or in the State of enforcement by a judge delegated by the Appeals Chamber.

2. The same three judges shall communicate the decision and the reasons for it to all those who participated in the review proceedings as soon as possible.

3. For the application of article 110, paragraph 5, three judges of the Appeals Chamber appointed by that Chamber shall review the question of reduction of sentence every three years, unless it establishes a shorter interval in its decision taken pursuant to article 110, paragraph 3. In case of a significant change in circumstances, those three judges may permit the sentenced person to apply for a review within the three-year period or such shorter period as may have been set by the three judges.

4. For any review under article 110, paragraph 5, three judges of the Appeals Chamber appointed by that Chamber shall invite written representations from the sentenced person or his or her counsel, the Prosecutor, the State of enforcement of any penalty under article 77 and any reparation order pursuant to article 75 and, to the extent possible, the victims or their legal representatives who participated in the proceedings. The three judges may also decide to hold a hearing.

5. The decision and the reasons for it shall be communicated to all those who participated in the review proceedings as soon as possible.

Section VI Escape

Rule 225 Measures under article 111 in the event of escape

1. If the sentenced person has escaped, the State of enforcement shall, as soon as possible, advise the Registrar by any medium capable of delivering a written record. The Presidency shall then proceed in accordance with Part 9.

2. However, if the State in which the sentenced person is located agrees to surrender him or her to the State of enforcement, pursuant to either international agreements or its national legislation, the State of enforcement shall so advise the Registrar in writing. The person shall be surrendered to the State of enforcement as soon as possible, if necessary in consultation with the Registrar, who shall provide all necessary assistance, including, if necessary, the presentation of requests for transit to the States concerned, in accordance with rule 207. The costs associated with the surrender of the sentenced person shall be borne by the Court if no State assumes responsibility for them.

3. If the sentenced person is surrendered to the Court pursuant to Part 9, the Court shall transfer him or her to the State of enforcement. Nevertheless, the Presidency may, acting on its own motion or at the request of the Prosecutor or of the initial State of enforcement and in accordance with article 103 and rules 203 to 206, designate another State, including the State to the territory of which the sentenced person has fled.

4. In all cases, the entire period of detention in the territory of the State in which the sentenced person was in custody after his or her escape and, where sub-rule 3 is applicable, the period of detention at the seat of the Court following the surrender of the sentenced person from the State in which he or she was located shall be deducted from the sentence remaining to be served.

DOCUMENT 55

Elements of Crime 2002
(footnotes omitted)
PCNICC/2000/I/Add I

Resolution F of the Final Act of the United Nations Diplomatic Conference of Plenipotentiaries on the Establishment of an International Criminal Court established the Preparatory Commission for the International Criminal Court (PCNICC) to prepare proposals for practical arrangements for the establishment and coming into operation of the Court, including draft texts of, inter alia, Rules of Procedure and Evidence **(Document 54)** *and Elements of Crime* **(Document 55)**. *Both of these draft texts were to be finalised before 30 June 2000. The draft Elements of Crime were considered by the PCNICC at its first to fifth sessions and the final text was adopted on time on 30 June 2000. The rules entered into force upon adoption at the first session of the Assembly of States Parties in New York from 3–10 September 2002.*

According to Article 9 of the Statute of the International Criminal Court **(Document 53)**, *the Elements of Crime are to 'assist the Court in the interpretation of Articles 6, 7 and 8 of the Statute'. The PCNICC was charged with preparing proposals for a provision on aggression, including the definition and Elements of Crime of aggression, although these do not form part of the Elements of Crime 2002. The Elements of Crime constitute part of the applicable law of the International Criminal Court (ICC) (ICC Statute, Article 21).*

According to the General Introduction, the Elements of Crime focus on the conduct, consequences and circumstances of each crime and, where necessary, a particular mental element as well as the contextual circumstances.

See also www.un.org/law/icc/prepcomm/report/prepreportdocs.htm.

General introduction

1. Pursuant to article 9, the following Elements of Crimes shall assist the Court in the interpretation and application of articles 6, 7 and 8, consistent with the Statute. The provisions of the Statute, including article 21 and the general principles set out in Part 3, are applicable to the Elements of Crimes.

2. As stated in article 30, unless otherwise provided, a person shall be criminally responsible and liable for punishment for a crime within the jurisdiction of the Court only if the material elements are committed with intent and knowledge. Where no reference is made in the Elements of Crimes to a mental element for any particular conduct, consequence or circumstance listed, it is understood that the relevant mental element, i.e., intent, knowledge or both, set out in article 30 applies. Exceptions to the article 30 standard, based on the Statute, including applicable law under its relevant provisions, are indicated below.

3. Existence of intent and knowledge can be inferred from relevant facts and circumstances.

4. With respect to mental elements associated with elements involving value judgment, such as those using the terms "inhumane" or "severe", it is not necessary that the perpetrator personally completed a particular value judgment, unless otherwise indicated.

5. Grounds for excluding criminal responsibility or the absence thereof are generally not specified in the elements of crimes listed under each crime.

6. The requirement of "unlawfulness" found in the Statute or in other parts of international law, in particular international humanitarian law, is generally not specified in the elements of crimes.

7. The elements of crimes are generally structured in accordance with the following principles:

- As the elements of crimes focus on the conduct, consequences and circumstances associated with each crime, they are generally listed in that order;
- When required, a particular mental element is listed after the affected conduct, consequence or circumstance;
- Contextual circumstances are listed last.

8. As used in the Elements of Crimes, the term "perpetrator" is neutral as to guilt or innocence. The elements, including the appropriate mental elements, apply, *mutatis mutandis,* to all those whose criminal responsibility may fall under articles 25 and 28 of the Statute.

9. A particular conduct may constitute one or more crimes.

10. The use of short titles for the crimes has no legal effect.

Article 6 Genocide
Introduction

- With respect to the last element listed for each crime:
- The term "in the context of" would include the initial acts in an emerging pattern;
- The term "manifest" is an objective qualification;

Notwithstanding the normal requirement for a mental element provided for in article 30, and recognizing that knowledge of the circumstances will usually be addressed in proving genocidal intent, the appropriate requirement, if any, for a mental element regarding this circumstance will need to be decided by the Court on a case-by-case basis.

Article 6(a) Genocide by killing
Elements

1. The perpetrator killed one or more persons.

2. Such person or persons belonged to a particular national, ethnical, racial or religious group.

3. The perpetrator intended to destroy, in whole or in part, that national, ethnical, racial or religious group, as such.

4. The conduct took place in the context of a manifest pattern of similar conduct directed against that group or was conduct that could itself effect such destruction.

Article 6(b) Genocide by causing serious bodily or mental harm
Elements

1. The perpetrator caused serious bodily or mental harm to one or more persons.

2. Such person or persons belonged to a particular national, ethnical, racial or religious group.

3. The perpetrator intended to destroy, in whole or in part, that national, ethnical, racial or religious group, as such.

4. The conduct took place in the context of a manifest pattern of similar conduct directed against that group or was conduct that could itself effect such destruction.

Article 6(c) Genocide by deliberately inflicting conditions of life calculated to bring about physical destruction
Elements

1. The perpetrator inflicted certain conditions of life upon one or more persons.

2. Such person or persons belonged to a particular national, ethnical, racial or religious group.

3. The perpetrator intended to destroy, in whole or in part, that national, ethnical, racial or religious group, as such.

4. The conditions of life were calculated to bring about the physical destruction of that group, in whole or in part.

5. The conduct took place in the context of a manifest pattern of similar conduct directed against that group or was conduct that could itself effect such destruction.

Article 6(d) Genocide by imposing measures intended to prevent births
Elements

1. The perpetrator imposed certain measures upon one or more persons.

2. Such person or persons belonged to a particular national, ethnical, racial or religious group.

3. The perpetrator intended to destroy, in whole or in part, that national, ethnical, racial or religious group, as such.

4. The measures imposed were intended to prevent births within that group.

5. The conduct took place in the context of a manifest pattern of similar conduct directed against that group or was conduct that could itself effect such destruction.

Article 6(e) Genocide by forcibly transferring children
Elements

1. The perpetrator forcibly transferred one or more persons

2. Such person or persons belonged to a particular national, ethnical, racial or religious group.

3. The perpetrator intended to destroy, in whole or in part, that national, ethnical, racial or religious group, as such.

4. The transfer was from that group to another group.

5. The person or persons were under the age of 18 years.

6. The perpetrator knew, or should have known, that the person or persons were under the age of 18 years.

7. The conduct took place in the context of a manifest pattern of similar conduct directed against that group or was conduct that could itself effect such destruction.

Article 7 Crimes against humanity
Introduction

1. Since article 7 pertains to international criminal law, its provisions, consistent with article 22, must be strictly construed, taking into account that crimes against humanity as defined in article 7 are among the most serious crimes of concern to the international community as a whole, warrant and entail individual criminal responsibility, and require conduct which is impermissible under generally applicable international law, as recognized by the principal legal systems of the world.

2. The last two elements for each crime against humanity describe the context in which the conduct must take place. These elements clarify the requisite participation in and knowledge of a widespread or systematic attack against a civilian population. However, the last element should not be interpreted as requiring proof that the perpetrator had knowledge of all characteristics of the attack or the precise details of the plan or policy of the State or organization. In the case of an emerging widespread or systematic attack against a civilian population, the intent clause of the last element indicates that this mental element is satisfied if the perpetrator intended to further such an attack.

3. "Attack directed against a civilian population" in these context elements is understood to mean a course of conduct involving the multiple commission of acts referred to in article 7, paragraph 1, of the Statute against any civilian population, pursuant to or in furtherance of a State or

organizational policy to commit such attack. The acts need not constitute a military attack. It is understood that "policy to commit such attack" requires that the State or organization actively promote or encourage such an attack against a civilian population.

Article 7(1)(a) Crime against humanity of murder
Elements
1. The perpetrator killed one or more persons.
2. The conduct was committed as part of a widespread or systematic attack directed against a civilian population.
3. The perpetrator knew that the conduct was part of or intended the conduct to be part of a widespread or systematic attack against a civilian population.

Article 7(1)(b) Crime against humanity of extermination
Elements
1. The perpetrator killed one or more persons, including by inflicting conditions of life calculated to bring about the destruction of part of a population.
2. The conduct constituted, or took place as part of, a mass killing of members of a civilian population.
3. The conduct was committed as part of a widespread or systematic attack directed against a civilian population.
4. The perpetrator knew that the conduct was part of or intended the conduct to be part of a widespread or systematic attack directed against a civilian population.

Article 7(1)(c) Crime against humanity of enslavement
Elements
1. The perpetrator exercised any or all of the powers attaching to the right of ownership over one or more persons, such as by purchasing, selling, lending or bartering such a person or persons, or by imposing on them a similar deprivation of liberty.
2. The conduct was committed as part of a widespread or systematic attack directed against a civilian population.
3. The perpetrator knew that the conduct was part of or intended the conduct to be part of a widespread or systematic attack directed against a civilian population.

Article 7(1)(d) Crime against humanity of deportation or forcible transfer of population
Elements
1. The perpetrator deported or forcibly transferred, without grounds permitted under international law, one or more persons to another State or location, by expulsion or other coercive acts.
2. Such person or persons were lawfully present in the area from which they were so deported or transferred.
3. The perpetrator was aware of the factual circumstances that established the lawfulness of such presence.
4. The conduct was committed as part of a widespread or systematic attack directed against a civilian population.
5. The perpetrator knew that the conduct was part of or intended the conduct to be part of a widespread or systematic attack directed against a civilian population.

Article 7(1)(e) Crime against humanity of imprisonment or other severe deprivation of physical liberty
Elements

1. The perpetrator imprisoned one or more persons or otherwise severely deprived one or more persons of physical liberty.

2. The gravity of the conduct was such that it was in violation of fundamental rules of international law.

3. The perpetrator was aware of the factual circumstances that established the gravity of the conduct.

4. The conduct was committed as part of a widespread or systematic attack directed against a civilian population.

5. The perpetrator knew that the conduct was part of or intended the conduct to be part of a widespread or systematic attack directed against a civilian population.

Article 7(1)(f) Crime against humanity of torture
Elements

1. The perpetrator inflicted severe physical or mental pain or suffering upon one or more persons.

2. Such person or persons were in the custody or under the control of the perpetrator.

3. Such pain or suffering did not arise only from, and was not inherent in or incidental to, lawful sanctions.

4. The conduct was committed as part of a widespread or systematic attack directed against a civilian population.

5. The perpetrator knew that the conduct was part of or intended the conduct to be part of a widespread or systematic attack directed against a civilian population.

Article 7(1)(g)-1 Crime against humanity of rape
Elements

1. The perpetrator invaded the body of a person by conduct resulting in penetration, however slight, of any part of the body of the victim or of the perpetrator with a sexual organ, or of the anal or genital opening of the victim with any object or any other part of the body.

2. The invasion was committed by force, or by threat of force or coercion, such as that caused by fear of violence, duress, detention, psychological oppression or abuse of power, against such person or another person, or by taking advantage of a coercive environment, or the invasion was committed against a person incapable of giving genuine consent

3. The conduct was committed as part of a widespread or systematic attack directed against a civilian population.

4. The perpetrator knew that the conduct was part of or intended the conduct to be part of a widespread or systematic attack directed against a civilian population.

Article 7(1)(g)-2 Crime against humanity of sexual slavery
Elements

1. The perpetrator exercised any or all of the powers attaching to the right of ownership over one or more persons, such as by purchasing, selling, lending or bartering such a person or persons, or by imposing on them a similar deprivation of liberty.

2. The perpetrator caused such person or persons to engage in one or more acts of a sexual nature.

3. The conduct was committed as part of a widespread or systematic attack directed against a civilian population.

4. The perpetrator knew that the conduct was part of or intended the conduct to be part of a widespread or systematic attack directed against a civilian population.

Article 7(1)(g)-3 Crime against humanity of enforced prostitution
Elements

1. The perpetrator caused one or more persons to engage in one or more acts of a sexual nature by force, or by threat of force or coercion, such as that caused by fear of violence, duress, detention, psychological oppression or abuse of power, against such person or persons or another person, or by taking advantage of a coercive environment or such person's or persons' incapacity to give genuine consent.

2. The perpetrator or another person obtained or expected to obtain pecuniary or other advantage in exchange for or in connection with the acts of a sexual nature.

3. The conduct was committed as part of a widespread or systematic attack directed against a civilian population.

4. The perpetrator knew that the conduct was part of or intended the conduct to be part of a widespread or systematic attack directed against a civilian population.

Article 7(1)(g)-4 Crime against humanity of forced pregnancy
Elements

1. The perpetrator confined one or more women forcibly made pregnant, with the intent of affecting the ethnic composition of any population or carrying out other grave violations of international law.

2. The conduct was committed as part of a widespread or systematic attack directed against a civilian population.

3. The perpetrator knew that the conduct was part of or intended the conduct to be part of a widespread or systematic attack directed against a civilian population.

Article 7(1)(g)-5 Crime against humanity of enforced sterilization
Elements

1. The perpetrator deprived one or more persons of biological reproductive capacity.

2. The conduct was neither justified by the medical or hospital treatment of the person or persons concerned nor carried out with their genuine consent

3. The conduct was committed as part of a widespread or systematic attack directed against a civilian population.

4. The perpetrator knew that the conduct was part of or intended the conduct to be part of a widespread or systematic attack directed against a civilian population.

Article 7(1)(g)-6 Crime against humanity of sexual violence
Elements

1. The perpetrator committed an act of a sexual nature against one or more persons or caused such person or persons to engage in an act of a sexual nature by force, or by threat of force or coercion, such as that caused by fear of violence, duress, detention, psychological oppression or abuse of power, against such person or persons or another person, or by taking advantage of a coercive environment or such person's or persons' incapacity to give genuine consent.

2. Such conduct was of a gravity comparable to the other offences in article 7, paragraph 1(g), of the Statute.

3. The perpetrator was aware of the factual circumstances that established the gravity of the conduct.

Article 7(1)(h) Crime against humanity of persecution
Elements

1. The perpetrator severely deprived, contrary to international law, one or more persons of fundamental rights.

2. The perpetrator targeted such person or persons by reason of the identity of a group or collectivity or targeted the group or collectivity as such.

3. Such targeting was based on political, racial, national, ethnic, cultural, religious, gender as defined in article 7, paragraph 3, of the Statute, or other grounds that are universally recognized as impermissible under international law.

4. The conduct was committed in connection with any act referred to in article 7, paragraph 1, of the Statute or any crime within the jurisdiction of the Court.

5. The conduct was committed as part of a widespread or systematic attack directed against a civilian population.

6. The perpetrator knew that the conduct was part of or intended the conduct to be part of a widespread or systematic attack directed against a civilian population.

Article 7(1)(i) Crime against humanity of enforced disappearance of person
Elements

1. The perpetrator:

   (a) Arrested, detained or abducted one or more persons; or

   (b) Refused to acknowledge the arrest, detention or abduction, or to give information on the fate or whereabouts of such person or persons.

2. (a) Such arrest, detention or abduction was followed or accompanied by a refusal to acknowledge that deprivation of freedom or to give information on the fate or whereabouts of such person or persons; or

   (b) Such refusal was preceded or accompanied by that deprivation of freedom.

3. The perpetrator was aware that:

   (a) Such arrest, detention or abduction would be followed in the ordinary course of events by a refusal to acknowledge that deprivation of freedom or to give information on the fate or whereabouts of such person or persons; or

   (b) Such refusal was preceded or accompanied by that deprivation of freedom.

4. Such arrest, detention or abduction was carried out by, or with the authorization, support or acquiescence of, a State or a political organization.

5. Such refusal to acknowledge that deprivation of freedom or to give information on the fate or whereabouts of such person or persons was carried out by, or with the authorization or support of, such State or political organization.

6. The perpetrator intended to remove such person or persons from the protection of the law for a prolonged period of time.

7. The conduct was committed as part of a widespread or systematic attack directed against a civilian population.

8. The perpetrator knew that the conduct was part of or intended the conduct to be part of a widespread or systematic attack directed against a civilian population.

Article 7(1)(j) Crime against humanity of apartheid
Elements

1. The perpetrator committed an inhumane act against one or more persons.

2. Such act was an act referred to in article 7, paragraph 1, of the Statute, or was an act of a character similar to any of those acts.

3.   The perpetrator was aware of the factual circumstances that established the character of the act.

4.   The conduct was committed in the context of an institutionalized regime of systematic oppression and domination by one racial group over any other racial group or groups.

5.   The perpetrator intended to maintain such regime by that conduct.

6.   The conduct was committed as part of a widespread or systematic attack directed against a civilian population.

7.   The perpetrator knew that the conduct was part of or intended the conduct to be part of a widespread or systematic attack directed against a civilian population.

Article 7(1)(k) Crime against humanity of other inhumane acts
Elements

1.   The perpetrator inflicted great suffering, or serious injury to body or to mental as physical health, by means of an inhumane act.

2.   Such act was of a character similar to any other act referred to in article 7, paragraph 1, of the Statute.

3.   The perpetrator was aware of the factual circumstances that established the character of the act.

4.   The conduct was committed as part of a widespread or systematic attack directed against a civilian population.

5.   The perpetrator knew that the conduct was part of or intended the conduct to be part of a widespread or systematic attack directed against a civilian population.

Article 8 War crimes
Introduction

The elements for war crimes under article 8, paragraph 2(c) and (e), are subject to the limitations addressed in article 8, paragraph 2(d) and (f), which are not elements of crimes. The elements for war crimes under article 8, paragraph 2, of the Statute shall be interpreted within the established framework of the international law of armed conflict including, as appropriate, the international law of armed conflict applicable to armed conflict at sea.

With respect to the last two elements listed for each crime:

There is no requirement for a legal evaluation by the perpetrator as to the existence of an armed conflict or its character as international or non-international;

In that context there is no requirement for awareness by the perpetrator of the facts that established the character of the conflict as international or non-international;

There is only a requirement for the awareness of the factual circumstances that established the existence of an armed conflict that is implicit in the terms "took place in the context of and was associated with".

Article 8(2)(a) Article 8(2)(a)(i) War crime of wilful killing
Elements

1.   The perpetrator killed one or more persons.

2.   Such person or persons were protected under one or more of the Geneva Conventions of 1949.

3.   The perpetrator was aware of the factual circumstances that established that protected status.

4.   The conduct took place in the context of and was associated with an international armed conflict.

5.   The perpetrator was aware of factual circumstances that established the existence of an armed conflict.

Article 8(2)(a)(ii)-1 War crime of torture
Elements

1. The perpetrator inflicted severe physical or mental pain or suffering upon one or more persons.

2. The perpetrator inflicted the pain or suffering for such purposes as: obtaining information or a confession, punishment, intimidation or coercion or for any reason based on discrimination of any kind.

3. Such person or persons were protected under one or more of the Geneva Conventions of 1949.

4. The perpetrator was aware of the factual circumstances that established that protected status.

5. The conduct took place in the context of and was associated with an international armed conflict.

6. The perpetrator was aware of factual circumstances that established the existence of an armed conflict.

Article 8(2)(a)(ii)-2 War crime of inhuman treatment
Elements

1. The perpetrator inflicted severe physical or mental pain or suffering upon one or more persons.

2. Such person or persons were protected under one or more of the Geneva Conventions of 1949.

3. The perpetrator was aware of the factual circumstances that established that protected status.

4. The conduct took place in the context of and was associated with an international armed conflict.

5. The perpetrator was aware of factual circumstances that established the existence of an armed conflict.

Article 8(2)(a)(ii)-3 War crime of biological experiments
Elements

1. The perpetrator subjected one or more persons to a particular biological experiment.

2. The experiment seriously endangered the physical or mental health or integrity of such person or persons.

3. The intent of the experiment was non-therapeutic and it was neither justified by medical reasons nor carried out in such person's or persons' interest.

4. Such person or persons were protected under one or more of the Geneva Conventions of 1949.

5. The perpetrator was aware of the factual circumstances that established that protected status.

6. The conduct took place in the context of and was associated with an international armed conflict.

7. The perpetrator was aware of factual circumstances that established the existence of an armed conflict.

Article 8(2)(a)(iii) War crime of wilfully causing great suffering
Elements

1. The perpetrator caused great physical or mental pain or suffering to, or serious injury to body or health of, one or more persons.

2. Such person or persons were protected under one or more of the Geneva Conventions of 1949.

3. The perpetrator was aware of the factual circumstances that established that protected status.

4. The conduct took place in the context of and was associated with an international armed conflict.

5. The perpetrator was aware of factual circumstances that established the existence of an armed conflict.

Article 8(2)(a)(iv) War crime of destruction and appropriation of property
Elements

1. The perpetrator destroyed or appropriated certain property.

2. The destruction or appropriation was not justified by military necessity.

3. The destruction or appropriation was extensive and carried out wantonly.

4. Such property was protected under one or more of the Geneva Conventions of 1949.

5. The perpetrator was aware of the factual circumstances that established that protected status.

6. The conduct took place in the context of and was associated with an international armed conflict.

7. The perpetrator was aware of factual circumstances that established the existence of an armed conflict.

Article 8(2)(a)(v) War crime of compelling service in hostile forces
Elements

1. The perpetrator coerced one or more persons, by act or threat, to take part in military operations against that person's own country or forces or otherwise serve in the forces of a hostile power.

2. Such person or persons were protected under one or more of the Geneva Conventions of 1949.

3. The perpetrator was aware of the factual circumstances that established that protected status.

4. The conduct took place in the context of and was associated with an international armed conflict.

5. The perpetrator was aware of factual circumstances that established the existence of an armed conflict.

Article 8(2)(a)(vi) War crime of denying a fair trial
Elements

1. The perpetrator deprived one or more persons of a fair and regular trial by denying judicial guarantees as defined, in particular, in the third and the fourth Geneva Conventions of 1949.

2. Such person or persons were protected under one or more of the Geneva Conventions of 1949.

3. The perpetrator was aware of the factual circumstances that established that protected status.

4. The conduct took place in the context of and was associated with an international armed conflict.

5. The perpetrator was aware of factual circumstances that established the existence of an armed conflict.

Article 8(2)(a)(vii)-1 War crime of unlawful deportation and transfer
Elements

1. The perpetrator deported or transferred one or more persons to another State or to another location.

2. Such person or persons were protected under one or more of the Geneva Conventions of 1949.

3. The perpetrator was aware of the factual circumstances that established that protected status.

4. The conduct took place in the context of and was associated with an international armed conflict.

5. The perpetrator was aware of factual circumstances that established the existence of an armed conflict.

Article 8(2)(a)(vii)-2 War crime of unlawful confinement
Elements

1. The perpetrator confined or continued to confine one or more persons to a certain location.

2. Such person or persons were protected under one or more of the Geneva Conventions of 1949.

3. The perpetrator was aware of the factual circumstances that established that protected status.

4. The conduct took place in the context of and was associated with an international armed conflict.

5. The perpetrator was aware of factual circumstances that established the existence of an armed conflict.

Article 8(2)(a)(viii) War crime of taking hostages
Elements

1. The perpetrator seized, detained or otherwise held hostage one or more persons.

2. The perpetrator threatened to kill, injure or continue to detain such person or persons.

3. The perpetrator intended to compel a State, an international organization, a natural or legal person or a group of persons to act or refrain from acting as an explicit or implicit condition for the safety or the release of such person or persons.

4. Such person or persons were protected under one or more of the Geneva Conventions of 1949.

5. The perpetrator was aware of the factual circumstances that established that protected status.

6. The conduct took place in the context of and was associated with an international armed conflict.

7. The perpetrator was aware of factual circumstances that established the existence of an armed conflict.

Article 8(2)(b)(i) War crime of attacking civilians
Elements

1. The perpetrator directed an attack.

2. The object of the attack was a civilian population as such or individual civilians not taking direct part in hostilities.

3. The perpetrator intended the civilian population as such or individual civilians not taking direct part in hostilities to be the object of the attack.

4. The conduct took place in the context of and was associated with an international armed conflict.

5. The perpetrator was aware of factual circumstances that established the existence of an armed conflict.

Article 8(2)(b)(ii) War crime of attacking civilian objects
Elements
1. The perpetrator directed an attack.
2. The object of the attack was civilian objects, that is, objects which are not military objectives.
3. The perpetrator intended such civilian objects to be the object of the attack.
4. The conduct took place in the context of and was associated with an international armed conflict.
5. The perpetrator was aware of factual circumstances that established the existence of an armed conflict.

Article 8(2)(b)(iii) War crime of attacking personnel or objects involved in a humanitarian assistance or peacekeeping mission
Elements
1. The perpetrator directed an attack.
2. The object of the attack was personnel, installations, material, units or vehicles involved in a humanitarian assistance or peacekeeping mission in accordance with the Charter of the United Nations.
3. The perpetrator intended such personnel, installations, material, units or vehicles so involved to be the object of the attack.
4. Such personnel, installations, material, units or vehicles were entitled to that protection given to civilians or civilian objects under the international law of armed conflict.
5. The perpetrator was aware of the factual circumstances that established that protection.
6. The conduct took place in the context of and was associated with an international armed conflict.
7. The perpetrator was aware of factual circumstances that established the existence of an armed conflict.

Article 8(2)(b)(iv) War crime of excessive incidental death, injury, or damage
Elements
1. The perpetrator launched an attack.
2. The attack was such that it would cause incidental death or injury to civilians or damage to civilian objects or widespread, long-term and severe damage to the natural environment and that such death, injury or damage would be of such an extent as to be clearly excessive in relation to the concrete and direct overall military advantage anticipated
3. The perpetrator knew that the attack would cause incidental death or injury to civilians or damage to civilian objects or widespread, long-term and severe damage to the natural environment and that such death, injury or damage would be of such an extent as to be clearly excessive in relation to the concrete and direct military advantage.
4. The conduct took place in the context of and was associated with an international armed conflict.
5. The perpetrator was aware of factual circumstances that established the existence of an armed conflict.

Article 8(2)(b)(v) War crime of attacking undefended places
Elements
1. The perpetrator attacked one or more towns, villages, dwellings or buildings.
2. Such towns, villages, dwellings or buildings were open for unresisted occupation.
3. Such towns, villages, dwellings or buildings did not constitute military objectives.

4. The conduct took place in the context of and was associated with an international armed conflict.

5. The perpetrator was aware of factual circumstances that established the existence of an armed conflict.

Article 8(2)(b)(vi) War crime of killing or wounding a person *hors de combat*
Elements

1. The perpetrator killed or injured one or more persons.

2. Such person or persons were *hors de combat*.

3. The perpetrator was aware of the factual circumstances that established this status.

4. The conduct took place in the context of and was associated with an international armed conflict.

5. The perpetrator was aware of factual circumstances that established the existence of an armed conflict.

Article 8(2)(b)(vii)-1 War crime of improper use of a flag of truce
Elements

1. The perpetrator used a flag of truce.

2. The perpetrator made such use in order to feign an intention to negotiate when there was no such intention on the part of the perpetrator.

3. The perpetrator knew or should have known of the prohibited nature of such use.

4. The conduct resulted in death or serious personal injury.

5. The perpetrator knew that the conduct could result in death or serious personal injury.

6. The conduct took place in the context of and was associated with an international armed conflict.

7. The perpetrator was aware of factual circumstances that established the existence of an armed conflict.

Article 8(2)(b)(vii)-2 War crime of improper use of a flag, insignia or uniform of the hostile party
Elements

1. The perpetrator used a flag, insignia or uniform of the hostile party.

2. The perpetrator made such use in a manner prohibited under the international law of armed conflict while engaged in an attack.

3. The perpetrator knew or should have known of the prohibited nature of such use.

4. The conduct resulted in death or serious personal injury.

5. The perpetrator knew that the conduct could result in death or serious personal injury.

6. The conduct took place in the context of and was associated with an international armed conflict.

7. The perpetrator was aware of factual circumstances that established the existence of an armed conflict.

Article 8(2)(b)(vii)-3 War crime of improper use of a flag, insignia or uniform of the United Nations
Elements

1. The perpetrator used a flag, insignia or uniform of the United Nations.

2. The perpetrator made such use in a manner prohibited under the international law of armed conflict.

3. The perpetrator knew of the prohibited nature of such use.

4. The conduct resulted in death or serious personal injury.

5. The perpetrator knew that the conduct could result in death or serious personal injury.

6. The conduct took place in the context of and was associated with an international armed conflict.

7. The perpetrator was aware of factual circumstances that established the existence of an armed conflict.

Article 8(2)(b)(vii)-4 War crime of improper use of the distinctive emblems of the Geneva Conventions
Elements

1. The perpetrator used the distinctive emblems of the Geneva Conventions.

2. The perpetrator made such use for combatant purposes in a manner prohibited under the international law of armed conflict.

3. The perpetrator knew or should have known of the prohibited nature of such use.

4. The conduct resulted in death or serious personal injury.

5. The perpetrator knew that the conduct could result in death or serious personal injury.

6. The conduct took place in the context of and was associated with an international armed conflict.

7. The perpetrator was aware of factual circumstances that established the existence of an armed conflict.

Article 8 (2)(b)(viii) The transfer, directly or indirectly, by the Occupying Power of parts of its own civilian population into the territory it occupies, or the deportation or transfer of all or parts of the population of the occupied territory within or outside this territory
Elements

1. The perpetrator:

   (a) Transferred, directly or indirectly, parts of its own population into the territory it occupies; or

   (b) Deported or transferred all or parts of the population of the occupied territory within or outside this territory.

2. The conduct took place in the context of and was associated with an international armed conflict.

3. The perpetrator was aware of factual circumstances that established the existence of an armed conflict.

Article 8(2)(b)(ix) War crime of attacking protected objects
Elements

1. The perpetrator directed an attack.

2. The object of the attack was one or more buildings dedicated to religion, education, art, science or charitable purposes, historic monuments, hospitals or places where the sick and wounded are collected, which were not military objectives.

3. The perpetrator intended such building or buildings dedicated to religion, education, art, science or charitable purposes, historic monuments, hospitals or places where the sick and wounded are collected, which were not military objectives, to be the object of the attack.

4. The conduct took place in the context of and was associated with an international armed conflict.

5. The perpetrator was aware of factual circumstances that established the existence of an armed conflict.

Article 8(2)(b)(x)-1 War crime of mutilation
Elements

1. The perpetrator subjected one or more persons to mutilation, in particular by permanently disfiguring the person or persons, or by permanently disabling or removing an organ or appendage.

2. The conduct caused death or seriously endangered the physical or mental health of such person or persons.

3. The conduct was neither justified by the medical, dental or hospital treatment of the person or persons concerned nor carried out in such person's or persons' interest

4. Such person or persons were in the power of an adverse party.

5. The conduct took place in the context of and was associated with an international armed conflict.

6. The perpetrator was aware of factual circumstances that established the existence of an armed conflict.

Article 8(2)(b)(x)-2 War crime of medical or scientific experiments
Elements

1. The perpetrator subjected one or more persons to a medical or scientific experiment.

2. The experiment caused death or seriously endangered the physical or mental health or integrity of such person or persons.

3. The conduct was neither justified by the medical, dental or hospital treatment of such person or persons concerned nor carried out in such person's or persons' interest.

4. Such person or persons were in the power of an adverse party.

5. The conduct took place in the context of and was associated with an international armed conflict.

6. The perpetrator was aware of factual circumstances that established the existence of an armed conflict.

Article 8(2)(b)(xi) War crime of treacherously killing or wounding
Elements

1. The perpetrator invited the confidence or belief of one or more persons that they were entitled to, or were obliged to accord, protection under rules of international law applicable in armed conflict.

2. The perpetrator intended to betray that confidence or belief.

3. The perpetrator killed or injured such person or persons.

4. The perpetrator made use of that confidence or belief in killing or injuring such person or persons.

5. Such person or persons belonged to an adverse party.

6. The conduct took place in the context of and was associated with an international armed conflict.

7. The perpetrator was aware of factual circumstances that established the existence of an armed conflict.

Article 8(2)(b)(xii) War crime of denying quarter
Elements

1. The perpetrator declared or ordered that there shall be no survivors.

2. Such declaration or order was given in order to threaten an adversary or to conduct hostilities on the basis that there shall be no survivors.

3. The perpetrator was in a position of effective command or control over the subordinate forces to which the declaration or order was directed.

4. The conduct took place in the context of and was associated with an international armed conflict.

5. The perpetrator was aware of factual circumstances that established the existence of an armed conflict.

Article 8(2)(b)(xiii) War crime of destroying or seizing the enemy's property
Elements

1. The perpetrator destroyed or seized certain property.

2. Such property was property of a hostile party.

3. Such property was protected from that destruction or seizure under the international law of armed conflict.

4. The perpetrator was aware of the factual circumstances that established the status of the property.

5. The destruction or seizure was not justified by military necessity.

6. The conduct took place in the context of and was associated with an international armed conflict.

7. The perpetrator was aware of factual circumstances that established the existence of an armed conflict.

Article 8(2)(b)(xiv) War crime of depriving the nationals of the hostile power of rights or actions
Elements

1. The perpetrator effected the abolition, suspension or termination of admissibility in a court of law of certain rights or actions.

2. The abolition, suspension or termination was directed at the nationals of a hostile party.

3. The perpetrator intended the abolition, suspension or termination to be directed at the nationals of a hostile party.

4. The conduct took place in the context of and was associated with an international armed conflict.

5. The perpetrator was aware of factual circumstances that established the existence of an armed conflict.

Article 8(2)(b)(xv) War crime of compelling participation in military operations
Elements

1. The perpetrator coerced one or more persons by act or threat to take part in military operations against that person's own country or forces.

2. Such person or persons were nationals of a hostile party.

3. The conduct took place in the context of and was associated with an international armed conflict.

4. The perpetrator was aware of factual circumstances that established the existence of an armed conflict.

Article 8(2)(b)(xvi) War crime of pillaging
Elements

1. The perpetrator appropriated certain property.

2. The perpetrator intended to deprive the owner of the property and to appropriate it for private or personal use.

3. The appropriation was without the consent of the owner.

4. The conduct took place in the context of and was associated with an international armed conflict.

5. The perpetrator was aware of factual circumstances that established the existence of an armed conflict.

Article 8(2)(b)(xvii) War crime of employing poison or poisoned weapons
Elements

1. The perpetrator employed a substance or a weapon that releases a substance as a result of its employment.

2. The substance was such that it causes death or serious damage to health in the ordinary course of events, through its toxic properties.

3. The conduct took place in the context of and was associated with an international armed conflict.

4. The perpetrator was aware of factual circumstances that established the existence of an armed conflict.

Article 8(2)(b)(xviii) War crime of employing prohibited gases, liquids, materials or devices
Elements

1. The perpetrator employed a gas or other analogous substance or device.

2. The gas, substance or device was such that it causes death or serious damage to health in the ordinary course of events, through its asphyxiating or toxic properties

3. The conduct took place in the context of and was associated with an international armed conflict.

4. The perpetrator was aware of factual circumstances that established the existence of an armed conflict.

Article 8(2)(b)(xix) War crime of employing prohibited bullets
Elements

1. The perpetrator employed certain bullets.

2. The bullets were such that their use violates the international law of armed conflict because they expand or flatten easily in the human body.

3. The perpetrator was aware that the nature of the bullets was such that their employment would uselessly aggravate suffering or the wounding effect.

4. The conduct took place in the context of and was associated with an international armed conflict.

5. The perpetrator was aware of factual circumstances that established the existence of an armed conflict.

Article 8(2)(b)(xx) War crime of employing weapons, projectiles or materials or methods of warfare listed in the Annex to the Statute
Elements

[Elements will have to be drafted once weapons, projectiles or material or methods of warfare have been included in an annex to the Statute.]

Article 8(2)(b)(xxi) War crime of outrages upon personal dignity
Elements

1. The perpetrator humiliated, degraded or otherwise violated the dignity of one or more persons.

2. The severity of the humiliation, degradation or other violation was of such degree as to be generally recognized as an outrage upon personal dignity.

3. The conduct took place in the context of and was associated with an international armed conflict.

4. The perpetrator was aware of factual circumstances that established the existence of an armed conflict.

Article 8(2)(b)(xxii)-1 War crime of rape
Elements

1. The perpetrator invaded the body of a person by conduct resulting in penetration, however slight, of any part of the body of the victim or of the perpetrator with a sexual organ, or of the anal or genital opening of the victim with any object or any other part of the body.

2. The invasion was committed by force, or by threat of force or coercion, such as that caused by fear of violence, duress, detention, psychological oppression or abuse of power, against such person or another person, or by taking advantage of a coercive environment, or the invasion was committed against a person incapable of giving genuine consent

3. The conduct took place in the context of and was associated with an international armed conflict.

4. The perpetrator was aware of factual circumstances that established the existence of an armed conflict.

Article 8(2)(b)(xxii)-2 War crime of sexual slavery
Elements

1. The perpetrator exercised any or all of the powers attaching to the right of ownership over one or more persons, such as by purchasing, selling, lending or bartering such a person or persons, or by imposing on them a similar deprivation of liberty.

2. The perpetrator caused such person or persons to engage in one or more acts of a sexual nature.

3. The conduct took place in the context of and was associated with an international armed conflict.

4. The perpetrator was aware of factual circumstances that established the existence of an armed conflict.

Article 8(2)(b)(xxii)-3 War crime of enforced prostitution
Elements

1. The perpetrator caused one or more persons to engage in one or more acts of a sexual nature by force, or by threat of force or coercion, such as that caused by fear of violence, duress, detention, psychological oppression or abuse of power, against such person or persons or another person, or by taking advantage of a coercive environment or such person's or persons' incapacity to give genuine consent.

2. The perpetrator or another person obtained or expected to obtain pecuniary or other advantage in exchange for or in connection with the acts of a sexual nature.

3. The conduct took place in the context of and was associated with an international armed conflict.

4. The perpetrator was aware of factual circumstances that established the existence of an armed conflict.

Article 8(2)(b)(xxii)-4 War crime of forced pregnancy
Elements

1. The perpetrator confined one or more women forcibly made pregnant, with the intent of affecting the ethnic composition of any population or carrying out other grave violations of international law.

2. The conduct took place in the context of and was associated with an international armed conflict.

3. The perpetrator was aware of factual circumstances that established the existence of an armed conflict.

Article 8(2)(b)(xxii)-5 War crime of enforced sterilization
Elements

1. The perpetrator deprived one or more persons of biological reproductive capacity.

2. The conduct was neither justified by the medical or hospital treatment of the person or persons concerned nor carried out with their genuine consent

3. The conduct took place in the context of and was associated with an international armed conflict.

4. The perpetrator was aware of factual circumstances that established the existence of an armed conflict.

Article 8(2)(b)(xxii)-6 War crime of sexual violence
Elements

1. The perpetrator committed an act of a sexual nature against one or more persons or caused such person or persons to engage in an act of a sexual nature by force, or by threat of force or coercion, such as that caused by fear of violence, duress, detention, psychological oppression or abuse of power, against such person or persons or another person, or by taking advantage of a coercive environment or such person's or persons' incapacity to give genuine consent.

2. The conduct was of a gravity comparable to that of a grave breach of the Geneva Conventions.

3. The perpetrator was aware of the factual circumstances that established the gravity of the conduct.

4. The conduct took place in the context of and was associated with an international armed conflict.

5. The perpetrator was aware of factual circumstances that established the existence of an armed conflict.

Article 8(2)(b)(xxiii) War crime of using protected persons as shields
Elements

1. The perpetrator moved or otherwise took advantage of the location of one or more civilians or other persons protected under the international law of armed conflict.

2. The perpetrator intended to shield a military objective from attack or shield, favour or impede military operations.

3. The conduct took place in the context of and was associated with an international armed conflict.

4. The perpetrator was aware of factual circumstances that established the existence of an armed conflict.

Article 8(2)(b)(xxiv) War crime of attacking objects or persons using the distinctive emblems of the Geneva Conventions
Elements

1. The perpetrator attacked one or more persons, buildings, medical units or transports or other objects using, in conformity with international law, a distinctive emblem or other method of identification indicating protection under the Geneva Conventions.

2. The perpetrator intended such persons, buildings, units or transports or other objects so using such identification to be the object of the attack.

3. The conduct took place in the context of and was associated with an international armed conflict.

4. The perpetrator was aware of factual circumstances that established the existence of an armed conflict.

Article 8(2)(b)(xxv) War crime of starvation as a method of warfare
Elements

1. The perpetrator deprived civilians of objects indispensable to their survival.

2. The perpetrator intended to starve civilians as a method of warfare.

3. The conduct took place in the context of and was associated with an international armed conflict.

4. The perpetrator was aware of factual circumstances that established the existence of an armed conflict.

Article 8(2)(b)(xxvi) War crime of using, conscripting or enlisting children
Elements

1. The perpetrator conscripted or enlisted one or more persons into the national armed forces or used one or more persons to participate actively in hostilities.

2. Such person or persons were under the age of 15 years.

3. The perpetrator knew or should have known that such person or persons were under the age of 15 years.

4. The conduct took place in the context of and was associated with an international armed conflict.

5. The perpetrator was aware of factual circumstances that established the existence of an armed conflict.

Article 8(2)(c)(i)-1 War crime of murder
Elements

1. The perpetrator killed one or more persons.

2. Such person or persons were either *hors de combat*, or were civilians, medical personnel, or religious personnel taking no active part in the hostilities.

3. The perpetrator was aware of the factual circumstances that established this status.

4. The conduct took place in the context of and was associated with an armed conflict not of an international character.

5. The perpetrator was aware of factual circumstances that established the existence of an armed conflict.

Article 8(2)(c)(i)-2 War crime of mutilation
Elements

1. The perpetrator subjected one or more persons to mutilation, in particular by permanently disfiguring the person or persons, or by permanently disabling or removing an organ or appendage.

2. The conduct was neither justified by the medical, dental or hospital treatment of the person or persons concerned nor carried out in such person's or persons' interests.

3. Such person or persons were either *hors de combat,* or were civilians, medical personnel or religious personnel taking no active part in the hostilities.

4. The perpetrator was aware of the factual circumstances that established this status.

5. The conduct took place in the context of and was associated with an armed conflict not of an international character.

6. The perpetrator was aware of factual circumstances that established the existence of an armed conflict.

Article 8(2)(c)(i)-3 War crime of cruel treatment
Elements

1. The perpetrator inflicted severe physical or mental pain or suffering upon one or more persons.

2. Such person or persons were either *hors de combat,* or were civilians, medical personnel, or religious personnel taking no active part in the hostilities.

3. The perpetrator was aware of the factual circumstances that established this status.

4. The conduct took place in the context of and was associated with an armed conflict not of an international character.

5. The perpetrator was aware of factual circumstances that established the existence of an armed conflict.

Article 8(2)(c)(i)-4 War crime of torture
Elements

1. The perpetrator inflicted severe physical or mental pain or suffering upon one or more persons.

2. The perpetrator inflicted the pain or suffering for such purposes as: obtaining information or a confession, punishment, intimidation or coercion or for any reason based on discrimination of any kind.

3. Such person or persons were either *hors de combat,* or were civilians, medical personnel or religious personnel taking no active part in the hostilities.

4. The perpetrator was aware of the factual circumstances that established this status.

5. The conduct took place in the context of and was associated with an armed conflict not of an international character.

6. The perpetrator was aware of factual circumstances that established the existence of an armed conflict.

Article 8(2)(c)(ii) War crime of outrages upon personal dignity
Elements

1. The perpetrator humiliated, degraded or otherwise violated the dignity of one or more persons.

2. The severity of the humiliation, degradation or other violation was of such degree as to be generally recognized as an outrage upon personal dignity.

3. Such person or persons were either *hors de combat,* or were civilians, medical personnel or religious personnel taking no active part in the hostilities.

4. The perpetrator was aware of the factual circumstances that established this status.

5. The conduct took place in the context of and was associated with an armed conflict not of an international character.

6. The perpetrator was aware of factual circumstances that established the existence of an armed conflict.

Article 8(2)(c)(iii) War crime of taking hostages
Elements

1. The perpetrator seized, detained or otherwise held hostage one or more persons.

2. The perpetrator threatened to kill, injure or continue to detain such person or persons.

3. The perpetrator intended to compel a State, an international organization, a natural or legal person or a group of persons to act or refrain from acting as an explicit or implicit condition for the safety or the release of such person or persons.

4. Such person or persons were either *hors de combat,* or were civilians, medical personnel or religious personnel taking no active part in the hostilities.

5. The perpetrator was aware of the factual circumstances that established this status.

6. The conduct took place in the context of and was associated with an armed conflict not of an international character.

7. The perpetrator was aware of factual circumstances that established the existence of an armed conflict.

Article 8(2)(c)(iv) War crime of sentencing or execution without due process
Elements

1. The perpetrator passed sentence or executed one or more persons.

2. Such person or persons were either *hors de combat,* or were civilians, medical personnel or religious personnel taking no active part in the hostilities.

3. The perpetrator was aware of the factual circumstances that established this status.

4. There was no previous judgment pronounced by a court, or the court that rendered judgment was not "regularly constituted", that is, it did not afford the essential guarantees of independence and impartiality, or the court that rendered judgment did not afford all other judicial guarantees generally recognized as indispensable under international law

5. The perpetrator was aware of the absence of a previous judgment or of the denial of relevant guarantees and the fact that they are essential or indispensable to a fair trial.

6. The conduct took place in the context of and was associated with an armed conflict not of an international character.

7. The perpetrator was aware of factual circumstances that established the existence of an armed conflict.

Article 8(2)(e)(i) War crime of attacking civilians
Elements

1. The perpetrator directed an attack.

2. The object of the attack was a civilian population as such or individual civilians not taking direct part in hostilities.

3. The perpetrator intended the civilian population as such or individual civilians not taking direct part in hostilities to be the object of the attack.

4. The conduct took place in the context of and was associated with an armed conflict not of an international character.

5. The perpetrator was aware of factual circumstances that established the existence of an armed conflict.

Article 8(2)(e)(ii) War crime of attacking objects or persons using the distinctive emblems of the Geneva Conventions
Elements

1. The perpetrator attacked one or more persons, buildings, medical units or transports or other objects using, in conformity with international law, a distinctive emblem or other method of identification indicating protection under the Geneva Conventions.

2. The perpetrator intended such persons, buildings, units or transports or other objects so using such identification to be the object of the attack.

3. The conduct took place in the context of and was associated with an armed conflict not of an international character.

4. The perpetrator was aware of factual circumstances that established the existence of an armed conflict.

Article 8(2)(e)(iii) War crime of attacking personnel or objects involved in a humanitarian assistance or peacekeeping mission
Elements

1. The perpetrator directed an attack.

2. The object of the attack was personnel, installations, material, units or vehicles involved in a humanitarian assistance or peacekeeping mission in accordance with the Charter of the United Nations.

3. The perpetrator intended such personnel, installations, material, units or vehicles so involved to be the object of the attack.

4. Such personnel, installations, material, units or vehicles were entitled to that protection given to civilians or civilian objects under the international law of armed conflict.

5. The perpetrator was aware of the factual circumstances that established that protection.

6. The conduct took place in the context of and was associated with an armed conflict not of an international character.

7. The perpetrator was aware of factual circumstances that established the existence of an armed conflict.

Article 8(2)(e)(iv) War crime of attacking protected object
Elements

1. The perpetrator directed an attack.

2. The object of the attack was one or more buildings dedicated to religion, education, art, science or charitable purposes, historic monuments, hospitals or places where the sick and wounded are collected, which were not military objectives.

3. The perpetrator intended such building or buildings dedicated to religion, education, art, science or charitable purposes, historic monuments, hospitals or places where the sick and wounded are collected, which were not military objectives, to be the object of the attack.

4. The conduct took place in the context of and was associated with an armed conflict not of an international character.

5. The perpetrator was aware of factual circumstances that established the existence of an armed conflict.

Article 8(2)(e)(v) War crime of pillaging
Elements

1. The perpetrator appropriated certain property.

2. The perpetrator intended to deprive the owner of the property and to appropriate it for private or personal use.

3. The appropriation was without the consent of the owner.

4. The conduct took place in the context of and was associated with an armed conflict not of an international character.

5. The perpetrator was aware of factual circumstances that established the existence of an armed conflict.

Article 8(2)(e)(vi)-1 War crime of rape
Elements

1. The perpetrator invaded the body of a person by conduct resulting in penetration, however slight, of any part of the body of the victim or of the perpetrator with a sexual organ, or of the anal or genital opening of the victim with any object or any other part of the body.

2. The invasion was committed by force, or by threat of force or coercion, such as that caused by fear of violence, duress, detention, psychological oppression or abuse of power, against such person or another person, or by taking advantage of a coercive environment, or the invasion was committed against a person incapable of giving genuine consent.

3. The conduct took place in the context of and was associated with an armed conflict not of an international character.

4. The perpetrator was aware of factual circumstances that established the existence of an armed conflict.

Article 8(2)(e)(vi)-2 War crime of sexual slavery
Elements

1. The perpetrator exercised any or all of the powers attaching to the right of ownership over one or more persons, such as by purchasing, selling, lending or bartering such a person or persons, or by imposing on them a similar deprivation of liberty.

2. The perpetrator caused such person or persons to engage in one or more acts of a sexual nature.

3. The conduct took place in the context of and was associated with an armed conflict not of an international character.

4. The perpetrator was aware of factual circumstances that established the existence of an armed conflict.

Article 8(2)(e)(vi)-3 War crime of enforced prostitution
Elements

1. The perpetrator caused one or more persons to engage in one or more acts of a sexual nature by force, or by threat of force or coercion, such as that caused by fear of violence, duress, detention, psychological oppression or abuse of power, against such person or persons or

another person, or by taking advantage of a coercive environment or such person's or persons' incapacity to give genuine consent.

2. The perpetrator or another person obtained or expected to obtain pecuniary or other advantage in exchange for or in connection with the acts of a sexual nature.

3. The conduct took place in the context of and was associated with an armed conflict not of an international character.

4. The perpetrator was aware of factual circumstances that established the existence of an armed conflict.

Article 8(2)(e)(vi)-4 War crime of forced pregnancy
Elements

1. The perpetrator confined one or more women forcibly made pregnant, with the intent of affecting the ethnic composition of any population or carrying out other grave violations of international law.

2. The conduct took place in the context of and was associated with an armed conflict not of an international character.

3. The perpetrator was aware of factual circumstances that established the existence of an armed conflict.

Article 8(2)(e)(vi)-5 War crime of enforced sterilization
Elements

1. The perpetrator deprived one or more persons of biological reproductive capacity.

2. The conduct was neither justified by the medical or hospital treatment of the person or persons concerned nor carried out with their genuine consent

3. The conduct took place in the context of and was associated with an armed conflict not of an international character.

4. The perpetrator was aware of factual circumstances that established the existence of an armed conflict.

Article 8(2)(e)(vi)-6 War crime of sexual violence
Elements

1. The perpetrator committed an act of a sexual nature against one or more persons or caused such person or persons to engage in an act of a sexual nature by force, or by threat of force or coercion, such as that caused by fear of violence, duress, detention, psychological oppression or abuse of power, against such person or persons or another person, or by taking advantage of a coercive environment or such person's or persons' incapacity to give genuine consent.

2. The conduct was of a gravity comparable to that of a serious violation of article 3 common to the four Geneva Conventions.

3. The perpetrator was aware of the factual circumstances that established the gravity of the conduct.

4. The conduct took place in the context of and was associated with an armed conflict not of an international character.

5. The perpetrator was aware of factual circumstances that established the existence of an armed conflict.

Article 8(2)(e)(vii) War crime of using, conscripting and enlisting children
Elements

1. The perpetrator conscripted or enlisted one or more persons into an armed force or group or used one or more persons to participate actively in hostilities.

2. Such person or persons were under the age of 15 years.

3. The perpetrator knew or should have known that such person or persons were under the age of 15 years.

4. The conduct took place in the context of and was associated with an armed conflict not of an international character.

5. The perpetrator was aware of factual circumstances that established the existence of an armed conflict.

Article 8(2)(e)(viii) War crime of displacing civilians
Elements

1. The perpetrator ordered a displacement of a civilian population.

2. Such order was not justified by the security of the civilians involved or by military necessity.

3. The perpetrator was in a position to effect such displacement by giving such order.

4. The conduct took place in the context of and was associated with an armed conflict not of an international character.

5. The perpetrator was aware of factual circumstances that established the existence of an armed conflict.

Article 8(2)(e)(ix) War crime of treacherously killing or wounding
Elements

1. The perpetrator invited the confidence or belief of one or more combatant adversaries that they were entitled to, or were obliged to accord, protection under rules of international law applicable in armed conflict.

2. The perpetrator intended to betray that confidence or belief.

3. The perpetrator killed or injured such person or persons.

4. The perpetrator made use of that confidence or belief in killing or injuring such person or persons.

5. Such person or persons belonged to an adverse party

6. The conduct took place in the context of and was associated with an armed conflict not of an international character.

7. The perpetrator was aware of factual circumstances that established the existence of an armed conflict.

Article 8(2)(e)(x) War crime of denying quarter
Elements

1. The perpetrator declared or ordered that there shall be no survivors.

2. Such declaration or order was given in order to threaten an adversary or to conduct hostilities on the basis that there shall be no survivors.

3. The perpetrator was in a position of effective command or control over the subordinate forces to which the declaration or order was directed.

4. The conduct took place in the context of and was associated with an armed conflict not of an international character.

5. The perpetrator was aware of factual circumstances that established the existence of an armed conflict.

Article 8(2)(e)(xi)-I War crime of mutilation
Elements

1. The perpetrator subjected one or more persons to mutilation, in particular by permanently disfiguring the person or persons, or by permanently disabling or removing an organ or appendage.

2. The conduct caused death or seriously endangered the physical or mental health of such person or persons.

3. The conduct was neither justified by the medical, dental or hospital treatment of the person or persons concerned nor carried out in such person's or persons' interest.

4. Such person or persons were in the power of another party to the conflict.

5. The conduct took place in the context of and was associated with an armed conflict not of an international character.

6. The perpetrator was aware of factual circumstances that established the existence of an armed conflict.

Article 8(2)(e)(xi)-2 War crime of medical or scientific experiments
Elements

1. The perpetrator subjected one or more persons to a medical or scientific experiment.

2. The experiment caused the death or seriously endangered the physical or mental health or integrity of such person or persons.

3. The conduct was neither justified by the medical, dental or hospital treatment of such person or persons concerned nor carried out in such person's or persons' interest.

4. Such person or persons were in the power of another party to the conflict.

5. The conduct took place in the context of and was associated with an armed conflict not of an international character.

6. The perpetrator was aware of factual circumstances that established the existence of an armed conflict.

Article 8(2)(e)(xii) War crime of destroying or seizing the enemy's property
Elements

1. The perpetrator destroyed or seized certain property.

2. Such property was property of an adversary.

3. Such property was protected from that destruction or seizure under the international law of armed conflict.

4. The perpetrator was aware of the factual circumstances that established the status of the property.

5. The destruction or seizure was not required by military necessity.

6. The conduct took place in the context of and was associated with an armed conflict not of an international character.

7. The perpetrator was aware of factual circumstances that established the existence of an armed conflict.

2. DOMESTIC

DOCUMENT 56

South African Promotion of National Unity and Reconciliation Act 1995 (as amended)

Act 95–34, 2 July 1995

The South African Promotion of National Unity and Reconciliation Act 1995 (the Act) was passed by the South African Parliament on 2 July 1995 and came fully into effect in stages on 1 December 1995, 10 April 1996 and 1 June 1996. It has been amended on two occasions, first by the Promotion of National Unity and Reconciliation Amendment Act 1995 (Act 95–87) and, secondly, by the Promotion of National Unity and Reconciliation Second Amendment Act 1997 (Act 97–84).

The Act was introduced to facilitate the transition from the internationally-condemned apartheid system to a fully functioning democratic system of government within South Africa. Particular focus was given to addressing human rights violations. The purpose of the Act is stated in the preamble which envisages the creation of a Truth and Reconciliation Commission which was itself made up of three committees: a Committee on Human Rights Violations; a Committee on Amnesty; and a Committee on Reparation and Rehabilitation.

The purpose of the Truth and Reconciliation Commission was to establish as complete a picture as possible of the causes, nature and extent of the gross violations of human rights from 1 March 1960 to the cut-off date of 10 May 1994 which was the date of President Mandela's inauguration; facilitating the granting of amnesties to persons making full disclosure of relevant facts; establishing and making known the fate or whereabouts of victims; and compiling a report providing as comprehensive an account as possible of the activities and findings of the commission. The commission was made up of 17 commissioners and was chaired by Archbishop Desmond Tutu. Each of the commissioners sat on one of the three committees alongside other individuals appointed by the commission.

The Committee on Human Rights Violations was charged with dealing with matters pertaining to investigations of gross violations of human rights (Section 3(3)(a)). The constitution and specific powers of the committee are stated in Chapter 3 of the Act and include the power to initiate inquiries, gather information, determine facts and record allegations and complaints of gross violations of human rights (Section 14(1)(a)). The Committee on Amnesty dealt with matters relating to amnesties (Section 3(3)(b)). Its constitution and specific powers are contained in Chapter 4 of the Act and include the power to grant amnesties where 'the act, omission or offence to which the application [for amnesty] relates is an act associated with a political objective committed in the course of the conflicts of the past' (Section 20(1)(b)) and where the applicant has made full disclosure of all relevant facts (Section 20(1)(c)). The Committee on Reparation and Rehabilitation was charged with dealing with matters referred to it regarding reparations (Section 3(3)(c)) (see also Chapter 5). Referrals to the Committee on Reparation and Rehabilitation could be made by the commission and by each of the other two committees (Section 25). Chapter 6 of the Act deals procedural matters relating to investigations and hearings by the commission.

The commission, which was based in Cape Town, South Africa, began its work on 16 December 1995 and presented its final report on 28 October 1998, although amnesty hearings and decisions continued until 2001. In total, 849 people were granted amnesty from a total of 7,112 applicants.

See Truth and Reconciliation Commission of South Africa Report *(5 volumes, 1998) and the comprehensive evaluation, published under the title* Truth and Reconciliation Commission of South Africa Final Report *as Volume 6 (2003).*

Act to provide for the investigation and the establishment of as complete a picture as possible of the nature, causes and extent of gross violations of human rights committed during the period from 1 March 1960 to the cut-off date contemplated in the Constitution, within or outside the Republic, emanating from the conflicts of the past, and the fate or whereabouts of the victims of such violations; the granting of amnesty to persons who make full disclosure of all the relevant facts relating to acts associated with a political objective committed in the course of the conflicts of the past during the said period; affording victims an opportunity to relate the violations they suffered; the taking of measures aimed at the granting of reparation to, and the rehabilitation and the restoration of the human and civil dignity of, victims of violations of human rights; reporting to the Nation about such violations and victims; the making of recommendations aimed at the prevention of the commission of gross violations of human rights; and for the said purposes to provide for the establishment of a Truth and Reconciliation Commission, a Committee on Human Rights Violations, a Committee on Amnesty and a Committee on Reparation and Rehabilitation; and to confer certain powers on, assign certain functions to and impose certain duties upon that Commission and those Committees; and to provide for matters connected therewith.

Since the Constitution of the Republic of South Africa, 1993 (Act No 200 of 1993), provides a historic bridge between the past of a deeply divided society characterized by strife, conflict, untold suffering and injustice, and a future founded on the recognition of human rights, democracy and peaceful co-existence for all South Africans, irrespective of colour, race, class, belief or sex;

And since is deemed necessary to establish the truth in relation to past events as well as the motives for and circumstances in which gross violations of human rights have occurred, and to make the findings known in order to prevent a repetition of such acts in future;

And since the Constitution states that the pursuit of national unity, the well-being of all South African citizens and peace require reconciliation between the people of South Africa and the reconstruction of society;

And since the Constitution states that there is a need for understanding but not for vengeance, a need for reparation but not for retaliation, a need for ubuntu but not for victimization;

And since the Constitution states that in order to advance such reconciliation and reconstruction amnesty shall be granted in respect of acts, omissions and offences associated with political objectives committed in the course of the conflicts of the past;

And since the Constitution provides that Parliament shall under the Constitution adopt a law which determines a firm cut-off date, which shall be a date after 8 October 1990 and before the cut-off date envisaged in the Constitution, and providing for the mechanisms, criteria and procedures, including tribunals, if any, through which such amnesty shall be dealt with;

Be it therefore enacted by the Parliament of the Republic of South Africa, as follows:

Chapter 1 Interpretation and application

Definitions

Section 1

1. In this Act, unless the context otherwise indicates:

    (i)   "act associated with a political objective" has the meaning ascribed thereto in section 20(2) and (3);

    (ii)   "article" includes any evidence, book, document, file, object, writing, recording or transcribed computer printout produced by any mechanical or electronic device or any device by means of which information is recorded, stored or transcribed;

    (iii)   "Commission" means the Truth and Reconciliation Commission established by section 2;

    (iv)   "commissioner" means a member of the Commission appointed in terms of section 7(2)(a);

    (v)   "committee" means the Committee on Human Rights Violations, the Committee on Amnesty or the Committee on Reparation and Rehabilitation, as the case may be;

    (vi)   "Constitution" means the Constitution of the Republic of South Africa, 1993 (Act No 200 of 1993);

    (vii)   "cut-off date" means the latest date allowed as the cut-off date in terms of the Constitution as set out under the heading "National Unity and Reconciliation";

    (viii) "former state" means any state or territory which was established by an Act of Parliament or by proclamation in terms of such an Act prior to the commencement of the Constitution and the territory of which now forms part of the Republic;

    (ix)   "gross violation of human rights" means the violation of human rights through:

            (a)   the killing, abduction, torture or severe ill-treatment of any person; or

            (b)   any attempt, conspiracy, incitement, instigation, command or procurement to commit an act referred to in paragraph (a), which emanated from conflicts of the past and which was committed during the period 1 March 1960 to the cut-off date within or outside the Republic, and the commission of which was advised, planned, directed, commanded or ordered, by any person acting with a political motive;

    (x)   "joint committee" means a joint committee of the Houses of Parliament appointed in accordance with the Standing Orders of Parliament for the purpose of considering matters referred to it in terms of this Act;

    (xi)   "Minister" means the Minister of Justice;

    (xii)   "prescribed" means prescribed by regulation made under section 40;

    (xiv)   "reparation" includes any form of compensation, *ex gratia* payment, restitution, rehabilitation or recognition;

    (xv)   "Republic" means the Republic of South Africa referred to in section 1.2 of the Constitution;

    (xvi)   "security forces" includes any full-time or part-time:

            (a)   member or agent of the South African Defence Force, the South African Police, the National Intelligence Service, the Bureau of State Security, the Department of Correctional Services, or any of their organs;

            (b)   member or agent of a defence force, police force, intelligence agency or prison service of any former state, or any of their organs;

    (xvii) "State" means the State of the Republic;

    (xviii) "subcommittee" means any subcommittee established by the Commission in terms of section 5(c);

(xix) "victims" includes:

    (a) persons who, individually or together with one or more persons, suffered harm in the form of physical or mental injury, emotional suffering, pecuniary loss or a substantial impairment of human rights

        (i) as a result of a gross violation of human rights; or

        (ii) as a result of an act associated with a political objective for which amnesty has been granted;

    (b) persons who, individually or together with one or more persons, suffered harm in the form of physical or mental injury, emotional suffering, pecuniary loss or a substantial impairment of human rights, as a result of such person intervening to assist persons contemplated in paragraph (a) who were in distress or to prevent victimization of such persons; and

    (c) such relatives or dependants of victims as may be prescribed.

2. For the purposes of sections 10.1, 2 and 3 and 11 and Chapters 6 and 7 "Commission" shall be construed as including a reference to "committee" or "subcommittee", as the case may be, and "Chairperson", "Vice-Chairperson" or "commissioner" shall be construed as including a reference to the chairperson, vice-chairperson or a member of a committee or subcommittee, as the case may be.

Chapter 2 Truth and Reconciliation Commission

Establishment and seat of Truth and Reconciliation Commission
Section 2

1. There is hereby established a juristic person to be known as the Truth and Reconciliation Commission.

2. The seat of the Commission shall be determined by the President.

Objectives of Commission
Section 3

1. The objectives of the Commission shall be to promote national unity and reconciliation in a spirit of understanding which transcends the conflicts and divisions of the past by:

    (a) establishing as complete a picture as possible of the causes, nature and extent of the gross violations of human rights which were committed during the period from 1 March 1960 to the cut-off date, including the antecedents, circumstances, factors and context of such violations, as well as the perspectives of the victims and the motives and perspectives of the persons responsible for the commission of the violations, by conducting investigations and holding hearings;

    (b) facilitating the granting of amnesty to persons who make full disclosure of all the relevant facts relating to acts associated with a political objective and comply with the requirements of this Act;

    (c) establishing and making known the fate or whereabouts of victims and by restoring the human and civil dignity of such victims by granting them an opportunity to relate their own accounts of the violations of which they are the victims, and by recommending reparation measures in respect of them;

    (d) compiling a report providing as comprehensive an account as possible of the activities and findings of the Commission contemplated in paragraphs (a), (b) and (c), and which contains recommendations of measures to prevent the future violations of human rights.

2. The provisions of subsection 1 shall not be interpreted as limiting the power of the Commission to investigate or make recommendations concerning any matter with a view to promoting or achieving national unity and reconciliation within the context of this Act.

3. In order to achieve the objectives of the Commission:

(a) the Committee on Human Rights Violations, as contemplated in Chapter 3, shall deal, among other things, with matters pertaining to investigations of gross violations of human rights;

(b) the Committee on Amnesty, as contemplated in Chapter 4, shall deal with matters relating to amnesty;

(c) the Committee on Reparation and Rehabilitation, as contemplated in Chapter 5, shall deal with matters referred to it relating to reparations;

(d) the investigating unit referred to in section 5(d) shall perform the investigations contemplated in section 28.4(a); and

(e) the subcommittees, referred to in subsection 5(c), shall exercise, perform and carry out the powers, functions and duties conferred upon, assigned to or imposed upon them by the Commission.

Functions of Commission
Section 4

The functions of the Commission shall be to achieve its objectives, and to that end the Commission shall:

(a) facilitate, and where necessary initiate or coordinate, inquiries into:

(i) gross violations of human rights, including violations which were part of a systematic pattern of abuse;

(ii) the nature, causes and extent of gross violations of human rights, including the antecedents, circumstances, factors, context, motives and perspectives which led to such violations;

(iii) the identity of all persons, authorities, institutions and organisations involved in such violations;

(iv) the question whether such violations were the result of deliberate planning on the part of the State or a former state or any of their organs, or of any political organisation, liberation movement or other group or individual; and

(v) accountability, political or otherwise, for any such violation;

(b) facilitate, and initiate or coordinate, the gathering of information and the receiving of evidence from any person, including persons claiming to be victims of such violations or the representatives of such victims, which establish the identity of victims of such violations, their fate or present whereabouts and the nature and extent of the harm suffered by such victims;

(c) facilitate and promote the granting of amnesty in respect of acts associated with political objectives, by receiving from persons desiring to make a full disclosure of all the relevant facts relating to such acts, applications for the granting of amnesty in respect of such acts, and transmitting such applications to the Committee on Amnesty for its decision, and by publishing decisions granting amnesty, in the Gazette;

(d) determine what articles have been destroyed by any person in order to conceal violations of human rights or acts associated with a political objective;

(e) prepare a comprehensive report which sets out its activities and findings, based on factual and objective information and evidence collected or received by it or placed at its disposal;

(f) make recommendations to the President with regard to:

(i) the policy which should be followed or measures which should be taken with regard to the granting of reparation to victims or the taking of other measures aimed at rehabilitating and restoring the human and civil dignity of victims;

    (ii) measures which should be taken to grant urgent interim reparation to victims;

(g) make recommendations to the Minister with regard to the development of a limited witness protection programme for the purposes of this Act;

(h) make recommendations to the President with regard to the creation of institutions conducive to a stable and fair society and the institutional, administrative and legislative measures which should be taken or introduced in order to prevent the commission of violations of human rights.

Powers of Commission
Section 5

In order to achieve its objectives and to perform its functions the Commission shall have the power to:

(a) determine the seat, if any, of every committee;

(b) establish such offices as it may deem necessary for the performance of its functions;

(c) establish subcommittees to exercise, carry out or perform any of the powers, duties and functions assigned to them by the Commission;

(d) conduct any investigation or hold any hearing it may deem necessary and establish the investigating unit referred to in section 28;

(e) refer specific or general matters to, give guidance and instructions to, or review the decisions of, any committee, subcommittee or the investigating unit with regard to the exercise of its powers, the performance of its functions and the carrying out of its duties, the working procedures which should be followed and the divisions which should be set up by any committee in order to deal effectively with the work of the committee: Provided that no decision, or the process of arriving at such a decision, of the Committee on Amnesty regarding any application for amnesty shall be reviewed by the Commission;

(f) direct any committee or subcommittee to make information which is has in its possession available to any other committee or subcommittee;

(g) direct the submission of and receive reports or interim reports from any committee, subcommittee or investigating unit;

(h) have the administrative and incidental work connected with the exercise of its powers, the execution of its duties or the performance of its functions carried out by persons:

    (i) employed or appointed by it;

    (ii) seconded to its service by any department of State at the request of the Commission and after consultation with the Public Service Commission;

    (iii) appointed by it for the performance of specified tasks;

(i) in consultation with the Minister and through diplomatic channels, obtain permission from the relevant authority of a foreign country to receive evidence or gather information in or from that country;

(j) enter into an agreement with any person, including any department of State, in terms of which the Commission will be authorized to make use of any of the facilities, equipment or personnel belonging to or under the control or in the employment of such person or department;

(k) recommend to the President that steps be taken to obtain an order declaring a person to be dead;

(l) hold meetings at any place within or outside the Republic;

(m) on its own initiative or at the request of any interested person inquire or investigate into any matter in terms of this Act, including the disappearance of any person or group of persons.

Certain powers shall be exercised in consultation with the Minister.

Section 6
Subject to the provisions of section 45, any power referred to in section 5(a), (b) and (c), and, if it is to be exercised outside the Republic, any power referred to in sections 5(d) and (1), 10.1 and 29.1, shall be exercised in consultation with the Minister.

Constitution of Commission
Section 7
1. The Commission shall consist of not fewer than 11 and not more than 17 commissioners, as may be determined by the President in consultation with the Cabinet.

2. (a) The President shall appoint the commissioners in consultation with the Cabinet.

    (b) The commissioners shall be fit and proper persons who are impartial and who do not have a high political profile: Provided that not more than two persons who are not South African citizens may be appointed as commissioners.

3. The President shall make the appointment of the commissioners known by proclamation in the Gazette.

4. The President shall designate one of the commissioners as the Chairperson, and another as the Vice-Chairperson, of the Commission.

5. A commissioner appointed in terms of subsection (2)(a) shall, subject to the provisions of subsections (6) and (7), hold office for the duration of the Commission.

6. A commissioner may at any time resign as commissioner by tendering his or her resignation in writing to the President.

7. The President may remove a commissioner from office on the grounds of misbehaviour, incapacity or incompetence, as determined by the joint committee and upon receipt of an address from the National Assembly and an address from the Senate.

8. If any commissioner tenders his or her resignation under subsection (6), or is removed from office under subsection 7, or dies, the President in consultation with the Cabinet, may fill the vacancy by appointing a person for the unexpired portion of the term of office of his or her predecessor or may allow the seat vacated as a result of a resignation, removal from office or death to remain vacant.

Principles to govern actions of Commission when dealing with victims
Section 11
When dealing with victims the actions of the Commission shall be guided by the following principles:

(a) Victims shall be treated with compassion and respect for their dignity;

(b) victims shall be treated equally and without discrimination of any kind, including race, colour, gender, sex, sexual orientation, age, language, religion, nationality, political or other opinion, cultural beliefs or practices, property, birth or family status, ethnic or social origin or disability;

(c) procedures for dealing with applications by victims shall be expeditious, fair, inexpensive and accessible;

(d) victims shall be informed through the press and any other medium of their rights in seeking redress through the Commission, including information of:

   (i) the role of the Commission and the scope of its activities;

   (ii) the right of victims to have their views and submissions presented and considered at appropriate stages of the inquiry;

(e) appropriate measures shall be taken in order to minimize inconvenience to victims and, when necessary, to protect their privacy, to ensure their safety as well as that of their families and of witnesses testifying on their behalf, and to protect them from intimidation;

(f) appropriate measures shall be taken to allow victims to communicate in the language of their choice;

(g) informal mechanisms for the resolution of disputes, including mediation, arbitration and any procedure provided for by customary law and practice shall be applied, where appropriate, to facilitate reconciliation and redress for victims.

Chapter 3 Investigation of Human Rights Violations

Committee on Human Rights Violations
Section 12

There is hereby established a committee to be known as the Committee on Human Rights Violations, which shall in this Chapter be referred to as the Committee.

Constitution of Committee
Section 13

1. The Committee shall consist of:

   (a) (i) a Chairperson; and

       (ii) two Vice-Chairpersons, who shall be commissioners designated by the Commission;

   (b) such other commissioners as may be appointed by the Commission; and

   (c) not more than ten other members.

2. The Commission shall appoint, as the members referred to in subsection 1(c), South African citizens who are fit and proper persons and broadly representative of the South African community and shall, when making such appointments, give preference to persons possessing knowledge of the content and application of human rights or of investigative or fact-finding procedures.

3. Any vacancies in the Committee shall be filled in accordance with this section.

Powers, duties and functions of Committee
Section 14

1. In addition to the powers, duties and functions conferred on, imposed upon and assigned to it in this Act, and for the purpose of achieving the objectives of the Commission, referred to in section 3.1(a), (c) and (d):

   (a) the Committee shall:

       (i) institute the inquiries referred to in section 4(a);

       (ii) gather the information and receive the evidence referred to in section 4(b);

       (iii) determine the facts contemplated in section 4(d);

       (iv) take into account the gross violations of human rights for which indemnity has been granted during the period between 1 March 1960 and the date of commencement of this Act or for which prisoners were released or had their sentences remitted for the sake of reconciliation and for the finding of peaceful solutions during that period;

       (v) record allegations and complaints of gross violations of human rights;

   (b) the Committee may:

       (i) collect or receive from any organisation, commission or person, articles relating to gross violations of human rights;

       (ii) make recommendations to the Commission with regard to the matters referred to in section 4(f), (g) or (h);

       (iii) make information which is in its possession available to a committee referred to in Chapter 4 or 5, a subcommittee or the investigating unit;

(iv) submit to the Commission interim reports indicating the progress made by the Committee with its activities or with regard to any other particular matter in terms of this Act;

(v) exercise the powers referred to in Chapters 6 and 7.

2. The Committee shall at the conclusion of its functions submit to the Commission a comprehensive report of all its activities and findings in connection with the performance of its functions and the carrying out of its duties in terms of this Act.

Referrals to Committee on Reparation and Rehabilitation
Section 15

1. When the Committee finds that a gross violation of human rights has been committed and if the Committee is of the opinion that a person is a victim of such violation, it shall refer the matter to the Committee on Reparation and Rehabilitation for its consideration in terms of section 26.

2. After a referral to the Committee on Reparation and Rehabilitation has been made by the Committee in terms of subsection (1), it shall, at the request of the Committee on Reparation and Rehabilitation, furnish that Committee with all the evidence and other information relating to the victim concerned or conduct such further investigation or hearing as the said Committee may require.

Chapter 4 Amnesty mechanisms and procedures

Committee on Amnesty
Section 16

There is hereby established a committee to be known as the Committee on Amnesty, which shall in this Chapter be referred to as the Committee.

Constitution of Committee
Section 17

1. The Committee shall consist of a Chairperson, a Vice-Chairperson and not more than 17 other members who are fit and proper persons, appropriately qualified, South African citizens and broadly representative of the South African community.

2. The President shall appoint the Chairperson, the Vice-Chairperson, one other person and, after consultation with the Commission, two commissioners as members of the Committee.

3. The Chairperson of the Committee shall be:

(a) a judge as defined in section 1(1) of the Judges' Remuneration and Conditions of Employment Act, 1989 (Act No 88 of 1989); or

(b) a judge who has been discharged from active service in terms of section 3 of the said Act.

4. Any vacancies in the Committee shall be filled in accordance with this section.

Applications for granting of amnesty
Section 18

1. Any person who wishes to apply for amnesty in respect of any act, omission or offence on the grounds that it is an act associated with a political objective, shall within 12 months from the date of the proclamation referred to in section 7.3, or such extended period as may be prescribed, submit such an application to the Commission in the prescribed form.

2. The Committee shall give priority to applications of persons in custody and shall prescribe measures in respect of such applications after consultation with the Minister and the Minister of Correctional Services.

Committee shall consider applications for Amnesty
Section 19

1. Upon receipt of any application for amnesty, the Committee may return the application to the applicant and give such directions in respect of the completion and submission of the application as may be necessary or request the applicant to provide such further particulars as it may deem necessary.

2. The Committee shall investigate the application and make such enquiries as it may deem necessary.

3. After such investigation,

   (a) the Committee may:

   (i) inform the applicant that the application, judged on the particulars or further particulars contained in the application or provided by the applicant or revealed as a result of enquiries made by the Committee, if any, does not relate to an act associated with a political objective;

   (ii) afford the applicant the opportunity to make a further submission; and

   (iii) decide whether the application, judged on the particulars referred to in subparagraph (i), and in such further submission, relates to such an act associated with a political objective, and if it is satisfied that the application does not relate to such an act, in the absence of the applicant and without holding a hearing refuse the application and inform the applicant accordingly; or

   (b) the Committee may, if it is satisfied that:

   (i) the requirements mentioned in section 20(i) have been complied with;

   (ii) there is no need for a hearing; and

   (iii) the act, omission or offence to which the application relates, does not constitute a gross violation of human rights, in the absence of the applicant and without holding a hearing, grant amnesty and inform the applicant accordingly.

4. If an application has not been dealt with in terms of subsection 3, the Committee shall conduct a hearing as contemplated in Chapter 6 and shall, subject to the provisions of section 33:

   (a) in the prescribed manner, notify the applicant and any victim or person implicated, or having an interest in the application, of the place where and the time when the application will be heard and considered;

   (b) inform the persons referred to in paragraph (a) of their right to be present at the hearing and to testify, adduce evidence and submit any article to be taken into consideration;

   (c) deal with the application in terms of section 20 or 21 by granting or refusing amnesty.

5. (a) The Committee shall, for the purpose of considering and deciding upon an application referred to in subsection 1, have the same powers as those conferred upon the Commission in section 5.1 and (m) and Chapters 6 and 7.

   (b) Notwithstanding the provisions of section 18.1, the Committee may consider jointly the individual applications in respect of any particular act, omission or offence to which such applications relate.

6. If the act, omission or offence which is the subject of an application under section 18 constitutes the ground of any claim in civil proceedings instituted against the person who submitted that application, the court hearing that claim may at the request of such person, if it is satisfied that the other parties to such proceedings have been informed of the request and afforded the opportunity to address the court or to make further submissions in this regard, suspend those proceedings pending the consideration and disposal of the application.

7. If the person who submitted an application under section 18 is charged with any offence constituted by the act or omission to which the application relates, or is standing trial upon a

charge of having committed such an offence, the Committee in consultation with the attorney-general concerned, may request the appropriate authority to postpone the proceedings pending the consideration and disposal of the application for amnesty.

8. (a) Subject to the provisions of section 33, the applications, documentation in connection therewith, further information and evidence obtained before and during an investigation by the Commission, the deliberations conducted in order to come to a decision or to conduct a hearing contemplated in section 33, shall be confidential.

    (b) Subject to the provisions of section 33, the confidentiality referred to in paragraph (a) shall lapse when the Commission decides to release such information or when the hearing commences.

Granting of amnesty and effect thereof
Section 20

1. If the Committee, after considering an application for amnesty, is satisfied that:

    (a) the application complies with the requirements of this Act;

    (b) the act, omission or offence to which the application relates is an act associated with a political objective committed in the course of the conflicts of the past in accordance with the provisions of subsections 2 and 3; and

    (c) the applicant has made a full disclosure of all relevant facts, it shall grant amnesty in respect of that act, omission or offence.

2. In this Act, unless the context otherwise indicates, "act associated with a political objective" means any act or omission which constitutes an offence or delict which, according to the criteria in subsection 3, is associated with a political objective, and which was advised, planned, directed, commanded, ordered or committed within or outside the Republic during the period 1 March 1960 to the cut-off date, by:

    (a) any member or supporter of a publicly known political organisation or liberation movement on behalf of or in support of such organisation or movement, bona fide in furtherance of a political struggle waged by such organisation or movement against the State or any former state or another publicly known political organisation or liberation movement;

    (b) any employee of the State or any former state or any member of the security forces of the State or any former state in the course and scope of his or her duties and within the scope of his or her express or implied authority directed against a publicly known political organisation or liberation movement engaged in a political struggle against the State or a former state or against any members or supporters of such organisation or movement, and which was committed bona fide with the object of countering or otherwise resisting the said struggle;

    (c) any employee of the State or any former state or any member of the security forces of the State or any former state in the course and scope of his or her duties and within the scope of his or her express or implied authority directed:

        (i) in the case of the State, against any former state; or

        (ii) in the case of a former state, against the State or any other former state, whilst engaged in a political struggle against each other or against any employee of the State or such former state, as the case may be, and which was committed bona fide with the object of countering or otherwise resisting the said struggle;

    (d) any employee or member of a publicly known political organisation or liberation movement in the course and scope of his or her duties and within the scope of his or her express or implied authority directed against the State or any former state or any publicly known political organisation or liberation movement engaged in a political struggle against that political organisation or liberation movement or against members of the security forces of the State or any former state or members or supporters of such publicly known political organisation or liberation movement, and which was committed bona fide in furtherance of the said struggle;

(e) any person in the performance of a coup d'etat to take over the government of any former state, or in any attempt thereto;

(f) any person referred to in paragraphs (b), (c) and (d), who on reasonable grounds believed that he or she was acting in the course and scope of his or her duties and within the scope of his or her express or implied authority;

(g) any person who associated himself or herself with any act or omission committed for the purposes referred to in paragraphs (a), (b), (c), (d), (e) and (f).

3. Whether a particular act, omission or offence contemplated in subsection 2 is an act associated with a political objective, shall be decided with reference to the following criteria:

(a) The motive of the person who committed the act, omission or offence;

(b) the context in which the act, omission or offence took place, and in particular whether the act, omission or offence was committed in the course of or as part of a political uprising, disturbance or event, or in reaction thereto;

(c) the legal and factual nature of the act, omission or offence, including the gravity of the act, omission or offence;

(d) the object or objective of the act, omission or offence, and in particular whether the act, omission or offence was primarily directed at a political opponent or State property or personnel or against private property or individuals;

(e) whether the act, omission or offence was committed in the execution of an order of, or on behalf of, or with the approval of, the organisation, institution, liberation movement or body of which the person who committed the act was a member, an agent or a supporter; and

(f) the relationship between the act, omission or offence and the political objective pursued, and in particular the directness and proximity of the relationship and the proportionality of the act, omission or offence to the objective pursued, but does not include any act, omission or offence committed by any person referred to in subsection 2 who acted:

(i) for personal gain:

Provided that an act, omission or offence by any person who acted and received money or anything of value as an informer of the State or a former state, political organisation or liberation movement, shall not be excluded only on the grounds of that person having received money or anything of value for his or her information; or

(ii) out of personal malice, ill-will or spite, directed against the victim of the acts committed.

4. In applying the criteria contemplated in subsection 3, the Committee shall take into account the criteria applied in the Acts repealed by section 48.

5. The Commission shall inform the person concerned and, if possible, any victim, of the decision of the Committee to grant amnesty to such person in respect of a specified act, omission or offence and the Committee shall submit to the Commission a record of the proceedings, which may, subject to the provisions of this Act, be used by the Commission.

6. The Committee shall forthwith by proclamation in the Gazette make known the full names of any person to whom amnesty has been granted, together with sufficient information to identify the act, omission or offence in respect of which amnesty has been granted.

7. (a) No person who has been granted amnesty in respect of an act, omission or offence shall be criminally or civilly liable in respect of such act, omission or offence and no body or organisation or the State shall be liable, and no person shall be vicariously liable, for any such act, omission or offence.

(b) Where amnesty is granted to any person in respect of any act, omission or offence, such amnesty shall have no influence upon the criminal liability of any other person contingent upon the liability of the first-mentioned person.

(c) No person, organisation or state shall be civilly or vicariously liable for an act, omission or offence committed between 1 March 1960 and the cut-off date by a person who is deceased, unless amnesty could not have been granted in terms of this Act in respect of such an act, omission or offence.

8. If any person:

   (a) has been charged with and is standing trial in respect of an offence constituted by the act or omission in respect of which amnesty is granted in terms of this section; or

   (b) has been convicted of, and is awaiting the passing of sentence in respect of, or is in custody for the purpose of serving a sentence imposed in respect of, an offence constituted by the act or omission in respect of which amnesty is so granted, the criminal proceedings shall forthwith upon publication of the proclamation referred to in subsection 6 become void or the sentence so imposed shall upon such publication lapse and the person so in custody shall forthwith be released.

9. If any person has been granted amnesty in respect of any act or omission which formed the ground of a civil judgment which was delivered at any time before the granting of the amnesty, the publication of the proclamation in terms of subsection 6 shall not affect the operation of the judgment in so far as it applies to that person.

10. Where any person has been convicted of any offence constituted by an act or omission associated with a political objective in respect of which amnesty has been granted in terms of this Act, any entry or record of the conviction shall be deemed to be expunged from all official documents or records and the conviction shall for all purposes, including the application of any Act of Parliament or any other law, be deemed not to have taken place: Provided that the Committee may recommend to the authority concerned the taking of such measures as it may deem necessary for the protection of the safety of the public.

Refusal of amnesty and effect thereof
Section 21

1. If the Committee has refused any application for amnesty, it shall as soon as practicable notify:

   (a) the person who applied for amnesty;

   (b) any person who is in relation to the act, omission or offence concerned, a victim; and

   (c) the Commission, in writing of its decision and the reasons for its refusal.

2. (a) If any criminal or civil proceedings were suspended pending a decision on an application for amnesty, and such application is refused, the court concerned shall be notified accordingly.

   (b) No adverse inference shall be drawn by the court concerned from the fact that the proceedings which were suspended pending a decision on an application for amnesty, are subsequently resumed.

Referrals to Committee on Reparation and Rehabilitation
Section 22

1. Where amnesty is granted to any person in respect of any act, omission or offence and the Committee is of the opinion that a person is a victim in relation to that act, omission or offence, it shall refer the matter to the Committee on Reparation and Rehabilitation for its consideration in terms of section 26.

2. Where amnesty is refused by the Committee and if it is of the opinion that:

   (a) the act, omission or offence concerned constitutes a gross violation of human rights; and

   (b) a person is a victim in the matter, it shall refer the matter to the Committee on Reparation and Rehabilitation for consideration in terms of section 26.

Chapter 5 Reparation and rehabilitation of victims

Committee on Reparation and Rehabilitation
Section 23

There is hereby established a committee to be known as the Committee on Reparation and Rehabilitation, which shall in this Chapter be referred to as the Committee.

Constitution of Committee
Section 24

1. The Committee shall consist of:

    (a) a Chairperson;

    (b) a Vice-Chairperson;

    (c) not more than five other members; and

    (d) in addition to the commissioners referred to in subsection 2, such other commissioners as may be appointed to the Committee by the Commission.

2. Commissioners designated by the Commission shall be the Chairperson and Vice-Chairperson of the Committee.

3. The Commission shall for the purpose of subsection 1(c) appoint as members of the Committee fit and proper persons who are appropriately qualified, South African citizens and broadly representative of the South African community.

4. Any vacancies in the Committee shall be filled in accordance with this section.

Powers, duties and functions of Committee
Section 25

1. In addition to the powers, duties and functions in this Act and for the purpose of achieving the Commission's objectives referred to in section 3.1(c) and (d):

    (a) the Committee shall:

        (i) consider matters referred to it by:

            (aa) the Commission in terms of section 5(e);

            (bb) the Committee on Human Rights Violations in terms of section 15.1; and

            (cc) the Committee on Amnesty in terms of section 22.1;

        (ii) gather the evidence referred to in section 4(b);

    (b) the Committee may:

        (i) make recommendations which may include urgent interim measures as contemplated in section 4(f)(ii), as to appropriate measures of reparation to victims;

        (ii) make recommendations referred to in section 4(h);

        (iii) prepare and submit to the Commission interim reports in connection with its activities;

        (iv) may exercise the powers referred to in section 5.1 and (m) and Chapters 6 and 7.

2. The Committee shall submit to the Commission a final comprehensive report on its activities, findings and recommendations.

Applications for reparation
Section 26

1. Any person referred to the Committee in terms of section 25.1(a)(i) may apply to the Committee for reparation in the prescribed form.

2. (a) The Committee shall consider an application contemplated in subsection 1 and may exercise any of the powers conferred upon it by section 25.

    (b) In any matter referred to the Committee, and in respect of which a finding as to whether an act, omission or offence constitutes a gross violation of human rights is required, the Committee shall refer the matter to the Committee on Human Rights Violations to deal with the matter in terms of section 14.

3. If upon consideration of any matter or application submitted to it under subsection 1 and any evidence received or obtained by it concerning such matter or application, the Committee is of the opinion that the applicant is a victim, it shall, having regard to criteria as prescribed, make recommendations as contemplated in section 25.1(b)(i) in an endeavour to restore the human and civil dignity of such victim.

Parliament to consider recommendations with regard to reparation of victims
Section 27

1. The recommendations referred to in section 4(f)(i) shall be considered by the President with a view to making recommendations to Parliament and making regulations.

2. The recommendations referred to in subsection 1 shall be considered by the joint committee and the decisions of the said joint committee shall, when approved by Parliament, be implemented by the President by making regulations.

3. The regulations referred to in subsection 2:

    (a) shall:

        (i)   determine the basis and conditions upon which reparation shall be granted;

        (ii) determine the authority responsible for the application of the regulations; and

    (b) may:

        (i)   provide for the revision and, in appropriate cases, the discontinuance or reduction of any reparation;

        (ii) prohibit the cession, assignment or attachment of any reparation in terms of the regulations, or the right to any such reparation;

        (iii) determine that any reparation received in terms of the regulations shall not form part of the estate of the recipient should such estate be sequestrated; and

        (iv) provide for any other matter which the President may deem fit to prescribe in order to ensure an efficient application of the regulations.

4. The joint committee may also advise the President in respect of measures that should be taken to grant urgent interim reparation to victims.

Chapter 6 Investigations and hearings by Commission

Commission may establish investigating unit
Section 28

1. The Commission may establish an investigating unit which shall consist of such persons, including one or more commissioners, as may be determined by the Commission.

2. The period of appointment of such members shall be determined by the Commission at the time of appointment, but such period may be extended or curtailed by the Commission.

3. The Commission shall appoint a commissioner as the head of the investigating unit.

4. (a) The investigating unit shall investigate any matter failing within the scope of the Commission's powers, functions and duties, subject to the directions of the Commission, and shall at the request of a committee investigate any matter failing within the scope of the powers, functions and duties of that committee, subject to the directions of the committee.

(b) The investigating unit shall in the performance of its functions follow such procedure as may be determined by the Commission or the committee concerned, as the case may be.

5. Subject to section 33, no article or information obtained by the investigating unit shall be made public, and no person except a member of the investigating unit, the Commission, the committee concerned or a member of the staff of the Commission shall have access to such article or information until such time as the Commission or the committee determines that it may be made public or until the commencement of any hearing in terms of this Act which is not held behind closed doors.

Powers of Commission with regard to investigations and hearings
Section 29

1. The Commission may for the purposes of or in connection with the conduct of an investigation or the holding of a hearing, as the case may be:

   (a) at any time before the commencement or in the course of such investigation or hearing conduct an inspection in loco;

   (b) by notice in writing call upon any person who is in possession of or has the custody of or control over any article or other thing which in the opinion of the Commission is relevant to the subject matter of the investigation or hearing to produce such article or thing to the Commission, and the Commission may inspect and, subject to subsection 3, retain any article or other thing so produced for a reasonable time;

   (c) by notice in writing call upon any person to appear before the Commission and to give evidence or to answer questions relevant to the subject matter of the hearing;

   (d) in accordance with section 32 seize any article or thing referred to in paragraph (b) which is relevant to the subject matter of the investigation or hearing.

2. A notice referred to in subsection 1 shall specify the time when and the place where the person to whom it is directed shall appear, shall be signed by a commissioner, shall be served by a member of the staff of the Commission or by a sheriff, by delivering a copy thereof to the person concerned or by leaving it at such person's last known place of residence or business, and shall specify the reason why the article is to be produced or the evidence is to be given.

3. If the Commission is of the opinion that the production of any article in the possession or custody or under the control of the State, any department of State, the Auditor-General or any Attorney-General may adversely affect any intended or pending judicial proceedings or the conduct of any investigation carried out with a view to the institution of judicial proceedings, the Commission shall take steps aimed at the prevention of any undue delay in or the disruption of such investigation or proceedings.

4. The Commission may require any person who in compliance with a requirement in terms of this section appears before it, to take the oath or to make an affirmation and may through the Chairperson or any member of the staff of the Commission administer the oath to or accept an affirmation from such person.

5. No person other than a member of the staff of the Commission or any person required to produce any article or to give evidence shall be entitled or be permitted to attend any investigation conducted in terms of this section, and the Commission may, having due regard to the principles of openness and transparency, declare that any article produced or information submitted at such investigation shall not be made public until the Commission determines otherwise or, in the absence of such a determination, until the article is produced at a hearing in terms of this Act, or at any proceedings in any court of law.

Procedure to be followed at investigations and hearings of Commission, committees and subcommittees
Section 30

1. The Commission and any committee or subcommittee shall in any investigation or hearing follow the prescribed procedure or, if no procedure has been prescribed, the procedure determined by the Commission, or, in the absence of such a determination, in the case of a committee or subcommittee the procedure determined by the committee or subcommittee, as the case may be.

2. If during any investigation by or any hearing before the Commission;

   (a) any person is implicated in a manner which may be to his or her detriment;

   (b) the Commission contemplates making a decision which may be to the detriment of a person who has been so implicated;

   (c) it appears that any person may be a victim, the Commission shall, if such person is available, afford him or her an opportunity to submit representations to the Commission within a specified time with regard to the matter under consideration or to give evidence at a hearing of the Commission.

Compellability of witnesses and inadmissibility of incriminating evidence given before Commission
Section 31

1. Any person who is questioned by the Commission in the exercise of its powers in terms of this Act, or who has been subpoenaed to give evidence or to produce any article at a hearing of the Commission shall, subject to the provisions of subsections 2, 3 and 5, be compelled to produce any article or to answer any question put to him or her with regard to the subject-matter of the hearing notwithstanding the fact that the article or his or her answer may incriminate him or her.

2. A person referred to in subsection 1 shall only be compelled to answer a question or to produce an article which may incriminate him or her if the Commission has issued an order to that effect, after the Commission:

   (a) has consulted with the attorney-general who has jurisdiction;

   (b) has satisfied itself that to require such information from such a person is reasonable, necessary and justifiable in an open and democratic society based on freedom and equality; and

   (c) has satisfied itself that such a person has refused or is likely to refuse to answer a question or produce an article on the grounds that such an answer or article might incriminate him or her.

3. Any incriminating answer or information obtained or incriminating evidence directly or indirectly derived from a questioning in terms of subsection 1 shall not be admissible as evidence against the person concerned in criminal proceedings in a court of law or before any body or institution established by or under any law: Provided that incriminating evidence arising from such questioning shall be admissible in criminal proceedings where the person is arraigned on a charge of perjury or a charge contemplated in section 39(d)(ii) of this Act or in section 319(3) of the Criminal Procedure Act, 1955 (Act No 56 of 1955).

4. Subject to the provisions of this section, the law regarding privilege as applicable to a witness summoned to give evidence in a criminal case in a court of law shall apply in relation to the questioning of a person in terms of subsection 1.

5 Any person appearing before the Commission by virtue of the provisions of subsection 1 shall be entitled to peruse any article referred to in that subsection, which was produced by him or her, as may be reasonably necessary to refresh his or her memory.

Entry upon premises, search for and seizure and removal of certain articles or other things
Section 32

1. Any commissioner, member of the staff of the Commission or police officer authorized thereto by a commissioner may on the authority of an entry warrant, issued in terms of subsection 2, enter upon any premises in or upon which any article or thing:

    (a) which is concerned with or is upon reasonable grounds suspected to be concerned with any matter which is the subject of any investigation in terms of this Act;

    (b) which contains, or is upon reasonable grounds suspected to contain, information with regard to any such matter, is or is upon reasonable grounds suspected to be, and may on the authority of a search warrant, issued in terms of subsection 2:

       (i) inspect and search such premises and there make such inquiries as he or she may deem necessary;

       (ii) examine any article or thing found in or upon such premises;

       (iii) request from the person who is in control of such premises or in whose possession or under whose control any article or thing is when it is found, or who is upon reasonable grounds believed to have information with regard to any article or thing, an explanation or information;

       (iv) make copies of or extracts from any such article found upon or in such premises;

       (v) seize any article or thing found upon or in such premises which he or she upon reasonable grounds suspects to be an article or thing mentioned in paragraph (a) or (b);

       (vi) after having issued a receipt in respect thereof remove any article or thing found on such premises and suspected upon reasonable grounds to be an article or thing mentioned in paragraph (a) or (b), and retain such article or thing for a reasonable period for the purpose of further examination or, in the case of such article, the making of copies thereof or extracts therefrom: Provided that any article or thing that has been so removed, shall be returned as soon as possible after the purpose of such removal has been accomplished.

2. An entry or search warrant referred to in subsection I shall be issued by a judge of the Supreme Court or by a magistrate who has jurisdiction in the area where the premises in question are situated, and shall only be issued if it appears to the judge or magistrate from information on oath that there are reasonable grounds for believing that an article or thing mentioned in paragraph (a) or (b) of subsection I is upon or in such premises, and shall specify which of the acts mentioned in paragraph (b)(i) to (vi) of that subsection may be performed thereunder by the person to whom it is issued.

3. A warrant issued in terms of this section shall be executed by day unless the person who issues the warrant authorizes the execution thereof by night at times which shall be reasonable, and any entry upon or search of any premises in terms of this section shall be conducted with strict regard to decency and order, including:

    (a) a person's right to, respect for and the protection of his or her dignity;

    (b) the right of a person to freedom and security; and

    (c) the right of a person to his or her personal privacy.

4. Any person executing a warrant in terms of this section shall immediately before commencing with the execution:

    (a) identify himself or herself to the person in control of the premises, if such person is present, and hand to such person a copy of the warrant or, if such person is not present, affix such copy to a prominent place on the premises;

    (b) supply such person at his or her request with particulars regarding his or her authority to execute such a warrant.

5. (a) Any commissioner, or any member of the staff of the Commission or police officer at the request of a commissioner, may without a warrant enter upon any premises, other than a private dwelling, and exercise the powers referred to in subsection 1(b)(i) up to and including (vi):

    (i) if the person who is competent to do so consents to such entry, search, seizure and removal; or

    (ii) if he or she upon reasonable grounds believes that;

        (aa) the required warrant will be issued to him or her in terms of subsection (2) if he or she were to apply for such warrant; and

        (bb) the delay caused by the obtaining of any such warrant would defeat the object of the entry, search, seizure and removal.

    (b) Any entry and search in terms of paragraph (a) shall be executed by day, unless the execution thereof by night is justifiable and necessary.

6. (a) Any person who may on the authority of a warrant issued in terms of subsection 2, or under the provisions of subsection 5, enter upon and search any premises, may use such force as may be reasonably necessary to overcome resistance to such entry or search.

    (b) No person may enter upon or search any premises unless he or she has audibly demanded admission to the premises and has notified the purpose of his or her entry, unless such person is upon reasonable grounds of the opinion that any article or thing may be destroyed if such admission is first demanded and such purpose is first notified.

7. If during the execution of a warrant or the conducting of a search in terms of this section, a person claims that an article found on or in the premises concerned contains privileged information and refuses the inspection or removal of such article, the person executing the warrant or conducting the search shall, if he or she is of the opinion that the article contains information which is relevant to the investigation and that such information is necessary for the investigation or hearing, request the registrar of the Supreme Court which has jurisdiction or his or her delegate, to seize and remove that article for safe custody until a court of law has made a ruling on the question whether the information concerned is privileged or not.

8. A warrant issued in terms of this section may be issued on any day and shall be of force until:

    (a) it is executed; or

    (b) it is cancelled by the person who issued it or, if such person is not available, by any person with like authority; or

    (c) the expiry of one month from the day of its issue; or

    (d) the purpose for the issuing of the warrant has lapsed, whichever may occur first.

Hearings of Commission to be open to public
Section 33

1. (a) Subject to the provisions of this section, the hearings of the Commission shall be open to the public.

    (b) If the Commission, in any proceedings before it, is satisfied that:

        (i) it would be in the interest of justice; or

        (ii) there is a likelihood that harm may ensue to any person as a result of the proceedings being open, it may direct that such proceedings be held behind closed doors and that the public or any category thereof shall not be present at such proceedings or any part thereof: Provided that the Commission shall permit any victim who has an interest in the proceedings concerned, to be present.

    (c) An application for proceedings to be held behind closed doors may be brought by a person referred to in paragraph (b) and such application shall be heard behind closed doors.

(d) The Commission may at any time review its decision with regard to the question whether or not the proceedings shall be held behind closed doors.

2. Where the Commission under subsection 1(b) on any grounds referred to in that subsection directs that the public or any category thereof shall not be present at any proceedings or part thereof, the Commission may, subject to the provisions of section 20.6:

(a) direct that no information relating to the proceedings, or any part thereof held behind closed doors, shall be made public in any manner;

(b) direct that no person may, in any manner, make public any information which may reveal the identity of any witness in the proceedings;

(c) give such directions in respect of the record of proceedings as may be necessary to protect the identity of any witness: Provided that the Commission may authorize the publication of so much information as it considers would be just and equitable.

Legal representation
Section 34

1. Any person questioned by an investigation unit and any person who has been subpoenaed or called upon to appear before the Commission is entitled to appoint a legal representative.

2. The Commission may, in order to expedite proceedings, place reasonable limitations with regard to the time allowed in respect of the cross-examination of witnesses or any address to the Commission.

3. The Commission may appoint a legal representative, at a tariff to be prescribed, to appear on behalf of the person concerned if it is satisfied that the person is not financially capable of appointing a legal representative himself or herself, and if it is of the opinion that it is in the interests of justice that the person be represented by a legal representative.

4. A person referred to in subsection 1 shall be informed timeously of his or her right to be represented by a legal representative.

Limited witness protection programme
Section 35

1. The Minister shall, in consultation with the Commission, promote the establishment of a witness protection programme in order to provide for the protection and safety of witnesses in any manner when necessary.

2. The witness protection programme contemplated in subsection 1 shall be prescribed by the President as soon as possible after the date referred to in section 7.3.

3. The regulations providing for a witness protection programme shall:

(a) provide for, among others, the appointment of a private person or the secondment of an official or employee of any department of State in terms of the Public Service Act 1994 (Proclamation No 103 of 1994), to act as the witness protector; and

(b) be Tabled in Parliament for approval.

4. (a) Until such time as the witness protection programme has been established the President may, in consultation with the Minister and the Commission, prescribe interim measures to be followed in order to provide for the protection and the safety of a witness: Provided that the provisions of section 185A of the Criminal Procedure Act 1977 (Act No 51 of 1977), shall, with the necessary changes, apply in the absence of such interim measures.

(b) The interim measures contemplated in paragraph (a) shall be Tabled in Parliament for approval.

5. In this section "witness" means a person who wishes to give evidence, gives evidence or gave evidence for the purposes of this Act and includes any member of his or her family or household whose safety is being threatened by any person or group of persons, whether known to him or her or not, as a result thereof.

Chapter 7 General provisions

Independence of Commission
Section 36

1. The Commission, its commissioners and every member of its staff shall function without political or other bias or interference and shall, unless this Act expressly otherwise provides, be independent and separate from any party, government, administration, or any other functionary or body directly or indirectly representing the interests of any such entity.

2. To the extent that any of the personnel of the entities referred to in subsection 1 may be involved in the activities of the Commission, such personnel will be accountable solely to the Commission.

3. (a) If at any stage during the course of proceedings at any meeting of the Commission it appears that a commissioner has or may have a financial or personal interest which may cause a substantial conflict of interests in the performance of his or her functions as such a commissioner, such a commissioner shall forthwith and fully disclose the nature of his or her interest and absent himself or herself from that meeting so as to enable the remaining commissioners to decide whether the commissioner should be precluded from participating in the meeting by reason of that interest.

   (b) Such a disclosure and the decision taken by the remaining commissioners shall be entered on the record of the proceedings.

4. If a commissioner fails to disclose any conflict of interest as required by subsection 3 and is present at a meeting of the Commission or in any manner participates in the proceedings, such proceedings in relation to the relevant matter shall, as soon as such non-disclosure is discovered, be reviewed and be varied or set aside by the Commission without the participation of the commissioner concerned.

5. Every commissioner and member of a committee shall:

   (a) notwithstanding any personal opinion, preference or party affiliation, serve impartially and independently and perform his or her duties in good faith and without fear, favour, bias or prejudice;

   (b) serve in a full-time capacity to the exclusion of any other duty or obligation arising out of any other employment or occupation or the holding of another office: Provided that the Commission may exempt a commissioner from the provisions of this paragraph.

6. No commissioner or member of a committee shall:

   (a) by his or her membership of the Commission, association, statement, conduct or in any other manner jeopardize his or her independence or in any other manner harm the credibility, impartiality or integrity of the Commission;

   (b) make private use of or profit from any confidential information gained as a result of his or her membership of the Commission or a committee; or

   (c) divulge any such information to any other person except in the course of the performance of his or her functions as such a commissioner or member of a committee.

Commission to decide on disclosure of identity of applicants and witnesses
Section 37

Subject to the provisions of sections 20.6, 33 and 35 the Commission shall, with due regard to the purposes of this Act and the objectives and functions of the Commission, decide to what extent, if at all, the identity of any person who made an application under this Act or gave evidence at the hearing of such application or at any other inquiry or investigation under this Act may be disclosed in any report of the Commission.

Confidentiality of matters and information
Section 38

1. Every commissioner and every member of the staff of the Commission shall, with regard to any matter dealt with by him or her, or information which comes to his or her knowledge in the exercise, performance or carrying out of his or her powers, functions or duties as such a commissioner or member, preserve and assist in the preservation of those matters which are confidential in terms of the provisions of this Act or which have been declared confidential by the Commission.

2. (a) Every commissioner and every member of the staff of the Commission shall, upon taking office, take an oath or make an affirmation in the form specified in subsection 6.

   (b) A commissioner shall take the oath or make the affirmation referred to in paragraph (a) before the Chairperson of the Commission or, in the case of the Chairperson, before the Vice-Chairperson.

   (c) A member of the staff of the Commission shall take the oath or make the affirmation referred to in paragraph (a) before a commissioner.

3. No commissioner shall, except for the purpose of the exercise of his or her powers, the performance of his or her functions or the carrying out of his or her duties or when required by a court of law to do so, or under any law, disclose to any person any information acquired by him or her as such a commissioner or while attending any meeting of the Commission.

4. Subject to the provisions of subsection 3 and sections 20.6 and 33, no person shall disclose or make known any information which is confidential by virtue of any provision of this Act.

5. No person who is not authorized thereto by the Commission shall have access to any information which is confidential by virtue of any provision of this Act.

6. For the purposes of this section the oath or affirmation shall be in the following form: "I, AB, hereby declare under oath/solemnly affirm that I understand and shall honour the obligation of confidentiality imposed upon me by any provision of the Promotion of National Unity and Reconciliation Act 1995, and shall not act in contravention thereof."

Offences and penalties
Section 39

Any person who:

(a) anticipates any finding of the Commission regarding an investigation in a manner calculated to influence its proceedings or such findings;

(b) does anything calculated improperly to influence the Commission in respect of any matter being or to be considered by the Commission in connection with an investigation;

(c) does anything in relation to the Commission which, if done in relation to a court of law, would constitute contempt of court;

   (i) hinders the Commission, any commissioner or member of the staff of the Commission in the exercise, performance or carrying out of its, his or her powers, functions or duties under this Act;

   (ii) wilfully furnishes the Commission, any such commissioner or member with any information which is false or misleading;

(e) (i) having been subpoenaed in terms of this Act, without sufficient cause fails to attend at the time and place specified in the subpoena, or fails to remain in attendance until the conclusion of the meeting in question or until excused from further attendance by the person presiding at that meeting, or fails to produce any article in his or her possession or custody or under his or her control;

(ii) having been subpoenaed in terms of this Act, without sufficient cause refuses to be sworn or to make affirmation as a witness or fails or refuses to answer fully and satisfactorily to the best of his or her knowledge and belief any question lawfully put to him or her; fails to perform any act as required in terms of sections 36.6 and 38;

(g) discloses any confidential information in contravention of any provision of this Act;

(h) destroys any article relating to or in anticipation of any investigation or proceedings in terms of this Act, shall be guilty of an offence and liable on conviction to a fine, or to imprisonment for a period not exceeding two years or to both such fine and such imprisonment.

DOCUMENT 57

The Netherlands/UK Agreement concerning a Scottish Trial in the Netherlands 1998
38 ILM 926 (1998)

This agreement was finalised on 18 September 1998.

Following the destruction of Pan Am Flight 103 over Lockerbie, Scotland, on 21 December 1988, with the death of 270 people, attempts were made through the Security Council to secure the surrender of two Libyans, Abdelbaset Ali Mohmed Megrahi and Al Amin Khalifa Fhimah, for trial in either Scotland or the United States: Security Council Resolutions 731 (1992), 748 (1992) and 883 (1993). This agreement between the Dutch and the British Governments to facilitate the trial in a neutral venue (the Netherlands) was appended in draft to a joint UK/US letter of 24 August 1998 (UN Doc S/1998/795) and was referred to and approved in para 3 of Security Council Resolution 1192 (1998). Its text was finalised and agreed on 18 September 1998.

In the words of Article 2: '[t]his Agreement regulates the sitting of the Scottish Court in the Netherlands and the matters arising out of the trial and the proper functioning of the Scottish Court.' Specifically, the Dutch Government undertook to make premises available for the Scottish court (Article 3(1)) for the duration of the trial and any appeal (Article 3(4)). These premises were declared to be inviolable (Article 5) and under 'the control and authority of the Scottish Court' (Article 6(1)). Internal security was to be the responsibility of the court, with external security falling to the Dutch authorities (Article 7(1)). The Scottish court was accorded legal (juridical) personality under Dutch law (Article 4), immunity from every form of legal process (Article 8) and exemption from a range of taxes and duties (Article 10). Special measures were agreed to allow Scottish advocates and solicitors to pursue their profession at the court (Article 15), and to permit the entry into the Netherlands of witnesses (Article 17) and international observers (Article 18). All the costs incurred by the Dutch government in meeting its obligations under the agreement were to be borne by the UK Government.

Late in 1998, the former NATO airbase at Camp Zeist, eight miles from Utrecht in central Holland, was identified as the court premises. The trial began on 3 May 2000 and concluded on 31 January 2001 with the conviction of Megrahi: HM Advocate v Megrahi and Fhimah *2000 SLT 1399; 40 ILM 582 (2001). His unsuccessful appeal concluded on 14 March 2002 (*Megrahi v HM Advocate *2002 JC 38; 2002 SLT 1473), whereafter the 100-acre site reverted to Dutch authority.*

See Grant, The Lockerbie Trial: A Documentary History *(2004).*

The Government of the Kingdom of the Netherlands and the Government of the United Kingdom of Great Britain and Northern Ireland,

Recalling that On 21 December 1988 Pan American World Airways flight 103 was bombed over Lockerbie in Scotland and 270 persons died;

Recalling that on 13 November 1991, following the presentation of a petition by the Procurator Fiscal for Dumfries, the Sheriff of South Strathclyde, Dumfries and Galloway in Scotland granted a warrant for the arrest of Abdelbaset Ali Mohmed Al Megrahi and Al Amin Khalifa Fhimah ("the accused") on charges of conspiracy to murder, murder and contravention of the Aviation Security Act 1982 of the United Kingdom of Great Britain and Northern Ireland;

Recalling that the Security Council of the United Nations, acting under Chapter VII of the United Nations Charter, in its Resolutions 748 (1992) and 883 (1993), demanded *inter alia* that Libya ensure the appearance of the accused for trial before a Scottish court;

Noting the letter of 24 August 1998 from the Permanent Representatives of the United Kingdom of Great Britain and Northern Ireland and of the United States of America to the Secretary-General of the United Nations proposing that the accused be tried before a Scottish Court sitting in the Kingdom of the Netherlands in accordance with the arrangements set out in that letter (Annex 1);

Having due regard to the decisions of the Security Council, acting under Chapter VII of the Charter of the United Nations, in its Resolution 1192 (1998) (Annex 2);

Whereas the Government of the Kingdom of the Netherlands and the Government of the United Kingdom of Great Britain and Northern Ireland wish to conclude an Agreement regulating the sitting of the Scottish Court in the Netherlands and all matters necessary for the proper functioning in the Netherlands of that Scottish Court for the purpose of the trial of the accused;

Have agreed as follows:

Article 1 Definitions

For the purposes of the present Agreement, the following definitions shall apply:

(a) "the host country" means the Kingdom of the Netherlands;

(b) "the Government" means the Government of the Kingdom of the Netherlands;

(c) "the competent authorities" means national, provincial, municipal and other competent authorities under the law of the host country;

(d) "Vienna Convention" means the Vienna Convention on Diplomatic Relations done at Vienna on 18 April 1961;

(e) "Procurator Fiscal" means the Procurator Fiscal for Dumfries and any person holding a commission from the Lord Advocate to act as Procurator Fiscal or Procurator Fiscal Depute for the purposes of the trial;

(f) "Sheriff" means a Sheriff of South Strathclyde, Dumfries and Galloway in Scotland and any officials of that Sheriffdom;

(g) "the accused" means Abdelbaset Ali Mohmed Al Megrahi and Al Amin Khalifa Fhimah, charged with the offences of conspiracy to murder, murder and contravention of the Aviation Security Act 1982 of the United Kingdom of Great Britain and Northern Ireland ("the offences") specified in the Procurator Fiscal s Petition upon which warrant for arrest was issued by the Sheriff of South Strathclyde, Dumfries and Galloway in Scotland on 3 November 1991:

(h) "Lord Advocate" means the Lord Advocate of Scotland and any officials, Advocate Deputes, Scottish police officers or other persons acting under his directions, or any person directly assisting him;

(i) "the trial" means the public trial of the accused in respect of the offences and any preliminary proceedings, investigative steps, preparations for the trial, preliminary hearings and appeals following service of the indictment, any determination of law or fact and the imposition of penal sanctions, and any appeal by the accused following conviction, all in accordance with Scots law and practice;

(j) "solicitors and advocates" means persons, being legally qualified in Scotland, instructed on behalf of the Lord Advocate or on behalf of the accused,

(k) "witnesses" means persons, including experts, cited to give evidence in the trial of the accused;

(l) "the Scottish Court" means the High Court of Justiciary (including that Scottish Court sitting in an appellate capacity) and the Sheriff Court, sitting in the Netherlands in accordance with the provisions of this Agreement;

(m) "Registrar" means the person designated as such by the Director of Scottish Courts Administration to act on his behalf;

(n) "international observers" means persons nominated, by the Secretary-General of the United Nations, to attend the public hearings, pursuant to arrangements between the Secretary-General and the Government of the United Kingdom;

(o) "the premises of the Scottish Court" means the complex of buildings and land, including installations and facilities, made available by the host country and maintained, occupied and used for the purpose of the trial, including detention of the accused;

(p) "the Parties" means the Government of the Kingdom of the Netherlands and the Government of the United Kingdom of Great Britain and Northern Ireland.

Article 2 Purpose and Scope of the Agreement

This Agreement regulates the sitting of the Scottish Court in the Netherlands and the matters arising out of the trial and the proper functioning of the Scottish Court.

Article 3 The Scottish Court

1. The Government undertakes to host the Scottish Court for the sole purpose, and for the duration, of the trial in the Netherlands. For this purpose the Government shall make available adequate premises for the trial. Within these premises the Scottish Court shall provide reasonable accommodation for persons with a legitimate interest in attending the public trial, including members of the families of the victims or their representatives.

2. The jurisdiction of the Scottish Court is limited to the trial.

3. The Government permits the detention of the accused for the purposes of the trial, and, in the event of conviction, pending their transfer to the United Kingdom, within the premises of the Scottish Court in accordance with Scots law and practice. The enforcement of all other sanctions involving the deprivation of liberty of persons within those premises is not permitted, except in so far as the Scottish Court orders:

   (a) the temporary detention of witnesses transferred in custody to the premises of the Scottish Court;

   (b) the temporary detention of witnesses in the course of their evidence;

   (c) the temporary detention of persons who may have committed offences within the premises of the Scottish Court, including contempt of court; and

   (d) the imprisonment of persons found guilty summarily of contempt of court.

4. The trial will be deemed to be ended when any of the following events, but not necessarily the same event, has occurred in relation to both accused:

   (a) the accused is acquitted;

   (b) the trial is discontinued by process of law preventing any further trial under Scots Law; or

   (c) any judgments of the Scottish Court following conviction have become final and conclusive.

Article 4 Juridical Personality of the Scottish Court

1. The Scottish Court shall possess in the host country full juridical personality. This shall, in particular, include the capacity:

    (a) to contract and to enter into exchanges of letters of understanding with the host country as envisaged in Article 27;

    (b) to acquire and dispose of movable and immovable property; and

    (c) to institute legal proceedings.

2. For the purpose of this article the Scottish Court shall be represented by the Registrar.

Article 5 Inviolability of the Premises of the Scottish Court

1. The premises of the Scottish Court shall be inviolable. The competent authorities shall take whatever action may be necessary to ensure that the Scottish Court shall not be dispossessed of all or any part of the premises of the Scottish Court without the express consent of the Scottish Court. The property, funds and assets of the Scottish Court, wherever located and by whomsoever held, shall be immune from search, seizure, requisition, confiscation, expropriation or any other form of interference, whether by executive, administrative, judicial or legislative action.

2. The competent authorities shall not enter the premises of the Scottish Court to perform any official duty, except with the express consent of, or at the request of, the Registrar or an official designated by him. Judicial actions and the service or execution of legal process, including the seizure of private property, shall not be enforced on the premises of the Scottish Court except with the consent of, and in accordance with conditions approved by, the Registrar.

3. In case of fire or other emergency requiring prompt protective action, or in the event that the competent authorities have reasonable cause to believe that such an emergency has occurred or is about to occur, on the premises of the Scottish Court, the consent of the Registrar, or an official designated by him, to any necessary entry into the premises of the Scottish Court shall be presumed if neither of them can be reached in time.

4. Subject to paragraphs 1, 2 and 3, the competent authorities shall take the necessary action to protect the premises of the Scottish Court against fire or other emergency.

5. The Scottish Court may expel or exclude from the premises of the Scottish Court persons whose presence is not considered conducive to the maintenance of order or the conduct of the trial.

Article 6 Law and Authority on the Premises of the Scottish Court

1. The premises of the Scottish Court shall be under the control and authority of the Scottish Court, as provided in this Agreement.

2. Except as otherwise provided in this Agreement, the laws and regulations of the host country shall apply within the premises of the Scottish Court.

3. The Scottish Court shall have the power to make regulations operative on the premises of the Scottish Court for the purpose of establishing therein the conditions in all respects necessary for the full execution of its functions. The Scottish Court shall promptly inform the competent authorities of regulations thus made in accordance with this paragraph. No law or regulation of the host country, which is inconsistent with a regulation of the Scottish Court, shall, to the extent of such inconsistency; be applicable within the premises of the Scottish Court.

4. Any dispute between the Scottish Court and the host country as to whether a regulation of the Scottish Court is authorised by this article, or as to whether a law or regulation of the host country is inconsistent with any regulation of the Scottish Court authorised by this article, shall be promptly settled by the procedure set out in Article 28. Pending such settlement, the regulation of the Scottish Court shall apply and the law or regulation of the host country shall

be inapplicable within the premises of the Scottish Court to the extent that the Scottish Court claims it to be inconsistent with its regulation.

Article 7 Protection of the Premises of the Scottish Court

1. The competent authorities shall have full responsibility for the external security of the premises of the Scottish Court. They shall exercise due diligence to ensure the security and protection of the Scottish Court and to ensure that the tranquility of the Scottish Court is not disturbed by the intrusion of persons or groups of persons from outside the premises of the Scottish Court or by disturbance in their immediate vicinity, and shall provide to the premises of the Scottish Court the appropriate protection as may be required.

2. If so requested by the Registrar, the competent authorities shall provide adequate police force necessary for the preservation of law and order within the premises of the Scottish Court or in the immediate vicinity thereof, and for the removal of persons therefrom.

Article 8 Immunity of the Scottish Courts

The Scottish Court, its funds, assets and other property, wherever located and by whomsoever held, shall enjoy immunity from every form of legal process, except insofar as in any particular case the Scottish Court has expressly waived its immunity. It is understood, however, that no waiver of immunity shall extend to any measure of execution.

Article 9 Inviolability of Archives and all Documents of the Scottish Court

The archives of the Scottish Court, and in general ail documents and materials made available, belonging to or used by it, wherever located in the host country and by whomsoever held, shall be inviolable.

Article 10 Exemption from Taxes and Duties

1. Within the scope of its official functions, the Scottish Court, its assets, income and other property, shall be exempt from all direct taxes, which include *inter alia* income tax, capital tax, corporation tax, as well as direct taxes levied by local and provincial authorities.

2. The Scottish Court shall:

    (a) on application be granted exemption from motor vehicle tax in respect of vehicles used for its official activities;

    (b) be exempt from all import duties and taxes in respect of goods, including publications and motor vehicles, whose import or export by the Scottish Court is necessary for the exercise of its official activities;

    (c) be exempt from value-added tax paid on any goods, including motor vehicles, or services of substantial value, which are necessary for its official activities. Such claims for exemption shall be made only in respect of goods or services supplied on a recurring basis or involving considerable expenditure;

    (d) be exempt from excise duty included in the price of alcoholic beverages, tobacco products and hydrocarbons, such as fuel oils and motor fuels, purchased by the Scottish Court and necessary for its official activities;

    (e) be exempt from the Tax on Private Passenger Vehicles and Motor Cycles (Belasting van personenauto sen motorrijwielen, BPM) with respect to motor vehicles for its official activities.

3. The exemptions provided for in paragraph 2(c) and (d) may be granted by way of a refund. The exemptions referred to in paragraph 2 shall be applied in accordance with the formal requirements of the host country. These requirements, however, shall not affect the general principles laid down in this article.

4. The provisions of this article shall not apply to taxes and duties which are considered to be charges for public utility services provided at a fixed rate according to the amount of services rendered and which can be specifically identified, described and itemised.

5. Goods acquired or imported under paragraph 2 shall not be sold, given away, or otherwise disposed of, except in accordance with conditions agreed upon with the Government.

Article 11 Communications Facilities

1. The Scottish Court shall enjoy, with respect to its official communications, treatment not less favourable than that accorded by the Government to any diplomatic mission in matters of establishment and operation, priorities, tariffs, charges on mail and cablegrams and teleprinter, facsimile, telephone and other communications, as well as rates for information to the press and radio.

2. No official correspondence or other communication of the Scottish Court shall be subject to censorship by the Government. Such immunity from censorship shall extend to printed matter, photographic and electronic data communications, and other forms of communications as may be used by the Scottish Court. The Scottish Court shall be entitled to use codes and to dispatch and receive correspondence and other material or communications either by courier or in sealed bags, all of which shall be inviolable and shall have the same privileges and immunities as diplomatic couriers and bags.

3. The Scottish Court shall have the right to operate radio and other telecommunications equipment, on frequencies allocated to it by the Government, between the premises of the Scottish Court and means of transport, within and outside the host country.

4. For the fulfilment of its purposes, the Scottish Court shall have the right to publish freely and without restrictions within the host country in conformity with this Agreement.

5. The provisions of this article shall apply also to the Lord Advocate.

Article 12 Public Services for the Premises of the Scottish Court

1. The competent authorities shall secure, on fair conditions and upon the request of the Registrar or made on his behalf, the public services needed for the premises of the Scottish Court such as, but not limited to, postal, telephone and telegraphic services, electricity, water, gas, sewage, collection of waste, fire protection, local transportation and cleaning of public streets.

2. In cases where electricity, water, gas or other services referred to m paragraph 1 are made available for the premises of the Scottish Court by the competent authorities, or where the prices thereof are under their control, the rates for such services shall not exceed the lowest comparable rates accorded to essential agencies and organs of the Government.

3. In case of *force majeure* resulting in a complete or partial disruption of the aforementioned services, the Scottish Court shall, for the performance of its functions, be accorded the priority given to essential agencies and organs of the Government.

4. Upon request of the competent authorities, the Registrar, or an official designated by him, shall make suitable arrangements to enable duly authorised representatives of the appropriate public services to inspect, repair, maintain, reconstruct and relocate utilities, conduits, mains and sewers on the premises of the Scottish Court under conditions which shall not unreasonably disturb the carrying out of the functions of the Scottish Court. Underground constructions may be undertaken by the competent authorities on the premises of the Scottish Court only after consultation with the Registrar, or an official designated by him, and under conditions which shall not disturb the carrying out of the functions of the Scottish Court.

Article 13 Emblem, Markings and Flag

The Scottish Court shall be entitled to display its emblem and markings, as well as the appropriate flag, on its premises.

Article 14 Privileges and Immunities Judges and Officials

1. The judges and officials of the Scottish Court, the Registrar, the Lord Advocate, the Sheriff and the Procurator Fiscal, shall enjoy the privileges, immunities and facilities accorded to diplomatic agents in accordance with the Vienna Convention.

2. The privileges and immunities are accorded to the judges and officials of the Scottish Court, the Registrar, the Lord Advocate, the Sheriff and the Procurator Fiscal in the interest of the Scottish Court and not for the personal benefit of the persons themselves. The right and duty to waive the immunity in any case where it can be waived without prejudice to the purposes for which it is accorded shall vest in the British Ambassador at The Hague.

Article 15 Solicitors and Advocates

1. The solicitors and advocates of the accused shall not be subjected by the host country to any measure which may affect the free and independent exercise of their functions under Scots law.

2. In particular, they shall be accorded:

   (a) exemption from immigration restrictions;

   (b) inviolability in respect of all documents relating to the exercise of their functions as solicitor or advocate of the accused;

   (c) immunity from criminal and civil jurisdiction in respect of words spoken or written and acts performed by them in their capacity as solicitor or advocate of the accuse(d) Such immunity shall continue to be accorded to them after termination of their functions as a solicitor or advocate of the accused.

3. The provisions of paragraph 2(a) and (b) shall apply also to persons directly assisting solicitors or advocates of the accused.

4. This article shall be without prejudice to such disciplinary rules as may be applicable to solicitors and advocates.

Article 16 The Accused

1. At the time of the arrival of the accused in the host country, the Government of the United Kingdom shall, in accordance with the relevant treaties, request the Government to transfer the accused to the premises of the Scottish Court for the purpose of the trial and to detain them pending their transfer, having regard to the requirements of United Nations Security Council Resolution 1192 (1998).

2. After their transfer to the premises of the Scottish Court the accused shall not be transferred to the territory of the United Kingdom. However, the Government of the United Kingdom may, after due notification to the Government, transfer the accused from the premises of the Scottish Court directly to the territory of the United Kingdom, but only:

   (a) for the purpose of trial by jury in Scotland, provided that the accused have given their written agreement, and have confirmed that agreement in person to the High Court of Justiciary in the presence of any counsel instructed by them, or

   (b) for the purpose of serving a custodial sentence imposed by the Scottish Court following the conviction of the accused.

3. The host country shall not exercise its criminal jurisdiction over the accused in respect of acts, omissions or convictions prior to their arrival in the host country. The immunity shall cease when the accused, being obliged to leave the territory of the host county, have not done so or, having left it, have returned.

4. The accused shall be obliged to leave the host country on:

   (a) the trial being discontinued by process of law preventing any further trial under Scots Law; or

   (b) their acquittal.

Article 17 Witnesses

1. The host country shall permit the entry into the Netherlands of witnesses for the sole purpose of attending the trial.

2. Where appropriate, the host country shall permit the transfer of a witness from the border of the host country to the premises of the Scottish Court in accordance with the relevant treaties and its national law.

3. For the purpose of paragraph 2, the Scottish Court may make requests for such transfer directly to the Ministry of Justice of the Kingdom of the Netherlands.

4. Upon request by the Lord Advocate or the Scottish Court, the host country shall provide for protection of a witness, in accordance with its law and practice.

5. Subject to paragraph 2, a witness shall not be prosecuted, detained or subjected to any other restriction of his or her personal liberty, by the authorities of the host country in respect of acts or convictions prior to his or her entry into the territory of the host country.

6. The immunity provided for in paragraph 5 shall cease on departure of the witness from the territory of the Netherlands, or following the elapse of 15 days from the date when his or her presence at the trial is no longer required and during which he or she has had an opportunity to leave the Netherlands and has not done so or, having left it, has returned, unless such return is required for the purposes of the trial.

7. Without prejudice to paragraph 4, a witness shall not be subjected by the host country to any measure which may affect the free and independent exercise of his or her functions.

Article 18 International Observers

The host country shall permit the entry into the territory of the Netherlands of international observers for the sole purpose of attending the trial. They shall not be subjected by the host country to any measure which may affect the free and independent exercise of their functions.

Article 19 Co-operation with the Competent Authorities

1. Without prejudice to their privileges and immunities, it is the duty of all persons enjoying such privileges and immunities to respect the laws and regulations of the host country. They also have the duty not to interfere in the internal affairs of the host country.

2. The Scottish Court shall co-operate at all times with the competent authorities to facilitate the proper administration of justice, secure the observance of police regulations and prevent the occurrence of any abuse of the privileges, immunities and facilities accorded under this Agreement.

3. The Scottish Court shall observe security directives issued by the host country, as well as directives of the competent authorities responsible for fire prevention regulations.

Article 20 Notification

1. The Registrar shall notify the Government of the names and status of persons referred to in this Agreement, other than members of the public, and of any change in their status. The provisions of this Agreement shall apply only to those persons who have been so notified.

2. The Registrar shall also notify the Government of the name and identity of any personnel entitled to carry firearms within the premises of the Scottish Court, as well as the name, type, calibre and serial number of the arm or arms at his or her disposition. The Registrar shall issue permits to be carried at all times by any personnel entitled to carry firearms within the premises of the Scottish Court.

Article 21 Entry, Exit and Movement within the Host Country

All persons notified by the Registrar to the Government in accordance with Article 20(1) shall have the right of unimpeded entry into, exit from and movement within the host country, as necessary for the purposes of the trial. They shall be granted facilities for speedy travel. Visas, entry permits or licences, where required, shall be granted free of charge and as promptly as possible. The same facilities shall be accorded to persons accompanying witnesses, provided that each such person has been notified by the Registrar to the Government.

Article 22 Identification Cards

At the request of the Registrar, the Government shall issue identification cards to persons notified by the Registrar in accordance with Article 20(1).

Article 23 Security, Safety and Protection of Persons referred to in this Agreement

Without prejudice to Article 17(4), the competent authorities shall, in accordance with the law and practice of the Netherlands, take effective and adequate action which may be required to ensure the appropriate security, safety and protection of persons referred to in this Agreement, indispensable for the proper functioning of the Scottish Court, free from interference of any kind.

Article 24 Costs

1. All costs:

    (a) relating to the establishment and sitting of the Scottish Court in the Netherlands, and

    (b) incurred by the host country relating to the sitting of the Scottish Court in the Netherlands, shall be borne by the Government of the United Kingdom.

2. The Government of the United Kingdom shall, in accordance with further arrangements made in and exchange of letters of understanding with the Government of the Netherlands, deposit in a designated account, prior to each quarter, the amount which the Ministry of Justice of the Netherlands estimates will be incurred by it in that quarter.

3. An accounting shall be supplied by the Government of all sums expended by it every quarter.

4. On the termination of this Agreement, the Government of the United Kingdom and the Government of the Netherlands shall agree a final accounting with regard to the costs incurred by the latter, and shall make any balancing payment which may be required.

Article 25 Legal Cooperation

Nothing in this Agreement shall prejudice the application of treaties on legal co-operation in criminal matters, except in so far as otherwise provided in this Agreement.

Article 26 Internal Security of the Host Country

Nothing in this Agreement shall affect the right of the host country to take such measures as it may consider necessary for the purpose of protecting its national security.

Article 27 Additional Arrangements

With a view to the practical application of this Agreement, letters of understanding may be exchanged between the Registrar and the designated representative of the Ministry of Justice of the Netherlands.

Article 28 Settlement of Disputes

Any dispute relating to the interpretation or application of this Agreement shall be resolved by consultation and negotiation between the Parties.

Article 29 Final Provisions

1. This Agreement shall enter into force on a date to be agreed by the Parties, provided that they may agree in the meantime to apply provisionally any of its provisions.

2. Subject to paragraph 3, this Agreement shall remain in force for one year from its entry into force, with the possibility of extending it by mutual agreement.

3. This Agreement shall terminate

    (a) on the day after the date of the end of the trial (as defined in Article 3(4)), and any person then detained or imprisoned in accordance with Article 3(3)(c) or (d) shall be released on that day, or

    (b) seven days after the date on which the Parties, after consultations with the Secretary-General of the United Nations, agree in an exchange of notes that there is no reasonable prospect of the trial taking place before the Scottish Court in the Netherlands as envisaged in this Agreement.

4. Termination following completion of the trial shall not affect:

    (a) those provisions of this Agreement which are required for the orderly termination of the operation of the Scottish Court, including the transfer of the accused in accordance with Article 16(2)(b); and

    (b) the continuation of the immunity from legal process in respect of words spoken or written or acts done in the capacity as solicitor or advocate of the accused.

5. This Agreement may be amended by mutual consent at any time at the request of either Party. With respect to the Kingdom of the Netherlands, this Agreement shall apply to the part of the Kingdom in Europe only.

DOCUMENT 58

Statute of the Iraqi Special Tribunal 2003
43 ILM 231 (2004)

The statute of the Iraqi Special Tribunal (IST) for Crimes Against Humanity was approved by the Iraqi Governing Council on 10 December 2003 and was signed into law by US ambassador Paul Bremer on behalf of the Coalition Provisional Authority on the same day.

The IST has jurisdiction over Iraqi nationals or residents of Iraq in relation to the crimes of genocide (Article 11), crimes against humanity (Article 12), war crimes (Article 13) and violations of certain Iraqi laws (Article 14) committed between 17 July 1968, the date when Saddam Hussein came to power, and 1 May 2003, the day on which US president George W Bush declared an end to major combat operations in Iraq.

The IST is to have its seat in Baghdad. It consists of one or more trial chambers composed of five permanent judges as well as an appeals chamber composed of nine permanent judges. The nationality of such judges is specified as Iraqi, (Article 28), but Article 4(d) envisages the appointment of some non-Iraqi judges. The members of the appeals chamber shall appoint the president of the IST.

The president of the IST is given overall control of the tribunal (Article 6(1)). However, the president is required to appoint non-Iraqi nationals to act in advisory capacities or as observers to the trial chambers and to the appeals chamber. Such individuals are specifically charged with 'providing assistance to the judges with respect to international law and the experience of similar tribunals (whether international or otherwise), and to monitor the protection by the IST of general due process of law standards' (Article 6(2)).

The statute also envisages the appointment of up to 20 IST investigative judges who are to investigate individuals for the commission of crimes falling within the jurisdiction of the IST (Article 7). Prosecutions are to be led by the prosecutions department, which consists of up to 20 prosecutors. Once again, the chief IST investigative judge and the chief prosecutor are required to appoint non-Iraqi nationals to act in advisory capacities or as observers.

The IST envisages individual criminal responsibility and no immunity is to be granted in respect of official status (Article 15). Rules of procedure and evidence are to be drafted by the president of the IST, who is to be guided by Iraqi criminal procedure law (Article 16). Applicable principles of criminal law are derived from Iraqi criminal law but, in interpreting Articles 11–13 of the statute, which deals with matters of international criminal law, the IST is to treat relevant decisions of international courts and tribunals as persuasive authority (Article 17). The statute further delimits rules on investigations and indictment (Articles 18–20); trial proceedings (Articles 21–24); and review and appeals proceedings (Articles 25–26). The enforcement of sentences is governed by Article 27, which provides that sentences are to be carried out by the legal system of Iraq in accordance with its laws, which provide for the possibility of the death penalty.

Section One The Establishment, Organization and Competence of the Tribunal

Part One Establishment and Competence of the Tribunal
Article 1

(a) A Tribunal is hereby established and shall be known as The Iraqi Special Tribunal (the "Tribunal"). The jurisdiction and functioning of the Tribunal and its associated bodies as defined in Article 3 below shall be governed by the provisions of this Statute. The Tribunal shall be an independent entity and not associated with any Iraqi government departments.

(b) The Tribunal shall have jurisdiction over any Iraqi national or resident of Iraq accused of the crimes listed in Articles 11 to 14 below, committed since July 17, 1968 and up until and including May 1, 2003, in the territory of the Republic of Iraq or elsewhere, including crimes committed in connection with Iraq's wars against the Islamic Republic of Iran and the State of Kuwait. This includes jurisdiction over crimes listed in Articles 12 and 13 committed against the people of Iraq (including its Arabs, Kurds, Turcomans, Assyrians and other ethnic groups, and its Shi'ites and Sunnis) whether or not committed in armed conflict.

(c) The Tribunal shall only have jurisdiction over natural persons.

Article 2

The Tribunal shall have its seat in the City of Baghdad, or, following a written proposal made by the President of the Tribunal, in any other Governorate in Iraq as determined by the Governing Council or the Successor Government.

Part Two Organization of the Tribunal
Article 3

(a) The Tribunal's judiciary shall consist of the following:

    1. one or more Trial Chambers;

2. an Appeals Chamber, which shall have the power to review the decisions of the Trial Chambers referred to above; and

3. the Tribunal Investigative Judges.

(b) The Tribunal will also have a Prosecutions Department.

(c) The Tribunal will also have an Administration Department,, which shall provide administrative services to the Tribunal's judiciary and the Prosecutions Department.

Part Three The Trial Chambers and the Appeals Chamber
Aricle 4

(a) The Chambers shall be composed of permanent independent judges, and independent reserve judges.

(b) Each Trial Chamber shall consist of five permanent judges.

(c) (i) The Appeals Chamber shall be composed of nine members. Once appointed the Appeals Chamber shall select one of its members to fill the position of President of the Appeals Chamber. No member of any Trial Chamber can simultaneously be a member of the Appeals Chamber or a Tribunal Investigative Judge.

(ii) The President of the Appeals Chamber shall also be the President of the Tribunal and will overview the administrative and financial aspects of the Tribunal.

(d) The Governing Council or the Successor Government, if it deems necessary, can appoint non-Iraqi judges who have experience in the crimes encompassed in this statute, and who shall be persons of high moral character, impartiality and integrity.

Part Four Qualification and Selection of the Judges
Article 5

(a) The permanent and reserve judges shall be persons of high moral character, impartiality and integrity who possess the qualifications required for appointment to the highest judicial offices. In the overall composition of the Chambers, due account shall be taken of the experience of the judges in criminal law and trial procedures.

(b) Iraqi candidates for permanent and reserve judges in the Trial Chambers need not be serving judges, and could be lawyers and jurists (who should also have the necessary experience and qualifications). Judges in the Appeals Chamber must be serving or former judges.

(c) Judges are to be nominated and appointed by the Governing Council or the Successor Government, after consultation with the Judicial Council.

(d) The permanent judges of each Trial Chamber shall elect a Presiding Judge from amongst their number, who shall oversee the work of the Trial Chamber as a whole.

(e) The permanent and reserve judges shall be appointed for a term of five years. The terms and conditions of service shall be those of the judges of the Iraqi judicial system as set out in the Law Number 160 of 1979 (Judicial Organization Law), save that matters of compensation shall be set by the Governing Council or the Successor Government in light of the increased risks associated with the position.

(f) 1. A judge shall be disqualified for any of the following reasons:

(i) He or she has a criminal record including a felony unless the felony is a political or false charge made by the Ba'ath Party regime;

(ii) He or she has made a material misrepresentation; or

(iii) He or she fails to carry out his or her duties without good reason.

2. The decision to disqualify a judge shall be taken by the majority of permanent judges of the Tribunal after conducting appropriate investigations.

3. The decision to disqualify the President shall be taken by the Governing Council or the Successor Government.

Part Five The Presidency of the Tribunal
Article 6

(a) The President shall:

    1. chair the proceedings of the Appeals Chamber.

    2. assign the judges to particular Trial Chambers;

    3. assign, from time to time, any reserve judges to a Trial Chamber; and

    4. have overall responsibility for the administration of the Tribunal.

(b) The President of the Tribunal shall be required to appoint non-Iraqi nationals to act in advisory capacities or as observers to the Trial Chambers and to the Appeals Chamber. The role of the non-Iraqi nationals shall be to provide assistance to the judges with respect to international law and the experience of similar tribunals (whether international or otherwise), and to monitor the protection by the Tribunal of general due process of law standards. In appointing such non-Iraqi experts, the President of the Tribunal shall be entitled to request assistance from the international community, including the United Nations.

(c) The non-Iraqi advisors and observers referred to in the above paragraph shall also be persons of high moral character, impartiality and integrity. In this regard, it would be preferable that such non-Iraqi advisor or observer shall have the following experience: (i) such person shall have acted in either a judicial or prosecutorial capacity in his or her respective country, or (ii) such person shall have experience in international war crimes trials or tribunals.

Part Six Tribunal Investigative Judges
Article 7

(a) The Tribunal Investigative Judges shall be appointed in order to investigate individuals for the commission of crimes stipulated in Articles 11 to 14.

(b) Tribunal Investigative Judges are to be nominated and appointed by the Governing Council or the Successor Government, after consultation with the Judicial Council.

(c) There shall be up to twenty permanent Tribunal Investigative Judges, and up to ten reserve investigative judges.

(d) The permanent and reserve investigative judges shall be persons of high moral character, impartiality and integrity who possess the qualifications required for appointment to the highest judicial offices. In the selection of investigative judges, due account shall be taken of the experience of the judges in criminal law and trial procedures.

(e) The Tribunal Investigative Judges shall be headed by a Chief Tribunal Investigative Judge, who shall be chosen by the Tribunal Investigative Judges from among them.

(f) The Chief Tribunal Investigative Judge shall assign cases to individual tribunal investigative judges.

(g) Each Office of the Tribunal Investigative Judge shall be composed of the Tribunal Investigative Judge and such other qualified staff as may be required.

(h) In accordance with Iraqi criminal procedure, each Tribunal Investigative Judge shall have the power to issue subpoenas, arrest warrants and indictments with respect to individuals that they are investigating.

(i) Each Tribunal Investigative Judge may gather evidence from whatever source he considers suitable.

(j) Each Tribunal Investigative Judge shall act independently as a separate organ of the Tribunal. He or she shall not seek or receive instructions from any Governmental Department, or from any other source, including the Governing Council or the Successor Government.

(k) The decisions or orders of the Tribunal Investigative Judge can be appealed to the Appeals Chamber within fifteen days of the notification or deemed notification of the decision.

(l) Each Tribunal Investigative Judge shall be appointed for a term of three years. The terms and conditions of service shall be those of the investigative judges of the Iraqi judicial system as set out in Law Number 160 of 1979 (Judicial Organization Law), save that matters of compensation shall be set by the Governing Council or the Successor Government in light of the increased risks associated with the position.

(m) 1. Any Tribunal Investigative Judge shall be disqualified for any of the following reasons:

    (i) He or she has a criminal record including a felony unless the felony is a political or false charge made by the Ba'ath Party regime;

    (ii) He or she has made a material misrepresentation; or

    (iii) He or she fails to carry out his or her duties without good reason.

  2. The decision to disqualify a Tribunal Investigative Judge shall be taken by the majority of permanent judges of the Tribunal, after conducting appropriate investigations.

(n) The Chief Tribunal Investigative Judge shall be required to appoint non-Iraqi nationals to act in advisory capacities or as observers to the Tribunal Investigative Judges. The role of the non-Iraqi nationals and observers shall be to provide assistance to the Tribunal Investigative Judges with respect to the investigations and prosecution of cases covered by the this Statute (whether in an international context or otherwise), and to monitor the protection by the Tribunal Investigative Judges of general due process of law standards. In appointing such advisors, the Chief Tribunal Investigative Judge shall be entitled to request assistance from the international community, including the United Nations.

(o) The non-Iraqi advisors and observers referred to in this Article shall also be persons of high moral character, impartiality and integrity. In this regard, it would be preferable that such non-Iraqi advisor or observer shall have the following experience: (i) such person shall have acted in either a judicial or prosecutorial capacity in his or her respective country, or (ii) such person shall have experience in international war crimes trials or tribunals.

Section Two Other Departments of the Tribunal

Part One The Prosecutions Department
Article 8

(a) The Prosecutions Department shall be responsible for the prosecution of persons responsible for crimes within the jurisdiction of the Tribunal.

(b) Each Prosecutor shall act independently. He or she shall not seek or receive instructions from any Governmental Department or from any other source, including the Governing Council or the Successor Government.

(c) The Prosecutions Department shall consist of up to twenty Prosecutors.

(d) Prosecutors are to be nominated and appointed by the Governing Council or the Successor Government after consultation with the Judicial Council.

(e) The Prosecution Department shall be headed by a Chief Prosecutor, who shall be selected from among the Prosecutors.

(f) 1. A prosecutor shall be disqualified for any of the following reasons:

    (i) He or she has a criminal record including a felony unless the felony is a political or false charge made by the Ba'ath Party regime;

    (ii) He or she has made a material misrepresentation; or

    (iii) He or she fails to carry out his or her duties without good reason.

  2. The decision to disqualify a Prosecutor shall be taken by the Chief Prosecutor, after conducting appropriate investigations.

(g) Each Office of the Prosecutor shall be composed of a Prosecutor and such other qualified staff as may be required.

(h) The Chief Prosecutor shall assign individual cases to a Prosecutor. Such Prosecutor shall have the right to be involved in the investigative stages of a case and shall be the individual who prosecutes such case, consistent with the powers granted to prosecutors pursuant to Law Number 23 of 1971 (Iraqi Criminal Procedure Law).

(i) Each Prosecutor shall be appointed for a term of three years. The terms and conditions of service shall be those of prosecutors of the Iraqi judicial system as set out in Law Number 159 of 1979 (The Law of Prosecutors), save that matters of compensation shall be set by the Governing Council or the Successor Government.

(j) The Chief Prosecutor shall be required to appoint non-Iraqi nationals to act in advisory capacities or as observers to the prosecutors. The role of the non-Iraqi nationals and observers shall be to provide assistance to the prosecutors of the Tribunal with respect to the investigations and prosecution of cases covered by this Statute (whether in an international context or otherwise), and to monitor the performance of the Prosecutor. In appointing such advisors, the Chief Prosecutor shall be entitled to request assistance from the international community, including the United Nations.

(k) The non-Iraqi advisors and observers referred to in this Article shall also be persons of high moral character, impartiality and integrity. In this regard, it would be preferable that such non-Iraqi adviser or observer shall have the following experience: (i) such person shall have acted in a prosecutorial capacity in his or her respective country, or (ii) such person shall have experience in international war crimes trials or tribunals.

Part Two The Administration Department
Article 9

(a) The Administration Department shall consist of a Director of the Administration Department and such other staff as may be required.

(b) The Administration Department shall be responsible for the administration and servicing of the Tribunal and the Prosecutions Department.

(c) The Director of the Administration Department shall initially be appointed by the Governing Council or the Successor Government. He or she shall serve for a three year term and be eligible for reappointment. The terms and conditions of service of the Director of the Administration Department shall be those of a General Director in an Iraqi government department.

(d) The staff of the Administration Department shall be appointed by the Director of the Administration Department.

(e) The Director of the Administration Department shall appoint a public relations expert to the position of spokesman of the Tribunal. Such spokesman shall give regular briefings to the press and the public at large with respect to the developments relating to the Tribunal.

Section Three Jurisdiction and Crimes

Part One Jurisdiction of the Tribunal
Article 10

The Tribunal shall have jurisdiction over any Iraqi national or resident of Iraq accused of the crimes listed in Articles 11–14, committed since July 17, 1968 and up and until May 1, 2003, in the territory of Iraq or elsewhere, namely:

(a) The crime of genocide;

(b) Crimes against humanity;

(c) War crimes; or

(d) Violations of certain Iraqi laws listed in Article 14 below.

Part Two The Crime of Genocide
Article 11

(a) For the purposes of this Statute and in accordance with the Convention on the Prevention and Punishment of the Crime of Genocide, dated December 9, 1948, as ratified by Iraq on January 20, 1959, "genocide" means any of the following acts committed with intent to destroy, in whole or in part, a national, ethnical, racial or religious group, as such:

1. killing members of the group;

2. causing serious bodily or mental harm to members of the group;

3. deliberately inflicting on the group conditions of life calculated to bring about its physical destruction in whole or in part;

4. imposing measures intended to prevent births within the group; and

5. forcibly transferring children of the group to another group.

(b) The following acts shall be punishable:

1. genocide;

2. conspiracy to commit genocide;

3. direct and public incitement to commit genocide;

4. attempt to commit genocide; and

5. complicity in genocide.

Part Three Crimes Against Humanity
Article 12

(a) For the purposes of this Statute, "crimes against humanity" means any of the following acts when committed as part of a widespread or systematic attack directed against any civilian population, with knowledge of the attack:

1. Murder;

2. Extermination;

3. Enslavement;

4. Deportation or forcible transfer of population;

5. Imprisonment or other severe deprivation of physical liberty in violation of fundamental norms of international law;

6. Torture;

7. Rape, sexual slavery, enforced prostitution, forced pregnancy, or any other form of sexual violence of comparable gravity;

8. Persecution against any identifiable group or collectivity on political, racial, national, ethnic, cultural, religious, gender or other grounds that are universally recognized as impermissible under international law, in connection with any act referred to in this paragraph or any crime within the jurisdiction of the Tribunal;

9. Enforced disappearance of persons; and

10. Other inhumane acts of a similar character intentionally causing great suffering, or serious injury to body or to mental or physical health.

(b) For the purposes of paragraph (a):

1. "Attack directed against any civilian population" means a course of conduct involving the multiple commission of acts referred to in the above paragraph against any civilian population, pursuant to or in furtherance of a state or organizational policy to commit such attack;

2. "Extermination" includes the intentional infliction of conditions of life, such as the deprivation of access to food and medicine, calculated to bring about the destruction of part of a population;

3. "Enslavement" means the exercise of any or all of the powers attaching to the right of ownership over a person and includes the exercise of such power in the course of trafficking in persons, in particular women and children;

4. "Deportation or forcible transfer of population" means forced displacement of the persons concerned by expulsion or other coercive acts from the area in which they are lawfully present, without grounds permitted under international law;

5. "Torture" means the intentional infliction of severe pain or suffering, whether physical or mental, upon a person in the custody or under the control of the accused; except that torture shall not include pain or suffering arising only from, inherent in, or incidental to lawful sanctions;

6. "Persecution" means the intentional and severe deprivation of fundamental rights contrary to international law by reason of the identity of the group or collectivity; and

7. "Enforced disappearance of persons" means the arrest, detention or abduction of persons by, or with the authorization, support or acquiescence of, the State or a political organization, followed by a refusal to acknowledge that deprivation of freedom or to give information on the fate or whereabouts of those persons, with the intention of removing them from the protection of the law for a prolonged period of time.

Part Four War Crimes
Article 13

For the purposes of this Statute, "war crimes" means:

(a) Grave breaches of the Geneva Conventions of 12 August 1949, namely, any of the following acts against persons or property protected under the provisions of the relevant Geneva Convention:

 1. Willful killing;

 2. Torture or inhuman treatment, including biological experiments;

 3. Willfully causing great suffering, or serious injury to body or health;

 4. Extensive destruction and appropriation of property, not justified by military necessity and carried out unlawfully and wantonly;

 5. Willfully denying the right of a fair trial to a prisoner of war or other protected person;

 6. Compelling a prisoner of war or other protected person to serve in the forces of a hostile power;

 7. Unlawful confinement;

 8. Unlawful deportation or transfer; and

 9. Taking of hostages.

(b) Other serious violations of the laws and customs applicable in international armed conflict, within the established framework of international law, namely, any of the following acts:

 1. Intentionally directing attacks against the civilian population as such or against individual civilians not taking direct part in hostilities;

 2. Intentionally directing attacks against civilians objects, that is, objects which are not military objectives;

 3. Intentionally directing attacks against personnel, installations, material, units or vehicles involved in a peacekeeping mission in accordance with the Charter of the United Nations or in a humanitarian assistance mission, as long as they are entitled to the protection given to civilians or civilian objects under the international law of armed conflict;

 4. Intentionally launching an attack in the knowledge that such attack will cause incidental loss of life or injury to civilians or damage to civilian objects which would be clearly excessive in relation to the concrete and direct overall military advantage anticipated;

5. Intentionally launching an attack in the knowledge that such attack will cause widespread, long-term and severe damage to the natural environment which would be clearly excessive in relation to the concrete and direct overall military advantage anticipated;

6. Attacking or bombarding, by whatever means, towns, villages, dwellings or buildings which are undefended and which are not military objectives;

7. Killing or wounding a combatant who, having laid down his arms or having no longer means of defense, has surrendered at discretion;

8. Making improper use of a flag of truce, of the flag or of the military insignia and uniform of the enemy or of the United Nations, as well as of the distinctive emblems of the Geneva Conventions, resulting in death or serious personal injury;

9. The transfer, directly or indirectly, by the Government of Iraq or any of its instrumentalities (including by an instrumentality of the Arab Socialist Ba'ath Party), of parts of its own civilian population into any territory it occupies, or the deportation or transfer of all or parts of the population of the occupied territory within or outside this territory;

10. Intentionally directing attacks against buildings that are dedicated to religion, education, art, science or charitable purposes, historic monuments, hospitals and places where the sick and wounded are collected, provided they are not military objectives;

11. Subjecting persons of another nation to physical mutilation or to medical or scientific experiments of any kind that are neither justified by the medical, dental or hospital treatment of the person concerned nor carried out in his or her interest, and which cause death to or seriously endanger the health of such person or persons;

12. Killing or wounding treacherously individuals belonging to the hostile nation or army;

13. Declaring that no quarter will be given;

14. Destroying or seizing the property of an adverse party unless such destruction or seizure be imperatively demanded by the necessities of war;

15. Declaring abolished, suspended or inadmissible in a court of law, or otherwise depriving, the rights and actions of the nationals of the adverse party;

16. Compelling the nationals of the hostile party to take part in the operations of war directed against their own country, even if they were in the belligerent's service before the commencement of the war;

17. Pillaging a town or place, even when taken by assault;

18. Employing poison or poisoned weapons;

19. Employing asphyxiating, poisonous or other gases, and all analogous liquids, materials or devices;

20. Employing bullets which expand or flatten easily in the human body, such as bullets with a hard envelope which does not entirely cover the core or is pierced with incisions;

21. Committing outrages upon personal dignity, in particular humiliating and degrading treatment;

22. Committing rape, sexual slavery, enforced prostitution, forced pregnancy, or any other form of sexual violence of comparable gravity;

23. Utilizing the presence of a civilian or other protected person to render certain points, areas or military forces immune from military operations;

24. Intentionally directing attacks against buildings, material, medical units and transport, and personnel using the distinctive emblems of the Geneva Conventions in conformity with international law;

25. Intentionally using starvation of civilians as a method of warfare by depriving them of objects indispensable to their survival, including willfully impeding relief supplies as provided for under international law; and

26. Conscripting or enlisting children under the age of fifteen years into the national armed forces or using them to participate actively in hostilities.

(c) In the case of an armed conflict, any of the following acts committed against persons taking no active part in the hostilities, including members of armed forces who have laid down their arms and those placed *hors de combat* by sickness, wounds, detention or any other cause:

  1. Violence to life and person, in particular murder of all kinds, mutilation, cruel treatment and torture;

  2. Committing outrages upon personal dignity, in particular humiliating and degrading treatment;

  3. Taking of hostages; and

  4. The passing of sentences and the carrying out of executions without previous judgment pronounced by a regularly constituted court, affording all judicial guarantees which are generally recognized as indispensable.

(d) Serious violations of the laws and customs of war applicable in armed conflict not of an international character, within the established framework of international law, namely, any of the following acts:

  1. Intentionally directing attacks against the civilian population as such or against individual civilians not taking direct part in hostilities;

  2. Intentionally directing attacks against buildings, material, medical units and transport, and personnel using the distinctive emblems of the Geneva Conventions in conformity with international law;

  3. Intentionally directing attacks against personnel, installations, material, units, or vehicles involved in a peacekeeping mission in accordance with the Charter of the United Nations or in a humanitarian assistance mission, as long as they are entitled to the protection given to civilians or civilian objects under the international law of armed conflict;

  4. Intentionally directing attacks against buildings that are dedicated to religion, education, art, science, or charitable purposes, historic monuments, hospitals and places where the sick and wounded are collected, provided they are not military objectives;

  5. Pillaging a town or place, even when taken by assault;

  6. Committing rape, sexual slavery, enforced prostitution, forced pregnancy, or any other form of sexual violence of comparable gravity;

  7. Conscripting or enlisting children under the age of fifteen years into armed forces or groups or using them to participate actively in hostilities;

  8. Ordering the displacement of the civilian population for reasons related to the conflict, unless the security of the civilians involved or imperative military reasons so demand;

  9. Killing or wounding treacherously a combatant adversary;

  10. Declaring that no quarter will be given;

  11. Subjecting persons who are in the power of another party to the conflict to physical mutilation or to medical or scientific experiments of any kind that are neither justified by the medical, dental or hospital treatment of the person concerned nor carried out in his or her interest, and which cause death to or seriously endanger the health of such person or persons; and

  12. Destroying or seizing the property of an adversary, unless such destruction or seizure be imperatively demanded by the necessities of the conflict.

Part Five Violations of Stipulated Iraqi Laws
Article 14

The Tribunal shall have the power to prosecute persons who have committed the following crimes under Iraqi law:

(a) For those outside the judiciary, the attempt to manipulate the judiciary or involvement in the functions of the judiciary, in violation, *inter alia*, of the Iraqi interim constitution of 1970, as amended;

(b) The wastage of national resources and the squandering of public assets and funds, pursuant to, *inter alia*, Article 2(g) of Law Number 7 of 1958, as amended; and

(c) The abuse of position and the pursuit of policies that may lead to the threat of war or the use of the armed forces of Iraq against an Arab country, in accordance with Article 1 of Law Number 7 of 1958, as amended.

Section Four Individual Criminal Responsibility

Article 15

(a) A person who commits a crime within the jurisdiction of this Tribunal shall be individually responsible and liable for punishment in accordance with this Statute.

(b) In accordance with this Statute, and the provisions of Iraqi criminal law, a person shall be criminally responsible and liable for punishment for a crime within the jurisdiction of the Tribunal if that person:

   1. Commits such a crime, whether as an individual, jointly with another or through another person, regardless of whether that other person is criminally responsible;

   2. Orders, solicits or induces the commission of such a crime which in fact occurs or is attempted;

   3. For the purpose of facilitating the commission of such a crime, aids, abets or otherwise assists in its commission or its attempted commission, including providing the means for its commission;

   4. In any other way contributes to the commission or attempted commission of such a crime by a group of persons acting with a common purpose. Such contribution shall be intentional and shall either:

       (i) Be made with the aim of furthering the criminal activity or criminal purpose of the group, where such activity or purpose involves the commission of a crime within the jurisdiction of the Tribunal; or

       (ii) Be made in the knowledge of the intention of the group to commit the crime;

   5. In respect of the crime of genocide, directly and publicly incites others to commit genocide;

   6. Attempts to commit such a crime by taking action that commences its execution by means of a substantial step, but the crime does not occur because of circumstances independent of the person's intentions. However, a person who abandons the effort to commit the crime or otherwise prevents the completion of the crime shall not be liable for punishment under this Statute for the attempt to commit that crime if that person completely and voluntarily gave up the criminal purpose.

(c) The official position of any accused person, whether as president, prime minister, member of the cabinet, chairman or a member of the Revolutionary Command Council, a member of the Arab Socialist Ba'ath Party Regional Command or Government (or an instrumentality of either) or as a responsible Iraqi Government official or member of the Ba'ath Party or in any other capacity, shall not relieve such person of criminal responsibility nor mitigate punishment. No person is entitled to any immunity with respect to any of the crimes stipulated in Articles 11 to 14.

(d) The fact that any of the acts referred to in Articles 11 to 14 of the present Statute was committed by a subordinate does not relieve his superior of criminal responsibility if he knew or had reason to know that the subordinate was about to commit such acts or had done so and the superior failed to take the necessary and reasonable measures to prevent such acts or to submit the matter to the competent authorities for investigation and prosecution.

(e) The fact that an accused person acted pursuant to an order of Government or of a superior shall not relieve him of criminal responsibility, but may be considered in mitigation of punishment if the Tribunal determines that justice so requires.

Section Five Rules of Procedure and Evidence

Article 16

The President of the Tribunal shall draft rules of procedure and evidence for the conduct of the pre-trial phase of the proceedings, trials and appeals, the admission of evidence, the protection of victims and witnesses and other appropriate matters (including regulations with respect to the disqualification of judges or prosecutors), where the applicable law, including this Statute does not, or does not adequately provide for a specific situation. He shall be guided by the Iraqi Criminal Procedure Law. Such rules shall be adopted by a majority of the permanent judges of the Tribunal.

Section Six General Principles of Criminal Law

Article 17

(a) Subject to the provisions of this Statute and the rules made thereunder, the general principles of criminal law applicable in connection with the prosecution and trial of any accused person shall be those contained: (i) in Iraqi criminal law as at July 17, 1968 (as embodied in The Baghdadi Criminal Code of 1919) for those offenses committed between July 17, 1968 and December 14, 1969; (ii) in Law Number 111 of 1969 (the Iraqi Criminal Code), as it was as of December 15, 1969, without regard to any amendments made thereafter, for those offenses committed between December 15, 1969 and May 1, 2003; and (iii) and in Law Number 23 of 1971 (the Iraqi Criminal Procedure Law).

(b) In interpreting Articles 11 to 13, the Trial Chambers and the Appellate Chamber may resort to the relevant decisions of international courts or tribunals as persuasive authority for their decisions.

(c) Grounds for exclusion of criminal responsibility under the said Iraqi Criminal Code shall be interpreted in a manner consistent with the Statute and with international legal obligations concerning the crimes within the jurisdiction of the Tribunal.

(d) The crimes stipulated in Articles 11 to 14 shall not be subject to any statute of limitations.

Section Seven Investigations and Indictment

Article 18

(a) The Tribunal Investigative Judge shall initiate investigations *ex-officio* or on the basis of information obtained from any source, particularly from the police, and governmental and non-governmental organizations. The Tribunal Investigative Judge shall assess the information received or obtained and decide whether there is sufficient basis to proceed.

(b) The Tribunal Investigative Judge shall have the power to question suspects, victims and witnesses, to collect evidence and to conduct on-site investigations. In carrying out these tasks, the Tribunal Investigative Judge may, as appropriate, request the assistance of the relevant governmental authorities concerned, who shall be required to provide full co-operation with the request.

(c) If questioned by a Tribunal Investigative Judge, the suspect shall be entitled to be assisted by counsel of his or her own choice, including the right to have legal assistance assigned to him or her without payment by him or her in any such case if he or she does not have sufficient means to pay for it. The suspect is entitled to have non-Iraqi legal representation, so long as the principal lawyer of such suspect is Iraqi.

(d) Upon a determination that a *prima facie* case exists, the Tribunal Investigative Judge shall prepare an indictment containing a concise statement of the facts and the crime or crimes with which the accused is charged under the Statute.

Part One Review of Indictment
Article 19

(a) If the Chief Tribunal Investigative Judge is satisfied that a *prima facie* case has been established by the Tribunal Investigative Judge, then he/she shall confirm the indictment. If not so satisfied, the indictment shall be dismissed without prejudice.

(b) Upon confirmation of an indictment, the Tribunal Investigative Judge may, at the request of the Chief Tribunal Investigative Judge, issue such orders and warrants for the arrest, detention, surrender or transfer of persons, and any other orders as may be required for the conduct of the trial.

Part Two Rights of the Accused
Article 20

(a) All persons shall be equal before the Tribunal.

(b) Everyone shall be presumed innocent until proven guilty before the Tribunal in accordance with the law.

(c) In the determination of any charge, the accused shall be entitled to a public hearing, having regard to the provisions of the Statute and the rules of procedure made hereunder.

(d) In the determination of any charge against the accused pursuant to the present Statute, the accused shall be entitled to a fair hearing conducted impartially and to the following minimum guarantees:

   1. to be informed promptly and in detail of the nature, cause and content of the charge against him;

   2. to have adequate time and facilities for the preparation of his defense and to communicate freely with counsel of his own choosing in confidence. The accused is entitled to have non-Iraqi legal representation, so long as the principal lawyer of such accused is Iraqi;

   3. to be tried without undue delay;

   4. to be tried in his presence, and to defend himself in person or through legal assistance of his own choosing; to be informed, if he does not have legal assistance, of this right; and to have legal assistance assigned to him, in any case where the interests of justice so require, and without payment by him in any such case if he does not have sufficient means to pay for it;

   5. to examine, or have examined, the witnesses against him and to obtain the attendance and examination of witnesses on his behalf under the same conditions as witnesses against him. The accused shall also be entitled to raise defences and to present other evidence admissible under this Statute and Iraqi law; and

   6. not to be compelled to testify against himself or to confess guilt, and to remain silent, without such silence being a consideration in the determination of guilt or innocence.

Section Eight Trial Proceedings

Article 21

(a) A person against whom an indictment has been issued shall, pursuant to an order or an arrest warrant of the Tribunal Investigative Judge, be taken into custody, immediately informed of the charges against him and transferred to the Tribunal.

(b) The Trial Chambers shall ensure that a trial is fair and expeditious and that proceedings are conducted in accordance with this Statute and the rules of procedure and evidence, with full respect for the rights of the accused and due regard for the protection of victims and witnesses.

(c) The Trial Chamber shall read the indictment, satisfy itself that the rights of the accused are respected, confirm that the accused understands the indictment, and instruct the accused to enter a plea.

(d) The hearings shall be public unless the Trial Chamber decides to close the proceedings in accordance with its rules of procedure and evidence. The decision to close the proceedings shall be exercised on a very limited basis.

Article 22

The Tribunal shall, in its rules of procedure and evidence, provide for the protection of victims and witnesses. Such protection measures shall take into account the rights of the accused and shall include, but shall not be limited to, the conduct of *in camera* proceedings and the protection of the identity of the victim or witness.

Article 23

(a) The Trial Chambers shall pronounce judgments and impose sentences and penalties on persons convicted of crimes within the jurisdiction of the Tribunal.

(b) The judgment shall be rendered by a simple majority of the judges of the Trial Chamber, and shall be delivered by the Trial Chamber in public. It shall be accompanied by a reasoned opinion in writing, to which separate or dissenting opinions may be appended.

Article 24

(a) The penalties that shall be imposed by the Tribunal shall be those prescribed by Iraqi law (especially Law Number 111 of 1969 of the Iraqi Criminal Code), save that for the purposes of this Tribunal, sentences of life imprisonment shall mean the remaining natural life of the person.

(b) Subject to paragraph (a) above, the penalties for crimes under Article 14 shall be those prescribed under the relevant provisions of Iraqi law.

(c) The penalty for crimes under Articles 11 to 13 shall be determined by the Trial Chambers, taking into account the factors contained in paragraphs (d) and (e) below.

(d) A person convicted of:

　1.　An offence involving murder or rape as defined under Iraqi law; or

　2.　An offence ancillary to such offence of murder or rape,

shall be dealt with as for an offence of, as the case may be, murder or rape or the corresponding ancillary offences in relation to murder or rape.

(e) The penalty for any crimes under Articles 11 to 13 which do not have a counterpart under Iraqi law shall be determined by the Trial Chambers taking into account such factors as the gravity of the crime, the individual circumstances of the convicted person and relevant international precedents.

(f) The Trial Chambers may order the forfeiture of proceeds, property or assets derived directly or indirectly from that crime, without prejudice to the rights of the *bona fide* third parties.

(g) In accordance with Article 307 of the Iraqi Criminal Procedure Code, the Tribunal has authority to confiscate any goods prohibited by law regardless of whether the case has been discharged for any lawful reason.

Section Nine Review and Appeals Proceedings

Part One Appellate Proceedings
Article 25

(a) The Appeals Chamber shall hear appeals from persons convicted by the Trial Chambers or from the Prosecutor on the following grounds:

　1.　an error on a question of law invalidating any decision;

　2.　an error of procedure; or

　3.　an error of material fact which has occasioned a miscarriage of justice.

(b) The Appeals Chamber may affirm, reverse or revise the decisions taken by the Trial Chambers.

(c) Where a verdict of acquittal is reversed by the Appeals Chamber, the case shall be referred back to a Trial Chamber for retrial.

Part Two Review Proceedings
Article 26

(a) Where a new fact has been discovered which was not known at the time of the proceedings before the Trial Chambers or the Appeals Chamber and which could have been a decisive factor in reaching the decision, the convicted person or the Prosecutor may submit to the Tribunal an application for review of the judgment.

(b) The Appeals Chamber shall reject the application if it considers it to be unfounded. If it determines that the application has merit, it may, as appropriate:

1. Reconvene the original Trial Chamber;

2. Constitute a new Trial Chamber; or

3. Retain jurisdiction over the matter,

with a view to, after hearing the parties, arriving at a determination on whether the judgment should be revised.

Section Ten Enforcement of Sentences

Article 27

Sentences shall be carried out by the legal system of Iraq in accordance with its laws.

Section Eleven General Principles and Other Matters

Article 28

The judges, investigative judges, prosecutors and the Director of the Administration Department shall be Iraqi nationals, except as provided for in Article 4(d).

Article 29

(a) The Tribunal and the national courts of Iraq shall have concurrent jurisdiction to prosecute persons for those offences prescribed in Article 14 that fall within the jurisdiction of the Tribunal.

(b) The Tribunal shall have primacy over all other Iraqi courts with respect to the crimes stipulated in Articles 11 to 13.

(c) At any stage of the procedure, the Tribunal may demand of any other Iraqi court to transfer any case being tried by it involving any crimes stipulated in Articles 11 to 14 to the Tribunal, and such court shall be required to transfer such case.

Article 30

(a) No person shall be tried before any other Iraqi court for acts for which he or she has already been tried by the Tribunal, in accordance with Articles 300 and 301 of the Iraqi Criminal Procedure Code.

(b) A person who has been tried by any Iraqi court for acts constituting crimes within the jurisdiction of the Tribunal may be subsequently tried by the Tribunal only if the Tribunal determines that the previous court proceedings were not impartial or independent, were designed to shield the accused from international or Iraqi criminal responsibility, or the case was not diligently prosecuted, provided that the requirements of Article 303 of the Iraqi Criminal Procedure Code are met or one of the conditions contained in Article 196 of the Iraqi Civil Procedure Code apply.

(c) In considering the penalty to be imposed on a person convicted of a crime under the present Statute, the Tribunal shall take into account the extent to which any penalty imposed by an Iraqi court on the same person for the same act has already been served.

Article 31

(a) The Tribunal, the judges, the Tribunal Investigative Judges, the Prosecutors, the Director of the Administration Department and their staffs shall have immunity from civil suits for their official acts.

(b) Other persons, including the accused, required at the seat of the Tribunal shall be accorded such treatment as is necessary for the proper functioning of the Tribunal.

Article 32

For purposes of this statute, the "Governing Council" shall mean the Governing Council of Iraq established on July 13, 2003. The powers conferred on the Governing Council in this Statute shall be transferred to the executive authority in any future government (the "Successor Government") established following the disbanding of the Governing Council.

Article 33

No officer, prosecutor, investigative judge, judge or other personnel of the Tribunal shall have been a member of the Ba'ath Party.

Article 34

Arabic shall be the official language of the Tribunal.

Article 35

The expenses of the Tribunal shall be borne by the regular budget of the Government of Iraq.

Article 36

The President of the Tribunal shall submit an annual report of the Tribunal to the Governing Council or the Successor Government.

Article 37

The Governing Council or the Successor Government has the powers to establish other rules and procedures in order to implement this Statute.

Article 38

This law shall become effective on the 10th day of December, 2003 and shall be published in the Official Gazette.

3. HYBRID

DOCUMENT 59

Law on the Establishment of Extraordinary Chambers in the Courts of Cambodia for the Prosecution of Crimes Committed during the Period of Democratic Kampuchea 2002 (as amended in 2004)

Reach Kram NS/RKM/0801/12 as amended by NS/RKM/1004/006

It is estimated that during the rule of the Khmer Rouge (the Communist Party of Kampuchea) from 1975 to 1979, the régime was responsible for between 1.7 and 2 million deaths. While the Khmer Rouge was overthrown in 1979 after an intervention by Vietnam, few efforts were made at the time to investigate the alleged atrocities. After many years of pressure, talks between the Government of Cambodia and the UN, aimed at bringing about the creation of a tribunal for the prosecution these crimes, began in 1997, leading to the adoption by the Cambodian National Assembly of the Law on the Establishment of Extraordinary Chambers in the Courts of Cambodia for the Prosecution of Crimes Committed During the Period of Democratic Kampuchea ('the Law') on 10 August 2002. The talks were suspended by the UN in February

2002 but recommenced in January 2003, leading to the signing of an agreement on 17 March 2003 on a draft framework for the creation of a tribunal (UN Doc A/57/769). On 27 October 2004, the Cambodian National Assembly and Senate approved the agreement and amendments to the Law. These amendments augmented the role of the Secretary-General and the international community and improved human rights' protections.

The Law is aimed at prosecuting only the senior leaders of the Khmer Rouge and those most responsible for the atrocities (Article 1) who are to be tried in special chambers of the existing Cambodian court structure consisting of the trial court and the Supreme Court (Article 2). The jurisdiction of the extraordinary chambers covers only the period between 17 April 1975 and 6 January 1979 and extends to specified crimes under the 1956 Penal Code of Cambodia (Article 3), the crime of genocide (Article 4), crimes against humanity (Article 5), grave breaches of the Geneva Convention 1949 (Article 6), the destruction of cultural property during armed conflict pursuant to the 1954 Hague Convention for Protection of Cultural Property in the Event of Armed Conflict (Article 7) and crimes against internationally protected persons pursuant to the Vienna Convention of 1961 on Diplomatic Relations (Article 8).

The trial court consists of five judges, three Cambodians, of whom one acts as president, and two foreign judges. The Supreme Court consists of seven judges, four Cambodians, of whom one acts as president, and three foreign judges (Article 9). Articles 10–13 govern the appointment of judges who are to be assisted by Cambodian and international staff 'as needed'. Prosecution of cases is to be undertaken by co-prosecutors, one Cambodian and one foreign (Article 16); Articles 17–22 govern their appointment and work. All investigations are to be undertaken by two co-investigating judges, one Cambodian and one foreign (Article 23); their appointment and work is governed by Articles 24–28. The Law provides for individual criminal responsibility and official rank does not relieve individuals of responsibility or mitigate punishment (Article 29). Articles 33–37 govern trial proceedings. Punishments are limited to imprisonment (Article 38) and no amnesties or pardons are to be granted (Article 40). The extraordinary chambers are to be located in Phnom Penh.

The extraordinary chambers are yet to be put into operation due to a failure to secure adequate financing. If and when they do come into operation, they will sit for a period of three years. Pol Pot, the Khmer Rouge leader, died in 1998 and only a handful of Khmer Rouge's top leaders remain alive.

Chapter I General Provisions

Article 1

The purpose of this law is to bring to trial senior leaders of Democratic Kampuchea and those who were most responsible for the crimes and serious violations of Cambodian penal law, international humanitarian law and custom, and international conventions recognized by Cambodia, that were committed during the period from 17 April 1975 to 6 January 1979.

Chapter II Competence

Article 2

Extraordinary Chambers shall be established in the existing court structure, the trial court and the Supreme Court, to bring to trial senior leaders of Democratic Kampuchea and those who were most responsible for the crimes and serious violations of Cambodian laws related to crimes, international humanitarian law and custom, and international conventions recognized by Cambodia, that were committed during the period from 17 April 1975 to 6 January 1979.

Senior leaders of Democratic Kampuchea and those who were most responsible for the above acts are hereinafter designated as "Suspects".

Article 3

The Extraordinary Chambers shall have the power to bring to trial all Suspects who committed any of these crimes set forth in the 1956 Penal Code, and which were committed during the period from 17 April 1975 to 6 January 1979:

- Homicide (Article 501, 503, 504, 505, 506, 507 and 508)
- Torture (Article 500)
- Religious Persecution (Articles 209 and 210)

The statute of limitations set forth in the 1956 Penal Code shall be extended for an additional 30 years for the crimes enumerated above, which are within the jurisdiction of the Extraordinary Chambers.

The penalty under Articles 209, 500, 506 and 507 of the 1956 Penal Code shall be limited to a maximum of life imprisonment, in accordance with Article 32 of the Constitution of the Kingdom of Cambodia, and as further stipulated in Articles 38 and 39 of this Law.

Article 4

The Extraordinary Chambers shall have the power to bring to trial all Suspects who committed the crimes of genocide as defined in the Convention on the Prevention and Punishment of the Crime of Genocide of 1948, and which were committed during the period from 17 April 1975 to 6 January 1979.

The acts of genocide, which have no statute of limitations, mean any acts committed with the intent to destroy, in whole or in part, a national, ethnical, racial or religious group as such:

- killing members of the group;
- causing serious bodily or mental harm to members of the group;
- deliberately inflicting on the group conditions of life calculated to bring about its physical destruction in whole or in part;
- imposing measures intended to prevent births within the group;
- forcibly transferring children from one group to another group.

The following acts shall be punishable under this Article:

- attempts to commit acts of genocide;
- conspiracy to commit acts of genocide;
- participation in acts of acts of genocide.

Article 5

The Extraordinary Chambers shall have the power to bring to trial all Suspects who committed crimes against humanity during the period 17 April 1975 to 6 January 1979.

Crimes against humanity, which have no statute of limitations, are any acts committed as part of a widespread or systematic attack against any civilian population, on national, political, ethnical, racial or religious grounds, such as:

- murder;
- extermination;
- enslavement;

- deportation;
- imprisonment;
- torture;
- rape;
- persecutions on political, racial, and religious grounds;
- other inhuman acts.

Article 6

The Extraordinary Chambers shall have the power to bring to trial all Suspects who committed or ordered the commission of grave breaches of the Geneva Convention of 12 August 1949, such as the following acts against persons or property protected under provisions of this Convention, and which were committed during the period 17 April 1975 to 6 January 1979:

- willful killing;
- torture or inhumane treatment;
- willfully causing great suffering or serious injury to body or health;
- destruction and serious damage to property, not justified by military necessity and carried out unlawfully and wantonly;
- compelling a prisoner of war or a civilian to serve in the forces of a hostile power;
- wilfully depriving a prisoner of war or civilian the rights of fair and regular trial;
- unlawful deportation or transfer or unlawful confinement of a civilian;
- taking civilians as hostages.

Article 7

The Extraordinary Chambers shall have the power to bring to trial all Suspects responsible for the destruction of cultural property during armed conflict pursuant to the 1954 Hague Convention for Protection of Cultural Property in the Event of Armed Conflict, and which were committed during the period from 17 April 1975 to 6 January 1979.

Article 8

The Extraordinary Chambers shall have the power to bring to trial all Suspects responsible for crimes against internationally protected persons pursuant to the Vienna Convention of 1961 on Diplomatic Relations, and which were committed during the period from 17 April 1975 to 6 January 1979.

Chapter III Composition of the Extraordinary Chambers

Article 9

The Trial Chamber shall be an Extraordinary Chamber composed of five professional judges, of whom three are Cambodian judges, with one as president, and two foreign judges; and before which the Co-Prosecutors shall present their cases. The president shall appoint one or more clerks of the court to participate.

The Supreme Court Chamber, which shall serve as both appellate chamber and final instance, shall be an Extraordinary Chamber composed of seven judges, of whom four are Cambodian judges, with one as president, and three foreign judges; and before which the Co-Prosecutors shall present their cases. The president shall appoint one or more clerks of the court to participate.

Chapter IV Appointment of Judges

Article 10

The judges of the Extraordinary Chambers shall be appointed from among the currently practising judges or are additionally appointed, in accordance with the existing procedures for appointment of judges, all of whom shall have high moral character, a spirit of impartiality and integrity, and experience, particularly in criminal law or international law, including international humanitarian law and human rights law.

Judges shall be independent in the performance of their functions, and shall not accept or seek any instructions from any government or any other source.

Article 11

The Supreme Council of the Magistracy shall appoint at least seven Cambodian judges to act as judges of the Extraordinary Chambers, and shall appoint reserve judges as needed, and shall also appoint the President of each of the Extraordinary Chambers from the above Cambodian judges so appointed, in accordance with the existing procedures for appointment of judges.

The reserve Cambodian judges shall replace the appointed Cambodian judges in case of their absence or withdrawal. These reserve judges may continue to perform their regular duties in their respective courts.

The Supreme Council of the Magistracy shall appoint at least five individuals of foreign nationality to act as foreign judges of the Extraordinary Chambers upon nomination by the Secretary-General of the United Nations.

The Secretary-General of the United Nations shall submit a list of not less than seven candidates for foreign judges to the Royal Government of Cambodia, from which the Supreme Council of the Magistracy shall appoint five sitting judges and at least two reserve judges. In addition to the foreign judges sitting in the Extraordinary Chambers and present at every stage of the proceedings, the President of the Chamber may, on a case-by-case basis, designate one or more reserve judges already appointed by the Supreme Council of the Magistracy to be present at each stage of the trial, and to replace a foreign judge if that judge is unable to continue sitting.

Article 12

All judges under this law shall enjoy equal status and rank according to each level of the Extraordinary Chambers.

Each judge under this law shall be appointed for the period of these proceedings.

Article 13

Judges shall be assisted by Cambodian and international staff as needed.

In choosing staff to serve as assistants and law clerks, the Director of the Office of Administration shall interview if necessary, and with the approval of the Cambodian judges by majority vote, hire staff who shall be appointed by the Royal Government of Cambodia. The Deputy Director of the Office of Administration shall be responsible for the recruitment and administration of all international staff. The number of assistants and law clerks shall be chosen in proportion to the Cambodian judges and foreign judges.

Cambodian staff shall be selected from Cambodian civil servants or other qualified nationals of Cambodia, if necessary.

Chapter V Decisions of the Extraordinary Chambers

Article 14

1. The judges shall attempt to achieve unanimity in their decisions. If this is not possible, the following shall apply:

    (a) a decision by the Extraordinary Chamber of the trial court shall require the affirmative vote of at least four judges;

    (b) a decision by the Extraordinary Chamber of the Supreme Court shall require the affirmative vote of at least five judges.

2. When there is no unanimity, the decision of the Extraordinary Chambers shall contain the views of the majority and the minority.

Article 15

The Presidents shall convene the appointed judges at the appropriate time to proceed with the work of the Extraordinary Chambers.

Chapter VI Co-Prosecutors

Article 16

All indictments in the Extraordinary Chambers shall be made by two prosecutors, one Cambodian and another foreign, who shall work together as Co-Prosecutors to prepare indictments against the Suspects in the Extraordinary Chambers.

Article 17

The Co-Prosecutors in the trial court shall have the right to appeal the verdict of the Extraordinary Chamber of the trial court.

Article 18

The Supreme Council of the Magistracy shall appoint Cambodian prosecutors and Cambodian reserve prosecutors as necessary from among the Cambodian professional judges.

The reserve prosecutors shall replace the regularly appointed prosecutors in case of their absence. These reserve prosecutors may continue to perform their regular duties in their respective courts.

One foreign prosecutor with the competence to appear in both Extraordinary Chambers shall be appointed by the Supreme Council of the Magistracy upon nomination by the Secretary-General of the United Nations.

The Secretary-General of the United Nations shall submit a list of at least two candidates for foreign Co-Prosecutor to the Royal Government of Cambodia, from which the Supreme Council of the Magistracy shall appoint one prosecutor and one reserve prosecutor.

Article 19

The Co-Prosecutors shall be appointed from among those individuals who are appointed in accordance with the existing procedures for selection of prosecutors who have high moral character and integrity and who are experienced in the conduct of investigations and prosecutions of criminal cases.

The Co-Prosecutors shall be independent in the performance of their functions and shall not accept or seek instructions from any government or any other source.

Article 20

The Co-Prosecutors shall prosecute in accordance with existing procedures in force. If these existing procedures do not deal with a particular matter, or if there is uncertainty regarding their interpretation or application or if there is a question regarding their consistency with international standards, the Co-Prosecutors may seek guidance in procedural rules established at the international level.

In the event of disagreement between the Co-Prosecutors the following shall apply:

The prosecution shall proceed unless the Co-Prosecutors or one of them requests within thirty days that the difference shall be settled in accordance with the following provisions.

The Co-Prosecutors shall submit written statements of facts and the reasons for their different positions to the Director of the Office of Administration.

The difference shall be settled forthwith by a Pre-Trial Chamber of five judges, three Cambodian judges appointed by the Supreme Council of the Magistracy, one of whom shall be President, and two foreign judges appointed by the Supreme Council of the Magistracy upon nomination by the Secretary-General of the United Nations. The appointment of the above judges shall follow the provisions of Article 10 of this Law.

Upon receipt of the statements referred to in the third paragraph, the Director of the Office of Administration shall immediately convene the Pre-Trial Chamber and communicate the statements to its members.

A decision of the Pre-Trial Chamber, against which there is no appeal, requires the affirmative vote of at least four judges. The decision shall be communicated to the Director of the Office of Administration, who shall publish it and communicate it to the Co-Prosecutors. They shall immediately proceed in accordance with the decision of the Chamber. If there is no majority, as required for a decision, the prosecution shall proceed.

In carrying out the prosecution, the Co-Prosecutors may seek the assistance of the Royal Government of Cambodia if such assistance would be useful to the prosecution, and such assistance shall be provided.

Article 21

The Co-Prosecutors under this law shall enjoy equal status and conditions of service according to each level of the Extraordinary Chambers.

Each Co-Prosecutor shall be appointed for the period of these proceedings.

In the event of the absence of the foreign Co-Prosecutor, he or she shall be replaced by the reserve Co-Prosecutor.

Article 22

Each Co-Prosecutor shall have the right to choose one or more deputy prosecutors to assist him or her with prosecution before the chambers. Deputy foreign prosecutors shall be appointed by the foreign Co-Prosecutor from a list provided by the Secretary-General.

The Co-Prosecutors shall be assisted by Cambodian and international staff as needed in their offices. In choosing staff to serve as assistants, the Director of the Office of Administration shall interview, if necessary, and with the approval of the Cambodian Co-Prosecutor, hire staff who shall be appointed by the Royal Government of Cambodia. The Deputy Director of the Office of Administration shall be responsible for the recruitment and administration of all foreign staff. The number of assistants shall be chosen in proportion to the Cambodian prosecutors and foreign prosecutors.

Cambodian staff shall be selected from Cambodian civil servants and, if necessary, other qualified nationals of Cambodia.

ChapterVII Investigations

Article 23

All investigations shall be the joint responsibility of two investigating judges, one Cambodian and another foreign, hereinafter referred to as Co-Investigating Judges, and shall follow existing procedures in force. If these existing procedures do not deal with a particular matter, or if there is uncertainty regarding their interpretation or application or if there is a question regarding their consistency with international standards, the Co-Investigating Judges may seek guidance in procedural rules established at the international level.

In the event of disagreement between the Co-Investigating Judges the following shall apply:

The investigation shall proceed unless the Co-Investigating Judges or one of them requests within thirty days that the difference shall be settled in accordance with the following provisions.

The Co-Investigating Judges shall submit written statements of facts and the reasons for their different positions to the Director of the Office of Administration.

The difference shall be settled forthwith by the Pre-Trial Chamber referred to in Article 20.

Upon receipt of the statements referred to in the third paragraph, the Director of the Office of Administration shall immediately convene the Pre-Trial Chamber and communicate the statements to its members.

A decision of the Pre-Trial Chamber, against which there is no appeal, requires the affirmative vote of at least four judges. The decision shall be communicated to the Director of the Office of Administration, who shall publish it and communicate it to the Co-Investigating Judges. They shall immediately proceed in accordance with the decision of the Pre-Trial Chamber. If there is no majority as required for a decision, the investigation shall proceed.

The Co-Investigating Judges shall conduct investigations on the basis of information obtained from any institution, including the Government, United Nations organs, or non-governmental organisations.

The Co-Investigating Judges shall have the power to question suspects and victims, to hear witnesses, and to collect evidence in accordance with existing procedures in force. In the event the Co-Investigating Judges consider it necessary to do so, they may issue an order requesting the Co-Prosecutors to interrogate the witnesses.

In carrying out the investigations, the Co-Investigating Judges may seek the assistance of the Royal Government of Cambodia, if such assistance would be useful to the investigation, and such assistance shall be provided.

Article 24

During the investigation, Suspects shall be unconditionally entitled to assistance of counsel of their own choosing, and to have legal assistance assigned to them free of charge if they cannot afford it, as well as the right to interpretation, as necessary, into and from a language they speak and understand.

Article 25

The Co-Investigating Judges shall be appointed from among the existing judges or from judges who are additionally appointed in accordance with the existing procedures for appointment of judges, who have high moral character, a spirit of impartiality and integrity, and who are experienced in criminal investigations. They shall be independent in the performance of their functions and shall not accept or seek instructions from any government or any other source.

Article 26

The Cambodian Co-Investigating Judge and the reserve Investigating Judges shall be appointed by the Supreme Council of the Magistracy from among the Cambodian professional judges.

The reserve Investigating Judges shall replace the regularly appointed Investigating Judges in case of their absence or withdrawal. The reserve Investigating Judges may continue to perform their regular duties in their respective courts.

The Supreme Council of the Magistracy shall appoint the foreign Co-Investigating Judge for the period of investigations, upon nomination by the Secretary-General of the United Nations.

The Secretary-General of the United Nations shall submit a list of at least two candidates for foreign Co-Investigating Judge to the Royal Government of Cambodia, from which the Supreme Council of the Magistracy shall appoint one sitting Investigating Judge and one reserve Investigating Judge.

Article 27

All Investigating Judges under this law shall enjoy equal status and conditions of service.

Each Investigating Judge shall be appointed for the period of the investigation.

In the event of the absence or withdrawal of the foreign Co-Investigating Judge, he or she shall be replaced by the reserve foreign Co-Investigating Judge.

Article 28

The Co-Investigating Judges shall be assisted by Cambodian and international staff as needed.

In choosing staff to serve as assistants, the Director of the Office of Administration shall comply with the provisions set forth in Article 13 of this law.

Chapter VIII Individual Responsibility

Article 29

Any Suspect who planned, instigated, ordered, aided and abetted, or committed the crimes referred to in articles 3, 4, 5, 6, 7 and 8 of this law shall be individually responsible for the crime.

The position or rank of any Suspect shall not relieve such person of criminal responsibility or mitigate punishment.

The fact that any of the acts referred to in Articles 3, 4, 5, 6, 7 and 8 of this law were committed by a subordinate does not relieve the superior of personal criminal responsibility if the superior had effective command and control or authority and control over the subordinate, and the superior knew or had reason to know that the subordinate was about to commit such acts or had done so and the superior failed to take the necessary and reasonable measures to prevent such acts or to punish the perpetrators.

The fact that a Suspect acted pursuant to an order of the Government of Democratic Kampuchea or of a superior shall not relieve the Suspect of individual criminal responsibility.

Chapter IX Office of Administration

Article 30

The staff of the judges, the investigating judges and prosecutors of the Extraordinary Chambers shall be supervised by an Office of Administration.

The Office of Administration shall have a Cambodian Director, a foreign Deputy Director and such other staff as necessary.

Article 31

The Director of the Office of Administration shall be appointed by the Royal Government of Cambodia for a two-year term and shall be eligible for reappointment.

The Director of the Office of Administration shall be responsible for the overall management of the Office of Administration, except in matters that are subject to United Nations rules and procedures.

The Director of the Office of Administration shall be selected from among those with significant experience in court administration and fluency in one of the foreign languages used in the Extraordinary Chambers, and shall be a person of high moral character and integrity.

The foreign Deputy Director shall be appointed by the Secretary-General of the United Nations and assigned by the Royal Government of Cambodia, and shall be responsible for the recruitment and administration of all international staff, as required by the foreign components of the Extraordinary Chambers, the Co-Investigating Judges, the Co-Prosecutors' Office, and the Office of Administration. The Deputy Director shall administer the resources provided through the United Nations Trust Fund.

The Office of Administration shall be assisted by Cambodian and international staff as necessary. All Cambodian staff of the Office of Administration shall be appointed by the Royal Government of Cambodia at the request of the Director. Foreign staff shall be appointed by the Deputy Director.

Cambodian staff shall be selected from the Cambodian civil service system and, if necessary, other qualified nationals of Cambodia.

Article 32

All staff assigned to the judges, Co-Investigating Judges, Co-Prosecutors, and Office of Administration shall enjoy the same working conditions according to each level of the Extraordinary Chambers.

Chapter X Trial Proceedings in the Extraordinary Chambers

Article 33

The Extraordinary Chambers of the trial court shall ensure that trials are fair and expeditious and are conducted in accordance with existing procedures in force, with full respect for the rights of the accused and for the protection of victims and witnesses. If these existing procedures do not deal with a particular matter, or if there is uncertainty regarding their interpretation or application or if there is a question regarding their consistency with international standards, the guidance may be sought in procedural rules established at the international level.

The Extraordinary Chambers of the trial court shall exercise their jurisdiction in accordance with international standards of justice, fairness and due process of law, as set out in Articles 14 and 15 of the 1966 International Covenant on Civil and Political Rights.

Suspects who have been indicted and arrested shall be brought to the Trial Chamber according to existing procedures in force. The Royal Government of Cambodia shall guarantee the security of the Suspects who appear before the court, and is responsible for taking measures for the arrest of the Suspects prosecuted under this law. Justice police shall be assisted by other law enforcement elements of the Royal Government of Cambodia, including the armed forces, in order to ensure that accused persons are brought into custody immediately.

Conditions for the arrest and the custody of the accused shall conform to existing law in force.

The Court shall provide for the protection of victims and witnesses. Such protection measures shall include, but not be limited to, the conduct of in camera proceedings and the protection of the victim's identity.

Article 34

Trials shall be public and open the representatives of foreign States, of the Secretary-General of the United Nations, of the media and of national and international non-government organizations unless in exceptional circumstances the Extraordinary Chambers decide to close the proceedings for good cause in accordance with existing procedures in force where publicity would prejudice the interests of justice.

Article 35

The accused shall be presumed innocent as long as the court has not given its definitive judgment.

In determining charges against the accused, the accused shall be equally entitled to the following minimum guarantees, in accordance with Article 14 of the International Covenant on Civil and Political Rights:

(a) To be informed promptly and in detail in a language that they understand of the nature and cause of the charge against them;

(b) To have adequate time for the preparation of their defence and to communicate with counsel of their own choosing;

(c) To be tried without delay;

(d) To be tried in their presence and to defend themselves in person or with the assistance of counsel of their own choosing, to be informed of this right and to have legal assistance assigned to them free of charge if they do not sufficient means to pay for it;

(e) To examine evidence against them and obtain the presentation and examination of evidence on their behalf under the same conditions as evidence against them;

(f) To have the free assistance of an interpreter if the accused cannot understand or does not speak the language used in the court;

(g) Not to be compelled to testify against themselves or to confess guilt.

Article 36

The Extraordinary Chamber of the Supreme Court shall decide appeals made by the accused, the victims, or the Co-Prosecutors against the decision of the Extraordinary Chamber of the trial court. In this case, the Supreme Court Chamber shall make final decisions on both issues of law and fact, and shall not return the case to the Extraordinary Chamber of the trial court.

Article 37

The provision of Article 33, 34 and 35 shall apply *mutatis mutandis* in respect of proceedings before the Extraordinary Chambers of the Supreme Court.

Chapter XI Penalties

Article 38

All penalties shall be limited to imprisonment.

Article 39

Those who have committed crimes as provided in Articles 3 4, 5, 6, 7 and 8 shall be sentenced to a prison term from five years to life imprisonment.

In addition to imprisonment, the Extraordinary Chamber of the trial court may order the confiscation of personal property, money, and real property acquired unlawfully or by criminal conduct.

The confiscated property shall be returned to the State.

Chapter XII Amnesty and Pardons

Article 40

The Royal Government of Cambodia shall not request an amnesty or pardon for any persons who may be investigated for or convicted of crimes referred to in Articles 3, 4, 5, 6, 7 and 8 of this law. The scope of any amnesty or pardon that may have been granted prior to the enactment of this Law is a matter to be decided by the Extraordinary Chambers.

Chapter XIII Status, Privileges and Immunities

Article 41

The foreign judges, the foreign Co-Investigating Judge, the foreign Co-Prosecutor and the Deputy Director of the Office of Administration, together with their families forming part of their household, shall enjoy all of the privileges and immunities, exemptions and facilities accorded to diplomatic agents in accordance with the 1961 Vienna Convention on Diplomatic Relations. Such officials shall enjoy exemption from taxation in Cambodia on their salaries, emoluments and allowances.

Article 42

1. Cambodian judges, the Co-Investigating Judge, the Co-Prosecutor, the Director of the Office of Administration and personnel shall be accorded immunity from legal process in respect of words spoken or written and all acts performed by them in their official capacity. Such immunity shall continue to be accorded after termination of employment with the Extraordinary Chambers, the Pre-Trial Chamber and the Office of Administration.

2. International personnel shall be accorded in addition:

   (a) immunity from legal process in respect of words spoken or written and all acts performed by them in their official capacity. Such immunity shall continue to be accorded after termination of employment with the Co-Investigating Judges, the Co-Prosecutors, the Extraordinary Chambers, the Pre-Trial Chamber and the Office of Administration.

   (b) immunity from taxation on salaries, allowances and emoluments paid to them by the United Nations;

   (c) immunity from immigration restriction;

   (d) the right to import free of duties and taxes, except for payment for services, their furniture and effects at the time of first taking up their official duties in Cambodia.

3. The counsel of a suspect or an accused who has been admitted as such by the Extraordinary Chambers shall not be subjected by the Government to any measure that may affect the free and independent exercise of his or her functions under the Law on the Establishment of the Extraordinary Chambers. In particular, the counsel shall be accorded:

   (a) immunity from personal arrest or detention and from seizure of personal baggage relating to his or her functions in the proceedings;

   (b) inviolability of all documents relating to the exercise of his or her functions as a counsel of a suspect or accused;

   (c) immunity from criminal or civil jurisdiction in respect of words spoken or written and acts performed in his or her capacity as counsel. Such immunity shall continue to be accorded after termination of their function as counsel of a suspect or accused.

4. The archives of the co-investigating judges, the co-prosecutors, the Extraordinary Chambers, the Pre-Trial Chamber and the Office of Administration and in general all documents and materials made available to, belonging to, or used by them, wherever located in the Kingdom of Cambodia and by whomsoever held, shall be inviolable for the duration of the proceedings.

Chapter XIV Location of the Extraordinary Chambers

Article 43

The Extraordinary Chambers established in the trial court and the Supreme Court shall be located in Phnom Penh.

Chapter XV Expenses and Salaries

Article 44

The expenses and salaries of the Extraordinary Chambers shall be as follows:

1. The expenses and salaries of the Cambodian administrative officials and staff, the Cambodian judges and reserve judges, investigating judges and reserve investigating judges, and prosecutors and reserve prosecutors shall be borne by the Cambodian national budget.

2. The expenses of the foreign administrative officials and staff, the foreign judges, the foreign Co-investigating judge and the foreign Co-prosecutor sent by the Secretary-General of the United Nations shall be borne by the United Nations Trust Fund.

3. The defence counsel may receive fees for mounting the defence.

4. The Extraordinary Chambers may receive additional assistance for their expenses from other voluntary funds contributed by foreign governments, international institutions, non-governmental organisations, and other persons wishing to assist the proceedings.

Chapter XVI Working Language

Article 45

The official working language of the Extraordinary Chambers shall be Khmer, English and French.

Chapter XVII Absence of Foreign Judges or Co-Prosecutors

Article 46

In order to ensure timely and smooth implementation of this law, in the event any foreign judges or foreign investigating judges or foreign prosecutors fail or refuse to participate in the Extraordinary Chambers, the Supreme Council of the Magistracy shall appoint other judges or investigating judges or prosecutors to fill any vacancies from the lists of foreign candidates provided for in Article 11, Article 18, and Article 26. In the event those lists are exhausted, and the Secretary-General of the United Nations does not supplement the lists with new candidates, or in the event that the United Nations withdraws its support from the Extraordinary Chambers, any such vacancies shall be filled by the Supreme Council of the Magistracy from candidates recommended by the Governments of Member States of the United Nations or from among other foreign legal personalities.

If, following such procedures, there are still no foreign judges or foreign investigating judges or foreign prosecutors participating in the work of the Extraordinary Chambers and no foreign candidates have been identified to occupy the vacant positions, then the Supreme Council of the Magistracy may choose replacement Cambodian judges, investigating judges or prosecutors.

Chapter XVIII Existence of the Court

Article 47

The Extraordinary Chambers in the courts of Cambodia shall be dissolved following the conclusion of these proceedings.

Article 47 bis

Following its ratification in accordance with the relevant provisions of the law of Kingdom of Cambodia regarding competence to conclude treaties, the Agreement between the United Nations and the Royal Government of Cambodia Concerning the Prosecution under Cambodian Law of Crime Committed during the period of Democratic Kampuchea, done at Phnom Penh on 6 June 2003, shall apply as law within the Kingdom of Cambodia.

DOCUMENT 60

Statute of the Special Court for Sierra Leone 2002
UN Doc S/2002/246

By Resolution 1315 (2000), the UN Security Council requested the Secretary-General to negotiate an agreement with the Government of Sierra Leone to create an independent special court to prosecute atrocities committed in the country during its civil conflict. The agreement was concluded on 16 January 2002 (UN Doc S/2002/246). The statute of the Special Court was annexed to the agreement as an integral part thereof.

The Special Court has jurisdiction over persons bearing the greatest responsibility for serious violations of international humanitarian law and Sierra Leonean law committed on the territory of Sierra Leone since 30 November 1996 (Article 1). The jurisdiction covers crimes against humanity (Article 2), violations of Article 3 common to the Geneva Conventions and of Additional Protocol II (Article 3), as well as other serious violations of international humanitarian law (Article 4) and specified crimes under Sierra Leonean law (Article 5). The statute provides for individual criminal responsibility and official rank does not relieve individuals of responsibility or mitigate punishment (Article 6). The Special Court does not have jurisdiction over individuals who were under the age of 15 at the time when alleged crimes were committed and special consideration is given to individuals who were between the ages of 15 and 18 at the relevant time (Article 7). The jurisdiction of the Special Court is concurrent with the national courts of Sierra Leone, but the Special Court has primacy over national courts (Article 8).

The Special Court consists of the chambers comprising one or more trial chambers and an appeals chamber, the prosecutor and the registry (Article 11). The trial chambers consist of three judges, one appointed by the Sierra Leonean Government and two by the UN Secretary-General. The appeals chamber is made up of five judges, two appointed by the Sierra Leonean Government and three by the UN Secretary-General. Each chamber appoints a presiding judge and the presiding judge of the appeals chamber serves as the president of the Special Court (Article 12). The Rules of Procedure and Evidence of the International Criminal Tribunal for Rwanda **(see Document 52)** *apply* mutatis mutandis *to the Special Court (Article 14). The prosecutor is appointed by the UN Secretary-General and is responsible for investigations and prosecutions (Article 15). Rights of the accused are delimited in Article 17 and punishments are to include imprisonment as well as forfeiture of property, proceeds and assets unlawfully acquired (Article 19). Articles 20 and 21 govern appeals and review proceedings.*

The Special Court sits in Freetown and has indicted 13 individuals. The deaths of two indictees led to the withdrawal of their indictments. Of the other 11 indictees, all bar two are in the custody of the Special Court. Cases against individuals associated with the three different groups involved in the civil conflict, the Civil Defence Forces (CDF), the Revolutionary United Front (RUF) and the Armed Forces Revolutionary Council (AFRC) have been consolidated into three trials. The CDF and RUF cases began in June 2004 and July 2004 respectively and the case against the AFRC began in March 2005.

See also www.sc-sl.org.

Having been established by an Agreement between the United Nations and the Government of Sierra Leone pursuant to Security Council resolution 1315 (2000) of 14 August 2000, the Special Court for Sierra Leone (hereinafter "the Special Court") shall function in accordance with the provisions of the present Statute.

Article 1 Competence of the Special Court

1. The Special Court shall, except as provided in subparagraph (2), have the power to prosecute persons who bear the greatest responsibility for serious violations of international humanitarian law and Sierra Leonean law committed in the territory of Sierra Leone since 30 November 1996, including those leaders who, in committing such crimes, have threatened the establishment of and implementation of the peace process in Sierra Leone.

2. Any transgressions by peacekeepers and related personnel present in Sierra Leone pursuant to the Status of Mission Agreement in force between the United Nations and the Government of Sierra Leone or agreements between Sierra Leone and other Governments or regional organizations, or, in the absence of such agreement, provided that the peacekeeping operations were undertaken with the consent of the Government of Sierra Leone, shall be within the primary jurisdiction of the sending State.

3. In the event the sending State is unwilling or unable genuinely to carry out an investigation or prosecution, the Court may, if authorized by the Security Council on the proposal of any State, exercise jurisdiction over such persons.

Article 2 Crimes against humanity

The Special Court shall have the power to prosecute persons who committed the following crimes as part of a widespread or systematic attack against any civilian population:

(a) Murder;

(b) Extermination;

(c) Enslavement;

(d) Deportation;

(e) Imprisonment;

(f) Torture;

(g) Rape, sexual slavery, enforced prostitution, forced pregnancy and any other form of sexual violence;

(h) Persecution on political, racial, ethnic or religious grounds;

(i) Other inhumane acts.

Article 3 Violations of Article 3 common to the Geneva Conventions and of Additional Protocol II

The Special Court shall have the power to prosecute persons who committed or ordered the commission of serious violations of article 3 common to the Geneva Conventions of 12 August

1949 for the Protection of War Victims, and of Additional Protocol II thereto of 8 June 1977. These violations shall include:

(a) Violence to life, health and physical or mental well-being of persons, in particular murder as well as cruel treatment such as torture, mutilation or any form of corporal punishment;

(b) Collective punishments;

(c) Taking of hostages;

(d) Acts of terrorism;

(e) Outrages upon personal dignity, in particular humiliating and degrading treatment, rape, enforced prostitution and any form of indecent assault;

(f) Pillage;

(g) The passing of sentences and the carrying out of executions without previous judgment pronounced by a regularly constituted court, affording all the judicial guarantees which are recognized as indispensable by civilized peoples;

(h) Threats to commit any of the foregoing acts.

Article 4 Other serious violations of international humanitarian law

The Special Court shall have the power to prosecute persons who committed the following serious violations of international humanitarian law:

(a) Intentionally directing attacks against the civilian population as such or against individual civilians not taking direct part in hostilities;

(b) Intentionally directing attacks against personnel, installations, material, units or vehicles involved in a humanitarian assistance or peacekeeping mission in accordance with the Charter of the United Nations, as long as they are entitled to the protection given to civilians or civilian objects under the international law of armed conflict;

(c) Conscripting or enlisting children under the age of 15 years into armed forces or groups or using them to participate actively in hostilities.

Article 5 Crimes under Sierra Leonean law

The Special Court shall have the power to prosecute persons who have committed the following crimes under Sierra Leonean law:

(a) Offences relating to the abuse of girls under the Prevention of Cruelty to Children Act, 1926 (Cap. 31):

   (i) Abusing a girl under 13 years of age, contrary to section 6;

   (ii) Abusing a girl between 13 and 14 years of age, contrary to section 7;

   (iii) Abduction of a girl for immoral purposes, contrary to section 12.

(b) Offences relating to the wanton destruction of property under the Malicious Damage Act, 1861:

   (i) Setting fire to dwelling - houses, any person being therein, contrary to section 2;

   (ii) Setting fire to public buildings, contrary to sections 5 and 6;

   (iii) Setting fire to other buildings, contrary to section 6.

Article 6 Individual criminal responsibility

1. A person who planned, instigated, ordered, committed or otherwise aided and abetted in the planning, preparation or execution of a crime referred to in articles 2 to 4 of the present Statute shall be individually responsible for the crime.

2. The official position of any accused persons, whether as Head of State or Government or as a responsible government official, shall not relieve such person of criminal responsibility nor mitigate punishment.

3. The fact that any of the acts referred to in articles 2 to 4 of the present Statute was committed by a subordinate does not relieve his or her superior of criminal responsibility if he or she knew or had reason to know that the subordinate was about to commit such acts or had done so and the superior had failed to take the necessary and reasonable measures to prevent such acts or to punish the perpetrators thereof.

4. The fact that an accused person acted pursuant to an order of a Government or of a superior shall not relieve him or her of criminal responsibility, but may be considered in mitigation of punishment if the Special Court determines that justice so requires.

5. Individual criminal responsibility for the crimes referred to in article 5 shall be determined in accordance with the respective laws of Sierra Leone.

Article 7 Jurisdiction over persons of 15 years of age

1. The Special Court shall have no jurisdiction over any person who was under the age of 15 at the time of the alleged commission of the crime. Should any person who was at the time of the alleged commission of the crime between 15 and 18 years of age come before the Court, he or she shall be treated with dignity and a sense of worth, taking into account his or her young age and the desirability of promoting his or her rehabilitation, reintegration into and assumption of a constructive role in society, and in accordance with international human rights standards, in particular the rights of the child.

2. In the disposition of a case against a juvenile offender, the Special Court shall order any of the following: care guidance and supervision orders, community service orders, counselling, foster care, correctional, educational and vocational training programmes, approved schools and, as appropriate, any programmes of disarmament, demobilization and reintegration or programmes of child protection agencies.

Article 8 Concurrent jurisdiction

1. The Special Court and the national courts of Sierra Leone shall have concurrent jurisdiction.

2. The Special Court shall have primacy over the national courts of Sierra Leone. At any stage of the procedure, the Special Court may formally request a national court to defer to its competence in accordance with the present Statute and the Rules of Procedure and Evidence.

Article 9 Non bis in idem

1. No person shall be tried before a national court of Sierra Leone for acts for which he or she has already been tried by the Special Court.

2. A person who has been tried by a national court for the acts referred to in articles 2 to 4 of the present Statute may be subsequently tried by the Special Court if:

    (a) The act for which he or she was tried was characterized as an ordinary crime; or

    (b) The national court proceedings were not impartial or independent, were designed to shield the accused from international criminal responsibility or the case was not diligently prosecuted.

3. In considering the penalty to be imposed on a person convicted of a crime under the present Statute, the Special Court shall take into account the extent to which any penalty imposed by a national court on the same person for the same act has already been served.

Article 10 Amnesty

An amnesty granted to any person falling within the jurisdiction of the Special Court in respect of the crimes referred to in articles 2 to 4 of the present Statute shall not be a bar to prosecution.

Article 11 Organization of the Special Court

The Special Court shall consist of the following organs:

(a) The Chambers, comprising one or more Trial Chambers and an Appeals Chamber;

(b) The Prosecutor; and

(c) The Registry.

Article 12 Composition of the Chambers

1. The Chambers shall be composed of not less than eight (8) or more than eleven (11) independent judges, who shall serve as follows:

    (a) Three judges shall serve in the Trial Chamber, of whom one shall be a judge appointed by the Government of Sierra Leone, and two judges appointed by the Secretary-General of the United Nations (hereinafter "the Secretary-General").

    (b) Five judges shall serve in the Appeals Chamber, of whom two shall be judges appointed by the Government of Sierra Leone, and three judges appointed by the Secretary-General.

2. Each judge shall serve only in the Chamber to which he or she has been appointed.

3. The judges of the Appeals Chamber and the judges of the Trial Chamber, respectively, shall elect a presiding judge who shall conduct the proceedings in the Chamber to which he or she was elected. The presiding judge of the Appeals Chamber shall be the President of the Special Court.

4. If, at the request of the President of the Special Court, an alternate judge or judges have been appointed by the Government of Sierra Leone or the Secretary-General, the presiding judge of a Trial Chamber or the Appeals Chamber shall designate such an alternate judge to be present at each stage of the trial and to replace a judge if that judge is unable to continue sitting.

Article 13 Qualification and appointment of judges

1. The judges shall be persons of high moral character, impartiality and integrity who possess the qualifications required in their respective countries for appointment to the highest judicial offices. They shall be independent in the performance of their functions, and shall not accept or seek instructions from any Government or any other source.

2. In the overall composition of the Chambers, due account shall be taken of the experience of the judges in international law, including international humanitarian law and human rights law, criminal law and juvenile justice.

3. The judges shall be appointed for a three-year period and shall be eligible for reappointment.

Article 14 Rules of Procedure and Evidence

1. The Rules of Procedure and Evidence of the International Criminal Tribunal for Rwanda obtaining at the time of the establishment of the Special Court shall be applicable *mutatis mutandis* to the conduct of the legal proceedings before the Special Court.

2. The judges of the Special Court as a whole may amend the Rules of Procedure and Evidence or adopt additional rules where the applicable Rules do not, or do not adequately, provide for a specific situation. In so doing, they may be guided, as appropriate, by the Criminal Procedure Act, 1965, of Sierra Leone.

Article 15 The Prosecutor

1. The Prosecutor shall be responsible for the investigation and prosecution of persons who bear the greatest responsibility for serious violations of international humanitarian law and crimes under Sierra Leonean law committed in the territory of Sierra Leone since 30 November 1996. The Prosecutor shall act independently as a separate organ of the Special

Court. He or she shall not seek or receive instructions from any Government or from any other source.

2. The Office of the Prosecutor shall have the power to question suspects, victims and witnesses, to collect evidence and to conduct on-site investigations. In carrying out these tasks, the Prosecutor shall, as appropriate, be assisted by the Sierra Leonean authorities concerned.

3. The Prosecutor shall be appointed by the Secretary-General for a three-year term and shall be eligible for re-appointment. He or she shall be of high moral character and possess the highest level of professional competence, and have extensive experience in the conduct of investigations and prosecutions of criminal cases.

4. The Prosecutor shall be assisted by a Sierra Leonean Deputy Prosecutor, and by such other Sierra Leonean and international staff as may be required to perform the functions assigned to him or her effectively and efficiently. Given the nature of the crimes committed and the particular sensitivities of girls, young women and children victims of rape, sexual assault, abduction and slavery of all kinds, due consideration should be given in the appointment of staff to the employment of prosecutors and investigators experienced in gender-related crimes and juvenile justice.

5. In the prosecution of juvenile offenders, the Prosecutor shall ensure that the child-rehabilitation programme is not placed at risk and that, where appropriate, resort should be had to alternative truth and reconciliation mechanisms, to the extent of their availability.

Article 16 The Registry

1. The Registry shall be responsible for the administration and servicing of the Special Court.

2. The Registry shall consist of a Registrar and such other staff as may be required.

3. The Registrar shall be appointed by the Secretary-General after consultation with the President of the Special Court and shall be a staff member of the United Nations. He or she shall serve for a three-year term and be eligible for re-appointment.

4. The Registrar shall set up a Victims and Witnesses Unit within the Registry. This Unit shall provide, in consultation with the Office of the Prosecutor, protective measures and security arrangements, counselling and other appropriate assistance for witnesses, victims who appear before the Court and others who are at risk on account of testimony given by such witnesses. The Unit personnel shall include experts in trauma, including trauma related to crimes of sexual violence and violence against children.

Article 17 Rights of the accused

1. All accused shall be equal before the Special Court.

2. The accused shall be entitled to a fair and public hearing, subject to measures ordered by the Special Court for the protection of victims and witnesses.

3. The accused shall be presumed innocent until proved guilty according to the provisions of the present Statute.

4. In the determination of any charge against the accused pursuant to the present Statute, he or she shall be entitled to the following minimum guarantees, in full equality:

    (a) To be informed promptly and in detail in a language which he or she understands of the nature and cause of the charge against him or her;

    (b) To have adequate time and facilities for the preparation of his or her defence and to communicate with counsel of his or her own choosing;

    (c) To be tried without undue delay;

    (d) To be tried in his or her presence, and to defend himself or herself in person or through legal assistance of his or her own choosing; to be informed, if he or she does not have legal assistance, of this right; and to have legal assistance assigned to him or her, in any case where the interests of justice so require, and without payment by him or her in any such case if he or she does not have sufficient means to pay for it;

(e) To examine, or have examined, the witnesses against him or her and to obtain the attendance and examination of witnesses on his or her behalf under the same conditions as witnesses against him or her;

(f) To have the free assistance of an interpreter if he or she cannot understand or speak the language used in the Special Court;

(g) Not to be compelled to testify against himself or herself or to confess guilt.

Article 18 Judgment

The judgment shall be rendered by a majority of the judges of the Trial Chamber or of the Appeals Chamber, and shall be delivered in public. It shall be accompanied by a reasoned opinion in writing, to which separate or dissenting opinions may be appended.

Article 19 Penalties

1. The Trial Chamber shall impose upon a convicted person, other than a juvenile offender, imprisonment for a specified number of years. In determining the terms of imprisonment, the Trial Chamber shall, as appropriate, have recourse to the practice regarding prison sentences in the International Criminal Tribunal for Rwanda and the national courts of Sierra Leone.

2. In imposing the sentences, the Trial Chamber should take into account such factors as the gravity of the offence and the individual circumstances of the convicted person.

3. In addition to imprisonment, the Trial Chamber may order the forfeiture of the property, proceeds and any assets acquired unlawfully or by criminal conduct, and their return to their rightful owner or to the State of Sierra Leone.

Article 20 Appellate proceedings

1. The Appeals Chamber shall hear appeals from persons convicted by the Trial Chamber or from the Prosecutor on the following grounds:

(a) A procedural error;

(b) An error on a question of law invalidating the decision;

(c) An error of fact which has occasioned a miscarriage of justice.

2. The Appeals Chamber may affirm, reverse or revise the decisions taken by the Trial Chamber.

3. The judges of the Appeals Chamber of the Special Court shall be guided by the decisions of the Appeals Chamber of the International Tribunals for the former Yugoslavia and for Rwanda. In the interpretation and application of the laws of Sierra Leone, they shall be guided by the decisions of the Supreme Court of Sierra Leone.

Article 21 Review proceedings

1. Where a new fact has been discovered which was not known at the time of the proceedings before the Trial Chamber or the Appeals Chamber and which could have been a decisive factor in reaching the decision, the convicted person or the Prosecutor may submit an application for review of the judgment.

2. An application for review shall be submitted to the Appeals Chamber. The Appeals Chamber may reject the application if it considers it to be unfounded. If it determines that the application is meritorious, it may, as appropriate:

(a) Reconvene the Trial Chamber;

(b) Retain jurisdiction over the matter.

Article 22 Enforcement of sentences

1. Imprisonment shall be served in Sierra Leone. If circumstances so require, imprisonment may also be served in any of the States which have concluded with the International Criminal Tribunal for Rwanda or the International Criminal Tribunal for the former Yugoslavia an agreement for the enforcement of sentences, and which have indicated to the Registrar of the Special Court their willingness to accept convicted persons. The Special Court may conclude similar agreements for the enforcement of sentences with other States.

2. Conditions of imprisonment, whether in Sierra Leone or in a third State, shall be governed by the law of the State of enforcement subject to the supervision of the Special Court. The State of enforcement shall be bound by the duration of the sentence, subject to article 23 of the present Statute.

Article 23 Pardon or commutation of sentences

If, pursuant to the applicable law of the State in which the convicted person is imprisoned, he or she is eligible for pardon or commutation of sentence, the State concerned shall notify the Special Court accordingly. There shall only be pardon or commutation of sentence if the President of the Special Court, in consultation with the judges, so decides on the basis of the interests of justice and the general principles of law.

Article 24 Working language

The working language of the Special Court shall be English.

Article 25 Annual Report

The President of the Special Court shall submit an annual report on the operation and activities of the Court to the Secretary-General and to the Government of Sierra Leone.

EXTRADITION

DOCUMENT 61

European Convention on Extradition 1957
359 UNTS 273; ETS No 24

This Convention was concluded under the auspices of the Council of Europe; it was opened for signature in Paris on 13 December 1957 and entered into force on 18 April 1960.

There are 45 parties, including all of the members of the Council of Europe except Monaco. Two non-Member States of the Council of Europe, Israel and South Africa, have ratified the Convention.

The process of extradition, whereby one State surrenders to another State, at its request, a person accused or convicted of a criminal offence against the laws of the requesting State, is normally enabled by means of bilateral treaty. However, in 1951, the Committee of Ministers of the Council of Europe began to examine the possibility of establishing a multilateral treaty setting down commonly agreed principles on extradition among the Member States of the Council of Europe.

The Contracting Parties agree to 'surrender to each other . . . all persons against whom the competent authorities of the requesting Party are proceeding for an offence or who are wanted by the said authorities for the carrying out of a sentence of detention order' (Article 1). An extraditable offence is defined in general terms as any offence which is punishable by a period of detention of at least one year (Article 2). The most controversial aspect of the Convention applies in relation to Article 3, which allows for the refusal of extradition if the offence is regarded by the requested party as a political offence. The Convention does not define what constitutes a political offence. However, the taking or attempted taking of the life of a head of State or a member of his family is excluded from the definition of a political offence (Article 3(3)). Further exclusions to the political offence exception were included in the First Additional Protocol to the Convention of 1975 **(Document 62)**. *Military offences are excluded from the Convention (Article 4) and the Convention provides that States may refuse the extradition of their nationals (Article 6). Article 11 provides for the possibility of non-extradition if the offence in respect of which the extradition is requested is punishable by the death penalty where the death penalty is not provided for in the law of the requested Party. However, refusal of extradition is not obligatory in such circumstances and the requested party can seek assurances that the death penalty will not be carried out.*

See also the Second Additional Protocol to the Convention of 1978 **(Document 63)**.

The governments signatory hereto, being members of the Council of Europe,

Considering that the aim of the Council of Europe is to achieve a greater unity between its members;

Considering that this purpose can be attained by the conclusion of agreements and by common action in legal matters;

Considering that the acceptance of uniform rules with regard to extradition is likely to assist this work of unification.

Article I Obligation to extradite

The Contracting Parties undertake to surrender to each other, subject to the provisions and conditions laid down in this Convention, all persons against whom the competent authorities of the requesting Party are proceeding for an offence or who are wanted by the said authorities for the carrying out of a sentence or detention order.

Article 2 Extraditable offences

1. Extradition shall be granted in respect of offences punishable under the laws of the requesting Party and of the requested Party by deprivation of liberty or under a detention order for a maximum period of at least one year or by a more severe penalty. Where a conviction and prison sentence have occurred or a detention order has been made in the territory of the requesting Party, the punishment awarded must have been for a period of at least four months.

2. If the request for extradition includes several separate offences each of which is punishable under the laws of the requesting Party and the requested Party by deprivation of liberty or under a detention order, but of which some do not fulfil the condition with regard to the amount of punishment which may be awarded, the requested Party shall also have the right to grant extradition for the latter offences.

3. Any Contracting Party whose law does not allow extradition for certain of the offences referred to in paragraph I of this article may, in so far as it is concerned, exclude such offences from the application of this Convention.

4. Any Contracting Party which wishes to avail itself of the right provided for in paragraph 3 of this article shall, at the time of deposit of its instrument of ratification or accession, transmit to the Secretary General of the Council of Europe either a list of the offences for which extradition is allowed or a list of those for which it is excluded and shall at the same time indicate the legal provisions which allow or exclude extradition. The Secretary General of the Council shall forward these lists to the other signatories.

5. If extradition is subsequently excluded in respect of other offences by the law of a Contracting Party, that Party shall notify the Secretary General. The Secretary General shall inform the other signatories. Such notification shall not take effect until three months from the date of its receipt by the Secretary General.

6. Any Party which avails itself of the right provided for in paragraphs 4 or 5 of this article may at any time apply this Convention to offences which have been excluded from it. It shall inform the Secretary General of the Council of such changes, and the Secretary General shall inform the other signatories.

7. Any Party may apply reciprocity in respect of any offences excluded from the application of the Convention under this article.

Article 3 Political offences

1. Extradition shall not be granted if the offence in respect of which it is requested is regarded by the requested Party as a political offence or as an offence connected with a political offence.

2. The same rule shall apply if the requested Party has substantial grounds for believing that a request for extradition for an ordinary criminal offence has been made for the purpose of prosecuting or punishing a person on account of his race, religion, nationality or political opinion, or that that person's position may be prejudiced for any of these reasons.

3. The taking or attempted taking of the life of a Head of State or a member of his family shall not be deemed to be a political offence for the purposes of this Convention.

4. This article shall not affect any obligations which the Contracting Parties may have undertaken or may undertake under any other international convention of a multilateral character.

Article 4 Military offences

Extradition for offences under military law which are not offences under ordinary criminal law is excluded from the application of this Convention.

Article 5 Fiscal offences

Extradition shall be granted, in accordance with the provisions of this Convention, for offences in connection with taxes, duties, customs and exchange only if the Contracting Parties have so decided in respect of any such offence or category of offences.

Article 6 Extradition of nationals

1. (a) A Contracting Party shall have the right to refuse extradition of its nationals.

   (b) Each Contracting Party may, by a declaration made at the time of signature or of deposit of its instrument of ratification or accession, define as far as it is concerned the term "nationals" within the meaning of this Convention.

   (c) Nationality shall be determined as at the time of the decision concerning extradition. If, however, the person claimed is first recognised as a national of the requested Party during the period between the time of the decision and the time contemplated for the surrender, the requested Party may avail itself of the provision contained in sub-paragraph a of this article.

2. If the requested Party does not extradite its national, it shall at the request of the requesting Party submit the case to its competent authorities in order that proceedings may be taken if they are considered appropriate. For this purpose, the files, information and exhibits relating to the offence shall be transmitted without charge by the means provided for in Article 12, paragraph 1. The requesting Party shall be informed of the result of its request.

Article 7 Place of commission

1. The requested Party may refuse to extradite a person claimed for an offence which is regarded by its law as having been committed in whole or in part in its territory or in a place treated as its territory.

2. When the offence for which extradition is requested has been committed outside the territory of the requesting Party, extradition may only be refused if the law of the requested Party does not allow prosecution for the same category of offence when committed outside the latter Party's territory or does not allow extradition for the offence concerned.

Article 8 Pending proceedings for the same offences

The requested Party may refuse to extradite the person claimed if the competent authorities of such Party are proceeding against him in respect of the offence or offences for which extradition is requested.

Article 9 Non bis in idem

Extradition shall not be granted if final judgment has been passed by the competent authorities of the requested Party upon the person claimed in respect of the offence or offences for which extradition is requested. Extradition may be refused if the competent authorities of the requested Party have decided either not to institute or to terminate proceedings in respect of the same offence or offences.

Article 10 Lapse of time

Extradition shall not be granted when the person claimed has, according to the law of either the requesting or the requested Party, become immune by reason of lapse of time from prosecution or punishment.

Article 11 Capital punishment

If the offence for which extradition is requested is punishable by death under the law of the requesting Party, and if in respect of such offence the death-penalty is not provided for by the law of the requested Party or is not normally carried out, extradition may be refused unless the requesting Party gives such assurance as the requested Party considers sufficient that the death-penalty will not be carried out.

Article 12 The request and supporting documents

1. The request shall be in writing and shall be communicated through the diplomatic channel. Other means of communication may be arranged by direct agreement between two or more Parties.

2. The request shall be supported by:

   (a) the original or an authenticated copy of the conviction and sentence or detention order immediately enforceable or of the warrant of arrest or other order having the same effect and issued in accordance with the procedure laid down in the law of the requesting Party;

   (b) a statement of the offences for which extradition is requested. The time and place of their commission, their legal descriptions and a reference to the relevant legal provisions shall be set out as accurately as possible; and

   (c) a copy of the relevant enactments or, where this is not possible, a statement of the relevant law and as accurate a description as possible of the person claimed, together with any other information which will help to establish his identity and nationality.

Article 13 Supplementary information

If the information communicated by the requesting Party is found to be insufficient to allow the requested Party to make a decision in pursuance of this Convention, the latter Party shall request the necessary supplementary information and may fix a time-limit for the receipt thereof.

Article 14 Rule of speciality

1. A person who has been extradited shall not be proceeded against, sentenced or detained with a view to the carrying out of a sentence or detention order for any offence committed prior to his surrender other than that for which he was extradited, nor shall he be for any other reason restricted in his personal freedom, except in the following cases:

   (a) when the Party which surrendered him consents. A request for consent shall be submitted, accompanied by the documents mentioned in Article 12 and a legal record of any statement made by the extradited person in respect of the offence concerned. Consent shall be given when the offence for which it is requested is itself subject to extradition in accordance with the provisions of this Convention;

   (b) when that person, having had an opportunity to leave the territory of the Party to which he has been surrendered, has not done so within 45 days of his final discharge, or has returned to that territory after leaving it.

2. The requesting Party may, however, take any measures necessary to remove the person from its territory, or any measures necessary under its law, including proceedings by default, to prevent any legal effects of lapse of time.

3. When the description of the offence charged is altered in the course of proceedings, the extradited person shall only be proceeded against or sentenced in so far as the offence under its new description is shown by its constituent elements to be an offence which would allow extradition.

Article 15 Re-extradition to a third state

Except as provided for in Article 14, paragraph 1.b, the requesting Party shall not, without the consent of the requested Party, surrender to another Party or to a third State a person surrendered to the requesting Party and sought by the said other Party or third State in respect of offences committed before his surrender. The requested Party may request the production of the documents mentioned in Article 12, paragraph 2.

Article 16 Provisional arrest

1. In case of urgency the competent authorities of the requesting Party may request the provisional arrest of the person sought. The competent authorities of the requested Party shall decide the matter in accordance with its law.

2. The request for provisional arrest shall state that one of the documents mentioned in Article 12, paragraph 2.a, exists and that it is intended to send a request for extradition. It shall also state for what offence extradition will be requested and when and where such offence was committed and shall so far as possible give a description of the person sought.

3. A request for provisional arrest shall be sent to the competent authorities of the requested Party either through the diplomatic channel or direct by post or telegraph or through the International Criminal Police Organisation (Interpol) or by any other means affording evidence in writing or accepted by the requested Party. The requesting authority shall be informed without delay of the result of its request.

4. Provisional arrest may be terminated if, within a period of 18 days after arrest, the requested Party has not received the request for extradition and the documents mentioned in Article 12. It shall not, in any event, exceed 40 days from the date of such arrest. The possibility of provisional release at any time is not excluded, but the requested Party shall take any measures which it considers necessary to prevent the escape of the person sought.

5. Release shall not prejudice re-arrest and extradition if a request for extradition is received subsequently.

Article 17 Conflicting requests

If extradition is requested concurrently by more than one State, either for the same offence or for different offences, the requested Party shall make its decision having regard to all the circumstances and especially the relative seriousness and place of commission of the offences, the respective dates of the requests, the nationality of the person claimed and the possibility of subsequent extradition to another State.

Article 18 Surrender of the person to be extradited

1. The requested Party shall inform the requesting Party by the means mentioned in Article 12, paragraph 1, of its decision with regard to the extradition.

2. Reasons shall be given for any complete or partial rejection.

3. If the request is agreed to, the requesting Party shall be informed of the place and date of surrender and of the length of time for which the person claimed was detained with a view to surrender.

4. Subject to the provisions of paragraph 5 of this article, if the person claimed has not been taken over on the appointed date, he may be released after the expiry of 15 days and shall in any case be released after the expiry of 30 days. The requested Party may refuse to extradite him for the same offence.

5. If circumstances beyond its control prevent a Party from surrendering or taking over the person to be extradited, it shall notify the other Party. The two Parties shall agree a new date for surrender and the provisions of paragraph 4 of this article shall apply.

Article 19 Postponed or conditional surrender

1. The requested Party may, after making its decision on the request for extradition, postpone the surrender of the person claimed in order that he may be proceeded against by that Party or, if

he has already been convicted, in order that he may serve his sentence in the territory of that Party for an offence other than that for which extradition is requested.

2. The requested Party may, instead of postponing surrender, temporarily surrender the person claimed to the requesting Party in accordance with conditions to be determined by mutual agreement between the Parties.

Article 20 Handing over of property

1. The requested Party shall, in so far as its law permits and at the request of the requesting Party, seize and hand over property:

   (a) which may be required as evidence, or

   (b) which has been acquired as a result of the offence and which, at the time of the arrest, is found in the possession of the person claimed or is discovered subsequently.

2. The property mentioned in paragraph 1 of this article shall be handed over even if extradition, having been agreed to, cannot be carried out owing to the death or escape of the person claimed.

3. When the said property is liable to seizure or confiscation in the territory of the requested Party, the latter may, in connection with pending criminal proceedings, temporarily retain it or hand it over on condition that it is returned.

4. Any rights which the requested Party or third parties may have acquired in the said property shall be preserved. Where these rights exist, the property shall be returned without charge to the requested Party as soon as possible after the trial.

Article 21 Transit

1. Transit through the territory of one of the Contracting Parties shall be granted on submission of a request by the means mentioned in Article 12, paragraph 1, provided that the offence concerned is not considered by the Party requested to grant transit as an offence of a political or purely military character having regard to Articles 3 and 4 of this Convention.

2. Transit of a national, within the meaning of Article 6, of a country requested to grant transit may be refused.

3. Subject to the provisions of paragraph 4 of this article, it shall be necessary to produce the documents mentioned in Article 12, paragraph 2.

4. If air transport is used, the following provisions shall apply:

   (a) when it is not intended to land, the requesting Party shall notify the Party over whose territory the flight is to be made and shall certify that one of the documents mentioned in Article 12, paragraph 2(a) exists. In the case of an unscheduled landing, such notification shall have the effect of a request for provisional arrest as provided for in Article 16, and the requesting Party shall submit a formal request for transit;

   (b) when it is intended to land, the requesting Party shall submit a formal request for transit.

5. A Party may, however, at the time of signature or of the deposit of its instrument of ratification of, or accession to, this Convention, declare that it will only grant transit of a person on some or all of the conditions on which it grants extradition. In that event, reciprocity may be applied.

6. The transit of the extradited person shall not be carried out through any territory where there is reason to believe that his life or his freedom may be threatened by reason of his race, religion, nationality or political opinion.

Article 22 Procedure

Except where this Convention otherwise provides, the procedure with regard to extradition and provisional arrest shall be governed solely by the law of the requested Party.

Article 23 Language to be used

The documents to be produced shall be in the language of the requesting or requested Party. The requested Party may require a translation into one of the official languages of the Council of Europe to be chosen by it.

Article 24 Expenses

1. Expenses incurred in the territory of the requested Party by reason of extradition shall be borne by that Party.

2. Expenses incurred by reason of transit through the territory of a Party requested to grant transit shall be borne by the requesting Party.

3. In the event of extradition from a non-metropolitan territory of the requested Party, the expenses occasioned by travel between that territory and the metropolitan territory of the requesting Party shall be borne by the latter. The same rule shall apply to expenses occasioned by travel between the non-metropolitan territory of the requested Party and its metropolitan territory.

Article 25 Definition of "detention order"

For the purposes of this Convention, the expression "detention order" means any order involving deprivation of liberty which has been made by a criminal court in addition to or instead of a prison sentence.

Article 28 Relations between this Convention and bilateral Agreements

1. This Convention shall, in respect of those countries to which it applies, supersede the provisions of any bilateral treaties, conventions or agreements governing extradition between any two Contracting Parties.

2. The Contracting Parties may conclude between themselves bilateral or multilateral agreements only in order to supplement the provisions of this Convention or to facilitate the application of the principles contained therein.

3. Where, as between two or more Contracting Parties, extradition takes place on the basis of a uniform law, the Parties shall be free to regulate their mutual relations in respect of extradition exclusively in accordance with such a system notwithstanding the provisions of this Convention. The same principle shall apply as between two or more Contracting Parties each of which has in force a law providing for the execution in its territory of warrants of arrest issued in the territory of the other Party or Parties. Contracting Parties which exclude or may in the future exclude the application of this Convention as between themselves in accordance with this paragraph shall notify the Secretary General of the Council of Europe accordingly. The Secretary General shall inform the other Contracting Parties of any notification received in accordance with this paragraph.

DOCUMENT 62

Additional Protocol to the European Convention on Extradition 1975

ETS No 86; 17 ILM 813 (1978)

The Additional Protocol to the European Convention on Extradition of 1957 (**Document 61**) *was opened for signature in Paris on 15 October 1975 and entered into force on 20 August 1979.*

There are 35 parties to the Additional Protocol, including South Africa but not Israel, the only other non-Members of the Council of Europe to ratify the 1957 Convention. The UK, France and Germany are among the 10 parties to the 1957 Convention that are not parties to the Additional Protocol.

The Additional Protocol is of particular importance in that it extends the exclusions to the political offence exception, provided for in Article 3 of the 1957 Convention, to include the crime of genocide and violations of the laws of war (Article 1).

See the Second Additional Protocol to the Convention of 1978 **(Document 63)**.

The member States of the Council of Europe, signatory to this Protocol,

Having regard to the provisions of the European Convention on Extradition opened for signature in Paris on 13 December 1957 (hereinafter referred to as "the Convention") and in particular Articles 3 and 9 thereof;

Considering that it is desirable to supplement these Articles with a view to strengthening the protection of humanity and of individuals,

Have agreed as follows:

Article 1
For the application of Article 3 of the Convention, political offences shall not be considered to include the following:

(a) the crimes against humanity specified in the Convention on the Prevention and Punishment of the Crime of Genocide adopted on 9 December 1948 by the General Assembly of the United Nations;

(b) the violations specified in Article 50 of the 1949 Geneva Convention for the Amelioration of the Condition of the Wounded and Sick in Armed Forces in the Field, Article 51 of the 1949 Geneva Convention for the Amelioration of the Condition of Wounded, Sick and Shipwrecked members of Armed Forces at Sea, Article 130 of the 1949 Geneva Convention relative to the Treatment of Prisoners of War and Article 147 of the 1949 Geneva Convention relative to the Protection of Civilian Persons in Time of War;

(c) any comparable violations of the laws of war having effect at the time when this Protocol enters into force and of customs of war existing at that time, which are not already provided for in the above-mentioned provisions of the Geneva Conventions.

Article 2
1. Article 9 of the Convention shall be supplemented by the following text, the original Article 9 of the Convention becoming paragraph 1 and the under-mentioned provisions becoming paragraphs 2, 3 and 4:

2. "The extradition of a person against whom a final judgment has been rendered in a third State, Contracting Party to the Convention, for the offence or offences in respect of which the claim was made, shall not be granted:

    (a) if the afore-mentioned judgment resulted in his acquittal;

    (b) if the term of imprisonment or other measure to which he was sentenced:

        (i) has been completely enforced;

        (ii) has been wholly, or with respect to the part not enforced, the subject of a pardon or an amnesty;

    (c) if the court convicted the offender without imposing a sanction.

3. However, in the cases referred to in paragraph 2, extradition may be granted:

(a) if the offence in respect of which judgment has been rendered was committed against a person, an institution or any thing having public status in the requesting State;

(b) if the person on whom judgment was passed had himself a public status in the requesting State;

(c) if the offence in respect of which judgment was passed was committed completely or partly in the territory of the requesting State or in a place treated as its territory.

4. The provisions of paragraphs 2 and 3 shall not prevent the application of wider domestic provisions relating to the effect of *ne bis in idem* attached to foreign criminal judgments."

DOCUMENT 63

Second Additional Protocol to the European Convention on Extradition 1978
ETS No 98

This Protocol to the European Convention on Extradition (**Document 61**) *was opened for signature in Paris on 17 March 1978 and entered into force on 5 June 1983.*

There are 38 parties to the Second Additional Protocol, including South Africa, the UK and Germany, but not France.

The Second Additional Protocol removes the so called double criminality rule in relation to fiscal offences recognising that States parties have differing fiscal regimes (Article 2). The most important provision of the Second Additional Protocol is Article 3, which permits a party to refuse extradition where a person has been prosecuted in absentia.

See the Additional Protocol to the Convention of 1975 (**Document 62**).

The member States of the Council of Europe, signatory to this Protocol,

Desirous of facilitating the application of the European Convention on Extradition opened for signature in Paris on 13 December 1957 (hereinafter referred to as "the Convention") in the field of fiscal offences;

Considering it also desirable to supplement the Convention in certain other respects,

Have agreed as follows:

Article 1
Paragraph 2 of Article 2 of the Convention shall be supplemented by the following provision:

"This right shall also apply to offences which are subject only to pecuniary sanctions."

Article 2
Article 5 of the Convention shall be replaced by the following provisions:

"Fiscal offences

1. For offences in connection with taxes, duties, customs and exchange extradition shall take place between the Contracting Parties in accordance with the provisions of the Convention if the offence, under the law of the requested Party, corresponds to an offence of the same nature.

2. Extradition may not be refused on the ground that the law of the requested Party does not impose the same kind of tax or duty or does not contain a tax, duty, custom or exchange regulation of the same kind as the law of the requesting Party."

Article 3

The Convention shall be supplemented by the following provisions:

"Judgments *in absentia*

1. When a Contracting Party requests from another Contracting Party the extradition of a person for the purpose of carrying out a sentence or detention order imposed by a decision rendered against him *in absentia,* the requested Party may refuse to extradite for this purpose if, in its opinion, the proceedings leading to the judgment did not satisfy the minimum rights of defence recognised as due to everyone charged with criminal offence. However, extradition shall be granted if the requesting Party gives an assurance considered sufficient to guarantee to the person claimed the right to a retrial which safeguards the rights of defence. This decision will authorise the requesting Party either to enforce the judgment in question if the convicted person does not make an opposition or, if he does, to take proceedings against the person extradited.

2. When the requested Party informs the person whose extradition has been requested of the judgment rendered against him in absentia, the requesting Party shall not regard this communication as a formal notification for the purposes of the criminal procedure in that State."

Article 4

The Convention shall be supplemented by the following provisions:

"Amnesty

Extradition shall not be granted for an offence in respect of which an amnesty has been declared in the requested State and which that State had competence to prosecute under its own criminal law."

Article 5

Paragraph 1 of Article 12 of the Convention shall be replaced by the following provisions:

"The request shall be in writing and shall be addressed by the Ministry of Justice of the requesting Party to the Ministry of Justice of the requested Party; however, use of the diplomatic channel is not excluded. Other means of communication may be arranged by direct agreement between two or more Parties."

DOCUMENT 64

European Council Framework Decision on the European Arrest Warrant and the Surrender Procedures between Member States 2002
Official Journal L190 18/07/2002

This legally binding Decision adopted on 13 June 2002 under Articles 31 and 34 of the Treaty on European Union effectively abolishes the traditional extradition system between Member States replacing it by mutual recognition of arrest warrants issues b Member States. The Decision entered into force on 7 August 2002 and was implemented on 31 December 2003.

The European Arrest Warrant unites the two procedures of arrest and surrender into a single judicial procedure. Execution of the arrest warrant is to be on the basis of mutual recognition (Article 1). The arrest warrant operates in respect of a list of 32 specific crimes where they are punishable by imprisonment for a maximum period of at least three years (Article 2) and includes mandatory (Article 3) and non-mandatory (Article 4) grounds for non-execution of arrest warrants. The content and form of the European arrest warrant is governed by Article 8 and surrender procedures are detailed in Chapter 2 (Articles 9–25).

As between the Member States of the European Union, the arrest warrant appears to limit a number of traditional extradition principles such as the requirement of double criminality (except as provided for in Article 2(4)), the political offence exception and the speciality rule (Article 27), as well as the rule by which States can refuse the surrender of their own nationals: see Article 31.

The Council of the European Union,

Having regard to the Treaty on European Union, and in particular Article 31(a) and (b) and Article 34(2)(b) thereof,

Having regard to the proposal from the Commission,

Having regard to the opinion of the European Parliament,

Whereas:

(1) According to the Conclusions of the Tampere European Council of 15 and 16 October 1999, and in particular point 35 thereof, the formal extradition procedure should be abolished among the Member States in respect of persons who are fleeing from justice after having been finally sentenced and extradition procedures should be speeded up in respect of persons suspected of having committed an offence.

(2) The programme of measures to implement the principle of mutual recognition of criminal decisions envisaged in point 37 of the Tampere European Council Conclusions and adopted by the Council on 30 November 2000, addresses the matter of mutual enforcement of arrest warrants.

(3) All or some Member States are parties to a number of conventions in the field of extradition, including the European Convention on Extradition of 13 December 1957 and the European Convention on the Suppression of Terrorism of 27 January 1977. The Nordic States have extradition laws with identical wording.

(4) In addition, the following three Conventions dealing in whole or in part with extradition have been agreed upon among Member States and form part of the Union *acquis*: the Convention of 19 June 1990 implementing the Schengen Agreement of 14 June 1985 on the gradual abolition of checks at their common borders (regarding relations between the Member States which are parties to that Convention), the Convention of 10 March 1995 on simplified extradition procedure between the Member States of the European Union and the Convention of 27 September 1996 relating to extradition between the Member States of the European Union.

(5) The objective set for the Union to become an area of freedom, security and justice leads to abolishing extradition between Member States and replacing it by a system of surrender between judicial authorities. Further, the introduction of a new simplified system of surrender of sentenced or suspected persons for the purposes of execution or prosecution of criminal sentences makes it possible to remove the complexity and potential for delay inherent in the present extradition procedures. Traditional cooperation relations which have prevailed up till now between Member States should be replaced by a system of free movement of judicial decisions in criminal matters, covering both pre-sentence and final decisions, within an area of freedom, security and justice.

(6) The European arrest warrant provided for in this Framework Decision is the first concrete measure in the field of criminal law implementing the principle of mutual recognition which the European Council referred to as the "cornerstone" of judicial cooperation.

(7) Since the aim of replacing the system of multilateral extradition built upon the European Convention on Extradition of 13 December 1957 cannot be sufficiently achieved by the Member States acting unilaterally and can therefore, by reason of its scale and effects, be better achieved at Union level, the Council may adopt measures in accordance with the principle of subsidiarity as referred to in Article 2 of the Treaty on European Union and Article 5 of the Treaty establishing the European Community. In accordance with the principle of proportionality, as set out in the latter Article, this Framework Decision does not go beyond what is necessary in order to achieve that objective.

(8) Decisions on the execution of the European arrest warrant must be subject to sufficient controls, which means that a judicial authority of the Member State where the requested person has been arrested will have to take the decision on his or her surrender.

(9) The role of central authorities in the execution of a European arrest warrant must be limited to practical and administrative assistance.

(10) The mechanism of the European arrest warrant is based on a high level of confidence between Member States. Its implementation may be suspended only in the event of a serious and persistent breach by one of the Member States of the principles set out in Article 6(1) of the Treaty on European Union, determined by the Council pursuant to Article 7(1) of the said Treaty with the consequences set out in Article 7(2) thereof.

(11) In relations between Member States, the European arrest warrant should replace all the previous instruments concerning extradition, including the provisions of Title III of the Convention implementing the Schengen Agreement which concern extradition.

(12) This Framework Decision respects fundamental rights and observes the principles recognised by Article 6 of the Treaty on European Union and reflected in the Charter of Fundamental Rights of the European Union, in particular Chapter VI thereof. Nothing in this Framework Decision may be interpreted as prohibiting refusal to surrender a person for whom a European arrest warrant has been issued when there are reasons to believe, on the basis of objective elements, that the said arrest warrant has been issued for the purpose of prosecuting or punishing a person on the grounds of his or her sex, race, religion, ethnic origin, nationality, language, political opinions or sexual orientation, or that that person's position may be prejudiced for any of these reasons. This Framework Decision does not prevent a Member State from applying its constitutional rules relating to due process, freedom of association, freedom of the press and freedom of expression in other media.

(13) No person should be removed, expelled or extradited to a State where there is a serious risk that he or she would be subjected to the death penalty, torture or other inhuman or degrading treatment or punishment.

(14) Since all Member States have ratified the Council of Europe Convention of 28 January 1981 for the protection of individuals with regard to automatic processing of personal data, the personal data processed in the context of the implementation of this Framework Decision should be protected in accordance with the principles of the said Convention,

Has adopted this Framework Decision:

Chapter 1 General Principles

Article 1 Definition of the European arrest warrant and obligation to execute it

1. The European arrest warrant is a judicial decision issued by a Member State with a view to the arrest and surrender by another Member State of a requested person, for the purposes of conducting a criminal prosecution or executing a custodial sentence or detention order.

2. Member States shall execute any European arrest warrant on the basis of the principle of mutual recognition and in accordance with the provisions of this Framework Decision.

3. This Framework Decision shall not have the effect of modifying the obligation to respect fundamental rights and fundamental legal principles as enshrined in Article 6 of the Treaty on European Union.

Article 2 Scope of the European arrest warrant

1. A European arrest warrant may be issued for acts punishable by the law of the issuing Member State by a custodial sentence or a detention order for a maximum period of at least 12 months or, where a sentence has been passed or a detention order has been made, for sentences of at least four months.

2. The following offences, if they are punishable in the issuing Member State by a custodial sentence or a detention order for a maximum period of at least three years and as they are defined by the law of the issuing Member State, shall, under the terms of this Framework Decision and without verification of the double criminality of the act, give rise to surrender pursuant to a European arrest warrant:

- participation in a criminal organisation,
- terrorism,
- trafficking in human beings,
- sexual exploitation of children and child pornography,
- illicit trafficking in narcotic drugs and psychotropic substances,
- illicit trafficking in weapons, munitions and explosives,
- corruption,
- fraud, including that affecting the financial interests of the European Communities within the meaning of the Convention of 26 July 1995 on the protection of the European Communities' financial interests,
- laundering of the proceeds of crime,
- counterfeiting currency, including of the euro,
- computer-related crime,
- environmental crime, including illicit trafficking in endangered animal species and in endangered plant species and varieties,
- facilitation of unauthorised entry and residence,
- murder, grievous bodily injury,
- illicit trade in human organs and tissue,
- kidnapping, illegal restraint and hostage-taking,
- racism and xenophobia,
- organised or armed robbery,
- illicit trafficking in cultural goods, including antiques and works of art,
- swindling,
- racketeering and extortion,
- counterfeiting and piracy of products,
- forgery of administrative documents and trafficking therein,
- forgery of means of payment,
- illicit trafficking in hormonal substances and other growth promoters,
- illicit trafficking in nuclear or radioactive materials,
- trafficking in stolen vehicles,
- rape,

– arson,

– crimes within the jurisdiction of the International Criminal Court,

– unlawful seizure of aircraft/ships,

– sabotage.

3. The Council may decide at any time, acting unanimously after consultation of the European Parliament under the conditions laid down in Article 39(1) of the Treaty on European Union (TEU), to add other categories of offence to the list contained in paragraph 2. The Council shall examine, in the light of the report submitted by the Commission pursuant to Article 34(3), whether the list should be extended or amended.

4. For offences other than those covered by paragraph 2, surrender may be subject to the condition that the acts for which the European arrest warrant has been issued constitute an offence under the law of the executing Member State, whatever the constituent elements or however it is described.

Article 3 Grounds for mandatory non-execution of the European arrest warrant

The judicial authority of the Member State of execution (hereinafter "executing judicial authority") shall refuse to execute the European arrest warrant in the following cases:

1. if the offence on which the arrest warrant is based is covered by amnesty in the executing Member State, where that State had jurisdiction to prosecute the offence under its own criminal law;

2. if the executing judicial authority is informed that the requested person has been finally judged by a Member State in respect of the same acts provided that, where there has been sentence, the sentence has been served or is currently being served or may no longer be executed under the law of the sentencing Member State;

3. if the person who is the subject of the European arrest warrant may not, owing to his age, be held criminally responsible for the acts on which the arrest warrant is based under the law of the executing State.

Article 4 Grounds for optional non-execution of the European arrest warrant

The executing judicial authority may refuse to execute the European arrest warrant:

1. if, in one of the cases referred to in Article 2(4), the act on which the European arrest warrant is based does not constitute an offence under the law of the executing Member State; however, in relation to taxes or duties, customs and exchange, execution of the European arrest warrant shall not be refused on the ground that the law of the executing Member State does not impose the same kind of tax or duty or does not contain the same type of rules as regards taxes, duties and customs and exchange regulations as the law of the issuing Member State;

2. where the person who is the subject of the European arrest warrant is being prosecuted in the executing Member State for the same act as that on which the European arrest warrant is based;

3. where the judicial authorities of the executing Member State have decided either not to prosecute for the offence on which the European arrest warrant is based or to halt proceedings, or where a final judgment has been passed upon the requested person in a Member State, in respect of the same acts, which prevents further proceedings;

4. where the criminal prosecution or punishment of the requested person is statute-barred according to the law of the executing Member State and the acts fall within the jurisdiction of that Member State under its own criminal law;

5. if the executing judicial authority is informed that the requested person has been finally judged by a third State in respect of the same acts provided that, where there has been sentence, the

sentence has been served or is currently being served or may no longer be executed under the law of the sentencing country;

6. if the European arrest warrant has been issued for the purposes of execution of a custodial sentence or detention order, where the requested person is staying in, or is a national or a resident of the executing Member State and that State undertakes to execute the sentence or detention order in accordance with its domestic law;

7. where the European arrest warrant relates to offences which:

    (a) are regarded by the law of the executing Member State as having been committed in whole or in part in the territory of the executing Member State or in a place treated as such; or

    (b) have been committed outside the territory of the issuing Member State and the law of the executing Member State does not allow prosecution for the same offences when committed outside its territory.

Article 5 Guarantees to be given by the issuing Member State in particular cases

The execution of the European arrest warrant by the executing judicial authority may, by the law of the executing Member State, be subject to the following conditions:

1. where the European arrest warrant has been issued for the purposes of executing a sentence or a detention order imposed by a decision rendered *in absentia* and if the person concerned has not been summoned in person or otherwise informed of the date and place of the hearing which led to the decision rendered *in absentia*, surrender may be subject to the condition that the issuing judicial authority gives an assurance deemed adequate to guarantee the person who is the subject of the European arrest warrant that he or she will have an opportunity to apply for a retrial of the case in the issuing Member State and to be present at the judgment;

2. if the offence on the basis of which the European arrest warrant has been issued is punishable by custodial life sentence or life-time detention order, the execution of the said arrest warrant may be subject to the condition that the issuing Member State has provisions in its legal system for a review of the penalty or measure imposed, on request or at the latest after 20 years, or for the application of measures of clemency to which the person is entitled to apply for under the law or practice of the issuing Member State, aiming at a non-execution of such penalty or measure;

3. where a person who is the subject of a European arrest warrant for the purposes of prosecution is a national or resident of the executing Member State, surrender may be subject to the condition that the person, after being heard, is returned to the executing Member State in order to serve there the custodial sentence or detention order passed against him in the issuing Member State.

Article 6 Determination of the competent judicial authorities

1. The issuing judicial authority shall be the judicial authority of the issuing Member State which is competent to issue a European arrest warrant by virtue of the law of that State.

2. The executing judicial authority shall be the judicial authority of the executing Member State which is competent to execute the European arrest warrant by virtue of the law of that State.

3. Each Member State shall inform the General Secretariat of the Council of the competent judicial authority under its law.

Article 7 Recourse to the central authority

1. Each Member State may designate a central authority or, when its legal system so provides, more than one central authority to assist the competent judicial authorities.

2. A Member State may, if it is necessary as a result of the organisation of its internal judicial system, make its central authority(ies) responsible for the administrative transmission and

reception of European arrest warrants as well as for all other official correspondence relating thereto. Member State wishing to make use of the possibilities referred to in this Article shall communicate to the General Secretariat of the Council information relating to the designated central authority or central authorities. These indications shall be binding upon all the authorities of the issuing Member State.

Article 8 Content and form of the European arrest warrant

1. The European arrest warrant shall contain the following information set out in accordance with the form contained in the Annex:

   (a) the identity and nationality of the requested person;

   (b) the name, address, telephone and fax numbers and e-mail address of the issuing judicial authority;

   (c) evidence of an enforceable judgment, an arrest warrant or any other enforceable judicial decision having the same effect, coming within the scope of Articles 1 and 2;

   (d) the nature and legal classification of the offence, particularly in respect of Article 2;

   (e) a description of the circumstances in which the offence was committed, including the time, place and degree of participation in the offence by the requested person;

   (f) the penalty imposed, if there is a final judgment, or the prescribed scale of penalties for the offence under the law of the issuing Member State;

   (g) if possible, other consequences of the offence.

2. The European arrest warrant must be translated into the official language or one of the official languages of the executing Member State. Any Member State may, when this Framework Decision is adopted or at a later date, state in a declaration deposited with the General Secretariat of the Council that it will accept a translation in one or more other official languages of the Institutions of the European Communities.

Chapter 2 Surrender Procedure

Article 9 Transmission of a European arrest warrant

1. When the location of the requested person is known, the issuing judicial authority may transmit the European arrest warrant directly to the executing judicial authority.

2. The issuing judicial authority may, in any event, decide to issue an alert for the requested person in the Schengen Information System (SIS).

3. Such an alert shall be effected in accordance with the provisions of Article 95 of the Convention of 19 June 1990 implementing the Schengen Agreement of 14 June 1985 on the gradual abolition of controls at common borders. An alert in the Schengen Information System shall be equivalent to a European arrest warrant accompanied by the information set out in Article 8(1). For a transitional period, until the SIS is capable of transmitting all the information described in Article 8, the alert shall be equivalent to a European arrest warrant pending the receipt of the original in due and proper form by the executing judicial authority.

Article 10 Detailed procedures for transmitting a European arrest warrant

1. If the issuing judicial authority does not know the competent executing judicial authority, it shall make the requisite enquiries, including through the contact points of the European Judicial Network(8), in order to obtain that information from the executing Member State.

2. If the issuing judicial authority so wishes, transmission may be effected via the secure telecommunications system of the European Judicial Network.

3. If it is not possible to call on the services of the SIS, the issuing judicial authority may call on Interpol to transmit a European arrest warrant.

4. The issuing judicial authority may forward the European arrest warrant by any secure means capable of producing written records under conditions allowing the executing Member State to establish its authenticity.

5. All difficulties concerning the transmission or the authenticity of any document needed for the execution of the European arrest warrant shall be dealt with by direct contacts between the judicial authorities involved, or, where appropriate, with the involvement of the central authorities of the Member States.

6. If the authority which receives a European arrest warrant is not competent to act upon it, it shall automatically forward the European arrest warrant to the competent authority in its Member State and shall inform the issuing judicial authority accordingly.

Article 11 Rights of a requested person

1. When a requested person is arrested, the executing competent judicial authority shall, in accordance with its national law, inform that person of the European arrest warrant and of its contents, and also of the possibility of consenting to surrender to the issuing judicial authority.

2. A requested person who is arrested for the purpose of the execution of a European arrest warrant shall have a right to be assisted by a legal counsel and by an interpreter in accordance with the national law of the executing Member State.

Article 12 Keeping the person in detention

When a person is arrested on the basis of a European arrest warrant, the executing judicial authority shall take a decision on whether the requested person should remain in detention, in accordance with the law of the executing Member State. The person may be released provisionally at any time in conformity with the domestic law of the executing Member State, provided that the competent authority of the said Member State takes all the measures it deems necessary to prevent the person absconding.

Article 13 Consent to surrender

1. If the arrested person indicates that he or she consents to surrender, that consent and, if appropriate, express renunciation of entitlement to the "speciality rule" referred to in Article 27(2), shall be given before the executing judicial authority, in accordance with the domestic law of the executing Member State.

2. Each Member State shall adopt the measures necessary to ensure that consent and, where appropriate, renunciation, as referred to in paragraph 1, are established in such a way as to show that the person concerned has expressed them voluntarily and in full awareness of the consequences. To that end, the requested person shall have the right to legal counsel.

3. The consent and, where appropriate, renunciation, as referred to in paragraph 1, shall be formally recorded in accordance with the procedure laid down by the domestic law of the executing Member State.

4. In principle, consent may not be revoked. Each Member State may provide that consent and, if appropriate, renunciation may be revoked, in accordance with the rules applicable under its domestic law. In this case, the period between the date of consent and that of its revocation shall not be taken into consideration in establishing the time limits laid down in Article 17. A Member State which wishes to have recourse to this possibility shall inform the General Secretariat of the Council accordingly when this Framework Decision is adopted and shall specify the procedures whereby revocation of consent shall be possible and any amendment to them.

Article 14 Hearing of the requested person

Where the arrested person does not consent to his or her surrender as referred to in Article 13, he or she shall be entitled to be heard by the executing judicial authority, in accordance with the law of the executing Member State.

Article 15 Surrender decision

1. The executing judicial authority shall decide, within the time-limits and under the conditions defined in this Framework Decision, whether the person is to be surrendered.

2. If the executing judicial authority finds the information communicated by the issuing Member State to be insufficient to allow it to decide on surrender, it shall request that the necessary supplementary information, in particular with respect to Articles 3 to 5 and Article 8, be furnished as a matter of urgency and may fix a time limit for the receipt thereof, taking into account the need to observe the time limits set in Article 17.

3. The issuing judicial authority may at any time forward any additional useful information to the executing judicial authority.

Article 16 Decision in the event of multiple requests

1. If two or more Member States have issued European arrest warrants for the same person, the decision on which of the European arrest warrants shall be executed shall be taken by the executing judicial authority with due consideration of all the circumstances and especially the relative seriousness and place of the offences, the respective dates of the European arrest warrants and whether the warrant has been issued for the purposes of prosecution or for execution of a custodial sentence or detention order.

2. The executing judicial authority may seek the advice of Eurojust when making the choice referred to in paragraph 1.

3. In the event of a conflict between a European arrest warrant and a request for extradition presented by a third country, the decision on whether the European arrest warrant or the extradition request takes precedence shall be taken by the competent authority of the executing Member State with due consideration of all the circumstances, in particular those referred to in paragraph 1 and those mentioned in the applicable convention.

4. This Article shall be without prejudice to Member States' obligations under the Statute of the International Criminal Court.

Article 17 Time limits and procedures for the decision to execute the European arrest warrant

1. A European arrest warrant shall be dealt with and executed as a matter of urgency.

2. In cases where the requested person consents to his surrender, the final decision on the execution of the European arrest warrant should be taken within a period of 10 days after consent has been given.

3. In other cases, the final decision on the execution of the European arrest warrant should be taken within a period of 60 days after the arrest of the requested person.

4. Where in specific cases the European arrest warrant cannot be executed within the time limits laid down in paragraphs 2 or 3, the executing judicial authority shall immediately inform the issuing judicial authority thereof, giving the reasons for the delay. In such case, the time limits may be extended by a further 30 days.

5. As long as the executing judicial authority has not taken a final decision on the European arrest warrant, it shall ensure that the material conditions necessary for effective surrender of the person remain fulfilled.

6. Reasons must be given for any refusal to execute a European arrest warrant.

7. Where in exceptional circumstances a Member State cannot observe the time limits provided for in this Article, it shall inform Eurojust, giving the reasons for the delay. In addition, a Member State which has experienced repeated delays on the part of another Member State in the execution of European arrest warrants shall inform the Council with a view to evaluating the implementation of this Framework Decision at Member State level.

Article 18 Situation pending the decision

1. Where the European arrest warrant has been issued for the purpose of conducting a criminal prosecution, the executing judicial authority must:

    (a) either agree that the requested person should be heard according to Article 19;

    (b) or agree to the temporary transfer of the requested person.

2. The conditions and the duration of the temporary transfer shall be determined by mutual agreement between the issuing and executing judicial authorities.

3. In the case of temporary transfer, the person must be able to return to the executing Member State to attend hearings concerning him or her as part of the surrender procedure.

Article 19 Hearing the person pending the decision

1. The requested person shall be heard by a judicial authority, assisted by another person designated in accordance with the law of the Member State of the requesting court.

2. The requested person shall be heard in accordance with the law of the executing Member State and with the conditions determined by mutual agreement between the issuing and executing judicial authorities.

3. The competent executing judicial authority may assign another judicial authority of its Member State to take part in the hearing of the requested person in order to ensure the proper application of this Article and of the conditions laid down.

Article 20 Privileges and immunities

1. Where the requested person enjoys a privilege or immunity regarding jurisdiction or execution in the executing Member State, the time limits referred to in Article 17 shall not start running unless, and counting from the day when, the executing judicial authority is informed of the fact that the privilege or immunity has been waived. The executing Member State shall ensure that the material conditions necessary for effective surrender are fulfilled when the person no longer enjoys such privilege or immunity.

2. Where power to waive the privilege or immunity lies with an authority of the executing Member State, the executing judicial authority shall request it to exercise that power forthwith. Where power to waive the privilege or immunity lies with an authority of another State or international organisation, it shall be for the issuing judicial authority to request it to exercise that power.

Article 21 Competing international obligations

This Framework Decision shall not prejudice the obligations of the executing Member State where the requested person has been extradited to that Member State from a third State and where that person is protected by provisions of the arrangement under which he or she was extradited concerning speciality. The executing Member State shall take all necessary measures for requesting forthwith the consent of the State from which the requested person was extradited so that he or she can be surrendered to the Member State which issued the European arrest warrant. The time limits referred to in Article 17 shall not start running until the day on which these speciality rules cease to apply. Pending the decision of the State from which the requested person was extradited, the executing Member State will ensure that the material conditions necessary for effective surrender remain fulfilled.

Article 22 Notification of the decision

The executing judicial authority shall notify the issuing judicial authority immediately of the decision on the action to be taken on the European arrest warrant.

Article 23 Time limits for surrender of the person

1. The person requested shall be surrendered as soon as possible on a date agreed between the authorities concerned.

2. He or she shall be surrendered no later than 10 days after the final decision on the execution of the European arrest warrant.

3. If the surrender of the requested person within the period laid down in paragraph 2 is prevented by circumstances beyond the control of any of the Member States, the executing and issuing judicial authorities shall immediately contact each other and agree on a new surrender date. In that event, the surrender shall take place within 10 days of the new date thus agreed.

4. The surrender may exceptionally be temporarily postponed for serious humanitarian reasons, for example if there are substantial grounds for believing that it would manifestly endanger the requested person's life or health. The execution of the European arrest warrant shall take place as soon as these grounds have ceased to exist. The executing judicial authority shall immediately inform the issuing judicial authority and agree on a new surrender date. In that event, the surrender shall take place within 10 days of the new date thus agreed.

5. Upon expiry of the time limits referred to in paragraphs 2 to 4, if the person is still being held in custody he shall be released.

Article 24 Postponed or conditional surrender

1. The executing judicial authority may, after deciding to execute the European arrest warrant, postpone the surrender of the requested person so that he or she may be prosecuted in the executing Member State or, if he or she has already been sentenced, so that he or she may serve, in its territory, a sentence passed for an act other than that referred to in the European arrest warrant.

2. Instead of postponing the surrender, the executing judicial authority may temporarily surrender the requested person to the issuing Member State under conditions to be determined by mutual agreement between the executing and the issuing judicial authorities. The agreement shall be made in writing and the conditions shall be binding on all the authorities in the issuing Member State.

Article 25 Transit

1. Each Member State shall, except when it avails itself of the possibility of refusal when the transit of a national or a resident is requested for the purpose of the execution of a custodial sentence or detention order, permit the transit through its territory of a requested person who is being surrendered provided that it has been given information on:

    (a) the identity and nationality of the person subject to the European arrest warrant;

    (b) the existence of a European arrest warrant;

    (c) the nature and legal classification of the offence;

    (d) the description of the circumstances of the offence, including the date and place.

    Where a person who is the subject of a European arrest warrant for the purposes of prosecution is a national or resident of the Member State of transit, transit may be subject to the condition that the person, after being heard, is returned to the transit Member State to serve the custodial sentence or detention order passed against him in the issuing Member State.

2. Each Member State shall designate an authority responsible for receiving transit requests and the necessary documents, as well as any other official correspondence relating to transit requests. Member States shall communicate this designation to the General Secretariat of the Council.

3. The transit request and the information set out in paragraph 1 may be addressed to the authority designated pursuant to paragraph 2 by any means capable of producing a written record. The Member State of transit shall notify its decision by the same procedure.

4. This Framework Decision does not apply in the case of transport by air without a scheduled stopover. However, if an unscheduled landing occurs, the issuing Member State shall provide the authority designated pursuant to paragraph 2 with the information provided for in paragraph 1.

5. Where a transit concerns a person who is to be extradited from a third State to a Member State this Article will apply *mutatis mutandis*. In particular the expression "European arrest warrant" shall be deemed to be replaced by "extradition request".

Chapter 3 Effects of the Surrender

Article 26 Deduction of the period of detention served in the executing Member State

1. The issuing Member State shall deduct all periods of detention arising from the execution of a European arrest warrant from the total period of detention to be served in the issuing Member State as a result of a custodial sentence or detention order being passed.

2. To that end, all information concerning the duration of the detention of the requested person on the basis of the European arrest warrant shall be transmitted by the executing judicial authority or the central authority designated under Article 7 to the issuing judicial authority at the time of the surrender.

Article 27 Possible prosecution for other offences

1. Each Member State may notify the General Secretariat of the Council that, in its relations with other Member States that have given the same notification, consent is presumed to have been given for the prosecution, sentencing or detention with a view to the carrying out of a custodial sentence or detention order for an offence committed prior to his or her surrender, other than that for which he or she was surrendered, unless in a particular case the executing judicial authority states otherwise in its decision on surrender.

2. Except in the cases referred to in paragraphs 1 and 3, a person surrendered may not be prosecuted, sentenced or otherwise deprived of his or her liberty for an offence committed prior to his or her surrender other than that for which he or she was surrendered.

3. Paragraph 2 does not apply in the following cases:

    (a) when the person having had an opportunity to leave the territory of the Member State to which he or she has been surrendered has not done so within 45 days of his or her final discharge, or has returned to that territory after leaving it;

    (b) the offence is not punishable by a custodial sentence or detention order;

    (c) the criminal proceedings do not give rise to the application of a measure restricting personal liberty;

    (d) when the person could be liable to a penalty or a measure not involving the deprivation of liberty, in particular a financial penalty or a measure in lieu thereof, even if the penalty or measure may give rise to a restriction of his or her personal liberty;

    (e) when the person consented to be surrendered, where appropriate at the same time as he or she renounced the speciality rule, in accordance with Article 13;

    (f) when the person, after his/her surrender, has expressly renounced entitlement to the speciality rule with regard to specific offences preceding his/her surrender. Renunciation shall be given before the competent judicial authorities of the issuing Member State and shall be recorded in accordance with that State's domestic law. The renunciation shall be drawn up in such a way as to make clear that the person has given it voluntarily and in full awareness of the consequences. To that end, the person shall have the right to legal counsel;

    (g) where the executing judicial authority which surrendered the person gives its consent in accordance with paragraph 4.

4. A request for consent shall be submitted to the executing judicial authority, accompanied by the information mentioned in Article 8(1) and a translation as referred to in Article 2. Consent shall be given when the offence for which it is requested is itself subject to surrender in accordance with the provisions of this Framework Decision. Consent shall be refused on the grounds referred to in Article 3 and otherwise may be refused only on the grounds referred to in Article 4. The decision shall be taken no later than 30 days after receipt of the request. For the situations mentioned in Article 5 the issuing Member State must give the guarantees provided for therein.

Article 28 Surrender or subsequent extradition

1. Each Member State may notify the General Secretariat of the Council that, in its relations with other Member States which have given the same notification, the consent for the surrender of a person to a Member State other than the executing Member State pursuant to a European arrest warrant issued for an offence committed prior to his or her surrender is presumed to have been given, unless in a particular case the executing judicial authority states otherwise in its decision on surrender.

2. In any case, a person who has been surrendered to the issuing Member State pursuant to a European arrest warrant may, without the consent of the executing Member State, be surrendered to a Member State other than the executing Member State pursuant to a European arrest warrant issued for any offence committed prior to his or her surrender in the following cases:

    (a) where the requested person, having had an opportunity to leave the territory of the Member State to which he or she has been surrendered, has not done so within 45 days of his final discharge, or has returned to that territory after leaving it;

    (b) where the requested person consents to be surrendered to a Member State other than the executing Member State pursuant to a European arrest warrant. Consent shall be given before the competent judicial authorities of the issuing Member State and shall be recorded in accordance with that State's national law. It shall be drawn up in such a way as to make clear that the person concerned has given it voluntarily and in full awareness of the consequences. To that end, the requested person shall have the right to legal counsel;

    (c) where the requested person is not subject to the speciality rule, in accordance with Article 27(3)(a), (e), (f) and (g).

3. The executing judicial authority consents to the surrender to another Member State according to the following rules:

    (a) the request for consent shall be submitted in accordance with Article 9, accompanied by the information mentioned in Article 8(1) and a translation as stated in Article 8(2);

    (b) consent shall be given when the offence for which it is requested is itself subject to surrender in accordance with the provisions of this Framework Decision;

    (c) the decision shall be taken no later than 30 days after receipt of the request;

    (d) consent shall be refused on the grounds referred to in Article 3 and otherwise may be refused only on the grounds referred to in Article 4. For the situations referred to in Article 5, the issuing Member State must give the guarantees provided for therein.

4. Notwithstanding paragraph 1, a person who has been surrendered pursuant to a European arrest warrant shall not be extradited to a third State without the consent of the competent authority of the Member State which surrendered the person. Such consent shall be given in accordance with the Conventions by which that Member State is bound, as well as with its domestic law.

Article 29 Handing over of property

1. At the request of the issuing judicial authority or on its own initiative, the executing judicial authority shall, in accordance with its national law, seize and hand over property which:

    (a) may be required as evidence, or

(b) has been acquired by the requested person as a result of the offence.

2. The property referred to in paragraph 1 shall be handed over even if the European arrest warrant cannot be carried out owing to the death or escape of the requested person.

3. If the property referred to in paragraph 1 is liable to seizure or confiscation in the territory of the executing Member State, the latter may, if the property is needed in connection with pending criminal proceedings, temporarily retain it or hand it over to the issuing Member State, on condition that it is returned.

4. Any rights which the executing Member State or third parties may have acquired in the property referred to in paragraph 1 shall be preserved. Where such rights exist, the issuing Member State shall return the property without charge to the executing Member State as soon as the criminal proceedings have been terminated.

Article 30 Expenses

1. Expenses incurred in the territory of the executing Member State for the execution of a European arrest warrant shall be borne by that Member State.

2. All other expenses shall be borne by the issuing Member State.

Chapter 4 General and Final Provisions

Article 31 Relation to other legal instruments

1. Without prejudice to their application in relations between Member States and third States, this Framework Decision shall, from 1 January 2004, replace the corresponding provisions of the following conventions applicable in the field of extradition in relations between the Member States:

(a) the European Convention on Extradition of 13 December 1957, its additional protocol of 15 October 1975, its second additional protocol of 17 March 1978, and the European Convention on the suppression of terrorism of 27 January 1977 as far as extradition is concerned;

(b) the Agreement between the 12 Member States of the European Communities on the simplification and modernisation of methods of transmitting extradition requests of 26 May 1989;

(c) the Convention of 10 March 1995 on simplified extradition procedure between the Member States of the European Union;

(d) the Convention of 27 September 1996 relating to extradition between the Member States of the European Union;

(e) Title III, Chapter 4 of the Convention of 19 June 1990 implementing the Schengen Agreement of 14 June 1985 on the gradual abolition of checks at common borders.

2. Member States may continue to apply bilateral or multilateral agreements or arrangements in force when this Framework Decision is adopted in so far as such agreements or arrangements allow the objectives of this Framework Decision to be extended or enlarged and help to simplify or facilitate further the procedures for surrender of persons who are the subject of European arrest warrants.

Member States may conclude bilateral or multilateral agreements or arrangements after this Framework Decision has come into force in so far as such agreements or arrangements allow the prescriptions of this Framework Decision to be extended or enlarged and help to simplify or facilitate further the procedures for surrender of persons who are the subject of European arrest warrants, in particular by fixing time limits shorter than those fixed in Article 17, by extending the list of offences laid down in Article 2(2), by further limiting the grounds for refusal set out in Articles 3 and 4, or by lowering the threshold provided for in Article 2(1) or (2).

The agreements and arrangements referred to in the second subparagraph may in no case affect relations with Member States which are not parties to them.

Member States shall, within three months from the entry into force of this Framework Decision, notify the Council and the Commission of the existing agreements and arrangements referred to in the first subparagraph which they wish to continue applying.

Member States shall also notify the Council and the Commission of any new agreement or arrangement as referred to in the second subparagraph, within three months of signing it.

3. Where the conventions or agreements referred to in paragraph 1 apply to the territories of Member States or to territories for whose external relations a Member State is responsible to which this Framework Decision does not apply, these instruments shall continue to govern the relations existing between those territories and the other Members States.

Article 34 Implementation

1. Member States shall take the necessary measures to comply with the provisions of this Framework Decision by 31 December 2003.

2. Member States shall transmit to the General Secretariat of the Council and to the Commission the text of the provisions transposing into their national law the obligations imposed on them under this Framework Decision. When doing so, each Member State may indicate that it will apply immediately this Framework Decision in its relations with those Member States which have given the same notification. The General Secretariat of the Council shall communicate to the Member States and to the Commission the information received pursuant to Article 7(2), Article 8(2), Article 13(4) and Article 25(2). It shall also have the information published in the Official Journal of the European Communities.

3. On the basis of the information communicated by the General Secretariat of the Council, the Commission shall, by 31 December 2004 at the latest, submit a report to the European Parliament and to the Council on the operation of this Framework Decision, accompanied, where necessary, by legislative proposals.

4. The Council shall in the second half of 2003 conduct a review, in particular of the practical application, of the provisions of this Framework Decision by the Member States as well as the functioning of the Schengen Information System.

DOCUMENT 65

Inter-American Convention on Extradition 1981
OASTS No 60; 20 ILM 723 (1981)

The Convention was concluded under the auspices of the Organization of American States (OAS); it was opened for signature in Caracas, Venezuela, on 25 February 1981 and entered into force on 28 March 1992.

While there are 14 signatories to the Convention, only six of these States are parties. The USA is not a party.

The States Parties agree to 'surrender to other States Parties that request their extradition persons who are judicially required for prosecution, are being tried, have been convicted or have been sentenced to a penalty involving deprivation of liberty' (Article 1). An extraditable offence is defined in general terms as any offence which is punishable by a period of detention of at least two years (Article 3). Article 4 provides grounds for denying extradition, including where the offence is a political offence as determined by the requested State, or where it can be inferred that persecution for reasons of race, religion or nationality is involved. The right of asylum is preserved by Article 6. Extradition is excluded in cases involving the death penalty (Article 9).

Reaffirming their goal of strengthening international cooperation in legal and criminal law matters, which was the inspiration for the agreements reached in Lima on March 27, 1879, in Montevideo on January 23, 1889, in Mexico City on January 28, 1902, in Washington on February 7, 1923, in Havana on February 20, 1928, in Montevideo on December 26, 1933, in Guatemala City on April 12, 1934, and in Montevideo on March 19, 1940;

Taking into consideration resolutions CVII of the Tenth Inter-American Conference (Caracas, 1954), VII of the Third Meeting of the Inter-American Council of Jurists (Mexico, 1956), IV of the Fourth Meeting of that Council (Santiago, Chile, 1959), and AG/RES.91 (II-0/72), 183 (V-0/75) and 310 (VII-0/77) of the General Assembly of the Organization of American States, as well as the draft Conventions proposed by the Inter-American Juridical Committee in 1954, 1957, 1973, and 1977;

Believing that the close ties and the cooperation that exist in the Americas call for the extension of extradition to ensure that crime does not go unpunished, and to simplify procedures and promote mutual assistance in the field of criminal law on a wider scale than provided for by the treaties in force, with due respect to the human rights embodied in the American Declaration of the Rights and Duties of Man and the Universal Declaration of Human Rights; and

Conscious that the fight against crime at the international level will enhance the fundamental value of justice in criminal law matters,

The Member States of the Organization of American States adopt the following Inter-American Convention on Extradition.

Article 1 Obligation to Extradite

The States Parties bind themselves, in accordance with the provisions of this Convention, to surrender to other States Parties that request their extradition persons who are judicially required for prosecution, are being tried, have been convicted or have been sentenced to a penalty involving deprivation of liberty.

Article 2 Jurisdiction

1. For extradition to be granted, the offense that gave rise to the request for extradition must have been committed in the territory of the requesting State.

2. When the offense for which extradition is requested has been committed outside the territory of the requesting State, extradition shall be granted provided the requesting State has jurisdiction to try the offense that gave rise to the request for extradition and to pronounce judgment thereon.

3. The requested State may deny extradition when it is competent, according to its own legislation, to prosecute the person whose extradition is sought for the offense on which the request is base(d) If it denies extradition for this reason, the requested State shall submit the case to its competent authorities and inform the requesting State of the result.

Article 3 Extraditable Offenses

1. For extradition to be granted, the offense for which the person is sought shall be punishable at the time of its commission, by reason of the acts that constitute it, disregarding extenuating circumstances and the denomination of the offense, by a penalty of not less than two years of deprivation of liberty under the laws of both the requesting State and the requested State. Where the principle of retroactivity of penal law exists, it shall be applied only when it is favorable to the offender.

2. If the extradition is to be carried out between States whose laws establish minimum and maximum penalties, the offense for which extradition is requested shall be punishable, under the

laws of the requesting and the requested States, by an average penalty of at least two years of deprivation of liberty. Average penalty is understood to be one-half of the sum of the minimum and maximum terms of each penalty of deprivation of liberty.

3. Where the extradition of an offender is requested for the execution of a sentence involving deprivation of liberty, the duration of the sentence still to be served must be at least six months.

4. In determining whether extradition should be granted to a State having a federal form of government and separate federal and state criminal legislation, the requested State shall take into consideration only the essential elements of the offense and shall disregard elements such as interstate transportation or use of the mails or other facilities of interstate commerce, since the sole purpose of such elements is to establish the jurisdiction of the federal courts of the requesting State.

Article 4 Grounds for Denying Extradition

Extradition shall not be granted:

1. When the person sought has completed his punishment or has been granted amnesty, pardon or grace for the offense for which extradition is sought, or when he has been acquitted or the case against him for the same offense has been dismissed with prejudice.

2. When the prosecution or punishment is barred by the statute of limitations according to the laws of the requesting State or the requested State prior to the presentation of the request for extradition.

3. When the person sought has been tried or sentenced or is to be tried before an extraordinary or *ad hoc* tribunal of the requesting State.

4. When, as determined by the requested State, the offense for which the person is sought is a political offense, an offense related thereto, or an ordinary criminal offense prosecuted for political reasons. The requested State may decide that the fact that the victim of the punishable act in question performed political functions does not in itself justify the designation of the offense as political.

5. When, from the circumstances of the case, it can be inferred that persecution for reasons of race, religion or nationality is involved, or that the position of the person sought may be prejudiced for any of these reasons.

6. With respect to offenses that in the requested State cannot be prosecuted unless a complaint or charge has been made by a party having a legitimate interest.

Article 5 Specific Offenses

No provision of this Convention shall preclude extradition regulated by a treaty or Convention in force between the requesting State and the requested State whose purpose is to prevent or repress a specific category of offenses and which imposes on such States an obligation to either prosecute or extradite the person sought.

Article 6 Right of Asylum

No provision of this Convention may be interpreted as a limitation on the right of asylum when its exercise is appropriate.

Article 7 Nationality

1. The nationality of the person sought may not be invoked as a ground for denying extradition, except when the law of the requested State otherwise provides.

2. In the case of convicted persons, the States Parties may negotiate the mutual surrender of nationals so that they may serve their sentences in the States of which they are nationals.

Article 8 Prosecution by the Requested State

If, when extradition is applicable, a State does not deliver the person sought, the requested State shall, when its laws or other treaties so permit, be obligated to prosecute him for the offense with which he is charged, just as if it had been committed within its territory, and shall inform the requesting State of the judgment handed down.

Article 9 Penalties Excluded

The States Parties shall not grant extradition when the offense in question is punishable in the requesting State by the death penalty, by life imprisonment, or by degrading punishment, unless the requested State has previously obtained from the requesting State, through the diplomatic channel, sufficient assurances that none of the above-mentioned penalties will be imposed on the person sought or that, if such penalties are imposed, they will not be enforced.

Article 10 Transmission of Request

The request for extradition shall be made by the diplomatic agent of the requesting State, or, if none is present, by its consular officer, or, when appropriate, by the diplomatic agent of a third State to which is entrusted, with the consent of the government of the requested State, the representation and protection of the interests of the requesting State. The request may also be made directly from government to government, in accordance with such procedure as the governments concerned may agree upon.

Article 11 Supporting Documents

1. The request for extradition shall be accompanied by the documents listed below, duly certified in the manner prescribed by the laws of the requesting State:

    (a) A certified copy of the warrant for arrest, or other document of like nature, issued by a competent judicial authority, or the *Ministerio Público* as well as a certified copy of evidence that, according to the laws of the requested State, is sufficient for the arrest and commitment for trial of the person sought. This last mentioned requirement shall not apply if the laws of the requesting State and of the requested State do not so provide. If the person has been tried and convicted of the offense by the courts of the requesting State, a certified verbatim copy of the final judgment shall suffice.

    (b) The text of the legal provisions that define and penalize the alleged crime, as well as those of the statute of limitations governing prosecution and punishment.

2. The request for extradition shall also be accompanied by the translation into the language of the requested State, if appropriate, of the documents enumerated in the previous paragraph, as well as by any personal data that will permit identification of the person sought, indication of his nationality, and, whenever possible, his location within the territory of the requested State, photographs, fingerprints, or any other satisfactory means of identification.

Article 12 Supplementary Information and Legal Assistance

1. The requested State, when it considers that the documents presented are insufficient, in accordance with the provisions of Article 11 of this Convention, shall so inform the requesting State as soon as possible. The requesting State shall correct any omissions or defects observed within a period of thirty days in the event the person sought is already detained or subject to precautionary measures. If, because of special circumstances, the requesting State is unable to correct the omissions or defects within that term, it may ask the requested State to extend the term by thirty days.

2. The requested State shall provide, at no cost to the requesting State, legal assistance to protect the interests of the requesting State before the competent authorities of the requested State.

Article 13 Rule of Speciality

1. A person extradited under this Convention shall not be detained, tried or punished in the territory of the requesting State for an offense, committed prior to the date of the request for extradition, other than that for which extradition has been granted unless:

    (a) That person leaves the territory of the requesting State after extradition and voluntarily returns to it; or

    (b) That person does not leave the territory of the requesting State within thirty days after being free to do so; or

    (c) The competent authority of the requested State consents to that person's detention, trial or punishment for another offense. In such case, the requested State may require the requesting State to submit the documents mentioned in Article 11 of this Convention.

2. When extradition has been granted, the requesting State shall inform the requested State of the final resolution of the case against the person extradited.

Article 14 Provisional Detention and Precautionary Measures

1. In urgent cases, a State Party may request by the means of communication provided for in Article 10 of this Convention, or any other such means, the detention of the person who is judicially required for prosecution, is being tried, has been convicted, or has been sentenced to a penalty involving deprivation of liberty, and may also request the seizure of the objects related to the offense. The request for provisional detention shall contain a statement of intention to present the formal request for the extradition of the person sought, a statement of the existence of a warrant of arrest or of a judgment of conviction against that person issued by a judicial authority, and a description of the offense. The request for provisional detention shall be the sole responsibility of the requesting State.

2. The requested State shall order provisional detention and, when appropriate, the seizure of objects and shall immediately inform the requesting State of the date on which provisional detention commenced.

3. If the request for extradition, accompanied by the documents referred to in Article 11 of this Convention, is not presented within sixty days of the date on which the provisional detention referred to in paragraph 1 of this article commenced, the person sought shall be set free.

4. After the period of time referred to in the preceding paragraph has expired, the detention of the person sought may not be again requested except upon presentation of the documents required under Article 11 of this Convention.

Article 15 Requests by more than One State

When the extradition is requested by more than one State for the same offense, the requested State shall give preference to the request of the State in which the offense was committed. If the requests are for different offenses, preference shall be given to the State seeking the individual for the offense punishable by the most severe penalty, in accordance with the laws of the requested State. If the requests involve different offenses that the requested State considers to be of equal gravity, preference shall be determined by the order in which the requests are received.

Article 16 Legal Rights and Assistance

1. The person sought shall enjoy in the requested State all the legal rights and guarantees granted by the laws of that State.

2. The person sought shall be assisted by legal counsel, and if the official language of the country is other than his own, he shall also be assisted by an interpreter.

Article 17 Communication of the Extradition Decision

The requested State shall promptly inform the requesting State of its decision on the request for extradition and the reasons for its approval or denial.

Article 18 *Non bis in idem*

Once the request for extradition of a person has been denied, a request may not be made again for the same offense.

Article 19 Surrender of the Person Sought and Delivery of Property

1. The surrender of the person sought to the agents of the requesting State shall be carried out at a place determined by the requested State. This place shall, if possible, be an airport from which direct international flights depart for the requesting State.

2. If the request for provisional detention or for extradition is accompanied by a request for the seizure of documents, money or other objects that result from the alleged offense or may serve as evidence, such objects shall be collected and deposited under inventory by the requested State for subsequent delivery to the requesting State when the extradition is granted and even though the extradition is impeded by *force majeure*, unless the law of the requested State forbids such delivery. In any event, the rights of third parties shall not be affected.

Article 20 Deferral of Surrender

1. When the person sought is being tried or is serving a sentence in the requested State for an offense other than that for which the extradition is requested, his surrender may be deferred until he is entitled to be set free by virtue of acquittal, completed service or commutation of sentence, dismissal, pardon, amnesty or grace. No civil suit that the person sought may have pending against him in the requested State may prevent or defer his surrender.

2. When the surrender of the person sought would, for reasons of health, endanger his life, his surrender may be deferred until it would no longer pose such a danger.

Article 21 Simplified Extradition

The requested State may grant extradition without a formal extradition proceeding if:

(a) Its laws do not expressly prohibit it;

(b) The person sought irrevocably consents in writing to the extradition after being advised by a judge or other competent authority of his right to a formal extradition proceeding and the protection afforded by such a proceeding.

Article 22 Period for Taking Custody of the Person Sought

If the extradition has been granted, the requesting State shall take custody of the person sought within a period of thirty days from the date on which he was placed at its disposal. If it does not take custody within that period, the person sought shall be set free and may not be subjected to a new extradition procedure for the same offense or offenses. This period, however, may be extended for thirty days if the requesting State is unable, owing to circumstances beyond its control, to take custody of the person sought and escort him out of the territory of the requested State.

Article 23 Custody

The agents of the requesting State who are in the territory of another State Party to take custody of a person whose extradition has been granted shall be authorized to have custody of him and escort him to the territory of the requesting State, provided, however, that such agents shall be subject to the jurisdiction of the State in which they are.

Article 24 Transit

1. If prior notification has been given from government to government through diplomatic or consular channels, the States Parties shall permit and cooperate in the transit through their territories of a person whose extradition has been granted under the custody of agents of the requesting State and/or the requested State, as the case may be, upon presentation of a copy of the order granting the extradition.

2. Such prior notification shall not be necessary when air transport is used and no landing is scheduled in the territory of the State Party that will be flown over.

Article 25 Expenses

Expenses incurred in the detention, custody, maintenance, and transportation of both the person extradited and of the objects referred to in Article 19 of this Convention shall be borne by the requested State up to the moment of surrender and delivery, and thereafter such expenses shall be borne by the requesting State.

Article 26 Waiver of Legalization

When the documents provided for in this Convention are communicated through the diplomatic or consular channel, or direct from government to government, their legalization shall not be required.

DOCUMENT 66

UN Model Treaty on Extradition 1990
UN Doc A/45/49; UN Doc A/RES/45/116; 30 ILM 1407 (1991)

The Model Treaty on Extradition was adopted by the UN General Assembly on 14 December 1990 in Resolution 45/116. In promulgating the Model Treaty, the General Assembly invited Member States 'if they have not yet established treaty relations with other States in the area of extradition, or if they wish to revise existing treaty relations, to take into account, whenever doing so, the Model Treaty on Extradition' (preamble). The General Assembly further urged all States to 'strengthen further international cooperation in criminal justice'.

The Model Treaty defines extraditable offences as those involving imprisonment of between one and two years (Article 2). It includes a number of mandatory grounds for refusal of extradition including, inter alia, the determination by the requested State that the offence is an offence of a political nature (Article 3), as well as optional grounds for refusal (Article 4). The Model Treaty allows for simplified extradition procedure (Article 6) and provisional arrest in case of urgency (Article 9). The Model Treaty preserves the speciality rule which ensures that an individual cannot be prosecuted for any offence other than the offence for which the extradition was granted or any other offence in respect of which the requested State consents (Article 14).

Article 1 Obligation to extradite

Each Party agrees to extradite to the other, upon request and subject to the provisions of the present Treaty, any person who is wanted in the requesting State for prosecution for an extraditable offence or for the imposition or enforcement of a sentence in respect of such an offence.

Article 2 Extraditable offences

1. For the purposes of the present Treaty, extraditable offences are offences that are punishable under the laws of both Parties by imprisonment or other deprivation of liberty for a maximum period of at least one/two year(s), or by a more severe penalty. Where the request for extradition relates to a person who is wanted for the enforcement of a sentence of imprisonment or other deprivation of liberty imposed for such an offence, extradition shall be granted only if a period of at least four/six months of such sentence remains to be served.

2. In determining whether an offence is an offence punishable under the laws of both Parties, it shall not matter whether:

    (a) The laws of the Parties place the acts or omissions constituting the offence within the same category of offence or denominate the offence by the same terminology;

    (b) Under the laws of the Parties the constituent elements of the offence differ, it being understood that the totality of the acts or omissions as presented by the requesting State shall be taken into account.

3. Where extradition of a person is sought for an offence against a law relating to taxation, customs duties, exchange control or other revenue matters, extradition may not be refused on the ground that the law of the requested State does not impose the same kind of tax or duty or does not contain a tax, customs duty or exchange regulation of the same kind as the law of the requesting State.

4. If the request for extradition includes several separate offences each of which is punishable under the laws of both Parties, but some of which do not fulfil the other conditions set out in paragraph 1 of the present article, the requested Party may grant extradition for the latter offences provided that the person is to be extradited for at least one extraditable offence.

Article 3 Mandatory grounds for refusal

Extradition shall not be granted in any of the following circumstances:

(a) If the offence for which extradition is requested is regarded by the requested State as an offence of a political nature;

(b) If the requested State has substantial grounds for believing that the request for extradition has been made for the purpose of prosecuting or punishing a person on account of that person's race, religion, nationality, ethnic origin, political opinions, sex or status, or that that person's position may be prejudiced for any of those reasons;

(c) If the offence for which extradition is requested is an offence under military law, which is not also an offence under ordinary criminal law;

(d) If there has been a final judgment rendered against the person in the requested State in respect of the offence for which the person's extradition is requested;

(e) If the person whose extradition is requested has, under the law of either Party, become immune from prosecution or punishment for any reason, including lapse of time or amnesty;

(f) If the person whose extradition is requested has been or would be subjected in the requesting State to torture or cruel, inhuman or degrading treatment or punishment or if that person has not received or would not receive the minimum guarantees in criminal proceedings, as contained in the International Covenant on Civil and Political Rights, article 14;

(g) If the judgment of the requesting State has been rendered in absentia, the convicted person has not had sufficient notice of the trial or the opportunity to arrange for his or her defence and he has not had or will not have the opportunity to have the case retried in his or her presence.

Article 4 Optional grounds for refusal

Extradition may be refused in any of the following circumstances:

(a) If the person whose extradition is requested is a national of the requested State. Where extradition is refused on this ground, the requested State shall, if the other State so requests, submit the case to its competent authorities with a view to taking appropriate action against the person in respect of the offence for which extradition had been requested;

(b) If the competent authorities of the requested State have decided either not to institute or to terminate proceedings against the person for the offence in respect of which extradition is requested;

(c) If a prosecution in respect of the offence for which extradition is requested is pending in the requested State against the person whose extradition is requested;

(d) If the offence for which extradition is requested carries the death penalty under the law of the requesting State, unless that State gives such assurance as the requested State considers sufficient that the death penalty will not be imposed or, if imposed, will not be carried out;

(e) If the offence for which extradition is requested has been committed outside the territory of either Party and the law of the requested State does not provide for jurisdiction over such an offence committed outside its territory in comparable circumstances;

(f) If the offence for which extradition is requested is regarded under the law of the requested State as having been committed in whole or in part within that State. Where extradition is refused on this ground, the requested State shall, if the other State so requests, submit the case to its competent authorities with a view to taking appropriate action against the person for the offence for which extradition had been requested;

(g) If the person whose extradition is requested has been sentenced or would be liable to be tried or sentenced in the requesting State by an extraordinary or ad hoc court or tribunal;

(h) If the requested State, while also taking into account the nature of the offence and the interests of the requesting State, considers that, in the circumstances of the case, the extradition of that person would be incompatible with humanitarian considerations in view of age, health or other personal circumstances of that person.

Article 5 Channels of communication and required documents

1. A request for extradition shall be made in writing. The request, supporting documents and subsequent communications shall be transmitted through the diplomatic channel, directly between the ministries of justice or any other authorities designated by the Parties.

2. A request for extradition shall be accompanied by the following:

    (a) In all cases,

       (i) As accurate a description as possible of the person sought, together with any other information that may help to establish that person's identity, nationality and location;

       (ii) The text of the relevant provision of the law creating the offence or, where necessary, a statement of the law relevant to the offence and a statement of the penalty that can be imposed for the offence;

    (b) If the person is accused of an offence, by a warrant issued by a court or other competent judicial authority for the arrest of the person or a certified copy of that warrant, a statement of the offence for which extradition is requested and a description of the acts or omissions constituting the alleged offence, including an indication of the time and place of its commission;

    (c) If the person has been convicted of an offence, by a statement of the offence for which extradition is requested and a description of the acts or omissions constituting the offence and by the original or certified copy of the judgment or any other document setting out the conviction and the sentence imposed, the fact that the sentence is enforceable, and the extent to which the sentence remains to be served;

(d) If the person has been convicted of an offence in his or her absence, in addition to the documents set out in paragraph 2 (c) of the present article, by a statement as to the legal means available to the person to prepare his or her defence or to have the case retried in his or her presence;

(e) If the person has been convicted of an offence but no sentence has been imposed, by a statement of the offence for which extradition is requested and a description of the acts or omissions constituting the offence and by a document setting out the conviction and a statement affirming that there is an intention to impose a sentence.

3. The documents submitted in support of a request for extradition shall be accompanied by a translation into the language of the requested State or in another language acceptable to that State.

Article 6 Simplified extradition procedure
The requested State, if not precluded by its law, may grant extradition after receipt of a request for provisional arrest, provided that the person sought explicitly consents before a competent authority.

Article 7 Certification and authentication
Except as provided by the present Treaty, a request for extradition and the documents in support thereof, as well as documents or other material supplied in response to such a request, shall not require certification or authentication.

Article 8 Additional information
If the requested State considers that the information provided in support of a request for extradition is not sufficient, it may request that additional information be furnished within such reasonable time as it specifies.

Article 9 Provisional arrest
1. In case of urgency the requesting State may apply for the provisional arrest of the person sought pending the presentation of the request for extradition. The application shall be transmitted by means of the facilities of the International Criminal Police Organization, by post or telegraph or by any other means affording a record in writing.

2. The application shall contain a description of the person sought, a statement that extradition is to be requested, a statement of the existence of one of the documents mentioned in paragraph 2 of article 5 of the present Treaty, authorizing the apprehension of the person, a statement of the punishment that can be or has been imposed for the offence, including the time left to be served and a concise statement of the facts of the case, and a statement of the location, where known, of the person.

3. The requested State shall decide on the application in accordance with its law and communicate its decision to the requesting State without delay.

4. The person arrested upon such an application shall be set at liberty upon the expiration of 40 days from the date of arrest if a request for extradition, supported by the relevant documents specified in paragraph 2 of article 5 of the present Treaty, has not been received. The present paragraph does not preclude the possibility of conditional release of the person prior to the expiration of the 40 days.

5. The release of the person pursuant to paragraph 4 of the present article shall not prevent rearrest and institution of proceedings with a view to extraditing the person sought if the request and supporting documents are subsequently received.

Article 10 Decision on the request

1. The requested State shall deal with the request for extradition pursuant to procedures provided by its own law, and shall promptly communicate its decision to the requesting State.

2. Reasons shall be given for any complete or partial refusal of the request.

Article 11 Surrender of the person

1. Upon being informed that extradition has been granted, the Parties shall, without undue delay, arrange for the surrender of the person sought and the requested State shall inform the requesting State of the length of time for which the person sought was detained with a view to surrender.

2. The person shall be removed from the territory of the requested State within such reasonable period as the requested State specifies and, if the person is not removed within that period, the requested State may release the person and may refuse to extradite that person for the same offence.

3. If circumstances beyond its control prevent a Party from surrendering or removing the person to be extradited, it shall notify the other Party. The two Parties shall mutually decide upon a new date of surrender, and the provisions of paragraph 2 of the present article shall apply.

Article 12 Postponed or conditional surrender

1. The requested State may, after making its decision on the request for extradition, postpone the surrender of a person sought, in order to proceed against that person, or, if that person has already been convicted, in order to enforce a sentence imposed for an offence other than that for which extradition is sought. In such a case the requested State shall advise the requesting State accordingly.

2. The requested State may, instead of postponing surrender, temporarily surrender the person sought to the requesting State in accordance with conditions to be determined between the Parties.

Article 13 Surrender of property

1. To the extent permitted under the law of the requested State and subject to the rights of third parties, which shall be duly respected, all property found in the requested State that has been acquired as a result of the offence or that may be required as evidence shall, if the requesting State so requests, be surrendered if extradition is granted.

2. The said property may, if the requesting State so requests, be surrendered to the requesting State even if the extradition agreed to cannot be carried out.

3. When the said property is liable to seizure or confiscation in the requested State, it may retain it or temporarily hand it over.

4. Where the law of the requested State or the protection of the rights of third parties so require, any property so surrendered shall be returned to the requested State free of charge after the completion of the proceedings, if that State so requests.

Article 14 Rule of speciality

1. A person extradited under the present Treaty shall not be proceeded against, sentenced, detained, re-extradited to a third State, or subjected to any other restriction of personal liberty in the territory of the requesting State for any offence committed before surrender other than:

    (a) An offence for which extradition was granted;

    (b) Any other offence in respect of which the requested State consents. Consent shall be given if the offence for which it is requested is itself subject to extradition in accordance with the present Treaty.

2. A request for the consent of the requested State under the present article shall be accompanied by the documents mentioned in paragraph 2 of article 5 of the present Treaty and a legal record of any statement made by the extradited person with respect to the offence.

3. Paragraph 1 of the present article shall not apply if the person has had an opportunity to leave the requesting State and has not done so within 30/45 days of final discharge in respect of the offence for which that person was extradited or if the person has voluntarily returned to the territory of the requesting State after leaving it.

Article 15 Transit

1. Where a person is to be extradited to a Party from a third State through the territory of the other Party, the Party to which the person is to be extradited shall request the other Party to permit the transit of that person through its territory. This does not apply where air transport is used and no landing in the territory of the other Party is scheduled.

2. Upon receipt of such a request, which shall contain relevant information, the requested State shall deal with this request pursuant to procedures provided by its own law. The requested State shall grant the request expeditiously unless its essential interests would be prejudiced thereby.

3. The State of transit shall ensure that legal provisions exist that would enable detaining the person in custody during transit.

4. In the event of an unscheduled landing, the Party to be requested to permit transit may, at the request of the escorting officer, hold the person in custody for 48 hours, pending receipt of the transit request to be made in accordance with paragraph 1 of the present article.

Article 16 Concurrent requests

If a Party receives requests for extradition for the same person from both the other Party and a third State it shall, at its discretion, determine to which of those States the person is to be extradited.

Article 17 Costs

1. The requested State shall meet the cost of any proceedings in its jurisdiction arising out of a request for extradition.

2. The requested State shall also bear the costs incurred in its territory in connection with the seizure and handing over of property, or the arrest and detention of the person whose extradition is sought.

3. The requesting State shall bear the costs incurred in conveying the person from the territory of the requested State, including transit costs.

Article 18 Final provisions

1. The present Treaty is subject to ratification, acceptance or approval. The instruments of ratification, acceptance or approval shall be exchanged as soon as possible.

2. The present Treaty shall enter into force on the thirtieth day after the day on which the instruments of ratification, acceptance or approval are exchanged.

3. The present Treaty shall apply to requests made after its entry into force, even if the relevant acts or omissions occurred prior to that date.

4. Either Contracting Party may denounce the present Treaty by giving notice in writing to the other Party. Such denunciation shall take effect six months following the date on which such notice is received by the other Party.

DOCUMENT 67

UK/US Extradition Treaty 2003
Cm 5821

The treaty was signed on 31 March 2003. It is to enter into force upon the exchange of the instruments of ratification (Article 23). At the present time, while the UK has ratified the treaty and implemented it into domestic law in the Extradition Act 2003, the USA has yet to ratify the treaty.

The treaty replaces an earlier extradition treaty between the UK and the USA of 1972 (UKTS No 16/1972). It defines an extraditable crime as one which is punishable under the laws of both States by imprisonment for one year or more (Article 2). It allows for the refusal of extradition in respect of a political offence (Article 4(1)). However, the Treaty includes a list of offences which 'shall not be considered political offences' (Article 4(2)). The treaty also excludes extradition for military offences which are not offences under the ordinary criminal law (Article 4(4)). Article 7 of the treaty governs the death penalty and is controversial inasmuch as it provides that the executive authorities of the requested State may refuse extradition as opposed to making refusal a requirement.

The most controversial aspect of the treaty relates to Article 8 on 'Extradition Procedures and Required Documents'. Under the 1972 Treaty, both States had been required to make out a prima facie case against the accused prior to extradition. Under the 2003 Treaty there is no specific requirement for the USA to make out a prima facie case. Both States are required only to provide a statement of the facts of the offence (Article 8(2)(b)). However, according to the terms of the Treaty, the UK is required also to provide 'such information as would provide a reasonable basis to believe that the person sought committed the offence for which extradition is requested' (Article 8(3)(c)).

Many of the provisions of the treaty exceed the comparable provisions of the Agreement on Extradition between the European Union and the United States of America of 2003 (**Document 68**). *The treaty has been strongly criticised by a number of human rights organisations.*

The Government of the United Kingdom of Great Britain and Northern Ireland and the Government of the United States of America,

Recalling the Extradition Treaty between the Government of the United States of America and the Government of the United Kingdom of Great Britain and Northern Ireland signed at London, June 8, 1972, as amended by the Supplementary Treaty between the two States, signed at Washington, June 25, 1985; and

Desiring to provide for more effective cooperation between the two States in the suppression of crime, and, for that purpose, to conclude a new treaty for the extradition of offenders;

Have agreed as follows:

Article 1 Obligation to Extradite
The Parties agree to extradite to each other, pursuant to the provisions of this Treaty, persons sought by the authorities in the Requesting State for trial or punishment for extraditable offenses.

Article 2 Extraditable Offenses
1. An offense shall be an extraditable offense if the conduct on which the offense is based is punishable under the laws in both States by deprivation of liberty for a period of one year or more or by a more severe penalty.

2. An offense shall also be an extraditable offense if it consists of an attempt or a conspiracy to commit, participation in the commission of, aiding or abetting, counseling or procuring the commission of, or being an accessory before or after the fact to any offense described in paragraph 1 of this Article.

3. For the purposes of this Article, an offense shall be an extraditable offense:

    (a) whether or not the laws in the Requesting and Requested States place the offense within the same category of offenses or describe the offense by the same terminology; or

    (b) whether or not the offense is one for which United States federal law requires the showing of such matters as interstate transportation, or use of the mails or of other facilities affecting interstate or foreign commerce, such matters being jurisdictional only.

4. If the offense has been committed outside the territory of the Requesting State, extradition shall be granted in accordance with the provisions of the Treaty if the laws in the Requested State provide for the punishment of such conduct committed outside its territory in similar circumstances. If the laws in the Requested State do not provide for the punishment of such conduct committed outside of its territory in similar circumstances, the executive authority of the Requested State, in its discretion, may grant extradition provided that all other requirements of this Treaty are met.

5. If extradition has been granted for an extraditable offense, it may also be granted for any other offense specified in the request if the latter offense is punishable by less than one year's deprivation of liberty, provided that all other requirements for extradition are met.

Article 3 Nationality

Extradition shall not be refused based on the nationality of the person sought.

Article 4 Political and Military Offenses

1. Extradition shall not be granted if the offense for which extradition is requested is a political offense.

2. For the purposes of this Treaty, the following offenses shall not be considered political offenses:

    (a) an offense for which both Parties have the obligation pursuant to a multilateral international agreement to extradite the person sought or to submit the case to their competent authorities for decision as to prosecution;

    (b) a murder or other violent crime against the person of a Head of State of one of the Parties, or of a member of the Head of State's family;

    (c) murder, manslaughter, malicious wounding, or inflicting grievous bodily harm;

    (d) an offense involving kidnapping, abduction, or any form of unlawful detention, including the taking of a hostage;

    (e) placing or using, or threatening the placement or use of, an explosive, incendiary, or destructive device or firearm capable of endangering life, of causing grievous bodily harm, or of causing substantial property damage;

    (f) possession of an explosive, incendiary, or destructive device capable of endangering life, of causing grievous bodily harm, or of causing substantial property damage;

    (g) an attempt or a conspiracy to commit, participation in the commission of, aiding or abetting, counseling or procuring the commission of, or being an accessory before or after the fact to any of the foregoing offenses.

3. Notwithstanding the terms of paragraph 2 of this Article, extradition shall not be granted if the competent authority of the Requested State determines that the request was politically motivated. In the United States, the executive branch is the competent authority for the purposes of this Article.

4. The competent authority of the Requested State may refuse extradition for offenses under military law that are not offenses under ordinary criminal law. In the United States, the executive branch is the competent authority for the purposes of this Article.

Article 5 Prior Prosecution

1. Extradition shall not be granted when the person sought has been convicted or acquitted in the Requested State for the offense for which extradition is requested.

2. The Requested State may refuse extradition when the person sought has been convicted or acquitted in a third state in respect of the conduct for which extradition is requested.

3. Extradition shall not be precluded by the fact that the competent authorities of the Requested State:

   (a) have decided not to prosecute the person sought for the acts for which extradition is requested;

   (b) have decided to discontinue any criminal proceedings which have been instituted against the person sought for those acts; or

   (c) are still investigating the person sought for the same acts for which extradition is sought.

Article 6 Statute of Limitations

The decision by the Requested State whether to grant the request for extradition shall be made without regard to any statute of limitations in either State.

Article 7 Capital Punishment

When the offense for which extradition is sought is punishable by death under the laws in the Requesting State and is not punishable by death under the laws in the Requested State, the executive authority in the Requested State may refuse extradition unless the Requesting State provides an assurance that the death penalty will not be imposed or, if imposed, will not be carried out.

Article 8 Extradition Procedures and Required Documents

1. All requests for extradition shall be submitted through the diplomatic channel.

2. All requests for extradition shall be supported by:

   (a) as accurate a description as possible of the person sought, together with any other information that would help to establish identity and probable location;

   (b) a statement of the facts of the offense(s);

   (c) the relevant text of the law(s) describing the essential elements of the offense for which extradition is requested;

   (d) the relevant text of the law(s) prescribing punishment for the offense for which extradition is requested; and

   (e) documents, statements, or other types of information specified in paragraphs 3 or 4 of this Article, as applicable.

3. In addition to the requirements in paragraph 2 of this Article, a request for extradition of a person who is sought for prosecution shall be supported by:

   (a) a copy of the warrant or order of arrest issued by a judge or other competent authority;

   (b) a copy of the charging document, if any; and

   (c) for requests to the United States, such information as would provide a reasonable basis to believe that the person sought committed the offense for which extradition is requested.

4. In addition to the requirements in paragraph 2 of this Article, a request for extradition relating to a person who has been convicted of the offense for which extradition is sought shall be supported by:

    (a) information that the person sought is the person to whom the finding of guilt refers;

    (b) a copy of the judgment or memorandum of conviction or, if a copy is not available, a statement by a judicial authority that the person has been convicted;

    (c) a copy of the sentence imposed, if the person sought has been sentenced, and a statement establishing to what extent the sentence has been carried out; and

    (d) in the case of a person who has been convicted in absentia, information regarding the circumstances under which the person was voluntarily absent from the proceedings.

Article 9 Authentication of Documents

The documents that support an extradition request shall be deemed to be authentic and shall be received in evidence in extradition proceedings without further proof if:

(a) regarding a request from the United States:

    (i) they are authenticated by the oath of a witness, or

    (ii) they purport to be signed by a judge, magistrate, or officer of the United States and they purport to be certified by being sealed with the official seal of the Secretary of State of the United States;

(b) regarding a request from the United Kingdom, they are certified by the principal diplomatic or principal consular officer of the United States resident in the United Kingdom, as provided by the extradition laws of the United States;

(c) regarding a request from a territory of the United Kingdom, they are certified either by the principal diplomatic or principal consular officer of the United States responsible for that territory; or

(d) regarding a request from either Party, they are certified or authenticated in any other manner acceptable under the law in the Requested State.

Article 10 Additional Information

If the Requested State requires additional information to enable a decision to be taken on the request for extradition, the Requesting State shall respond to the request within such time as the Requested State requires.

Article 11 Translation

All documents submitted under this Treaty by the Requesting State shall be in English or accompanied by a translation into English.

Article 12 Provisional Arrest

1. In an urgent situation, the Requesting State may request the provisional arrest of the person sought pending presentation of the request for extradition. A request for provisional arrest may be transmitted through the diplomatic channel or directly between the United States Department of Justice and such competent authority as the United Kingdom may designate for the purposes of this Article

2. The application for provisional arrest shall contain:

    (a) a description of the person sought;

    (b) the location of the person sought, if known;

    (c) a brief statement of the facts of the case including, if possible, the date and location of the offense(s);

(d) a description of the law(s) violated;

(e) a statement of the existence of a warrant or order of arrest or a finding of guilt or judgment of conviction against the person sought; and

(f) a statement that the supporting documents for the person sought will follow within the time specified in this Treaty.

3. The Requesting State shall be notified without delay of the disposition of its request for provisional arrest and the reasons for any inability to proceed with the request.

4. A person who is provisionally arrested may be discharged from custody upon the expiration of sixty (60) days from the date of provisional arrest pursuant to this Treaty if the executive authority of the Requested State has not received the formal request for extradition and the documents supporting the extradition request as required in Article 8. For this purpose, receipt of the formal request for extradition and supporting documents by the Embassy of the Requested State in the Requesting State shall constitute receipt by the executive authority of the Requested State.

5. The fact that the person sought has been discharged from custody pursuant to paragraph 4 of this Article shall not prejudice the subsequent re-arrest and extradition of that person if the extradition request and supporting documents are delivered at a later date.

Article 13 Decision and Surrender

1. The Requested State shall promptly notify the Requesting State of its decision on the request for extradition. Such notification should be transmitted directly to the competent authority designated by the Requesting State to receive such notification and through the diplomatic channel.

2. If the request is denied in whole or in part, the Requested State shall provide reasons for the denial. The Requested State shall provide copies of pertinent judicial decisions upon request.

3. If the request for extradition is granted, the authorities of the Requesting and Requested States shall agree on the time and place for the surrender of the person sought.

4. If the person sought is not removed from the territory of the Requested State within the time period prescribed by the law of that State, that person may be discharged from custody, and the Requested State, in its discretion, may subsequently refuse extradition for the same offense(s).

Article 14 Temporary and Deferred Surrender

1. If the extradition request is granted for a person who is being proceeded against or is serving a sentence in the Requested State, the Requested State may temporarily surrender the person sought to the Requesting State for the purpose of prosecution. If the Requested State requests, the Requesting State shall keep the person so surrendered in custody and shall return that person to the Requested State after the conclusion of the proceedings against that person, in accordance with conditions to be determined by mutual agreement of the States.

2. The Requested State may postpone the extradition proceedings against a person who is being prosecuted or who is serving a sentence in that State. The postponement may continue until the prosecution of the person sought has been concluded or until such person has served any sentence imposed.

Article 15 Requests for Extradition Made by Several States

If the Requested State receives requests from two or more States for the extradition of the same person, either for the same offense or for different offenses, the executive authority of the

Requested State shall determine to which State, if any, it will surrender the person. In making its decision, the Requested State shall consider all relevant factors, including but not limited to:

(a) whether the requests were made pursuant to a treaty;

(b) the place where each offense was committed;

(c) the gravity of the offenses;

(d) the possibility of any subsequent extradition between the respective Requesting States; and

(e) the chronological order in which the requests were received from the respective Requesting States.

Article 16 Seizure and Surrender of Property

1. To the extent permitted under its law, the Requested State may seize and surrender to the Requesting State all items in whatever form, and assets, including proceeds, that are connected with the offense in respect of which extradition is granted. The items and assets mentioned in this Article may be surrendered even when the extradition cannot be effected due to the death, disappearance, or escape of the person sought.

2. The Requested State may condition the surrender of the items upon satisfactory assurances from the Requesting State that the property will be returned to the Requested State as soon as practicable. The Requested State may also defer the surrender of such items if they are needed as evidence in the Requested State.

Article 17 Waiver of Extradition

If the person sought waives extradition and agrees to be surrendered to the Requesting State, the Requested State may surrender the person as expeditiously as possible without further proceedings.

Article 18 Rule of Specialty

1. A person extradited under this Treaty may not be detained, tried, or punished in the Requesting State except for:

(a) any offense for which extradition was granted, or a differently denominated offense based on the same facts as the offense on which extradition was granted, provided such offense is extraditable, or is a lesser included offense;

(b) any offense committed after the extradition of the person; or

(c) any offense for which the executive authority of the Requested State waives the rule of specialty and thereby consents to the person's detention, trial, or punishment. For the purpose of this subparagraph:

    (i) the executive authority of the Requested State may require the submission of the documentation called for in Article 8; and

    (ii) the person extradited may be detained by the Requesting State for 90 days, or for such longer period of time as the Requested State may authorize, while the request for consent is being processed.

2. A person extradited under this Treaty may not be the subject of onward extradition or surrender for any offense committed prior to extradition to the Requesting State unless the Requested State consents.

3. Paragraphs 1 and 2 of this Article shall not prevent the detention, trial, or punishment of an extradited person, or the extradition of the person to a third State, if the person:

(a) leaves the territory of the Requesting State after extradition and voluntarily returns to it; or

(b) does not leave the territory of the Requesting State within 20 days of the day on which that person is free to leave.

4. If the person sought waives extradition pursuant to Article 17, the specialty provisions in this Article shall not apply.

Article 19 Transit

1. Either State may authorize transportation through its territory of a person surrendered to the other State by a third State or from the other State to a third State. A request for transit shall contain a description of the person being transported and a brief statement of the facts of the case. A person in transit shall be detained in custody during the period of transit.

2. Authorization is not required when air transportation is used by one State and no landing is scheduled on the territory of the other State. If an unscheduled landing does occur, the State in which the unscheduled landing occurs may require a request for transit pursuant to paragraph 1 of this Article, and it may detain the person until the request for transit is received and the transit is effected, as long as the request is received within 96 hours of the unscheduled landing.

Article 20 Representation and Expenses

1. The Requested State shall advise, assist, and appear on behalf of, the Requesting State in any proceedings in the courts of the Requested State arising out of a request for extradition or make all necessary arrangements for the same.

2. The Requesting State shall pay all the expenses related to the translation of extradition documents and the transportation of the person surrendered. The Requested State shall pay all other expenses incurred in that State in connection with the extradition proceedings.

3. Neither State shall make any pecuniary claim against the other State arising out of the arrest, detention, examination, or surrender of persons under this Treaty.

Article 21 Consultation

The Parties may consult with each other in connection with the processing of individual cases and in furtherance of efficient implementation of this Treaty.

Article 22 Application

1. This Treaty shall apply to offenses committed before as well as after the date it enters into force.

2. This Treaty shall apply:

    (a) in relation to the United Kingdom: to Great Britain and Northern Ireland, the Channel Islands, the Isle of Man; and to any territory for whose international relations the United Kingdom is responsible and to which this agreement has been extended by agreement of the Parties; and

    (b) to the United States of America.

3. The application of this Treaty to any territory in respect of which extension has been made in accordance with paragraph 2 of this Article may be terminated by either State giving six months' written notice to the other through the diplomatic channel.

4. A request by the United States for the extradition of an offender who is found in any of the territories to which this Treaty applies in accordance with paragraph 2 of this Article may be made to the Governor or other competent authority of that territory, who may take the decision himself or refer the matter to the Government of the United Kingdom for its decision. A request on the part of any of the territories to which this Treaty applies in accordance with paragraph 2 of this Article for the extradition of an offender who is found in the United States of America may be made to the Government of the United States by the Governor or other competent authority of that territory.

DOCUMENT 68

Agreement on Extradition between the European Union and the United States of America 2003
Official Journal L181/27 19/07/2003; 43 ILM 749 (2004)

The agreement was concluded at Washington, DC, on 25 June 2003, the Member States of the European Union having previously agreed to the signing of the agreement by Council Decision of 6 June 2003 (2003/516/EC). The agreement, together with the Agreement on Mutual Legal Assistance between the European Union and the United States of America 2003 **(Document 74)**, *is intended to provide additional tools to both the EU and the USA to combat terrorism, organised crime and other serious forms of criminality. Both agreements have been severely criticised by human rights organisations as weakening traditional protections for the individual.*

The agreement is intended to enhance existing relationships between Member States of the EU and the USA (Article 1). The agreement is to be applied by both the EU and the USA 'in relation to bilateral extradition treaties between the Member States and the USA, in force at the time of the entry into force of [the] Agreement'. Certain of the provisions of the agreement are intended to replace provisions in existing bilateral treaties, others are to be applied in the absence of existing bilateral treaty provisions and yet others are to be applied in addition to bilateral treaty provisions (Article 3). Article 3 also requires that the EU ensures that new Member States having extradition treaties with the USA comply with the provisions of the agreement.

The agreement defines an extraditable crime as one punishable by a maximum period of imprisonment of one year or more (Article 4). It includes provisions relating to transmission and authentication of documents (Article 5), for the possibility of provisional arrest (Articles 6–7) and for temporary surrender (Article 9). The agreement also provides for a simplified extradition procedure where the person being sought consents. The agreement contains a specific provision on the death penalty which allows for extradition where the punishment is the death penalty on condition that the penalty is not carried out (Article 13). The agreement is to be reviewed at least every five years (Article 21).

The European Union and the United States of America,

Desiring further to facilitate cooperation between the European Union Member States and the United States of America,

Desiring to combat crime in a more effective way as a means of protecting their respective democratic societies and common values,

Having due regard for rights of individuals and the rule of law,

Mindful of the guarantees under their respective legal systems which provide for the right to a fair trial to an extradited persoxn, including the right to adjudication by an impartial tribunal established pursuant to law,

Desiring to conclude an Agreement relating to the extradition of offenders,

Have agreed as follows:

Article 1 Object and Purpose

The Contracting Parties undertake, in accordance with the provisions of this Agreement, to provide for enhancements to cooperation in the context of applicable extradition relations between the Member States and the United States of America governing extradition of offenders.

Article 2 Definitions

1. "Contracting Parties" shall mean the European Union and the United States of America.

2. "Member State" shall mean a Member State of the European Union.

3. "Ministry of Justice" shall, for the United States of America, mean the United States Department of Justice; and for a Member State, its Ministry of Justice, except that with respect to a Member State in which functions described in Articles 3, 5, 6, 8 or 12 are carried out by its Prosecutor General, that body may be designated to carry out such function in lieu of the Ministry of Justice in accordance with Article 19, unless the United States and the Member State concerned agree to designate another body.

Article 3 Scope of application of this Agreement in relation to bilateral extradition treaties with Member States

1. The European Union, pursuant to the Treaty on European Union, and the United States of America shall ensure that the provisions of this Agreement are applied in relation to bilateral extradition treaties between the Member States and the United States of America, in force at the time of the entry into force of this Agreement, under the following terms:

   (a) Article 4 shall be applied in place of bilateral treaty provisions that authorise extradition exclusively with respect to a list of specified criminal offences;

   (b) Article 5 shall be applied in place of bilateral treaty provisions governing transmission, certification, authentication or legalisation of an extradition request and supporting documents transmitted by the requesting State;

   (c) Article 6 shall be applied in the absence of bilateral treaty provisions authorising direct transmission of provisional arrest requests between the United States Department of Justice and the Ministry of Justice of the Member State concerned;

   (d) Article 7 shall be applied in addition to bilateral treaty provisions governing transmission of extradition requests;

   (e) Article 8 shall be applied in the absence of bilateral treaty provisions governing the submission of supplementary information; where bilateral treaty provisions do not specify the channel to be used, paragraph 2 of that Article shall also be applied;

   (f) Article 9 shall be applied in the absence of bilateral treaty provisions authorising temporary surrender of persons being proceeded against or serving a sentence in the requested State;

   (g) Article 10 shall be applied, except as otherwise specified therein, in place of, or in the absence of, bilateral treaty provisions pertaining to decision on several requests for extradition of the same person;

   (h) Article 11 shall be applied in the absence of bilateral treaty provisions authorising waiver of extradition or simplified extradition procedures;

   (i) Article 12 shall be applied in the absence of bilateral treaty provisions governing transit; where bilateral treaty provisions do not specify the procedure governing unscheduled landing of aircraft, paragraph 3 of that Article shall also be applied;

   (j) Article 13 may be applied by the requested State in place of, or in the absence of, bilateral treaty provisions governing capital punishment;

   (k) Article 14 shall be applied in the absence of bilateral treaty provisions governing treatment of sensitive information in a request.

2. (a) The European Union, pursuant to the Treaty on European Union, shall ensure that each Member State acknowledges, in a written instrument between such Member State and the

United States of America, the application, in the manner set forth in this Article, of its bilateral extradition treaty in force with the United States of America.

(b) The European Union, pursuant to the Treaty on European Union, shall ensure that new Member States acceding to the European Union after the entry into force of this Agreement and having bilateral extradition treaties with the United States of America, take the measures referred to in subparagraph (a).

(c) The Contracting Parties shall endeavour to complete the process described in subparagraph (b) prior to the scheduled accession of a new Member State, or as soon as possible thereafter. The European Union shall notify the United States of America of the date of accession of new Member States.

3. If the process described in paragraph 2(b) is not completed by the date of accession, the provisions of this Agreement shall apply in the relations between that new Member State and the United States of America as from the date on which they have notified each other and the European Union of the completion of their internal procedures for that purpose.

Article 4 Extraditable offences

1. An offence shall be an extraditable offence if it is punishable under the laws of the requesting and requested States by deprivation of liberty for a maximum period of more than one year or by a more severe penalty. An offence shall also be an extraditable offence if it consists of an attempt or conspiracy to commit, or participation in the commission of, an extraditable offence. Where the request is for enforcement of the sentence of a person convicted of an extraditable offence, the deprivation of liberty remaining to be served must be at least four months.

2. If extradition is granted for an extraditable offence, it shall also be granted for any other offence specified in the request if the latter offence is punishable by one year's deprivation of liberty or less, provided that all other requirements for extradition are met.

3. For the purposes of this Article, an offence shall be considered an extraditable offence:

(a) regardless of whether the laws in the requesting and requested States place the offence within the same category of offences or describe the offence by the same terminology;

(b) regardless of whether the offence is one for which United States federal law requires the showing of such matters as interstate transportation, or use of the mails or of other facilities affecting interstate or foreign commerce, such matters being merely for the purpose of establishing jurisdiction in a United States federal court; and

(c) in criminal cases relating to taxes, customs duties, currency control and the import or export of commodities, regardless of whether the laws of the requesting and requested States provide for the same kinds of taxes, customs duties, or controls on currency or on the import or export of the same kinds of commodities.

4. If the offence has been committed outside the territory of the requesting State, extradition shall be granted, subject to the other applicable requirements for extradition, if the laws of the requested State provide for the punishment of an offence committed outside its territory in similar circumstances. If the laws of the requested State do not provide for the punishment of an offence committed outside its territory in similar circumstances, the executive authority of the requested State, at its discretion, may grant extradition provided that all other applicable requirements for extradition are met.

Article 5 Transmission and authentication of documents

1. Requests for extradition and supporting documents shall be transmitted through the diplomatic channel, which shall include transmission as provided for in Article 7.

2. Documents that bear the certificate or seal of the Ministry of Justice, or Ministry or Department responsible for foreign affairs, of the requesting State shall be admissible in

extradition proceedings in the requested State without further certification, authentication, or other legalisation.

Article 6 Transmission of requests for provisional arrest

Requests for provisional arrest may be made directly between the Ministries of Justice of the requesting and requested States, as an alternative to the diplomatic channel. The facilities of the International Criminal Police Organisation (Interpol) may also be used to transmit such a request.

Article 7 Transmission of documents following provisional arrest

1. If the person whose extradition is sought is held under provisional arrest by the requested State, the requesting State may satisfy its obligation to transmit its request for extradition and supporting documents through the diplomatic channel pursuant to Article 5(1), by submitting the request and documents to the Embassy of the requested State located in the requesting State. In that case, the date of receipt of such request by the Embassy shall be considered to be the date of receipt by the requested State for purposes of applying the time limit that must be met under the applicable extradition treaty to enable the person's continued detention.

2. Where a Member State on the date of signature of this Agreement, due to the established jurisprudence of its domestic legal system applicable at such date, cannot apply the measures referred to in paragraph 1, this Article shall not apply to it, until such time as that Member State and the United States of America, by exchange of diplomatic note, agree otherwise.

Article 8 Supplemental information

1. The requested State may require the requesting State to furnish additional information within such reasonable length of time as it specifies, if it considers that the information furnished in support of the request for extradition is not sufficient to fulfil the requirements of the applicable extradition treaty.

2. Such supplementary information may be requested and furnished directly between the Ministries of Justice of the States concerned.

Article 9 Temporary surrender

1. If a request for extradition is granted in the case of a person who is being proceeded against or is serving a sentence in the requested State, the requested State may temporarily surrender the person sought to the requesting State for the purpose of prosecution.

2. The person so surrendered shall be kept in custody in the requesting State and shall be returned to the requested State at the conclusion of the proceedings against that person, in accordance with the conditions to be determined by mutual agreement of the requesting and requested States. The time spent in custody in the territory of the requesting State pending prosecution in that State may be deducted from the time remaining to be served in the requested State.

Article 10 Requests for extradition or surrender made by several States

1. If the requested State receives requests from the requesting State and from any other State or States for the extradition of the same person, either for the same offence or for different offences, the executive authority of the requested State shall determine to which State, if any, it will surrender the person.

2. If a requested Member State receives an extradition request from the United States of America and a request for surrender pursuant to the European arrest warrant for the same person, either for the same offence or for different offences, the competent authority of the requested

Member State shall determine to which State, if any, it will surrender the person. For this purpose, the competent authority shall be the requested Member State's executive authority if, under the bilateral extradition treaty in force between the United States and the Member State, decisions on competing requests are made by that authority; if not so provided in the bilateral extradition treaty, the competent authority shall be designated by the Member State concerned pursuant to Article 19.

3. In making its decision under paragraphs 1 and 2, the requested State shall consider all of the relevant factors, including, but not limited to, factors already set forth in the applicable extradition treaty, and, where not already so set forth, the following:

    (a) whether the requests were made pursuant to a treaty;

    (b) the places where each of the offences was committed;

    (c) the respective interests of the requesting States;

    (d) the seriousness of the offences;

    (e) the nationality of the victim;

    (f) the possibility of any subsequent extradition between the requesting States; and

    (g) the chronological order in which the requests were received from the requesting States.

Article 11 Simplified extradition procedures

If the person sought consents to be surrendered to the requesting State, the requested State may, in accordance with the principles and procedures provided for under its legal system, surrender the person as expeditiously as possible without further proceedings. The consent of the person sought may include agreement to waiver of protection of the rule of specialty.

Article 12 Transit

1. A Member State may authorise transportation through its territory of a person surrendered to the United States of America by a third State, or by the United States of America to a third State. The United States of America may authorise transportation through its territory of a person surrendered to a Member State by a third State, or by a Member State to a third State.

2. A request for transit shall be made through the diplomatic channel or directly between the United States Department of Justice and the Ministry of Justice of the Member State concerned. The facilities of Interpol may also be used to transmit such a request. The request shall contain a description of the person being transported and a brief statement of the facts of the case. A person in transit shall be detained in custody during the period of transit.

3. Authorisation is not required when air transportation is used and no landing is scheduled on the territory of the transit State. If an unscheduled landing does occur, the State in which the unscheduled landing occurs may require a request or transit pursuant to paragraph 2. All measures necessary to prevent the person from absconding shall be taken until transit is effected, as long as the request for transit is received within 96 hours of the unscheduled landing.

Article 13 Capital punishment

Where the offence for which extradition is sought is punishable by death under the laws in the requesting State and not punishable by death under the laws in the requested State, the requested State may grant extradition on the condition that the death penalty shall not be imposed on the person sought, or if for procedural reasons such condition cannot be complied with by the requesting State, on condition that the death penalty if imposed shall not be carried out. If the requesting State accepts extradition subject to conditions pursuant to this Article, it shall comply with the conditions. If the requesting State does not accept the conditions, the request for extradition may be denied.

Article 14 Sensitive information in a request

Where the requesting State contemplates the submission of particularly sensitive information in support of its request for extradition, it may consult the requested State to determine the extent to which the information can be protected by the requested State. If the requested State cannot protect the information in the manner sought by the requesting State, the requesting State shall determine whether the information shall nonetheless be submitted.

Article 15 Consultations

The Contracting Parties shall, as appropriate, consult to enable the most effective use to be made of this Agreement, including to facilitate the resolution of any dispute regarding the interpretation or application of this Agreement.

Article 16 Temporal application

1. This Agreement shall apply to offences committed before as well as after it enters into force.

2. This Agreement shall apply to requests for extradition made after its entry into force. Nevertheless, Articles 4 and 9 shall apply to requests pending in a requested State at the time this Agreement enters into force.

Article 17 Non-derogation

1. This Agreement is without prejudice to the invocation by the requested State of grounds for refusal relating to a matter not governed by this Agreement that is available pursuant to a bilateral extradition treaty in force between a Member State and the United States of America.

2. Where the constitutional principles of, or final judicial decisions binding upon, the requested State may pose an impediment to fulfilment of its obligation to extradite, and resolution of the matter is not provided for in this Agreement or the applicable bilateral treaty, consultations shall take place between the requested and requesting States.

Article 18 Future bilateral extradition treaties with Member States

This Agreement shall not preclude the conclusion, after its entry into force, of bilateral Agreements between a Member State and the United States of America consistent with this Agreement.

Article 19 Designation and notification

The European Union shall notify the United States of America of any designation pursuant to Article 2(3) and Article 10(2), prior to the exchange of written instruments described in Article 3(2) between the Member States and the United States of America.

Article 20 Territorial application

1. This Agreement shall apply:

   (a) to the United States of America;

   (b) in relation to the European Union to:

   – Member States,

   – territories for whose external relations a Member State has responsibility, or countries that are not Member States for whom a Member State has other duties with respect to external relations, where agreed upon by exchange of diplomatic note between the Contracting Parties, duly confirmed by the relevant Member State.

2. The application of this Agreement to any territory or country in respect of which extension has been made in accordance with subparagraph (b) of paragraph 1 may be terminated by either Contracting Party giving six months' written notice to the other Contracting Party through the diplomatic channel, where duly confirmed between the relevant Member State and the United States of America.

Article 21 Review

The Contracting Parties agree to carry out a common review of this Agreement as necessary, and in any event no later than five years after its entry into force. The review shall address in particular the practical implementation of the Agreement and may also include issues such as the consequences of further development of the European Union relating to the subject matter of this Agreement, including Article 10.

Article 62 Review

MUTUAL ASSISTANCE

DOCUMENT 69

European Convention on Mutual Assistance in Criminal Matters 1959
ETS No 30

The Convention was concluded under the auspices of the Council of Europe; it was opened for signature in Strasbourg, Austria, on 20 April 1959 and entered into force on 9 April 1960.

There are 43 parties, including all of the members of the Council of Europe except Monaco. Andorra, Bosnia and Herzegovina and San Marino have each signed the Convention, but have not yet ratified it. One non-Member State of the Council of Europe, Israel, has ratified the treaty. The Convention has been supplemented by an Additional Protocol of 1978 **(Document 70)** *and a Second Additional Protocol of 2001* **(Document 71)**.

The Convention is intended to allow Contracting Parties to provide to one another the greatest degree of mutual assistance in criminal matters (Article 1). Such assistance is excluded in relation to military offences (Article 1(2)) and in relation to any matter which the requested Party considers involves a political offence or is contrary to its essential interests (Article 2). Assistance is envisaged over the execution of letters rogatory in relation to procuring evidence or transmitting articles to be produced in evidence, records or documents (Articles 3–6), and in relation to the service of writs, and records of judicial verdicts including the appearance of witnesses, experts and prosecuted persons (Articles 7–12). The procedure for such assistance is governed by Articles 14–20.

The governments signatory hereto, being members of the Council of Europe,

Considering that the aim of the Council of Europe is to achieve greater unity among its members;

Believing that the adoption of common rules in the field of mutual assistance in criminal matters will contribute to the attainment of this aim;

Considering that such mutual assistance is related to the question of extradition, which has already formed the subject of a Convention signed on 13th December 1957,

Have agreed as follows:

Chapter I General provisions

Article I

1. The Contracting Parties undertake to afford each other, in accordance with the provisions of this Convention, the widest measure of mutual assistance in proceedings in respect of offences the punishment of which, at the time of the request for assistance, falls within the jurisdiction of the judicial authorities of the requesting Party.

2. This Convention does not apply to arrests, the enforcement of verdicts or offences under military law which are not offences under ordinary criminal law.

Article 2

Assistance may be refused:

(a) if the request concerns an offence which the requested Party considers a political offence, an offence connected with a political offence, or a fiscal offence;

(b) if the requested Party considers that execution of the request is likely to prejudice the sovereignty, security, *ordre public* or other essential interests of its country.

Chapter II Letters rogatory

Article 3

1. The requested Party shall execute in the manner provided for by its law any letters rogatory relating to a criminal matter and addressed to it by the judicial authorities of the requesting Party for the purpose of procuring evidence or transmitting articles to be produced in evidence, records or documents.

2. If the requesting Party desires witnesses or experts to give evidence on oath, it shall expressly so request, and the requested Party shall comply with the request if the law of its country does not prohibit it.

3. The requested Party may transmit certified copies or certified photostat copies of records or documents requested, unless the requesting Party expressly requests the transmission of originals, in which case the requested Party shall make every effort to comply with the request.

Article 4

On the express request of the requesting Party the requested Party shall state the date and place of execution of the letters rogatory. Officials and interested persons may be present if the requested Party consents.

Article 5

1. Any Contracting Party may, by a declaration addressed to the Secretary General of the Council of Europe, when signing this Convention or depositing its instrument of ratification or accession, reserve the right to make the execution of letters rogatory for search or seizure of property dependent on one or more of the following conditions:

   (a) that the offence motivating the letters rogatory is punishable under both the law of the requesting Party and the law of the requested Party;

   (b) that the offence motivating the letters rogatory is an extraditable offence in the requested country;

   (c) that execution of the letters rogatory is consistent with the law of the requested Party.

   Where a Contracting Party makes a declaration in accordance with paragraph I of this article, any other Party may apply reciprocity.

Article 6

1. The requested Party may delay the handing over of any property, records or documents requested, if it requires the said property, records or documents in connection with pending criminal proceedings.

2. Any property, as well as original records or documents, handed over in execution of letters rogatory shall be returned by the requesting Party to the requested Party as soon as possible unless the latter Party waives the return thereof.

Chapter III Service of writs and records of judicial verdicts – Appearance of witnesses, experts and prosecuted persons

Article 7

1. The requested Party shall effect service of writs and records of judicial verdicts which are transmitted to it for this purpose by the requesting Party. Service may be effected by simple transmission of the writ or record to the person to be served. If the requesting Party expressly so requests, service shall be effected by the requested Party in the manner provided for the service of analogous documents under its own law or in a special manner consistent with such law.

2. Proof of service shall be given by means of a receipt dated and signed by the person served or by means of a declaration made by the requested Party that service has been effected and stating the form and date of such service. One or other of these documents shall be sent immediately to the requesting Party. The requested Party shall, if the requesting Party so requests, state whether service has been effected in accordance with the law of the requested Party. If service cannot be effected, the reasons shall be communicated immediately by the requested Party to the requesting Party.

3. Any Contracting Party may, by a declaration addressed to the Secretary General of the Council of Europe, when signing this Convention or depositing its instrument of ratification or accession, request that service of a summons on an accused person who is in its territory be transmitted to its authorities by a certain time before the date set for appearance. This time shall be specified in the aforesaid declaration and shall not exceed 50 days. This time shall be taken into account when the date of appearance is being fixed and when the summons is being transmitted.

Article 8

A witness or expert who has failed to answer a summons to appear, service of which has been requested, shall not, even if the summons contains a notice of penalty, be subjected to any punishment or measure of restraint, unless subsequently he voluntarily enters the territory of the requesting Party and is there again duly summoned.

Article 9

The allowances, including subsistence, to be paid and the travelling expenses to be refunded to a witness or expert by the requesting Party shall be calculated as from his place of residence and shall be at rates at least equal to those provided for in the scales and rules in force in the country where the hearing is intended to take place.

Article 10

1. If the requesting Party considers the personal appearance of a witness or expert before its judicial authorities especially necessary, it shall so mention in its request for service of the summons and the requested Party shall invite the witness or expert to appear. The requested Party shall inform the requesting Party of the reply of the witness or expert.

2. In the case provided for under paragraph 1 of this article the request or the summons shall indicate the approximate allowances payable and the travelling and subsistence expenses refundable.

3. If a specific request is made, the requested Party may grant the witness or expert an advance. The amount of the advance shall be endorsed on the summons and shall be refunded by the requesting Party.

Article 11

1. A person in custody whose personal appearance as a witness or for purposes of confrontation is applied for by the requesting Party shall be temporarily transferred to the territory where the hearing is intended to take place, provided that he shall be sent back within the period stipulated by the requested Party and subject to the provisions of Article 12 in so far as these are applicable.

   Transfer may be refused:

   (a) if the person in custody does not consent;

   (b) if his presence is necessary at criminal proceedings pending in the territory of the requested Party;

   (c) if transfer is liable to prolong his detention, or

   (d) if there are other overriding grounds for not transferring him to the territory of the requesting Party.

2. Subject to the provisions of Article 2, in a case coming within the immediately preceding paragraph, transit of the person in custody through the territory of a third State, Party to this Convention, shall be granted on application, accompanied by all necessary documents, addressed by the Ministry of Justice of the requesting Party to the Ministry of Justice of the Party through whose territory transit is requested. A Contracting Party may refuse to grant transit to its own nationals.

3. The transferred person shall remain in custody in the territory of the requesting Party and, where applicable, in the territory of the Party through which transit is requested, unless the Party from whom transfer is requested applies for his release.

Article 12

1. A witness or expert, whatever his nationality, appearing on a summons before the judicial authorities of the requesting Party shall not be prosecuted or detained or subjected to any other restriction of his personal liberty in the territory of that Party in respect of acts or convictions anterior to his departure from the territory of the requested Party.

2. A person, whatever his nationality, summoned before the judicial authorities of the requesting Party to answer for acts forming the subject of proceedings against him, shall not be prosecuted or detained or subjected to any other restriction of his personal liberty for acts or convictions anterior to his departure from the territory of the requested Party and not specified in the summons.

3. The immunity provided for in this article shall cease when the witness or expert or prosecuted person, having had for a period of fifteen consecutive days from the date when his presence is no longer required by the judicial authorities an opportunity of leaving, has nevertheless remained in the territory, or having left it, has returned.

Chapter IV Judicial records

Article 13

1. A requested Party shall communicate extracts from and information relating to judicial records, requested from it by the judicial authorities of a Contracting Party and needed in a criminal matter, to the same extent that these may be made available to its own judicial authorities in like case.

2. In any case other than that provided for in paragraph 1 of this article the request shall be complied with in accordance with the conditions provided for by the law, regulations or practice of the requested Party.

Chapter V Procedure

Article 14

1. Requests for mutual assistance shall indicate as follows:

   (a) the authority making the request,

   (b) the object of and the reason for the request,

   (c) where possible, the identity and the nationality of the person concerned, and

   (d) where necessary, the name and address of the person to be served.

2. Letters rogatory referred to in Articles 3, 4 and 5 shall, in addition, state the offence and contain a summary of the facts.

Article 15

1. Letters rogatory referred to in Articles 3, 4 and 5 as well as the applications referred to in Article 11 shall be addressed by the Ministry of Justice of the requesting Party to the Ministry of Justice of the requested Party and shall be returned through the same channels.

2. In case of urgency, letters rogatory may be addressed directly by the judicial authorities of the requesting Party to the judicial authorities of the requested Party. They shall be returned together with the relevant documents through the channels stipulated in paragraph 1 of this article.

3. Requests provided for in paragraph 1 of Article 13 may be addressed directly by the judicial authorities concerned to the appropriate authorities of the requested Party, and the replies may be returned directly by those authorities. Requests provided for in paragraph 2 of Article 13 shall be addressed by the Ministry of Justice of the requesting Party to the Ministry of Justice of the requested Party.

4. Requests for mutual assistance, other than those provided for in paragraphs 1 and 3 of this article and, in particular, requests for investigation preliminary to prosecution, may be communicated directly between the judicial authorities.

5. In cases where direct transmission is permitted under this Convention, it may take place through the International Criminal Police Organisation (Interpol).

6. A Contracting Party may, when signing this Convention or depositing its instrument of ratification or accession, by a declaration addressed to the Secretary General of the Council of Europe, give notice that some or all requests for assistance shall be sent to it through channels other than those provided for in this article, or require that, in a case provided for in paragraph 2 of this article, a copy of the letters rogatory shall be transmitted at the same time to its Ministry of Justice.

7. The provisions of this article are without prejudice to those of bilateral agreements or arrangements in force between Contracting Parties which provide for the direct transmission of requests for assistance between their respective authorities.

Article 16

1. Subject to paragraph 2 of this article, translations of requests and annexed documents shall not be required.

2. Each Contracting Party may, when signing or depositing its instrument of ratification or accession, by means of a declaration addressed to the Secretary General of the Council of Europe, reserve the right to stipulate that requests and annexed documents shall be addressed to it accompanied by a translation into its own language or into either of the official languages of the Council of Europe or into one of the latter languages, specified by it. The other Contracting Parties may apply reciprocity.

3. This article is without prejudice to the provisions concerning the translation of requests or annexed documents contained in the agreements or arrangements in force or to be made between two or more Contracting Parties.

Article 17

Evidence or documents transmitted pursuant to this Convention shall not require any form of authentication.

Article 18

Where the authority which receives a request for mutual assistance has no jurisdiction to comply therewith, it shall, *ex officio,* transmit the request to the competent authority of its country and shall so inform the requesting Party through the direct channels, if the request has been addressed through such channels.

Article 19

Reasons shall be given for any refusal of mutual assistance.

Article 20

Subject to the provisions of Article 10, paragraph 3, execution of requests for mutual assistance shall not entail refunding of expenses except those incurred by the attendance of experts in the territory of the requested Party or the transfer of a person in custody carried out under Article 11.

Chapter VI Laying of information in connection with proceedings

Article 21

1. Information laid by one Contracting Party with a view to proceedings in the courts of another Party shall be transmitted between the Ministries of Justice concerned unless a Contracting Party avails itself of the option provided for in paragraph 6 of Article 15.

2. The requested Party shall notify the requesting Party of any action taken on such information and shall forward a copy of the record of any verdict pronounced.

3. The provisions of Article 16 shall apply to information laid under paragraph 1 of this article.

Chapter VII Exchange of information from judicial records

Article 22

Each Contracting Party shall inform any other Party of all criminal convictions and subsequent measures in respect of nationals of the latter Party, entered in the judicial records. Ministries of Justice shall communicate such information to one another at least once a year. Where the person concerned is considered a national of two or more other Contracting Parties, the information shall be given to each of these Parties, unless the person is a national of the Party in the territory of which he was convicted.

Chapter VIII Final provisions

Article 23

1. Any Contracting Party may, when signing this Convention or when depositing its instrument of ratification or accession, make a reservation in respect of any provision or provisions of the Convention.

2. Any Contracting Party which has made a reservation shall withdraw it as soon as circumstances permit. Such withdrawal shall be made by notification to the Secretary General of the Council of Europe.

3. A Contracting Party which has made a reservation in respect of a provision of the Convention may not claim application of the said provision by another Party save in so far as it has itself accepted the provision.

Article 24

A Contracting Party may, when signing the Convention or depositing its instrument of ratification or accession, by a declaration addressed to the Secretary General of the Council of Europe, define what authorities it will, for the purpose of the Convention, deem judicial authorities.

Article 26

1. Subject to the provisions of Article 15, paragraph 7, and Article 16, paragraph 3, this Convention shall, in respect of those countries to which it applies, supersede the provisions of any treaties, conventions or bilateral agreements governing mutual assistance in criminal matters between any two Contracting Parties.

2. This Convention shall not affect obligations incurred under the terms of any other bilateral or multilateral international convention which contains or may contain clauses governing specific aspects of mutual assistance in a given field.

3. The Contracting Parties may conclude between themselves bilateral or multilateral agreements on mutual assistance in criminal matters only in order to supplement the provisions of this Convention or to facilitate the application of the principles contained therein.

4. Where, as between two or more Contracting Parties, mutual assistance in criminal matters is practised on the basis of uniform legislation or of a special system providing for the reciprocal application in their respective territories of measures of mutual assistance, these Parties shall, notwithstanding the provisions of this Convention, be free to regulate their mutual relations in this field exclusively in accordance with such legislation or system. Contracting Parties which, in accordance with this paragraph, exclude as between themselves the application of this Convention shall notify the Secretary General of the Council of Europe accordingly.

DOCUMENT 70

Additional Protocol to the European Convention on Mutual Assistance in Criminal Matters 1978
ETS No 99

The Additional Protocol to the European Convention on Mutual Assistance in Criminal Matters of 1959 **(Document 69)** *was concluded under the auspices of the Council of Europe; it was opened for signature in Strasbourg, Austria, on 17 March 1978 and entered into force on 12 April 1982.*

Thirty-nine of the 46 Member States of the Council of Europe are party to the Additional Protocol. Two States, Switzerland and Malta, have signed but not yet ratified the Additional Protocol. Israel, which is the only non-Member State of the Council of Europe which is party to the 1959 Convention, is not a party to the Additional Protocol.

The most important provision of the Additional Protocol excludes the operation of Article 2(1) of the 1959 Convention in relation political offences between the parties to the Additional Protocol (Article 1).

See also the Second Additional Protocol to the European Convention on Mutual Assistance in Criminal Matters of 2001 **(Document 71)**.

The member States of the Council of Europe, signatory to this Protocol,

Desirous of facilitating the application of the European Convention on Mutual Assistance in Criminal Matters opened for signature in Strasbourg on 20th April 1959 (hereinafter referred to as "the Convention") in the field of fiscal offences;

Considering it also desirable to supplement the Convention in certain other respects,

Have agreed as follows:

Chapter I

Article 1

The Contracting Parties shall not exercise the right provided for in Article 2.a of the Convention to refuse assistance solely on the ground that the request concerns an offence which the requested Party considers a fiscal offence.

Article 2

1. In the case where a Contracting Party has made the execution of letters rogatory for search or seizure of property dependent on the condition that the offence motivating the letters rogatory is punishable under both the law of the requesting Party and the law of the requested Party, this condition shall be fulfilled, as regards fiscal offences, if the offence is punishable under the law of the requesting Party and corresponds to an offence of the same nature under the law of the requested Party.

2. The request may not be refused on the ground that the law of the requested Party does not impose the same kind of tax or duty or does not contain a tax, duty, customs and exchange regulation of the same kind as the law of the requesting Party.

Chapter II

Article 3

The Convention shall also apply to:

(a) the service of documents concerning the enforcement of a sentence, the recovery of a fine or the payment of costs of proceedings;

(b) measures relating to the suspension of pronouncement of a sentence or of its enforcement, to conditional release, to deferment of the commencement of the enforcement of a sentence or to the interruption of such enforcement.

Chapter III

Article 4

Article 22 of the Convention shall be supplemented by the following text, the original Article 22 of the Convention becoming paragraph 1 and the below-mentioned provisions becoming paragraph 2:

"2. Furthermore, any Contracting Party which has supplied the above-mentioned information shall communicate to the Party concerned, on the latter's request in individual cases, a copy of the convictions and measures in question as well as any other information relevant thereto in order to enable it to consider whether they necessitate any measures at national level. This communication shall take place between the Ministries of Justice concerned."

Chapter IV

Article 9

The provisions of this Protocol are without prejudice to more extensive regulations in bilateral or multilateral agreements concluded between Contracting Parties in application of Article 26, paragraph 3, of the Convention.

Article 10

The European Committee on Crime Problems of the Council of Europe shall be kept informed regarding the application of this Protocol and shall do whatever is needful to facilitate a friendly settlement of any difficulty which may arise out of its execution.

DOCUMENT 71

Second Additional Protocol to the European Convention on Mutual Assistance in Criminal Matters 2001

ETS No 182

The Second Additional Protocol to the European Convention on Mutual Assistance in Criminal Matters 1959 (**Document 69**) *was concluded under the auspices of the Council of Europe; it was opened for signature on 8 November 2001 and entered into force on 1 February 2004.*

Only 10 of the 46 Member States of the Council of Europe are party to the Second Additional Protocol, which compares unfavourably with the 43 parties to the Convention itself and 39 parties to the Additional Protocol of 1978 (**Document 70**). *Nineteen other States, including the UK and France, have signed but not yet ratified the Second Additional Protocol.*

The Second Additional Protocol seeks to amend certain of the provisions of the original Convention. Further, it seeks to make use of technological advances including use of video technology (Article 9) and telephone conferencing (Article 10). This extensive instrument effects a major clarification and amplification of the extent and modalities of European mutual assistance. The Second Additional Protocol provides, inter alia, for temporary transfer of detained persons (Article 13), cross-border observation of suspects in respect of certain criminal offences (Article 17), covert investigations (Article 19) and the temporary creation of joint investigation teams (Article 20).

The member States of the Council of Europe, signatory to this Protocol,

Having regard to their undertakings under the Statute of the Council of Europe;

Desirous of further contributing to safeguard human rights, uphold the rule of law and support the democratic fabric of society;

Considering it desirable to that effect to strengthen their individual and collective ability to respond to crime;

Decided to improve on and supplement in certain aspects the European Convention on Mutual Assistance in Criminal Matters done at Strasbourg on 20 April 1959 (hereinafter referred to as "the Convention"), as well as the Additional Protocol thereto, done at Strasbourg on 17 March 1978;

Taking into consideration the Convention for the Protection of Human Rights and Fundamental Freedoms, done at Rome on 4 November 1950, as well as the Convention for the Protection of Individuals with regard to Automatic Processing of Personal Data, done at Strasbourg on 28 January 1981,

Have agreed as follows:

Chapter I

Article I Scope

Article 1 of the Convention shall be replaced by the following provisions:

"1. The Parties undertake promptly to afford each other, in accordance with the provisions of this Convention, the widest measure of mutual assistance in proceedings in respect of offences the punishment of which, at the time of the request for assistance, falls within the jurisdiction of the judicial authorities of the requesting Party.

2. This Convention does not apply to arrests, the enforcement of verdicts or offences under military law which are not offences under ordinary criminal law.

3. Mutual assistance may also be afforded in proceedings brought by the administrative authorities in respect of acts which are punishable under the national law of the requesting or the requested Party by virtue of being infringements of the rules of law, where the decision may give rise to proceedings before a court having jurisdiction in particular in criminal matters.

4. Mutual assistance shall not be refused solely on the grounds that it relates to acts for which a legal person may be held liable in the requesting Party."

Article 2 Presence of officials of the requesting Party

Article 4 of the Convention shall be supplemented by the following text, the original Article 4 of the Convention becoming paragraph 1 and the provisions below becoming paragraph 2:

"2. Requests for the presence of such officials or interested persons should not be refused where that presence is likely to render the execution of the request for assistance more responsive to the needs of the requesting Party and, therefore, likely to avoid the need for supplementary requests for assistance."

Article 3 Temporary transfer of detained persons to the territory of the requesting Party

Article 11 of the Convention shall be replaced by the following provisions:

"1. A person in custody whose personal appearance for evidentiary purposes other than for standing trial is applied for by the requesting Party shall be temporarily transferred to its territory, provided that he or she shall be sent back within the period stipulated by the requested Party and subject to the provisions of Article 12 of this Convention, in so far as these are applicable.

Transfer may be refused if:

(a) the person in custody does not consent;

(b) his or her presence is necessary at criminal proceedings pending in the territory of the requested Party;

(c) transfer is liable to prolong his or her detention, or

(d) there are other overriding grounds for not transferring him or her to the territory of the requesting Party.

2. Subject to the provisions of Article 2 of this Convention, in a case coming within paragraph 1, transit of the person in custody through the territory of a third Party, shall be granted on

application, accompanied by all necessary documents, addressed by the Ministry of Justice of the requesting Party to the Ministry of Justice of the Party through whose territory transit is requested. A Party may refuse to grant transit to its own nationals.

3. The transferred person shall remain in custody in the territory of the requesting Party and, where applicable, in the territory of the Party through which transit is requested, unless the Party from whom transfer is requested applies for his or her release."

Article 4 Channels of communication

Article 15 of the Convention shall be replaced by the following provisions:

"1. Requests for mutual assistance, as well as spontaneous information, shall be addressed in writing by the Ministry of Justice of the requesting Party to the Ministry of Justice of the requested Party and shall be returned through the same channels. However, they may be forwarded directly by the judicial authorities of the requesting Party to the judicial authorities of the requested Party and returned through the same channels.

2. Applications as referred to in Article 11 of this Convention and Article 13 of the Second Additional Protocol to this Convention shall in all cases be addressed by the Ministry of Justice of the requesting Party to the Ministry of Justice of the requested Party and shall be returned through the same channels.

3. Requests for mutual assistance concerning proceedings as mentioned in paragraph 3 of Article 1 of this Convention may also be forwarded directly by the administrative or judicial authorities of the requesting Party to the administrative or judicial authorities of the requested Party, as the case may be, and returned through the same channels.

4. Requests for mutual assistance made under Articles 18 and 19 of the Second Additional Protocol to this Convention may also be forwarded directly by the competent authorities of the requesting Party to the competent authorities of the requested Party.

5. Requests provided for in paragraph 1 of Article 13 of this Convention may be addressed directly by the judicial authorities concerned to the appropriate authorities of the requested Party, and the replies may be returned directly by those authorities. Requests provided for in paragraph 2 of Article 13 of this Convention shall be addressed by the Ministry of Justice of the requesting Party to the Ministry of Justice of the requested Party.

6. Requests for copies of convictions and measures as referred to in Article 4 of the Additional Protocol to the Convention may be made directly to the competent authorities. Any Contracting State may, at any time, by a declaration addressed to the Secretary General of the Council of Europe, define what authorities it will, for the purpose of this paragraph, deem competent authorities.

7. In urgent cases, where direct transmission is permitted under this Convention, it may take place through the International Criminal Police Organisation (Interpol).

8. Any Party may, at any time, by a declaration addressed to the Secretary General of the Council of Europe, reserve the right to make the execution of requests, or specified requests, for mutual assistance dependent on one or more of the following conditions:

   (a) that a copy of the request be forwarded to the central authority designated in that declaration;

   (b) that requests, except urgent requests, be forwarded to the central authority designated in that declaration;

   (c) that, in case of direct transmission for reasons of urgency, a copy shall be transmitted at the same time to its Ministry of Justice;

   (d) that some or all requests for assistance shall be sent to it through channels other than those provided for in this article.

9. Requests for mutual assistance and any other communications under this Convention or its Protocols may be forwarded through any electronic or other means of telecommunication

provided that the requesting Party is prepared, upon request, to produce at any time a written record of it and the original. However, any Contracting State, may by a declaration addressed at any time to the Secretary General of the Council of Europe, establish the conditions under which it shall be willing to accept and execute requests received by electronic or other means of telecommunication.

10. The provisions of this article are without prejudice to those of bilateral agreements or arrangements in force between Parties which provide for the direct transmission of requests for assistance between their respective authorities."

Article 5 Costs

Article 20 of the Convention shall be replaced by the following provisions:

"1. Parties shall not claim from each other the refund of any costs resulting from the application of this Convention or its Protocols, except:

(a) costs incurred by the attendance of experts in the territory of the requested Party;

(b) costs incurred by the transfer of a person in custody carried out under Articles 13 or 14 of the Second Additional Protocol to this Convention, or Article 11 of this Convention;

(c) costs of a substantial or extraordinary nature.

2. However, the cost of establishing a video or telephone link, costs related to the servicing of a video or telephone link in the requested Party, the remuneration of interpreters provided by it and allowances to witnesses and their travelling expenses in the requested Party shall be refunded by the requesting Party to the requested Party, unless the Parties agree otherwise.

3. Parties shall consult with each other with a view to making arrangements for the payment of costs claimable under paragraph 1(c) above.

4. The provisions of this article shall apply without prejudice to the provisions of Article 10, paragraph 3, of this Convention."

Article 6 Judicial authorities

Article 24 of the Convention shall be replaced by the following provisions:

"Any State shall at the time of signature or when depositing its instrument of ratification, acceptance, approval or accession, by means of a declaration addressed to the Secretary General of the Council of Europe, define what authorities it will, for the purpose of the Convention, deem judicial authorities. It subsequently may, at any time and in the same manner, change the terms of its declaration."

Chapter II

Article 7 Postponed execution of requests

1. The requested Party may postpone action on a request if such action would prejudice investigations, prosecutions or related proceedings by its authorities.

2. Before refusing or postponing assistance, the requested Party shall, where appropriate after having consulted with the requesting Party, consider whether the request may be granted partially or subject to such conditions as it deems necessary.

3. If the request is postponed, reasons shall be given for the postponement. The requested Party shall also inform the requesting Party of any reasons that render impossible the execution of the request or are likely to delay it significantly.

Article 8 Procedure

Notwithstanding the provisions of Article 3 of the Convention, where requests specify formalities or procedures which are necessary under the law of the requesting Party, even if unfamiliar to the requested Party, the latter shall comply with such requests to the extent that the action sought is not contrary to fundamental principles of its law, unless otherwise provided for in this Protocol.

Article 9 Hearing by video conference

1. If a person is in one Party's territory and has to be heard as a witness or expert by the judicial authorities of another Party, the latter may, where it is not desirable or possible for the person to be heard to appear in its territory in person, request that the hearing take place by video conference, as provided for in paragraphs 2 to 7.

2. The requested Party shall agree to the hearing by video conference provided that the use of the video conference is not contrary to fundamental principles of its law and on condition that it has the technical means to carry out the hearing. If the requested Party has no access to the technical means for video conferencing, such means may be made available to it by the requesting Party by mutual agreement.

3. Requests for a hearing by video conference shall contain, in addition to the information referred to in Article 14 of the Convention, the reason why it is not desirable or possible for the witness or expert to attend in person, the name of the judicial authority and of the persons who will be conducting the hearing.

4. The judicial authority of the requested Party shall summon the person concerned to appear in accordance with the forms laid down by its law.

5. With reference to hearing by video conference, the following rules shall apply:

    (a) a judicial authority of the requested Party shall be present during the hearing, where necessary assisted by an interpreter, and shall also be responsible for ensuring both the identification of the person to be heard and respect for the fundamental principles of the law of the requested Party. If the judicial authority of the requested Party is of the view that during the hearing the fundamental principles of the law of the requested Party are being infringed, it shall immediately take the necessary measures to ensure that the hearing continues in accordance with the said principles;

    (b) measures for the protection of the person to be heard shall be agreed, where necessary, between the competent authorities of the requesting and the requested Parties;

    (c) the hearing shall be conducted directly by, or under the direction of, the judicial authority of the requesting Party in accordance with its own laws;

    (d) at the request of the requesting Party or the person to be heard, the requested Party shall ensure that the person to be heard is assisted by an interpreter, if necessary;

    (e) the person to be heard may claim the right not to testify which would accrue to him or her under the law of either the requested or the requesting Party.

6. Without prejudice to any measures agreed for the protection of persons, the judicial authority of the requested Party shall on the conclusion of the hearing draw up minutes indicating the date and place of the hearing, the identity of the person heard, the identities and functions of all other persons in the requested Party participating in the hearing, any oaths taken and the technical conditions under which the hearing took place. The document shall be forwarded by the competent authority of the requested Party to the competent authority of the requesting Party.

7. Each Party shall take the necessary measures to ensure that, where witnesses or experts are being heard within its territory, in accordance with this article, and refuse to testify when under an obligation to testify or do not testify according to the truth, its national law applies in the same way as if the hearing took place in a national procedure.

8. Parties may at their discretion also apply the provisions of this article, where appropriate and with the agreement of their competent judicial authorities, to hearings by video conference involving the accused person or the suspect. In this case, the decision to hold the video conference, and the manner in which the video conference shall be carried out, shall be subject

to agreement between the Parties concerned, in accordance with their national law and relevant international instruments. Hearings involving the accused person or the suspect shall only be carried out with his or her consent.

9. Any Contracting State may, at any time, by means of a declaration addressed to the Secretary General of the Council of Europe, declare that it will not avail itself of the possibility provided in paragraph 8 above of also applying the provisions of this article to hearings by video conference involving the accused person or the suspect.

Article 10 Hearing by telephone conference

1. If a person is in one Party's territory and has to be heard as a witness or expert by judicial authorities of another Party, the latter may, where its national law so provides, request the assistance of the former Party to enable the hearing to take place by telephone conference, as provided for in paragraphs 2 to 6.

2. A hearing may be conducted by telephone conference only if the witness or expert agrees that the hearing take place by that method.

3. The requested Party shall agree to the hearing by telephone conference where this is not contrary to fundamental principles of its law.

4. A request for a hearing by telephone conference shall contain, in addition to the information referred to in Article 14 of the Convention, the name of the judicial authority and of the persons who will be conducting the hearing and an indication that the witness or expert is willing to take part in a hearing by telephone conference.

5. The practical arrangements regarding the hearing shall be agreed between the Parties concerned. When agreeing such arrangements, the requested Party shall undertake to:

   (a) notify the witness or expert concerned of the time and the venue of the hearing;

   (b) ensure the identification of the witness or expert;

   (c) verify that the witness or expert agrees to the hearing by telephone conference.

6. The requested Party may make its agreement subject, fully or in part, to the relevant provisions of Article 9, paragraphs 5 and 7.

Article 11 Spontaneous information

1. Without prejudice to their own investigations or proceedings, the competent authorities of a Party may, without prior request, forward to the competent authorities of another Party information obtained within the framework of their own investigations, when they consider that the disclosure of such information might assist the receiving Party in initiating or carrying out investigations or proceedings, or might lead to a request by that Party under the Convention or its Protocols.

2. The providing Party may, pursuant to its national law, impose conditions on the use of such information by the receiving Party.

3. The receiving Party shall be bound by those conditions.

4. However, any Contracting State may, at any time, by means of a declaration addressed to the Secretary General of the Council of Europe, declare that it reserves the right not to be bound by the conditions imposed by the providing Party under paragraph 2 above, unless it receives prior notice of the nature of the information to be provided and agrees to its transmission.

Article 12 Restitution

1. At the request of the requesting Party and without prejudice to the rights of bona fide third parties, the requested Party may place articles obtained by criminal means at the disposal of the requesting Party with a view to their return to their rightful owners.

2. In applying Articles 3 and 6 of the Convention, the requested Party may waive the return of articles either before or after handing them over to the requesting Party if the restitution of such articles to the rightful owner may be facilitated thereby. The rights of bona fide third parties shall not be affected.

3. In the event of a waiver before handing over the articles to the requesting Party, the requested Party shall exercise no security right or other right of recourse under tax or customs legislation in respect of these articles.

4. A waiver as referred to in paragraph 2 shall be without prejudice to the right of the requested Party to collect taxes or duties from the rightful owner.

Article 13 Temporary transfer of detained persons to the requested Party

1. Where there is agreement between the competent authorities of the Parties concerned, a Party which has requested an investigation for which the presence of a person held in custody on its own territory is required may temporarily transfer that person to the territory of the Party in which the investigation is to take place.

2. The agreement shall cover the arrangements for the temporary transfer of the person and the date by which the person must be returned to the territory of the requesting Party.

3. Where consent to the transfer is required from the person concerned, a statement of consent or a copy thereof shall be provided promptly to the requested Party.

4. The transferred person shall remain in custody in the territory of the requested Party and, where applicable, in the territory of the Party through which transit is requested, unless the Party from which the person was transferred applies for his or her release.

5. The period of custody in the territory of the requested Party shall be deducted from the period of detention which the person concerned is or will be obliged to undergo in the territory of the requesting Party.

6. The provisions of Article 11, paragraph 2, and Article 12 of the Convention shall apply *mutatis mutandis*.

7. Any Contracting State may at any time, by means of a declaration addressed to the Secretary General of the Council of Europe, declare that before an agreement is reached under paragraph 1 of this article, the consent referred to in paragraph 3 of this article will be required, or will be required under certain conditions indicated in the declaration.

Article 14 Personal appearance of transferred sentenced persons

The provisions of Articles 11 and 12 of the Convention shall apply *mutatis mutandis* also to persons who are in custody in the requested Party, pursuant to having been transferred in order to serve a sentence passed in the requesting Party, where their personal appearance for purposes of review of the judgment is applied for by the requesting Party.

Article 15 Language of procedural documents and judicial decisions to be served

1. The provisions of this article shall apply to any request for service under Article 7 of the Convention or Article 3 of the Additional Protocol thereto.

2. Procedural documents and judicial decisions shall in all cases be transmitted in the language, or the languages, in which they were issued.

3. Notwithstanding the provisions of Article 16 of the Convention, if the authority that issued the papers knows or has reasons to believe that the addressee understands only some other language, the papers, or at least the most important passages thereof, shall be accompanied by a translation into that other language.

4. Notwithstanding the provisions of Article 16 of the Convention, procedural documents and judicial decisions shall, for the benefit of the authorities of the requested Party, be accompanied

by a short summary of their contents translated into the language, or one of the languages, of that Party.

Article 16 Service by post

1. The competent judicial authorities of any Party may directly address, by post, procedural documents and judicial decisions, to persons who are in the territory of any other Party.

2. Procedural documents and judicial decisions shall be accompanied by a report stating that the addressee may obtain information from the authority identified in the report, regarding his or her rights and obligations concerning the service of the papers. The provisions of paragraph 3 of Article 15 above shall apply to that report.

3. The provisions of Articles 8, 9 and 12 of the Convention shall apply *mutatis mutandis* to service by post.

4. The provisions of paragraphs 1, 2 and 3 of Article 15 above shall also apply to service by post.

Article 17 Cross-border observations

1. Police officers of one of the Parties who, within the framework of a criminal investigation, are keeping under observation in their country a person who is presumed to have taken part in a criminal offence to which extradition may apply, or a person who it is strongly believed will lead to the identification or location of the above-mentioned person, shall be authorised to continue their observation in the territory of another Party where the latter has authorised cross-border observation in response to a request for assistance which has previously been submitted. Conditions may be attached to the authorisation.

   On request, the observation will be entrusted to officers of the Party in whose territory it is carried out.

   The request for assistance referred to in the first sub-paragraph must be sent to an authority designated by each Party and having jurisdiction to grant or to forward the requested authorisation.

2. Where, for particularly urgent reasons, prior authorisation of the other Party cannot be requested, the officers conducting the observation within the framework of a criminal investigation shall be authorised to continue beyond the border the observation of a person presumed to have committed offences listed in paragraph 6, provided that the following conditions are met:

   (a) the authorities of the Party designated under paragraph 4, in whose territory the observation is to be continued, must be notified immediately, during the observation, that the border has been crossed;

   (b) a request for assistance submitted in accordance with paragraph 1 and outlining the grounds for crossing the border without prior authorisation shall be submitted without delay.

   Observation shall cease as soon as the Party in whose territory it is taking place so requests, following the notification referred to in (a) or the request referred to in (b) or where authorisation has not been obtained within five hours of the border being crossed.

3. The observation referred to in paragraphs 1 and 2 shall be carried out only under the following general conditions:

   (a) The officers conducting the observation must comply with the provisions of this article and with the law of the Party in whose territory they are operating; they must obey the instructions of the local responsible authorities.

   (b) Except in the situations provided for in paragraph 2, the officers shall, during the observation, carry a document certifying that authorisation has been granted.

   (c) The officers conducting the observation must be able at all times to provide proof that they are acting in an official capacity.

(d) The officers conducting the observation may carry their service weapons during the observation, save where specifically otherwise decided by the requested Party; their use shall be prohibited save in cases of legitimate self-defence.

(e) Entry into private homes and places not accessible to the public shall be prohibited.

(f) The officers conducting the observation may neither stop and question, nor arrest, the person under observation.

(g) All operations shall be the subject of a report to the authorities of the Party in whose territory they took place; the officers conducting the observation may be required to appear in person.

(h) The authorities of the Party from which the observing officers have come shall, when requested by the authorities of the Party in whose territory the observation took place, assist the enquiry subsequent to the operation in which they took part, including legal proceedings.

4. Parties shall at the time of signature or when depositing their instrument of ratification, acceptance, approval or accession, by means of a declaration addressed to the Secretary General of the Council of Europe, indicate both the officers and authorities that they designate for the purposes of paragraphs 1 and 2 of this article. They subsequently may, at any time and in the same manner, change the terms of their declaration.

5. The Parties may, at bilateral level, extend the scope of this article and adopt additional measures in implementation thereof.

6. The observation referred to in paragraph 2 may take place only for one of the following criminal offences:

   – assassination;
   – murder;
   – rape;
   – arson;
   – counterfeiting;
   – armed robbery and receiving of stolen goods:
   – extortion;
   – kidnapping and hostage taking;
   – traffic in human beings;
   – illicit traffic in narcotic drugs and psychotropic substances;
   – breach of the laws on arms and explosives;
   – use of explosives;
   – illicit carriage of toxic and dangerous waste;
   – smuggling of aliens;
   – sexual abuse of children.

Article 18 Controlled delivery

1. Each Party undertakes to ensure that, at the request of another Party, controlled deliveries may be permitted on its territory in the framework of criminal investigations into extraditable offences.

2. The decision to carry out controlled deliveries shall be taken in each individual case by the competent authorities of the requested Party, with due regard to the national law of that Party.

3. Controlled deliveries shall take place in accordance with the procedures of the requested Party. Competence to act, direct and control operations shall lie with the competent authorities of that Party.

4. Parties shall at the time of signature or when depositing their instrument of ratification, acceptance, approval or accession, by means of a declaration addressed to the Secretary General of the Council of Europe, indicate the authorities that are competent for the purposes of this article. They subsequently may, at any time and in the same manner, change the terms of their declaration.

Article 19 Covert investigations

1. The requesting and the requested Parties may agree to assist one another in the conduct of investigations into crime by officers acting under covert or false identity (covert investigations).

2. The decision on the request is taken in each individual case by the competent authorities of the requested Party with due regard to its national law and procedures. The duration of the covert investigation, the detailed conditions, and the legal status of the officers concerned during covert investigations shall be agreed between the Parties with due regard to their national law and procedures.

3. Covert investigations shall take place in accordance with the national law and procedures of the Party on the territory of which the covert investigation takes place. The Parties involved shall co-operate to ensure that the covert investigation is prepared and supervised and to make arrangements for the security of the officers acting under covert or false identity.

4. Parties shall at the time of signature or when depositing their instrument of ratification, acceptance, approval or accession, by means of a declaration addressed to the Secretary General of the Council of Europe, indicate the authorities that are competent for the purposes of paragraph 2 of this article. They subsequently may, at any time and in the same manner, change the terms of their declaration.

Article 20 Joint investigation teams

1. By mutual agreement, the competent authorities of two or more Parties may set up a joint investigation team for a specific purpose and a limited period, which may be extended by mutual consent, to carry out criminal investigations in one or more of the Parties setting up the team. The composition of the team shall be set out in the agreement.

   A joint investigation team may, in particular, be set up where:

   (a) a Party's investigations into criminal offences require difficult and demanding investigations having links with other Parties;

   (b) a number of Parties are conducting investigations into criminal offences in which the circumstances of the case necessitate co-ordinated, concerted action in the Parties involved.

   A request for the setting up of a joint investigation team may be made by any of the Parties concerned. The team shall be set up in one of the Parties in which the investigations are expected to be carried out.

2. In addition to the information referred to in the relevant provisions of Article 14 of the Convention, requests for the setting up of a joint investigation team shall include proposals for the composition of the team.

3. A joint investigation team shall operate in the territory of the Parties setting up the team under the following general conditions:

   (a) the leader of the team shall be a representative of the competent authority participating in criminal investigations from the Party in which the team operates. The leader of the team shall act within the limits of his or her competence under national law;

   (b) the team shall carry out its operations in accordance with the law of the Party in which it operates. The members and seconded members of the team shall carry out their tasks under the leadership of the person referred to in sub-paragraph a, taking into account the conditions set by their own authorities in the agreement on setting up the team;

(c) the Party in which the team operates shall make the necessary organisational arrangements for it to do so.

4. In this article, members of the joint investigation team from the Party in which the team operates are referred to as "members", while members from Parties other than the Party in which the team operates are referred to as "seconded members".

5. Seconded members of the joint investigation team shall be entitled to be present when investigative measures are taken in the Party of operation. However, the leader of the team may, for particular reasons, in accordance with the law of the Party where the team operates, decide otherwise.

6. Seconded members of the joint investigation team may, in accordance with the law of the Party where the team operates, be entrusted by the leader of the team with the task of taking certain investigative measures where this has been approved by the competent authorities of the Party of operation and the seconding Party.

7. Where the joint investigation team needs investigative measures to be taken in one of the Parties setting up the team, members seconded to the team by that Party may request their own competent authorities to take those measures. Those measures shall be considered in that Party under the conditions which would apply if they were requested in a national investigation.

8. Where the joint investigation team needs assistance from a Party other than those which have set up the team, or from a third State, the request for assistance may be made by the competent authorities of the State of operation to the competent authorities of the other State concerned in accordance with the relevant instruments or arrangements.

9. A seconded member of the joint investigation team may, in accordance with his or her national law and within the limits of his or her competence, provide the team with information available in the Party which has seconded him or her for the purpose of the criminal investigations conducted by the team.

10. Information lawfully obtained by a member or seconded member while part of a joint investigation team which is not otherwise available to the competent authorities of the Parties concerned may be used for the following purposes:

(a) for the purposes for which the team has been set up;

(b) subject to the prior consent of the Party where the information became available, for detecting, investigating and prosecuting other criminal offences. Such consent may be withheld only in cases where such use would endanger criminal investigations in the Party concerned or in respect of which that Party could refuse mutual assistance;

(c) for preventing an immediate and serious threat to public security, and without prejudice to sub-paragraph (b) if subsequently a criminal investigation is opened;

(d) for other purposes to the extent that this is agreed between Parties setting up the team.

11. This article shall be without prejudice to any other existing provisions or arrangements on the setting up or operation of joint investigation teams.

12. To the extent that the laws of the Parties concerned or the provisions of any legal instrument applicable between them permit, arrangements may be agreed for persons other than representatives of the competent authorities of the Parties setting up the joint investigation team to take part in the activities of the team. The rights conferred upon the members or seconded members of the team by virtue of this article shall not apply to these persons unless the agreement expressly states otherwise.

Article 21 Criminal liability regarding officials

During the operations referred to in Articles 17, 18, 19 or 20, unless otherwise agreed upon by the Parties concerned, officials from a Party other than the Party of operation shall be regarded as officials of the Party of operation with respect to offences committed against them or by them.

Article 22 Civil liability regarding officials

1. Where, in accordance with Articles 17, 18, 19 or 20, officials of a Party are operating in another Party, the first Party shall be liable for any damage caused by them during their operations, in accordance with the law of the Party in whose territory they are operating.

2. The Party in whose territory the damage referred to in paragraph 1 was caused shall make good such damage under the conditions applicable to damage caused by its own officials.

3. The Party whose officials have caused damage to any person in the territory of another Party shall reimburse the latter in full any sums it has paid to the victims or persons entitled on their behalf.

4. Without prejudice to the exercise of its rights vis-à-vis third parties and with the exception of paragraph 3, each Party shall refrain in the case provided for in paragraph 1 from requesting reimbursement of damages it has sustained from another Party.

5. The provisions of this article shall apply subject to the proviso that the Parties did not agree otherwise.

Article 23 Protection of witnesses

Where a Party requests assistance under the Convention or one of its Protocols in respect of a witness at risk of intimidation or in need of protection, the competent authorities of the requesting and requested Parties shall endeavour to agree on measures for the protection of the person concerned, in accordance with their national law.

Article 24 Provisional measures

1. At the request of the requesting Party, the requested Party, in accordance with its national law, may take provisional measures for the purpose of preserving evidence, maintaining an existing situation or protecting endangered legal interests.

2. The requested Party may grant the request partially or subject to conditions, in particular time limitation.

Article 25 Confidentiality

The requesting Party may require that the requested Party keep confidential the fact and substance of the request, except to the extent necessary to execute the request. If the requested Party cannot comply with the requirement of confidentiality, it shall promptly inform the requesting Party.

Article 26 Data protection

1. Personal data transferred from one Party to another as a result of the execution of a request made under the Convention or any of its Protocols, may be used by the Party to which such data have been transferred, only:

   (a) for the purpose of proceedings to which the Convention or any of its Protocols apply;

   (b) for other judicial and administrative proceedings directly related to the proceedings mentioned under (a);

   (c) for preventing an immediate and serious threat to public security.

2. Such data may however be used for any other purpose if prior consent to that effect is given by either the Party from which the data had been transferred, or the data subject.

3. Any Party may refuse to transfer personal data obtained as a result of the execution of a request made under the Convention or any of its Protocols where:

   – such data is protected under its national legislation; and

   – the Party to which the data should be transferred is not bound by the Convention for the Protection of Individuals with regard to Automatic Processing of Personal Data, done at Strasbourg on 28 January 1981, unless the latter Party undertakes to afford such protection to the data as is required by the former Party.

4. Any Party that transfers personal data obtained as a result of the execution of a request made under the Convention or any of its Protocols may require the Party to which the data have been transferred to give information on the use made with such data.

5. Any Party may, by a declaration addressed to the Secretary General of the Council of Europe, require that, within the framework of procedures for which it could have refused or limited the transmission or the use of personal data in accordance with the provisions of the Convention or one of its Protocols, personal data transmitted to another Party not be used by the latter for the purposes of paragraph I unless with its previous consent.

Article 27 Administrative authorities
Parties may at any time, by means of a declaration addressed to the Secretary General of the Council of Europe, define what authorities they will deem administrative authorities for the purposes of Article I, paragraph 3, of the Convention.

Article 28 Relations with other treaties
The provisions of this Protocol are without prejudice to more extensive regulations in bilateral or multilateral agreements concluded between Parties in application of Article 26, paragraph 3, of the Convention.

Article 29 Friendly settlement
The European Committee on Crime Problems shall be kept informed regarding the interpretation and application of the Convention and its Protocols, and shall do whatever is necessary to facilitate a friendly settlement of any difficulty which may arise out of their application.

DOCUMENT 72

Inter-American Convention on Mutual Assistance in Criminal Matters 1992
OASTS No 75

This Convention was concluded under the auspices of the Organization of American States; it was opened for signature at Nassau, Bahamas, on 23 May 1992 and entered into force on 14 April 1996.

Eighteen of the 34 member States of the OAS are parties to the Convention, including the USA, although 15 of these have become parties since 2001. A further five member States have signed the Convention but are yet to ratify it.

The Convention envisages mutual co-operation between States parties in relation to investigations, prosecutions and proceedings (Article 2). Except in relation to immobilisation and sequestration of property, and searches and seizures, there is no requirement of double criminality (Article 5). The Convention applies only to offences that are punishable by a sentence of imprisonment of one year or more (Article 6) and excludes military crimes (Article 8). Assistance may be refused at the determination of the requested State in a number of cases, including discriminatory prosecutions and political prosecutions. Chapter II of the Convention deals with the processing and execution of requests for assistance, including search, seizure, attachment and surrender of property (Article 13), and measures for securing assets (Articles 14–15). Chapter III deals with service of judicial decisions, judgments and verdicts and appearances of witnesses and expert witnesses (Articles 17–23). Chapter IV governs transmittal of information and records and Chapter V deals with procedure.

See the Optional Protocol to the Inter-American Convention on Mutual Assistance in Criminal Matters of 1993 (**Document 73**).

Whereas:

The Charter of the Organization of American States, in Article 2.e, establishes that an essential objective of the American states is "to seek the solution of political, juridical, and economic problems that may arise among them"; and

The adoption of common rules in the field of mutual assistance in criminal matters will contribute to the attainment of this goal,

The Member States of the Organization of American States

Do hereby adopt the following Inter-American Convention on Mutual Assistance in Criminal Matters:

Chapter I General provisions

Article I Purpose of the convention
The states parties undertake to render to one another mutual assistance in criminal matters, in accordance with the provisions of this convention.

Article 2 Scope and application of the convention
The states parties shall render to one another mutual assistance in investigations, prosecutions, and proceedings that pertain to crimes over which the requesting state has jurisdiction at the time the assistance is requested.

This convention does not authorize any state party to undertake, in the territory of another state party, the exercise of jurisdiction or the performance of functions that are placed within the exclusive purview of the authorities of that other party by its domestic law.

This convention applies solely to the provision of mutual assistance among states parties. Its provisions shall not create any right on the part of any private person to obtain or exclude any evidence or to impede execution of any request for assistance.

Article 3 Central authority
Each state shall designate a central authority at the time of signature or ratification of this convention or accession hereto.

The central authorities shall be responsible for issuing and receiving requests for assistance.

The central authorities shall communicate directly with one another for all purposes of this convention.

Article 4
In view of the diversity of the legal systems of the states parties, the assistance to which this convention refers shall be based upon requests for cooperation from the authorities responsible for criminal investigation or prosecution in the requesting state.

Article 5 Double criminality
The assistance shall be rendered even if the act that gives rise to it is not punishable under the legislation of the requested state.

When the request for assistance pertains to the following measures: (a) immobilization and sequestration of property and (b) searches and seizures, including house searches, the requested state may decline to render the assistance if the act that gives rise to the request is not punishable under its legislation.

Article 6

For the purposes of this convention, the act that gives rise to the request must be punishable by one year or more of imprisonment in the requesting state.

Article 7 Scope of application

The assistance envisaged under this convention shall include the following Procedures among others:

(a) notification of rulings and judgments;

(b) taking of testimony or statements from persons;

(c) summoning of witnesses and expert witnesses to provide testimony;

(d) immobilization and sequestration of property, freezing of assets, and assistance in procedures related to seizures;

(e) searches or seizures;

(f) examination of objects and places;

(g) service of judicial documents;

(h) transmittal of documents, reports, information, and evidence;

(i) ransfer of detained persons for the purpose of this convention; and

(j) any other procedure provided there is an agreement between the requesting state and the requested state.

Article 8 Military crimes

This convention shall not apply to crimes subject exclusively to military legislation.

Article 9 Refusal of assistance

The requested state may refuse assistance when it determines that:

(a) The request for assistance is being used in order to prosecute a person on a charge with respect to which that person has already been sentenced or acquitted in a trial in the requesting or requested state;

(b) The investigation has been initiated for the purpose of prosecuting, punishing, or discriminating in any way against an individual or group of persons for reason of sex, race, social status, nationality, religion, or ideology;

(c) The request refers to a crime that is political or related to a political crime, or to a common crime prosecuted for political reasons;

(d) The request has been issued at the request of a special or ad hoc tribunal;

(e) Public policy (*ordre public*), sovereignty, security, or basic public interests are prejudiced; and

(f) The request pertains to a tax crime. Nevertheless, the assistance shall be granted if the offense is committed by way of an intentionally incorrect statement, whether oral or written, or by way of an intentional failure to declare income derived from any other offense covered by this convention for the Purpose of concealing such income.

Chapter II Requests for assistance, processing and execution

Article 10 Requests for assistance

Requests for assistance issued by the requesting state shall be made in writing and shall be executed in accordance with the domestic law of the requested state.

The procedures specified in the request for assistance shall be fulfilled in the manner indicated by the requesting state insofar as the law of the requested state is not violated.

Article 11

The requested state may postpone the execution of any request that has been made to it, with an explanation of its grounds for doing so, if it is necessary to continue an investigation or proceeding in progress in the requested state.

Article 12

Documents and objects delivered in compliance with a request for assistance shall be returned to the requested state as soon as possible, unless the latter decides otherwise.

Article 13 Search, seizure, attachment, and surrender of property

The requested state shall execute requests for search, seizure, attachment, and surrender of any items, documents, records, or effects, if the competent authority determines that the request contains information that justifies the proposed action. That action shall be subject to the procedural and substantive law of the requested state.

In accordance with the provisions of this convention, the requested state shall determine, according to its law, what requirements must be met to protect the interests held by third parties in the items that are to be transferred.

Article 14 Measures for securing assets

The central authority of any party may convey to the central authority of any other party information it has on the existence of proceeds, fruits, or instrumentalities of a crime in the territory of that other party.

Article 15

The parties shall assist each other, to the extent permitted by their respective laws, in precautionary measures and measures for securing the proceeds, fruits, and instrumentalities of the crime.

Article 16 Date, place and modality of the execution of the request for assistance

The requested state shall set the date and place for execution of the request for assistance and may so inform the requesting state.

Officials and interested parties of the requesting state or their representatives may, after informing the central authority of the requested state, be present at and participate in the execution of the request for assistance, to the extent not prohibited by the law of the requested state, and provided that the authorities of the requested state have given their express consent thereto.

Chapter III Service of judicial decisions, judgments, and verdicts, and appearance of witnesses and expert witnesses

Article 17

At the request of the requesting state, the requested state shall serve notice of decisions, judgments, or other documents issued by the competent authorities of the requesting state.

Article 18 Testimony in the requested state

At the request of the requesting state, any person present in the requested state shall be summoned to appear before a competent authority, in accordance with the law of the requested state, to give testimony or to provide documents, records, or evidence.

Article 19 Testimony in the requesting state

When the requesting state requests that a person appear in its territory to give testimony or a report, the requested state shall invite the witness or expert witness to appear voluntarily, without the use of threats or coercive measures, before the appropriate authority in the requesting state. If deemed necessary, the central authority of the requested state may make a written record of the individual's willingness to appear in the requesting state. The central authority of the requested state shall promptly inform the central authority of the requesting state of the response of the person.

Article 20 Transfer of person subject to criminal proceedings

A person subject to criminal proceedings in the requested state whose presence in the requesting state is needed for purposes of assistance under this convention shall be transferred temporarily to the requesting state for that purpose if the person and the requested state consent to the transfer.

A person subject to criminal proceedings in the requesting state whose presence in the requested state is needed for purposes of assistance under this convention shall be transferred temporarily to the requested state if the person consents and both states agree.

The actions set forth above may be denied for the following reasons, among others:

(a) the individual in custody or serving a sentence refuses to consent to the transfer:

(b) as long as his presence is necessary in an investigation or criminal proceeding that is under way in the jurisdiction to which he is subject at the time;

(c) there are other considerations, whether legal or of another nature, as determined by the competent authority of the requested or requesting state.

For purposes of this article:

(a) the receiving state shall have the authority and the obligation to keep the transferred person in physical custody unless otherwise indicated by the sending state;

(b) the receiving state shall return the transferred person to the sending state as soon as circumstances permit or as otherwise agreed by the central authorities of the two states;

(c) the sending state shall not be required to initiate extradition proceedings for the return of the transferred person;

(d) the transferred person shall receive credit toward service of the sentence imposed in the sending state for time served in the receiving state; and

(e) the length of time spent by the person in the receiving state shall never exceed the period remaining for service of the sentence or 60 days, whichever is less, unless the person and both states agree to an extension of time.

Article 21 Transit

The states parties shall render cooperation, to the extent possible, for travel through their territory of the persons mentioned in the preceding article, provided that the respective central authority has been given due advance notice and that such persons travel in the custody of agents of the requesting state.

Such prior notice shall not be necessary when air transportation is used and no regular landing is scheduled in the territory of the state party or states parties to be overflown.

Article 22 Safe-conduct

The appearance or transfer of the person who agrees to render a statement or to testify under the provisions of this convention shall require, if the person or the sending state so requests prior to such appearance or transfer, that the receiving state grant safe-conduct under which the person, while in the receiving state, shall not:

(a) be detained or prosecuted for offenses committed prior to his departure from the territory of the sending state;

(b) be required to make a statement or to give testimony in proceedings not specified in the request; or

(c) be detained or prosecuted on the basis of any statement he makes, except in case of contempt of court or perjury.

The safe-conduct specified in the preceding paragraph shall cease when the person voluntarily prolongs his stay in the territory of the receiving state for more than 10 days after his presence is no longer necessary in that state, as communicated to the sending state.

Article 23

In connection with witnesses or expert witnesses, documents containing the relevant questions, interrogatories, or questionnaires shall be forwarded to the extent possible or necessary.

Chapter IV Transmittal of information and records

Article 24

In cases where assistance is carried out under this convention, the requested state, upon request and in accordance with its domestic procedure, shall make available to the requesting state a copy of the public documents, records, or information held by the government agencies or departments of the requested state.

The requested state may make available copies of any document, record, or other information held by a government agency or department of that state that is not public in nature, to the same extent as and subject to the same conditions under which they would be made available to its own judicial authorities or to others responsible for application of the law. The requested state, at its own discretion, may deny, in whole or in part, any request made under the provisions of this paragraph.

Article 25 Limitation on the use of information or evidence

The requesting state may not disclose or use any information or evidence obtained in the course of application of this convention for purposes other than those specified in the request for assistance without prior consent from the central authority of the requested state.

In exceptional cases, if the requesting state needs to disclose and use, in whole or in part, the information or evidence for purposes other than those specified, it shall request authorization therefor from the requested state, which, at its discretion, may accede to or deny that request in whole or in part.

The information or evidence that must be disclosed and used to the extent necessary for proper fulfillment of the procedure or formalities specified in the request shall not be subject to the authorization requirement set forth in this article.

When necessary, the requested state may ask that the information or evidence provided remain confidential according to conditions specified by the central authority. If the requesting party is unable to accede to such request, the central authorities shall confer in order to define mutually acceptable terms of confidentiality.

Chapter V Procedure

Article 26

Requests for assistance shall contain the following details:

(a) the crime to which the procedure refers; a summary description of the essential facts of the crime, investigation, or criminal proceeding in question; and a description of the facts to which the request refers;

(b) proceeding giving rise to the request for assistance, with a precise description of such proceeding;

(c) where pertinent, a description of any proceeding or other special requirement of the requesting state;

(d) a precise description of the assistance requested and any information necessary for the fulfillment of that request.

When the requested state is unable to comply with a request for assistance, it shall return the request to the requesting state with an explanation of the reason therefor.

The requested state may request additional information when necessary for fulfillment of the request under its domestic law or to facilitate such fulfillment.

When necessary, the requesting state shall proceed in accordance with the provisions of the last paragraph of Article 24 of this convention.

Article 27

Documents processed through the central authorities in accordance with this convention shall be exempt from certification or authentication.

Article 28

Requests for assistance and the accompanying documentation must be translated into an official language of the requested state.

Article 29

The requested state shall be responsible for all regular costs of executing a request in its territory, except for those listed below, which shall be borne by the requesting state:

(a) fees for expert witnesses; and

(b) travel costs and other expenses related to the transportation of persons from the territory of one state to that of the other.

If it appears that the processing of the request might entail unusual costs, the states parties shall confer to determine the terms and conditions under which the assistance could be rendered.

Article 30

To the extent that they find it useful and necessary for furthering the implementation of this convention, the states parties may exchange information on matters related to its application.

Article 31

The domestic law of each party shall govern liability for damages arising from the acts of its authorities in the execution of this Convention.

Neither party shall be liable for damages that may arise from the acts committed by the authorities of the other party in the formulation or execution of a request under this Convention.

Chapter VI Final clauses

Article 36

This convention shall not be interpreted as affecting or restricting obligations in effect under any other international, bilateral, or multilateral convention that contains or might contain clauses governing specific aspects of international criminal judicial assistance, wholly or in part, or more favorable practices which those states might observe in the matter.

DOCUMENT 73

Optional Protocol related to the Inter-American Convention on Mutual Assistance in Criminal Matters 1993
OASTS No 77

The Optional Protocol was concluded under the auspices of the Organization of American States and is attached to the Inter-American Convention on Mutual Assistance in Criminal Matters 1992 **(Document 72)**; *it was opened for signature at Managua, Nicaragua, on 11 June 1993 and entered into force on 7 April 2002.*

There are only five State parties to the Optional Protocol, including the USA.

The Optional Protocol deals specifically with tax crimes.

The member states of the Organization of American States,

Bearing in mind the Inter-American Convention on Mutual Assistance in Criminal Matters adopted at Nassau on May 23, 1992 (hereinafter referred to as "the Convention"),

Have agreed to adopt the following Optional Protocol related to the Inter-American Convention on Mutual Assistance in Criminal Matters:

Article 1
The states parties to this Protocol shall not exercise the right provided for in Article 9.f of the Convention to refuse a request for assistance solely on the ground that the request concern a tax crime in any case in which the request is from another state party to this Protocol.

Article 2
The states parties to this Protocol, when acting as a requested state under the Convention, shall not decline assistance which requires the measures referred to in Article 5 of the Convention, if the act specified in the request corresponds to a tax crime of the same nature under the laws of the requested state.

DOCUMENT 74

Agreement on Mutual Legal Assistance between the European Union and the United States of America 2003
Official Journal L181/34 19/07/2003; 43 ILM 758 (2004)

This agreement was concluded at Washington, DC, on 25 June 2003, the Member States of the European Union having previously agreed to the signing of the agreement by Council Decision of 6 June 2003 (2003/516/EC). The agreement, together with the Agreement on Extradition between the European Union and the United States of America 2003 **(Document 68)**, *was intended to provide additional tools to both the EU and the USA to combat terrorism, organised crime and other serious forms of criminality. Both agreements have been severely criticised by human rights organisations as weakening traditional protections for the individual.*

The agreement is intended to enhance co-operation and mutual legal assistance between the EU and the USA (Article 1). The agreement envisages application of its provisions in relation to bilateral mutual assistance treaties between the Member States of the EU and the USA and requires the EU to ensure that new Member States having mutual assistance treaties with the USA comply with the provisions of the agreement (Article 3).

Key provisions include Articles 4, 5, 6 and 9. The agreement envisages the sharing of banking information on suspects (Article 4) and the creation of joint investigative teams (Article 5). It also provides for the possibility of video conferencing for the hearing of witness testimony (Article 6). Protection on personal and other data is provided for in Article 9.

The European Union and the United States of America,

Desiring further to facilitate cooperation between the European Union Member States and the United States of America,

Desiring to combat crime in a more effective way as a means of protecting their respective democratic societies and common values,

Having due regard for rights of individuals and the rule of law,

Mindful of the guarantees under their respective legal systems which provide an accused person with the right to a fair trial, including the right to adjudication by an impartial tribunal established pursuant to law,

Desiring to conclude an Agreement relating to mutual legal assistance in criminal matters,

Have agreed as follows:

Article 1 Object and purpose

The Contracting Parties undertake, in accordance with the provisions of this Agreement, to provide for enhancements to cooperation and mutual legal assistance.

Article 2 Definitions

1. "Contracting Parties" shall mean the European Union and the United States of America.

2. "Member State" shall mean a Member State of the European Union.

Article 3 Scope of application of this Agreement in relation to bilateral mutual legal assistance treaties with Member States and in the absence thereof

1. The European Union, pursuant to the Treaty on European Union, and the United States of America shall ensure that the provisions of this Agreement are applied in relation to bilateral mutual legal assistance treaties between the Member States and the United States of America, in force at the time of the entry into force of this Agreement, under the following terms:

    (a) Article 4 shall be applied to provide for identification of financial accounts and transactions in addition to any authority already provided under bilateral treaty provisions;

    (b) Article 5 shall be applied to authorise the formation and activities of joint investigative teams in addition to any authority already provided under bilateral treaty provisions;

    (c) Article 6 shall be applied to authorise the taking of testimony of a person located in the requested State by use of video transmission technology between the requesting and requested States in addition to any authority already provided under bilateral treaty provisions;

    (d) Article 7 shall be applied to provide for the use of expedited means of communication in addition to any authority already provided under bilateral treaty provisions;

(e) Article 8 shall be applied to authorise the providing of mutual legal assistance to the administrative authorities concerned, in addition to any authority already provided under bilateral treaty provisions;

(f) subject to Article 9.4 and 5, Article 9 shall be applied in place of, or in the absence of bilateral treaty provisions governing limitations on use of information or evidence provided to the requesting State, and governing the conditioning or refusal of assistance on data protection grounds;

(g) Article 10 shall be applied in the absence of bilateral treaty provisions pertaining to the circumstances under which a requesting State may seek the confidentiality of its request.

2. (a) The European Union, pursuant to the Treaty on European Union, shall ensure that each Member State acknowledges, in a written instrument between such Member State and the United States of America, the application, in the manner set forth in this Article, of its bilateral mutual legal assistance treaty in force with the United States of America.

(b) The European Union, pursuant to the Treaty on European Union, shall ensure that new Member States acceding to the European Union after the entry into force of this Agreement, and having bilateral mutual legal assistance treaties with the United States of America, take the measures referred to in subparagraph (a).

(c) The Contracting Parties shall endeavour to complete the process described in subparagraph (b) prior to the scheduled accession of a new Member State, or as soon as possible thereafter. The European Union shall notify the United States of America of the date of accession of new Member States.

3. (a) The European Union, pursuant to the Treaty on European Union, and the United States of America shall also ensure that the provisions of this Agreement are applied in the absence of a bilateral mutual legal assistance treaty in force between a Member State and the United States of America.

(b) The European Union, pursuant to the Treaty on European Union, shall ensure that such Member State acknowledges, in a written instrument between such Member State and the United States of America, the application of the provisions of this Agreement.

(c) The European Union, pursuant to the Treaty on European Union, shall ensure that new Member States acceding to the European Union after the entry into force of this Agreement, which do not have bilateral mutual legal assistance treaties with the United States of America, take the measures referred to in subparagraph (b).

4. If the process described in paragraph 2(b) and 3(c) is not completed by the date of accession, the provisions of this Agreement shall apply in the relations between the United States of America and that new Member State as from the date on which they have notified each other and the European Union of the completion of their internal procedures for that purpose.

5. The Contracting Parties agree that this Agreement is intended solely for mutual legal assistance between the States concerned. The provisions of this Agreement shall not give rise to a right on the part of any private person to obtain, suppress, or exclude any evidence, or to impede the execution of a request, nor expand or limit rights otherwise available under domestic law.

Article 4 Identification of bank information

1. (a) Upon request of the requesting State, the requested State shall, in accordance with the terms of this Article, promptly ascertain if the banks located in its territory possess information on whether an identified natural or legal person suspected of or charged with a criminal offence is the holder of a bank account or accounts. The requested State shall promptly communicate the results of its enquiries to the requesting State.

(b) The actions described in subparagraph (a) may also be taken for the purpose of identifying:

(i) information regarding natural or legal persons convicted of or otherwise involved in a criminal offence;

    (ii)   information in the possession of non-bank financial institutions; or

    (iii) financial transactions unrelated to accounts.

2.   A request for information described in paragraph 1 shall include:

   (a) the identity of the natural or legal person relevant to locating such accounts or transactions; and

   (b) sufficient information to enable the competent authority of the requested State to:

     (i)   reasonably suspect that the natural or legal person concerned has engaged in a criminal offence and that banks or non-bank financial institutions in the territory of the requested State may have the information requested; and

     (ii) conclude that the information sought relates to the criminal investigation or proceeding;

   (c) to the extent possible, information concerning which bank or non-bank financial institution may be involved, and other information the availability of which may aid in reducing the breadth of the enquiry.

3.   Requests for assistance under this Article shall be transmitted between:

   (a) central authorities responsible for mutual legal assistance in Member States, or national authorities of Member States responsible for investigation or prosecution of criminal offences as designated pursuant to Article 15(2); and

   (b) national authorities of the United States responsible for investigation or prosecution of criminal offences, as designated pursuant to Article 15(2).

The Contracting Parties may, following the entry into force of this Agreement, agree by Exchange of Diplomatic Note to modify the channels through which requests under this Article are made.

4.   (a) Subject to subparagraph (b), a State may, pursuant to Article 15, limit its obligation to provide assistance under this Article to:

     (i)   offences punishable under the laws of both the requested and requesting States;

     (ii) offences punishable by a penalty involving deprivation of liberty or a detention order of a maximum period of at least four years in the requesting State and at least two years in the requested State; or

     (iii) designated serious offences punishable under the laws of both the requested and requesting States.

   (b) A State which limits its obligation pursuant to subparagraph (a)(ii) or (iii) shall, at a minimum, enable identification of accounts associated with terrorist activity and the laundering of proceeds generated from a comprehensive range of serious criminal activities, punishable under the laws of both the requesting and requested States.

5.   Assistance may not be refused under this Article on grounds of bank secrecy.

6.   The requested State shall respond to a request for production of the records concerning the accounts or transactions identified pursuant to this Article, in accordance with the provisions of the applicable mutual legal assistance treaty in force between the States concerned, or in the absence thereof, in accordance with the requirements of its domestic law.

7.   The Contracting Parties shall take measures to avoid the imposition of extraordinary burdens on requested States through application of this Article. Where extraordinary burdens on a requested State nonetheless result, including on banks or by operation of the channels of communications foreseen in this Article, the Contracting Parties shall immediately consult with a view to facilitating the application of this Article, including the taking of such measures as may be required to reduce pending and future burdens.

Article 5 Joint investigative teams

1. The Contracting Parties shall, to the extent they have not already done so, take such measures as may be necessary to enable joint investigative teams to be established and operated in the respective territories of each Member State and the United States of America for the purpose of facilitating criminal investigations or prosecutions involving one or more Member States and the United States of America where deemed appropriate by the Member State concerned and the United States of America.

2. The procedures under which the team is to operate, such as its composition, duration, location, organisation, functions, purpose, and terms of participation of team members of a State in investigative activities taking place in another State's territory shall be as agreed between the competent authorities responsible for the investigation or prosecution of criminal offences, as determined by the respective States concerned.

3. The competent authorities determined by the respective States concerned shall communicate directly for the purposes of the establishment and operation of such team except that where the exceptional complexity, broad scope, or other circumstances involved are deemed to require more central coordination as to some or all aspects, the States may agree upon other appropriate channels of communications to that end.

4. Where the joint investigative team needs investigative measures to be taken in one of the States setting up the team, a member of the team of that State may request its own competent authorities to take those measures without the other States having to submit a request for mutual legal assistance. The required legal standard for obtaining the measure in that State shall be the standard applicable to its domestic investigative activities.

Article 6 Video conferencing

1. The Contracting Parties shall take such measures as may be necessary to enable the use of video transmission technology between each Member State and the United States of America for taking testimony in a proceeding for which mutual legal assistance is available of a witness or expert located in a requested State, to the extent such assistance is not currently available. To the extent not specifically set forth in this Article, the modalities governing such procedure shall be as provided under the applicable mutual legal assistance treaty in force between the States concerned, or the law of the requested State, as applicable.

2. Unless otherwise agreed by the requesting and requested States, the requesting State shall bear the costs associated with establishing and servicing the video transmission. Other costs arising in the course of providing assistance (including costs associated with travel of participants in the requested State) shall be borne in accordance with the applicable provisions of the mutual legal assistance treaty in force between the States concerned, or where there is no such treaty, as agreed upon by the requesting and requested States.

3. The requesting and requested States may consult in order to facilitate resolution of legal, technical or logistical issues that may arise in the execution of the request.

4. Without prejudice to any jurisdiction under the law of the requesting State, making an intentionally false statement or other misconduct of the witness or expert during the course of the video conference shall be punishable in the requested State in the same manner as if it had been committed in the course of its domestic proceedings.

5. This Article is without prejudice to the use of other means for obtaining of testimony in the requested State available under applicable treaty or law.

6. This Article is without prejudice to application of provisions of bilateral mutual legal assistance agreements between Member States and the United States of America that require or permit the use of video conferencing technology for purposes other than those described in paragraph 1, including for purposes of identification of persons or objects, or taking of investigative statements. Where not already provided for under applicable treaty or law, a State may permit the use of video conferencing technology in such instances.

Article 7 Expedited transmission of requests

Requests for mutual legal assistance, and communications related thereto, may be made by expedited means of communications, including fax or e-mail, with formal confirmation to follow where required by the requested State. The requested State may respond to the request by any such expedited means of communication.

Article 8 Mutual legal assistance to administrative authorities

1. Mutual legal assistance shall also be afforded to a national administrative authority, investigating conduct with a view to a criminal prosecution of the conduct, or referral of the conduct to criminal investigation or prosecution authorities, pursuant to its specific administrative or regulatory authority to undertake such investigation. Mutual legal assistance may also be afforded to other administrative authorities under such circumstances. Assistance shall not be available for matters in which the administrative authority anticipates that no prosecution or referral, as applicable, will take place.

2. (a) Requests for assistance under this Article shall be transmitted between the central authorities designated pursuant to the bilateral mutual legal assistance treaty in force between the States concerned, or between such other authorities as may be agreed by the central authorities.

    (b) In the absence of a treaty, requests shall be transmitted between the United States Department of Justice and the Ministry of Justice or, pursuant to Article 15.1, comparable Ministry of the Member State concerned responsible for transmission of mutual legal assistance requests, or between such other authorities as may be agreed by the Department of Justice and such Ministry.

3. The Contracting Parties shall take measures to avoid the imposition of extraordinary burdens on requested States through application of this Article. Where extraordinary burdens on a requested State nonetheless result, the Contracting Parties shall immediately consult with a view to facilitating the application of this Article, including the taking of such measures as may be required to reduce pending and future burdens.

Article 9 Limitations on use to protect personal and other data

1. The requesting State may use any evidence or information obtained from the requested State:

    (a) for the purpose of its criminal investigations and proceedings;

    (b) for preventing an immediate and serious threat to its public security;

    (c) in its non-criminal judicial or administrative proceedings directly related to investigations or proceedings:

        (i)   set forth in subparagraph (a); or

        (ii)   for which mutual legal assistance was rendered under Article 8;

    (d) for any other purpose, if the information or evidence has been made public within the framework of proceedings for which they were transmitted, or in any of the situations described in subparagraphs (a), (b) and (c); and

    (e) for any other purpose, only with the prior consent of the requested State.

2. (a) This Article shall not prejudice the ability of the requested State to impose additional conditions in a particular case where the particular request for assistance could not be complied with in the absence of such conditions. Where additional conditions have been imposed in accordance with this subparagraph, the requested State may require the requesting State to give information on the use made of the evidence or information.

    (b) Generic restrictions with respect to the legal standards of the requesting State for processing personal data may not be imposed by the requested State as a condition under subparagraph (a) to providing evidence or information.

3. Where, following disclosure to the requesting State, the requested State becomes aware of circumstances that may cause it to seek an additional condition in a particular case, the requested State may consult with the requesting State to determine the extent to which the evidence and information can be protected.

4. A requested State may apply the use limitation provision of the applicable bilateral mutual legal assistance treaty in lieu of this Article, where doing so will result in less restriction on the use of information and evidence than provided for in this Article.

5. Where a bilateral mutual legal assistance treaty in force between a Member State and the United States of America on the date of signature of this Agreement, permits limitation of the obligation to provide assistance with respect to certain tax offences, the Member State concerned may indicate, in its exchange of written instruments with the United States of America described in Article 3.2, that, with respect to such offences, it will continue to apply the use limitation provision of that treaty.

Article 10 Requesting State's request for confidentiality

The requested State shall use its best efforts to keep confidential a request and its contents if such confidentiality is requested by the requesting State. If the request cannot be executed without breaching the requested confidentiality, the central authority of the requested State shall so inform the requesting State, which shall then determine whether the request should nevertheless be executed.

Article 11 Consultations

The Contracting Parties shall, as appropriate, consult to enable the most effective use to be made of this Agreement, including to facilitate the resolution of any dispute regarding the interpretation or application of this Agreement.

Article 12 Temporal application

1. This Agreement shall apply to offences committed before as well as after it enters into force.

2. This Agreement shall apply to requests for mutual legal assistance made after its entry into force. Nevertheless, Articles 6 and 7 shall apply to requests pending in a requested State at the time this Agreement enters into force.

Article 13 Non-derogation

Subject to Article 4.5 and Article 9.2(b), this Agreement is without prejudice to the invocation by the requested State of grounds for refusal of assistance available pursuant to a bilateral mutual legal assistance treaty, or, in the absence of a treaty, its applicable legal principles, including where execution of the request would prejudice its sovereignty, security, ordre public or other essential interests.

Article 14 Future bilateral mutual legal assistance treaties with Member States

This Agreement shall not preclude the conclusion, after its entry into force, of bilateral Agreements between a Member State and the United States of America consistent with this Agreement.

Article 15 Designations and notifications

1. Where a Ministry other than the Ministry of Justice has been designated under Article 8.2(b), the European Union shall notify the United States of America of such designation prior to the exchange of written instruments described in Article 3.3 between the Member States and the United States of America.

2. The Contracting Parties, on the basis of consultations between them on which national authorities responsible for the investigation and prosecution of offences to designate pursuant to Article 4.3, shall notify each other of the national authorities so designated prior to the

exchange of written instruments described in Article 3.2 and 3 between the Member States and the United States of America. The European Union shall, for Member States having no mutual legal assistance treaty with the United States of America, notify the United States of America prior to such exchange of the identity of the central authorities under Article 4(3).

3. The Contracting Parties shall notify each other of any limitations invoked under Article 4(4) prior to the exchange of written instruments described in Article 3(2) and (3) between the Member States and the United States of America.

Article 17 Review

The Contracting Parties agree to carry out a common review of this Agreement no later than five years after its entry into force. The review shall address in particular the practical implementation of the Agreement and may also include issues such as the consequences of further development of the European Union relating to the subject matter of this Agreement.

MISCELLANEOUS

DOCUMENT 75

INTERPOL Constitution 1956
www.interpol.int/Public/ICPO/LegalMaterials/Constitution

Originally created in 1923 as the International Criminal Police Commission, the organisation changed its name to the International Police Criminal Organisation (INTERPOL) by virtue of Article 1 of its constitution which, together with the general regulations of INTERPOL, was adopted by the organisation's General Assembly at its 25th session in Vienna in 1956 and took immediate effect.

There are 182 Member States of INTERPOL.

INTERPOL's aims are to 'ensure and promote the widest possible mutual assistance between all criminal police authorities' (Article 2). INTERPOL is specifically forbidden from undertaking any intervention or activities of a political, military, religious or racial character (Article 3).

INTERPOL consists of the General Assembly (Articles 6–14), the Executive Committee (Articles 15–24), the General Secretariat (Articles 25–30), the National Central Bureaus (Articles 31–33), and the Advisers (Articles 34–37).

The headquarters of INTERPOL are in Lyon, France. INTERPOL deals primarily with issues relating to terrorism, organised crime, drug-related crimes, financial and high-tech crimes, trafficking in human beings and fugitive investigation support.

See www.interpol.int.

General Provisions

Article 1
The Organization called the "INTERNATIONAL CRIMINAL POLICE COMMISSION" shall henceforth be entitled: "THE INTERNATIONAL CRIMINAL POLICE ORGANIZATION – INTERPOL".

Its seat shall be in France.

Article 2
Its aims are:

1. To ensure and promote the widest possible mutual assistance between all criminal police authorities within the limits of the laws existing in the different countries and in the spirit of the "Universal Declaration of Human Rights".

2. To establish and develop all institutions likely to contribute effectively to the prevention and suppression of ordinary law crimes.

Article 3
It is strictly forbidden for the Organization to undertake any intervention or activities of a political, military, religious or racial character.

Article 4

Any country may delegate as a Member to the Organization any official police body whose functions come within the framework of activities of the Organization.

The request for membership shall be submitted to the Secretary General by the appropriate governmental authority.

Membership shall be subject to approval by a two-thirds majority of the General Assembly.

Structure and Organization

Article 5

The International Criminal Police Organization – Interpol – shall comprise:

- The General Assembly;
- The Executive Committee;
- The General Secretariat;
- The National Central Bureaus;
- The Advisers.

The General Assembly

Article 6

The General Assembly shall be the body of supreme authority in the Organization. It is composed of delegates appointed by the Members of the Organization.

Article 7

Each Member may be represented by one or several delegates; however, for each country there shall be only one delegation head, appointed by the competent governmental authority of that country.

Because of the technical nature of the Organization, Members should attempt to include the following in their delegations:

(a) High officials of departments dealing with police affairs;

(b) Officials whose normal duties are connected with the activities of the Organization;

(c) Specialists in the subjects on the agenda.

Article 8

The functions of the General Assembly shall be the following:

(a) To carry out the duties laid down in the Constitution;

(b) To determine principles and lay down the general measures suitable for attaining the objectives of the Organization as given in Article 2 of the Constitution;

(c) To examine and approve the general programme of activities prepared by the Secretary General for the coming year;

(d) To determine any other regulations deemed necessary;

(e) To elect persons to perform the functions mentioned in the Constitution;

(f) To adopt resolutions and make recommendations to Members on matters with which the Organization is competent to deal;

(g) To determine the financial policy of the Organization;

(h) To examine and approve any agreement to be made with other organizations.

Article 9

Members shall do all within their power, in so far as is compatible with their own obligations, to carry out the decisions of the General Assembly.

Article 10

The General Assembly of the Organization shall meet in ordinary session every year. It may meet in extraordinary session at the request of the Executive Committee or of the majority of Members.

Article 11

1. The General Assembly may, when in session, set up special committees for dealing with particular matters.

2. It may also decide to hold regular conferences between two General Assembly sessions.

Article 12

1. At the end of each session, the General Assembly shall choose the place where it will meet for its next session.

2. The General Assembly may also decide where it will meet for its session in two years time, if one or more countries have issued invitations to host that session.

3. If circumstances make it impossible or inadvisable for a session to be held in the chosen meeting place, the General Assembly may decide to choose another meeting place for the following year.

Article 13

Only one delegate from each country shall have the right to vote in the General Assembly.

Article 14

Decisions shall be made by a simple majority except in those cases where a two-thirds majority is required by the Constitution.

The Executive Committee

Article 15

The Executive Committee shall be composed of the President of the Organization, the three Vice-Presidents and nine Delegates.

The thirteen members of the Executive Committee shall belong to different countries, due weight having been given to geographical distribution.

Article 16

The General Assembly shall elect, from among the delegates, the President and three Vice-Presidents of the Organization.

A two-thirds majority shall be required for the election of the President; should this majority not be obtained after the second ballot, a simple majority shall suffice.

The President and Vice-Presidents shall be from different continents.

Article 17

The President shall be elected for four years. The Vice-Presidents shall be elected for three years. They shall not be immediately eligible for re-election either to the same posts or as Delegates on the Executive Committee.

If, following the election of a President, the provisions of Article 15 (paragraph 2) or Article 16 (paragraph 3) cannot be applied or are incompatible, a fourth Vice-President shall be elected so that all four continents are represented at the Presidency level.

If this occurs, the Executive Committee will, for a temporary period, have fourteen members. The temporary period shall come to an end as soon as circumstances make it possible to apply the provisions of Articles 15 and 16.

Article 18

The President of the Organization shall:

(a) Preside at meetings of the Assembly and the Executive Committee and direct the discussions;

(b) Ensure that the activities of the Organization are in conformity with the decisions of the General Assembly and the Executive Committee;

(c) Maintain as far as is possible direct and constant contact with the Secretary General of the Organization.

Article 19

The nine Delegates on the Executive Committee shall be elected by the General Assembly for a period of three years. They shall not be immediately eligible for re-election to the same posts.

Article 20

The Executive Committee shall meet at least once each year on being convened by the President of the Organization.

Article 21

In the exercise of their duties, all members of the Executive Committee shall conduct themselves as representatives of the Organization and not as representatives of their respective countries.

Article 22

The Executive Committee shall:

(a) Supervise the execution of the decisions of the General Assembly;

(b) Prepare the agenda for sessions for the General Assembly;

(c) Submit to the General Assembly any programme of work or project which it considers useful;

(d) Supervise the administration and work of the Secretary General;

(e) Exercise all the powers delegated to it by the General Assembly.

Article 23

In case of resignation or death of any of the members of the Executive Committee, the General Assembly shall elect another member to replace him and whose term of office shall end on the same date as his predecessor's. No member of the Executive Committee may remain in office should he cease to be a delegate to the Organization.

Article 24

Executive Committee members shall remain in office until the end of the session of the General Assembly held in the year in which their term of office expires.

The General Secretariat

Article 25

The permanent departments of the Organization shall constitute the General Secretariat.

Article 26

The General Secretariat shall:

(a) Put into application the decisions of the General Assembly and Executive Council;

(b) Serve as an international centre in the fight against ordinary crime;

(c) Serve as a technical and information centre;

(d) Ensure the efficient administration of the Organization;

(e) Maintain contact with national and international authorities, whereas questions relative to the search for criminals shall be dealt with through National Central Bureaus;

(f) Produce any publications which may be considered useful;

(g) Organize and perform secretarial work at the sessions of the General Assembly, the Executive Council and any other body of the Organization;

(h) Draw up a draft programme of work for the coming year for the consideration and approval of the General Assembly and the Executive Committee;

(i) Maintain as far as is possible direct and constant contact with the President of the Organization.

Article 27

The General Secretariat shall consist of the Secretary General and a technical and administrative staff entrusted with the work of the Organization.

Article 28

The appointment of the Secretary General shall be proposed by the Executive Committee and approved by the General Assembly for a period of five years. He may be re-appointed for other terms but must lay down office on reaching the age of sixty-five, although he may be allowed to complete his term of office on reaching this age.

He must be chosen from among persons highly competent in police matters.

In exceptional circumstances, the Executive Committee may propose at a meeting of the General Assembly that the Secretary General be removed from office.

Article 29

The Secretary General shall engage and direct the staff, administer the budget, and organize and direct the permanent departments, according to the directives decided upon by the General Assembly or Executive Committee.

He shall submit to the Executive Committee or the General Assembly any propositions or projects concerning the work of the Organization.

He shall be responsible to the Executive Committee and the General Assembly.

He shall have the right to take part in the discussions of the General Assembly, the Executive Committee and all other dependent bodies.

In the exercise of his duties, he shall represent the Organization and not any particular country.

Article 30

In the exercise of their duties, the Secretary General and the staff shall neither solicit nor accept instructions from any government or authority outside the Organization. They shall abstain from any action which might be prejudicial to their international task.

Each Member of the Organization shall undertake to respect the exclusively international character of the duties of the Secretary General and the staff, and abstain from influencing them in the discharge of their duties.

All Members of the Organization shall do their best to assist the Secretary General and the staff in the discharge of their functions.

National Central Bureaus

Article 31

In order to further its aims, the Organization needs the constant and active co-operation of its Members, who should do all within their power which is compatible with the legislations of their countries to participate diligently in its activities.

Article 32

In order to ensure the above co-operation, each country shall appoint a body which will serve as the National Central Bureau. It shall ensure liaison with:

(a) The various departments in the country;

(b) Those bodies in other countries serving as National Central Bureaus;

(c) The Organizations General Secretariat.

Article 33

In the case of those countries where the provisions of Article 32 are inapplicable or do not permit of effective centralized co-operation, the General Secretariat shall decide, with these countries, the most suitable alternative means of co-operation.

The Advisers

Article 34

On scientific matters, the Organization may consult "Advisers".

Article 35

The role of the Advisers shall be purely advisory.

Article 36

Advisers shall be appointed for three years by the Executive Committee. Their appointment will become definite only after notification by the General Assembly.

They shall be chosen from among those who have a world-wide reputation in some field of interest to the Organization.

Article 37

An Adviser may be removed from office by decision of the General Assembly.

Budget and Resources

Article 38

The Organization's resources shall be provided by:

(a) The financial contributions from Members;

(b) Gifts, bequests, grants and other resources after these have been accepted or approved by the Executive Committee.

Article 39

The General Assembly shall establish the basis of Members' subscriptions and the maximum annual expenditure according to the estimate provided by the Secretary General.

Article 40

The draft budget of the Organization shall be prepared by the Secretary General and submitted for approval to the Executive Committee.

It shall come into force after acceptance by the General Assembly.

Should the General Assembly not have had the possibility of approving the budget, the Executive Committee shall take all necessary steps according to the general outlines of the preceding budget.

Relations with other Organizations

Article 41

Whenever it deems fit, having regard to the aims and objects provided in the Constitution, the Organization shall establish relations and collaborate with other intergovernmental or non-governmental international organizations.

The general provisions concerning the relations with international, intergovernmental or non-governmental organizations will only be valid after their approval by the General Assembly.

The Organization may, in connection with all matters in which it is competent, take the advice of non-governmental international, governmental national or non-governmental national organizations.

With the approval of the General Assembly, the Executive Committee or, in urgent cases, the Secretary General may accept duties within the scope of its activities and competence either from other international institutions or organizations or in application of international conventions.

Application, Modification and Interpretation of the Constitution

Article 42

The present Constitution may be amended on the proposal of either a Member or the Executive Committee.

Any proposal for amendment to this Constitution shall be communicated by the Secretary General to Members of the Organization at least three months before submission to the General Assembly for consideration.

All amendments to this Constitution shall be approved by a two-thirds majority of the Members of the Organization.

Article 43

The French, English and Spanish texts of this Constitution shall be regarded as authoritative.

Article 44

The application of this Constitution shall be determined by the General Assembly through the General Regulations and Appendices, whose provisions shall be adopted by a two-thirds majority.

Temporary Measures

Article 45

All bodies representing the countries mentioned in Appendix I shall be deemed to be Members of the Organization unless they declare through the appropriate governmental authority that they cannot accept this Constitution. Such a declaration should be made within six months of the date of the coming into force of the present Constitution.

Article 46

At the first election, lots will be drawn to determine a Vice-President whose term of office will end a year later.

At the first election, lots will be drawn to determine two Delegates on the Executive Committee whose term of office will end a year later, and two others whose term of office will end two years later.

Article 47

Persons having rendered meritorious and prolonged services in the ranks of the ICPC may be awarded by the General Assembly honorary titles in corresponding ranks of the ICPO.

Article 48

All property belonging to the International Criminal Police Commission are transferred to the International Criminal Police Organization.

Article 49

In the present Constitution:

"Organization", wherever it occurs, shall mean the International Criminal Police Organization;

"Constitution", wherever it occurs, shall mean the Constitution of the International Criminal Police Organization;

"Secretary General" shall mean the Secretary General of the International Criminal Police Organization;

"Committee" shall mean the Executive Committee of the Organization;

"Assembly" or "General Assembly" shall mean the General Assembly of the Organization;

"Member" or "Members" shall mean a Member or Members of the International Criminal Police Organization as mentioned in Article 4 of the Constitution;

"delegate" (in the singular) or "delegates" (in the plural) shall mean a person or persons belonging to a delegation or delegations as defined in Article 7;

"Delegate" (in the singular) or "Delegates" (in the plural) shall mean a person or persons elected to the Executive Committee in the conditions laid down in Article 19.

Appendix I

List of States to which the Provisions of Article 45 of the Constitution shall Apply:

Argentina, Australia, Austria, Belgium, Brazil, Burma, Cambodia, Canada, Ceylon, Chile, Colombia, Costa Rica, Cuba, Denmark, Dominican Republic, Egypt, Eire, Finland, France, Federal German Republic, Greece, Guatemala, India, Indonesia, Iran, Israel, Italy, Japan, Jordan, Lebanon, Liberia, Libya, Luxembourg, Mexico, Monaco, Netherlands, Netherlands Antilles, New Zealand, Norway, Pakistan, Philippines, Portugal, Saar, Saudi Arabia, Spain, Sudan, Surinam, Sweden, Switzerland, Syria, Thailand, Turkey, United Kingdom of Great Britain and Northern Ireland, United States of America, Uruguay, Venezuela, Yugoslavia.

DOCUMENT 76

Principles of International Co-operation in the Detection, Arrest, Extradition and Punishment of Persons Guilty of War Crimes and Crimes Against Humanity 1973
UN Doc A/9030/Add 1; UN Doc A/RES/3074 (XXVIII)

These Principles were adopted on 3 December 1973 by the UN General Assembly in Resolution 3074 (XXVIII).

These non-binding principles provide for co-operation between States in relation to the prevention and suppression of war crimes and crimes against humanity, in the detection, arresting and bringing to trial of accused persons and in the collection of information and evidence. Despite their vintage and brevity, these Principles assert a duty on States to prosecute those who commit war crimes and crimes against humanity (paras 1, 5, 8–9).

The General Assembly,

Recalling its resolutions 2583 (XXIV) of 15 December 1969, 2712 (XXV) of 15 December 1970, 2840 (XXVI) of 18 December 1971 and 3020(XXVII) of 18 December 1972,

Taking into account the special need for international action in order to ensure the prosecution and punishment of persons guilty of war crimes and crimes against humanity,

Having considered the draft principles of international co-operation in the detection, arrest, extradition and punishment of persons guilty of war crimes and crimes against humanity,

Declares that the United Nations, in pursuance of the principles and purposes set forth in the Charter concerning the promotion of co-operation between peoples and the maintenance of international peace and security, proclaims the following principles of international co-operation in the detection, arrest, extradition and punishment of persons guilty of war crimes and crimes against humanity:

1. War crimes and crimes against humanity, wherever they are committed, shall be subject to investigation and the persons against whom there is evidence that they have committed such crimes shall be subject to tracing, arrest, trial and, if found guilty, to punishment.

2. Every State has the right to try its own nationals for war crimes and crimes against humanity.

3. States shall co-operate with each other on a bilateral and multilateral basis with a view to halting and preventing war crimes and crimes against humanity, and shall take the domestic and international measures necessary for that purpose.

4. States shall assist each other in detecting, arresting and bringing to trial persons suspected of having committed such crimes and, if they are found guilty, in punishing them.

5. Persons against whom there is evidence that they have committed war crimes and crimes against humanity shall be subject to trial and, if found guilty, to punishment, as a general rule in the countries in which they committed those crimes. In that connection, States shall co-operate on questions of extraditing such persons.

6. States shall co-operate with each other in the collection of information and evidence which would help to bring to trial the persons indicated in paragraph 5 above and shall exchange such information.

7. In accordance with article 1 of the Declaration on Territorial Asylum of 14 December 1967, States shall not grant asylum to any person with respect to whom there are serious reasons for considering that he has committed a crime against peace, a war crime or a crime against humanity.

8. States shall not take any legislative or other measures which may be prejudicial to the international obligations they have assumed in regard to the detection, arrest, extradition and punishment-of persons guilty of war crimes and crimes against humanity.

9. In co-operating with a view to the detection, arrest and extradition of persons against whom there is evidence that they have committed war crimes and crimes against humanity and, if found guilty, their punishment, States shall act in conformity with the provisions of the Charter of the United Nations and of the Declaration on Principles of International Law concerning Friendly Relations and Co-operation among States in accordance with the Charter of the United Nations.

DOCUMENT 77

Convention on the Non-Applicability of Statutory Limitations on War Crimes and Crimes Against Humanity 1968
754 UNTS 73; 8 ILM 68 (1969)

The Convention was adopted on 26 November 1968 as an annex to UN General Assembly Resolution 2391 (XXIII) and entered into force on 11 November 1970.

There are 48 parties to the Convention. Neither the UK nor the USA is party to the Convention.

The Convention requires State parties to amend their domestic law (Article IV) in order that no statutory limitation apply in relation to war crimes and crimes against humanity which include, for the purposes of the Convention, inhuman acts resulting from the policy of apartheid and the crime of genocide (Article I). The Convention applies to crimes committed by 'representatives of State authority' as well as to private individuals (Article II). It requires States to take measures to permit the extradition of persons accused of such crimes (Article III), but this obligation is stated in vague terms.

The States Parties to the present Convention,

Recalling resolutions of the General Assembly of the United Nations 3 (I) of 13 February 1946 and 170 (II) of 31 October 1947 on the extradition and punishment of war criminals, resolution 95 (I) of 11 December 1946 affirming the principles of international law recognized by the Charter of the International Military Tribunal, Nurnberg, and the judgment of the Tribunal, and resolutions 2184(XXI) of 12 December 1966 and 2202(XXI) of 16 December 1966 which expressly condemned as crimes against humanity the violation of the economic and political rights of the indigenous population on the one hand and the policies of apartheid on the other,

Recalling resolutions of the Economic and Social Council of the United Nations 1074 D (XXXIX) of 28 July 1965 and 1158 (XLI) of 5 August 1966 on the punishment of war criminals and of persons who have committed crimes against humanity,

Noting that none of the solemn declarations, instruments or conventions relating to the prosecution and punishment of war crimes and crimes against humanity made provision for a period of limitation,

Considering that war crimes and crimes against humanity are among the gravest crimes in international law,

Convinced that the effective punishment of war crimes and crimes against humanity is an important element in the prevention of such crimes, the protection of human rights and fundamental freedoms, the encouragement of confidence, the furtherance of co-operation among peoples and the promotion of international peace and security,

Noting that the application to war crimes and crimes against humanity of the rules of municipal law relating to the period of limitation for ordinary crimes is a matter of serious concern to world public opinion, since it prevents the prosecution and punishment of persons responsible for those crimes,

Recognizing that it is necessary and timely to affirm in international law, through this Convention, the principle that there is no period of limitation for war crimes and crimes against humanity, and to secure its universal application,

Have agreed as follows:

Article I

No statutory limitation shall apply to the following crimes, irrespective of the date of their commission:

(a) War crimes as they are defined in the Charter of the International Military Tribunal, Nuremberg, of 8 August 1945 and confirmed by resolutions 3(1) of 13 February 1946 and 95(I) of 11 December 1946 of the General Assembly of the United Nations, particularly the "grave breaches" enumerated in the Geneva Conventions of 12 August 1949 for the protection of war victims;

(b) Crimes against humanity whether committed in time of war or in time of peace as they are defined in the Charter of the International Military Tribunal, Nuremberg, of 8 August 1945 and confirmed by resolutions 3(I) of 13 February 1946 and 95(I) of 11 December 1946 of the General Assembly of the United Nations, eviction by armed attack or occupation and inhuman acts resulting from the policy of apartheid, and the crime of genocide as defined in the 1948 Convention on the Prevention and Punishment of the Crime of Genocide, even if such acts do not constitute a violation of the domestic law of the country in which they were committed.

Article II

If any of the crimes mentioned in article I is committed, the provisions of this Convention shall apply to representatives of the State authority and private individuals who, as principals or accomplices, participate in or who directly incite others to the commission of any of those crimes, or who conspire to commit them, irrespective of the degree of completion, and to representatives of the State authority who tolerate their commission.

Article III

The States Parties to the present Convention undertake to adopt all necessary domestic measures, legislative or otherwise, with a view to making possible the extradition, in accordance with international law, of the persons referred to in article II of this Convention.

Article IV

The States Parties to the present Convention undertake to adopt, in accordance with their respective constitutional processes, any legislative or other measures necessary to ensure that statutory or other limitations shall not apply to the prosecution and punishment of the crimes referred to in articles I and 2 of this Convention and that, where they exist, such limitations shall be abolished.

DOCUMENT 78

The Princeton Principles on Universal Jurisdiction 2001
Princeton Project on Universal Jurisdiction (2001);
www.princeton.edu/~lapa/principles.html

The Principles constitute a private attempt 'to clarify and bring order to an increasingly important area of international criminal law: prosecutions for serious crimes under international law in national courts based on universal jurisdiction, absent traditional links to the victims or perpetrators of crimes' (preface). In addition to Princeton University, the Principles were sponsored by the International Commission of Jurists, the American Association for the International Commission of Jurists, the Netherlands Institute of Human Rights and the Urban Morgan Institute for Human Rights.

The Principles were drafted by a drafting committee and then considered by an international group of jurists who met at Princeton University from 25–27 January 2001. The Principles were then circulated to human rights organisations around the world, many of which made comment on the Principles.

Universal jurisdiction is boldly stated to apply in relation to seven crimes: piracy, slavery, war crimes, crimes against peace, crimes against humanity, genocide and torture (Principle 2). More controversially, Principle 3 requires that domestic courts exercise jurisdiction over such crimes even without domestic authority, while Principle 5 purports to remove all forms of immunity, including State and diplomatic immunity in respect of such crimes. The Principles call upon States to enact the necessary legislation in order to give effect to the Principles. The Principles do not, in their entirety, reflect international practice and are to be viewed as aspirational.

The participants in the Princeton Project on Universal Jurisdiction propose the following principles for the purposes of advancing the continued evolution of international law and the application of international law in national legal systems:

Principle 1 Fundamentals of Universal Jurisdiction

1. For purposes of these Principles, universal jurisdiction is criminal jurisdiction based solely on the nature of the crime, without regard to where the crime was committed, the nationality of the alleged or convicted perpetrator, the nationality of the victim, or any other connection to the state exercising such jurisdiction.

2. Universal jurisdiction may be exercised by a competent and ordinary judicial body of any state in order to try a person duly accused of committing serious crimes under international law as specified in Principle 2.1, provided the person is present before such judicial body.

3. A state may rely on universal jurisdiction as a basis for seeking the extradition of a person accused or convicted of committing a serious crime under international law as specified in Principle 2.1 provided that it has established a prima facie case of the person's guilt and that the person sought to be extradited will be tried or the punishment carried out in accordance with international norms and standards on the protection of human rights in the context of criminal proceedings.

4. In exercising universal jurisdiction or in relying upon universal jurisdiction as a basis for seeking extradition, a state and its judicial organs shall observe international due process norms including but not limited to those involving the rights of the accused and victims, the fairness of the proceedings, and the independence and impartiality of the judiciary (hereinafter referred to as "international due process norms").

5. A state shall exercise universal jurisdiction in good faith and in accordance with its rights and obligations under international law.

Principle 2 Serious Crimes Under International Law

1. For purposes of these Principles, serious crimes under international law include: (1) piracy; (2) slavery; (3) war crimes; (4) crimes against peace; (5) crimes against humanity; (6) genocide; and (7) torture.

2. The application of universal jurisdiction to the crimes listed in paragraph 1 is without prejudice to the application of universal jurisdiction to other crimes under international law.

Principle 3 Reliance on Universal Jurisdiction in the Absence of National Legislation

With respect to serious crimes under international law as specified in Principle 2.1, national judicial organs may rely on universal jurisdiction even if their national legislation does not specifically provide for it.

Principle 4 Obligation to Support Accountability

1. A state shall comply with all international obligations that are applicable to: prosecuting or extraditing persons accused or convicted of crimes under international law in accordance with a legal process that complies with international due process norms, providing other states investigating or prosecuting such crimes with all available means of administrative and judicial assistance, and under-taking such other necessary and appropriate measures as are consistent with international norms and standards.

2. A state, in the exercise of universal jurisdiction, may, for purposes of prosecution, seek judicial assistance to obtain evidence from another state, provided that the requesting state has a good faith basis and that the evidence sought will be used in accordance with international due process norms.

Principle 5 Immunities

With respect to serious crimes under international law as specified in Principle 2.1, the official position of any accused person, whether as head of state or government or as a responsible government official, shall not relieve such person of criminal responsibility nor mitigate punishment.

Principle 6 Statutes of Limitations

Statutes of limitations or other forms of prescription shall not apply to serious crimes under international law as specified in Principle 2.1.

Principle 7 Amnesties

1. Amnesties are generally inconsistent with the obligation of states to provide accountability for serious crimes under international law as specified in Principle in 2.1.

2. The exercise of universal jurisdiction with respect to serious crimes under international law as specified in Principle 2(1) shall not be precluded by amnesties which are incompatible with the international legal obligations of the granting state.

Principle 8 Resolution of Competing National Jurisdictions

Where more than one state has or may assert jurisdiction over a person and where the state that has custody of the person has no basis for jurisdiction other than the principle of universality, that state or its judicial organs shall, in deciding whether to prosecute or extradite, base their decision on an aggregate balance of the following criteria:

(a) multilateral or bilateral treaty obligations;

(b) the place of commission of the crime;

(c) the nationality connection of the alleged perpetrator to the requesting state;

(d) the nationality connection of the victim to the requesting state;

(e) any other connection between the requesting state and the alleged perpetrator, the crime, or the victim;

(f) the likelihood, good faith, and effectiveness of the prosecution in the requesting state;

(g) the fairness and impartiality of the proceedings in the requesting state;

(h) convenience to the parties and witnesses, as well as the availability of evidence in the requesting state; and

(i) the interests of justice.

Principle 9 *Non Bis In Idem* Double Jeopardy

1. In the exercise of universal jurisdiction, a state or its judicial organs shall ensure that a person who is subject to criminal proceedings shall not be exposed to multiple prosecutions or punishment for the same criminal conduct where the prior criminal proceedings or other accountability proceedings have been conducted in good faith and in accordance with international norms and standards. Sham prosecutions or derisory punishment resulting from a conviction or other accountability proceedings shall not be recognized as falling within the scope of this Principle.

2. A state shall recognize the validity of a proper exercise of universal jurisdiction by another state and shall recognize the final judgment of a competent and ordinary national judicial body or a competent international judicial body exercising such jurisdiction in accordance with international due process norms.

3. Any person tried or convicted by a state exercising universal jurisdiction for serious crimes under international law as specified in Principle 2.1 shall have the right and legal standing to raise before any national or international judicial body the claim of non bis in idem in opposition to any further criminal proceedings.

Principle 10 Grounds for Refusal of Extradition

1. A state or its judicial organs shall refuse to entertain a request for extradition based on universal jurisdiction if the person sought is likely to face a death penalty sentence or to be subjected to torture or any other cruel, degrading, or inhuman punishment or treatment, or if it is likely that the person sought will be subjected to sham proceedings in which international due process norms will be violated and no satisfactory assurances to the contrary are provided.

2. A state which refuses to extradite on the basis of this Principle shall, when permitted by international law, prosecute the individual accused of a serious crime under international law as specified in Principle 2.1 or extradite such person to another state where this can be done without exposing him or her to the risks referred to in paragraph 1.

Principle 11 Adoption of National Legislation

A state shall, where necessary, enact national legislation to enable the exercise of universal jurisdiction and the enforcement of these Principles.

Principle 12 Inclusion of Universal Jurisdiction in Future Treaties

In all future treaties, and in protocols to existing treaties, concerned with serious crimes under international law as specified in Principle 2(1), states shall include provisions for universal jurisdiction.

Principle 13 Strengthening Accountability and Universal Jurisdiction

1. National judicial organs shall construe national law in a manner that is consistent with these Principles.

2. Nothing in these Principles shall be construed to limit the rights and obligations of a state to prevent or punish, by lawful means recognized under international law, the commission of crimes under international law.

3. These Principles shall not be construed as limiting the continued development of universal jurisdiction in international law.

Principle 14 Settlement of Disputes

1. Consistent with international law and the Charter of the United Nations, states should settle their disputes arising out of the exercise of universal jurisdiction by all available means of

peaceful settlement of disputes and in particular by submitting the dispute to the International Court of Justice.

2. Pending the determination of the issue in dispute, a state seeking to exercise universal jurisdiction shall not detain the accused person nor seek to have that person detained by another state unless there is a reasonable risk of flight and no other reasonable means can be found to ensure that person's eventual appearance before the judicial organs of the state seeking to exercise its jurisdiction.

DOCUMENT 79

Guidelines of the Counter-Terrorism Committee for the Conduct of its Work 2001
UN Doc S/AC.40/2001/CRP.1

The Counter-Terrorism Committee (CTC) was established by the UN Security Council in Resolution 1373 (2001) of 28 September 2001 **(Document 27)** *in the immediate aftermath of the 9/11 terrorist attacks on the USA. According to para 6 of that resolution, the CTC, which consists of all the members of the Security Council, is 'to monitor the implementation' of the resolution through examining reports submitted by States on steps they have taken to implement the resolution. The guidelines were adopted by the CTC on 16 October 2001. The mandate of the CTC has been augmented, as part of a 'revitalization' process, with power to undertake visits to States (para 6 of Security Council Resolution 1566 (2004) of 8 October 2004).*

See www.un.org/Docs/sc/committees/1373.

1. The Counter-Terrorism Committee

(a) The Committee of the Security Council established by paragraph 6 of Security Council resolution 1373 (2001) of 28 September 2001 will be known as the Counter-Terrorism Committee.

(b) The Committee will monitor implementation of resolution 1373 (2001), in accordance with paragraphs 6 and 7 of that resolution.

(c) The guiding principles of the Committee's work will be co-operation, transparency and even-handedness.

2. Composition of the Committee

(a) The Committee will consist of all Members of the Security Council.

(b) The Chairman of the Committee will be appointed by the Security Council, and will be the Permanent Representative of a Member of the Security Council.

(c) The Chairman will chair meetings of the Committee. When he is unable to chair a meeting, he will nominate a chairman to act on his behalf.

(d) The Secretariat of the Committee will be provided by the Secretariat of the United Nations.

(e) The Chairman of the Committee will be assisted by Vice Chairmen of the Committee who will be appointed by the Security Council.

(f) The Chairman and Vice Chairmen will make the necessary preparations for meetings of the Committee in order to ensure its proper and effective functioning.

3. Meetings of the Committee

(a) Meetings of the Committee will be convened at any time the Chairman deems necessary, or at the request of a Member of the Committee.

(b) 24 hours notice will normally be given of any meeting of the Committee.

(c) The Committee will meet in closed session, unless it decides otherwise.

(d) The Committee may invite any member of the United Nations to participate in the discussion of any question brought before the Committee in which the interests of that Member are specifically affected.

(e) The Committee may invite members of the Secretariat or other persons whom it considers competent for the purpose to supply it with appropriate expertise or information or to give it other assistance in examining matters within its competence.

(f) The Chairman will invite the experts of the Committee to attend meetings as appropriate.

4. Documentation and Agenda

(a) The Chairman, in conjunction with the Secretariat, will circulate a provisional Agenda before a meeting of the Committee.

(b) The Chairman, in conjunction with the Secretariat, will circulate documents and papers to members of the Committee.

5. Information Supplied to the Committee

(a) The Committee will consider information relevant to its work not only from all States, but also from any other sources in a position to provide such information, including international organisations and institutions, non-governmental organisations and individuals.

(b) The information received by the Committee will be kept confidential if the provider so requests or if the Committee so decides.

(c) The Committee will establish such arrangements as are necessary with other intergovernmental organisations and bodies, particularly those in the United Nations system, operating in areas relevant to the work of the Committee, for the provision of information relevant to the work of the Committee.

6. Reports Submitted Pursuant to Paragraph 6

Reports submitted by States pursuant to paragraph 6 of resolution 1373 (2001) will be circulated as documents of the Security Council.

7. Decision-making

(a) The Committee will reach decisions by consensus of its members. If consensus cannot be reached on a particular issue, the Chairman will undertake such further consultations as may facilitate agreement. If, after these consultations, consensus still cannot be reached, the matter will be submitted to the Security Council.

(b) Where the Committee agrees, decisions may be taken by a written procedure. In such cases the Chairman will circulate to all members of the Committee the proposed decision of the Committee, and will request members of the Committee to indicate their objection to the proposed decision within 48 hours (or in urgent situations, such shorter period as the Chairman shall determine). If no objection is received within such a period, the decision will be deemed adopted.

8. Transparency in the Work of the Committee

The Chairman, and as appropriate the Vice Chairmen, in consultation with the Committee, will hold regular briefings of Member States and of the media to explain and publicise the work of the Committee.

9. Reports to the Security Council

The Committee will submit regular reports, including recommendations as necessary, to the Security Council on the implementation of SCR 1373 (2001), either orally or in writing, as requested by the Security Council, or where the Committee deems it necessary to submit a report to the Security Council.